Hitler's Prisons

Hitler's Prisons

Legal Terror in Nazi Germany

Nikolaus Wachsmann

Yale University Press
New Haven and London

Copyright © 2004 by Nikolaus Wachsmann

All rights reserved. This book may not be reproduced in whole or in part, in any form (beyond that copying permitted by Sections 107 and 108 of the U.S. Copyright Law and except by reviewers for the public press) without written permission from the publishers.

For information about this and other Yale University Press publications, please contact:
U.S. Office: sales.press@yale.edu   yalebooks.com
Europe Office: sales@yaleup.co.uk   www.yalebooks.co.uk

Set in Minion by SNP Best-set Typesetter Ltd., Hong Kong
Printed in Great Britain by St. Edmundsbury Press Ltd, Bury St. Edmunds

ISBN 0–300–10250–x

Library of Congress Control Number   2003021218

A catalogue record for this book is available from the British Library.

10 9 8 7 6 5 4 3 2 1

Contents

List of Plates viii
List of Figures x
Acknowledgements xi
List of Abbreviations xiv
Map of German penal institutions xvi

Introduction 1

Part I Setting the Scene 15

Chapter 1 The Weimar Prison, 1918–33 17

Crime and Correction *18* · The Prison and the Public *36* · Fighting the 'Incorrigible' *46* · The Prison in Crisis *54*

Part II Enforcing Legal Terror, 1933–39 65

Chapter 2 Inside the Nazi Prison 67

Terror, Crime and Punishment *68* · Hitler's Jurists and the Prison *71* · Everyday Life behind Bars *83* · Prison Camps *101*

Chapter 3 The Campaign against 'Community Aliens'   112

Political Resistance and Repression 113 · 'Dangerous Habitual Criminals' and Security Confinement 128 · Sex Crimes, Castration and Homosexuality 139 · The Sterilisation of Prisoners 149 · German Jews and Legal Terror 156

Chapter 4 The Nazi Web of Terror   165

The Rise of the Police and the SS 165 · Conflict and Compromise: the Law and the Police 171 · Denouncing Prisoners to the Police 176 · Prisons and Concentration Camps 184

Part III Escalating Legal Terror, 1939–45   189

Chapter 5 Law in Wartime   191

Terror on the Home Front, 1939–41 192 · The Legal System under Attack, 1942 208 · Total War and Extermination, 1942–44 218

Chapter 6 Prison Conditions: from Bad to Worse   227

Prisons as Penal Factories 228 · Life and Death in Prisons 237 · Torment in Prison Camps 248

Chapter 7 Privilege and Punishment   257

'National Comrades' behind Bars 258 · Soldiers as Prisoners – Prisoners as Soldiers 262 · Foreign Political Prisoners 269 · Enforcing Racial Policy: Polish Prisoners 274

Chapter 8 Killing Prisoners   284

'Annihilation through Labour': the View from Above 284 · 'Annihilation through Labour': the View from Below 299 · Extending the Killings: 'Asocials' and the Disabled 306 · Capital Punishment 314

Chapter 9 Final Defeat   319

The Last Stand of Nazi Terror 319 · Prison Evacuations 323 · Chaos, Murder, Liberation 331

Part IV Aftermath 339

Chapter 10 The Nazi Prison in Perspective 341

Bloody Hands, Clean Conscience: Nazi Jurists and Postwar
Justice *341* · Back to Work: Prison Officials in West Germany *347* ·
East Germany and the Perversion of the Law *356* · Special Path?
A Comparative View *361*

Conclusion 372

Figures 392

Notes 404

Bibliography 488

Index 523

Plates

between pages 142 and 143

1. Hitler at the Landsberg am Lech fortress, 1924. (Bundesarchiv Koblenz, Bild 146/1970/050/23)
2. The Straubing prison doctor Theodor Viernstein conducting a criminal-biological examination of an inmate, c. 1925. (JVA Straubing)
3. Privileged inmates play handball at Untermaßfeld, mid- to late 1920s. (ThHStAW, Thüringisches Justizministerium Nr. 1572)
4. Lessons for prisoners from a social worker at Untermaßfeld, mid- to late 1920s. (ThHStAW, Thüringisches Justizministerium Nr. 1572)
5. Warders practice ju-jitsu at Straubing, mid-1920s. (JVA Straubing)
6. Exercise for privileged inmates at Straubing, 1925. (JVA Straubing)
7. Inmates during their daily exercise at Aichach, 1931. (Ullstein Bild, photo by Wolfgang Weber)
8. Carpet-weaving at Aichach, 1931. (Ullstein Bild, photo by Wolfgang Weber)
9. Hanns Kerrl visits the Jüterbog training camp, c. 1933–34. (Bundesarchiv Koblenz, Bild 102/14899)
10. German dignitaries at the 1935 International Prison and Penitentiary Congress in Berlin. (Bundesarchiv Koblenz, Bild 183/1988/0810/501)
11. Franz Gürtner, 1937. (Bundesarchiv Koblenz, Bild 146/1986/130/05)
12. Rudolf Marx, c. 1934. (Bundesarchiv Berlin, R 3001/alt R22/Pers. 67687)
13. Wilhelm Crohne, 1937. (Bundesarchiv Berlin, R 3001/alt R22/Pers. 53759)
14. Prison guards relaxing at Emsland, c. 1935–36. (Dokumentations- und Informationszentrum Emslandlager, Papenburg)
15. Emsland camp inmates labouring on the moor, c. 1938–39. (Dokumentations- und Informationszentrum Emslandlager, Papenburg)

Plates   ix

16. Illustration from a propaganda article 'Sex Fiends and Criminals', 1939. (*Neues Volk* 4, vol. 7 (1939), p. 19)
17. Rosa S. at Aichach, 1935. (Staatsarchiv München, Justizvollzugsanstalten Nr. 13693)
18. Magdalena S. at Aichach, 1936. (Staatsarchiv München, Justizvollzugsanstalten Nr. 10514)

between pages 302 and 303

19. Hitler's speech at the Reichstag, 26 April 1942. (Bundesarchiv Koblenz, Bild 183/J 01258)
20. Hitler with Curt Rothenberger and Otto-Georg Thierack, 20 August 1942. (Bundesarchiv Koblenz, Bild 146/85/106/21)
21. Curt Rothenberger and Otto-Georg Thierack take over from the former State Secretaries Franz Schlegelberger and Roland Freisler at the Reich Ministry of Justice, 26 August 1942. (Bundesarchiv Koblenz, Bild 183/J 3166)
22. Roland Freisler, c. 1944. (Bundesarchiv Koblenz, Bild 183/64425/001)
23. Karl Engert. (Bundesarchiv Berlin, R 3001/alt R 22/Pers. 55262)
24. Inside the Brandenburg-Görden penitentiary, c. 1930–40. (Bildarchiv Preußischer Kulturbesitz, Berlin, 2003)
25. Prisoners producing army uniforms at Brandenburg-Görden, c. 1942. (*Arbeit und Strafvollzug in dem Zuchthaus Brandenburg-Görden*, Bundesarchiv Filmarchiv, copyright Transit Film)
26. Inmates from the Duisburg-Hamborn prison sorting coal at a nearby pit, 1943. (Nordrhein-Westfälisches Hauptstaatsarchiv, Gerichte Rep. 321/406)
27. Two Brandenburg-Görden prisoners in security confinement sorting buttons, c. 1942. (*Arbeit und Strafvollzug in dem Zuchthaus Brandenburg-Görden*, Bundesarchiv Filmarchiv, copyright Transit Film)
28. The Czech political prisoner Bretislaus Krejsa, 1942. (Thüringisches Staatsarchiv Meiningen, Zuchthaus Untermaßfeld Nr. 752)
29. Czech prisoner Josef Kopal, 1943. (Thüringisches Staatsarchiv Meiningen, Zuchthaus Untermaßfeld Nr. 718)
30. Petty criminal Richard Franke, 1940. (Thüringisches Staatsarchiv Meiningen, Zuchthaus Untermaßfeld Nr. 311)
31. Inmates carrying stones up the 'stairs of death' at Mauthausen concentration camp, 1942. (United States Holocaust Memorial Museum, photo 15622)
32. After the massacre of inmates at the Sonnenburg penitentiary, 1945. (Editions saint-paul, Luxembourg)
33. An Allied officer talks to three liberated prisoners at the Werl penitentiary, 11 April 1945. (IWM, Film 3568)
34. Officials from the Werl penitentiary hand over their keys, 11 April 1945. (IWM, Film 3569)
35. The guillotine at the Plötzensee prison, 1945. (Landesarchiv Berlin, Photo 71 425)
36. Former legal officials on trial at Nuremberg, 1947. (Ullstein Bild)

Figures

1. Inmate numbers in German penal institutions, 1924–44 … 392
2. Inmate numbers (per day) in German penal institutions and SS concentration camps, 1934–45 (selected dates) … 394
3. Inmate numbers in penal institutions in the Altreich, 1933–44 … 394
4. Inmate numbers in penal institutions in the incorporated territory in Eastern Europe, 1940–44 … 396
5. Gender balance in German penal institutions, 1934–43 … 396
6. Deaths in the Emsland prison camp, 1934–45 … 398
7. Number of sentences by the People's Court, 1934–45 … 398
8. Number of defendants before the special courts in Frankfurt am Main, Braunschweig and Düsseldorf, 1933–45 … 400
9. 'Preventive and rehabilitative measures' (based on the Habitual Criminals Law) ordered by German courts, 1934–43 … 400
10. Number of death sentences by judicial courts in the territory of the Third Reich, 1933–45 … 402

Acknowledgements

It is with the greatest pleasure that I thank all those who have contributed to this project.

This book began its life in the very stimulating and welcoming atmosphere of Birkbeck College (University of London), and I want to thank my former colleagues there. Most of *Hitler's Prisons* was written during my time as a Research Fellow at Downing College (Cambridge), which provided a perfect environment for research and writing. I am deeply grateful to the masters, fellows and staff. The book was completed after I moved to the University of Sheffield, where I received vital support from my colleagues in the history department. I owe special thanks to my students in London, Cambridge and Sheffield, who have helped to shape my thinking about German history. I should also like to thank the *Journal of Modern History*, *The Historical Journal* and Princeton University Press, all of which previously published material I have drawn on for individual sections in Chapters 1, 3 and 8.

I have received great help and expert guidance in the archives and libraries I consulted in Germany and Britain. I am grateful to all the staff for their support. My individual debts are too great to list here, but I want to take this opportunity to express my particular gratitude to Sabine Gresens and Torsten Zarwel at the Bundesarchiv in Berlin, Katharina Witter in Meiningen, Frau Graupner in Weimar and Reinhard Weber of the Staatsarchiv in Munich. In addition, I want to thank Fietje Ausländer from the Emsland Documentation Centre for providing me with important information and photographs. I have also gained crucial information from documents held by the German legal authorities. I should like to thank Oberstaatsanwalt Richter in Kiel for his help in this respect. Above all, I am grateful to Richter Schneider and Staatsanwalt Riedel from the Central Agency for the Solution of National-Socialist Crimes in Ludwigsburg for their tireless support.

I also want to thank those who have helped me gain a deeper understanding of the realities of prison life. Erich Viehöfer set up an illuminating visit to the prison museum in Ludwigsburg and also kindly sent me several documents. Governor Schwämmlein led me through the penal institution in Untermaßfeld and answered many questions. Hauptlehrer Friedolin Resch from the penal institution in Straubing has been especially generous with his assistance, showing me around the institution twice and also providing me with many valuable photographs and documents.

My work has benefited in many ways from discussion or correspondence with scholars and historians, including Omer Bartov, Wolfgang Burgmair, Michael Burleigh, Chris Clark, Nick Coleman, Jennifer Evans, Henry Friedlander, Stephen Garton, Neil Gregor, Elizabeth Harvey, Tobias Jersak, Helmut Kramer, Oliver Liang, Peter Longerich, Kai Naumann, Christina Vanja and Matthias Weber. I am also grateful to the participants at the Modern German History Seminar in London, where some of the ideas presented here first took shape. I have received several pieces of important advice from Heinz Müller-Dietz. My warmest thanks also go to Jane Caplan, who has greatly encouraged and supported my research from the start. Richard Wetzell kindly invited me to stimulating conferences in Florence and Washington. I have also learned much from Robert Gellately, who asked me to attend a conference on social outsiders (organised with Nathan Stoltzfus) which provided a lot of food for thought. Peter Kitson and Zoë Laidlaw kindly helped me with the presentation of the figures at the end of the book. Finally, I have had inspiring discussions over many years with Stefan Schurr, who also sent me copies of several articles and books.

Much of my research and writing has been made possible by support from different institutions. I want to acknowledge the generous help given by the British Academy, the University of London and the Institute of Historical Research in London. I am especially grateful for crucial assistance from the Harry Frank Guggenheim Foundation, which has enabled me to complete my work.

It has been a pleasure to publish this book with Yale University Press. I am deeply indebted to Robert Baldock for taking on this project, and for all his advice and calm support throughout. Beth Humphries has done a very good job copy-editing the manuscript. Ewan Thompson and Margot Levy helped with the index. The transition of the book from my computer to the printers has been greatly eased by the professionalism of Candida Brazil, Diana Yeh and the rest of the team at Yale.

Acknowledgements xiii

Many colleagues and friends have generously left off from their own research to read parts of this book. Pertti Ahonen, Constantine Brancovan, Jörg Morré, Christian Müller, Corey Ross and Dan Vyleta (who also translated an article from the Czech for me) all read sections of the manuscript, often at short notice. Their comments have been very useful and have benefited the book significantly. I am especially grateful to Richard Overy and Lucy Riall, who read most of the material presented in Parts I and II, and gave me incisive feedback. Among many other things, they made me think harder about the comparative dimension of Nazi penal policy. Kristin Semmens kindly agreed to read the entire manuscript and did much to make the overall argument tighter. A very special word of thanks is due to Andreas Fleiter. His knowledge of German prison policy, his advice on the literature and, above all, his extensive comments on the manuscript were invaluable.

I am very grateful to Sir Ian Kershaw and Jeremy Noakes, whose work on Nazi Germany I admired long before I embarked on my own research. Their encouragement has meant a lot to me, and both have cast their expert eyes over the manuscript, helping greatly to improve it. Most of all I have to thank Richard J. Evans, who accompanied this book all the way from its inception. I have profited immensely from his scholarship and intellect. His comments were always to the point and his support could not have been more generous.

I am very fortunate to have received so much help from my family and friends. During my various research trips, I enjoyed the hospitality of Christian Kirschstein, Christoph and Joachim Ruckhäberle, Robyn Schulkowsky, Patrik Schwarz and Ines Langelüddecke, Matthias Tischer, and Friederike and Max von Trott. My debt to Michael Metzger is of a very special order and goes far beyond his immense practical help. And my very supportive family in Munich made it possible for me to live and work in the UK in the first place. I am deeply grateful to Christa, Sebastian, Gabriele and Michael. Sebastian also helped to locate several important books, while my father read the manuscript, making many valuable suggestions.

My greatest debt is to Tracey McGeagh, who has lived with this book as long as I have. She gave me much needed strength and also had to put up with long periods when I was buried deep into my research. And despite her own busy schedule and the fact that she has – thank God – no specialist interest in Nazi prisons, she always took the time to discuss my ideas and to read my work, making countless crucial improvements. I want to thank her for all her support, understanding and love. I could never have written this book without her.

N.W.

Abbreviations

AV	Allgemeine Verfügung (General Decree)
BA Berlin	Bundesarchiv Berlin
BayHStA	Bayerisches Hauptstaatsarchiv
BDC	Berlin Document Centre
BlGefK	*Blätter für Gefängniskunde*
BLHA	Landeshauptarchiv Brandenburg
BNSDJ	Bund Nationalsozialistischer Deutscher Juristen (Association of National Socialist German Jurists)
DJV	Deutsche Zentralverwaltung für Justiz (Central German Judicial Administration)
GDR	German Democratic Republic
GStA	Generalstaatsanwalt (General State Prosecutor)
GStA PK	Geheimes Staatsarchiv Preußischer Kulturbesitz
HHStAW	Hessisches Hauptstaatsarchiv
HStAD-Kalkum	Nordrhein-Westfälisches Hauptstaatsarchiv, Zweigarchiv Schloss Kalkum
IfZ	Institut für Zeitgeschichte, München
IKV	Internationale Kriminalistische Vereinigung (International Union of Penal Law)
IMT	*The Trial of the Major War Criminals before the International Military Tribunal*
JVA	Justizvollzugsanstalt (Penal Institution)
KPD	Kommunistische Partei Deutschlands (German Communist Party)
LaB	Landesarchiv Berlin
MdRfW	*Monatsblätter des Deutschen Reichszusammenschlusses für Gerichtshilfe, Gefangenen- und Entlassenenfürsorge der freien Wohlfahrtspflege*

MGGE	*Monatsblätter für Gerichtshilfe, Gefangenen- und Entlassenenfürsorge*
MKG	*Mitteilungen der Kriminalbiologischen Gesellschaft*
MPIP-HA	Max-Planck-Institut für Psychiatrie, Historisches Archiv
MSchriftKrim	*Monatsschrift für Kriminalpsychologie und Strafrechtsreform* (between 1937 and 1944: *Kriminalbiologie*; since 1953: *Kriminologie*)
NKVD	People's Commissariat of Internal Affairs
NN	Nacht und Nebel (Night and Fog)
NRW	Nordrhein-Westfalen (North-Rhine Westphalia)
NSDAP	Nationalsozialistische Deutsche Arbeiter Partei (Nazi Party)
OLG	Oberlandesgericht (Higher State Court)
PRO	Public Record Office
RJM	Reichsjustizministerium (Reich Ministry of Justice)
RSHA	Reichssicherheitshauptamt (Reich Security Head Office)
SA	Sturmabteilung (Storm Troop)
SD	Sicherheitsdienst (Security Service)
SED	Sozialistische Einheitspartei Deutschlands (Socialist Unity Party)
SL	Strafvollzugsmuseum Ludwigsburg
Sopade	*Deutschland-Berichte der Sozialdemokratischen Partei Deutschlands*
SPD	Sozialdemokratische Partei Deutschlands (German Social Democratic Party)
SS	Schutzstaffel (lit. Protection Squad)
StAMü	Staatsarchiv München
StK	Staatsanwaltschaft Kiel
ThHStAW	Thüringisches Hauptstaatsarchiv
ThSTA Mgn.	Thüringisches Staatsarchiv Meiningen
VfZ	*Vierteljahreshefte für Zeitgeschichte*
WL	Wiener Library
ZfStrVo	*Zeitschrift für Strafvollzug und Straffälligenhilfe*
ZStL	Zentrale Stelle der Landesjustizverwaltungen in Ludwigsburg
ZStW	*Zeitschrift für die gesamte Strafrechtswissenschaft*

Selected German prisons, penitentiaries and prison camps (c. August 1941)

This map includes all penal institutions with an official maximum capacity of 500 or more inmates in the territory where the German prison service operated in August 1941. In addition, a few selected smaller institutions have been included as well (Cottbus, Eisenach, Glatz, Gräfentonna, Innsbruck, Kattowitz, Königsberg, Leitmeritz, Linz, Luckau, Luxemburg, Posen, Prague-Pankratz, Preußisch Stargard, Rendsburg, Rottenburg, Schweidnitz, Sosnowitz, Tapiau, Teschen). Four cities contained more than one penal institution with a maximum capacity of 500 or more: Berlin (Moabit, Lehrter Straße, Plötzensee and Tegel), Graz (remand prison and penal institution), Hamburg (remand prison and Fuhlsbüttel) and Leipzig (remand prison and Kleinmeusdorf). Following the invasion of the Soviet Union, the German prison authorities also apparently administered, for some time, institutions in the Bialystok district. The names on the map are, for the most part, those used by the German authorities at the time.

Introduction

Asked to name the sites of imprisonment in Hitler's Germany, most people would point to concentration camps, and no further. These SS camps have become symbols of Nazi repression, and indeed of the Third Reich as a whole. There is very little awareness that there were other places of confinement in Nazi Germany, run by the traditional legal system rather than the SS. In fact, several million men and women were held in judicial confinement in prisons, penitentiaries and prison camps between 1933 and 1945. As this book reveals, during most of the Third Reich, such penal institutions actually held more inmates than the concentration camps. It is these convicts who are at the heart of this study.

Hitler's Prisons contributes to a social history of punishment in the Third Reich. It is not a narrow institutional history of imprisonment, but looks at legal terror from many different perspectives, illuminating the largely unknown world of Nazi prisons. It explores the inmates' everyday lives, looking at prison labour, living conditions, discipline and violence. Particular attention is paid to prisoners excluded from Nazi society as dangerous 'community aliens', on political, racial and criminological grounds. This highlights the fate of some of the last forgotten victims of the Third Reich, including so-called 'dangerous habitual criminals', who became the victims of a systematic programme of mass extermination during the war. This study also adds to the history of other Nazi victims, including Jews, Poles, political opponents, Jehovah's Witnesses and homosexuals. These different prisoners are not presented as a faceless and nameless mass. Rather, many individual experiences have been woven into the narrative and, wherever possible, the prisoners speak for themselves.

The general focus is on adult inmates serving sentences in the larger penal institutions administered by the regular legal apparatus.[1] There were two main types of imprisonment handed down by judges in Nazi Germany. Most common were prison (*Gefängnis*) sentences, with terms ranging from one day to five years. In practice, most prison sentences lasted less than one year, at least before the outbreak of war. The second main type of legal confinement was the penitentiary (*Zuchthaus*) sentence, which explicitly aimed to dishonour offenders, stigmatising them even after their release. Penitentiary sentences were generally harsher and much longer than prison sentences, with one year the minimum duration (life sentences, though, were very rare). In 1935, 28 per cent of all defendants sentenced to imprisonment in a penitentiary had to serve three years or more.[2] At the end of June 1935, there was a total of 107,162 inmates in all the German penal institutions (including young offenders): 48,778 of them were serving prison sentences and 27,888 penitentiary sentences.[3] The great majority of these prisoners were held in 'special institutions' (*besondere Anstalten*), so called because they had a full-time governor. In 1935, there was a total of 167 such larger penal institutions, which could lock up, on average, around 450 prisoners each. Aside from prisons and penitentiaries, there were many mixed penal institutions, which held a combination of inmates (including, for example, offenders sentenced to prison and penitentiary terms, and inmates on remand) on separate wings. In addition, there was one large prison camp at that time, also run by the legal authorities.[4]

Nazi penal institutions are not viewed in isolation in this study. Carceral institutions have sometimes been described in the sociological literature as 'total institutions', virtually divorced from the outside world.[5] While this perspective offers valuable insights into the institutional life of the inmates, it is not really concerned with the way in which it was shaped by wider forces. But the life of prisoners in Nazi Germany was profoundly influenced by social, economic and political change on the outside. Therefore, the book situates the prison in the broader context of the Nazi dictatorship, exploring various general themes, such as Nazi ideology, criminology, resistance and dissent, criminality, the police and concentration camps, and extermination policy. Most importantly, it examines different aspects of the German legal apparatus and sentencing. After all, prisons were part of the legal system and it was the judges who ultimately determined who would end up inside. Timing was of crucial importance here, as the Second World War dramatically radicalised legal terror.

Exploring prisons and penal policy, this book also addresses several broader questions about Nazi terror. One is the function of the legal system in the Third Reich. How important was it for the establishment and maintenance of the Nazi dictatorship? Have historians been justified in overlooking penal institutions? This also raises questions about the way in which legal terror operated.

To what extent was Hitler involved in shaping it? And how much room did the legal officials have for their own initiatives?

A further crucial issue concerns the relationship between the legal apparatus (with its penal institutions) and the police and SS (with the concentration camps). Many historians draw a very sharp line between the two, inspired by the structural analysis advanced by the émigré German lawyer and political scientist Ernst Fraenkel in his 1941 book *The Dual State* (discussed in the conclusion).[6] Fraenkel's influence is most obvious, perhaps, in the work of the legal historian Lothar Gruchmann, who has described the Third Reich as a Dual State, consisting of the Normative State, which included the regular court system and administered justice on the basis of fundamental legal principles, and the Prerogative State, with the police and SS as its most powerful agencies, which relied on 'organised extra-normative force' to implement the 'will of the Führer'. According to Gruchmann, the relationship between the two was characterised by competition, friction and conflict, with the SS and police interfering in judicial affairs and usurping legal power, overpowering the weaker legal system. The judicial authorities, at least under Reich Minister of Justice Franz Gürtner (1933–41), generally tried to maintain the rule of law, aiming to prevent a descent into an arbitrary police state. Of course, they were not without blame, Gruchmann allows. Sympathetic to the 'national' goals of Nazism, the legal authorities did not at first oppose various illegal measures, regarding them as temporary phenomena that would disappear after the establishment of the new regime. Once they realised that the state of emergency was to be a permanent feature of Nazi rule, it was too late. Any compromises legal officials made in the following years, aimed at preserving the law, only helped to undermine it further. And in the face of the extra-normative activities of the police, they were essentially 'powerless' anyway. The result, Gruchmann concludes, was the defeat of the legal system: it suffered more and more police interference, while any attempts to legally regulate police activities failed miserably.[7] This study will evaluate whether this general view holds up, focusing on the development of the prison system in the Third Reich.

Hitler's Prisons also touches on the link between Nazi terror and the German population. Some early works after the war portrayed Nazi Germany as a strictly regimented totalitarian society, with the population cowed into total submission by an omnipotent terror apparatus.[8] This picture has since been comprehensively revised. The most recent attempt to provide a history of consent and coercion in the Third Reich has been made by the historian Robert Gellately. Like others before him, Gellately argues that Nazi repression was very selective and did not touch the great majority of the population until the last months of the war, when 'German-on-German terror' finally became the order of the day. Nazi terror, he emphasises, was conducted with remarkable openness because the Nazis believed that it would win them public approval, tapping into the hostility of law-abiding 'good citizens' towards minorities. This strategy worked: 'the Germans generally turned out to be proud and pleased that Hitler and his henchmen were putting away certain kinds of people who did not fit in, or who were regarded as "outsiders", "asocials", "useless eaters", or "criminals"'. Crucially, Gellately adds, many 'ordinary' Germans not only supported Nazi terror passively, but actually helped make it possible with a 'flood of denunciations' to the police. In this way, 'many ordinary people served as the eyes and ears of the police', with the police tending to operate merely as a reactive force. Gellately here draws on his earlier groundbreaking work on the Gestapo, which aimed to undermine the picture of an all-knowing and ever-present Gestapo, replacing it with that of Germany as a self-policing society.[9] Some of these general conclusions will be examined in this book, focusing on the legal apparatus and those individuals caught up in it.

A final broader theme concerns the continuities and discontinuities between the pre-Nazi period and the Third Reich, a topic that has been controversially discussed by historians for many decades and from many different perspectives.[10] What was the impact of Nazism on the prison system and the officials of the preceding Weimar Republic? To what extent was prison life in the Third Reich shaped by the mainstream criminology and penal policy of the earlier, democratic period? Clearly, these questions are important for any assessment of the nature of the Nazi prison. But they cannot be answered as long as the history of the Weimar prison service remains a blank page. After the Second World War, Weimar was often seen as little more than a prologue to the Nazi regime. Indeed, some historical research was motivated purely by the desire to search for the roots of Nazi policies in the previous era. But such a search was not seen as a rewarding exercise by historians in the case of the Weimar prison, presumably because the prison in the Third Reich was, until very recently, of no interest either. To fill this gap and to set the scene for the exploration of the Nazi prison, this book provides the first in-depth analysis of imprisonment in the Weimar Republic.[11]

All these concerns have shaped the structure of the book. Following brief comments on the historiography and the source material (below), the narrative opens with an investigation of the German prison in the pre-Nazi years, which forms the first part of the book (Chapter 1). Attention then turns to the Third Reich. To take account of the immense changes during the Second World War, the discussion is divided between the prewar and the war period. Part II opens with a general exploration of life behind bars before the outbreak of war (Chapter 2). Next, it details the fate of many of those individuals labelled as 'community aliens' (Chapter 3). The following chapter places Nazi legal terror in the broader context of the development of the regime, examining in particular the relationship between police and legal system (Chapter 4). The same general theme is taken up again at the beginning of Part III, which deals with the escalation of legal terror during the Second World War (Chapter 5). This is followed by a detailed account of the impact of war on conditions inside prisons, penitentiaries and prison camps (Chapter 6). Next, the focus is narrowed again, to explore the fate of individual groups of prisoners singled out for differential treatment. In the war, this could range from transfer to special army formations to extermination in concentration camps (Chapters 7 and 8). The final chapter then details the chaos, evacuations and murders in penal institutions during the collapse of Nazi Germany in 1945 (Chapter 9). In the last part, *Hitler's Prisons* addresses some of the wider themes. The conclusion returns to the broader questions introduced at the beginning of the study. Before that, the book offers some thoughts for further discussion, contrasting the Nazi prison with prisons in the Soviet Union and the West, and examining the legacy of Nazi legal terror in postwar Germany (Chapter 10).

The Nazi Prison in History

Hitler's prisons played an important role in Nazi terror – but we know very little about them. General books about the Nazi dictatorship almost invariably ignore them altogether. Reading these works, it seems as if prisons had not existed at all. Even large encyclopaedias boasting thousands of facts about the Third Reich fail to mention details about the prison system. The same is true for studies which are concerned more narrowly with Nazi terror. Even specialist studies of the legal apparatus itself have ignored the prison system. At the very best, the reader can hope for a couple of pages with some basic information.[12] More commonly, studies of the Nazi legal system simply stop outside the prison gates. Lothar Gruchmann's monumental work *Justiz im Dritten Reich* (Justice in the Third Reich), to mention the most obvious example, contains no discussion of the prison system, despite its length of almost 1,300 pages.

Only a small number of studies have actually been devoted to the Nazi prison system. Outside Germany, virtually nothing has been published on the topic since the end of the war.[13] Even inside Germany, the Nazi prison has remained largely uncharted territory, even though some small progress has been made in recent years. The few studies published in West Germany up to the end of the 1980s generally fell into the narrow field of legal history, drily enumerating and comparing prison regulations and statutes.[14] With the exception of two studies on the Emsland prison camp, no real attempt was made to shed any light on life inside penal institutions.[15] There was slightly more interest coming from East Germany, which resulted in the publication of studies containing some useful material.[16] But on the whole, they offered limited insights. Their uncritical focus was on the Communist prisoners, who were hailed as martyrs – typical of attempts in East Germany to exploit Communist resistance in the past to legitimise the present-day dictatorship.[17]

It was only in the 1990s that new historical studies offered further glimpses of life in Hitler's prisons. These included a handful of articles with valuable case studies of individual institutions.[18] Other research has explored specific aspects of the Nazi prison, such as youth prisons and the role of prison chaplains.[19] Some historians have also tried to draw a more general picture of the prison service in the Third Reich. An interdisciplinary project at the University of Saarbrücken has made the most important contribution to date, culminating in the publication in 1996 of the first and only full-length study, by the historian Rainer Möhler.[20] But all this research is very much in its infancy and there are still enormous gaps in our knowledge.

How can one explain this relative silence about Hitler's prisons? To start with, historians concerned with imprisonment in Nazi Germany have inevitably turned to the concentration camps. This is easily understandable. The concentration camps were specific expressions of Nazi terror, unlike prisons which had already existed before. And during the war, the camps became sites of Nazi genocide. This is true both of the death camps of the Holocaust with their gas chambers and of concentration camps where the inmates were beaten to death, drowned, shot or killed through infernal conditions and slave labour. After the war, historians were initially slow to explore the organisation and reality of the concentration camps. In 1964, the German historian Martin Broszat noted in the introduction to his masterly account of the camp system that, while the camps were frequently mentioned in political-historical discourse, 'there still exists little concrete knowledge about them'.[21] Much has changed since then. Since the late 1970s, a large number of academic books and articles has been published on individual camps and different aspects of the camp reality. In addition, several important studies have appeared on more general aspects of the development and organisation of the camps.[22] As we shall see in this book, the concentration camps were much more lethal than prisons and penitentiaries. But this did not mean that these penal institutions were humanely administered safe havens which had 'nothing to do with the concentration camps', as former prison officials claimed after the war.[23]

Another likely reason for the lack of research into penal institutions is the prevailing focus on innocent victims of the Nazi regime. Historical research and public memory has concentrated on Jews and political opponents of the regime, and more recently also on the mentally ill, homosexuals and other persecuted groups. Compared with these millions of men, women and children, some convicts make rather more awkward victims. Of course, a large number of them were also innocent in our eyes, persecuted on racial grounds or for their political views. But many others were criminals convicted of offences still punishable today. 'Ordinary' criminality, such as property offences and violent crimes, did not vanish in Nazi Germany, and most of the offenders were taken to penal institutions. Inevitably, theirs is a morally ambiguous tale. They cannot be described solely as innocent victims of racial madness or as brave anti-Fascists. Nor can they be depicted as romantic rebels or social revolutionaries, as some historians have done with bandits and poachers of the early modern period. But their persecution must not be forgotten either. Ignoring the fate of criminal offenders means ignoring a central element of repression in the Third Reich. In addition, a number of 'ordinary' criminal offenders were subject to exorbitant punishment and brutal, unlawful violence in the Third Reich. And such crimes against criminals are still crimes.[24]

Finally, historians interested specifically in the history of the German prison have ignored the Third Reich in favour of earlier periods, focusing instead on the 'birth' (or, more accurately, the 'rebirth') of the prison in the eighteenth and nineteenth centuries.[25] Before this time, other punitive measures were more widespread. Public, ritualistic and extremely violent punishments, such as the scaffold, mutilation and branding, were dominant in early modern Europe. But gradually, these open and symbolic acts of shaming and dishonouring aimed at the body of the offender were replaced with imprisonment away from the gaze of the public. By the middle of the nineteenth century, the prison had developed into the central form of punishment. In this process, the character of the prison was transformed, too. In early prisons, discipline had often been lax and inmates mingled freely with each other, as well as with family and friends from the outside. But during the nineteenth century, the prison was increasingly turned into a strict institution dominated by rigid rules. And while the early prisons had been houses of correction for a vast variety of individuals, including the mentally ill and debtors, the modern prison belongs exclusively to the sphere of criminal justice. This process of specialisation also took place inside penal institutions, with the setting up of special wings or institutions for young offenders, women, remand prisoners and others.[26] It is this transformation of punishment, set in the context of the emerging modern world, which has been the subject of several celebrated studies, the most influential being Michel Foucault's *Surveiller et punir* (Discipline and Punish), first published in 1975. Foucault here described the prison as a paradigm of bourgeois society, which he saw as being driven by the desire to eradicate the slightest deviation from what it prescribed as normative behaviour. The aim of this 'carceral society' was to discipline, dominate and, if necessary, transform the behaviour of individuals by introducing strict rules of conduct and constant surveillance into prisons, as well as into schools and factories.[27] Inevitably, many of the general features of the modern prison as described by Foucault and others can be detected in Germany. But this modern prison is, of course, an archetype. In practice, the history of the prison has been fractured, full of changes, contradictions and ruptures, and this book explores what was distinctive about the Nazi prison.

The Nazi Legal System in History

As already mentioned, a comprehensive study of the Nazi prison must look far beyond the prison walls, above all to penal policy and the courts. Inevitably, such an approach raises important questions about the role of the legal system in the Third Reich. In the first decades after the war, the widespread assumption in West Germany was that the legal apparatus had played a rather insignificant part in Nazi repression and may even have become a victim of the regime itself. True, there were a few pioneering studies in the late 1950s and 1960s which exposed the complicity of the legal administration in Nazi terror.[28] But other studies argued that judges and other officials could not really be blamed, in keeping with the myth that the German professional classes had been largely innocent of any involvement in atrocities. Only a fraction of legal officials had been true Nazis, it was claimed. The fact that many others had seemingly fallen in line with the regime as well was explained away with reference to the positivist legal tradition in Germany, which was said to have forced them to apply the law regardless of their own moral convictions. On top of that, the argument continued, jurists were crushed by the totalitarian strength of the Nazi dictatorship. Ultimately, they had not been perpetrators but victims of the regime. In this vein, the former president of the West German Federal Supreme Court, Hermann Weinkauff, concluded in 1968 that each legal official had been on his own – 'a helpless prey for the terrorist pressure of state and party'.[29] This apologetic picture is not unconnected to the fact that the legal history of the Third Reich was largely written by jurists, some of whom had themselves served in Nazi Germany. Weinkauff, for example, had been appointed to the Supreme Court (*Reichsgericht*) in 1937, and continued his career after the war, like so many of his colleagues.

More recently, a different view of the Nazi legal apparatus has emerged. Particularly since the 1980s, a number of important works published in Germany have painted a more nuanced picture of the judiciary. A new generation of jurists has written about the Nazi past from a more critical perspective, reflecting the wider change in the German political climate. At the same time, historians have no longer been content to leave the history of the Nazi legal system to jurists. This growing concern of historians with the role of judges, state prosecutors and other legal officials arose partly out of the general attack on the conception of the Third Reich as a rigidly structured monolithic whole in which orders always flowed from top to bottom. Detailed research into the workings and structure of the regime revealed the more complex, 'polycratic' reality of the Nazi dictatorship, highlighting the participation in Nazi repression of many Germans in the state bureaucracy, the army, industry and many other sectors of society.

This new research helped to pave the way for two important general histories of the legal apparatus in the Third Reich. Lothar Gruchmann's monumental work, mentioned above, was first published in 1988 and represents a great scholarly achievement. It serves as an indispensable guide to the legal system under the Nazis, covering in immense detail the development of the legal administration, its officials, new legislation and many aspects of the relationship between the legal system, the police and the regime. The second study was Ralph Angermund's *Deutsche Richterschaft* (German Judiciary), published in 1990 and still the most stimulating account of the judiciary in the Third Reich. Angermund not only drew a sharp picture of the legal officials and their motivation, but also dealt in some detail with the treatment of individual groups of defendants before the courts.[30] However, both studies inevitably left significant gaps. For example, Gruchmann's study did not really deal with sentencing, and stopped at Reich Minister Gürtner's death in early 1941, leaving out most of the crucial years during the Second World War.

Some of these remaining gaps have now been filled by research published since the 1990s, which has also opened up important new perspectives. Several of these studies have been sponsored by German state and regional Ministries of Justice, in a belated attempt to examine their own history critically.[31] Much of this recent work has been about the sentencing policy of individual courts, above all the People's Court and various special courts, while some historians have also published larger studies of penal policy in entire regional districts.[32] Other historians have focused on the application of individual laws or the persecution of individual groups of offenders.[33] Unfortunately, this research has seldom been received outside the narrow circle of legal historians. General books on the Third Reich still tend to marginalise the legal apparatus, perhaps with the exception of the People's Court, notorious for the trials of the men behind the 20 July 1944 bomb plot on Hitler's life.

Ignorance about the Nazi legal system is particularly common outside Germany. Here, most of the new research remains unknown. Hardly any studies have been translated. Even the seminal works by Gruchmann and Angermund are not available in English.[34] Only a few English-speaking historians have made use of at least some of this recent German literature in their accounts of Nazi terror.[35] Even fewer have made original contributions themselves to the history of the law in Nazi Germany.[36] Instead, their focus has been on the political police (Gestapo). In the same way as camps came to epitomise imprisonment in the Third Reich, the Gestapo (and the SS) symbolise the Nazi apparatus of repression. Thus, over the last decades, a large number of valuable empirical studies have appeared, exploring the reality of the police persecution of Jews, Poles and political opponents in different regions of the Third Reich.[37] But there was more to Nazi terror than the police and this book will paint a fuller picture, drawing together many of the recent studies of the Nazi legal system for the first time.

Sources

The dearth of research into Hitler's prisons stands in sharp contrast to the mass of available source material. Whilst a large number of SS and police files were destroyed before the end of the war, a vast quantity of documents about the legal apparatus has survived. Looking at the central prison administration, the Federal Archive in Berlin holds hundreds of relevant files from the Reich Ministry of Justice, which controlled the German prison service between 1935 and 1945. These files cover most aspects of the Nazi prison, from inmate labour to draft laws, from religious services to clothing. At the same time, the Federal Archive holds personal files of ministerial and regional prison officials, their Nazi party membership files and the official diary of Hitler's longest-serving Minister of Justice, Franz Gürtner. In addition, this archive contains unpublished prison statistics and important documents about the influence on the prison service of other powerful Nazi agencies, including the SS and the police. Further relevant documents about the Nazi prison are held in other archives. Many of them were collected after the war, in preparation for trials of former prison officials, both before the Allied court in Nuremberg and before West German judges. Much of the evidence collected by German courts is documented in the Central Agency for the Solution of National-Socialist Crimes (Zentrale Stelle der Landesjustizverwaltungen zur Aufklärung nationalsozialistischer Verbrechen), based in Ludwigsburg. During the various postwar judicial investigations, the authorities also interrogated several former leading German prison officials. These transcripts, like many other documents used here for the first time, help to illuminate those developments in the Nazi prison which remain murky in the surviving written documentation – either because the Nazi officials had been careful not to incriminate themselves by committing illegal policies to paper, or because they had destroyed the relevant material in the last months of the war.

Taken together, these different sources offer a fairly comprehensive overview of the general running of the prison service in the Third Reich. They also contain some information about life inside individual penal institutions. But they are more valuable in indicating the general direction of prison policy. In order to gain a deeper insight into the realities of life behind bars, it is necessary also to draw on other sources. One obvious way to investigate life inside Hitler's prisons is to study recollections of former inmates, published after the war.[38] But while some of these memoirs contain powerful descriptions, one has to be conscious of their limitations. Apart from the obvious problems arising from sources written often decades after the events they depict, the writers were not representative of the inmate population as a whole. Most of the accounts are written by rather well-educated political prisoners. But the majority of inmates were poorly educated men and women serving time for common crimes. It is naturally more difficult to reconstruct the experiences of these offenders; after all, individuals convicted of theft rarely wrote memoirs.

To study aspects of everyday life in penal institutions, I have drawn above all on regional and local documents. This includes the documents collected and produced by the general state prosecution offices in the different German judicial districts (35 by early 1941). These agencies held much crucial information, as they served as the connection point between the Reich Ministry of Justice and individual penal institutions all over the country. Many of these documents are still available in state archives in Germany (and elsewhere) and for this study I have examined three districts in some detail (Munich, Jena and Düsseldorf). Most importantly, I have studied three individual penal institutions in depth, examining administrative files, personal files of officials and many hundreds of individual inmate files (for reasons of data protection, the names of inmates are often abbreviated in this study). Of course, the prisoner files were put together by the authorities and have to be read critically. Also, the files often remain silent on several important aspects of prison life, such as the relations between inmates. Still, prisoner files – sometimes several hundred pages long and containing requests, complaints and censored letters by the inmates – are among the most valuable sources for exploring their world.

The three penal institutions chosen as case studies for this book are quite distinct from each other. They differ in terms of the size, age and location, as well as in the prisoners they held. The first case study is the Untermaßfeld penitentiary, situated on the edge of a small village in the Werra valley in Thuringia. A former castle, Untermaßfeld was one of the oldest sites used for imprisonment in Germany, a convoluted construction quite removed from the Panopticon, the nineteenth-century ideal of total supervision through rational prison architecture (with four cell blocks radiating from a tower in the middle, from where officials could monitor all the cells). Untermaßfeld was a medium-sized penitentiary for men, with space for some 545 inmates (in 1935). Often hailed in the 1920s as the most progressive of all German penal institutions, Untermaßfeld makes an especially interesting example of the changes in prison life under the Nazis. Also, it held many different groups of prisoners in the Third Reich, including a higher proportion of Czech political prisoners than most other German penal institutions.

The second case study, Brandenburg-Görden, west of Berlin, was built during the Weimar Republic in an idyllic spot, surrounded by pinewoods, fruit trees and gardens, all hidden from the view of most prisoners. Known among some prisoners as the 'German Sing-Sing', the institution first opened its gates in December 1931. Once it was fully completed in 1935, it was designed to accommodate up to 1,800 prisoners, making it the largest German penal institution at this time. It was also one of the most modern prison buildings in Germany, which had mixed results for the inmates. The halls in the cell blocks were well ventilated and lit, thanks to the glass roofs. All cells were fitted with electric lamps and the association cells also contained toilets. However, the prison was designed for maximum security, using the latest technology. To prevent escape, all the roofs and courtyards could be floodlit. In addition, there were armed officials in watchtowers on each corner, equipped with searchlights. And to maximise control inside the building, an electric alarm system had been installed. In the Third Reich, Brandenburg-Görden held male prisoners only, including various groups of particular interest to the regime. Above all, it contained a very large proportion of political prisoners, largely Communist activists from nearby Berlin, and it also had a special wing for inmates singled out as 'dangerous habitual criminals'.[39]

Finally, I have examined the Aichach penal institution in Bavaria, situated just outside a small town near Augsburg. Aichach was one of the few institutions reserved exclusively for women. The prison population in the Third Reich was dominated by men. In the summer of 1937, the ratio of male to female prisoners was more than 10:1. This dropped sharply during the war, but even then men easily outnumbered women (see Figure 5, pp. 396–7). As a result, male prisoners were traditionally seen as the norm. The rules and regulations, written by male officials, contained only a few special provisions for women. One study concluded in 1927 that male and female prisoners were treated alike 'almost to an absurd degree'.[40] This might suggest that a study of Nazi prisons could concentrate on men only – just as many studies of prisons in other countries have done. However, gender is clearly an important aspect in the history of punishment.[41] And as the study of the Aichach institution demonstrates, there were indeed some significant differences to institutions reserved for men. Aichach itself was a fairly modern building, opened in 1909 and largely modelled on the Panopticon. As in most other German penal institutions, prisoners were held either in single or in association cells. Equipped for 443 prisoners (1935), Aichach held women convicted of all types of offence and sentenced to various forms of imprisonment. For example, the inmate population on 12 August 1937 included 305 penitentiary inmates, 83 adult prison inmates (and some young offenders), 97 women classified as 'dangerous habitual criminals' and another 50 women in workhouse confinement.[42]

In addition to these three case studies, I have drawn on a variety of contemporary sources about other penal institutions. To start with, I have used a vast collection of documents about the Emsland prison camp, published in three volumes in 1983. The Nazi legal authorities set up several such large-scale prison camps for men. The Emsland camp was by far the biggest of them all, holding some 9,500 male inmates in 1938, and the published documents about this camp give a detailed picture of the conditions inside, which were among the worst of all sites of legal imprisonment.[43] Another central source are the contemporary accounts of left-wing political prisoners from institutions all over Nazi Germany, which were collected by the Social Democratic Party in exile between 1934 and 1940.[44] Finally, I have used published material about the Nazi prison from newspapers and specialist journals. The Nazi prison was not completely hidden from view, a fact which raises more questions about the wider function of Nazi terror. But before legal terror in Nazi Germany can be explored, attention will turn to the Weimar period, which left an ambivalent inheritance for Hitler's prisons.

Part I Setting the Scene

1 The Weimar Prison, 1918–33

In the Third Reich, it was customary to pour scorn on the Weimar prison. The prison was ridiculed and attacked for having been soft on criminals and perverted by pedagogical illusions. Otto-Georg Thierack, who later served as Hitler's Minister of Justice, in 1936 described the Weimar prison service as 'stupid' and 'crazy'. Inmates had been much better off than civilians on the outside, Thierack alleged, with an abundance of food, music, games and fun.[1] Prison officials themselves were among the loudest critics of the Weimar prison. In the spring of 1933, only a few months after Hitler's appointment as Chancellor had finally finished off the Weimar Republic, a leading journal of prison officials demanded a clean break with the past. The list of wishes, which included some 13 detailed demands, began as follows:

> In the first place, the sentimental humanitarianism and weakness in the face of ordinary criminals has to stop. Imprisonment has to become fair but strict. As regards the aim of punishment, retribution and deterrence have to be emphasised above the betterment and education of criminal offenders. The improvement of discipline in the penal institutions has to be pursued with every possible means.[2]

As we shall see, the picture of the Weimar prison as a hotel for pampered criminals had already been popular on the nationalist right in the last years of Weimar. In the early 1930s, enemies of the republic, including the Nazis, pointed to the prison as typical of the weakness of liberalism and promised to restore law and order in an authoritarian state.

This chapter will look beyond this politically motivated caricature of the Weimar prison, exploring the reality of prison policy and life inside. The Weimar Republic, built on the ruins of the defeat of the First World War, lasted only 14 years, a short time marked by latent civil war, social upheaval and economic disaster. In this brief period, the prison underwent significant changes. Life behind bars was profoundly shaped by events on the outside, such as the fall of the old Imperial order during the revolution of 1918, the hyper-inflation of 1922–23, the expansion of social policy, and the rise of Nazism to power in the early 1930s. The Weimar years were full of contradictions: a time of change and conservatism, optimism and despair, radical reform and missed opportunities, humanitarian dreams and authoritarian initiatives. It was also a time which left important legacies for the Nazi period – not least in penal policy.

The Weimar period has arguably been captured most imaginatively by the late Detlev Peukert, whose analysis continues to stimulate historians of German social and penal policy.[3] Broadly speaking, Peukert, like a number of other historians, challenged the claim that the Third Reich was the product of enduring pre-modern structures and traditions in Germany. Instead, he saw Nazism emerge in a thoroughly modern society undergoing a massive crisis.[4] Peukert argued that the study of Weimar was vital as it saw 'the emergence of the world we inhabit today'. 'In less than a decade and a half,' he noted, 'virtually every social and intellectual initiative we think of as modern was formulated or put into practice. And yet . . . no sooner had modern ideas been put into effect than they came under attack, were revoked or began to collapse.' Modern social policy, Peukert claimed, had a Janus face: 'care for the reformables and exclusion of the incorrigibles'. However, Peukert suggested that during the 1920s the question of selection and exclusion had still been marginal. Instead, this period was characterised by 'pedagogical dreams of omnipotence'. It was only during the disastrous crisis in the last years of Weimar, according to Peukert, that this utopian vision was reconceptualised in negative terms, 'identifying, segregating, and disposing of those individuals who are "abnormal" or "sick" '. This demand for selection and eradication, Peukert concluded, then shaped the approach towards social outsiders in Nazi Germany, where it gained 'unprecedented operational licence'.[5] In the following sections, we shall see whether the prison system fits into this general view of Weimar history.

Crime and Correction

Weimar was always obsessed with crime. The flourishing tabloid press and illustrated magazines, eager to increase circulation, surpassed one another with sensational stories about members of the criminal underworld. Countless articles were devoted to confidence tricksters, clever bank robbers and daring thieves. Some of the criminals became famous among the general population – men such as the 'cat burglar' Emil Strauß, who came to prominence after stealing burglary tools from an exhibition in the Berlin police museum. Murders and sex crimes were covered in particularly gruesome detail in the Weimar press, which was unencumbered by the stricter censorship of previous decades. Trials were reported in great depth and the newspapers printed ever more lurid reports of executions, including eyewitness accounts of the last moments in the life of the condemned criminal. This curiosity about and revulsion from crime and the underworld were reflected in Weimar culture in general, featuring prominently in pulp fiction, novels, plays, films and paintings. The fixation on crime was intensified by modern police methods, which tried to involve the public in solving crimes. In the capital Berlin, at the time the world's third largest city, the press was informed of every murder that took place, and during intermissions cinemas even showed photos of wanted criminals.[6] In short, crime seemed to be everywhere.

Alarm about criminality was already widespread at the birth of the Weimar Republic. In part, this was a reflection of real changes in criminality. In the months following the armistice, soldiers returning from the front committed many armed robberies and thefts. Violent crimes increased sharply. Among the most infamous cases was the deliberate derailment of a passenger train on 20 January 1919 by Otto Perleberg, who then proceeded to rob the passengers. Eighteen people were killed and more than 300 were hurt. Armed criminal gangs roamed the countryside, raiding farms and shops and spreading terror among the population. The Dresden Army Command noted in July 1919 that the situation in one district was 'reminiscent of the period after the Thirty Years War'.[7]

In the following years, Weimar was hit by a crime wave. In the early 1920s, inflation increasingly rendered the German currency worthless, driving vast numbers of people to property crime. Recorded theft reached new heights, and the total number of people convicted of criminal offences more than doubled, increasing from 348,247 in 1919 to 823,902 in 1923, at the climax of the catastrophic hyper-inflation. According to one astute observer, writing in the late 1920s, nothing had been safe: 'Dogs and cats are taken away, light bulbs are screwed out in corridors, brass plates are removed from entrance doors, even the dustbins left outside for the waste collection disappear.'[8] The desperate circumstances which led many Germans to break the law are all too manifest in the condition in which they arrived in the penal institutions. The Social Democrat newspaper *Vorwärts* reported that, of 100 men committed to Plötzensee (Berlin) prison in 1921, 50 arrived without a shirt, 60 without shoes and 80 without socks.[9]

The crime wave inevitably led to a rapid increase in prisoners. During the war, prisoner numbers had remained rather low and postwar amnesties reduced them still further. But this quickly changed, and by 1920 penal institutions all over Germany were reporting a serious lack of space. Inmate numbers continued to rise as inflation progressed. The average monthly population in Bavarian penitentiaries, for example, more than doubled between 1919 and 1923.[10] There can be no doubt that by 1923 the number of prisoners held each day in German penal institutions well exceeded 100,000.

Many Germans saw the crime wave as a symptom of the disintegration of society. Defeat in the First World War had come as a great shock to them. But they had no time to catch their breath after this 'national catastrophe'. In the years after the war, many Germans were gripped by a deep anxiety about the apparent collapse of the social, political and moral order. Everywhere they looked, they saw signs that appeared to presage the breakdown of authority and traditional values. They pointed to the increase in sexual promiscuity and venereal disease, the delinquent behaviour of the young, the spread of 'pulp literature', inflation, political unrest, the increasing rates of divorce and illegitimate births – all these real and imagined developments were taken as evidence of the collapse of a previously orderly society.[11]

To overcome the deep postwar crisis and reconstruct the moral and social order, many observers believed that far-reaching state intervention was urgently required. In practice, this intervention took different forms. There was cross-party support for the extension of the welfare state and the principle of rehabilitation in social policy in order to bring about a 'regeneration' of the population. The new constitution, approved in 1919, guaranteed a lengthy list of basic social rights and the Weimar Republic saw a rapid growth in public health provision and housing. The desire to rebuild the nation also heightened the importance of education. There were extensive debates about education in the 1920s, both in the public sphere and in academia, and the demand for reform left its mark on schools, social work, reformatories, asylums and adult education. But the reconstruction of Germany was to be achieved not just through progressive social policy. At the same time, a variety of repressive and prohibitive measures were put forward, or implemented. This ranged from the 1926 Law to Protect Young People from Harmful and Obscene Publications (*Schund- und Schmutzgesetz*), to debates about the sterilisation of 'degenerates'. The aim to safeguard society also affected the draft for a Correctional Custody Law (*Bewahrungsgesetz*), which envisaged the internment of non-criminal social outsiders such as alcoholics, prostitutes and the homeless.[12] This emphasis on both reform and repression was mirrored in Weimar penal policy.

The postwar debate about crime and penal policy was influenced by the ideas of the so-called modern school of criminal law, which had emerged during the

German Empire. For much of the nineteenth century, the criminal justice system in Germany, as in many other European states, had been characterised by deterrence and retribution. The aim of punishment was seen as the infliction of an appropriate measure of pain on the offender, corresponding to the severity of the crime committed. This conception of punishment had been advocated by the so-called classical school of criminal law. Aiming at the protection of the individual from arbitrary punishment by the state, it demanded that each crime should carry a fixed penalty, to be determined *a priori*. Thus, punishment would be uniform and predictable. Offenders were seen as rational individuals who had wilfully disobeyed the law, and the threat of punishment was intended to deter them. It was this conception of punishment that influenced the Prussian Criminal Code of 1851, based on the principle of general prevention.[13] But in the last decades of the nineteenth century, a different approach to punishment gained ground, focusing increasingly on the offender. Punishment should fit the criminal, it was argued, not the crime. And while the classical school had called for the punishment of criminal acts committed in the past, the new doctrine looked ahead, seeing punishment as a means of protecting society against future criminal behaviour.

The rise of the modern school of criminal law in the nineteenth century has to be seen, not least, in the context of the extension of the medical paradigm into the criminal justice system. In the nineteenth century, rapid progress was made in the fight against a number of illnesses, such as cholera. As a consequence, the expectation emerged that rational methods used to detect, cure and prevent such illnesses could also be used to solve social problems. The activities of doctors were extended, to examinations in schools and to the control of sexual diseases. This interventionist approach influenced penal policy. It was increasingly thought that crime, just like physical diseases, could be combated and, to some degree, eliminated. As a consequence, crime was conceptualised in the language of medical diagnosis, distinguishing between different 'types' of criminals. The most fundamental differentiation was made between criminal offenders who could be 'healed' and those who were beyond help. Among the most influential writers on crime were a number of trained doctors, such as Emil Kraepelin, the doyen of German psychiatry, who described crime as 'an illness of the social body' and explained: 'just like a doctor, we have to regard as our first and foremost duty the prevention of crime. In addition, we have to reform the criminal as far as possible, as well as to incapacitate the incorrigible.'[14]

The leading protagonist of the modern school of criminal law in Imperial Germany was the liberal law professor Franz von Liszt, whose writings had a lasting impact well beyond his death in 1919. Liszt had summarised his demand for special prevention in 1882 as the 'incapacitation of incorrigibles, reformation of reformables'. Many 'reformable offenders', Liszt argued, might be 'saved' by a regime based on discipline, work and basic education – like many other criminal law reformers, he remained vague about the details of this programme of rehabilitation. Liszt also called for the incapacitation of all 'incorrigible habitual criminals', which he deemed 'one of the most pressing tasks at present'. For these offenders, rehabilitation was useless. It would also be madness to let them 'loose on the public like a wild beast' after their imprisonment. How was this to be avoided? At the beginning of the nineteenth century, some German states had singled out inmates regarded as particularly dangerous and deported them as far as Siberia or Brazil. But by the time Liszt was writing, deportation had been abolished in Germany, even though it was still periodically discussed. Instead, Liszt suggested that 'incorrigible' criminals should be isolated indefinitely under an extremely harsh disciplinarian regime in special institutions, in almost all cases until their death. Essentially, they would be imprisoned not for what they had done, but for what they would do.[15] This dual approach of reform and repression left its stamp on German penal policy during the Empire, and later had a significant impact on the various Weimar drafts for a new criminal code.[16] It also influenced prison policy.

Reform and the Prison

The idea of the prison as a rehabilitative institution was not new. The claim that imprisonment could reform inmates has proven to be one of its most powerful and enduring ideological justifications. Of course, the actual method of 'reform' has been the subject of much controversy, ever since the 'birth of the prison'. Reform has been interpreted in very different ways, including strict discipline, prisoner autonomy and therapy. Indeed, the almost infinite adaptability of the concept of the 'reformative prison' helps to explain its enduring appeal. Once a certain approach to prisoner reform was thought to have been discredited, for example, because of high rates of recidivism, it was superseded by another. Mostly, the cause for the failure of reform was located not in the prison as an institution, but in the 'wrong' methods employed. In this way, the ideal of the reformative prison has survived, despite the fact that, in practice, it has largely proved unable to keep its promise, irrespective of the methods used. Nevertheless, as we shall see, the changing conceptions of 'reform' still had important consequences for the everyday life of the inmates.

Starting in the late eighteenth century, religiously inspired prison reformers such as John Howard in England attacked the contemporary prison as dirty, noisy, smelly and disorderly. They demanded that prisons become more utilitarian, geared towards the reform of the inmate through a regime based on order, productive labour and religious instruction. The calls for a transformation of the prison along these lines were echoed in nineteenth-century Germany. In the face of growing social protest and property crime, linked to the social change accompanying industrialisation, German reformers argued that the prison should aim to better inmates and curb recidivism by instilling into them discipline, cleanliness, a strict work ethic and Christian virtues. This programme of rehabilitation, it was argued in Germany and elsewhere, could best be achieved by separating prisoners from one another. Not only would inmates be removed from the depraved influence of others, it was thought, but isolation might force them to confront their guilt, the first step towards redemption. There were heated discussions about the practical details of this policy. The debate focused on two different systems, pioneered in the US in the 1820s. Under the so-called Pennsylvania system, first introduced in the Eastern Penitentiary near Philadelphia, prisoners were held in solitary confinement at all times. By contrast, in Auburn (New York) the inmates were only separated at night. During the day, they worked and ate together, but were forbidden to talk and even to look at each other. In the 1830s and 1840s, the North American debate about the virtues and defects of both systems reached Europe, with the separate system as practised in Pennsylvania emerging victorious. But its realisation, with some modifications, proceeded at a rather slow pace in Germany in the second half of the nineteenth century. The building of new penal institutions (or the alteration of existing ones) to accommodate prisoners in single cells, such as in Bruchsal (Baden) and Moabit (Berlin), was costly. And the ideological dominance of the strict solitary ideal began to be questioned, with some growing support for group confinement towards the end of prison sentences. Still, by 1905 over 60 per cent of the average daily inmate population in Prussian prisons were held in solitary confinement. Prison officials often tried to prevent these inmates from establishing any contact with one another. In a number of institutions, rows of single cells had been constructed in chapels to separate inmates even during the services.[17]

The reality of imprisonment in German penal institutions at the turn of the century did not live up to the intentions of the prison reformers. True, there were gradual improvements in health care, hygiene and food provision, which contributed to a fall in inmate mortality. And corporal punishment and other excessive forms of physical punishment were gradually abolished in the second half of the nineteenth century. Unrestrained physical violence by warders was also generally frowned upon.[18] But the reforms created a cruel system of isolation and depersonalisation for most prisoners. Life inside German penal institutions was characterised above all by uniform and strict discipline. Michel Foucault has emphasised the parallels between prison and military discipline, pointing to the meticulous rules set out even for the most insignificant aspects of everyday life, the strict timetables and the exactly prescribed gestures and movements expected of the individual, all of which aimed at turning inmates into 'docile bodies'.[19] In German penal institutions, the daily routine was often strictly regimented in this way. The officials' clothing even imitated the soldier's uniform and it was common for inmates, when addressing the warders, to click their heels and place their hands on the trouser seam. When officials entered a cell, inmates were forced to rise, stand to attention and state their name, offence and length of sentence.[20]

The militarisation of prison life was achieved in part by the employment of ex-soldiers. As in many other countries, the male German prison officials were often recruited from the army. In Imperial Germany, former soldiers acquired the right to state employment after lengthy military service. In practice, better qualified ex-soldiers applied for higher paid and less demanding jobs with the state railway system or the postal service; the prison service was left to the rest. Basic education, no criminal record and a strong physical build were the sole requirements for employment as a warder (for the small number of female warders, the main criteria for hiring were physical fitness and basic schooling, as in the case of men, as well as some knowledge of housekeeping and needlework or the like; a number of the applicants were daughters of prison officials). The leading prison officials still made a virtue of the influx of ex-soldiers. As the prominent Prussian prison administrator Karl Krohne explained in his extensive manual on the prison system, which influenced several generations of German officials, soldiers had internalised many skills required for the prison service: 'The adjustment to order, punctuality, cleanliness, discipline in giving and receiving orders, fearlessness, personal courage . . .'.[21]

Of course, not all warders lived up to this ideal. An English prison commissioner, visiting several German penal institutions in 1922, disapproved of the attitude of some warders, whom he described as

> slovenly in dress, frequently in need of razor and clothes-brush, their buttons are rarely bright, their boots bear the mud of yesterday. They do not move briskly, but lean against the wall and smoke in unexpected publicity, are casual in the locking of doors and prone to eat sausage when speaking to their superior.[22]

Nevertheless, most German prison officials did enforce strict discipline, just as their superiors expected. The official guidelines in Prussia reminded warders in 1902 that 'through the punishment, the prisoner should be made to feel his wrongdoing . . .'.[23] There was little room here for the individual treatment of prisoners. As one legal official put it in 1904: 'The prison official is no pedagogue, no teacher; he is . . . an official who, like the soldier during war, has to fulfil the task of inflicting evil on his fellow humans, because the public good demands it.'[24]

Before the First World War, there had already been growing criticism that the contemporary prison service, with its emphasis on deterrence and retribution, completely failed to rehabilitate inmates. Critics associated with the modern school of criminal law pointed to the large number of recidivists. Some criminologists offered more detailed critiques. Gustav Radbruch, who in the early 1920s played an important role as the Social Democrat (SPD) Reich Minister of Justice in drafting new national prison guidelines (together with his subordinate Erwin Bumke, later president of the Supreme Court), argued in 1911 that the rule of silence and solitary confinement crippled the life of inmates and made their resocialisation less likely.[25] Some former inmates also raised their voices, complaining that supposedly reformative measures in practice only caused suffering: solitary confinement was often physically and mentally ruinous, the rule of silence alienated prisoners from human interaction, and the exhausting, monotonous and mindless prison labour left inmates with a general revulsion for all forms of work. The anarchist Sepp Oerter, who had served eight years in the Münster penitentiary around the turn of the century, concluded in his published account of his time behind bars: 'I have the feeling that the treatment in the penitentiary was supposed to wear me out physically, destroy me mentally, and make me morally intolerable for the world'.[26]

The demand for a different approach to prison reform quickly gained momentum after the First World War. This was strengthened by the general extension of welfare policies in the 1920s, the rise of social work and the introduction of new methods into other total institutions such as mental asylums and workhouses. Prison reformers saw their project as being part of what one of them called the 'great pedagogic wave' which swept over Germany at the time.[27] The postwar crime wave also amplified calls for alternative policies. After all, many criminal offenders in the early 1920s were not recidivists, but had previously been law-abiding citizens. Their crimes were greeted with understanding and even sympathy by sections of the general population, who blamed the desperate economic and social crisis for the rise in crime. Such offenders, penal reformers argued, had to be reintegrated into society after their release, with the help of new measures. In addition, the crime wave raised doubts about the deterrent effect of the prison. Even the threat of strict imprisonment, it seemed, was unable to prevent the population from committing more and more crimes.[28]

The changed political realities also played some part. In November 1918, after Emperor Wilhelm II was forced to abdicate, the Social Democrats were in power for the first time in German history. In the following years, the SPD – the largest party until 1932 – remained a key player on the political stage, both at national and regional level. This had some impact on prison policy, as the party was largely sympathetic to the calls for education and prison reform, and explicitly rejected the principle of retribution and the use of brutal disciplinary punishments.[29] But party politics were not all decisive. Prison administrators of different political persuasions shared the view that the old prison had partially failed. While they did not want to abandon it completely, a new start was needed, they felt, to help overcome the deep social, political and moral crisis which appeared to engulf Germany.

The principle of rehabilitation featured prominently in the Weimar prison regulations. On a national level, it was first stressed for young offenders in the Juvenile Court Law (16 February 1923). A few months later, it was enshrined in the national prison guidelines for adult prisoners (*Grundsätze für den Vollzug von Freiheitsstrafen*) of 7 June. These guidelines were not passed by the Reichstag, but by representatives of the individual German states, for the Weimar prison service was still federated. Following unification, from 1871 all the German territories had come under the same criminal code, but prisons continued to be administered by the individual states, according to different regulations. During the Empire, all the various states could agree upon were some very limited, non-binding principles for prison administration, passed in 1897. It was these principles which were replaced in 1923. Even though the new guidelines did not have the force of law, they resulted in far-reaching changes in the administrative regulations of the states, which now resembled each other more closely. Still, the prison service in the 1920s and early 1930s continued to be run by the federated states.

According to the 1923 guidelines, the aim of imprisonment was that 'the prisoners, as far as necessary, should be accustomed to order and work and morally strengthened in such a way that they do not re-offend'. But how was rehabilitation to be achieved? In the first place, the prison officials were instructed to treat inmates in a 'humane' way. Disciplinary punishment regarded as particularly cruel, such as detention in a dark cell, was abolished. And the prewar prison regime based on absolute silence and excessive military discipline was rejected. These changes had been foreshadowed by reforms introduced in the immediate postwar period in several German states, such as Prussia and Thuringia, controlled by the Social Democrats. Still, the 1923 national prison guidelines made few concrete proposals for prisoner rehabilitation. All inmates under the age of 30 were to receive lessons to improve their general knowledge and their vocational skills. And the introduction of the so-called stages system was encouraged in order to aid the inmates' 'moral advancement'. The stages system rewarded individual inmates for their 'progress' by transferring them to a higher stage, where they enjoyed more privileges. This was not an entirely novel suggestion in Germany – there had been some trials since the early nineteenth century, most importantly in the Wittlich prison for juvenile delinquents just before the First World War – but it had failed to gain widespread support at a time when deterrence and the solitary ideal were dominant. This changed in the Weimar Republic. Some German states had already introduced the stages system in the early 1920s, and by 1926 it had been realised in all of them (only inmates with longer sentences, generally one year or more, were eligible for the stages system).[30]

The 'Model Penitentiary'

The emphasis on rehabilitation left some marks on life behind bars in the 1920s. But a lot depended on how the guidelines were implemented, and here there were significant differences between the German states. The most far-reaching proposals were put forward by the Study Group for Prison Reform (*Arbeitsgemeinschaft für Reform des Strafvollzugs*), formed in 1923 by a group of university teachers, prison officials and civil servants. Their political background was pro-republican and they included supporters of the liberal and Catholic parties, as well as Social Democrats and socialists. Beyond that, they were united by their belief in the ideals of the German youth movement and in the new approaches to education pioneered in reform pedagogy before the First World War. Thus, the Study Group demanded that character-building exercises and creative stimulation by inspirational teachers were to take the place of purely mechanical and military forms of discipline. Only by awarding prison inmates more freedom and personal responsibility, it was argued, could they become law-abiding citizens after their release. Key figures in the Study Group included the liberal Professor for Criminal Law in Hamburg, Moritz Liepmann, and Lothar Frede, who had been appointed by the progressive left-wing government in Thuringia in 1922 as head of the prison service, a position he retained even after power shifted to the right two years later. Thuringia soon became one of the centres of prison reform in Germany, as Frede tried to implement many of the policies advanced by the Study Group.[31]

In the 1920s, the Untermaßfeld penitentiary, the second-largest Thuringian penal institution, was often singled out as a 'model' institution. A brief case study of Untermaßfeld will highlight the aims of the Study Group. The most obvious change in this penitentiary in the early 1920s was a change of personnel. The Study Group argued that the reformative prison needed trained educators. Consequently, the Untermaßfeld prison chaplain was removed and replaced by three social workers (one for each of the three stages of the new progressive system), who were subordinated to the new, reform-minded governor.

Life in Untermaßfeld, a penitentiary for men only, was structured around the stages system. On arrival, the inmates (who included a high proportion of particularly violent offenders) were put on stage one, which also contained those demoted from higher stages for disciplinary offences, and those who, in the officials' eyes, had not yet responded to the educational measures. Over one-third of inmates were held on this stage. They spent their spare time in solitude in single cells and did not qualify for any privileges. If they were promoted to stage two, the prisoners acquired greater freedom and responsibility. Stage two was open to most prisoners, even those with lengthy disciplinary records. About half of the inmate population were classed as stage two. Here, school lessons were conducted by the social worker for small groups and the inmates spent some of their spare time unsupervised, playing board games, singing in the choir, playing in the orchestra, listening to the radio or performing plays. Sports were also popular and the inmates sometimes played local teams from outside. The prisoners were actively involved in writing and producing the prison newspaper, a unique innovation in Germany. On stage three, seen as a preparation for life at liberty, inmates were given an even larger degree of autonomy. Their leisure time was unsupervised, their cells were unlocked and had no iron bars. Among the most controversial innovations was the permission granted for prisoners to walk in the woods outside the prison walls, accompanied only by the unarmed governor (and sometimes a social worker).

Life in Untermaßfeld changed in other ways, too, in the 1920s. The Study Group argued that inmates were imprisoned citizens and should be awarded legal status, a demand which had been championed before the First World War by the Frankfurt law professor Berthold Freudenthal, another leading figure in the Study Group. Before the war, inmates were almost entirely subjected to the whims of the prison administration. The few rights awarded on paper, such as the right to complain, were largely worthless in practice. To give some status to the inmates, disciplinary tribunals were set up in Untermaßfeld, consisting of prison officials and inmate representatives (elected by prisoners on stages two and three). True, the final decision about any disciplinary punishment still rested with the governor, but he often appears to have followed the views of the other members of the tribunal. Finally, the Study Group called for modernisation of forced prison labour. Most inmates were employed in their cells, in repetitive and dirty labour, or in workshops with antiquated equipment. The Study Group demanded that this approach should be replaced with measures aimed at helping the largely untrained prisoners to develop skills useful on the labour market after their release. To realise this aim, a limited company was set up in Untermaßfeld, with the governor acting as company director. Modern machines were introduced into agricultural production and into some workshops, supervised by trained craftsmen. Some inmates could now learn a trade.[32]

The reform project in Untermaßfeld was never uncontested. Most importantly, many of the warders violently opposed the policies introduced in the 1920s and wanted to return to the old-style prison service. Almost overnight, they were expected to treat prisoners no longer as obedient subjects but as individuals with specific educational needs, a task for which they had no training, sympathy or aptitude. A number of warders tried for years to derail the reform project. In 1928, the most vocal Untermaßfeld warder openly stated their opposition in a letter to the Thuringian Ministry of Justice, demanding that the military virtues of 'drill, order and discipline' should take precedence.[33] The warders had already displayed their contempt several years earlier, when almost all of them boycotted new courses on the reformative prison service; instead, they had attended a course in Japanese wrestling techniques, making clear where their priorities lay. The warders felt threatened by the change in the prisoners' status and resented being held accountable in prison tribunals. Also, the reforms increased their workload. Under the old system, prisoners could be treated literally by the rulebook. But individualisation was labour-intensive and the warders – who were poorly paid and already overworked – were now expected to take on many further duties. Finally, the experienced warders deeply resented the influence of the newly employed social workers, who were often half their age and fresh out of university. The Thuringian branch of the Association of Prison Warders insisted in 1925 that the battle-scarred warders had more to offer than the naïve social workers: 'knowledge gained from experience alone is decisive for the practice of the prison service'.[34] The warders even complained that Lothar Frede, who was in his early thirties when he took over the Thuringian prison administration, was too inexperienced for his job. But Frede and the senior officials in Untermaßfeld insisted on the implementation of the new policies and, by the late 1920s, had won over at least some of the warders.

What should one make of the reforms in Untermaßfeld? For many years, the history of the prison was written as a success story, progressing inevitably from primitive cruelty to enlightened benevolence. But this narrative has since been effectively challenged, and the revisionist critique has to be taken into account when evaluating the reforms in Untermaßfeld in the 1920s.[35] Certainly, the Untermaßfeld reforms should not be depicted as an unmitigated triumph of humane policies. Disciplinary punishment often remained strict and the general living conditions were poor (see below). Nevertheless, the impact of the reforms was significant. In a number of ways, the new policies contained the seeds of the German prison today. This is obvious in the shift from religious instruction, so prominent in prisons in the nineteenth century, to social work. The roots of the contemporary prison are also evident in the strengthening of the status of prison inmates, the measures designed to help prisoners learn practical skills, and the introduction of more individual freedom at the expense of strict military discipline. Clearly, the policies of the Study Group and the reality of life in the Untermaßfeld penitentiary were part of what Detlev Peukert characterised as the era of 'classical modernity', when modern ideas in social policy were first devised and partially implemented.[36] But, as we shall see, the Untermaßfeld experience was not typical of imprisonment in Germany as a whole.

Reluctant Reformers

The policies introduced in Untermaßfeld were matched in only a few other states, such as Saxony and Hamburg, where the prison administration was also in the hands of progressive officials. But in most German penal institutions, life was transformed slowly. In some states, such as reactionary Bavaria, the prison administrators themselves had remained sceptical about many of the new proposals. Instead, the Bavarian prison administration put considerable emphasis on traditional methods of 'reform' such as religious instruction. As early as April 1921, the Bavarian Ministry of Justice urged prison governors to use every opportunity to 'sprinkle the good seeds of religion and a moral education into the hearts of the prisoners . . .'.[37] In some other German states the prison administration was more open to change but faced considerable administrative problems. The senior ministerial officials in Prussia, still controlled by the Social Democrats, eventually showed themselves willing in the late 1920s to experiment with more innovative policies, such as the 'half-open' principle, which would have allowed selected prisoners to take up jobs outside the prison. But in practice this shift in prison policy had a limited impact, not least because the reforms in Prussia were held back by the sheer size of the prison system: in 1927 there were over 1,000 penal institutions in Prussia (including 37 holding more than 500 inmates), compared to only 69 in Thuringia. And these Prussian institutions were not even controlled directly by the Ministry of Justice, as in other German states, but by 13 regional prison service offices (*Strafvollzugsämter*), set up in different districts in 1923 (and dissolved again under the Nazis).[38]

In fact, the Untermaßfeld experience was not even altogether typical of Thuringia in the 1920s. While the Untermaßfeld governor was busy implementing the ideals of the Study Group – even noting down the birthday of inmates so that he could personally congratulate them – his colleague in Ichtershausen, the largest prison in Thuringia, pursued a quite different line. The prison was led by an official of the old school, the former police and army officer Max Vollrath. Of course, Vollrath implemented various prison reforms; given the instructions by his superiors, he had little choice. But life in Ichtershausen was very much shaped by his army experience and his disciplinarian beliefs. A right-wing *völkisch* nationalist and open anti-Semite, Vollrath despised some of the social workers and he frequently addressed the inmates as scoundrels, bums, arseholes or worse. On one occasion, he lectured the prisoners: 'You swine, if you didn't wank so much, you wouldn't be so cold.' Vollrath also handed out significantly harsher disciplinary punishments than his colleague in Untermaßfeld, even though inmates in prisons were supposed to be treated less strictly than those in penitentiaries.[39]

In contrast to institutions like Untermaßfeld, there was no shake-up among the local prison officials in most German states. Limited attempts were made to train prison warders and only a few reform-minded officials were employed as governors and social workers. In 1927, Thuringia, Saxony and Hamburg held some 12 per cent of all German prisoners but employed 55 of the 58 social workers in penal institutions. Prussia, by contrast, held well over half of all the prisoners but only engaged one part-time social worker. On the whole, the German prison service still relied on teachers and prison chaplains to 'reform' the inmates. In 1927, there were 864 state-employed chaplains (125 of them full-time) and 150 teachers (122 of them full-time) working in all the penal institutions.[40]

Prison life remained largely in the hands of officials subscribing to a more traditional understanding of crime and imprisonment. Most German prison governors were strict and autocratic disciplinarians, emphasising the importance of deterrence and retribution – concepts which had been central during their study of law (many of the prison governors were law graduates; others were trained doctors or chaplains). The appointment of governors was supposedly guided by Karl Krohne's dictum that 'a good prison governor is not trained or taught, but found'.[41] In reality, this phrase served as an excuse for the employment of many men with poor degrees and few qualities. For the prison administration could not afford to be very choosy, due to the low social status of a career as a prison official. Many governors compensated for the lack of social standing on the outside by demanding complete subservience on the inside. Once appointed, they wielded almost total power, dominating practically every aspect of the prisoners' and the other officials' lives. They clearly enjoyed their power and a number of them felt, in the words of one official, like a 'little king'.[42]

Many governors had served as officers in the army, often in the First World War, and used this as their model. The infatuation with all things military was taken to the extreme by Franz Kohl, governor of the Straubing penitentiary, who was famous for wearing an imaginary uniform complete with a general's shoulder straps.[43] The governors ensured that the military atmosphere behind bars was preserved in the 1920s. In most penal institutions inmates still had to stand to attention and take off their caps when they met the warders and other officials. Military discipline extended not only to prisoners, but also to prison officials. It was not unusual for warders to salute the governor, who often left them little room for their own initiative. One governor typically liked to remind his subordinates that 'no nail is put into the wall without my prior written consent'.[44]

Not surprisingly, the governors were rather critical of the immediate postwar prison reforms and the national prison guidelines of 1923. Most governors unsuccessfully opposed the permanent abolition of the harshest available disciplinary punishments (in particular detention in a dark cell). They also often supported the dishonourable custom of shaving the penitentiary inmates' hair and beards – a ritual which many prisoners experienced as particularly humiliating – which was eventually restricted in the 1923 national prison guidelines.[45] Some governors even publicly mocked the ideals of the Study Group. In a speech at the 1927 conference of the Association of German Prison Officials, the Remscheid-Lüttringhausen governor Pollitz warned his colleagues about the current 'exaggeration of the pedagogical point of view', which he caricatured as the demand to give prisoners a spoonful of 'betterment' every couple of hours. Pollitz added, 'We can't go into the cell and say: "Come here, now you will be educated, now I will reform you".'[46]

Any acknowledgement by the governors of the need for radical reform would have amounted to an admission of the bankruptcy of the prison system they had supported for most of their professional lives. Contrary to what Detlev Peukert implied in his work, 'pedagogical dreams of omnipotence' were apparently only dreamt of by a small minority of Weimar officials. While many governors occasionally used progressive language, they still clung to the traditional prison regime based on military discipline. Curt Bondy, one of the leading members of the Study Group, highlighted this practice with unusual candour at a meeting of the Association of German Prison Officials in 1930:

> We speak completely openly today and you won't blame me for saying: you have taken over our terminology, namely the terminology of psychology. If someone speaks of love and comradeship and self-education, then this is understood by the different generations in a completely different way . . .

There was a 'very marked gap', Bondy concluded, between 'the old and the new direction'.[47]

The same gap existed between the aims of the few social workers in penal institutions and many of the experienced prison teachers. To start with, the total amount of schooling for prisoners was still strictly limited: on average, Prussian penitentiary inmates in 1927 spent only about twice as much time in classes as in detention cells for disciplinary offences. And the education they did receive often had little practical value, failing to address their needs as the inmates themselves perceived them. Prisoners repeatedly declared that they wanted to learn practical skills such as writing and accounting, as this might boost their prospects of employment on the outside. But a number of teachers were sceptical about the possibility of teaching adults such basic skills. Ignoring the fact that most inmates had received only very rudimentary schooling, one prison teacher dismissively remarked that 'anyone who has failed to learn multiplication tables, the basics of arithmetic and spelling in ten years as a child, will not learn it as an adult either'. Instead of practical skills, many teachers believed that they should implant discipline, religious devotion and nationalism in the prisoners.[48]

Many prison chaplains, too, clung on to these traditional goals of prison policy. Generally employed by the state and not the church, they reacted critically to aspects of the prison reforms advanced in the 1920s, arguing that the new policies did not force prisoners to confront their moral failings and guilt. In addition, the chaplains were clearly concerned that social workers would eventually edge them out of the penal institutions – just as traditional religious welfare organisations in the Weimar Republic at large feared that their moral and religious conception of charity was being pushed aside by the secular welfare state. The chaplains pointed to several warning signs: Thuringia had already removed all prison chaplains employed by the state, Hamburg had initiated a similar policy, and the SPD and the Communists repeatedly demanded the restriction of their role elsewhere.[49]

Most German prison warders, just like their colleagues in Untermaßfeld, also had little time for new policies aimed at prisoner rehabilitation. Instead, warders often continued to enforce strict military order, as they had done for many years. Many Weimar warders had started out in the Empire. For example, the average age of the 20 most senior warders working in the Ichtershausen prison in 1927 was 50 years, and they had been employed in the prison service for more than 20 years. A number of warders treated inmates differently after the war, but most, it seems, continued to put their trust in the old-style prison.[50] The attitude of the German prison warders proved a constant source of frustration for the Study Group for Prison Reform. The reformers' misgivings were summed up in the liberal *Vossische Zeitung* in 1929, which concluded that:

> there won't be a modern prison service in Prussia as long as 50- and 60-year-old officials in gendarme uniforms with a sabre at their side understand the realisation of the modern prison service as nothing more than the strictest maintenance of a 'discipline', which has a damnable likeness to purely military discipline.[51]

The warders' criticism of progressive prison policies was most forceful in institutions such as Untermaßfeld, which had actually introduced extensive reforms. But any such opposition from local prison officials did not mean that life in penal institutions remained unchanged.

Life Inside

Conditions in penal institutions improved from the mid-1920s. In part, this was not the result of prison policy, but of a temporary improvement in the economic climate. Criminal convictions, in particular for property crime, declined after the introduction of the new *Rentenmark* in November 1923, which stabilised the currency and put an end to the hyper-inflation. In some areas, crime rates fell very quickly. In Hamburg, for example, the number of thefts reported to the police fell by more than half in only one year, from 58,379 (1923) to 28,625 (1924). Also, sentencing by German courts became somewhat less strict in the second half of the 1920s.[52] As a result, total prisoner numbers in Germany fell drastically. The average daily number of inmates probably halved in the space of just four years, plummeting from around 110,000 in 1924 to around 54,000 in 1928 (see Figure 1, pp. 392–3). This resulted in better living standards inside. Less space was needed for the imprisonment of offenders and many dilapidated prisons, penitentiaries and above all small jails were closed down.[53] Fewer inmates meant that more resources could be distributed among the remaining prisoners. In addition, some states increased the yearly subsidies for penal institutions. Buildings were improved and inmates received better provisions. While meat had often been absent from the diet in many penal institutions in the early 1920s, inmates now received several small portions per week. All these developments contributed to an improvement in the general health of inmates and a decline in the death rate.[54]

But despite all of this, living conditions were still often poor. Much depended on the condition of the individual institution, especially its age, a factor which was in many ways as important as the outlook of the local prison officials. For example, cells in the Straubing penitentiary, built at the turn of the century, boasted water toilets, central heating and electric lights.[55] Consequently, the inmates in Straubing, situated deep in reactionary Bavaria, enjoyed significantly better general conditions than prisoners in the 'model' penitentiary in Untermaßfeld. Originally a medieval castle, Untermaßfeld was rebuilt after 1813 as a penal institution. By the mid-1920s, some parts of the building were in ruins. Four out of five cells had neither artificial light nor proper heating. Prisoners often could not wash in the mornings as the water in their wash bowls had turned to ice. To keep warm, they went to bed fully clothed immediately after the lock-in. As in most other German penal institutions, the inmates had to use worn-out buckets as toilets and the characteristic smell of the institution was that of urine and excrement.[56] Some of the older penal institutions were renovated in the 1920s, when central heating and sanitary improvement were introduced, but others continued to be without running water, a sewage system, adequate heating or electric light.

Among the most important changes for offenders serving longer sentences in the 1920s was the new stages system. Those prisoners who did reach stage two, maybe about half of all those who were eligible, now enjoyed previously unknown privileges, which were largely determined by the state prison administration, not the local officials. The privileges could include extra rations and permission to talk at certain times, as well as some sports activities, theatre and music, as in Untermaßfeld. But not all prisoners welcomed the stages system. In Bavaria, for example, its introduction meant that most inmates were initially worse off than they had been before. Placed on the lowest stage, they were now excluded from virtually all privileges. Bavarian penitentiary inmates on this stage were not allowed to buy extra rations, were banned from speaking with each other and could only receive one visit of 15 minutes every three months. All this was very much in line with the broader aims of the Bavarian prison administration, which had seen the stages system all along as a way of making conditions harsher for many inmates.[57] The creation of a formal hierarchy also caused tensions among the inmates. While inmates elevated to the higher stages appreciated their privileges, prisoners stuck on the lowest stage were jealous and resentful.[58]

Local prison officials generally adjusted to the stages system. True, many opposed certain privileges in the system, assuming that they made imprisonment too soft and pampered the inmates. Other officials resented the added work they caused. One inmate recalled that warders 'groaned when they had to turn off the light at six cells one hour later'.[59] At the same time, though, the governors saw that the stages system could accommodate their disciplinarian views, as even those inmates later promoted first had to spend a mandatory period under the harsh conditions of stage one. Upgrading an inmate to a higher stage as a reward for good behaviour, together with the threat of demotion for breaking the rules, also functioned as highly effective disciplining tools. Finally, the local officials were pleased that the pedagogical thrust of the progressive stages system as envisaged by the Study Group was largely ignored. Only a few penal institutions introduced elements of prisoner autonomy, prisoner representatives or prison tribunals, and none followed the Thuringian example of co-opting prisoners for these tribunals.[60]

Overall, despite some important changes, the structure of the German prison system was not radically transformed in the 1920s. There was a significant degree of continuity with the prewar years, personified by the local prison officials themselves. These officials were critical of individual aspects of Weimar prison policy, such as some of the privileges granted by the stage system, and they remained sceptical about claims that a new approach could rehabilitate the inmates. Instead, they largely continued to believe in the traditional prison regime. In the last years of the Weimar Republic, this attitude would lead a number of prison officials to call for a more authoritarian prison policy, a demand which was shared by the rising Nazi movement. But in the second half of the 1920s, such open and sustained opposition was still limited to states such as Thuringia and Hamburg which had actually introduced more extensive changes.

The Prison and the Public

The Weimar penal system became a central focus for politicians and journalists. There had already been some public interest in the prison in the nineteenth and early twentieth centuries. For example, there had been protests by the working-class movement during the Empire about the treatment of journalists and politicians, sentenced under the Socialist Law (1878–90) or for offences such as lese-majesty or blasphemy.[61] But the prison had never been an important topic and largely remained hidden from the public eye. With the German revolution at the end of the First World War, this changed.

German penal institutions were in the thick of the revolution. The initial trigger for the revolution had been the suicidal plan by the German navy to fight one last-ditch battle with the British. Some crews, unwilling to sacrifice themselves, mutinied. In early November 1918, protests spread to more and more soldiers and civilians and in a matter of days engulfed much of Germany. Tens of thousands took to the streets and so-called workers' and soldiers' councils were set up all over the country. Penal institutions were one of the targets for the revolutionary masses. It is well known that the French and the Russian revolutions were accompanied by raids on state prisons, symbols of the repressive power of the old regime. In this respect, the German revolution was no exception. Starting in early November 1918, numerous prisons and penitentiaries throughout Germany were attacked. Many were targeted during the night by agitated crowds led by armed soldiers. The immediate aim of the revolutionaries was the release of selected inmates, such as army prisoners and political prisoners. However, in the frenzied atmosphere of the raids, many more escaped. In some judicial districts, half of all the inmates were freed. But the revolutionaries were not completely indiscriminate, and prisoners held for particularly violent crimes were often left inside. The raids were accompanied by the looting of bread and other goods and the symbolic destruction of prison property, such as the weapons of the warders. Still, many raids passed without excessive violence. Prison governors recognised that it would not be possible to defend the institutions and cooperated with the representatives of the workers' and soldiers' councils in freeing the prisoners. In turn, the revolutionaries often tried to be on their best behaviour. In one case, several hundred soldiers gained entry to a prison after first politely ringing the doorbell – reminiscent of Lenin's barbed comment that German revolutionaries first bought a platform ticket before they dared to occupy a station.[62] In the wake of these attacks, some governors pleaded for greater police and military protection, as well as more weapons. The Straubing governor asked the Bavarian Ministry of Justice in January 1919 for hand grenades, signal flares, gas bombs, rifles, bayonets and 10,000 rounds of ammunition. Most of his demands were fulfilled.[63]

Politics and the Prison

The prison remained a political symbol in the following months and years, above all because of the escalation of political violence and the blatant political bias of the German judiciary. The first years of the Weimar Republic were marked by extreme political unrest. From the start, many Germans refused to accept the legitimacy of the new order. Socialists and Communists attacked the state from the left, claiming that it had betrayed the true aims of the revolution. Extreme nationalists and supporters of the far right also fought the hated democracy, not least for signing the despised Treaty of Versailles. Determined activists and paramilitary forces took matters into their own hands. The experience of the First World War and the revolution had transformed political culture: violence was now accepted as a political tool, and Germany experienced a wave of unrest, uprisings and assassinations between 1919 and 1923. In short, a new 'paradigm of violence' was established, which further added to the general sense of dislocation and crisis.[64]

The legal system was ultimately responsible for dealing with the perpetrators of political disorder and violence. But many German judges were anything but impartial. Authoritarian, nationalist and largely opposed to the new democratic regime, they had some political sympathy for the radical right-wing activists who attacked the republic. Often, these counter-revolutionaries were let off very lightly, even for brutal violence and murder. In contrast, the judges cracked down with extreme vigour on radical left-wingers, triggering heated protests in the press, parliament and on the streets against what Communists and socialists called 'class justice'. But the judges were not deterred and German penal institutions in the early 1920s filled up with left-wing radicals who often faced very long sentences under poor conditions.[65] The biased treatment of political offenders often extended from the court room to prisons and penitentiaries.

Counter-revolutionaries sentenced to imprisonment frequently enjoyed lenient treatment. Their imprisonment was often short, and served in rather cosy conditions. One of these radical right-wing activists was Adolf Hitler. His first taste of the Weimar prison system came in 1922, when he was sentenced to three months in prison for the violent disruption of a meeting by one of the Nazis' political rivals. On 24 June 1922, he started his sentence in Munich's Stadelheim prison. Hitler, at that time still little more than a local beerhall agitator, was handled with kid gloves by the prison staff. The deputy governor of Stadelheim, who had only recently heard one of Hitler's speeches, was eager to ensure that Hitler was comfortable. Instead of the standard tiny cell, he was housed in a spacious former sick-room with two large windows. He was allowed to conduct his party business freely, writing and receiving many letters and meeting with his supporters. He was released on 27 July 1922, with two months of his sentence suspended against good behaviour in the future.[66]

Hitler was back behind bars the following year, arrested in the wake of the disastrous failure of the Nazi putsch in Munich on 8–9 November 1923. Together with his accomplices, he was tried in February and March 1924, by the same nationalist judge who had sentenced him back in 1922. Hitler was allowed to turn the trial into a propaganda show for the Nazis and his subsequent punishment, only five years' imprisonment for high treason, flew in the face of all legal standards. This time, he did not even have to serve his sentence in a regular prison or penitentiary. Instead, he was sentenced to imprisonment in a fortress (*Festungshaft*), an 'honourable' form of detention which was handed out extremely rarely by judges, restricted to a few individuals guilty of duelling or certain political offences. In most cases, life in a fortress had little to do with imprisonment and actually resembled house arrest. According to the regulations, inmates could keep their own clothes and many of their belongings. They could even have their own catering, including wine and beer. The inmates were more or less free to do what they wanted, as the rooms were generally unlocked and there was no obligation to work (they did not even have to clean their own rooms). They could also receive as many visitors from the outside as they pleased. Hitler was taken to the Landsberg am Lech fortress, where he held court in a comfortable and spacious room with panoramic views, dictating parts of *Mein Kampf* to fellow inmate Rudolf Heß. Hitler was treated with great sympathy by the prison staff, who bent over backwards to make his time as pleasant as possible. As it happened, he did not have much time to sample the comforts of Landsberg. Thanks to the Bavarian judiciary, he was granted parole in late 1924, even though he still had almost four years of his sentence left to serve. This decision had been influenced by the enthusiastic reports of the Landsberg governor about Hitler's supposedly exemplary conduct. He was released on 20 December 1924, seen off by his congenial jailers.[67]

It was not just prominent radical right-wing prisoners like Hitler who received special consideration. Rank-and-file militants on the right could also expect favours. One of them was Rudolf Höß, later the first commandant of Auschwitz. In March 1924, Höß, at the time a follower of the extreme right-wing Freikorps leader, Gerhard Roßbach, received a 10-year penitentiary sentence for his participation in the vicious killing of a suspected Communist informer (Martin Bormann had also been involved in the killing). Höß was committed to the Brandenburg penitentiary on 9 April 1924 as a 'delinquent motivated by conviction' – a provision introduced in the national prison guidelines of 1923 which stipulated that offenders whose main motive had been moral, religious or political qualified for special privileges inside. Höß also benefited from the political bias of some of the local prison officials. According to his own account, he was the first inmate in the Brandenburg penitentiary to be promoted to stage three of the progressive system. The light in his cell was kept on until 10 p.m., he was allowed to write a letter every two weeks and was given an easy job in the administration of the institution. Unlike other inmates, Höß also received visits from individuals not related to him, including Gerhard Roßbach himself. And while other prisoners (even on stage three) were only sometimes allowed to accept one small box of presents at Christmas, Höß received lavish gifts including sausages, butter, cheese and sweets, not just for Christmas, but also on his birthday and his name-day. Contrary to prison regulations, he was even allowed to subscribe to radical right-wing publications. After an amnesty was passed in the Reichstag with support from the radical left and right on 14 July 1928, Höß was released, more than five years before the official end of his sentence.[68]

While local prison officials often indulged radical right-wing militants, most of them had little time for left-wing activists. They had already felt contempt for the left before the war. Most governors were nationalist, authoritarian and monarchist, and like other members of the German middle class they harboured a deep distrust of the working class and its political organisations. Prison chaplains, too, were largely national-conservatives, offended not only by the political views of the left but also by its atheism. And prison teachers had traditionally seen themselves as guardians of nationalism and the monarchy against political subversion.[69] The postwar experiences intensified the loathing many local prison officials felt for the left. Not only did they oppose the political aims of the revolution, but they were directly affected by it, with prison raids bringing chaos and confusion to their strictly regimented institutions. There was a widespread conviction on the German right that the revolutionaries, often labelled 'November criminals', were traitors who had broken the law. Indeed, many local officials saw little difference between common criminals and revolutionaries. Distinctions between these two groups had already become blurred on the German right in the nineteenth century, with the right-wing press claiming, after the 1848 revolution as well as in subsequent political upheavals, that there was a close link between criminality and revolution. This view was reinforced by the events of 1918–19. Franz Kohl, the Straubing governor and respected member of the executive of the Association of German Prison Officials, spoke for many of his colleagues when he warned that Communists welcomed the liberation of thieves, rapists and murderers, because they would be useful to the revolution. In 1919, Kohl left no doubt about what should be done with Communist revolutionaries: 'These hyenas need to be locked up behind bars and in cages.'[70] Even after the end of the Weimar revolutionary crisis, many observers continued to posit a close connection between Communists and criminality, pointing, for example, to the supposedly high crime rates in Communist neighbourhoods and to the alleged Communist sympathies among criminal gangs.[71] Another manifestation of this trend was the way in which left-wing revolutionaries were classified by prison officials and leading psychiatrists as 'inferiors' and 'psychopaths,' labels previously reserved for common criminals (see below).[72]

Left-wing prisoners were embittered by the leniency shown to the radical right, which stood in such contrast to their own treatment. Not only did left-wing prisoners often receive very lengthy sentences, but the judges generally denied them the special status of 'delinquents motivated by conviction'. On 1 July 1927, only a total of 111 inmates in all German penal institutions were classified in this way.[73] The left-wing radicals were incensed further by the heavy-handed approach of many local prison officials. Often, especially in the early 1920s, the frustration of the inmates erupted. Hunger strikes and other disturbances were common. Officials in 15 larger German penal institutions claimed to have witnessed no fewer than 51 riots and serious attacks on warders between 1919 and 1924. Many inmates, political prisoners and others, were severely injured or killed during such incidents. Thousands more were sentenced by the courts to further terms of imprisonment for rioting.[74] These tensions inside penal institutions were intensified by the very poor living conditions. For instance, on 28 March 1920 most of the inmates of the Brandenburg (Berlin) penitentiary escaped. Several were shot dead during the escape and almost all others were quickly recaptured. Asked about his motives for escaping, one prisoner replied: 'The food was appalling. For weeks, we got no potatoes and the fish which was dished up all the time stank seven miles up wind.'[75]

Prisoners and the Public Sphere

Nevertheless, left-wing radicals often received better treatment than many other prisoners, despite the political bias of most judges, governors and warders. To a large extent, this was due to the pressure put on the prison service from the outside. Campaigns in the left-wing press often focused on the treatment of prominent political activists. One of them was Felix Fechenbach, the former private secretary of the left-wing revolutionary Kurt Eisner, Bavarian Minister President until his assassination by a right-wing fanatic in February 1919. Fechenbach himself had been arrested during the counter-revolution in Bavaria, and in a farcical trial in 1922 was sentenced for treason to 11 years in a penitentiary. He served his sentence, until his early release in December 1924, in the Ebrach penitentiary in Bavaria. The left-wing papers were full of the 'Fechenbach case', with headlines such as 'Fechenbach under torture', and his fate was also raised in the Reichstag. In his prison memoirs, published in 1925, Fechenbach later recalled that this public pressure had brought him benefits:

he was quickly moved to stage two and later stage three, with all the extra privileges this entailed. In addition, he received more letters than other prisoners, got a regular newspaper and was treated better than previously by the governor.[76]

Individual *causes célèbres* were also taken up by left-wing pressure groups. Among the most influential was the German League for Human Rights (Deutsche Liga für Menschenrechte) which included many prominent lawyers, journalists and artists. The League was the leading opposition group to the death penalty in the Weimar Republic and also campaigned for better conditions in penal institutions. In 1927, the League's General Secretary, Kurt Großmann declared that 'the prison service today is still barbaric and unworthy of a republic'. The League was involved in several high-profile campaigns which aimed to highlight the fate of individual prisoners, including the pacifist publicist Carl von Ossietzky.[77]

The left-wing press, above all the Communist papers, also ceaselessly criticised the conditions of imprisonment of less prominent political prisoners, especially in the period of revolutionary unrest in the early 1920s. Just as the extreme left-wing (and right-wing) parties in the Weimar Republic shamelessly exploited trials for their own political ends – with a dedicated team of lawyers determined to use every trick to dramatise the proceedings – so, too, did they instrumentalise the imprisoned activists.[78] The hunger strikes and riots by political prisoners in the early years of the Weimar Republic were eagerly seized upon by the radical left. The main motivation was not concern for the prisoners, but the desire to destabilise the Weimar Republic further. Sensationalised reports appeared in the Communist press and became the basis for extremely heated exchanges in parliament.

Often, the Communists grossly exaggerated the suffering of the prisoners. For example, when 120 prisoners convicted for their part in a left-wing uprising in central Germany in March 1921 went on hunger strike in the Lichtenburg penitentiary on 12 November 1921, their cause was immediately taken up by the radical left. The Communist paper *Rote Fahne* (Red Flag) screamed about the 'horrific pangs of death' suffered by the Lichtenburg prisoners, and Communist Party (KPD) deputies in the Reichstag painted an apocalyptic picture of their agony. In reality, as a commission of Reichstag deputies established during a visit to Lichtenburg, the state of health of the inmates had been painted in colours far blacker than reality. According to an SPD commission member, the only people apparently suffering from hunger-induced hallucinations were not the inmates but the Communist journalists of the *Rote Fahne*. This case was no anomaly. In the early 1920s, similar incidents occurred in other penal institutions, with the Communists repeatedly attacking the treatment of political prisoners.[79] Communist deputies in federated diets and the Reichstag often visited inmates, with one functionary making some 35 visits in the space of only nine months. There was also a large and well-organised pressure group for Communist prisoners, part of the KPD welfare organisation Rote Hilfe (Red Help). Set up in 1921, Rote Hilfe claimed a membership of 285,000 ten years later and owned several publishing houses, which printed various books attacking the supposed barbarism and torture inside penal institutions.[80]

Political controversy about conditions in prisons and penitentiaries became somewhat less heated in the second half of the 1920s. Against the odds, the young republic survived the first years of crisis and entered a brief period of comparative stability from 1924. Most parties, save the Communists, seemed to share at least some common ground about the general direction of the prison service, even though there were clear party-political differences: right-wing nationalists repeatedly stressed the continued importance of retribution, while some SPD deputies demanded the further extension of the educational principle.[81] Still, criticism by most politicians was largely confined to individual instances of incompetence or maltreatment.[82]

But imprisonment remained very much in the public eye, not least because several left-wing prisoners, who had been committed during the early years of crisis, were now released and promptly published books about their experiences. Prison memoirs seem to have been a rather popular genre in the nineteenth century, and there are numerous accounts by ex-convicts covering the German Empire. But never before had there been such a rush of publications as in the second half of the 1920s. Generally, these memoirs painted a bleak picture of life inside. While they often acknowledged that at least some officials had behaved humanely and fairly, and that political prisoners had sometimes got favourable treatment, the accounts generally attacked the mindless military discipline, strict punishment, monotonous labour and poor hygienic conditions. Felix Fechenbach, for example, described the 'suffering, life-draining and degradation' experienced by common criminals in the penitentiary.[83] Fechenbach, like other well-known left-wing activists with personal experience of imprisonment (such as Ernst Toller, Erich Mühsam and Erich Zeigner), also described his experiences in detail at the public meetings of the German League for Human Rights.

Another influential account by a former prisoner was that of Max Hoelz, published in 1929. A maverick on the edges of the Communist movement, Hoelz had became a *bête noire* of the bourgeoisie and a celebrated working-class hero as military leader of the March 1921 uprising in central Germany. The uprising was quickly and brutally put down and Hoelz was sentenced in June 1921 to life imprisonment in a penitentiary. During his imprisonment, his case was taken up by the famous journalist Egon Erwin Kisch, and Hoelz also received public support from prominent figures such as Bertolt Brecht, Martin Buber, Otto Dix and Albert Einstein.[84] After his release in July 1928, Hoelz wrote a colourful and highly polemical memoir of his time behind bars and his constant run-ins with the authorities. On virtually every single page, Hoelz attacked the 'revolting' food, the 'appalling' smells, the 'terrible' hygienic conditions, or the mental and physical cruelty of the prison officials, which had driven him, by his count, to several hunger strikes and one suicide attempt.[85]

One of the most controversial works on prison life was written by Karl Plättner, who had also participated in the March 1921 uprising. Unlike Hoelz, he had managed to evade the police and subsequently led numerous organised 'expropriation raids' on banks and the like, apparently in the expectation that this would further the revolution. Plättner was finally arrested in February 1922 and sentenced in late 1923 to ten years' imprisonment in a penitentiary. Released on 17 July 1928 (under the same amnesty which set free Rudolf Höß and Max Hoelz), Plättner published *Eros in the Penitentiary* in 1929, drawing on his own experiences, as well as on medical literature. Plättner graphically detailed the physical and mental effects of a life of enforced celibacy, as well as compensatory sexual acts in prison, ranging from various forms of masturbation, homosexual sex and exhibitionism, to sodomising animals. As a solution, Plättner demanded the 'right of natural intercourse' by allowing visits from the outside and the abolition of the gender separation in German penal institutions. Plättner's book was an instant popular success; the first edition of 15,000 was sold within one year.[86] It was quickly at the centre of a heated public debate. The problems that imprisonment caused for the prisoners' sexuality, which were also debated at the time in relation to inmates in reformatories, lent themselves to highly sensationalist and titillating treatment and at times threatened to overshadow all other issues relating to prison life.[87]

Autobiographical accounts by former political prisoners were accompanied by books written by journalists and social workers sympathetic to the demands for better living conditions.[88] The boom of factual accounts in the second half of the 1920s also inspired a number of novels that included attacks on the legal system and the poor conditions in penal institutions.[89] Such criticism was not confined to the written word. Several films critical of imprisonment were released as well. In the late 1920s, German theatres also put on plays attacking the prison service. This was part of a wider trend which saw the production of real-life dramas, often based on fact, which highlighted contemporary social problems.[90] Great controversy was caused in January 1930 by the performance of *Amnestie* in Berlin, written by none other than Karl Maria Finkelnburg, the president of the Berlin district prison administration. Finkelnburg, who was soon to retire, was an exception among the senior Prussian prison officials. A very experienced former governor and administrator (Finkelnburg had been appointed in 1913 as head of the Prussian prison service in the Interior Ministry, succeeding Karl Krohne), he was a founding member of the Study Group for Prison Reform.[91] Finkelnburg developed a reputation for taking prisoners and their complaints seriously, and, unusual for a man in his position, repeatedly took the side of the prisoners against local governors or warders. He made no secret of his convictions. 'The more I considered the individuality [of the prisoners],' Finkelnburg explained in the press, 'the more humane my thinking became in the majority of cases.'[92] In his play *Amnestie*, the penal system was portrayed as corrupting the inmates, rather than reforming them, and was personified as a narrow-minded and disciplinarian prison governor who opposes any attempts to rehabilitate inmates as 'nonsense'. The play received a standing ovation and the reaction in the left-wing press was enthusiastic. The SPD paper *Vorwärts* reported that there was 'hardly anyone among the 2,000 visitors at the Volksbühne who had not been shocked to the very core'.[93]

Criticism of the fate of prisoners featured time and again in newspapers, books, plays and films. All this pressure, part of the wider criticism of the Weimar judiciary by the left, was ultimately aimed at forcing prison officials to improve conditions. It certainly had some impact. When considering an application or a request by a prisoner, the officials had to bear in mind that a negative decision might lead to public protest or a legal challenge. The main beneficiaries of this were the political prisoners, who could rely on the greatest support from the outside – much to the annoyance of some of the other prisoners, who also demanded better treatment.[94] Political prisoners often fared better and were over-represented in the higher stages of the system.[95] The left-wing pressure groups were well aware of their influence. According to Rote Hilfe officials, 'it is our experience that a political prisoner who receives a letter from a deputy and gets advice for his complaints or legal affairs is treated completely differently by the top local prison officials than if he only has private postal contact with his relatives'. Of 119 petitions sent to the prison administrations between November 1930 and October 1931, half were classified by the Rote Hilfe as a success.[96]

But this influence of the public sphere left a dangerous legacy. For persistent outside scrutiny and criticism of life behind bars caused great anger among local officials, further alienating them from the Weimar prison. Many felt maligned, victimised and constantly under attack. Following accusations in the press or in books, these officials were often forced to explain themselves to their superiors. The officials deeply resented this and protested against the 'invented or exaggerated' accounts of their critics. According to Max Hoelz, the governor in the Groß-Strehlitz penitentiary 'went completely berserk' as soon as anyone as much as mentioned the League for Human Rights.[97]

The anger of the local prison officials focused above all on prisoner complaints. In the Imperial period, senior prison administrators had generally dismissed those complaints that were passed on by the governors. Not only were such formal prisoner complaints often ignored, they could even result in punishment. As one official explained in 1914: if somebody puts 'filthy' or 'slanderous' remarks into a complaint, 'he will naturally be severely punished'.[98] But in the Weimar Republic, complaints were dealt with more conscientiously by senior civil servants, mindful of potential criticism in the press and parliament. Local officials saw the growing willingness of their superiors to approve inmate demands and complaints as seriously undermining their position and claimed that they were being victimised by the prisoners. In reality, such claims were wildly exaggerated. There was a relative increase of prisoner complaints in this period, as more and more inmates believed that it was worth raising their voices in protest. But this increase was nowhere near as large as some of the officials claimed. For example, the leading prison administrator in the Breslau district (Prussia) publicly alleged that there had been up to 6,000 prisoner complaints per year in his district, when the statistics showed the real figure to be about a tenth of that.[99] And local prison officials still had enormous power over the inmates. In some institutions, complaints were not passed on, or inmates were not given enough paper to write their complaint. Other officials certified inmates as 'feeble minded', 'psychopaths' or 'alcoholics' to discredit them or deprive them of their right to complain. Also, inmates were occasionally still punished by the authorities if they dared to complain.[100] Nevertheless, despite opposition on the part of local officials and the reluctance of many prison administrators to award more rights to inmates, complaints were taken more seriously, thanks to pressure from outside.

But the public sphere did not function, as has been implied by some historians, only as a check on the disciplining power of officials in carceral institutions.[101] In German states where more far-reaching prison reforms were introduced, the right-wing press actually claimed that the penitentiary was turned into a sanatorium. In Thuringia, for example, local journalists pointed to the supposed pampering of inmates with food, music and sports in the Untermaßfeld penitentiary.[102] Such accusations, almost as old as the prison itself, were not yet as virulent as they were to become during the depression. Still, they were present in most of Germany. Articles in right-wing newspapers described penal institutions as a mix between a five-star hotel and an amusement park, with smoking room, tennis club and gourmet meals. While the prisoners were enjoying life to the full, these articles charged, ordinary and honest citizens had to work hard, without being able to afford similar luxuries.[103] In addition, the Weimar press raised the question of what should be done with those prisoners who supposedly could not be educated. In 1927, the conservative *Kreuzzeitung* charged that the pampering of 'professional criminals' with care, good food, leisure and games was 'almost grotesque'. Lifelong confinement was the safest and cheapest option: 'For in "security confinement", there is no cinema, no football clubs, there is only work.'[104] This view was of course not confined to the right-wing press. It reflected intense debates taking place at the time among prison officials and criminologists, which are outlined in the next section.

Fighting the 'Incorrigible'

In Weimar Germany, countless newspaper articles, pamphlets and books featured the 'incorrigible criminal'. There was widespread agreement that certain criminals were destined to commit further offences. Of course, not everybody believed in the 'incorrigible'. Some members of the Study Group for Prison Reform argued that it was simply absurd to speak of 'incorrigibles' as long as no real attempts were made to rehabilitate inmates in penal institutions.[105] But most observers dismissed these arguments as naïve delusions. Their conviction that some individuals would always re-offend was very well established. Just before the First World War, for example, Prussian prison officials had judged nine out of ten recidivist penitentiary inmates as likely to commit further offences. In almost all cases, the officials justified their views with reference to the inmates' supposed 'incorrigibility'.[106] And with recidivism seemingly on the increase, the hunt for the 'incorrigible' intensified in the Weimar years.[107]

So how was the 'incorrigible criminal' constructed? The detection of the 'incorrigible' was a crucial element in the search for the causes of crime, and this quest had greatly intensified in the late nineteenth century. As we have seen, the modern school of criminal law had conceived of crime no longer as a predominantly moral failing on the part of a fully autonomous individual, but in more deterministic terms. Criminology, which emerged in this period as an academic discipline, focused on the environmental, physical and psychological factors that were said to drive criminal behaviour. One of the most influential biological explanations of the 'incorrigible' was advanced by the Italian doctor Cesare Lombroso, above all in his *L'Uomo delinquente* (The Criminal Man), first published in 1876. These criminals, Lombroso argued, exhibited specific bodily peculiarities. They were 'abnormal beings who bear certain physical attributes of our ancestors, of monkeys and carnivors . . .', biological throwbacks to an earlier time. It was Lombroso's pupil Enrico Ferri who came up with the famous phrase to describe this offender: a 'born criminal'.[108]

Lombroso's fame soon spread to Germany and the influence of his theories on popular conceptions of crime should not be underestimated. Some local prison officials were under the spell of the 'born criminal' for many decades. For example, in a lecture in 1921, the governor of the Landsberg penal institution explained to warders that the 'born criminal' was distinguished by an accumulation of many of the following physical signs:

Abnormal skull shape (dog's head, ape skull). Receding forehead. Unusually low forehead. Strong protruding upper jaw. Unusual order of the teeth. Joined-up eyebrows. Misshapen (sticking out) ears; unusual earlobes. Left-handedness. Unusual formation of the palate. Excess fingers and toes.[109]

This blind faith in the significance of physical features, it has to be said, was by no means universally shared. In fact, Lombroso's theory about the 'born criminal' was largely rejected in the emerging criminological scene in Germany.[110] However, many observers there still believed that endogenous factors did play an important role in creating 'incorrigibles'. While 'occasional criminals' might commit offences due to exceptional environmental pressures, biological factors were often regarded as decisive in stimulating the criminal drive of the 'incorrigibles'.

The 'incorrigible criminal' was often – but not always – described as standing between fully developed mental illness and sanity; non-normative behaviour was thus stigmatised as biologically abnormal. This link between the 'incorrigible' and mental 'inferiority' had already been made during the Empire. Franz von Liszt, for example, had described criminals as part of the 'degenerate and mostly hereditarily burdened people', a term which, for Liszt, also included beggars, vagrants, prostitutes and other social outsiders. Liszt was drawing here on the concept of degeneration, advanced by the French psychiatrist Bénédict Augustin Morel in the middle of the nineteenth century. According to Morel, individuals whose behaviour deviated from the 'norm' had acquired moral deficiencies or diseases, which were passed on to their children. Fear of degeneration in this period was linked to the growing insecurity among the bourgeoisie in the face of the challenges of the emerging modern world. Crime, alcoholism and mental illness all seemed to be on the increase, and were perceived as a danger to the foundation of society. But the spread of degeneracy was not regarded as inevitable. Degeneracy was seen by Liszt and others as a predisposition, which could be combated, for example, by social policies. But in the case of 'incorrigible' criminals, Liszt believed, it had become irreversible.[111] When describing criminals in the 1920s, the term 'degenerate' (or 'inferior') was often dropped in favour of 'psychopath', which at the time had a more scientific ring and also gained popularity in other Western countries at the time. In Germany, the term was advanced above all by Kurt Schneider, a professor at the psychiatric hospital of the University of Cologne, who regarded psychopathic traits as generally hereditary and famously defined 'psychopaths' as 'abnormal personalities, who suffer from their abnormality, or from whose abnormality society suffers', a definition which could be applied to many criminal offenders as well as to other social outsiders.[112]

The belief in some link between mental abnormality and chronic criminal behaviour was adhered to by a cross-section of the political spectrum in the Weimar Republic. True, many left-wing activists believed that criminality was the result of exploitation by the capitalist system. But some prominent Social Democrats, including the one-time Reich Minister of Justice Gustav Radbruch, thought otherwise. Radbruch, a former pupil of Franz von Liszt, argued that certain criminals were 'incorrigible' on account of their hereditary 'inferiority'. The debate on the left was also influenced by the socialist publicist Oda Olberg who differentiated sharply between criminal offences committed out of necessity by the impoverished working class, and those perpetrated by the so-called *Lumpenproletariat*. This was nothing new. Since the nineteenth century, leading socialist intellectuals (including Marx and Engels) and SPD functionaries had drawn a clear line between the labour movement and these outcasts of society, who were dismissed because of their supposedly immoral lifestyle (including prostitution and alcoholism), and their alleged sympathies for the reactionary political order. Crucially, Olberg charged that this *Lumpenproletariat* was defined in biological rather than in social terms. It consisted mainly of 'degenerates, of imbeciles or psychopaths' – the 'waste from all social sections'.[113] Still, mental abnormality alone proved no reliable guide to the 'incorrigible': not all 'psychopathic' criminals were regarded as 'incorrigible', and not all 'incorrigibles' were branded as mentally abnormal.

In their continued search for the 'incorrigible', German criminologists constructed two very different types of criminal. The first were the 'habitual' criminals, characterised as drifting into small-time criminality because they were weak and driven by primitive urges – a sure sign, in the criminologists' eyes, of their mental abnormality. Their recidivism was taken as a mark of their 'incorrigibility', following Franz von Liszt, who had argued that the majority of recidivists were 'incorrigible'. According to the senior Prussian prison official Werner Gentz, the criminality of these offenders 'does not lie in the area of big, sensational offences. They are dangerous less because of the values they damage or destroy in each instance, but because of the continued series of thefts, fraud, begging, vagrancy, sex offences, prostitution.' This focus on the social destructiveness of 'habitual' offenders led some Weimar criminologists to describe them as part of the 'asocials', another term widely used to label deviant groups seen as a burden on society, including the mentally ill, drug addicts and the 'work-shy'.[114]

The second criminal type associated with the 'incorrigible' was the 'professional' (or 'anti-social') criminal, who was considered to be more dangerous. Often described as unusually intelligent, they had little in common with the 'habitual criminal'. The construction of the 'professional criminal' left a deep impression on criminologists, prison and police officials, and the general public. Arguably the most influential publication was *Der Berufsverbrecher*

(The Professional Criminal, 1926) by the senior police official Robert Heindl. In his lurid book, Heindl claimed that these offenders did not drift into crime, but actively pursued it as their chosen vocation: 'Like bankers going to the stock market every day,' Heindl wrote, 'the professional crooks frequent their meeting places to control the balance of supply and demand.' Between photos of gruesome crime scenes and public executions, which no doubt contributed to the book's popularity, Heindl presented his own particularly unrefined typology of dangerous, trained, and highly specialised criminals.[115]

It was often assumed that 'professional criminals' worked hand in hand, hatching their plans in shady pubs or clubs. Such criminal associations, so-called *Ringvereine*, were real enough. They existed mainly in Berlin and largely controlled prostitution in the capital. But the clubs were not as dangerous as many observers imagined. Overall, they had at best no more than a few thousand members, and their primary function was not criminal activity but the provision of a social framework for ex-convicts excluded from mainstream society. Indeed, the criminal clubs closely mirrored the structures of mainstream bourgeois clubs and associations, down to the annual balls and the pedantic club statutes stipulating fines for those who arrived late at meetings.[116]

Targeting the 'Incorrigible'

Most commentators believed that dangerous 'incorrigibles' had to be interned even after the end of their prison or penitentiary sentence, possibly for life. As we have seen, this demand had been put forward by the modern school of criminal law from the late nineteenth century. It had quickly gained popularity among German psychiatrists, prison officials and legal officials. This was reflected in the drafts of a new criminal code. Indefinite detention for a minor offence ran contrary to the basic principle of the classical school that the punishment ought to fit the crime, and the preliminary draft of a criminal code (*Vorentwurf*) of 1909, drawn up under the chairmanship of a conservative civil servant, still ignored it.[117] But only four years later, the climate had changed sufficiently for so-called security confinement (*Sicherungsverwahrung*) of dangerous 'professional and habitual criminals' to be included in the next official draft of a criminal code, a step later hailed by liberal criminologists.[118]

In the 1920s, there was overwhelming support for security confinement. There was cross-party approval for this policy and even the Social Democrats, who expressed some concerns, ultimately supported the measure. Driven by their general 'therapeutic enthusiasm', the SPD came to see security confinement as potentially educative.[119] A similar position was taken by some members of the Study Group, who believed that the measure would allow the long-term education of prisoners who could not be rehabilitated during the normal terms of imprisonment. However, this vision of security confinement as a reformative policy was rejected by many other observers, who regarded the vast majority of potential inmates as 'incorrigible'. The prisoners would have to be safely interned either until they died or until they posed no more risk to society, for example, because their health had seriously deteriorated.[120] In any case, security confinement featured in all the Weimar drafts for a criminal code, but it was never realised, due to the failure of the Weimar politicians to implement the new Criminal Code. It remained a paper proposal until 1933.

Many German prison officials agreed that, as long as security confinement had not become law, 'incorrigible' prisoners should at least face particularly strict treatment. The stages system was ideally suited to fulfil this demand: while 'reformables' would advance to the comparatively better conditions on the higher stages, 'incorrigibles' would remain under the harsh conditions of the lowest stage. This repressive function of the stages system had been emphasised by prison officials right from the start. It was realised most comprehensively by the Bavarian prison administration, well known at the time for its strict approach. The Bavarian directive of 3 November 1921, which first introduced the stages system, already declared that 'incorrigible prisoners' had to be treated as strictly as possible: 'during their treatment the aim of retribution and deterrence in punishment cannot be stressed enough. There is no doubt at all that it is these prisoners in particular who have been treated far too leniently in penal institutions in the past.'[121] This meant that prison officials had to single out 'incorrigible prisoners' to ensure that they remained on the lowest stage. Apparently, most officials at first relied on their gut feeling when making their decisions.

But in July 1923, the Bavarian prison administration announced that a 'scientifically reliable basis' was required for the classifications of inmates. Prison doctors were asked to conduct criminal-biological investigations of inmates, a term first used in 1888 by Franz von Liszt.[122] Such investigations were typical for the widespread expectation at the time that social problems could be fully understood by applying objective methods. Parts of the examinations, revised in 1925, dealt with the physical appearance (including exact measurements of the head size and spread of body hair) and the biological make-up of the offender (including questions about instances of criminality and mental illness among relatives). The investigations were also concerned with the offender's social milieu. Finally, the prison doctors had to send forms with requests for further information to police stations, town councils, school authorities and church officials. At the heart of the investigations stood the so-called social prognosis of the offender's 'reformability', to be used for the stages system.[123] The different investigations were collected in the new Criminal-Biological Centre (Kriminalbiologische Sammelstelle). From here, they were passed on to state prosecutors, courts, the police and mental asylums, placing penal institutions firmly in the wider framework of the carceral society. At the same time, the information was used by criminologists in their studies of criminal behaviour, in line with Michel Foucault's observation that 'the prisons must be conceived as places for the formation of clinical knowledge about the convicts'.[124]

The criminal-biological examinations of prisoners in Bavaria were soon modified to solve two problems which had emerged. Firstly, some local prison officials resented the new powers which the investigations gave doctors. Secondly, only a very small number of new prisoners were actually examined, as most doctors were unable or unwilling to invest the time required for the detailed investigations. Therefore, in December 1927 the Bavarian prison authorities introduced so-called psychological-sociological questionnaires. These simplified versions of the criminal-biological forms were filled in by prison chaplains, by teachers and other senior officials, for those new inmates not investigated by the prison doctors.[125] Soon the Bavarian prison chaplains and teachers had become the harshest judges of all, classifying some 38.5 per cent of all examined inmates as 'incorrigible' (the prison doctors regarded 36.1 per cent as 'incorrigible').[126] Prisoners with this classification often faced the harsh conditions of stage one for their entire sentence. It is hardly surprising, then, that some of them tried to undermine the examinations by lying about their family background, keeping silent when asked whether they came from 'broken homes' or whether their parents were alcoholics.[127]

The Bavarian investigations were not without critics in Weimar Germany, both among criminologists and prison officials.[128] But there were a number of leading prison officials that strongly supported the Bavarian model. Otto Weissenrieder, the influential chairman of the Association of German Prison Officials, was among the admirers of the examinations, declaring: 'I have to confess openly that if scientists tell me that it is possible to put my judgement on a firm basis, then I am thankful for this'.[129] These feelings were broadly shared by prison administrators in various German states; and Saxony, Hamburg and Prussia all carried out criminal-biological investigations rather similar to those in Bavaria.[130] In Berlin after 1929, prisoners effectively regarded as 'incorrigible', following a criminal-biological examination conducted centrally in the Moabit remand prison, could be taken into a wing of the Plötzensee penal institution set aside for inmates euphemistically described as 'those most difficult to educate'.[131] This was greatly welcomed by many, including members of the Study Group such as Karl Maria Finkelnburg, the progressive president of the Berlin prison administration, who supported special institutions 'for the most anti-social elements, with a particularly bleak social prognosis'.[132]

The criminal-biological examinations give an important insight into prison officials' construction of the 'incorrigible' in the Weimar Republic. The authority of the examinations derived from the claim that they were based on neutral observation. But under the veneer of scientific objectivity, the examinations largely reflected the prejudices of the prison officials, characterised by unproved allegations, moralising assumptions, and the reduction of deviant behaviour to biological determinism. Prison officials were particularly inclined to write off individuals who had most manifestly failed to conform to the moral, political and social values of bourgeois society. Like many other criminal offenders, most of the inmates judged 'incorrigible' had grown up in unstable families in urban centres, which had long been regarded by prison officials as cesspools of depravity and degeneration. The officials highlighted the offenders' unsettled lifestyle, homelessness, alcoholism and their 'abnormal' sexual appetite. Many offenders had only ever held casual jobs and were described as 'work-shy'. 'He is a person who since his youth has never got used to regular work,' the Moabit prison doctor commented on Albert M., 'and then unscrupulously commits thefts when he lacks subsistence'. What really set the 'incorrigibles' apart from most other offenders was their very high rate of recidivism, often viewed as evidence of 'incorrigibility'. On average, each inmate examined in Moabit had 14 previous convictions. The focus on recidivism made petty property offenders much more likely to be judged 'incorrigible' than others, such as sex offenders or violent criminals. Most of their offences had consisted of minor thefts, which meant that they received comparatively short sentences of imprisonment or jail (or even fines) and therefore had more opportunities to accumulate additional offences than prisoners serving long-term sentences for more serious crimes. Of course, this focus on property offenders had a great tradition in Germany. They had long been seen as dangerous threats to the established social order, part of the 'asocial' and 'degenerate' sub-proletariat.[133]

Classification as an 'incorrigible' could influence more than the treatment of prisoners during their sentence. The label also stuck after their release. Ex-convicts in Germany faced great difficulties anyway. In a period of sustained economic instability and high unemployment, many inmates were released with nothing more than a stern lecture by the governor, a few Reichsmark in earnings from prison labour, and a one-way train ticket in their pocket. They had little prospect of finding regular work, not least because of the strong suspicion they faced from the general public. As one prisoner complained, most people viewed former prisoners 'as if they were dealing with wild animals'. Not surprisingly, many former prisoners soon broke the law again. One recidivist, on trial for theft in 1925, explained that 'once you are released from the penal institution, you are without money, job and accommodation. If you end up before the court again, then you are incorrigible.'[134] Financial and logistical support from religious prisoners' aid organisations and state authorities was often restricted to ex-convicts regarded as 'reformable', if it was forthcoming at all.[135]

The position of 'incorrigible' ex-inmates was made even more difficult by police measures enforced after the prisoner's release. For reasons of efficiency, the police traditionally concentrated on those it regarded as likely to re-offend. Police officials had a large arsenal of weapons available in their 'fight' against these ex-convicts. They could deny former inmates the right to settle in their home town and even deprive them of the right to hold a driving licence. Those ex-convicts who did find a job sometimes lost it as a result of the continual and unannounced visits by the police, which also made it difficult for them to find accommodation; most landlords were reluctant to rent to former prisoners. Clearly, these police practices contributed to the inability of some released inmates to stay on the straight and narrow and thus played a role in the creation of the 'incorrigible criminal'. In this way, the classification as 'incorrigible' became a self-fulfilling prophecy.[136]

Finally, some 'incorrigible' inmates were detained even after the end of their sentence of imprisonment, foreshadowing security confinement. Detention for supposedly 'work-shy' ex-convicts in a workhouse had been practised in Germany for a long time (see Chapter 3). This practice was extended by the Bavarian authorities on 16 July 1926, when the Law for the Combating of Gypsies, Travellers and the Work-shy was passed. In part, this legislation aimed at the exclusion of Sinti and Roma ('Gypsies') from Bavarian society by criminalising their lifestyle. But it also threatened 'incorrigible habitual criminals' with 'correctional post-detention' in a workhouse, which could last up to two years.[137] The Bavarian prison administration welcomed this measure and instructed governors to provide the police with material about 'incorrigible' offenders who were coming to the end of their sentence.[138] A number of Bavarian prison officials were happy to cooperate, as can be illustrated by the case of Johann W., an unskilled labourer with numerous convictions for property offences. In 1929, after he reached the end of his most recent sentence in the Straubing penitentiary, the Munich police asked the prison officials for an assessment of the inmate. In response, the officials compiled a report, concluding that Johann W. was an 'incorrigible habitual criminal . . . who leads a parasitic existence'. Johann W. was not freed but instead held by the Bavarian authorities for 16 more months in the workhouse in Rebdorf, even though he was not guilty of any new offences.[139]

Important aspects of the Weimar prison in the 1920s clearly run counter to the evolution of social policy as depicted by historians such as Detlev Peukert. As we have seen, Peukert suggested that the 1920s were dominated by the belief in the power of education to transform individuals, which still overshadowed attempts to pursue more repressive policies against the 'unfit'. But such optimism was not dominant in penal policy. As has been noted, many prison officials were sceptical about new policies which claimed to rehabilitate prisoners. Furthermore, the isolation of the 'incorrigible' was in fact a central concern of prison policy: criminologists and prison officials throughout the 1920s tirelessly tried to identify the 'incorrigible' and intensively debated the measures put forward to combat these offenders. Their exclusion was perceived to be essential, complementing any measures introduced to rehabilitate the 'reformable'. Criminologists and prison officials insisted that if released offenders committed a further offence, despite the efforts to reform them during imprisonment, this was an indication of the inmates' 'incorrigibility' – ignoring both the grim social realities which faced ex-convicts on the outside and the fact that not much had changed inside penal institutions. During the crisis that gripped the Weimar Republic in the early 1930s, the familiar call for the 'incapacitation of the incorrigible' grew louder than ever.

The Prison in Crisis

The Weimar obsession with crime reached fever pitch in the last years of the republic. Many Germans were convinced that a surge in crime was sweeping across the country, one more symptom of the general breakdown of society in the early 1930s. The previous years had done little to solve deep-seated structural economic and political problems in Germany, and these tensions came to the fore during the crisis which finally brought the republic to its knees. Germany was hit harder than any other Western state by the dramatic global economic crisis following the New York Stock Exchange crash of 29 October 1929. The immediate consequence of the depression was a dramatic rise in unemployment, which soared to 5.6 million registered unemployed by 1932 (30 per cent of the population). The economic collapse exposed the frailty of a political system that had lacked popular legitimacy even during the preceding brief period of comparative stability. Voters rapidly turned to the radical parties on the far left and right, above all to the Nazi party (NSDAP), which achieved its national breakthrough in the elections of September 1930 and became the largest party in the July 1932 elections, setting Germany on the road to authoritarianism.[140]

There were some changes in criminality in the last years of Weimar. To start with, political violence intensified once more. Political radicalisation was accompanied by attacks on prominent party officials and violent disruptions of rallies in almost all German towns and cities. In countless street battles, troops of Nazi brownshirts (SA) and left-wing paramilitaries attacked each other, leaving hundreds of activists dead and injuring many more. Nazi members could sometimes count on the sympathies of police officials. But the police did, on the whole, try to crack down on open violence and restore order. Thousands of party activists were arrested and convictions rose substantially.

Prison sentences for breach of the public peace (§ 125), for example, increased more than tenfold, from 230 (1929) to 2,962 (1932).[141] Some common criminal offences were on the rise, too, as the economic crisis contributed to another increase in property crime. This was true, in particular, for thefts and robberies. Recorded figures for 'serious theft', for example, increased by 80 per cent between 1928 and 1932. Many of the offenders were recidivists. During the crisis, former convicts found it harder than most to find subsistence. Hopes of getting paid employment were smaller than ever before, as even state and municipal authorities now generally refused to employ released inmates. As one female offender, with numerous sentences for property offences, openly explained to the Aichach prison officials in 1930: '[I] have to rely on myself and find no assistance anywhere. I don't yet know how I shall avoid my offences in future, as I don't yet know what I shall live on.' Hardly surprisingly, she was back in Aichach a few months after her release, once again convicted of theft.[142]

Despite these developments, one cannot speak of a crime wave. In fact, the total number of persons convicted by German courts fell slightly after 1930. Of course, these figures should not be taken as an accurate reflection of the crime rate, as they fail to account for any changes in policing and sentencing. Still, they indicate that there was no dramatic increase in crime, in contrast to the early years of Weimar. As a result, there was no explosion of prisoner numbers, even though they did creep up. The inmate population as a whole grew from about 50,000 in 1930 to about 63,000 in 1932 (see Figure 1, pp. 392–3). The figure for 1932 was in no way exceptional, equalling the prison population in 1927, when economic conditions had been significantly better. As we shall see below, the rise in inmate numbers during the depression was less a reflection of an increase in crime than the result of stricter sentencing by the courts.

Crime and Punishment

In many ways, the popular panic about law and order was not surprising. To start with, political violence was not hidden from the public, as were most other crimes, but often took place in broad daylight. Many Germans witnessed the street battles for themselves, which strengthened their conviction that crime and disorder were on the rampage. In addition, reports about crime in the Weimar media became ever more alarmist, reflecting the general sense of anxiety at the time. This was the case, not least, for the reporting of capital crimes. The most spectacular case was that of the 'Düsseldorf vampire' Peter Kürten, a sadistic serial sex killer arrested and tried in 1931. His name reverberated loudly in the public arena and dominated the press for weeks, with newspapers carrying countless reports of the proceedings, interviews with witnesses, photos and drawings. While the press agreed to leave out much of the gruesome details of the murders, it still offered its readers lurid descriptions. Part of the public fascination with this particular case stemmed from the discrepancy between Kürten's petty-bourgeois appearance and his gruesome crimes. Underneath his 'respectable' exterior, several papers noted, lurked a degenerate 'beast' which had to be killed. There was overwhelming public pressure for Kürten's execution. By now the death sentence had been virtually abolished, with only three executions in Germany between 1928 and 1930. But the Kürten case gave fresh impetus to the critics of this trend, indicating a more general shift towards a harsher penal policy in the last years of Weimar. Eventually Kürten was sentenced to death and executed in July 1931.[143]

Much was written during the depression about the 'incorrigible criminal'. Some observers pointed to new criminological studies to prove that hereditary factors were the main cause of criminality.[144] Others claimed that there was now conclusive evidence that vast numbers of criminals were 'incorrigible'. The irrepressible Straubing prison doctor Theodor Viernstein, the greatest champion of criminal-biology in Bavaria, argued in several speeches in 1930 that examinations of prisoners had proved that no less than half of them were essentially 'incorrigible'. Viernstein admitted privately that his conclusions were not derived from scientific research, however spurious (three years earlier, he had still claimed that at least two-thirds of inmates were 'reformable'), but from his conviction that in a time of crisis the 'strictest selection' of prisoners was paramount. Still, the figure of '50 per cent incorrigibles' was seized upon in criminological journals and the popular press.[145] Other prison officials also felt more and more surrounded by 'incorrigibles', not least because of the increase of prisoners with previous sentences. Not only were penal institutions filling up with recidivists, but many of them were repeat property offenders, the criminal 'type' most readily associated with the 'incorrigible'.

Above all, it was the 'professional criminal' who loomed large in public perceptions of criminality during the last years of Weimar. Stories about 'professional criminals' and their supposedly close-knit organisations, the *Ringvereine*, appeared more frequently than before in the press, popular books and films. Under headlines such as 'Under the Spell of the Horror of the *Ringvereine*', the right-wing local press in Berlin published one sensationalised story after another about the criminal clubs, simultaneously feeding the growing moral panic and the public fascination with crime. The criminals' supposed reign of terror, often described as symptomatic of the moral decay in the Weimar Republic, was contrasted in the press with the repeated failure of the police to bring successful prosecutions against the ex-convicts. The fixation with the organised criminal underground was reflected in other popular media. For example, in Fritz Lang's 1931 masterpiece *M*, a serial child sex murderer, played by the mesmerising Peter Lorre, is hunted down, tried and sentenced to death by the leaders of the Berlin underworld, desperate to end the disruption of their criminal activities caused by the police search for the murderer. The film, released immediately after the Kürten trial, reflected both the widespread fear of the 'degenerate' criminal and the popular image of the tightly structured and extensive criminal underworld.

In real life, probably the most famous 'professional criminals' in this period were the Berlin brothers Franz and Erich Sass. Charged by the police on numerous occasions as clever thieves and safe-crackers, they were the prime suspects for one of the most spectacular burglaries of the time, the cleaning out of almost all the safes of the Disconto-Bank in Berlin in 1929. But the police could not find enough evidence against the brothers and had to let them go, much to their chagrin. This release was greeted with derision by the press, which lapped up the failures of the police and the capers of the Sass brothers, who even held a press conference to celebrate their freedom. The press continued to cover the contest between the police and the two brothers, who managed to escape serious punishment for their various suspected offences. Together with their lawyer, they clearly delighted in playing the criminal justice system, claiming to have no knowledge of any illegal activities and taking full advantage of all the legal loopholes. For example, when they were arrested in December 1932 on suspicion of planning to break into a house, the brothers claimed that they had not wanted to break in to steal, but merely to hide their burglary tools in the cellar of the house. The police could not prove them wrong and had to set them free once again.[146]

The moral panic about crime strengthened calls for tougher measures. This was linked to the changing political climate in Germany, as the drift to the far right was accompanied by demands for a more authoritarian approach to punishment. The supposed crime wave was blamed on the weakness of the liberal system, accused of protecting the individual criminal rather than the general public. The cult of the individual in liberalism had made penal policy too soft, it was argued, unable to fight dangerous criminals like the Sass brothers. This attack came, not least, from the ever more powerful Nazi movement. As in other policy areas, the Nazis had no coherent programme for penal policy. But remarks by the party leaders left no doubt about their general views. Throughout the Weimar Republic, they called for an extension of the death penalty, to rid the 'national community' of racial and political threats, as well as common crime. The Nazis strongly attacked Weimar penal policy. In 1929, Hitler charged that 'Marxism had made its baleful influence felt in the German judicial system in that humanitarianism was misused and blindly applied to penal policy'.[147]

These demands for stricter penal policy also found widespread support within the legal profession. A growing number of officials and academics joined in the attack on the 'soft' and 'liberalistic' penal system. This was quickly picked up by the press, which reported on the 'dispute over the new criminal law'.[148] There was an obvious political dimension to this. Attacking the penal system meant attacking the Weimar Republic, which had remained unpopular with the mostly authoritarian and nationalist legal officials. This antipathy was very much shared by younger officials, who had just left university. Most German students vigorously rejected the Weimar Republic and instead pushed for a nationalist and strictly hierarchical order centred around the idea of the German *Volk*.[149] In their attack on Weimar penal policy, the critical jurists drew on new criminological research to substantiate their claims. Particularly important was Franz Exner's 1931 study of sentencing policy. Exner, a leading German criminologist, showed that sentencing in Germany had become more lenient over the previous decades: judges resorted less to penitentiary and prison sentences and used more fines. Exner explained this trend by pointing to the growing tendency among judges to see individual criminals as driven by factors outside their own making, such as hereditary disposition, education and environment.[150] The critics of Weimar attacked this 'exaggerated humanity' which 'effectively glorified crime', blaming it for the perceived crime wave in the early 1930s.[151] No doubt, these considerations also influenced German judges, who passed stricter sentences than before. At the height of the depression, they handed down almost as many prison sentences as fines, reversing the trend towards more fines of the previous years.[152]

At the same time, there were also urgent calls for the introduction of 'security confinement'. In the early 1930s, the failure to introduce this measure was highlighted by the opponents of the Weimar Republic as another example of the weakness of the liberal state. Many police officials blamed the liberal system for their unsuccessful and humiliating attempts to break up the *Ringvereine* and to prosecute the Sass brothers, and stepped up pressure for the introduction of more radical policies against 'professional criminals'.[153] Support also came from criminologists and prison officials, who were alarmed by the apparent ubiquitousness of the 'incorrigible criminal'. Dangerous 'incorrigibles', it was argued with even more urgency than before, had to be taken into security confinement. For example in 1932 the National Association of Catholic Prison Teachers demanded that a law to allow security confinement of 'habitual' and 'professional' criminals should be quickly passed, as this was 'one of the most pressing tasks of the present day'.[154]

These demands were rather typical responses to the Weimar crisis, echoed in many other areas of social policy. Exclusion of 'incurables' and the 'undeserving' became ever more central in social policy. A growing number of psychiatrists, social workers and politicians demanded introduction of the sterilisation of 'degenerates'. In November 1932, the government also decreed that children or youths should be excluded from correctional education when there was no prospect of success.[155]

The call for measures against 'incorrigible' criminals and for a more authoritarian penal policy was probably made most effectively by two young legal academics, Georg Dahm and Friedrich Schaffstein, in their *Liberales oder autoritäres Strafrecht?* (Liberal or Authoritarian Criminal Law?), published in early 1933. Dahm and Schaffstein stressed the primacy of strict punishment and general prevention. But they also reserved a place for the modern school of criminal law. Thus, they demanded the introduction of the 'permanent security confinement of incorrigible habitual and professional criminals', typically blaming the liberal system for the failure to introduce this measure. Dahm and Schaffstein also supported the rehabilitation of 'reformables'. But while they took note of the work of prison reformers in Thuringia, their vision of reform was crucially different from that of the Study Group: inmates should not be turned into law-abiding citizens of a liberal state, but should be taught the 'idea of the national community', not least through strict military discipline. Obviously, this vision of penal policy had a strong political thrust. For Dahm and Schaffstein envisaged that it would be implemented in an authoritarian and nationalist regime, which would replace the despised liberal one. These hopes for the fall of the Weimar Republic and the advent of a more authoritarian penal policy were soon to be fulfilled.[156]

Attacking the Weimar Prison

Criticism of Weimar penal policy – fuelled by the panic about crime, the economic collapse and the rise of the Nazis – did not stop at the prison gates. In the last years of the Weimar Republic there were sustained public complaints, especially from the right, that prisoners were treated far too leniently. Some of this criticism, not surprisingly, came from the Nazi movement. Nazi thinking on the prison was illuminated in an article in *Der Strafvollzug* (The Prison Service), a specialist journal for prison officials. After the Prussian elections of April 1932, in which the NSDAP emerged as the largest party, the editors asked the party for its views on imprisonment. In response, the NSDAP made clear that retribution and deterrence had to move back into the centre, at the expense of reform and education. The party attacked all 'weakness' and 'sentimental humanitarianism' towards common criminals, employing terminology popular among the many critics of the Weimar penal system. The leniency of the prison regime manifested itself, according to the NSDAP, both in the stages system, and in the fact that not enough distinction was being made between the prison and the dishonouring penitentiary sentence.[157]

Other right-wing politicians did not want to be put in the shade by the Nazis' hard-line stance, and also launched fierce attacks on the supposedly lavish provisions in penal institutions. Meanwhile, newspapers diagnosed the 'bankruptcy of the modern prison service'. This criticism centred around the well-rehearsed charge that prison reforms had gone too far, providing criminals with much better conditions than the mass of ordinary Germans. In a time of severe economic crisis, it was argued, inmates in penal institutions had to be among the first to have their belt tightened. Of course, the descriptions of the supposedly lavish prison life were generally still based on nothing more than wild exaggerations or outright fabrications. But the image of the Weimar prison as an amusement park apparently struck a chord with readers.[158] Even the most trivial issues could cause great controversy, such was the agitated mood of the early 1930s. For instance, in January 1932 the regional newspaper *Meininger Tageblatt* published a poem that alleged, among other things, that the Untermaßfeld governor had just bought a new grand piano for the inmates at a cost of 2,000 marks. The poem concluded:

> Now everything in the penitentiary is complete!
> Only afternoon dance and ballet would make it more neat!
> We outside? We're made gloomy about the hardship that has arisen.
> Until we perhaps end up, too, in the prison!

In reality, the piano had been bought for half the price some five years earlier. But this did not stop the poem from being picked up by many other Thuringian papers, as well as by the state diet.[159]

Perhaps the most vitriolic attack on the Weimar prison came from Ernst Siefert, an elderly professor at the University of Halle. In a pamphlet, Siefert blamed what he regarded as the ills of the modern world in general, and the Weimar Republic in particular – atheism, liberalism, Communism, socialism, humanism, pacifism, and so on – for the fact that the Prussian prison service was in 'a chronic crisis with constant danger of a catastrophe'. Prison officials had lost all their authority, Siefert claimed, and prisoners had become pampered, profane, undisciplined, brash and coarse, making life hell for the officials with their constant disobedience and 'grotesque' flood of 'evil-minded' complaints. Siefert's alternative programme was purely reactionary: 'one has to turn back the wheel of evolution in a determined way'. His ideal was the prewar German prison system, overseen by the all-powerful governor and dominated by order, retribution, deterrence and Christian morals.[160]

Legal officials played a leading role in the assault on prison policy. The professional association of Prussian state prosecutors, for example, in 1932 demanded cuts in prisoner provisions and rights, and a general 'limitation of exaggerated measures of education and reform'.[161] Numerous criminologists, academics and other 'experts' made the same point, castigating the prison system for having become too soft. Pastor Heinrich Seyfarth, the General Secretary of the umbrella group of German prisoners' aid organisations and a highly respected commentator on prison policy, repeatedly demanded the rooting out of the 'exaggerated and dangerous humanity' which had undermined the 'seriousness of punishment'. He called for a return to the trusted values of discipline, obedience and belief in God.[162]

Some of the harshest criticism came from local prison officials. As we have seen, they often supported the old-style prison and now urged that inmate privileges had to be cut back. Supposedly excessive privileges included walks outside the prison, musical instruments, additional rations, theatre productions and much more. The remaining privileges, it was argued, had to be restricted to the select few prisoners who really were deserving, that is, 'reformable'. The prison officials justified their demands as responses to growing public criticism of the prison and to the economic crisis. But the demands also built upon the long-term dissatisfaction of local prison officials. Clearly, they saw the social and political crisis in the early 1930s as a good opening for rooting out some of the policies they had disagreed with for some time, such as certain privileges, the handling of prisoner complaints and outside scrutiny of the prison.

The officials were keen to make these complaints known to the wider public. The chaplain of the Rheinbach penitentiary, for example, openly stated in 1932: 'We oppose the burden put on the prison service by privileges which spoil and mollycoddle people, rather than teaching them moderation and self-control.' Already one year earlier, the Association of Prison Warders had called for cuts to the inmates' right to complain as well as more 'discipline and order in the institutions'.[163]

Some senior prison officials joined in the attack. Richard Degen, the head of the Bavarian prison administration, announced on 18 January 1930 to his colleagues from other German states that Bavaria would restructure its stages system. Degen said that his high hopes for prisoner rehabilitation had been crushed. He claimed that practical experience and the criminal-biological investigations had shown that the 'great mass' of inmates with a 'disadvantageous disposition' could not be educated after all. In the light of these findings, Degen argued, a much stricter selection had to be made: 'By doing this, we push unnecessary ballast out of the way, which only impedes our intensive attention to the really reformable prisoners.'[164]

The criticism of prison policy did not go unchallenged. There were still more moderate voices and the SPD, the strongest defender of the Weimar Republic, continued to support aspects of the reformist prison service. Individual prison officials and criminologists opposed demands for the stricter treatment of inmates, and pointed out that there was a massive gap between the prison service as portrayed in the public debate, and the reality of life inside the institutions. Also, they stressed, the newly introduced policies had not made life more pleasant for the prisoners at all. On the contrary, the new privileges meant more responsibility: the more freedom the inmates had, the more they had to learn to control their desires.[165]

Nevertheless, the general trend was towards a more authoritarian prison policy. The reformers in the Study Group recognised this and were on the defensive. They complained that 'today, it is almost considered good manners . . . to ridicule the "emotional exaggeration of the reform ideal" by Liepmann, Freudenthal and other leaders of prison reform'.[166] Moritz Liepmann and Berthold Freudenthal were easy targets for their critics. They had died in 1928 and 1929 respectively, and were badly missed by their younger admirers. By 1932, the Study Group was weighed down by pessimism. The sense of crisis was caused not just by external attack on their views, but also by their own growing doubts about the attainability of their ideals. The reformers admitted that they were still unsure how best to treat criminals. They had also faced occasional resistance from the prisoners themselves, becoming painfully aware that some inmates did not necessarily agree with the aims and methods used to 'reform' them. Also, educating adults, as the reformers understood it, meant helping them to educate themselves. However, this required voluntary and free participation, conditions they knew to be absent from penal institutions.[167] The growing loss of heart by members of the Study Group was also reflected in the way in which they now fell into line with the chorus which demanded immediate measures against 'professional' and 'habitual' criminals.[168]

But what was the impact of all of this on life behind bars? The economic crisis and the attack on Weimar penal policy certainly left an imprint on penal institutions. To start with, the prison service was directly affected by the depression, which led to the gradual dismantling of the Weimar welfare state. Its ideological principles came under attack, and unemployment benefits, pensions and welfare payments were drastically reduced. Expenditure on social outsiders such as prisoners, the mentally ill and youths in reformatories was also cut back. Reductions in state subsidies, as well as the diminishing revenue from prison labour due to rising inmate unemployment, led to cuts in the basic provision for prisoners such as clothing, food and health care.[169]

The ideological backlash against aspects of Weimar prison policy also had consequences for prisons and penitentiaries. In Bavaria, which already boasted one of the strictest prison regimes, access to the higher stages of the progressive system was systematically restricted further, in line with the intentions of the prison administration. By the end of 1932, about four out of five prisoners in the stages system were held on the harsh stage one. The progressive system in Bavaria became the privilege of a very small minority of inmates.[170] Political upheaval in the early 1930s also shaped prison life. The unrest fuelled tensions between different groups of highly politicised inmates, as well as between inmates and warders. The radical parties used their growing popular support to force the prison administration into concessions for their supporters behind bars. The Hamburg NSDAP, for example, pressurised the judicial administration in 1932 into allowing prisoners to subscribe to the local Nazi newspaper.[171] Even more importantly, numerous political activists were actually released from late 1932 onwards to rejoin the mayhem and violence on the outside, following an amnesty on 20 December 1932.[172]

Those few penal institutions which had introduced far-reaching reforms in the 1920s were particularly vulnerable to attack. This was part of what Detlev Peukert described as the 'crisis of classical modernity', when recently launched progressive policies were attacked and started to crumble. Similar developments occurred in other carceral institutions at the same time. In workhouses, policies pioneered in the 1920s, including the employment of social workers, were abolished. And in mental asylums, new measures such as outpatient care and 'active therapy' were scaled down, as the asylums reverted to more custodial practices.[173]

The attack on the rehabilitative prison was most pronounced in Thuringia, the centre of the Study Group. This was linked directly to the transformation of the regional political landscape. Following its victory in the 31 July 1932 Thuringian state elections, the Nazi party controlled the government, and with it the prison administration.[174] Soon, it was decided that the prison service should be brought into line with more authoritarian conceptions of punishment. Attention focussed on the 'model' penitentiary in Untermaßfeld. At the time, the institution was run by the 35-year-old governor Albert Krebs, who had started out in the penitentiary nine years earlier as a social worker. Like other prison social workers, Krebs had been active in the German youth movement and had studied in Frankfurt with Christian Jasper Klumker, who held the first chair in Germany for social work. During the crisis in the early 1930s, Krebs had tried to preserve many of the policies introduced in recent years: social workers were still on the payroll, prison tribunals continued to operate and the majority of inmates still progressed to the higher stages of the stages system.[175] All this made Krebs very conspicuous to the Nazis. In late 1932, a NSDAP deputy demanded in a letter to the new Nazi Minister of Justice that he should 'get rid, without mercy, of the prison service built up under red rule in Thuringia'. The Nazi activist claimed that prison inmates enjoyed 'unbelievable luxury' and urged that reformers like Krebs had to 'disappear'. He supported his attack with a list of alleged irregularities in Untermaßfeld, secretly compiled by local prison officials still keen to oust the reformers.[176] The material supplied against Krebs proved to be insubstantial. But this could not stop the Ministry of Justice. On 21 January 1933, nine days before Hitler's appointment as Chancellor, Krebs was informed that the Nazi sympathiser Johannes Gericke, who had only recently been appointed as prison doctor, would take over from him as governor.[177] Gericke, in a symbolic break with his predecessor, later sold the controversial prison piano.[178] Krebs was not the only casualty among the Thuringian prison officials after the regional Nazi takeover in 1932. The governor of the Eisenach youth prison, Curt Bondy, a key figure of the Study Group, was dismissed in December 1932.[179] At around the same time, the architect of the Thuringian prison service, Lothar Frede, was transferred to a different position in the judiciary.[180] Thus the three senior prison officials associated with the Study Group for Prison Reform in Thuringia had been removed even before the Nazis came to power in Germany.

Overall, the trend in penal policy during the depression was towards stricter treatment. There were loud calls by journalists, politicians and prison officials for cuts in prison provisions and a return to stricter treatment. But most of these critics cannot simply be described as reactionaries. Only a few wanted to return to the prewar prison service. Most critics also strongly supported the introduction of measures against dangerous 'incorrigible' criminals. This 'dark side' of modern penal policy, which was pursued with more vigour than ever during the depression, eclipsed hopes for the rehabilitation of offenders. The twin demands for the stricter treatment of prisoners and for special policies against 'incorrigibles' left an important legacy for the Nazi prison.

Part II Enforcing Legal Terror, 1933–39

2 Inside the Nazi Prison

When the Nazis talked about the prison, they could often draw on personal experiences. Numerous rank-and-file members had been held in penal institutions in the Weimar years, during the period they later glorified as the 'time of struggle'. The same was true for several leading figures of the party who, thanks to the sympathies of the German judiciary and the prison staff, had often experienced the Weimar prison at its most relaxed – spacious cells, lax discipline, decent food and easy access to the outside. Little wonder that they later claimed that imprisonment was too soft, advocating a harsh penal policy after Hitler became Reich Chancellor on 30 January 1933. Nazi expectations of the prison were summed up early on by Hermann Göring, in a speech on 18 May 1933: 'Punishment can only protect and deter by being harmful, and at the same time educate – where reform is still possible – through adjustment and order.'[1]

So how did penal institutions change under the Nazis? This chapter examines the reality of life behind bars, exploring the attitudes of state and local legal officials, the general treatment and living conditions of inmates, and forced labour – looking at prisons, penitentiaries and the new, large-scale prison camps. First of all, though, it is necessary to sketch a broad outline of Nazi repression between 1933 and the start of the Second World War in 1939.

Terror, Crime and Punishment

From the beginning, terror was a principal feature of the Third Reich. Of course, not the entire population was targeted directly. Nazi society was divided into friend and foe. On the one hand, 'national comrades' were supposed to be protected by the state and encouraged to procreate, with the ultimate aim of creating a socially, politically and racially regimented community, an image incessantly perpetuated by Nazi propaganda. 'Community aliens', on the other hand, had to be singled out and removed from Nazi society. Hitler made clear that all those who did not, or could not, fit in had to be brutally attacked. In a speech before the Reichstag on 23 March 1933, in the debate that marked the official end of parliamentarism in Germany, Hitler demanded that 'in future, treason against the country and the *Volk* should be burned out with barbaric ruthlessness'. His announcement was greeted with ecstatic applause by the deputies.[2] Of course, such threats also served as a warning to 'national comrades' not to step out of line. Deterrence was always a central element of Nazi policy.

Until 1939, repression took various forms, including stigmatisation, social exclusion, detention and sterilisation. Terror involved a great number of different agencies. The most important among them, in the eyes of the Nazi leadership, were the police and the SS. Hitler saw the police apparatus as the main force in the fight against all 'community aliens' and put his weight behind the ruthless and increasingly unshackled police. In the Weimar Republic, police powers had been strictly circumscribed. An arrested person could only be held briefly by the police. Ultimately, it was the legal system which was responsible for the initial incarceration (in a remand prison), the trial and the subsequent imprisonment (in prisons or penitentiaries) of a criminal offender. This changed in the Third Reich. From 1933, arrested individuals could be held indefinitely in police custody – without trial or any other involvement of the legal authorities. In the prewar years, the police made extensive use of these new powers, locking up tens of thousands of political opponents, 'professional criminals', 'asocials' and other deviants. Most of these prisoners were taken to newly set up concentration camps, run by the SS – places of confinement which were independent of the traditional prison apparatus run by the legal authorities (this development is described in more detail in Chapter 4).

In contrast with the unwavering support given to the police, leading Nazis felt ambiguous about the legal apparatus and often held it in low esteem. Already in the Weimar Republic, as we have seen, many Nazis had made no secret of their contempt for the legal system, dismissing it as biased in favour of criminals and the left, slow to dispense punishment and overly bureaucratic.[3] Hitler's distrust of the traditional court system did not diminish in the

Third Reich and was shared by a lot of other Nazi officials. The weekly newspaper of the SS leadership *Das schwarze Korps*, for example, orchestrated a determined campaign against legal officials, accusing them of being reactionary and soft on crime.[4]

But, for all Hitler's distaste for the law, the regular legal system continued to operate right until the German capitulation in May 1945. The Third Reich did not become an all-out police state. Leading Nazis occasionally even made public gestures of support for the legal system, at least in the early years of the dictatorship. Hitler himself publicly promised in his speech on 23 March 1933 that the German judges were irremovable. At the same time, though, he also expected the legal system to fall into line with his general wishes, demanding 'elasticity' in sentencing. Crucially, Hitler and other senior Nazis stressed that judges were ultimately answerable to the 'national community', not to abstract legal principles. The only guideline for judges, it was said, was the welfare of the German people, and the mythical 'will of the national community' was frequently invoked to justify brutal punishment. That this 'will' was in reality nothing more than the will of the Nazi leaders, or more precisely Hitler's own, was not seen as a contradiction. After all, the 'will of the Führer' was regarded as the embodiment of the 'will of the people'. Hermann Göring made this point crystal clear in a speech to Prussian state prosecutors in the summer of 1934: 'The law and the will of the Führer are one'.[5]

The legal apparatus was an essential element of Nazi terror. It played a central role in the criminalisation of political dissent and the politicisation of common crime. Trials were not completely hidden from the public. On the contrary, the Nazi media were full of news about court cases and sentences. One key message was that the Nazis were winning the battle against crime. It was claimed that offences were down and that the streets were safe again, following the supposed crime wave in the last Weimar years. These reports, no doubt, were welcomed by many Germans.[6] Indeed, the belief that the Nazis had beaten crime lived on in the memory of many Germans long after the defeat of 1945, held up as one of Hitler's supposedly positive achievements, together inevitably with the *Autobahnen*.[7]

But crime did not disappear in Nazi Germany. The image of the Third Reich as a virtually crime-free society was completely fictitious. Statistics used by the Nazis to back up their claim that crime had fallen sharply after they took power provide no reliable guide to criminality in Nazi Germany. For the real number of criminal offences was certainly significantly higher than these figures suggest. First of all, the official crime statistics were incomplete.[8] More importantly, the statistics ignore offences not prosecuted because of Nazi amnesties. The first amnesty, drafted by the Reich Ministry of Justice and passed on 21 March 1933, was overtly political and applied to crimes committed 'during the fight for the national uprising of the German people'. In all, more than 7,100 judicial proceedings were quashed – thousands of serious, violent crimes went unpunished. The main focus of the three subsequent amnesties (7 August 1934, 23 April 1936, 30 April 1938) was on minor criminal acts. Under the first two of these amnesties alone, almost 720,000 judicial proceedings were quashed against individuals accused of non-political offences.[9] In addition, thousands of crimes against 'community aliens' never came before the courts, even though they were not covered by amnesties, because the crimes were backed by the regime itself. These included, for example, brutal crimes inside concentration camps and almost all of the destruction, violence and murder wreaked during the anti-Jewish pogrom in November 1938.[10] Even so, the conclusion that crime as a whole – as defined by the Nazis – probably *increased* in the prewar period is also questionable.[11] There is actually some reason to believe that ordinary criminality declined before the war, even though this fall was much less pronounced than Nazi propaganda claimed. Given the general improvement in the economic climate in these years, compared to the crisis years of Weimar, such a trend would not be entirely surprising.[12]

What is beyond dispute is that judicial punishment was often significantly harder than in the years before the Third Reich. To start with, sentencing for certain common crimes became stricter. The linchpin of legislation against criminal offenders was the new Law against Dangerous Habitual Criminals and on Preventive and Rehabilitative Measures (Habitual Criminals Law) of 24 November 1933, which introduced significantly stricter punishment for certain repeat offenders and gave courts sweeping new powers to order the indefinite detention of selected recidivists, vagrants, beggars, mentally ill individuals as well as sex offenders, who could also be castrated. At the same time, the German judges eagerly used existing legislation and new laws to crack down on many other supposed enemies of the Nazi regime. The courts were heavily involved in the assault on real or imagined political opponents. Throughout the Third Reich, hundreds of thousands of individuals were persecuted as political enemies, either before regular courts or before new special courts. The defendants were charged with a great variety of offences, ranging from mere grumbling about the regime to active political resistance. Simultaneously, the courts played a crucial role in enforcing key elements of Nazi racial policy, targeting social and racial outsiders. Thus, the legal system played its part in the harassment and persecution of the German Jews. Also, many more homosexual men were sentenced by the courts than prior to the Nazi takeover (for details on sentencing, see Chapter 3).

The result of legal terror was an explosion of inmate numbers in prisons and penitentiaries. In 1933, the first year of Nazi rule, the average daily number of inmates in all Prussian penal institutions rose to 56,928, up 50 per cent compared with the previous year. Numbers elsewhere in Germany shot up, too. In

Hamburg, the number of prisoners actually doubled, from 1,702 inmates (31 December 1932) to 3,401 (31 December 1933).[13] By the summer of 1934, inmate numbers in the whole of Germany already topped 100,000 and numbers continued to grow in 1935 and 1936 – far outstripping concentration camp inmates (see Figures 1 & 2, pp. 392–5). Prisoner numbers reached their prewar high on the last day of February 1937, with a total of 122,305 inmates.[14] To be sure, not all of them were in captivity on account of Nazi penal policy. But we can estimate that maybe around 50,000 inmates would not have been held under the Weimar legal system. Their imprisonment was the direct result of stricter sentences and new laws in the Third Reich.[15] Only in the late 1930s did numbers in penal institutions begin to decline, with the daily inmate population fluctuating between 100,000 and 108,000.[16] Still, even at that time penal institutions held significantly more inmates than the SS concentration camps. In short, the court and prison systems became key instruments of Nazi repression. This would have been impossible without the cooperation of the German legal officials.

Hitler's Jurists and the Prison

The Nazi legal apparatus remained largely in the hands of the same officials who had been in charge in Weimar. Most of them came from a rather similar social and political background: middle-class, national-conservative and resolutely anti-republican. Having kept their distance from the state in the Weimar Republic, they welcomed the revival of nationalism, authoritarianism and militarism in the Third Reich. The great majority of German judges, prosecutors and other senior legal officials broadly supported the new regime. They may not have greeted the 'seizure of power' with the Hitler salute, but they welcomed it with open arms. Professional organisations of legal officials quickly dissolved themselves in 1933, with individual members joining the Association of National Socialist German Jurists (BNSDJ). Support for the regime was reflected in the rush to join the Nazi party, which cannot be dismissed as entirely opportunistic. Party membership among legal officials was already particularly high in 1933, and by 1938 more than half the German judges and prosecutors were members of the Nazi party.[17]

Continuity with the Weimar years was epitomised by Franz Gürtner, who headed the Reich Ministry of Justice for most of Hitler's reign. Before 1933, Gürtner, like most Weimar legal officials, had not been a Nazi supporter. But as a national-conservative and a follower of the radical right-wing German National People's Party, he was sympathetic to many of the Nazis' aims. He, too, believed in the establishment of a strong authoritarian state and was an unrelenting opponent of Weimar parliamentary democracy. This had not damaged his career in the 1920s. On the contrary, Gürtner, born in 1881, had served as Minister of Justice in reactionary Bavaria from 1922, before being appointed by Chancellor von Papen as Reich Minister of Justice on 2 June 1932. When Hitler became Chancellor on 30 January 1933, Gürtner kept his job.[18]

Why did Hitler retain Gürtner, rather than replace him with a loyal Nazi? To start with, it should be recalled that Hitler, in early 1933, was not yet in total control. His appointment had been the result of behind-the-scenes manoeuvres by a small clique at the top of the German state, who believed that Hitler would be little more than a figurehead, with conservatives and nationalists actually in the driving seat.[19] Fatally underestimating the Nazis, they initially believed that this strategy might be successful. After all, Hitler's first cabinet only included two other Nazis. The remaining ministers, like Gürtner, were generally members or sympathisers of other right-wing interest groups and parties. In Gürtner's case, Hitler's coalition partners had expressed the hope that he would remain in office. Also, as an able and determined jurist, Gürtner was held in high regard by the conservative judicial establishment, whose support Hitler initially required. But Hitler also held on to Gürtner because he had repeatedly shown his willingness in the past to accommodate authoritarian policies.

On the whole, Gürtner did not disappoint. In penal policy, he saw much common ground with the Nazis. He shared the Nazis' hostility to all political movements on the left, including the moderate trade union movement and the Social Democrats, and also pushed for a hard line against 'professional criminals'. True, Gürtner's repeated defence of the authority of the legal system caused some conflict, as we shall see later. But the rule of law was not sacrosanct for him. Crucially, Gürtner accepted that vital national interests – as defined by Hitler as head of state – had precedence over the rule of law. Time and time again, Gürtner supported unlawful measures and even murders, because they had been declared by Hitler as crucial for the survival of the state.

Reich Minister Gürtner's deference to the new rulers was openly displayed at the very beginning of the Third Reich, in the aftermath of the Reichstag fire of 27 February 1933. The fire had been intended as a protest against the new German government by the Dutch loner Marinus van der Lubbe, a former Communist. The hysterical reaction by the Nazi leadership had serious implications for the legal apparatus. Not only were the powers of the police dramatically extended in the aftermath of the fire (see Chapter 4), but Hitler also issued the first serious challenge to traditional legal principles. For, while van der Lubbe could legally only be sentenced to imprisonment in a penitentiary, Hitler declared in a cabinet meeting on 7 March 1933 that it was vital that van der Lubbe was executed. At first, the officials in the Reich Ministry of Justice were reluctant to agree to such a blatant breach of the elementary legal principle *nulla poena sine lege* (no punishment without law). State Secretary Franz

Schlegelberger, an experienced official who had served in the Reich Ministry of Justice since 1921, warned that the retrospective application of the death penalty would result in 'confusion of the general understanding of right and wrong'. But, in the end, the Reich Ministry of Justice fulfilled Hitler's demand and drafted a law (soon known as the Lex van der Lubbe) which was published on 29 March 1933. Franz Gürtner justified the law as vital for the successful fight against 'international terrorism', and the Supreme Court (Reichsgericht) duly made use of the law to sentence van der Lubbe to death.[20] The Lex van der Lubbe set a fateful precedent. Once the legal authorities had accepted that the wishes of the political leadership could take precedence over legal principle, it became all the more difficult to resist any future demands by the regime to sacrifice the rule of law. In practice, German legal officials quickly became used to bending the law, and in 1935 the principle *nulla poena sine lege* was completely abolished. Courts could now even convict persons who had not broken any specific law, if they 'deserve punishment according to the basic idea of a criminal law and healthy popular feeling'.[21]

After the consolidation of the Nazi dictatorship, Hitler's national-conservative allies became increasingly dispensable, and in the second half of the 1930s, key politicians and generals were replaced by loyal Nazis. Not so Franz Gürtner. His accommodating attitude helps to explain why he was allowed to remain in office, serving the Third Reich until his death on 29 January 1941.

Like Gürtner, most legal officials also simply continued their careers after the Nazi takeover. Of course, this is not to say that there were no changes in legal personnel from 1933 onwards. A number of legal officials were sent into early retirement, moved to other posts or summarily dismissed. The Nazis had lost no time during the 'seizure of power' to introduce measures aimed at regimenting state and society. One key policy was the purging of Jews and suspected political opponents from the civil service, introduced in the euphemistically entitled Law for the Restoration of the Professional Civil Service of 7 April 1933. Because only a small number of German Jews had been appointed as judges or state prosecutors and because the great majority of other legal officials were regarded as politically sound, the overall number of dismissed officials was low. In Prussia, for example, only 225 of all the 6,284 judges and state prosecutors were sacked in 1933–34 because they were Jewish or because of their political convictions. The rest stayed in their posts. There was even more continuity in the Reich Ministry of Justice, where not one of the senior officials was removed for political reasons.[22]

Changes among the legal officials in 1933 were most obvious at the top of the Ministries of Justice in individual German states. Almost immediately after the Reichstag elections of 5 March 1933, the NSDAP had taken control of those federated states which had not yet been in its hands.[23] In several key states, the Ministry of Justice, and with it the administration of the prison service, was soon controlled by Nazi supporters. In Prussia, Hanns Kerrl, a long-standing NSDAP activist and since 1932 president of the Prussian parliament, took over the Ministry of Justice at the end of March 1933.[24] Kerrl proved a transitional figure and left much of the initiative to his right-hand man and personal friend, Roland Freisler. A Nazi lawyer and deputy in the Reichstag, Freisler had been appointed as a senior official to the Prussian Ministry of Justice in March 1933 and was promoted to State Secretary on 1 June 1933.[25] Like other leading Nazi officials, Freisler sharply attacked Weimar penal policy and promised that, in the Third Reich, punishment would 'hurt'. He saw criminal law both as a political tool to remove opponents of the regime, and as an instrument of racial policy, protecting the *Volk* against 'degenerates'.[26]

Prussia was not the only German state led by new legal officials. In Saxony, the former state prosecutor Otto-Georg Thierack was elevated to the position of acting Minister of Justice. And in Bavaria, the Ministry of Justice was taken over on 10 March 1933 by the 32-year-old committed Nazi activist Hans Frank. As a young man, in 1919 and 1920, Frank had belonged to a notorious *völkisch* and anti-Semitic secret group, the Thule Society. Soon after, he switched his allegiance to the fledgling Nazi party and actively participated in the Hitler putsch on 8–9 November 1923. A trained jurist, Hans Frank became the leading Nazi lawyer in the Weimar years, defending countless activists, including Hitler himself. Once Hitler was in power, Frank tried to make his mark as the loudest voice on legal matters in the Nazi party, heading the BNSDJ and the Academy for German Law. 'In accordance with the will of the Führer,' Frank claimed in 1934, 'I have decided for years what National Socialism is in the sphere of law.' Such boasts could not disguise the fact that Frank's political influence was, in reality, strictly limited. Still, he continued to advance his vision for the Nazi legal system, coining the famous phrase: 'Justice is whatever is useful for the German people' – often cited as the epitome of the Nazi disdain for the law. Not surprisingly, Frank also distinguished himself as a supporter of harsh punishment. He called for the ruthless repression of all 'community aliens', exclaiming that: 'The National Socialist state does not negotiate with criminals, it knocks them to the ground.' Punishment in the Third Reich, he added, filled 'the criminal underworld with fear, but the law-abiding citizen with calm'.[27]

The Ministries of Justice in the different German states were closed down soon after this initial process of restructuring. The establishment of the Nazi dictatorship involved the centralisation of federated administrative structures. The first, and most thorough, process of centralisation occurred in the legal sphere, between February 1934 and April 1935. Only now, in the Third Reich, did the Reich Minister of Justice gain full authority over the administration of justice in Germany. The staunch Nazi Hans Frank had hoped that this process would work in his favour, helping him to gain control of legal policy. But Hitler instead supported the traditional legal apparatus under Reich Minister Gürtner, thwarting Frank's ambitions. Accordingly, the centralisation of the legal system initially weakened the direct influence of top Nazi officials on the justice system: with the closure of the federated Ministries of Justice, activists such as Kerrl, Frank and Thierack lost their posts (Thierack soon returned to high legal office). Power shifted to the Reich Ministry of Justice, controlled largely by experienced national-conservative officials from the Weimar period like Franz Gürtner. Of course, the process of centralisation also brought some changes within the Reich Ministry of Justice. In October 1934, it was amalgamated with the Prussian Ministry of Justice (some non-Prussian civil servants were also appointed later). The combination of established Reich officials and those from Prussia was most obvious in the case of Franz Schlegelberger and Roland Freisler, the two State Secretaries. While Freisler (whose brief included the prison service) was a committed Nazi supporter, the national-conservative Franz Schlegelberger was a respected career civil servant who had been appointed as State Secretary back in 1931. But this background did not prevent Schlegelberger from playing a leading role in the destruction of the rule of law in the Third Reich, as we shall see later.[28]

Prison Officials and the New Regime

Prison policy in the Third Reich was shaped by the call for stricter punishment. This demand was voiced by most legal officials, starting with Reich Minister Franz Gürtner at the very top. Gürtner had already demonstrated his hard-line views during his tenure as Bavarian Minister of Justice. In 1923, during the drafting of the national prison guidelines, Gürtner had fought a losing battle to prevent the abolition of the harshest disciplinary punishment: detention in a dark cell. Its abolition, Gürtner had argued, would result in an 'unacceptable loss of discipline', a claim not borne out by the continued strict control of prisoners in subsequent years.[29] And in 1930, in the early stages of the collapse of the Weimar Republic, it had been Gürtner who had ordered that prisoners in Bavaria had to be treated even more harshly.[30] As Reich Minister of Justice, Gürtner reaffirmed his views and described attempts to reform every inmate as 'madness'. But he also believed that certain prisoners could be rehabilitated, echoing the modern school of criminal law: 'the more ruthlessly the incorrigible and incurable elements are eliminated from the community of the people, the more the community has to look after those who, while having done wrong, have the honest will to return to the community of their people'.[31] But Gürtner showed little inclination to get involved in the details of the prison service, exhibiting the typical lack of interest of most legal officials. Until the late 1930s, the same was true to a large degree of State Secretary Roland Freisler, who nevertheless made it clear from the start which approach he favoured, demanding in a speech in 1933 that the prison had to become a 'house of horror'.[32]

The civil servants in the Reich Ministry of Justice in Berlin enjoyed considerable influence over the direction of the prison service, in particular from 1 January 1935, when they officially took over the administration of the German prison system, putting a formal end to the federated states' control.[33] Who were these officials? The department for the administration of criminal justice and the prison system was headed by Wilhelm Crohne. A strict disciplinarian, Crohne was a proponent of harsh punishment directed at the 'elimination', as he called it, of those who continued to work against the new regime. In the Weimar Republic, Crohne had served as a relatively senior regional judge (*Landgerichtsdirektor*) in Berlin. Like many German judges, Crohne's sympathies were firmly with the anti-republican, anti-Semitic and authoritarian right. In fact, he was so open about his views that he had even been criticised by his superiors, both for making racist remarks in court and for his blatant political bias. The latter had been particularly obvious during a high-profile trial in 1928 of the pacifist journalist Carl von Ossietzky, who later described Crohne as 'using the judicial superiority like a rubber truncheon, which constantly silences whoever else dares to talk'. In April 1933 Crohne was appointed as a senior official to the Prussian Ministry of Justice. His subsequent rise in the Third Reich (culminating in his appointment as vice-president of the People's Court in November 1942) was certainly helped by his party connections: he had joined the NSDAP on 1 September 1932, shortly after an earlier ban on NSDAP membership for Prussian legal officials had been lifted.[34]

Unlike Crohne, most senior prison officials in the Reich Ministry of Justice did not owe their position to sympathies with the Nazis, even though many of them later joined the party. Often, they were experienced officials from the Weimar Republic, who had held leading positions in penal institutions before being appointed to the prison administration of one of the German states. Four of the six most senior civil servants in April 1936 had come from the Prussian Ministry of Justice, while the other two had previously worked in the Ministries of Justice in Bavaria and Saxony. A typical representative of these officials was Crohne's direct subordinate, Rudolf Marx, who headed the section for prison administration from 1935. Marx, born in 1880, had served as governor in several penal institutions from 1916 before being appointed to the Prussian Ministry of Justice in 1929, at a time when Prussia was still ruled by the SPD. Marx joined the SA in January 1934, but despite his attempts, he was never admitted to the NSDAP. According to his postwar testimony, he had never belonged to any party: 'I have always considered myself only as an expert'.[35] Marx's deputy was Edgar Schmidt, born in 1886, who had also been governor in various penal institutions in the 1920s. A widely respected official, Schmidt was appointed to the Prussian Ministry of Justice in 1927. Like Marx, he was not an early Nazi follower. Schmidt had been a member of the Catholic Centre Party in the Weimar Republic, and only joined the NSDAP in May 1937.[36] In short, the two top prison officials in Berlin were not fanatical Nazis.

For the administration of penal policy in the regions, the officials in Berlin relied above all on the general state prosecutors, one in each of the judicial districts (initially 26, growing to 35 by early 1941). Once the state Ministries of Justice had been abolished in 1935, it was the job of these general state prosecutors to act as a link between the Reich Ministry of Justice and local legal officials. The general state prosecutors were responsible for all aspects of penal policy in their districts, including the prisons. They supervised and controlled the individual institutions in their district and were also the recipients of complaints and suggestions by the prison governors. Issues of particular importance were passed on by the general state prosecutors to the Reich Ministry of Justice. In turn, the ministry issued directives and regulations to the general state prosecutors, who then disseminated the information among the local officials.

The general state prosecutors, like other senior legal officials, came from national-conservative backgrounds and sympathised with many aims of the Nazi regime. There had been significant changes among the officials in 1933, with more than half of them newly appointed that year. These changes appear to have been linked in part to the balance of power in the individual states before Hitler's appointment as chancellor. In reactionary Bavaria, all four general state prosecutors stayed in office in 1933. By contrast, only four of the 14 in Prussia kept their jobs. In general, the legal authorities considered the wishes of the party when selecting officials as general state prosecutors, while opposing the appointment of individuals regarded as professionally unqualified. By early 1941, all general state prosecutors carried a NSDAP membership card. However, three out of four were not 'old comrades' but had joined the party in 1933 or later.[37]

The civil servants in the Reich Ministry of Justice and the general state prosecutors supported a harsher prison policy. Edgar Schmidt complained in 1933 that, in the Weimar period, 'atonement and retribution became terms which disappeared from the prison regulations'. By contrast, 1933 was hailed as the year of the renaissance of the prison service, when discipline returned to the penal institutions. Rehabilitation, one of the buzz-words of the 1920s, was marginalised. In so far as penal institutions were still supposed to educate inmates at all, these efforts were to be limited to a few 'reformables'. The main objective was the protection of the 'national community', to be achieved by stricter punishment. This was emphasised once more by Edgard Schmidt in 1934, in an address to a delegation of British prison officials: 'The programme of the penal law rings like steel. The fight of the State against crime and against the enemies of the people is stern, and the penal law in this conflict is a weighty and effective weapon of the State. He who will not hear must feel.'[38] After several other lectures by German officials, as well as visits to individual penal institutions, the British visitors concluded that the guiding principle of the German prison was indeed harsh treatment: 'The modern German system seems definitely to subordinate any question of reformative and educational treatment of the individual to a strict enforcement of discipline intended to leave unpleasant recollections in the mind of the prisoner.'[39]

The emphasis on stricter treatment and selection in the prison service was naturally welcomed from below. After all, such a policy had been demanded by many local prison officials for some time. As we have seen, they had been at the forefront of calls for a tougher prison regime in the early 1930s, hoping that this would make their jobs less labour-intensive and restore their total power over the prisoners. In the summer of 1933, the prison officials' journal *Der Strafvollzug* declared that all officials welcomed the shift of emphasis in the Third Reich: they were pleased 'that the offenders would learn, once more, to regard the penal institutions as houses of punishment and not as rest homes'. At least 80 per cent of officials, the article added, had always opposed the prison reforms of the 1920s.[40]

Not surprisingly, most local and regional prison officials made a seamless transition to the Third Reich. True, a small number of governors, warders, chaplains and others regarded as politically or racially suspect, or as unacceptable because of their close links to the prison reform movement, were dismissed, and the Study Group for Prison Reform was disbanded.[41] The year 1933 also saw the removal of several regional prison administrators who were regarded as implicated in the Weimar reforms. In Hamburg, several officials lost their jobs, including the head of the prison service, who was temporarily put into one of the institutions he used to run. His old job was taken by a leading local Nazi activist, a plumber with no experience of prison administration.[42] And in the Prussian Ministry of Justice, three of the seven senior administrators were removed from their posts. One of them was Werner Gentz, whose dismissal had been demanded in the *Völkischer Beobachter* in late March 1933, on the grounds that Gentz was a Jew, a member of the SPD paramilitary organisation, a pacifist and the official responsible for introducing the 'humane' prison service in Prussia – a pretty extensive selection of all that the NSDAP detested.[43] But the great majority of local prison officials remained in office after the 'seizure of power'. Out of a total of 46 governors in Prussia in 1931–32, 39 were still in office in 1935. It is unclear how many of the other seven governors were dismissed for political or racial reasons. Even the small number of warders who had supported more radical reforms in the 1920s, or those who had supported the SPD, often remained in their posts.[44] Overall, the composition of the local prison officials was probably changed more decisively by the gradual employment of Nazi activists as prison warders (see below), than by any dismissals.

Officials inside penal institutions did not sit on their hands waiting for policy to change from above. On the contrary, after the Nazi takeover, many local prison officials redoubled their calls for a stricter prison service. They obviously saw the 'seizure of power' as a good opportunity to put their stamp on prison policy. Often, they started with a ritual denunciation of the Weimar prison. Prison governors again and again repeated the claim that attempts to rehabilitate inmates in the Weimar years had gone too far. Too many privileges had become available and the 'circle of those [regarded as] open to education had been too large', as one governor put it.[45] Local officials outdid one another in running down the Weimar years. Typically, one chaplain exclaimed in June 1933 that the 'new order' marked the end of the 'era of weak and sickly humanity . . .'.[46]

Local officials bombarded their superiors with detailed suggestions for the restructuring of the prison service. This included the demand that all warders should be equipped with rubber truncheons and be allowed to use them without restriction against ill-disciplined inmates.[47] Other officers argued that lazy inmates should be punished by a cut in their rations, invoking an old maxim of prison officials: 'He who does not work, also should not eat.'[48] Officials also argued, like some leading Nazis, that the difference between prison and penitentiary had to be stressed more clearly, to redress attempts by prison reformers in the 1920s to diminish the dishonourable nature of the penitentiary sentence.[49] Finally, prison officials urged once more that the inmates' right to complain had to be cut back, their rallying cry since the 1920s. As Otto Weissenrieder, still chairman of the Association of German Prison Officials, alleged in 1933, the right to complain had led to the 'defamation and unjust suspicion of officials by the most inferior prisoners and the uncritical acceptance and political use of their complaints by Socialist and Communist deputies, with extensive consequences for the accused officials'.[50] All this was now supposed to change.

Prison Regulations

Prison regulations in Germany were revised soon after the Nazis came to power – hardly surprising, given the widespread consensus that a stricter regime was required. Initially, the extent of these changes differed from state to state. In Bavaria, which had pursued a particularly harsh policy in the Weimar Republic, changes were marginal. One leading Bavarian prison official noted with satisfaction in the spring of 1933 that no transformation was necessary because 'Bavaria kept a distance from the extreme direction of the educational prison service. This is best proven by the not infrequent complaints by prisoners in Bavaria about too strict treatment and unpleasant diet.' This sense of continuity was mirrored among the ministerial prison officials, who remained in office in 1933.[51] In contrast, Saxony had implemented more far-reaching policies in the 1920s. The new Saxon Minister of Justice Otto-Georg Thierack made sure that those measures were quickly abolished in the spring of 1933: prison tribunals were scrapped, the inmates' right to complain or write letters was greatly reduced, and social workers were either sacked or transferred. The position of prison social worker was later abolished by the Reich Ministry of Justice in 1936. By the late spring of 1933, there were few traces of the 1920s reform spirit left in the Saxony regulations.[52]

The Prussian Ministry of Justice also introduced measures in spring 1933 to make life behind bars more unpleasant. And on 1 August 1933, a whole new set of prison regulations were introduced in Prussia. Life inside was to become as austere as possible: 'privileges during imprisonment should be a very special exception'. The new regulations also stressed the dishonourable function of the penitentiary by introducing a new disciplinary punishment. Previously, the harshest punishment had been aggravated detention (*verschärfter Arrest*), which allowed the governor to imprison the inmate in detention cells for up to four weeks without a bed or exercise in the yard, receiving only bread and water. However, on every third day spent in detention, these additional penalties were dropped. Such 'good third days' were now abolished in the new so-called strict detention (*strenger Arrest*) in Prussian penitentiaries.[53] The Prussian Ministry of Justice was quick to draw public attention to the new direction in prison policy, clearly convinced that this would be popular with 'respectable' Germans and would deter potential criminals. The Minister of Justice Hanns Kerrl personally presented the new prison regulations to the press on 2 August 1933, warning that the aim was 'to awaken the unqualified desire in the prisoner never to return into such a house'. The Nazi press welcomed this hard line. Already in April 1933, the *Völkischer Beobachter* claimed that the Prussian measures spelled 'bad news for professional criminals'. Joseph Goebbels' *Der Angriff* greeted the new prison regulations in August 1933, stating that the 'madness' was now over when the state 'spent more money on the parasite of the racial body than on a decent person, who had become unemployed through no fault of his own'.[54]

The developments in the individual German states culminated in the national prison regulations of 14 May 1934. Already, one year earlier, during a meeting of the various German Ministers of Justice, it had been decided that the 1923 prison guidelines had to be overhauled and brought into line with the new approach.[55] Soon the civil servants in the Reich Ministry of Justice submitted a draft, which was discussed by the leading state prison officials and officials from the Reich Ministry of Justice on 5 and 6 October 1933 in Darmstadt. The final version was passed as a directive on 14 May 1934.[56] During the discussions in Darmstadt, the senior prison officials agreed that expiation, deterrence and retribution were central elements of the prison service. Consequently, the instruction to prison officials in the 1923 guidelines to treat inmates in a 'humane' manner was replaced in the 1934 regulations with the demand that imprisonment had to be a 'painful evil'. This spirit was reflected in several of the new rules. To start with, disciplinary punishment was exacerbated: regular detention (up to four weeks) was now always aggravated and strict detention (up to one week), recently introduced in Prussia, was extended to penitentiaries all over Germany. Inmates' right to complain was restricted: governors were no longer obliged to receive inmates who wished to raise a complaint, and written complaints had to comply with very strict formal rules. Furthermore, the officials at the Darmstadt meeting decided to abolish volunteer prison visitors, who had been introduced in some German states in the early years of the Weimar Republic. Finally, while the pedagogical justification of the prison was not abandoned completely, the officials agreed that certain policies in the past had obviously gone too far. Elements of prisoner autonomy, walks outside the building and brief holidays from imprisonment were banned, while school lessons in penal institutions were cut back and brought into line with Nazi ideology. The lessons, just like books available in the prison libraries, were to teach nationalist beliefs and turn the prisoners into 'able parts of the national community'.[57]

At the time, the 14 May 1934 prison regulations were described by German prison officials as a dramatic break with the 'sentimental humanitarianism' of the past, and the Nazi state was hailed as a saviour from the liberal aberrations of the Weimar Republic. Simultaneously, the significance of the new regulations was emphasised by the anti-Nazi opposition, as part of their general attack on the Third Reich. The SPD in exile, for example, claimed that the regulations were a return to primitive barbarism, a 'step back by at least 100 years'.[58]

However, the new regulations did not completely break with the Weimar period. First of all, the great majority of individual rules from the 1923 prison guidelines were taken over unchanged in 1934. And those changes that were made did not reinvent the prison. Some were little more than cosmetic (for example, volunteer prison visitors had either been ineffective or non-existent anyway). Others were deeply rooted in the criticism of prison policy which had grown ever louder in the last years of the Weimar Republic. Finally, while the regulations were stricter than before, they did not return to the 1830s. Corporal punishment, to name but one example, was not reintroduced in 1934. Indeed, some prison officials felt that the new regulations did not turn the clock back far enough and demanded the restoration of corporal punishment and further cuts to inmates' rights.

Demands for even stricter regulations were controversially debated in the following years, during the process of drafting a national prison law, a proposal that had been on the agenda since the late nineteenth century. In the Third Reich, it was envisaged that such a law would be enacted in conjunction with a new criminal code, under discussion from November 1933 by an official committee led by Franz Gürtner. On 28 January 1935, a commission for a prison law met for the first time, consisting of ministerial and regional legal officials and the respected Professor of Criminal Law, August Schoetensack. The commission members apparently agreed on some measures to make imprisonment harder, including the reintroduction of detention in a dark cell as a disciplinary punishment and the shaving of penitentiary inmates' hair. But there was no consensus on how much stricter the prison service could become, with some members warning that it should not be turned into pure harassment. For example, several officials supported the reduction of inmates' rations in the initial stages of their imprisonment, but this was strongly opposed by others, such as the head of the Reich prison administration, Rudolf Marx: 'It is being assessed at the moment whether today's diet is sufficient. In my view, the prisoner's health would definitely be harmed if he received even less than now.'[59]

Another ongoing issue of contention was corporal punishment. This had been brought up by a panel set up by Hans Frank's Academy for German Law, which also tried to shape the new criminal law. Frank's group had suggested the possibility of reintroducing corporal punishment for male penitentiary inmates sentenced to life.[60] Such suggestions could count on the support of some local prison officials. In February 1935, for example, the governor of Gräfentonna complained to his superiors about the inmate Anna K. who often soiled her cell. The best remedy, he claimed, was a 'thrashing, a proper and sound thrashing. Unfortunately, corporal punishment is not allowed.'[61] One might have expected the official ministerial commission to approve of corporal punishment, too. After all, several of its members were also part of Hans Frank's rival group. Instead, it was rejected by leading ministerial officials including Rudolf Marx. Officials like Marx were not driven by humanitarian motives. Rather, they believed that corporal punishment was inefficient, or even counter-productive.[62] This belief had been shared by leading German prison officials for decades, contributing to the gradual abolition of corporal punishment in penal institutions in the second part of the nineteenth century. The view that corporal punishment was worse than useless had been put forward forcefully by Karl Krohne in his influential 1889 manual on prison administration: beatings did not break strong-willed prisoners, Krohne had argued, but only instilled hatred into them. It turned those who were beaten into heroes among the other inmates, while demeaning and brutalising the warders who carried out the violence. Instead, Krohne had advocated the extensive use of disciplinary punishments away from the gaze of fellow inmates, such as food cuts, the withdrawal of the bed and complete isolation. It was disciplinary punishments like these which remained central to imprisonment in the Third Reich.[63]

In the end, the plans for a prison law came to nothing, as the new Criminal Code itself was never implemented. The Code was debated in cabinet in 1937, but was undermined by Hans Frank who continued his attempts to influence criminal law. Most importantly, Hitler showed no desire to implement a new criminal code that would have limited his own freedom of action. By retaining the old Code, any disregard by the Nazis for the legal norms could be excused with reference to its 'liberalistic' and 'individualist' orientation.[64] Even so, the commission's discussions of a prison law were significant, as they demonstrate that senior officials were still unsure of exactly how harshly the inmates should be treated in future. At the same time, it should not be forgotten that there was a broad consensus for a harsher prison service, which had resulted in stricter regulations in 1933–34.

But what was the impact of these regulations on the lives of individual prisoners? Some officials in the Third Reich were quick to claim that the harsher rules had greatly improved discipline. In December 1934, officials in the Bavarian Ministry of Justice noted that 'all governors agree that the basic aims of the stricter prison service, expiation and deterrence, significantly improve the behaviour of prisoners and therefore order in the institutions'.[65] The next section examines the reality behind such statements. For life inside penal institutions in the prewar period was not just determined by general regulations. It was shaped by the complex interplay of political, economic and social reality, directives by the central prison administration, the actions and initiatives of local prison governors, and by the individual inmates.

Everyday Life behind Bars

Some local prison officials in Nazi Germany were clearly drunk with their own disciplinary power. One of them was the Ichtershausen prison governor Max Vollrath, who mused in 1936: 'I think if a prisoner dreams of me at night, he stands to attention in bed.'[66] Strict discipline did mark most aspects of life behind bars. Of course, exhaustive rules governing the behaviour of prisoners had already existed in the 1920s. But in the Third Reich prison life became even more militarised. In October 1933, a newspaper report described the military exercises of inmates in the Plötzensee prison: 'One – two – three and four! Left parades forward, right parades forward! Down! The sand splashes – at the double, march, march, march!' Previously, the Plötzensee prisoners had been allowed sports and games in the yard.[67] Instead of games, a number of penal institutions now introduced explicit military training (*Wehrsport*) – at a time when the whole of German society was becoming increasingly militarised. In the Luckau penitentiary, inmates even had to parade with wooden rifles. Such exercises were not ordered centrally in Berlin, but were introduced by local officials. In some penal institutions they were mandatory; in others voluntary, in which case almost no inmate participated. The interaction of officials and prisoners also still copied military forms, probably more so than in the 1920s. The constant pressure on prisoners to demonstrate their total submission followed them everywhere. In Brandenburg-Görden, the prisoners even had to salute passing warders during the daily procedure of emptying and cleaning their chamber-pots.[68]

Many local prison officials, often themselves former soldiers, welcomed the further militarisation and praised its influence on inmates' discipline. One senior warder in Berlin claimed that: 'Just like in the army, where the spirit of the drill ground is taken back into the barrack itself, in prisons, too, the spirit of the drill exercises, if performed in a military way . . . is taken by the prisoners back into the institution . . . '.[69] But not all officials agreed with this. One governor argued that many prisons and penitentiaries had gone too far and had become miniature military establishments, with embarrassing results: 'When a number of prisoners in prison clothes, which are generally not in a very good state, practise the goose-step with a poor posture or try to march in review, following a military command, this only gives a ridiculous impression . . . '.[70] This view was echoed by the female governor of the wing for women in the Waldheim penitentiary in Saxony. In the Weimar period, military rituals had been less widespread in penal institutions for women. Apparently, this began to change in the Third Reich, and the Waldheim governor complained in the journal of the Association of German Prison Officials that the imitation of military traditions by female inmates was 'simply ridiculous'.[71] This statement was harshly criticised in the same journal one year later by a colleague, the female governor of the Hohenleuben institution for young female prisoners, who insisted that 'for women, the necessity for strict education in a military fashion is called for, too, in the present-day'.[72] Female prisoners were not supposed to be exempted.

But penal institutions in Nazi Germany did not always live up to the disciplinarian ideal perpetuated in newspapers, speeches, prison journals and the regulations. The gap between this ideal and the reality was often an unintended consequence of the new penal policies. As it turned out, the strict sentencing of the German courts undermined strict discipline inside, because massive overcrowding, the direct result of the courts' eagerness, made it more difficult to control the prisoners and also increased tensions between inmates. Some prison authorities responded by ordering daily searches of the cells. More warders were equipped with guns and even prison chaplains took part in shooting practice to foil escape attempts.[73] But lack of space and shortages of personnel made it difficult to keep tight control. The Brandenburg-Görden penitentiary in early October 1934 was designed for no more than 1,100 men (the building was not yet complete), yet it had to accommodate 1,918 prisoners. As only a few new officers had been employed, due to a lack of funds, in many wards of the penitentiary two officials were now responsible for supervising 250 inmates. 'It should be perfectly clear,' the Brandenburg-Görden governor warned, 'that correct observation, searches in cells, regular control of the bars, continued and constant supervision and, at the end of the day, security, is now out of the question.'[74] In the 1920s, successful escapes by inmates had become less frequent, thanks to the introduction of central alarm systems into penal institutions and the modernisation of police methods used to arrest escaped convicts. But this trend was reversed in the Third Reich, partly because of overcrowding. The governor in Untermaßfeld reported in 1936 that one in eight of the inmates currently held had already made escape attempts.[75]

The ideal of strict military discipline was further subverted by the employment of militant Nazis as prison warders. From 1933, Nazi activists were enlisted as assistant warders inside penal institutions. In part, this was a response to the rapid increase of inmate numbers, but the policy was also designed to dampen the social-revolutionary fervour of SA men by integrating them into the state.[76] By the mid-1930s, there were already well over a thousand such 'old fighters' working in penal institutions.[77]

Many of them were later taken on as regular warders.[78] The experienced regular warders and governors often complained about the undisciplined conduct of the 'old fighters', who were, despite their tag, in fact often much younger than the middle-aged regular prison officials. Many of the 'old fighters' had no military training and apparently took a rather casual approach, playing pranks on their colleagues, refusing to follow orders, joking with the inmates and selling them tobacco, stealing, arriving late for duty, or falling asleep while on guard. After two assistant warders had spied on him in the toilet, the Ichtershausen governor Vollrath, himself an old soldier, exclaimed: 'Gentlemen, the prison service needs conscientious men, not silly boys.'[79]

The employment of 'old fighters' also occasionally threatened to undermine the military hierarchy among the prison officials. To be sure, the 'old fighters' constituted only a minority among the around 8,700 prison warders (in 1938), and institutional power rested very much in the hands of the experienced regular officials.[80] But the Nazi activists enlisted as assistant warders at times used their political clout to challenge the status quo. Sometimes arriving for duty wearing their SS or SA outfit, rather than the warder's uniform, they drew on their party connections to undermine their superiors. In some cases, such campaigns succeeded. In March and April 1933, the governor in Brandenburg-Görden employed nine SS and SA members as assistant warders. Soon after their appointment, these men sent detailed complaints to the Prussian Minister of Justice, Kerrl and also to Göring. They alleged that inmates were spoiled and that 'Marxist offenders' were treated even better than others because some warders and the governor had sympathy for their views. Governor Dr Rudolf Schwerdtfeger defended himself against these accusations. His right-wing credentials were attested to by a senior prison administrator and, regarding the treatment of inmates, Schwerdtfeger made clear that 'the Spartan simplicity of the furnishings of the cells has already been realised, in accordance with the wishes of the Minister of Justice'. Initially, Schwerdtfeger remained in his job, but claims about his political unreliability resurfaced in the following years, and in 1937 the governor, suffering from illness, was granted early retirement by the Reich Ministry of Justice.[81] Such conflicts between established local officials and junior Nazi officials became less pronounced after the establishment of the Nazi dictatorship, when the 'old fighters' lost political leverage. The organisations of prison officials had already been coordinated in 1933, either dissolved completely or merged into Hans Frank's BNSDJ.[82] And in the following years, more and more experienced members of the prison service joined the Nazi movement. Opportunistic considerations played a part here. Experienced prison officials were well aware that failure to join could lead to attacks by Nazi activists and might also stand in the way of promotion.[83]

The subversion of the prison rules by some of the new Nazi warders did not always work in favour of the inmates. For a number of 'old fighters' were quick to beat prisoners, despite this being strictly forbidden except in cases of self-defence. One of them, an assistant warder in Untermaßfeld, repeatedly hit prisoners for no reason. When asked by the Ministry of Justice to explain himself, he openly bragged about his actions: 'I am supposed to have beaten a prisoner. Yes, that is what I did. I have given a young guy, who was disobedient and rude to me, a smack in the face. Today, he is one of the most obedient prisoners.'[84] Gratuitous beatings by warders had already occurred in the Weimar prison service, but it is almost certain that such violence increased in the Nazi period. The employment of Nazi warders was one factor. Another was the fact that there was no outside scrutiny of the prison – in contrast to the Weimar years, when newspapers, pressure groups and politicians had still kept an eye on life inside. In addition, an increasing number of penal institutions, including those reserved for women, were being equipped with rubber truncheons. A number of officials were happy to use their new weapons: inmates all over Germany reported that prisoners were pushed and beaten. According to SPD sources, most inmates in the Flensburg prison had 'smashed faces' when they saw visitors.[85] Inmates in Untermaßfeld were also repeatedly beaten in this way. One prisoner suffering from paralysis was hunted by warders across the prison yard with truncheons until he soiled his trousers.[86]

At the same time, senior prison officials, keen to maintain the prison rules, repeatedly criticised random violence against inmates. The Hamburg general state prosecutor reminded his officials in February 1939 that:

> Discipline and order can also be maintained without shoves and punches or swearwords. Of course, every attack on an official and every form of resistance has to be broken with determination, if need be with the rubber truncheon. But any additional punch or shove is a criminal offence.[87]

These were not entirely idle threats, as the prosecution of officials at the Luckau penitentiary, which had prompted the above letter, demonstrates. The governor of Luckau, Dr Rudolf Seitler, a former Freikorps fighter who had joined the prison service in August 1932, repeatedly tortured inmates, in particular those who had attempted to escape. In some respects, this was not entirely unusual. It had been a common practice for local prison officials all over Germany for many decades to assault inmates who had unsuccessfully tried to flee. Escapes could have serious disciplinary consequences for the officials and the beatings were intended as a warning to other inmates. Such beatings, it seems, were tacitly condoned by many governors and ministerial officials – not least, presumably, because a legal loophole meant that prisoners could not be charged by the courts for escaping.[88] What was unusual in governor Seitler's case was his personal involvement. Thus, on 16 September 1938, Seitler himself beat up an inmate who had tried to escape. He then ordered a warder to hit the inmate with a truncheon. After the prisoner had been locked up for seven days in a cold and damp detention cell, the governor set other prisoners upon him, and they viciously beat him up again. On the next day, the injured man was taken into detention for a full four weeks. This, and similar incidents, finally brought down governor Seitler. He was arrested in late 1938 and sentenced in February 1939 to seven months' imprisonment for causing grievous bodily harm. The fate of warders guilty of torturing prisoners in Luckau depended upon their seniority. Assistant warders, working on contract only, were quickly dismissed, but senior warders merely received small fines and remained as civil servants in the prison service – highlighting the half-heartedness with which the legal authorities dealt with violent behaviour among prison personnel.[89]

On the whole, while brutal attacks on inmates such as those in Luckau also occurred elsewhere, they were not yet endemic in prisons and penitentiaries (life in new prison camps is discussed below). Some inmates reported no such incidents at all.[90] Most warders were former soldiers who had been drilled for years to follow the prison regulations slavishly, which outlawed random brutality. In any case, the punishments listed in the prison regulations already gave the officials ample opportunity to discipline prisoners in a perfectly legal way. As we have seen, the new regulations introduced strict detention for penitentiary inmates, and at least some governors soon made extensive use of this new measure: in the Aichach penitentiary, almost one in four of all disciplinary offences committed by female inmates in 1939 was punished with strict detention.[91] However, this did not mean that disciplinary punishment was now entirely different to that in the 1920s. Such punishment in Weimar had often been frequent and strict. In 1929, almost two-thirds of all disciplinary offences in Prussian penitentiaries were punished with aggravated detention, the strictest penalty then available, which often had to be served in soiled clothes and freezing temperatures. Some German governors had even continued to use punishments such as manacling and detention in a dark cell, which had officially been outlawed.[92]

'Reform' and Propaganda

In the prison officials' eyes, harsh treatment of inmates promised a whole range of benefits. Apart from retribution, deterrence and strict discipline, it was also said to 'reform' prisoners. As we have seen, the vision of the prison as reformative was central to its success. It also, at least officially, remained an aspiration in the Third Reich. Hitler himself had noted in *Mein Kampf* that 'the born criminal is and will remain a criminal; but many people, who only have a certain inclination towards criminal behaviour, can still become valuable parts of the national community with the help of the right kind of education'.[93] However, it was clear in the Nazi prison that any 'education' – often equated with repression anyway – was subordinated to the ideals of expiation and deterrence. The prison regulations in 1933 and 1934 shifted the emphasis away from reform. This was reflected in the brief training courses for prison warders. While candidates in the Stuttgart district in the early 1930s still had to answer the question, 'Which personal qualities are necessary for the warder as teacher?', in the Third Reich the first essay was written on 'Commanding and obeying in the penal institution'.[94]

The inmates most affected by this shift were once again those in the few German states which had actually pioneered more extensive reforms in the 1920s. Elsewhere, the most important change was arguably the phasing out of the stages system. Introduced with great pedagogical ambitions in the Weimar years, it was now clearly out of step with the direction of prison policy. In Nazi Germany the benefits of the higher stages were reduced, and also limited to ever fewer prisoners. In Bavaria, the proportion of inmates on the two higher stages in several penal institutions for men had already fallen below 6 per cent by 1934.[95] Some privileges and benefits were now awarded without promotion to stages two or three. The stages system was virtually dead even before it was officially abandoned in German penal institutions for adults in July 1940.

In place of the abandoned policies of the 1920s, there were some attempts to use Nazi propaganda to turn prisoners into members of the 'national community'. These efforts had a limited impact. To be sure, inmates occasionally had to listen to radio speeches by Nazi leaders and they also came across Nazi ideology in prison newspapers, produced without any meaningful contribution from the inmates. Prison libraries were cleansed, from 1933 onwards, of books written by pacifist, left-wing and Jewish authors (some blacklisted books were withdrawn only during the war), and replaced by works in the Nazi canon.[96] But inmates were not forced to read such Nazi books or articles and most prisoners were touched only marginally by Nazi ideology, a fact criticised by the Gestapo.[97]

The prison authorities concentrated their efforts on inmates judged especially promising for indoctrination. In particular, those inmates attending prison school were exposed to Nazi ideology. Some teachers lectured on Nazi racial theory, while others read out articles from the Nazi daily *Völkischer Beobachter*. Such propaganda dominated the curriculum. In Aichach, the inmates admitted to prison school received five hours of lessons per month. This included three and a half hours of politics, singing German songs and studying 'German ways and customs'. By contrast, only one and a half hours were spent on writing and reading. Even the teaching of such practical skills was used for propaganda purposes, with reading lessons concentrating on 'German literature', which could include propagandists such as Alfred Rosenberg and Joseph Goebbels.[98]

Such attempts to 're-educate' selected prisoners apparently met with relatively little success. Of course, a number of prisoners claimed conversion to the Nazi cause and expressed their devotion to Hitler in their letters home.[99] Some of them certainly believed in the Third Reich. There is no reason to think that prisoners were completely immune to the 'Hitler myth' that had gripped most Germans in this period.[100] However, in many cases prisoners' letters were probably rather more pragmatic attempts to curry favour with the officials. Prisoners knew that their letters were vetted by the authorities and that a 'patriotic character' was one of the benchmarks by which they were judged. By praising the Third Reich, inmates hoped to gain better treatment, early release or avoid being sent to a concentration camp after completion of their sentence. The prison authorities, for their part, were uneasy about some aspects of the inmates' show of support for the Nazi cause. The Ministry of Justice in Saxony informed penal institutions as early as August 1933 that inmates should not be allowed to practise the Hitler salute.[101] The salute, senior Bavarian officials agreed, had to remain the privilege of the 'free German man'.[102]

In any case, mere lip-service to the regime was generally not enough to gain early release, and it seems that the legal authorities only rarely rewarded an inmate's supposed political conversion. Overall, a more substantial commitment to the Nazi cause was required. An untold number of convicted Nazi activists were released after having served only a fraction of their sentence. This included many SA and SS men who had been sentenced to lengthy spells in prison for violent crimes. Sometimes it was Hitler himself who intervened to ensure their early release.[103]

Another subtle change to the Weimar prison was that, at least in the early years of the Third Reich, slightly greater emphasis was placed on religious instruction. At the start of the Third Reich, prison chaplains hoped that religion, and with it their own role in penal institutions, would be strengthened, following concern that their status might be eroded by the Weimar prison reforms. They were not completely disappointed. Above all, this was probably a sign of the influence of the national-conservative officials in the Reich Ministry of Justice, who had traditionally seen Christianity as central to inmate rehabilitation. Most importantly, prison inmates were forced to attend religious services. Refusal to do so could lead to disciplinary punishment. This had been a general policy in the German Empire, when it was regarded as indispensable for the moral awakening of 'criminal sinners'. But this requirement had been abolished in 1920, as it was incompatible with the right to religious freedom enshrined in the new Weimar constitution.[104]

However, there was no religious revival in penal institutions in the Third Reich. Due to the anti-Christian current in Nazism, particularly zealous believers among the prison officials were regarded with some suspicion. At least one religious fanatic, Johannes Muntau, was actually removed as a regional prison administrator, apparently on account of his religious views.[105] The religious services in Nazi prisons were far removed from the ideal of some officials – solemn occasions where inmates were confronted with their guilt. In reality, many inmates saw the services as a good opportunity to barter and gossip. A few chaplains critical of the Nazi dictatorship used the services for political subversion: some allowed inmates to engage in political debates during the weekly religious instruction while others included covert criticisms of the regime in their sermons, until they were denounced to the authorities.[106]

Living Conditions

Looking at the general provision for prisoners, it is clear that life in German penal institutions became worse after the Nazi takeover. To start with, the prison diet, already reduced in previous years, was cut further. According to SPD sources, expenditure on food for penitentiary inmates was cut in real terms by half between 1932 and 1935. While this was surely exaggerated, the quality of food definitely deteriorated.[107] Before the First World War, the aim of prison nutrition had been to provide what had been scientifically determined as the physiological minimum, and that as cheaply as possible. Inmates were not supposed to derive any pleasure from eating. In the 1920s, there had been some attempts to change this and offer food which was both nutritious and more appetising. While this practice did not disappear entirely in the Nazi prison, prisoners' diet did get worse.[108] In the Third Reich, numerous penal institutions were competing with each other to keep spending as low as possible.[109] There had been a long-standing belief that the standard of living of prisoners had to be lower than that of the poorest sections of the population, for reasons of deterrence. This was now enshrined in the new Prussian prison regulations, a provision welcomed in the Nazi press.[110] But food cuts were not just the result of this ideological approach by the prison officials. Germany as a whole experienced shortages, with the price of basic foodstuffs such as fat and potatoes increasing sharply. Once again, it was inmates in 'total institutions' that were hit particularly hard. Coffee, tea, rice and lentils became practically impossible for prison officials to purchase, making the prison diet even more monotonous.[111]

Many prisoners were plagued by hunger. One inmate in the Brieg penitentiary described typical rations in 1936 as consisting of 'a lot of watery vegetables, $\frac{1}{2}$ litre in the morning, $\frac{3}{4}$ litre at lunchtime and evenings. With it, one gets a piece of dry bread. As all this food is prepared without fat, each inmate gets 50 grams of fat per day. Meat is served only once a week.'[112] In the same year, SPD informers reported from the Plötzensee prison that 'it is so bad that inmates, to pacify their hunger, pick up mouldy bits of bread from the bins'.[113] In the second half of the 1930s, numerous local prison officials warned that poor nutrition had led to significant weight loss and also noted the rise in skin disease among inmates.[114] At a meeting in March 1938, several general state prosecutors argued that the rations were no longer sufficient, especially as inmates were now often performing exhausting labour.[115] In response, the Reich Ministry of Justice permitted governors to serve more meat and fish in the evenings.[116] Most inmates benefited under these regulations, but complaints about malnourishment continued. In June 1938, the Vechta prison doctor urged a further increase in provisions so that the prisoners could eat their fill at least once a day.[117]

Inmates' health was also affected by massive overcrowding. Most German prisoners shared their cells at night with one or more others. At times, there were 16 inmates sharing cells designed for only four.[118] While no new prisons were built in the Nazi period, several larger penal institutions (or wings) which had been closed in the 1920s because they were decaying and unhygienic, were quickly reopened to make space for the influx of prisoners into the system.[119] Other institutions converted various spaces into additional cells. In the Aichach institution for women, for example, the gymnasium was transformed into an associated cell in 1934.[120] Conditions were not uniformly bad all over

Germany, but in many prisons and penitentiaries overcrowding had serious consequences. Inmates were dirty as trips to the shower rooms were restricted and clothing was changed infrequently. In the Waldheim penitentiary, around 100 men were forced into a large community cell, which, according to one prisoner, 'literally stank like a rabbit cage'.[121]

There were serious epidemics and many cells were infested with bugs. Many prison officials did not approve of these conditions. They habitually insisted on the maintenance of spotlessness in the cells and corridors, which had long been seen as an important ingredient in reforming prisoners. This meticulous order was now upset. In addition, prison officials themselves were affected by the poor conditions, as they had to work in these reeking institutions. In the summer of 1935, the governor of the Remscheid-Lüttringhausen penitentiary complained about conditions in many cells: 'In this heat, three prisoners lie together in a small normal cell. This results in unbearable fumes, especially if the prisoners have to wear the same clothes, day and night, for 14 days.'[122] Overcrowding only eased in the late 1930s, when the overall rate of convictions declined. This affected women more than men, as the number of female prisoners fell much more quickly and sharply, from 9,563 (31 December 1937) to just 5,793 (30 July 1938). It seems likely that by the summer of 1938, penal institutions for women held slightly less inmates than their official maximum capacity – for the first time since 1933.[123]

Most prison inmates could not expect competent treatment in case of illness. Medical care in Nazi prisons was largely characterised by negligence, lack of supplies and brutality. This had not been very different before 1933. Of course, health care for prisoners had slowly improved during the German Empire, as part of the general drive to turn the prison into a more effective machine of punishment and reform. But officials had ensured that improvements did not undermine the severity of punishment. In his manual on prison administration, Karl Krohne had reminded prison officials that 'the discipline of the institution takes precedence over the health of the offender'. Krohne added that 'the sick prisoner is, in the first place, a convict, and only then a patient'.[124] This attitude characterised the approach of German prison doctors for decades. They often had little time for prisoners and dismissed sick inmates as cheats and malingerers. To be sure, health care gradually continued to improve in the Weimar years. But prison regulations still aimed at little more than the provision of a minimum of care, and even these basic rules were often not fully implemented. For example, while the prison guidelines of 1923 stipulated that all of the larger penal institutions had to have a full-time doctor, only seven of the 37 penal institutions in Prussia with a capacity for 500 or more inmates actually employed a full-time doctor in 1927.[125] Even these full-time doctors often had little time for inmates and examined them superficially, if at all. Some doctors only worked a few hours each day in the institution. The rest of their time was spent in private surgeries.[126]

Pregnant prisoners also suffered from poor medical care. In the Weimar years, legal officials had been told to avoid imprisoning offenders during the last months of their pregnancy. While this rule remained valid in Nazi Germany, it was often disregarded and births behind bars remained frequent. In the women's prison in Berlin, 13 of the 210 women imprisoned in September 1938 were looking after their babies, and another 14 were pregnant. In Aichach, there were 34 births in 1935 and 1936 alone.[127] Prison doctors in the Third Reich (and indeed before) often lacked sufficient medical knowledge or were indifferent to these women, while some female warders on duty in sick bays had not received proper training as midwives.[128]

The treatment of pregnant women exemplified the way in which female inmates continued to be neglected. They played little role in the considerations of the leading prison officials, all of whom were men (only during the war did the first woman, Frau Marquard-Ibbeken, join the prison administration in the Reich Ministry of Justice). In 1935, only six of the 167 'special penal institutions' (that is, those with a full-time governor) were reserved for women only. Most female prisoners were held in one of the 92 institutions largely intended for men, where they would generally occupy small wings, separated from the male prisoners.[129] Here, official duties, except bathing and body searching, were still often carried out by the male warders.[130] The vast majority of senior local prison officials were male. Some of the institutions reserved for women were led by female governors (their number further increased during the war), but these were exceptions. Male doctors, for example, had successfully fought against the involvement of women in their profession since the turn of the century. And even though qualified female doctors applied for jobs, the male-dominated prison administration apparently preferred men.[131]

One prison doctor who profited from this gender bias was Dr Ludwig Schemmel, who had joined the Aichach penal institution for women in 1931. Like many of his colleagues, Schemmel simultaneously worked as a general practitioner, limiting the time he spent inside the institution. When he did encounter the prisoners, Dr Schemmel often treated them with barely concealed contempt. He ordered inmates to take off their shoes while waiting for their turn, in order to protect the floor covers (a common practice in many other institutions, too). Prisoners, already sick, had to stand on the cold floor for long periods.[132] When they were finally seen by Dr Schemmel, they were sometimes greeted with verbal and physical abuse. According to one penitentiary inmate, the doctor told her in 1938: 'I don't care if you rot away'.[133] It was not just Aichach prisoners who were distressed by his behaviour. A few of the female warders were concerned enough to send two anonymous letters to the

Munich general state prosecutor in the late 1930s. They wrote that Schemmel 'takes sensual pleasure from assaulting and torturing the prisoners and he has many opportunities here to satisfy his lust. During almost every report at the doctor's, prisoners are slapped in the face or pulled around by their hair.' The Aichach warders believed that the male governor condoned this treatment. The same was evidently true for the prison administration, for Schemmel was allowed to continue to work in the penal institution.[134]

Brutal behaviour by prison doctors occurred in many other penal institutions in the Third Reich. But even those doctors who took their duties more seriously found it difficult to provide adequate treatment, due to financial constraints. Despite the massive increase in inmate numbers there was often no money for more personnel. And seriously ill inmates who had been operated on in a state hospital were often transported back to prison as soon as they could be moved, in order to minimise the fee which the prison administration had to pay the hospital.[135] In addition, prison officials were instructed to feed sick inmates the same food as healthy ones whenever possible. Special rations could be handed out, but the doctors were asked 'to exercise the greatest economy both in permitting diet for the sick and in allowing any additional diet'.[136]

On the whole, conditions in penal institutions declined in the Third Reich. Prisoners were worse off than before and they also effectively lost the ability to protest against their treatment. Appeals to the outside world were virtually impossible. Prisoners who tried to use illicit channels to complain about their treatment were brutally disciplined. Willi O., a prisoner in Untermaßfeld, was punished with four weeks' detention (one week with only water and bread) after prison officials discovered a letter he intended to smuggle outside, in which he complained about his poor state of health. According to a fellow inmate, Willi O. lost 12 kilos during his detention.[137] In Nazi Germany, ever fewer inmates made complaints, much to the delight of the prison officials. Prison governors in the Hamm district noted with great satisfaction in November 1934 that the sharp decline in prisoner complaints had significantly improved the 'job satisfaction of the officials'.[138]

However, one must not overlook the similarities between prison life in Nazi Germany and the period before 1933. Conditions had often been poor and discipline strict throughout the 1920s, while the trend towards harsher punishment had already become evident in the last years of the Weimar Republic. In some ways, life in penal institutions before the Second World War resembled prison life in Imperial Germany. The stricter treatment of prisoners, the limitation of the right to complain, reluctance to experiment with innovative reforms, smaller rations, greater stress on religious instruction – all these measures were welcomed by reactionary prison officials who had rejected some of the more progressive aspects of the Weimar prison. But it would be wrong to picture the Nazi prison as purely reactionary. After all, it was in the Third Reich that policies against 'incorrigible' inmates were introduced, finally realising this long-standing demand of the modern school of criminal law. And as the rest of this chapter will show, in the field of prison labour, the prison service in the Nazi dictatorship also slowly began to leave the past behind.

Forced Labour

Forced labour was traditionally at the heart of imprisonment. In Weimar Germany, there had been three main types of labour. Firstly, there was domestic work in the direct service of the penal institution itself, washing clothes, preparing food and so on. Secondly, a number of prisoners worked for state offices, for instance, producing furniture for other penal institutions. Finally, prisoners were forced to work for private companies or individuals. Often, these companies would buy finished goods from the penal institution or set up workshops inside, overseen jointly by their employees and the warders. In other cases, prisoners were temporarily contracted to companies or individuals such as farmers during the harvest. Such labour was a source of income for the prison authorities, but any financial gains were far outweighed by the yearly state subsidies for the penal institutions. As for the prisoners, they had no legal right to be paid for their labour, but only qualified for a so-called 'reward'. In 1927, this amounted on average to the paltry sum of 0.16 Reichsmark per day (civilian industrial workers earned around 5 Reichsmark) – less than a quarter of what the prison administration was paid by private contractors for the prisoners' labour. Small as this 'reward' was, the prisoners did not even receive all of it immediately. Instead, the authorities kept half of it or more, only handing it over as a lump sum to the inmate on the day of release. The rest could be used by inmates during their imprisonment. Some inmates chose to send small amounts of money home to support their families, others applied to buy a few extra provisions, such as bread, pencils, soap and toothpaste.[139]

The Nazi prison was initially characterised not by forced labour, but by prisoner unemployment. During the depression unemployment had quickly spread to the penal institutions, in particular in states such as Prussia where large numbers of inmates had been employed by private enterprises. The proportion of inmates without work in all Prussian penal institutions rose from 35.8 per cent (1930) to 55.2 per cent (1932). Unemployment was lower in institutions for long-term prisoners, especially women, who were traditionally more engaged in domestic work than male prisoners (see below).[140] In the Third Reich unemployment as a whole soon dropped sharply, from 4.8 million in 1933 to 2.7 million in the following year. By 1936, it had fallen almost to the

1928 level, boosting the popularity of the new regime in general, and Hitler in particular.[141] But penal institutions were only gradually affected. In July 1934, almost half of the just over 100,000 inmates were not working.[142] As late as November 1934, Wilhelm Crohne in the Reich Ministry of Justice referred to 'catastrophic unemployment in the institutions'.[143]

On balance, most inmates undoubtedly welcomed the lack of work. True, they were often bored and also could not earn money to buy themselves extra provisions. But at least they were not forced to perform often dreary and exhausting prison labour and, in a number of penal institutions, they could even spend their days together. One male prisoner in Groß-Strehlitz reported that the inmates passed most of their time 'in community rooms with about 20 men in each one. Here, one can read and play. The penitentiary administration has provided each room with some board games (chess and halma) . . . .'[144] Another prisoner, sharing his cell with only one other inmate, recalled after the war that 'I read from early to late . . . German classical authors and philosophers. I was as happy as one can be in a penitentiary'.[145]

How can the continued high levels of prisoner unemployment in the early years of the Third Reich be explained? In part, they were caused by prisoners being barred from government initiatives to reduce unemployment on the outside, such as work-creation schemes. In addition, there was presumably pressure on employers to fill vacant jobs first with free workers, rather than with prisoners. The ideological obsessions of some prison officials also helped to keep inmates out of work. This was true particularly in Prussia, where the Ministry of Justice in 1933–34 was in the hands of the committed Nazis Hanns Kerrl and Roland Freisler. Already in 1933, they were demanding that all links between penal institutions and Jewish companies should be severed. Other German states warned that this would increase unemployment among inmates, but the Prussian prison administration went ahead anyway.[146] Furthermore, in November 1933 it ordered that more prison labour should be limited to manual labour, in order to create work opportunities on the outside.[147]

Unemployment amongst convicts only declined markedly in the mid-1930s when the economic recovery finally reached the prisons. Also, a number of previously unemployed prisoners were now occupied with land cultivation in new prisoner camps run by the Reich Ministry of Justice (examined in the next section). And even though work was still hard to come by in some penal institutions, by 1935–36 only one in every three prisoners was out of work.[148] This decline continued in the following years and by March 1938 four out of five prisoners were working. In view of the fact that this figure included inmates unable to work and those rarely occupied with labour (see below), it is clear that practically all inmates judged fit for work, and serving sentences in prisons or penitentiaries, were now employed.[149] Once more, work dominated most days spent by convicted offenders in prisons and penitentiaries. Prisoners were generally forced to work all day Monday to Saturday, only briefly interrupted by lunch and exercise in the yard. One prisoner, held in the Werl penitentiary in the mid-1930s, described the rigid daily routine followed in many German penal institutions, with some modifications, at that time: '6 a.m. get up, 6.30 a.m. coffee distribution, 7 a.m. start of work, from 8–8.30 a.m. exercise in the yard . . . then back to work . . . After the lunchbreak from 12–1 p.m., work again until 6 p.m. After dinner, depart at 7.30 p.m. to the dormitories'.[150]

Increasingly, prison labour in the Third Reich was influenced by Nazi ideology – as was the German economy as a whole, which was being transformed into a racist, militarist command economy. This development was marked by the Four-Year Plan, introduced in the autumn of 1936. Its goal had been outlined by Hitler in August 1936 in a secret memorandum, in which he demanded that the German army and economy be ready for war within four years. He called for rapid rearmament and the build-up of military resources. This policy was to be accompanied by an increase in economic self-sufficiency, reducing the need for imports. This emphasis on self-sufficiency was one of the 'lessons' Hitler thought he had learned from the First World War. Germany, he believed, had to become independent of the world market, so that it could not be hurt again by a blockade. Autarky was proclaimed as a goal for industry, which was to intensify the production of fuel and synthetic rubber, and also for agriculture. Hitler noted that it was 'our duty to use any arable land that may become available either for human or animal foodstuffs or for the cultivation of fibrous materials'. He delegated responsibility for executing the plan to Hermann Göring.[151]

At first, the increasing mobilisation of the German economy for war had little effect on prison labour. The Reich Ministry of Justice did remind prison officials that autarky was a central aim of the Four-Year Plan, encouraging the recycling of raw materials in penal institutions and demanding production increases in agriculture and land cultivation. But in practice the leading prison administrators in this period simply seemed relieved that the inmates were now back at work and showed no urgency to transform prison labour. On the whole, work inside prisons and penitentiaries in the mid-1930s was probably little different in comparison to the Weimar period.

To put this into perspective, it is necessary to have a more detailed look at German prisoner labour before 1933. In Imperial Germany, prison inmates had often been employed in their own cells in repetitive and dirty labour, with fixed quotas to be produced each day. Repeated failure to achieve the quota was often punished, a practice which remained common in the Weimar and the Nazi prison. Inmates in prison workshops had generally used outdated equipment. Many prison officials had opposed the introduction of modern machinery, partly because they feared that this would lessen the suffering of the inmates during forced labour, and thus undermine the deterrent effect of imprisonment as a whole. They were not alone in their views. Private companies, artisans and trade unions also frequently criticised competition from prison labour, attacks which had accompanied the modern prison from the start, not just in Germany. As a result, German penal institutions, at least according to one observer, had 'used production methods which can hardly be encountered any more in private enterprises in the Balkans and in deepest Russia...'.[152] In the early 1920s, up to ten inmates were still occupied in several Prussian institutions with turning a great wheel that powered a chainsaw, which could easily have been operated by a small electric motor.[153]

There had been some change in prison labour in the 1920s, as we have already seen in the case of Untermaßfeld. Modern production methods were slowly introduced into more prison workshops, championed by some senior prison officials and politicians as an important rehabilitative measure.[154] By the mid-1920s, around half of the bakeries and laundries in penal institutions were equipped with some form of machinery. The same was true for around one-third of all smithies and carpentry workshops. At the same time, an increasing number of inmates were allowed to take apprentice examinations as carpenters, tailors or shoemakers, though attempts to extend such activities further were often thwarted by artisans' associations.[155]

But this gradual introduction of new techniques of production often stopped at penal institutions for women, few of which used modern technology. Instead, most female prisoners were engaged in manual domestic labour. In institutions they shared with men, for example, women had to carry out many chores for the male prisoners, such as mending their clothes. Prison officials had an obvious ideological justification for this: domestic work was supposed to turn female prisoners into home-makers. Many prison officials and criminologists believed that these women had been led to crime by deviating from the bourgeois ideal of the sexually passive housewife and mother, and needed to be moulded according to this model.[156] Prison teacher Anni Dimpfl in Aichach summarised the main themes of her lessons in 1928: 'The woman, the soul of the family; the faithful companion of the man; the loving mother of the children; the hard working and reliable housewife, either as lady or as maid.'[157] Of course, these aims were not relevant to the experiences of most female offenders, only a minority of whom were married. Most belonged to the poorest sections of society and had to fend for themselves, despite lacking qualifications.[158] For most of these women, the bourgeois ideal of the woman as housewife was unattainable and possibly also undesirable.

In the early years of the Third Reich, the general organisation of labour inside penal institutions remained deeply rooted in Weimar practice. In summer 1937, the single most prominent occupation of inmates, carried out by about one in every six prisoners, was work in the service of the penal institution. Slightly fewer inmates were employed in pasting paper bags and weaving mats, occupations as typical of prison labour in Germany as the manufacturing of mailbags in English prisons and the production of car licence tags in US prisons in this period.[159] In some cases, German prison officials simply adapted the classification of prison labour to Nazi ideology and the Four-Year Plan, without changing its actual content. For instance, in 1937 dozens of inmates in the Brandenburg-Görden penitentiary were occupied in recycling threads and strings, a particularly hard and painful task. Trying to untie hundreds of small knots with a sharp metal stick, the inmates often hurt themselves, especially as they had to work fast to achieve the daily quota, for which they were awarded a mere 0.04 Reichsmark. Other inmates had to spend their days tying recycled pieces of string together. According to a former prisoner, one 'took a thread, and another one and makes a knot, a sailor's knot. Then a new thread and again a knot. Thread, knot – thread, knot! Millions of knots!' The same jobs had already been carried out in the Weimar period, but now the Brandenburg-Görden officials boasted that each inmate recycled around 10 kilos per month, preserving precious raw materials and saving foreign exchange.[160]

Prison labour also mostly continued to be handed out regardless of inmates' qualifications. The ruthless persecution of political opponents of the Nazis by the courts meant that penal institutions filled up with SPD supporters and union members, who, in contrast to most other prison inmates, had often learned a trade.[161] But initially the prison authorities made no effort to exploit this skilled labour force. According to State Secretary Freisler, only 1,300 of the around 8,000 trained metal workers in penal institutions were actually doing metalwork.[162] Often, inmates were simply moved from one occupation to the next, depending on which workshop required inmates, with little regard for efficient production.

This approach only changed as war came closer. In the spring of 1938, the Reich Ministry of Justice introduced a whole new range of policies aimed at bringing prison labour more into line with the Four-Year Plan. This shift resulted partly from pressure by other state and municipal offices, which demanded the employment of prisoners in new work projects or to fill positions that had been left vacant as a result of the labour shortage of the late 1930s. Evidently, leading Nazi officials regarded prisoners as a cheap source of labour which could be tapped into at any given moment. Prison officials were snowed under with requests for the supply of prisoners as forced labourers. Inmates were in demand as agricultural labourers, construction workers, railway workers, mechanics and garbage collectors.[163] Other considerations also played a part in the attempts to restructure prison labour. Following the expansion of the police state, officials in the Ministry of Justice became increasingly aware that it was vital for the prison system to be seen to operate in line with Nazi principles. As we shall see, leading police officials had begun to demand that any inmates in penal institutions, who were supposedly not treated according to Nazi ideology, should be transferred to the SS camps instead. Restructuring prison labour according to the Four-Year Plan therefore meant that the Ministry officials in Berlin could present the prison system as operating in accordance with Nazi ideology and resist police pressure to hand over inmates.[164]

Prison labour was to be transformed in 1938 in different ways. To start with, the Reich Ministry of Justice aimed to increase the number of prisoners available for work. State Secretary Roland Freisler promised that he would ensure 'that even the last state prisoner will be used for hard labour, as long as he is partially able to work'. Consequently, the old provision that remand prisoners were not obliged to work was abolished on 23 March 1938 and inmates in jails serving very short sentences were also increasingly forced to work.[165] Also, the employment of prisoners in labour outside the walls of prisons and penitentiaries was to be increased. Prisoners were to be used in road construction, land cultivation projects, harvest work and other projects regarded as vital for the Four-Year Plan.[166] Furthermore, prison officials were urged to increase the productivity of prison labour. The proportion of prisoners officially allowed to work in the domestic service of each institution was reduced to 7 per cent of the inmate population. In August 1939, this was reduced further, to just 5 per cent. Any unproductive labour was to be replaced with work essential for the Four-Year Plan, with inmates employed according to their skills. Manual labour was to be supplanted by machines, a significant shift in emphasis. As late as November 1936, the ministerial official in charge of prison labour, Sigmund Nörr, had told the general state prosecutors that productivity was not of primary importance in penal institutions. Machines should only be purchased in special circumstances. Two years later, however, Freisler reversed this policy, insisting that in those institutions where 'more modern machines have been cleared away in recent years, they should be used again to improve the productivity of labour'.[167] Finally, the inmates' output was to be increased. Brutal pressure was already applied in penal institutions to force inmates to work, and they were punished and insulted if they failed to reach their quota. Fear made many inmates work faster. Some regular builders, working side by side with prisoners on an extension to the Untermaßfeld penitentiary in 1937, complained about the speed with which the inmates carried out their tasks. But in 1938, officials were encouraged to rely not only on the 'stick', but to use positive incentives to make the inmates work even more.

Special rewards could be introduced for hard workers, including better food, more frequent baths and cigarette breaks. And, in future, decisions regarding the early release of an inmate could be based partly on the prisoner's diligence.[168]

Prison labour in Nazi Germany demonstrates once more the influence of outside factors on life behind bars. From the mid-1930s, large-scale unemployment among prisoners diminished, following the economic recovery. And in the late 1930s, prison labour was increasingly influenced by Nazi ideology, as the state prison system was beginning to be integrated into the economic drive to prepare Germany for war. Even though its overall contribution remained small, prison labour was increasingly seen as part of the national economy.

The various measures introduced in the late 1930s did not change prison labour overnight. But they had at least some impact. To begin with, more prisoners were forced to work than ever before. According to the Reich Ministry of Justice, the proportion of employed inmates among all prisoners (excluding those unable to work) increased to up to 95 per cent during 1938.[169] In addition, between May and December 1938 alone, some 93 prison workshops for private contractors regarded as inefficient were closed, and work in a further 167 such workshops was scaled down.[170] Most importantly, more and more prisoners were employed on the outside. Many inmates were transported from their prison or penitentiary to building sites every morning, or were confined in permanent satellite camps affiliated to penal institutions. In some prisons and penitentiaries, more inmates were working outside than inside by the late 1930s. In total, at least 20,000 prisoners in Germany worked outside the walls of penal institutions every day by spring 1938. Almost 12,000 of them (men only) were held in large prison camps, under especially harsh conditions.[171]

Prison Camps

Nazi Germany was a land of camps. During the Second World War, there were at least 17 different types of camp, including death camps, concentration camps, police camps and camps for delinquent youths, Sinti and Roma, Jews, foreign workers and many other victims of Nazism. Most of these camps were set up during the escalation of Nazi terror after 1939.[172] But a number had already been built before war broke out. These included several large-scale prison camps, arguably the most striking innovation in Nazi prison policy before the Second World War. Crucially, such prison camps were not part of the SS concentration camp apparatus. Like regular prisons and penitentiaries, they were penal institutions run by the criminal justice system. The legal authorities in Nazi Germany controlled their own camps.

The first new prison camp had been set up under the control of the Prussian Ministry of Justice in the area north and west of Papenburg, along the River Ems near the Dutch border. Cultivation of the moors in the Emsland, which had been going on for decades, intensified in the Third Reich. Initially, the moors were chosen as the site for concentration camps, set up in 1933 and guarded by SS and SA men. Steam ploughs, which had previously been used on the moors, were often discarded and the prisoners, who later included prominent inmates such as Carl von Ossietzky, were forced to carry out the hard work manually, supposedly in order to 're-educate' them through brutal physical labour. In spring 1934, the Prussian Ministry of Justice took over two of the camps in the Emsland, Börgermoor and Neusustrum. The remaining concentration camp inmates were held in Esterwegen, which was eventually also left to the prison authorities.[173] As in most penal institutions, common criminals made up the majority of the inmate population in the Emsland prison camp. In the prewar period, only about one in ten prisoners had been convicted as political opponents.[174]

At the time, the initiative by the Prussian legal authorities promised to solve two urgent problems facing the prison administration. Transferring prisoners to new prison camps would ease the massive overcrowding inside regular penal institutions. Simultaneously, it would cut down on unemployment among prisoners. But the officials could see many other advantages. Forcing prisoners to cultivate the moors appealed to the Prussian authorities as it was exhausting manual work, and thus in line with the emphasis on punitive prison life. In addition, it was non-competitive and would provoke no criticism from small businesses and artisans. Finally, the cultivation of the moors also fitted into the Nazis' 'blood and soil' ideology. The judicial authorities stressed that the prison camps would help 'to satisfy the people's hunger for land and create a new peasantry'.[175]

Prison camps and labour outside penal institutions were not entirely original ideas. Outside labour had been introduced in Prussia in the mid-nineteenth century, even though it was apparently used rather rarely. Nevertheless, by the turn of the century, farming and the cultivation of forests and moors were undertaken by prisoners in several German states. Some officials supported this work, partly because they argued that once inmates had become used to working the land, these prisoners could move to rural workers' colonies after their release, thus 'cleansing' the cities.[176] Looking at the Weimar years, close to 1,500 penitentiary inmates had been employed on average per day (1926) in Prussia in the cultivation of land, a form of prisoner employment also championed by the SPD and the Communists. Many prisoners working on the outside returned to penal institutions in the evening. Others were held permanently in barracks and large farmsteads, such as some 300 prisoners working on the moors in the Ems area.[177] Similar work had been carried out in other German states. For example, between 1913 and 1929 the Straubing penitentiary had run a satellite camp for up to 80 prisoners based in the Benediktbeuern monastery. The prisoners here were occupied in moor cultivation, as well as building paths and helping farmers during the harvest.[178]

The most obvious difference between these early camps and Nazi prison camps was size. In 1937, the Emsland camp of the Reich Ministry of Justice included seven sub-camps in the area around Papenburg, filled with around 8,800 prisoners.[179] Prison camps soon became part of Nazi planning for war, following the emphasis on autarky in agriculture in the Four-Year Plan. Göring's office, one of the most powerful agencies in the late 1930s, stressed that such work was important to increase German self-sufficiency, a goal threatened by the growing shortage of workers. 'Therefore, it is absolutely vital,' a Four-Year Plan official wrote to the Reich Ministry of Justice, 'that the workers missing ... in the cultivation of land are replaced by state prisoners.'[180] Nazi leaders also approved of the Emsland camp, which regularly featured in the press. Hitler himself had taken notice of the camp early on. Indeed, he was so impressed that he commissioned his favourite architect Albert Speer to design a communal building for the camp warders in 1936. In February 1937, Hitler received a group of Emsland warders and promised them another communal building. Hitler wanted to demonstrate his support for the camp publicly and ordered that his meeting with the warders be reported in the press.[181]

Always keen to secure support from the Nazi leadership, the Reich Ministry of Justice proclaimed prison camps to be the future of imprisonment. Roland Freisler, for example, described the Emsland camp in November 1936 as the 'most modern part of the prison service'.[182] In the second half of the 1930s, the prison authorities quickly set up or extended further camps for the cultivation of land. Because of the very hard physical labour expected of the inmates, these camps were limited to male prisoners, just like the Emsland camp. The prison camp Rodgau was opened in April 1938. Following a request by the Reich Ministry for Food and Agriculture, in cooperation with the office for the Four-Year Plan, the prison authorities agreed to send 3,500 inmates to Rodgau, which consisted of a former workhouse in Dieburg and several satellite camps. By December 1938, more than 1,000 prisoners were already working in the camp, on river regulation and the building of paths and bridges. The main project was the building of a sewer system linking Frankfurt am Main and Offenbach to large surrounding areas of farmland, in order to increase the fertility of the land.[183] Another prison camp was the one in Oberems in Gütersloh. This camp had already existed in the pre-Nazi period and was now extended. Around 1,000 prisoners were held here from 1937 onwards in 27 satellite camps, each consisting of solid houses resembling the farmhouses in the area. Prisoners were forced to cultivate wasteland and improve the fertility of fields.[184] More prisoners were toiling in several camps along the Rivers Elbe and Saale, occupied with river regulation in the rocky terrain and with the construction of locks. This work had been going on for some time when it was stepped up from 1936 onwards. Many hundreds more inmates were taken there and new camps were set up, with the main camp situated in Griebo near Coswig (Anhalt).[185] In order to fill these new prison camps with sufficient inmates, the Reich Ministry of Justice set quotas for individual districts, specifying how many male prisoners had to be transferred from other penal institutions. In 1938 the Ministry relaxed the rules governing which prisoners were classified as suitable for outside work, to increase the pool of eligible prisoners.[186] The transfer of inmates to the camps meant that prisons and penitentiaries lost many of their most able workers. Inmates left behind were often those judged too weak to perform hard physical labour.

In their enthusiasm for land cultivation, officials in the Reich Ministry of Justice also decided to enlarge the Emsland camp further. In July 1938, they announced that another 10,000 prisoners were to be transferred there by the following spring. More barracks were built, with the aim of housing a total of 19,000 prisoners. These ambitious plans for the extension of the Emsland camp were never realised. In the late 1930s the annual number of inmates in the Emsland camp actually declined from 9,500 (1938) to 9,234 (1939). In part, this was due to the overall fall in prisoner numbers in Germany in the last years before the outbreak of war, reducing the number of inmates available for outside work. In addition, the Emsland camp was now competing for inmates with other prison camps. Also, by the late 1930s, it had become obvious that the immediate benefits from land cultivation such as that carried out around Papenburg were negligible. At a time when too few agricultural labourers were working on existing fertile fields, the use of prisoners to develop even more land seemed increasingly pointless.[187]

The failure of the plans to extend the Emsland camp was also indicative of a shift in Nazi war planning. Long-term projects such as land cultivation lost their appeal as war seemed increasingly imminent. After Hitler had successfully established his dictatorship, Nazi foreign policy became markedly more aggressive. In a secret speech on 5 November 1937, Hitler outlined Germany's foreign policy aims. Autarky, he now claimed, could not be obtained with regard to food or the economy as a whole. Thus, in order to 'preserve the racial community', Germany required more living space, which could be achieved 'only by the use of force'.[188] Convicts were assigned a small part in the preparation for Germany's military campaign. One specific goal mentioned by Hitler in his secret speech was the destruction of Czechoslovakia. Hitler felt that his opportunity had arrived in late spring 1938. On 30 May 1938, he informed his military leaders that 'it is my unalterable decision to smash Czechoslovakia by military action in the near future'.[189] Hitler demanded that this war should be carried out with 'lightning speed'. In preparation for such an attack, the so-called Ostmarkstraße, under construction since 1935, was to be completed as soon as possible. This road, today a popular tourist route, was to run for around 250 kilometres parallel to the Czech border, from Passau to Hof, and was intended for the use of military vehicles during the invasion.[190] To deter other powers from intervening, Hitler ordered the building of the Westwall: between May 1938 and September 1939, over 600 kilometres of fortifications were built on Germany's western border, from Switzerland to the area around Aachen.[191]

Both these projects, the Ostmarkstraße and the Westwall, were originally to be carried out with the help of prisoners. At the height of the Czech crisis, on 28 August 1938, Hitler ordered that, within 14 days, inmates from the Emsland prison camp should be put to work at the Westwall. The Reich Ministry of Justice went into frantic overdrive to fulfil this demand. By 10 September 1938, around 3,000 prisoners, from the Emsland camp and other penal institutions, had already been transferred. In anticipation of the arrival of many thousands more, over 100 barracks had been dismantled in the Emsland camp and taken away. But on the same day, Hitler reversed his earlier orders, possibly because the deployment of criminal offenders would have undermined the propaganda attempt to present the Westwall as a historic project of the Nazi community, carried out by 'national comrades' in the Labour Service and other Nazi organisations.[192]

In contrast, convicts were used in the construction of the Ostmarkstraße. Due to labour shortages and the urgency of the project, the General Inspector for German Road Construction demanded in early summer 1938 that prisoners be made available. Following an agreement with the Reich Ministry of Justice on 18 June 1938, the prison camp Bayerische Ostmark was set up, divided into six different sub-camps, each holding between 200 and 300 men (mainly penitentiary inmates). The camps were built like construction workers' barracks, surrounded by barbed wire, guard dogs and watchtowers manned by guards with machine-guns. But soon after the camps had been set up, the Ostmarkstraße lost its strategic importance. In October 1938, following the Munich agreement, the neighbouring Sudetenland fell to Nazi Germany, and in March 1939 German troops occupied the rest of western Czechoslovakia. By the time construction work was finally stopped in 1941, only around 150 kilometres of road had been built.[193]

The proliferation of prison camps and outside prison labour increased the visibility of Nazi terror. Since the nineteenth century, punishment had largely taken place away from the public gaze. This was still true in the Third Reich, at least in the prewar years. Even so, the growth of large-scale outside labour inevitably increased the points of contact between the population and prisoners, undermining the regulations which strictly prohibited any such contact. Some civilians found shrewd ways of communicating with the prisoners. Relatives of inmates in the Ostmarkstraße camp, for instance, disguised themselves as tourists, to contact prisoners on the construction sites.[194] The general population in the areas surrounding the camps apparently felt ambivalent about the prisoners. Inhabitants around the Ostmarkstraße camp were clearly concerned about their presence as they had been described by some officials as the 'scum' of various penal institutions. In particular, the population was frightened by the high numbers of escapes.[195] But, according to Walter N., a Communist prisoner taken to the Ostmarkstraße camp in August 1938, some locals also showed their sympathy for the prisoners, secretly throwing them food or tobacco. Such gestures were greatly appreciated.[196] And even though outside labour such as road construction and land cultivation was physically very hard, some inmates initially welcomed it – keen to swap the monotonous life behind grey prison walls for work in the open countryside, and tempted by the significantly better pay.[197] But the reality inside the prison camps failed to live up to these expectations and many inmates, suffering from brutal treatment, were soon desperate to return to the prisons and penitentiaries.

Life Inside

Life for inmates in the prison camps was, on the whole, worse than inside the regular penal institutions. This was especially the case in the Emsland camp. Prisoner testimonies and postwar investigations paint a picture of brutal labour, random violence and sadistic torture. Inmates were constantly beaten with fists and feet, dog whips, sticks and rifle butts. Some had their teeth knocked out and their faces disfigured. Others were maimed by dogs or forced by warders to eat faeces. A number of inmates were beaten to death or shot, without judicial sanction. One prisoner, who had been transported back to a prison, described life in the Emsland camp as 'hell'.[198]

How can this brutality in the Emsland camp be explained? Most decisive was the unique organisation of the camp. When the first camps in the Emsland were taken over from the SA, the judicial authorities also took on SA guards from the dissolved camps. At first, these men, already used to resorting to brutal violence, were solely responsible for the supervision of inmates. Later, this function was increasingly taken over by regular warders inside the camp, while the SA commandos guarded the inmates when they worked outside the barbed wire. However, there was no clear dividing line between prison officials and SA, as numerous SA guards were employed as regular warders.[199] This overlap between party and state was personified by the commander of the Emsland camp, Werner Schäfer, who was both an SA-Standartenführer and a senior judicial official subordinated to the Reich prison administration in Berlin. Schäfer, a hard-line Nazi who had struggled in the Weimar years as a police and bank official, rapidly moved up the hierarchy in the Third Reich. In spring 1933, he became commandant of the Oranienburg concentration camp, before the Prussian Minister of Justice Hanns Kerrl, impressed with his brutal reign, offered him the position as head of the Emsland camp. As a result, the largest German prison camp was run by an SA brute.[200]

Inmates in the Emsland camp were beaten and maltreated from the moment of their arrival at the local railway station. Every day was characterised by violence. In summer, the inmates had to get up in the barracks at 5 a.m. and make their beds according to fantastically pedantic rules, just as in concentration camps. Using planks of wood and strings, the beds had to have sharp edges like boxes. If the inmates failed to do this, they were often attacked by their fellow inmates. Mirroring the so-called *Kapo* system in concentration camps, the Emsland authorities used selected inmates in the running of the camp, for instance, as barrack supervisors. The Emsland officials secured their support by granting them privileges, such as better food and lighter work. Often, these inmates were even more brutal than the guards. After a quick wash and a meagre breakfast, prisoners had to assemble at 7 a.m. for inspection, where they were again subjected to kicks, slaps and beatings. Afterwards, they were marched out on the moor, where they worked until about 5 p.m., with one half-hour break for lunch. During work, prisoners were beaten for not working fast enough or if they failed to achieve the daily quota. The guards also punished any one who broke the rules, such as by secretly eating a bit of bread or going to the toilet without permission. Inmates were not only beaten but also had to endure other maltreatment. The inventiveness of the guards in devising ever more cruel punishments knew few limits. When inmate B. failed to salute one of the camp guards, the guard shouted: 'I will teach you how to salute' and ordered the prisoner to march past, arms at his side and eyes fixed on the guard, until he hit the wall of a nearby barrack. This was repeated several times until the man bled from his forehead and nose.[201] Resistance could be deadly. In early 1938, prisoner W. refused to touch a wheel smeared all over with faeces. When forced to obey, he gripped the wheel, saying that he only did so in order to hit the warder in the face with his dirty hands. The official ordered the prisoner to turn around, and shot him dead.[202]

Inmates singled out by the guards were not only punished on the spot, but could also be sent to a punishment battalion (*Strafkompanie*), sometimes for several months. Here, they had to carry out particularly hard or dirty work, aggravated by senseless rules designed to increase their suffering (for instance, prisoners were forced to push heavy wheelbarrows through the sand, rather than using the streets) and by especially brutal treatment. Inmate P. gave a vivid description of the conditions:

> In Aschendorf [camp] I came into the punishment battalion, because I couldn't work due to weakness. Was tortured. Had to dance with arms held high [referred to by inmates as the 'bear-dance', where they had to turn around in a circle until they collapsed]. Was kicked in behind and balls. Had involuntary discharge from both parts. Feet got inflamed and legs were swollen all the way up to the body. Then into the hospital.[203]

Most inmates were frightened to complain about their treatment, as those brave enough to do so were routinely beaten up. This fear remained even after they had been transferred to other penal institutions. One penitentiary inmate, who was asked to describe his experiences in the Emsland camp by the state prosecution service in late 1937, explained that he had been 'in punishment battalion, because I had a file. There, I was repeatedly hit by warders in the face and kicked in the behind. Had to strip naked and stand up to the navel in faeces in [the] latrine, and that three times.' Having recounted his treatment, the prisoner added: 'I don't want to complain'.[204]

A number of inmates in the Emsland camp tried to kill themselves in desperation. Others were shot dead as they tried to flee. Those who were recaptured were beaten and sometimes tied up and put on show as a deterrent to other prisoners. As a last resort, many inmates seriously injured themselves, severing fingers or putting out eyes, hoping that they would be classified as unable to work on the moor and sent back to a regular penal institution. In a seven-week period in late summer 1937, the authorities recorded more than 40 such injuries in one of the sub-camps alone. But such self-inflicted wounds did not necessarily put an end to an inmate's imprisonment in the Emsland camp. Many had to remain there, suffering one month's detention and two months in the punishment battalion, labouring in the moor despite their often horrific injuries.[205] Overall, life in the Emsland camp was significantly worse than inside almost all other penal institutions. But appalling as these conditions were, they were still preferable to those which prevailed in the SS concentration camps, as we shall see later (Chapter 4).

Crucially, the officials in the Reich Ministry of Justice, including Reich Minister Franz Gürtner, were well aware of the violence in the Emsland camp. Brutal measures such as the punishment battalions had even been officially approved in Berlin. The legal authorities showed little desire to put a stop to other savage assaults against prisoners in the camp. If individual cases of beatings and torture reached the state prosecution authorities, they were routinely dismissed. Not a single one of the 45 judicial investigations of prisoner maltreatment started between 1935 and 1937 actually came to trial.[206] The only serious attempt to establish closer control over the camp was made in 1938, when the Reich Ministry of Justice initiated disciplinary proceedings against the commandant of the camp, Werner Schäfer. The charges against him were investigated in court, which found that maltreatment of prisoners had taken place frequently. However, the judges, under pressure from the Nazi party, concluded that Schäfer himself could not really be blamed for this and merely reprimanded him. In November 1938, Reich Minister Gürtner personally visited the Emsland camp to bring the episode to an end. After he had praised the assembled SA troops for their service, he informed the ecstatic crowd that Schäfer would be reinstated as commandant (he served until 1942).[207] Subsequently, the Reich Ministry restricted itself to minor rebukes of Schäfer's regime. In the judgement of historians of the Emsland camp, the legal authorities passively accepted the brutal conditions and thus became the 'decorative façade of the repressive system'.[208] The attitude of ministerial officials is illuminated most clearly by their plans to enlarge the Emsland camp further in the late 1930s, even though they knew that this meant delivering even more prisoners to a regime of terror.

Little is known about life in other prison camps run by the Reich Ministry of Justice. Conditions there may have been somewhat less extreme than in the Emsland camp. Warders were generally drawn from established penal institutions, and appear not to have been as prone to relentless physical violence as many of the SA guards in the Emsland camp. The other prison camps aimed above all at mercilessly exploiting the inmates' labour power. 'The daily quota,' one prisoner reported, who had toiled in a quarry in the Griebo camp, 'could only be achieved by exerting all one's strength.'[209] The Rodgau camp commandant ordered warders to act immediately against all 'openly lazy' prisoners.[210] Inmates in the Ostmarkstraße camp had to fell trees and cut stones in quarries, constantly driven on by the prison warders and foremen of construction companies engaged on the site.[211]

But there are reports of random brutality and violence from these camps, too. In the sub-camp Verl, part of the prison camp Oberems, inmates were brutally beaten and sadistically tortured by warders and *Kapos*, especially if they failed to fulfil their quota. One inmate who collapsed during work was forced to stand still for the rest of the day, wearing all his equipment, and stare into the sun. Several inmates were driven to suicide or beaten to death. When prisoner W. collapsed during work on 6 August 1937, assistant warder K. brutally beat him up until the inmate lost consciousness. When W. came to his senses three hours later, warder K. aimed his rifle at him, whereupon the inmate collapsed again. K. then ordered that the prisoner be thrown into a cold bath. On the following day, W. repeatedly lost his balance and vomited. The camp doctor refused to give him any treatment, describing him as a psychopath. W. died one day later. The reaction of the prison authorities to such incidents, if they were reported at all, is instructive. Only in the late summer of 1937, after the suicide attempt of another Verl inmate, did the Hamm general state prosecutor Hans Semler, a committed Nazi, investigate conditions in the camp. The assistant warder K. and the prison doctor were subsequently put on trial. K. was eventually sentenced to seven years in a penitentiary. But the doctor was acquitted and no action at all was taken against any other senior prison warders in Verl.[212] In short, while murderous violence against inmates in prison camps could result in prosecution, brutal treatment and neglect of inmates was apparently often tolerated.

Physical violence against prisoners was not the only feature of prison camps which subverted the regulations. Any individual treatment of inmates, still officially part of the rules, was an impossibility in these large camps. Almost no inmate was employed in the trade he had learned and school lessons were reduced to occasional propaganda lectures. Structuring the camps according to the requirements of the work process also undermined the separation of inmates according to their 'reformability' and some prison officials were concerned that communal life in the barracks might corrupt the inmates.[213] In addition, relaxation of the rules governing who could be sent to the camps meant that those who were regarded by many officials as 'dangerous', such as political prisoners and homosexuals, were now more difficult to separate from others.

The high number of escapes from the prison camps, even more pronounced than those from other penal institutions, further subverted penal ideology. With the growth of the prison camp system, the total number of escapes by convicts in Germany increased rapidly, from 449 (1936) to 763 (1938).[214] Working in the open countryside provided good opportunities for escape. For instance, the Ostmarkstraße was built, in some areas, through very dense woodland, and prisoners could easily jump into the undergrowth and run away. One prisoner estimated that in his sub-camp, 75 of the 250 prisoners escaped over a four-month period (official police figures were lower).[215] The authorities reacted by tightening up discipline and security. New watchtowers and searchlights were installed and more warders were deployed. Inmates suspected of planning to escape were forced to wear special outfits to single them out and shoes designed to make escapes more difficult.[216] But prisoners continued to flee from the camps, driven by hunger, exhaustion and fear.

The prison officials were well aware that outside labour undermined important aspects in the regulations. But this did not stop them from supporting it, pointing to the ideological importance of such work. The Jena general state prosecutor concluded in February 1939 that if 'one cannot speak any more of a prison service of the old type, then this has to be accepted in the interest of the Four-Year Plan'.²¹⁷ In part, the prison officials clearly hoped that this would increase the standing and credibility of the prison regime in the eyes of the Nazi leadership. This ideological approach to prison labour, and the prison in general, was to become ever more pronounced during the Second World War.

3 The Campaign against 'Community Aliens'

Legal terror did not hit all suspected offenders in the same way. Sentences varied greatly and life behind bars differed according to a variety of factors such as age, length of sentence, type of offence, ethnicity and gender. It is impossible to reconstruct the experiences of all offenders here. One of the most relevant lines of inquiry is the examination of the fate of those singled out for special treatment as 'community aliens', a term applied by the authorities to a multitude of individuals including 'racial aliens', political prisoners and various criminal offenders regarded as particularly dangerous (such as persistent property offenders and sex offenders). Of course, there was a considerable overlap in Nazi thinking about these different groups, with criminal, racial and political categories often merging into one. To start with, Jews were not only seen as a 'racial danger', they were also described as the political enemies of Nazism behind Communism and liberalism, and as a criminal menace blamed for much common crime. Political prisoners, for their part, were also often labelled as common criminals, not least in order to smear the political opposition at large. In addition, common criminals were also described as 'racial threats' on account of their supposed 'degeneracy', and as political threats, suspected of making common cause with the revolutionaries in 1918. However, despite these overlaps, the legal authorities still pursued a range of distinct policies – both in the courts and inside penal institutions – against specific groups of 'community aliens'.

Political Resistance and Repression

Initially, the main targets of the Nazi regime were its political opponents. In particular, Hitler and his supporters were driven by violent hatred of the left-wing parties, and attacks on the KPD and the SPD had featured prominently in Nazi propaganda in the Weimar Republic. In a private speech in Hamburg in February 1926, Hitler had declared that

> when we win, Marxism will be completely destroyed; we, too, don't know tolerance. We won't have peace until the last newspaper is destroyed, the last organisation is finished, the last educational institution is removed and the last Marxist is converted or exterminated. There is nothing in between.[1]

This declaration of war had the backing of many Germans. It was the perception of the Nazi party as the most determined force against the left which was crucial in winning the NSDAP massive popular support from 1929, helping to sweep Hitler into office. Once in power, the Nazis were quick to realise their threats. Police terror exploded (Chapter 4) and many of those arrested soon found themselves in the hands of Hitler's jurists.

Political Offences and the Courts

Nazi Germany was soon overflowing with political prisoners. According to the internal statistics, at the end of June 1935 some 14,963 convicted political prisoners were held in penal institutions, with another 7,972 in remand prisons. The figure remained high in the following years. Between 1936 and 1937, on average, around 14,100 political offenders were held in penal institutions every day, with another 5,800 individuals awaiting trial.[2] These figures are significantly higher than those of political opponents inside SS concentration camps at this time, demonstrating once more the importance of legal terror. But who, exactly, ended up in penal institutions?

By no means all the political prisoners had been sentenced for organised resistance aimed at undermining the regime. The Nazis also classified grumbling and dissent as political opposition, even if it had not been intended as a political challenge to the regime. This was the result of the total claim of Nazism on society. Aiming at the creation of a completely regimented 'national community', it extended the political into the private sphere. All forms of non-conformist behaviour could be interpreted as attacks on the state, including complaints about living conditions or jokes about Hitler's sex life. As Ian Kershaw has commented, the 'age-old sport of venting spleen on the government, whatever its colour, was turned by the Nazis into punishable crime'. Of course, such essentially private gestures were quite different from political resistance in the more narrow sense of the term. Grumbling and other criticism generally concerned specific aspects of the Nazi dictatorship. This could go hand in hand with support for other elements of Nazi rule, such as the aggressive foreign policy or the 'Hitler myth'. It was obviously not the same as the fundamental opposition of Communists and other ideological enemies of Nazism.[3]

The legal basis for the persecution of dissent was a decree drafted in March 1933 by the Reich Ministry of Justice, following criticism in the cabinet that the legal system was not acting radically enough against opponents of the government. In the cabinet meeting on 21 March 1933, State Secretary Schlegelberger, standing in for Gürtner, dismissed this criticism by assuring his colleagues that the legal system would support 'in the most energetic manner' all measures which aimed at protecting the state against 'treason and high treason'. To prove his point, Schlegelberger presented the decree, which was passed on the very same day (Decree of the Reich President for the Defence against Malicious Attacks against the Government of the National Uprising). From now on, any person found guilty of making or passing on 'a statement of a factual nature which is untrue or grossly exaggerated' and which might cause 'serious damage' to the welfare or reputation of the government and the parties and organisations behind it, could be sentenced to prison or penitentiary. The decree was replaced on 20 December 1934 by the Law against Malicious Attacks on State and Party, which extended the regulations to include private comments even if they were not statements 'of a factual nature'.[4]

The trials were left to new special courts (*Sondergerichte*), also set up on 21 March 1933, which were to gain notoriety during the war. In each judicial district, one special court was established, staffed with professional judges selected by the legal authorities. No doubt, they were partially chosen for their political reliability, and the great majority belonged to the Nazi party. But, once again, there were only a few 'old comrades' among them. The judges were supposed to execute summary justice. Basic legal principles, such as the right of the defendant to present evidence and to appeal, were thrown out in the quest for 'swift justice'. In Nazi legal literature, the special courts were hailed as weapons to 'render harmless', 'eradicate' and 'exterminate' the political enemy. However, this was not really reflected in the practice of the courts, as political offences regarded as more serious were soon handled exclusively by more senior courts. Consequently, the function of the special courts changed.

For most of the prewar years, the special courts concentrated on the persecution of essentially harmless remarks. Most defendants had been denounced for criticising or grumbling about the Nazi leadership, about economic and social conditions or about particular measures taken by the regime. Some remarks contained astute criticism of the regime, others were no more than wild rumours and gossip. Most of the defendants, who were overwhelmingly male, had not set out to take a political stance against the regime. In fact, the defendant's tongue had often been loosened by alcohol: almost one-third of all defendants tried by the Frankfurt special court for 'malicious attacks' had been denounced for remarks they had made in a pub. As regards their social background, most defendants belonged to more disadvantaged sections of society. But 'malicious attacks' were not simply a lower-class phenomenon, as defendants also included white-collar workers, landowners, professors and many others. They came from diverse political backgrounds. Most had no political affiliation, but even Nazi party members were not exempt from prosecution. The circle of those persecuted for critical remarks was 'extremely heterogeneous' (Bernward Dörner). This does not mean, of course, that defendants were all treated equally. Looking at their political affiliation, it appears that a number of Nazi supporters received more lenient sentences and were more likely to be pardoned than many others. Class also played some part, with members of the working class generally punished harder than others, probably because they often sympathised with the political left. Those who were convicted generally received prison sentences of less than one year, with the average length probably about five to six months. Thus, custodial sentences were often not very long. But they were frequent. In 1933, some 3,744 individuals were convicted (largely to prison) for making 'malicious attacks', and the number of sentences rose further in the following years.[5]

Active resistance to the regime came overwhelmingly from the left, in particular from the Communists. In the spring of 1933, the Gestapo reported that the KPD had been almost entirely destroyed. This judgement proved to be premature. Many tens of thousands of former members were willing to continue their work and to maintain the party structures, at almost any cost. Communist cells which had been uncovered were often rebuilt and membership fees were still collected. Leaflets, pamphlets and newspapers were printed, often in print runs of several thousands, and distributed all over Germany. Most Communist activists were driven by the belief that the Nazi regime was heading for inevitable collapse and would be swept aside, bringing about a Soviet-style regime to Germany. Blinded by this illusion, they greatly underestimated the strength and popular support for the Nazis, not least among the working class. Not surprisingly, the impact of this open Communist resistance in the early years of the Nazi regime was minimal. However, it proved extremely dangerous for the activists. Many Communists were put under strict surveillance and were relentlessly pursued by the police. They often made easy targets: the production of leaflets proved a very risky business, while the maintenance of formal party structures meant that the arrest of one key figure often led to the destruction of an entire underground group. Other left-wing activists operated somewhat differently from the Communists. Most former Social

Democrats withdrew into their private lives, even though they often kept loose contacts with former comrades. Only a rather small number of SPD supporters were willing to engage in more open resistance. More pragmatic than most Communist activists, they largely confined themselves to affirming their political convictions in small groups. Thanks to this low-profile and more defensive approach, the SPD was initially more successful in evading detection. This was also true for members of the many smaller left-wing splinter groups, who generally restricted themselves to the ideological instruction of their members.[6]

German judges played a key role in the Nazi war against political resistance. Anti-Nazi activists arrested by the police on suspicion of treason or high treason (the former implied an attack on the external security of the state, the latter on internal security; in practice, there was often some overlap between the two) were generally turned over to the legal authorities. Most cases were then dealt with by political senates set up in ten of the 26 Higher State Courts.[7] Not surprisingly, the majority of individuals accused of high treason apparently had links to the Communist movement. In fact, in some judicial districts, almost all such cases between 1933 and 1939 involved Communist supporters.[8] Most judges needed no invitation to crack down on the Communists. Their hatred of the radical left was deep-seated and, in a number of cases, had already led them to bend the law in the Weimar Republic in order to guarantee particularly brutal sentences. In the Third Reich, the judges were given official licence to pass even harsher sentences. They had considerable latitude, as the extensions of the legal definition of treason and high treason meant that the term could soon be applied to all forms of political opposition to the regime. On 28 February 1933, a decree conceived and drafted by the Reich Ministry of Justice had introduced stricter sentences. Further regulations followed, which were pulled together in a new law on 24 April 1934. This law allowed even more severe penalties for these offences, which were also defined more extensively. High treason was now regarded not just as an attack on the rulers, but on the entire 'national community', and as such demanded especially harsh sentences.[9] Certain privileges for political offenders – left over from the Weimar years – were quickly abolished in Nazi Germany. The special treatment of 'delinquents motivated by conviction' was abandoned, as was the possibility of imprisonment in a fortress (the 'honourable' form of detention) for defendants found guilty of treason or high treason.[10]

Convictions for political resistance increased dramatically in Nazi Germany. In 1932, the last year of Weimar, just 66 defendants were sentenced to imprisonment for 'preparation of high treason'. In 1933, according to the same official statistics, the German courts sentenced 1,652 individuals to imprisonment for this offence.[11] In the following years, the courts cracked down even harder on political opponents. The toughest sentences were passed in the Hamm judicial district in the industrial Ruhr area, where the Communists had traditionally had a strong following. Between 1934 and 1938, the Hamm judges convicted no fewer than 12,000 persons of high treason.[12] Many were sentenced in groups, rather than in individual trials. There were numerous mass trials, with hundreds of defendants. One trial of the illegal Social Democrat organisation in northern Bavaria, before the Nuremberg Higher State Court in early 1935, involved some 171 defendants.[13] Many of those convicted faced lengthy spells behind bars. In the Karlsruhe district, for example, those found guilty of high treason received an average sentence of 25 months' imprisonment (1933).[14]

Cases of treason and high treason regarded as particularly serious were dealt with by the People's Court (*Volksgerichtshof*), established in April 1934, which took over jurisdiction for these offences from the Supreme Court. The People's Court had been set up on the initiative of Hitler and other senior Nazis, who were dissatisfied with the time it had taken the Supreme Court to sentence Marinus van der Lubbe to death for torching the Reichstag (the judicial proceedings had lasted more than nine months, culminating in van der Lubbe's execution on 10 January 1934). The new court soon made its force felt. Between 1934 and 1939, around 3,000 individuals were tried, overwhelmingly German nationals. Most were convicted of left-wing (largely Communist) opposition to the Nazis. Sentencing was harsh, reflecting the supposed seriousness of the offences tried before the People's Court. With the death penalty being used only in exceptional cases, the great majority of those convicted of political opposition received lengthy penitentiary sentences, averaging six years.

The People's Court was a brutally effective weapon in the fight against resistance. But the court should not be pictured as a 'revolutionary tribunal' that was not a 'true part of the justice system'.[15] To be sure, the Nazi leaders had hoped that the new court would come closer to their ideal of summary justice, and the political resolve of the court was to be enhanced by the inclusion of lay judges, nominated by the army and the police, as well as the Nazi party and its organisations. But leading posts were reserved for professional judges, hand-picked by the Reich Ministry of Justice. Political considerations played some part here. Most of the judges were members of the Nazi party, starting at the very top with Otto-Georg Thierack, who served as president of the court for most of its existence (1936–42). But, apart from Thierack, relatively few other officials had joined the party before 1933. Only a small number were 'old comrades' and professional criteria such as legal experience played an important role in their selection. It should also be mentioned that the use of special courts, including lay judges, for political offences was not a total break with past legal practice in Germany.[16]

Conviction rates for political resistance dropped significantly only in the second half of the 1930s. For example, cases of high treason fell by more than 35 per cent in 1937 compared to the previous year.[17] By this point, much of the active left-wing resistance had been destroyed, while former activists on the outside were intimidated by Nazi terror and resigned to the apparent futility of resistance. Economic recovery and aggressive Nazi foreign policy had enhanced the popularity of the regime, and Hitler in particular, and had deprived the resistance of further recruits. The Communists could no longer ignore the fact that the German working class was evidently not moving towards revolution: in the Saar region, dejected Communists complained as early as 1935 that they would no longer work 'for the stupid proletarians – all the effort is in vain'. Gradually, more and more Communist supporters withdrew from organised resistance and retreated into informal, decentralised and conspiratorial networks, often based on individual friendships.[18]

As a result, there was 'extraordinarily little political dissidence' inside Germany during the period that many Germans later remembered as the 'good years' before the war.[19] Far fewer individuals were now charged with offences such as printing and distributing leaflets or collecting party membership fees. And in the whole of Germany, sentences for high treason continued to fall dramatically towards the end of the 1930s, from 5,255 (1937) to 1,126 (1939), according to the internal crime statistics.[20] This contributed to the sharp decline in inmates classified as political prisoners: the number fell to 11,265 inmates at the end of December 1938 – down from almost 23,000 at the end of June 1935.[21]

Political Prisoners

As we have seen, prisons and penitentiaries rapidly filled up with political prisoners from 1933 onwards. The great majority of those sentenced for active resistance had ties to the left-wing opposition. The most basic observation one can make about their life behind bars is that they were not treated uniformly. Not all of them were regarded as dangerous enemies of the regime. Just as Hitler had distinguished between 'Marxists' who could be reformed and those who had to be 'exterminated', many prison officials stressed that a number of political offenders were not yet lost to the 'national community'. In theory, the prison governor was to be informed whether an offender was regarded by the authorities as harmless (*Mitläufer*) or dangerous (*Aktivist*), drawing on distinctions between political prisoners which had sometimes been applied in a rather similar fashion in the early years of the Weimar Republic.[22]

Political activists judged 'dangerous' were supposed to be isolated inside penal institutions. This had been pursued by some local officials from early 1933, and it was also the policy pushed by the Reich Ministry of Justice, which warned of the dangers resulting from the 'confinement of trained former Communist functionaries with other prisoners . . .'.[23] As a result, some prominent political opponents of the Nazis, including Ernst Thälmann, the leader of the German Communist Party, were held for years in strict solitary confinement. At times, they were manacled even at night and during their exercise in the yard.[24] Such treatment was not reserved for leading political functionaries. Some activists sentenced for violence against the Nazis were also singled out. The Communist Josef Kandulski had been serving a penitentiary sentence since 1931 in Brandenburg-Görden for his part in the killing of the SA thug Horst Wessel, who was celebrated as a martyr in Nazi propaganda.[25] After the 'seizure of power', Kandulski quickly lost his privileged status as a 'delinquent motivated by conviction' and was put into strict solitary confinement: 'I am not allowed to have contact with any human being,' he complained in a censored letter in October 1933, 'therefore I have to go alone to the daily exercise, wash alone, go to the toilet, shower alone etc.' In the same month, he was punished with two weeks' detention for allegedly whistling the Internationale. In 1935, instead of being released at the end of his sentence, he was kept in a penal institution, after he had been retrospectively sentenced to security confinement. On the first page of his new prisoner file, an official noted in red pen: 'Involved in Horst Wessel Murder! . . . Enemy of the State!'[26]

Meanwhile, several penal institutions set out to 're-educate' some of the other political prisoners. In the early euphoria of Nazi rule, some eager officials were absolutely determined to win over selected left-wing opponents for the new regime, setting up talks and films to bring Nazi ideology to the prisoners. A few institutions even introduced special courses to win over young political prisoners. But this clumsy and heavy-handed propaganda was generally doomed to failure. Most local prison officials soon admitted the futility of indoctrinating well-read and committed political prisoners, and special courses were quickly abandoned again. Indeed, attempts to win over inmates to the Nazi cause sometimes backfired spectacularly. Propaganda speeches were noisily subverted by political prisoners, who also took these opportunities to exchange news and information. Political prisoners also used the Marxist quotations in Alfred Rosenberg's Nazi propaganda tract *Myth of the Twentieth Century*, now stocked in most prisons and penitentiaries, for their own political discussions.[27]

This was not the only obvious failure of Nazi policy regarding political prisoners. It also proved impossible, in practice, to isolate all supposedly dangerous inmates, despite reminders by the Reich Ministry of Justice. Single cells were in high demand and short supply, not only because of overcrowding, but also because governors had been instructed to reserve single cells for sick inmates, homosexuals, prisoners who had tried to escape and inmates with life sentences. As a result, political prisoners were often put into cells with non-political offenders. Elsewhere, they even shared cells with their comrades. One governor complained in 1935 that 'the majority of admissions are political prisoners who are supposed to be separated immediately. But I have to jam two and three of them together.' Thus, he could not prevent the inmates 'giving each other further Communist instruction'.[28] It also proved impossible to prevent contact between political inmates during work, especially in penal institutions with a high proportion of political offenders such as Brandenburg-Görden, where at one stage more than half the inmates were serving sentences for high treason. This situation became even more difficult from the late 1930s onwards, when the demand that prisoners should be isolated clashed with the growing desire to exploit their labour power.[29] Local prison officials repeatedly complained that it was the unavoidable contacts between political prisoners which made any attempts at re-education impossible.[30]

Looking at the everyday life of left-wing political prisoners, much depended on the individual officials they encountered. Luck played an important part here. The prisoners had little to fear from the small group of warders who had been close to the left in the Weimar years. In the Luckau penitentiary, eight warders were singled out after the war for having treated the political prisoners well. Six of them were former SPD members.[31] It is not surprising that these officials were inclined to act leniently towards political prisoners. Of course, their attitude to other inmates was not necessarily the same. For example, the hospital warder Kraffelt in Brandenburg-Görden was a former SPD supporter and did not attack political prisoners. Yet he acted with great brutality against criminal offenders.[32] But while some political prisoners were treated decently by officials, this was by no means always the case.

Some local officials left no doubt about their boundless hatred of left-wing prisoners. When the Communist Max K. arrived in the Untermaßfeld penitentiary in 1934, sentenced for his involvement in the underground movement, one senior prison official noted: 'He is an utterly dogged and stubborn Communist . . . K. should really have been shot, because he will always be active for Communism, as soon as he has the opportunity.'[33] Nazi activists newly employed as warders were among the most brutal officials. In a sample of 20 'old fighters' chosen by the Reich Ministry of Justice as regular warders in 1935, no fewer than nine had been injured, often severely, in street battles and brawls with Communists or the Weimar police.[34] These violent men now had total power over individuals against whom they had fought on the streets not long before. Political prisoners reported that these Nazi warders were a lot more brutal than the majority of more experienced prison warders, who were apparently more likely to stick to the prison rules.[35]

Perhaps surprisingly, many left-wing prisoners received rewards for good behaviour and other benefits.[36] Even some prominent inmates were granted the same privileges open to other inmates. This included the former Communist Reichstag deputy Karl Elgas. He had been taken to the Luckau penitentiary in September 1934, to serve a three-year sentence for organising the underground movement in Breslau. The Luckau authorities regarded him as a 'dangerous' activist, and he was duly isolated. Still, he was allowed to keep his own razor and he received photos, French and English textbooks, pencils and paper from his relatives, who could visit for 30 minutes every three months.[37] Even more importantly, political inmates obtained many privileged and influential positions inside the institutions. They were better trained and educated than most criminal offenders. Some prison officials felt that political inmates deserved better treatment, thanks to their higher social standing: this meant that they could be usefully employed in more responsible positions. A number of warders also believed that political prisoners were better suited than others to ensure the smooth running of the prison service. As one warder explained: 'I was always pleased when I only had politicals in my commando. They were disciplined and didn't pull any jobs, like theft', a view – whether true or not – evidently shared by some of his colleagues.[38] In Brandenburg-Görden, political prisoners worked as so-called trusties (for example, handing out food to other inmates) and clerks on several wings of the penitentiary, in the doctor's office, in various workshops, in the library and even in the prison administration.[39]

One of these privileged political prisoners in Brandenburg-Görden was Walter Schwerdtfeger, who had been sentenced to life imprisonment by the People's Court in 1935. Having shown his reliability in several favoured positions, Schwerdtfeger was eventually appointed as clerk in the joiner's workshop in the war. His experience here was quite different from that of the great mass of inmates. He was a prisoner, Schwerdtfeger himself noted, 'who is no longer shouted at, because he is needed'. He worked in an office with fresh air and flowers on his desk, and his work was not physically demanding. Well-connected and earning more money than other prisoners, Schwerdtfeger also had access to better food and clothes, partly gained by bribing the warders. For his birthday, he and his privileged co-workers managed to get hold of two bottles of wine, liqueur, cake and sweets. He had become, he recalled, 'a kind of penitentiary dandy'.[40] Like political prisoners who served as *Kapos* in concentration camps, some inmates in penal institutions also used their influence to distribute benefits among their political friends. For example, they tried to fix the prison officials' choice of trusties. And, as one Communist inmate boasted, who had been responsible for the distribution of bread, jam and fat in the Waldheim penitentiary: 'the criminals only received one or two extra portions. I gave some more portions to the comrades'.[41]

After the war, many former left-wing prisoners stressed the supposed unity of political inmates inside Nazi penal institutions. One former inmate remembered this spirit: 'We political prisoners shared one thing: the strong feeling of solidarity, comradeship and belonging, irrespective of age or political direction.' Another inmate referred to the political prisoners as one 'big family'.[42] In fact, they did not form a close-knit community. Many had little more in common than their label as political offenders. It is well known that the German working-class movement during the Weimar Republic was deeply split into Social Democrats and Communists. The mutual antipathy and open hatred of these party activists, which had undermined working-class resistance to the Nazis, was not easily overcome in the prisons and penitentiaries of the Third Reich. Hence, some underground groups formed by political prisoners were open only to those who had been active in the Communist movement.[43] Even prisoners of the same political persuasion fell out with one another. According to Gestapo reports, the Communist prisoners in Luckau penitentiary were divided into two camps, with rival activists excluding each other from the party for ideological deviation.[44]

The spirit of political prisoners was further undermined by political events on the outside. For example, Communist and other left-wing inmates were shocked and confused by the non-aggression pact between Nazi Germany and the Soviet Union signed on 23 August 1939. Prison officials lost no time in informing the inmates of this event, grasping any opportunity to unsettle them. The national prison newspaper carried a front-page photo of Foreign Minister Joachim von Ribbentrop's reception at Moscow airport, reporting that he had been welcomed by a Red Army orchestra playing the *Horst-Wessel-Lied*. One prison warder triumphantly showed other press reports to the inmates, apparently adding: 'There you are. The Russians are going with the Führer and you are the losers . . . .'[45] Even hardline functionaries were stunned. The former KPD Reichstag deputy Fritz Selbmann later recalled that when a warder had gleefully told him the news, he was 'at first speechless in the true meaning of the word and must have made a rather helpless expression'. Selbmann spent a sleepless night digesting this 'absurd' turn of events.[46]

In their memoirs, former political prisoners also often pointed to their resistance activities behind bars. Such claims are difficult to assess. To start with, Gestapo reports about the activities of underground prisoner groups have to be examined with caution. Leading police officials had a strong motive for exaggerating the danger of political resistance inside penal institutions, as they clearly hoped that this might result in political prisoners being transferred to concentration camps.[47] A number of former political prisoners after the war exaggerated their activities as well. This is true, in particular, of memoirs by former inmates published in East Germany. The main thrust of these books is the glorification of imprisoned Communists and their anti-Fascist struggle. For example, most of the 1975 publication about the Brandenburg-Görden penitentiary, characteristically entitled *Broken Chains*, deals with the 'illegal party organisation'. Among other things, the book claims that Communist prisoners had set up an operational party machine, fit for action, which had sabotaged the work process and liberated fellow Communists from solitary confinement.[48] But these claims were dismissed by former Brandenburg-Görden prisoners who had settled in the West after the war. They recalled that sabotage in the workshops had been impossible and that the party organisation had been ineffective, unable even to direct political discussions among inmates.[49] Finally, it is clear that by no means all political prisoners were keen to continue their resistance activities behind bars. One former inmate in the Zwickau penitentiary informed the SPD in exile in 1938 that, while political prisoners still looked out for each other, they were no longer engaging in political debates, afraid of being transported as 'incorrigible' to a concentration camp at the end of their sentence: 'Most of them long for their families and don't want anything more to do with politics.'[50]

Having said this, a number of political prisoners did participate in underground activities. A few inmates had already been primed before their imprisonment to set up political organisations in case they were arrested. A Communist pamphlet published in exile in 1934 gave practical tips on how best to survive interrogation and imprisonment and, following Lenin, it stylised the concentration camps and penitentiaries as 'universities of the proletarian revolution'.[51] Open resistance and defiance in penal institutions, such as hunger strikes or go-slows, were rare, since the inmates knew that detection was likely and draconian punishment would follow. Most inmates restricted themselves to occasional political discussions and the repetition of political slogans. Probably most important was the exchange of news, both about life outside and about the fate of other political activists. Prisoners gained information from Nazi newspapers and occasionally also from hidden radios or from the warders. This information was transmitted verbally or in written notes, either through the trusties or directly during exercise, work, doctors' visits, church services, showers or the ritual of emptying the toilet buckets. Inmates also left political messages in books on loan from the prison library, which were then distributed to other inmates. Some political prisoners not only exchanged information, they also distributed chewing tobacco and other items, helping out long-term prisoners or inmates without privileges.[52] Such gestures of solidarity were an important psychological support for the political prisoners. Unlike inmates imprisoned for criminal offences, who often had to fend for themselves (there is little evidence for the existence of gangs, so prevalent in contemporary prisons), political prisoners could share their fears and needs with some of their comrades.

Contact with the outside was rather more difficult to maintain for the political prisoners. In the early years of the Nazi dictatorship, the Communist Rote Hilfe was still active underground. But it was greatly reduced in strength and more successful in helping families of imprisoned Communists than the prisoners themselves. Smuggling information out of penal institutions also proved complicated. Even so, some prisoners bribed warders to take letters out of the prison. Others hid political references in their letters. To carry on their agitation against the regime, Communist prisoners in Amberg and Ludwigsburg even slipped small papers with political slogans into envelopes and coffee filters they were making, to surprise unsuspecting shoppers on the outside.[53]

Political activity by the convicts was brutally persecuted. While it posed no real threat to the prison authorities or the Nazi regime, it helped inmates to maintain some sense of fraternity and undermined the regime's claim to total control. Punishment was very harsh. To start with, inmates could expect strict disciplinary punishment. And, if the local governor was keen to demonstrate his commitment to the Nazi cause, the matter did not end there. Local prison officials had numerous sanctions available to them. In some cases, they ensured that the prisoners would be taken into police custody after the end of their sentence. Thus, the Waldheim governor made certain that a group of inmates who had maintained a one-hour silence in memory of the Communist leaders Karl Liebknecht and Rosa Luxemburg would eventually be sent to a concentration camp. In other cases, prisoners were reported for further sentencing to the courts. For example, after warders surprised several inmates in the Hamm prison as they marched in a circle with brooms shouldered like rifles, singing the Internationale, the local officials referred their case to the courts.[54] Before the war, such court cases generally ended with further sentences of imprisonment. After 1939, courts also sometimes imposed the death penalty on prisoners reported for making 'defeatist' comments.[55]

Punishment of prisoners for offences committed on the inside often rested on information supplied by fellow inmates. It is known that such denunciations took place inside many places of confinement in Nazi Germany, even though the academic literature on concentration camps, for example, continues to shy away from this taboo subject.[56] As regards penal institutions, denunciations by inmates clearly proved an important source of information for the authorities, as they had done before the Third Reich. In a number of cases, reports by prisoners alerted the authorities to disciplinary offences, such as theft or secret contacts between prisoners.[57] Looking at denunciations for political offences, some of the betrayers were official informers, recruited by the Nazi regime. More often, prisoners denounced fellow inmates on their own initiative, hoping to gain privileges or early release. Some denouncers were themselves political prisoners, delivering their former comrades to the authorities. Others were criminal offenders, which contributed to the already widespread animosity of political prisoners towards these inmates.[58]

Political prisoners often referred to regular criminal inmates with open hatred, both in contemporary and in postwar accounts (the same is true of descriptions of criminals by political concentration camp inmates). Criminals were pictured as brutal bullies and unscrupulous spies for the authorities, who received more privileges and better jobs: 'The criminal has less character, sometimes lacks all character and pursues his own advantage wherever he can,' one former political prisoner wrote after the war.[59] But the relationship between political and regular criminal prisoners was a great deal more complex than this. Crucially, the criminal prisoners formed no cohesive group. While some political prisoners clearly did suffer greatly from the actions of individual criminal inmates, others formed close bonds. In addition, as we have just seen, a number of political prisoners actually gained privileges and benefits themselves. Clearly, political prisoners were not generally disadvantaged as a group.

So why were criminals described with such contempt? Many political prisoners saw themselves as part of the 'respectable' working class, which since the nineteenth century had distanced itself from the disorderly lifestyle and criminal activity associated with the 'underworld'. Having been imprisoned for active resistance against the regime, many political prisoners felt morally and intellectually superior to common criminals. Political inmates often shared the widespread social and racial prejudice against deviants, and were alienated by what they saw as the coarse language and lack of manners of some criminals. The political prisoner Walter Hammer, for instance, recalled after the war that the worst aspect of his punishment had been 'to be lumped together with dangerous professional criminals and to be reduced to being a criminal yourself. What ugly faces, what meanness in spirit and action!'[60] Hammer's reference to the criminal's 'ugly face' was probably no coincidence. Some political prisoners believed in biological differences between themselves and common criminals, subscribing to the persistent popular belief that the 'habitual criminals' could be identified by physical signs. Hence, one political prisoner noted that, in the case of serious criminals, 'their animal nature is already evident in their faces'.[61] Such views were shared by leading prison officials, with deadly consequences during the Second World War.

Jehovah's Witnesses

So far, the focus of this section has been on politically motivated resistance to the Nazi regime. But the legal authorities also targeted the religious opposition. This included Catholic and Protestant priests, who bravely spoke out against Nazism. But the total number of priests convicted by the courts remained rather small. Most were treated relatively leniently, at least compared to other defendants, and often had their cases dismissed before they came to trial. To some extent, this may have been linked to the sympathies of the judges for men who shared, as they did, the values of the German bourgeoisie.

Another important factor was that priests were well integrated into respectable society, and a number of judges were presumably keen not to escalate existing tensions between the regime and the churches by cracking down on popular clergymen.[62] However, the courts were much less forgiving in the case of other religiously motivated non-conformist behaviour. This was true, above all, in the case of the Jehovah's Witnesses.

In 1933, individual German states outlawed the Jehovah's Witnesses as 'enemies of the state', with a national ban following in 1935. Their persecution could build on a tradition of prejudice and paranoia against Jehovah's Witnesses on the *völkisch* right. In the Third Reich, this persecution became state policy. Having sworn the oath of loyalty to Jehovah, the believers refused to acknowledge the claim to total control of society by Hitler and the Nazi dictatorship. The believers, who included a large proportion of women, did not practise the Hitler salute, boycotted political demonstrations, organisations and elections and the men also refused to serve in the German army after general conscription was introduced in 1935. Their response to harassment by SA thugs and the police was expressed in growing criticism of the Nazi regime and open resistance in the form of leaflet actions. This reached a climax after an international Jehovah's Witness conference in Lucerne (Switzerland) in 1936, when a resolution critical of Nazi Germany was passed and was soon distributed inside Germany. The Nazi regime saw the Lucerne resolution and the leaflets as open provocation, which resulted in radical repression of the sect, with mass police arrests in 1936 and 1937.

Many Jehovah's Witnesses arrested by the police were tried by special courts. Not surprisingly, the number of such court cases increased rapidly in 1936 and 1937, following the wave of police arrests. This was particularly dramatic in Saxony, the main base of the Jehovah's Witnesses in Germany. In 1937, some 60 per cent of all cases dealt with by the Freiberg special court in Saxony involved Jehovah's Witnesses. Sentencing by the special courts was influenced above all by the role the defendant had played within the sect: those who had merely attended bible lessons received a few months in prison, while leading officials sometimes received the maximum sentence of five years. There were significant variations in sentencing between different courts, leading to police criticism of supposedly too lenient sentences. In a meeting on 18 June 1937 with senior regional legal officials, Wilhelm Crohne from the Reich Ministry of Justice stressed that the maximum sentence was not imposed often enough by the judges. In a colossal overestimation of public support for the sect, Crohne added that he believed that they numbered one to two million in Germany. The Jehovah's Witnesses, Crohne added, were an 'absolutely seditious organisation', subverted by the Communists, a view shared by Reich Minister of Justice Franz Gürtner. The German judges responded and soon there were few police criticisms of the court sentences. In all, according to one postwar estimate, a total of 6,000 Jehovah's Witnesses were convicted between 1933 and 1945, receiving prison sentences averaging over two years.[63]

The prison authorities developed no clear strategy for dealing with these imprisoned Jehovah's Witnesses. As we have seen, prison regulations stated that inmates thought to have a harmful influence on others were to be isolated. But this rule was apparently not uniformly applied to Jehovah's Witnesses. For a number of governors felt that they were not dangerous enemies of the state but rather harmless 'fools', an opinion also expressed by some senior legal officials and Nazi leaders. Other leading officials, such as the Dresden general state prosecutor, advocated that they should be divided into two groups. At the June 1937 meeting of legal officials in Berlin, he suggested that officials should differentiate between 'functionaries' who were to be isolated in single cells, and the harmless remaining inmates, who should be tempted away from the sect during their imprisonment – a strategy similar to that applied to certain left-wing prisoners.[64]

One local prison official who took plans to brainwash Jehovah's Witnesses seriously was governor Dr Heinz Brandstätter in Eisenach. In the Weimar Republic, he had been a social worker in the Ichtershausen prison and remained an outspoken champion of the Study Group for Prison Reform until 1933. Unlike some of his Thuringian colleagues, Brandstätter was not dismissed and quickly switched his allegiance to the Nazi regime. He was promoted to governor, and in 1938 he focused his efforts on a group of Jehovah's Witnesses imprisoned in Eisenach. Brandstätter intended to 'dissuade them from their wrong ideas by systematic treatment' in order to 'win them for the Third Reich as useful parts of the national community'. The inmates had to attend special instructions and were also regularly indoctrinated in their cells. After only one year, Brandstätter broke off the experiment, claiming that the prisoners were now needed for important work projects. But the real reason was probably that his attempt to indoctrinate the inmates had proved unsuccessful.[65] Officials like Brandstätter quickly realised how difficult it was to indoctrinate individuals who saw their punishment as a divine test of their faith in God. The Ichtershausen prison teacher concluded that training the Jehovah's Witnesses was among 'the most difficult, tedious and thankless types of ideological indoctrination of political prisoners'.[66] In the light of these experiences, some prison officials did not even try to re-educate them, but instead aimed to break them with strict treatment.[67]

Once convicted, Jehovah's Witnesses often continued their opposition to the Nazi regime, arguably more openly than any other group of prisoners. Those who did so often paid a heavy price. A number of Jehovah's Witnesses extended their general refusal to serve the Nazi state to prison labour. Local prison officials, perplexed by the principled stance, answered in the only way they knew – with harsh sanctions. In 1936, a Jehovah's Witness in the Ichtershausen prison was punished for three consecutive months with detention for his continual refusal to work. Exasperated, governor Vollrath noted that the prisoner would probably have to spend another 120 weeks in detention, until the final completion of his sentence. Vollrath knew of no other solution 'because a pigheaded prisoner must not be allowed to succeed'.[68]

In extreme cases, inmates even went on hunger strike. In March 1938, Otto Grasshof was sentenced to four years' imprisonment. As a Jehovah's Witness, he had refused military service and had tried to convince a young man to follow his example. Serving his sentence for this 'crime' in the Wolfenbüttel prison, Grasshof tried in vain to appeal against the judgment, which he dismissed as a 'rape of true Christians'. In the meantime, the state authorities continued their campaign against him, evicting his family from their home and taking his children into care (Grasshof's wife was also held in prison as a Jehovah's Witness). In November 1938, Grasshof, who had already been punished several times with detention, started a hunger strike. The prison authorities responded by brutally force-feeding him. Grasshof eventually died in early 1940, weighing less than 40 kilograms.[69] Such tragic cases, however, did not diminish the determination of judges and prison officials to crush opponents of the regime. The officials displayed similar zeal against many other offenders, including petty criminals.

'Dangerous Habitual Criminals' and Security Confinement

The call for harsher punishment of 'habitual criminals' had grown increasingly loud in the Weimar years, amplified, as we have seen, by the popular obsession with crime and the spectre of the 'incorrigible' criminal. New measures such as indefinite confinement were urged by most legal officials. But due to the failure of the Weimar politicians to implement a new criminal code, these measures had never become law – to the great frustration of the officials. After the Nazis came to power, they quickly seized the opportunity. Aware that strict measures against 'habitual offenders' would find approval among the Nazi leaders, the national-conservative officials in the Reich Ministry of Justice under Franz Gürtner realised that the time was right for introducing the law. A draft was completed by autumn 1933, and following some debate and alterations, the Habitual Criminals Law was published on 24 November 1933.[70] German legal officials and jurists were delighted with the law, which was deeply indebted to earlier drafts – demonstrating the continuity in this field of penal policy with the Weimar period. Robert von Hippel, a highly respected professor of criminal law and the venerable honorary chairman of the Association of German Prison Officials, hailed the law as 'a great and long aspired-to . . . step forward'. Meanwhile, prison governors praised it 'with deep satisfaction' as a 'major achievement' which 'exactly expressed the sentiments of us prison practitioners'. Prison chaplains were equally pleased.[71]

The Habitual Criminals Law

The first part of the Habitual Criminals Law (§ 20a) introduced much stricter sentences for repeat offenders. If a defendant was judged to be a 'dangerous habitual criminal', who had already been sentenced twice to at least six months' imprisonment, it became mandatory for the judges to pass harsher sentences of up to 15 years in a penitentiary. Even if the offender had never been imprisoned before, the court could pass such a sentence if the accused had committed at least three offences. Crucially, the law did not provide any definition of who exactly was a 'dangerous habitual criminal'. It was left to the judges to decide whether the offender had committed the crimes due to a 'criminal disposition'.[72] For the first time, criminological 'types' were punished by law, bolstering the standing of criminal-biology. One senior Reich Ministry of Justice official explained that the Habitual Criminals Law drew directly on the 'results of modern criminal-biology'.[73]

This was one reason for the initial expansion of criminal-biology in the Third Reich. Activists such as Theodor Viernstein had the backing of senior legal officials such as Franz Gürtner and immediately after the Nazi takeover staked a claim to play a central role in the implementation of ruthless measures against 'incorrigibles'.[74] Soon, criminal-biology was taught at more German universities and was extended to additional penal institutions. In 1937, criminal-biological examinations were coordinated on a national level. Officials in over 70 penal institutions were asked to focus on selected inmates, including those considered potentially dangerous or 'incorrigible'. The completed reports were passed to the newly set up central criminal-biological collection offices. From here, the information could be sent to criminal courts and other authorities.[75] But the impact of criminal-biology should not be overestimated, as the examinations were often severely hampered by understaffing, time pressure and lack of resources. After the outbreak of war in September 1939, examinations were further scaled down, until they were officially abandoned in February 1942 in all German penal institutions for adults.[76]

The second part of the Habitual Criminals Law contained so-called Preventive and Rehabilitative Measures (§ 42). In spite of its title, the only supposedly 'rehabilitative' measure was the rather rarely applied provision that offenders convicted of an act committed due to their habitual consumption of drugs or alcohol could be sent to a detoxification centre after imprisonment.[77] All other measures were openly repressive, for example, detention in a workhouse for individuals sentenced for offences such as vagrancy, begging and prostitution. This detention followed directly on the completion of an initial sentence of imprisonment (§ 42d). In itself, the transport of social outsiders to a workhouse after imprisonment was nothing new. By the nineteenth century, many German states had introduced so-called 'correctional post-detention' (*korrektionelle Nachhaft*), later included in the Criminal Code of 1871. Following a formal ruling by a judge, the police authorities could hold certain petty offenders in a workhouse for up to two years after their release from a penal institution. What was new in the 1933 Habitual Criminals Law was that this measure was now dealt with by the courts alone, without police involvement. Detention in a workhouse became purely a matter for the legal authorities. In addition, the detention of individuals who had already been to a workhouse once before was no longer limited to two years. This meant that many of the detained beggars and homeless persons could now be held indefinitely. They were classified as 'asocial', 'work-shy' and 'parasites', terms used to justify their permanent removal from the Nazi 'national community' to institutions characterised by hard labour and small rations.[78] By the end of 1939, German judges had already sent over 7,500 persons to workhouse detention (see Figure 9, pp. 400–1).

The most prominent 'preventive' measure in the Habitual Criminals Law – and the focus of this section – was the indefinite security confinement (*Sicherungsverwahrung*) of 'dangerous habitual criminals'. Given that numerous historians have mistaken this as a police measure, it is worth stressing at the outset that it had nothing to do with the police.[79] Security confinement was ordered by the regular courts and prisoners were held in institutions run by the legal system. Judges could send offenders to security confinement if this was deemed 'in the interests of public safety' (§ 42e). This judgment was normally passed in conjunction with a custodial sentence in prisons or penitentiaries. After the completion of the sentence of imprisonment, the offender was taken into security confinement. Here, the prisoner would remain 'for as long as he [or she] presents a danger to the community', as the official legal justification put it.[80] In effect, this meant that 'dangerous habitual criminals' were now punished twice by the courts, first in prison, then in security confinement.[81]

Many German judges made eager use of security confinement. Obviously, much depended on what they regarded as the 'interests of public safety'. There were different views on this. In the Weimar Republic, prominent commentators such as Robert Heindl had argued that security confinement should apply only to the hard-core of truly dangerous 'professional criminals', whom he regarded as responsible for much criminal activity.[82] Heindl's work had clearly impressed Reich Minister of Justice Franz Gürtner. When Gürtner presented the new law to the public in November 1933, he stressed that it was specifically designed to fight Heindl's 'professional criminals' who, according to Gürtner, had made theft or fraud their vocation. In line with Heindl's work, Gürtner claimed that there were no more than 800 or 1,000 such criminals in the whole of Germany.[83]

But most other legal officials supported a more wide-ranging application of security confinement. This had already been envisaged by the modern school of criminal law in the late nineteenth century. Franz von Liszt, for one, had claimed that at least half of all the inmates in penal institutions were 'incorrigible habitual criminals'. Among those he singled out for indefinite confinement were many relatively harmless petty offenders, such as individuals sentenced for the third time for theft or damage to property. Liszt's views had been echoed in the Weimar Republic, with numerous criminologists arguing that security confinement should target not only the criminal elite, but also many 'habitual criminals', including beggars, small-time thieves, pick-pockets, pimps and impostors. Many prison officials had agreed. In July 1927, they classified 12,030 of the 51,727 inmates in penal institutions (excluding remand prisons) as 'habitual offenders' and 4,000 as candidates for security confinement.[84] Once security confinement had become law in the Third Reich, it quickly became clear that many German judges followed the more extensive interpretation. Between 1934 and 1939, German courts passed at least 9,689 sentences of security confinement – ten times more than had been envisaged by Franz Gürtner (see Figure 9, pp. 400–1).

Sentences to security confinement were greatly influenced by local prison officials, especially early on. These officials were asked to report inmates currently serving prison or penitentiary terms to the courts for retrospective sentences. Denouncing inmates to the state prosecution service gave new powers to local prison officials, and raised their status inside the legal apparatus. Retrospective sentencing (not included in the Weimar drafts for security confinement) had been put forward during the discussions of the Habitual Criminals Law in October 1933 by the Bavarian and Prussian Ministries of Justice. Of course, this broke once more with the rule *nulla poena sine lege*. When this principle had first been undermined in the Third Reich, with the Lex van der Lubbe in March 1933, there had been some resistance by leading legal officials against such a fundamental breach of traditional legal norms (see Chapter 2). Just six months later, such scruples had been set aside.[85] Many prison governors embraced retrospective security confinement. Indeed, some were so keen that they denounced a large proportion of their prison population. The Straubing officials proposed around 28 per cent of their inmates for retrospective sentencing, and the Brandenburg-Görden officials a staggering 37 per cent. By no means all of these applications were successful, as the courts proved to be more measured than the frenzied prison officials. Still, the input of these local officials was crucial. In 1934, 2,367 of all 3,723 individuals sentenced to security confinement were convicted retrospectively, many of whom had been put forward by penal institutions.[86]

Many convicts were crushed as well as shocked by the introduction of security confinement. This measure, together with other policies that came into effect in 1934 (see below), caused massive anxiety among the prison population. Officials in the Bavarian Ministry of Justice noted with satisfaction that inmates now 'try to present themselves in the best possible light to prevent, if possible, further harm being done to them'.[87] A few even persuaded warders to testify to their good character.[88] Some inmates also directly petitioned the courts. In August 1934, the governor of the Remscheid-Lüttringhausen penitentiary, asked for his views by the prosecution authorities, proposed the inmate Gustav T. for retrospective sentencing. The governor characterised him as a 'work-shy, unscrupulous ... unstable person of weak character' and labelled him as 'persistent habitual thief'. The state prosecution service agreed and applied to the courts for Gustav T. to be sentenced. Gustav T. appealed to the court:

> I deny that I am an 'incorrigible thief'. W[h]en I committed my offences I was still very young and barely aware of my crimes[,] crimes which repulse me today and which I will definitely not commit again. During almost all of my thefts I was suffering hardship [and] during my last thefts which I committed in 1930 I rarely took more than I needed to live.

The judges ignored this plea. Sentencing him to security confinement in September 1934, the court noted that he 'is a dangerous habitual criminal who will not be reformed by imprisonment, however strict'.[89]

Dangerous Criminals?

Security confinement usually followed the completion of a custodial sentence in a prison or penitentiary. Initially, most prisoners taken to security confinement were held in small wards set up inside existing penal institutions, which also held other inmates at the same time. In 1935, only a few hundred of the around 2,000 security-confined prisoners were held in an institution reserved exclusively for them. All the others were imprisoned in one of 25 special wings inside prisons or penitentiaries. But soon, thanks to the fervour of German legal officials, this decentralised system was no longer enough to cope with the influx of prisoners. The number of inmates in the wards increased steadily and, in December 1936, the Reich Ministry of Justice restructured the system. Three penal institutions were now designated exclusively for security confinement (Gräfentonna, Rendsburg and Werl), with some additional wards in other institutions (such as Brandenburg-Görden, Aichach and Tapiau). By 31 January 1939 there were 4,326 inmates in security confinement. Many thousands more had also been sentenced to security confinement, but were still serving their prior prison or penitentiary sentences.[90]

Who were these individuals sentenced to security confinement? Prison officials and criminologists in Nazi Germany always described them as 'dangerous', sometimes adding that they were 'human ruins' and 'the scum of the criminal class'.[91] But such statements were more revealing of the officials' mind-set than the prisoners' social background. For the inmates were not, by and large, very menacing criminals. In fact, of all the men and women in security confinement on 1 January 1937, only 7.7 per cent had been sentenced to security confinement for violent or sex crimes. By contrast, 86.1 per cent had been convicted of theft or fraud.[92] Most of them were recidivist petty property offenders like Gustav T. Many had been born around the turn of the century, in large families in deprived urban centres, and had spent practically all of their adult life under conditions of severe economic instability and unprecedented levels of unemployment, highest among their generation. They were poorly equipped to sustain themselves in the perpetual economic crisis of the Weimar Republic. Often, they had gained no adequate education or vocational training. If they had worked at all, they had been engaged in poorly paid casual labour, which was vulnerable to fluctuations in the market. Many had relied on small-time property crimes for subsistence, often very minor crimes involving the theft of bicycles, coats or small amounts of food and money. With each new conviction, they became more likely to offend again, not least because of the widespread public resentment against ex-convicts and the police supervision of recidivists. On average, each inmate had 14 previous convictions at the time of being sentenced to security confinement in the Third Reich, accumulated over a long period since the 1920s or even earlier. The sheer number of convictions meant that many offenders had spent very large parts of their adult life in prisons and penitentiaries. In a sample of 135 inmates with an average age of 43 years, sentenced retrospectively in the Hamburg area, each had already spent 21 years behind bars. Such lengthy spells of imprisonment made it difficult to maintain social relations with the outside world. Those who still had contact with relatives or partners could not always count on their support. Some were relieved by the prospect of lifelong detention for the 'black sheep' in their family. Others wrote to the prison administration to stop the inmates sending letters, fearing that association with them could harm their standing in the Third Reich.[93]

Clearly, the security confined were rather similar to those singled out as 'incorrigible' in the Weimar Republic – another example of the way in which Weimar criminology and penal practice helped to shape Nazi policy. In some cases, officials actually targeted identical individuals in Weimar and the Third Reich, as the example of Karl Kakuschky demonstrates. Born in 1899, he had left school after only one year and took various casual jobs. At a young age, he came into conflict with the law and was taken to a reformatory. During the 1920s, he was frequently imprisoned for minor property offences. For example, in 1928 he was sentenced to 18 months' imprisonment for the theft of three bicycles. By this stage, he had already spent seven years of his life behind bars. He was released in January 1930, after the depression had hit Germany, with no prospect of finding employment, only 20 Reichsmark in his pocket, and a suit, coat and hat paid for by the prison. Only a few months later, in April 1930, Kakuschky re-offended, again stealing a bicycle. Even though the court acknowledged his economic hardship, it still sentenced him to 11 months' imprisonment. After he had been classified by prison doctors in Moabit as a 'habitual criminal', he was committed to the wing reserved 'for those most difficult to educate' in Plötzensee prison. Released in April 1931, he was readmitted to Plötzensee in February 1932 for the theft of a coat, and again in the following year for the theft of a bell and some glue, among other items. He was never released again. Once security confinement had become law on 1 January 1934, he was retrospectively sentenced. According to the prison officials in Brandenburg-Görden, where he was held, Kakuschky exhibited many typical characteristics of the security confined: 'poor educational circumstances, breaking off an apprenticeship, irregular labour, early criminality, many convictions, especially quick recidivism; plus his penchant for alcohol'.[94] Ultimately, an individual like Karl Kakuschky was persecuted not as a highly dangerous criminal menace, but as a social deviant, unwilling or unable to conform. Security confinement was not just a weapon of criminal policy, but of Nazi racial and social policy – permanently removing outsiders and 'biological inferiors' from the 'national community'.[95]

The vast majority of inmates in security confinement were men. By 1 January 1937, there were 3,121 men in security confinement, compared to only 137 women. This gender imbalance is not very surprising. After all, women accounted for only a small number of persistent offenders and they were also traditionally less likely than men to receive the harshest available penal sanctions. But those women who were sentenced to security confinement did not differ much in social background or types of offence committed from their male counterparts. The vast majority of women were also sentenced to security confinement for property offences, proportionally even slightly more than men. Apparently, a number of these women had worked as prostitutes and had previous convictions for stealing from men they had slept with.[96] A typical case was Rosa S., who was arrested in August 1934, after she had stolen 40 Reichsmark from the pocket of an unskilled labourer with whom she had had sex. S. was tried as a 'dangerous habitual criminal', following a long tradition in Germany of classifying prostitutes as part of the criminal underworld. The prosecutor cited a previous court sentence which had described her as early as 1927 as a 'debased and dangerous street-whore'. Only security confinement, he argued, could protect the public from her. The court agreed, and Rosa S. was sentenced to 16 months' imprisonment and subsequent security confinement.

Asked in 1936 about her plans for the future, she wrote: 'Most of all, I do not want to come back here . . . I will buy myself a sewing-machine a.[nd] 1 bed . . . I want to patch a.[nd] sew a.[nd] embroider'. But she was never released again.[97]

Conditions in security confinement were always meant to be strict. Many criminologists had argued in the past that 'habitual criminals' deserved a very harsh disciplinarian regime. Some of the most extreme proposals had come from Franz von Liszt, who had demanded as early as 1880 that such prisoners should be exposed to 'military sternness without further ado and as cheap as possible, even if these characters perish. Corporal punishment essential . . . To give [the inmate] food, air, exercise etc. according to economical principles would be an abuse of the taxpayer.'[98] But other observers had opposed such a harsh line and suggested instead that the security confined should receive special privileges. After all, it was argued, most such inmates would be confined until their death anyway.[99] In Nazi Germany, such disagreements were not immediately resolved. At a meeting of senior prison officials in October 1933, the Prussian representative demanded that the offenders should be treated as harshly as penitentiary inmates. But other officials argued that more lenient treatment would help to improve discipline in security confinement.[100] In the Habitual Criminals Law, the latter position was dominant. It stated clearly that there was no room for expiation and retribution, and that privileges should be made available as long as this did not increase the likelihood of escapes.[101] But by the time administrative guidelines for security confinement were published on 14 May 1934, the tone had changed. The emphasis on preventing escapes was now used to justify 'merciless' treatment, for example, by extending the disciplinary punishment of strict detention from penitentiaries to security confinement.[102]

Overall, life in security confinement most closely resembled the regimen inside penitentiaries. True, the inmates could enjoy a few more privileges, such as writing more letters and receiving more visits.[103] But in many other ways they were worse off, as the prison administration introduced a host of repressive measures justified with reference to the supposed danger of the inmates. Bavarian prison officials were instructed in December 1933 to prevent any escape attempt 'without mercy'. Warders were also ordered to shoot rather than manhandle when attacked by an inmate. Such rules had the desired result: by 30 April 1938, there had been only 19 escapes from security confinement.[104] Some local officials insisted on maintaining very sharp discipline. The Gräfentonna governor, for example, demanded that the prisoners had to be forced at all times to follow orders 'immediately and unconditionally'. To cement this spirit of total compliance, he was particularly keen on military exercises such as marching in formation.[105] Strict treatment was reflected in disciplinary punishments. In the penal institution in Aichach, which contained wings for penitentiary inmates and the security confined, it was the latter who were treated more harshly. Not only were they more likely to be disciplined, they were also punished more severely.[106]

The health of the security confined deteriorated more rapidly than that of most other prisoners. In part, this was a result of hard prison labour. At first, many security confined were occupied with dirty work such as mat-weaving in their cells, because they were banned from outside labour for security reasons, and from contact with prison or penitentiary inmates in the workshops.[107] But following the setting up of separate institutions for the security confined and the general attempt by the prison authorities in the late 1930s to make prison labour more productive, officials tried to use the prisoners more effectively. The rules governing outside labour were relaxed and in 1939 the Reich Ministry of Justice even decided to send some security-confined inmates to the Emsland prison camp.[108]

But attempts to exploit the security confined were often restricted by their poor health. They found it particularly hard to fulfil the strict work quotas because they were significantly older than other inmates. On average, well over one in four inmates in security confinement was 50 years old or older. In Aichach, the average age of the women in security confinement was 54. Prison officials repeatedly complained about the poor state of health of these inmates. At a meeting of prison officials on the eve of the outbreak of war in August 1939, the Straubing governor protested that the offenders recently committed to his institution had been 'such bad material' that 189 of them could only do the easiest types of work.[109] Reich Minister Gürtner himself was well aware of these concerns. In the same month, he acknowledged that about one in five of the security-confined prisoners was barely able to work on account of old age or illness.[110]

The security-confined inmates also suffered from serious psychological problems. Most other convicts could focus their mind on the day of their release, however far that might be in the future. The security confined, by contrast, served open-ended sentences. The Brandenburg-Görden prison doctor noted in 1938 that this uncertainty about their release put the prisoners under severe pressure. Not only did they hardly ever leave their cells, but they lived with the expectation that this would probably never change. As a result, there were many cases of illness, self-mutilation and weight loss. Some two-thirds of the inmates in Brandenburg-Görden lost weight without suffering from a physical illness. One of them wrote to his wife in October 1939 that to describe himself as nothing but skin and bones would still be 'flattery'.[111] Depression was widespread. One prisoner in Aichach, Franziska K., who had accumulated numerous convictions for minor thefts, wrote to her family (in a letter censored by the authorities): 'My dear ones, I am totally embittered, sitting here and not knowing why and for how long a[nd] still be treated as a convict. I, I will lose my mind if this goes on like that . . . alone a[nd] forsaken I have to sit here a[nd] waste away, this is a <u>slow suicide</u>.'[112] The uncertainty also greatly unsettled some of their families and friends on the outside.[113]

The pressures of indefinite detention led to several cases of mental breakdown. Magdalena S. was committed to the security confinement wing in the Aichach penal institution in June 1936. Thirty-three years of age at the time, she had accumulated 16 minor convictions, generally for theft and prostitution. Initially, she submitted to the strict order, as she had done during most of her previous terms of imprisonment. But after being castigated by an official for not being industrious enough, she stopped working and refused to clean her cell. She told the officials: 'I cannot bear this life any longer, I cannot say yes to everything and I cannot obey any more'. The authorities answered with force. By October 1938, Magdalena S. had already spent at least 147 days in aggravated detention and 21 days in strict detention. Locked away for long periods, mostly without a bed or fresh air and often subsisting on nothing but water and stale bread, Magdalena S. deteriorated both mentally and physically. In the following years, she acted in an increasingly disturbed manner, throwing faeces at warders, ripping her clothes and mattress into pieces, cutting off her hair, grunting and screaming. The only response the prison officials could think of was to increase her punishment. When she was not in the prison hospital because of malnourishment, she was locked into one of the Aichach detention cells.[114]

Release

Most security confined believed that, one day, they would be released again. Until the war, this remained at least a possibility. According to the Habitual Criminals Law, each sentence would be reviewed by the courts at least every three years. Inmates could be set free if the courts no longer considered them a danger to society.[115] But the great majority of prisoners hoped in vain. Already in 1936, State Secretary Freisler had told the general state prosecutors that he could not, in general, accept the release of inmates. Many legal officials also subscribed to this view.[116] Prisoners were hit very hard by the court's rejection of their release. One Aichach inmate, Hedwig J., wrote to her sister in two censored letters in March 1937: 'I won't do another 3 years here . . . I have stolen, but I will rather do myself in, my dear sister, than be buried alive for that in here.'[117] Officials in Werl noted that the rejection of release led to extreme reactions. In recent weeks, the officials reported in September 1937, seven items had been swallowed by inmates, one prisoner had almost completely blinded himself by poking a pencil into his eyes and another had apparently lost his mind.[118] The officials in the Ministry of Justice in Berlin were not overly concerned about such incidents. One civil servant coldly noted that cases of self-mutilation and suicide attempts among inmates refused release were consequences which had to be tolerated.[119]

In 1938, the Reich Ministry of Justice further tightened up the conditions for releasing security-confined inmates, in response to growing competition with the police in the 'fight against habitual criminals' in this period (see Chapter 4). In an official publication entitled 'Urgent Questions of Security Confinement', State Secretary Freisler re-emphasised that release should be used sparingly. Any show of compassion for the inmates amounted to 'cruelty towards the whole *Volk*'.[120] And in a decree signed by Gürtner, the Reich Ministry of Justice stressed that inmates who had committed their offences because of 'irreversible hereditary characteristics' should always be excluded from release. In addition, the state prosecution service was instructed to oppose all those releases not approved by local prison officials.[121] This further cut the number of releases, as governors rarely supported the inmates, presumably because they feared that they would be held responsible if the prisoner re-offended.

Still, some inmates were released. By 30 April 1938, 701 former inmates had been set free, while 3,886 were still imprisoned.[122] The criteria used by the courts to free prisoners remained rather unclear. Many officials agreed that good conduct on the inside was irrelevant, as it could give no indication of future behaviour on the outside. But in the absence of an infallible mechanism for predicting their behaviour, some officials fell back on judging their conduct – probably one of the reasons why most of the security confined submitted to the punishing discipline, clinging to the hope that this might persuade the officials to support their release.[123] Other factors influencing the judges (and the governors' reports to the courts) were a positive assessment of the offender's social environment on the outside, as well as serious biological changes to the offender's body, caused by senility, incurable illness or castration, which in the view of the officials made future offences impossible.[124] Finally, inmates sentenced retrospectively apparently had a better chance of being released than others, presumably because some officials harboured doubts about the fairness of this particular measure.[125]

In most cases, the courts made release from security confinement conditional on the inmates obeying very strict regulations. In one typical case, an ex-inmate who had been sentenced for picking pockets was not allowed to leave her home town without prior police approval, had to stay at home at night, hand over keys to her rooms to the police, and was not permitted to enter large shops, where it was feared she might steal goods.[126] Every aspect of the former inmate's life was strictly regulated by the courts and police. One ex-prisoner was released on the condition that he moved in with his brother and accepted any job offered to him by the job centre. Others were forced to move to special institutions set up for released inmates, and forbidden to visit their friends or children. Often, the prison governors themselves also kept up the pressure on their former inmates to lead exemplary lives.[127] Some former inmates were even forbidden from getting married, after the Marriage Health Law of 18 October 1935 had banned marriages of 'undesirables'. According to the official commentary on the law, this term applied to individuals who tended to exhibit 'severe psychopathy, psychosis or criminal and dangerous social behaviour'. Some former security-confined inmates' prospective spouses were evaluated, to determine whether the marriage would be in the interests of the 'racial community'.[128]

In view of these strict controls, it is hardly surprising that many former inmates were again committed to security confinement. For release was conditional and could be revoked at any time. Often, former prisoners were re-arrested almost as soon as they had been set free.[129] Overall, it seems likely that half or more were taken back to security confinement.[130] Many former inmates simply re-offended. For example, Willy Leske was caught in November 1937, only shortly after his release, stealing in the Kaufhaus des Westens, Berlin's largest department store. Leske was drunk and pleaded in vain with the store detective to let him go. The court saw his offence as final proof of his 'considerable danger to the national community', and sentenced him to three years in a penitentiary with subsequent security confinement.[131] In a number of other cases, former inmates were readmitted not because they had committed more offences, but simply because they failed to conform to the norms set by the officials for their work life and private conduct. Numerous former inmates were accused of being 'work-shy'. Despite the fact that police surveillance made it difficult to find steady employment, failure to do so was seen as further evidence of the offenders' nature as 'habitual criminals'. Others were re-committed after they had dared to criticise publicly the brutal treatment and harsh conditions in security confinement.[132] None of these prisoners had any hope of ever being freed again.

Sex Crimes, Castration and Homosexuality

In the Weimar years, a spate of gruesome sex crimes – reported in lurid and extensive detail by the media – had helped to stoke up fear and anxiety among the German population. Nazi propaganda was quick to exploit these crimes politically, blaming the 'perverse' individualism and 'immoral' liberalism of the Weimar years. As an article in the publication of the NSDAP Office for Racial Policy (see Illustration 16) later put it, this atmosphere had 'inevitably created those sex fiends, who tried to corrupt and destroy our *Volk* from within'. Even worse, the article charged, convicted offenders had not been punished but, instead, pampered in 'luxury appartments', because they were regarded as pitiable victims of their environment. All this had changed in the Third Reich, the article concluded, where the offenders were now treated 'especially hard'.[133] Punishment for various sex offences did indeed become stricter in Nazi Germany. And once in power, the Nazis searched for increasingly radical policies, determined to prove themselves champions of law and order.

Among the most extreme proposals was castration. This was not an entirely new idea. It had already been discussed in the Weimar Republic, with a small number of voluntary castrations actually being performed, following petitions by individual sex offenders to the authorities.[134] Naturally, the issue of forcible castration had been controversial in the Weimar years. Many commentators had remained sceptical, unsure whether such operations would have any lasting effect on the criminal activities of sex offenders. Some warned about the physical and psychological damage caused by the operations. In the end castration was not included in any of the Weimar drafts for a Habitual Criminals Law.[135] Still, support for the measure had grown in the years before the Nazis came to power, driven not least by the massive media circus surrounding the trial and execution of the 'Düsseldorf vampire' Peter Kürten in 1931.[136]

Shortly after the Nazi takeover, a number of state officials and criminologists argued that the moment had come for the forcible castration of sex offenders.[137] This view was shared by some leading government officials. For example, the 1933 draft by the Reich Ministry of Interior for a sterilisation law included provisions for the castration of certain sex offenders. These were dropped only after Reich Minister of Justice Gürtner personally demanded that any such decisions be left to the legal authorities. But the issue was not yet off the table. On the day the Sterilisation Law was passed by the cabinet, 14 July 1933, Hitler asked Gürtner to draw up a law for the 'castration of dangerous sex offenders'. Gürtner probably used Hitler's intervention to speed up the introduction of the Habitual Criminals Law, adding castration to the catalogue of so-called preventive and rehabilitative measures. Thus, according to the Habitual Criminals Law of 24 November 1933, courts could now order the castration (*Entmannung*, literally emasculation) of 'dangerous sex criminals' over the age of 20. This measure could be applied to men who were sentenced to at least six months behind bars and had already been sentenced once before to imprisonment for a sex offence, or men who were sentenced for two separate offences to a total of at least one year's imprisonment. The law was not meant to cover all the sex offences listed in the German Criminal Code. Reich Minister Gürtner had emphasised that since little was known about the efficacy of castration 'a certain caution' was necessary. In the end, castrations were restricted to paedophiles, rapists and exhibitionists.[138] According to official statistics, some 1,808 men were sentenced to forcible castration between 1934 and December 1939 (see Figure 9, pp. 400–1). Internal statistics in the Reich

Ministry of Justice put these figures even higher, counting some 2,079 forcible castrations carried out in penal institutions up to the end of 1939.[139]

Prison officials participated prominently in the castration of sex offenders. Local officials could put forward imprisoned sex offenders for retrospective sentencing, an addition to the law which had been suggested by Reich Minister of the Interior, Wilhelm Frick.[140] A number of prison officials were not reluctant to use their new powers. They saw castration not only as a means of preventing further crimes, but also as a eugenic measure. The Wuppertal prison doctor Neuhaus, for example, claimed in an expert report that 'castration is the measure which rescues the people from this sex criminal; at the same time, it functions as a sterilisation measure and, thirdly, it replaces security confinement, which would otherwise be necessary . . .'.[141] The involvement of the prison officials is evident in the sentencing figures. In 1934, well over half of all the 613 men sentenced by German courts were already serving prison or penitentiary terms and were sentenced retrospectively to castration.[142] Had it not been for the reluctance of some judges to hand out this measure, the number of castrated convicts would have been higher still.[143] The number of retrospective sentences declined after 1934, as most inmates regarded as 'dangerous sex offenders' had by now been castrated. With this decline, the overall number of men sentenced to castration also fell, reaching an average of less than 210 per year between 1937 and 1939 (see Figure 9).

The great majority of castrated men were convicted for sexual assaults on children. According to the official crime statistics for 1934 to 1936, more than seven of every ten men sentenced to castration had been convicted of this crime. As incest was excluded from the castration law, many of these castrated men came from outside the family network and had committed their offences in public places.[144] One of them was the carpenter Max W., born in 1876. He had numerous convictions for particularly brutal sex crimes, including the rape of his own daughter. In July 1933 he was committed to Untermaßfeld, sentenced to five years in a penitentiary after sexually abusing a 12-year-old girl for a period of over a year. Governor Gericke proposed him for retrospective castration in February 1934: 'One can be certain that once he is castrated, W. will not have any more sensations which drive him to sex crimes.' The judges accepted this argument and Max W. was castrated soon after.[145] Other sex offences figured much less prominently in cases of castration, a reflection of the significantly higher absolute number of convicted paedophiles. Even so, some men were sentenced to castration for rape or attempted rape. As in the castration of paedophiles, these cases involved violent men whose castration would have found widespread support among the population. But castration was also directed at defendants convicted of indecent exposure, offences which involved no direct physical attack on women or children. Nevertheless, it appears that more of these offenders than rapists were castrated in Nazi Germany.[146]

Regarding their social background, the vast majority of the castrated sex offenders came from the most impoverished sections of the population. In a sample of some 114 castrated men, close to half were unskilled workers. Most men were aged between 30 and 50, but youth or old age did not deter the courts from deciding on castration. Many of the offenders had accumulated a number of previous convictions for sex offences. However, this was not a necessary condition and a number of men were first-time offenders.[147]

Most of the operations were performed shortly after the offender had been sentenced by the courts. Otherwise, an official in the Bavarian Ministry of Justice explained, the temptation for the prisoner to escape would increase, as he 'wants not only to win his freedom, but also to preserve his manhood'.[148] These castrations were carried out either in hospital wards of penal institutions or in selected hospitals.[149] During the operation, the testicles and epididymis were removed through an incision under the scrotum. For the surgeons, this operation soon became routine. In the Moabit prison, a total of 111 castrations were carried out in the first nine months after the law came into force. The Moabit doctor boasted that he could perform the entire operation in exactly eight minutes, declaring it 'the cheapest method' of protecting the community.[150] Following the guidelines in the semi-official instructions to doctors, castration was generally performed under local anaesthetic.[151] Sometimes, the offenders had to be manacled, but only when they became too agitated or violent did doctors use general anaesthetic. Hamburg prison officials reported in November 1935 that 17 of 80 castrated men had been operated on under general anaesthetic. Two of them were beaten to get them on to the operating table.[152]

German legal officials knew that castration had consequences for offenders. In the statement accompanying the law of 24 November 1933, the Ministry of Justice in Berlin noted that while the operation would lead in some cases to 'serious damage of body and mind', this had to be accepted 'in the overriding interests of the general public'.[153] In order to monitor the effects of castration, the Reich Ministry of Justice ordered doctors to carry out detailed examinations of castrated men at regular intervals after the operation.[154] However, this did not always prove possible as released inmates could not yet be forced to submit to these examinations. Friedrich K., for instance, refused to cooperate, telling the authorities that 'after they had already mutilated him, they should at least leave him in peace now'.[155]

Even so, prison doctors and criminologists were able to put together detailed studies of the castrated men. A number of men complained of physical pain for years after the operation. Some felt aches and occasional paralysis in their lower limbs. Others developed layers of fat and were prone to profuse perspiration. Several men lost their body hair and started to develop breasts. Other

1. Hitler enjoys the comfortable conditions during his brief imprisonment in the Landsberg am Lech fortress in 1924 following the failure of his attempted putsch.

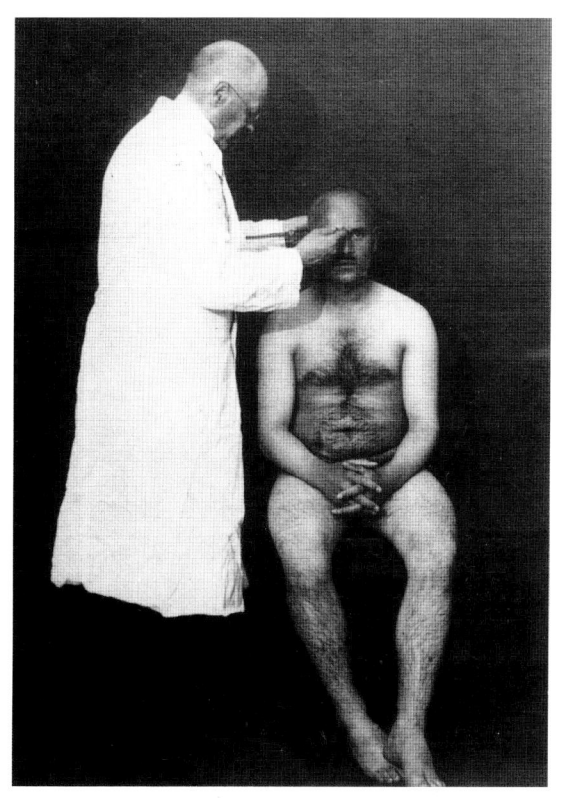

2. The Straubing prison doctor, Theodor Viernstein, conducting a criminal-biological examination of an inmate, c. 1925.

3. Untermaßfeld in the Weimar Republic: privileged inmates play handball in the prison reformers' model institution, mid- to late 1920s.

4. Lessons for prisoners from a social worker in the Untermaßfeld penitentiary, mid- to late 1920s.

5. Straubing in the Weimar Republic: warders practice ju-jitsu, mid-1920s.

6. Strictly regimented exercise for privileged inmates in the Straubing penitentiary, 1925.

7. Aichach in the Weimar Republic: inmates at the bottom of the stages system during their daily exercise, 1931. The women had to keep a distance of five steps to prevent them from talking to one another.

8. Carpet-weaving by hand in the Aichach penal institution, 1931.

9. Following the Nazi 'seizure of power', the law is symbolically hanged as new Prussian Minister of Justice Hanns Kerrl (centre) visits the training camp Jüterbog, which was set up for prospective German jurists, c. 1933–34.

10. The German dignitaries at the 1935 International Prison and Penitentiary Congress in Berlin. From the right: Reich Minister of Justice Franz Gürtner, Propaganda Minister Joseph Goebbels, President of the Academy for German Law Hans Frank, State Secretary Roland Freisler.

11. Reich Minister of Justice Franz Gürtner (centre), October 1937. A national-conservative, Gürtner served from 1932 until his death on 29 January 1941.

12. Rudolf Marx, c. 1934. Marx headed the prison administration in the Reich Ministry of Justice between 1935 and 1943.

13. Wilhelm Crohne, 1937. Crohne was Marx's hard-line superior in the Reich Ministry until 1942, when he became vice-president of the notorious People's Court.

14. Emsland camp prison guards relaxing, c. 1935–36. On the wall the motto reads: 'Loyalty is the Core of Honour'.

15. Emsland camp inmates labouring on the moor, c. 1938–39.

16. An illustration from a propaganda article, 'Sex Fiends and Criminals' in a publication of the Nazi Party Office for Racial Policy, 1939.

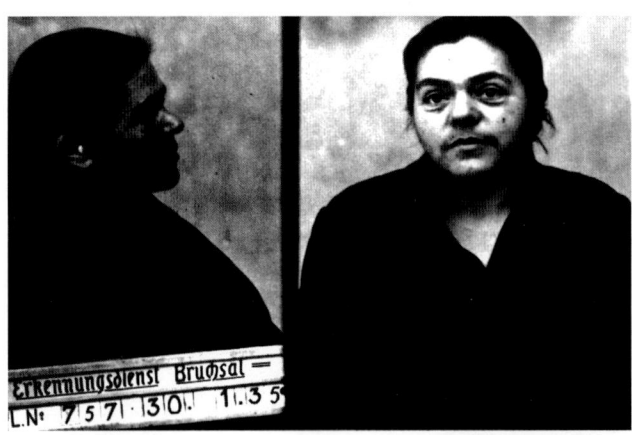

17. Rosa S., 1935. She was sentenced in 1934 to indefinite security confinement after stealing 40 Marks. In 1943, she was taken from the Aichach penal institution to a concentration camp for 'annihilation through labour'.

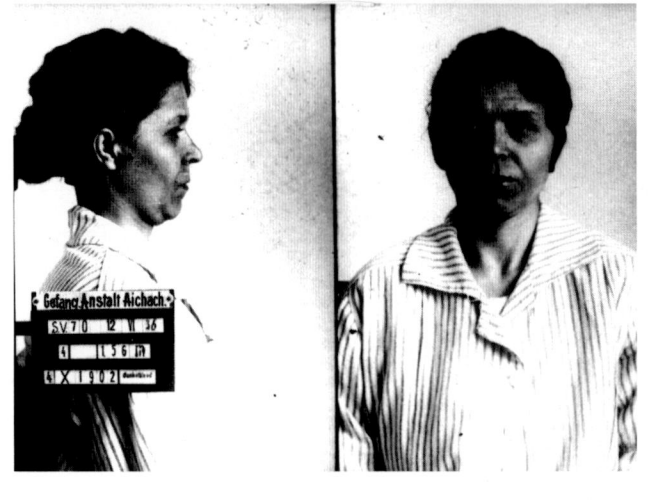

18. Magdalena S., 1936. Another Aichach prisoner held in security confinement following minor offences, she was also later included in the 'annihilation through labour' programme, as were more than 20,000 other prison inmates.

reports noted that castrated inmates were phlegmatic, tired and depressed, and that they were irritable because they were mocked by the other prisoners. Some, such as a 70-year-old man with 12 previous convictions for begging and six sentences for sexual assaults on children, committed suicide immediately after the operation.[156] Reports of the castrations were not hidden from the public. On the contrary, cases were openly discussed in newspapers and in legal and medical journals, which sometimes even carried 'before and after' photographs of castrated men.[157] But prison officials and criminologists were not especially interested in the after-effects for the offenders. Rather, they focused on the question of whether castration actually prevented new offences. This, after all, had been the justification for its introduction.

In the Third Reich, very optimistic conclusions about the social effects of castration were reached. By the late 1930s and early 1940s, the estimated rate of recidivism among castrated offenders was between 2 and 5 per cent.[158] It was also argued that there were 'beneficial' side-effects of the operation, with suggestions that inmates had become more productive. Such claims confirmed the expectations of psychiatrists such as Max Mikorey, the head doctor of the Munich psychiatric hospital, who in a leading legal journal drew a revealing parallel in 1935 with the animal world: 'through castration, the uncontrollable stallion and the wild bull are transformed into the docile gelding and the patient ox. Correspondingly, one can expect that the castrated [men] will generally be easier to incorporate into the great working process of the nation.'[159] Similar claims for the disciplinary and economic benefits of castration had been made for several decades by mental asylum officials in other Western countries.[160]

But some commentators in Nazi Germany remained more sceptical about the supposedly beneficial effects of the operation. Prison doctors warned their colleagues to treat assurances by castrated men that they had lost all sexual desire with caution. After all, most offenders realised that any other admission would only prolong their imprisonment.[161] The criminologist Johannes Lange, who generally welcomed the castration of sex offenders, also argued that the operation did not necessarily put an end to their sexual activities.[162] In exceptional cases, castrated men themselves admitted to the authorities that they still masturbated and had sexual intercourse. One man openly told the Cologne prison authorities that he had erections and ejaculations 'just like before'.[163] Such statements are confirmed by recent research which has concluded that more than 40 per cent of castrated men remain sexually active.[164] Uncertainty about the effects of castration was reflected in the decision of the Reichsgericht in 1935 to allow the simultaneous sentence of castration and security confinement. While early supporters of castration had envisaged the operation as an alternative to imprisonment, judges could now decide on both measures, if they expected the individual to re-offend even after being castrated.[165]

However, doubts over the impact of castration on the future behaviour of sex offenders could do little to dampen the widespread enthusiasm for the operation. Only during the war did the number of sentences begin to decline (see Figure 9, pp. 400–1). But this was probably not the result of growing scepticism. Rather, it was influenced by the fact that numerous potential offenders had now been drafted into the army. In addition, some of those German men guilty of sex offences were now executed rather than castrated, under the new wartime legislation. Faith in the benefits of castration remained high. Before the war, some observers even suggested that the operation should be extended to other offenders. Several prison officials picked homosexuals as targets for forcible castration.[166] Such calls had some influence on the treatment of arrested homosexuals.

Homosexuals and Legal Terror

The Third Reich cracked down with great force on all behaviour seen as sexually deviant. The Nazi leadership was determined to improve the 'racial health' of the nation and to persecute any behaviour that threatened to undermine the 'battle for the birth rate'. Many victims of this Nazi terror were homosexual men, singled out for their particularly 'immoral' and 'degenerate' behaviour.[167] One of the most obsessive homophobes was also one of the most powerful men in the Third Reich: SS and police leader Heinrich Himmler. In a speech to SS officials on 18 February 1937, Himmler warned that homosexuals had 'upset the sexual balance-sheet of Germany' by failing to produce children. In the long run, this would result 'in a catastrophe . . . the end of the Germanic world'.[168] In the Third Reich, many tens of thousands of homosexual men were arrested by Himmler's police. Crucially, most of them were then handed over for sentencing to the regular courts. This meant that arrested homosexuals were far more likely to end up in prisons or penitentiaries than in concentration camps. It has been estimated that, in all, some 10,000–15,000 homosexuals were taken to concentration camps. By contrast, around 100,000 served time in penal institutions.[169]

Once more, the legal apparatus was deeply involved in enforcing Nazi racial policy. To be sure, homosexual sex had been illegal in Germany long before the Nazi takeover in 1933. Thus, according to § 175 of the German Criminal Code of 1871, 'an unnatural sex act committed between persons of male sex' was punishable by imprisonment.[170] But conviction rates had remained relatively low in the pre-Nazi period. And, especially in the Weimar years, the criminalisation of homosexuality was controversially debated. Associations formed by homosexuals and left-liberal political activists campaigned for the abolition of § 175, a demand which was narrowly supported in 1929 by the Committee for Criminal Law in the Reichstag (this had no legislative consequences, though). At the same time, conservative politicians fought hard to introduce even harsher penalties.[171] It was this latter trend which became dominant in the Third Reich. Repression of homosexuals was stepped up in the early stages of Nazi rule. The German police, as well as the SA and SS, attacked the homosexual subculture which had flourished in larger German cities in the 1920s. Well-known meeting places, such as bars, night-clubs, baths and public toilets were raided or closed down, and homosexual magazines and clubs disappeared.[172] In the wake of this, the number of prison sentences for homosexual sex increased, rising from 464 (1932) to 575 (1933) and 635 (1934).[173] But this proved to be nothing more than the prelude to the dramatic assault by the Nazi state on homosexuals.

It was Adolf Hitler who personally called for an intensification of the persecution of homosexuals, following his decision in the summer of 1934 to have the homosexual SA leader Ernst Röhm murdered. During the Nazi rise to power, the brownshirts in the SA had been a vital force. But by 1934 they had become a growing threat to Hitler's rule. Widely unpopular even among Nazi supporters, the ambitions of SA leader Röhm were also viewed with great suspicion by the German army. On 30 June 1934, Hitler finally acted, in a state of frenzy because of false claims of an imminent putsch. A wave of murderous violence was unleashed in the so-called 'Night of the Long Knives', leaving an estimated 150 to 200 people dead, among them SA leaders, other suspected opponents and former rivals of Hitler. SA leader Röhm was shot in the prison in Stadelheim on 1 July 1934. In the aftermath of these murders, much was made in Nazi propaganda of Röhm's sexual orientation. Of course, this had been no secret and had previously been tolerated by Hitler. But the regime, keen to shift attention away from the real motives for the killings, emphasised the homosexuality of Röhm and other SA men, playing to the prejudices of the German public.[174]

The murder of Ernst Röhm provided the backdrop for the radical criminalisation of homosexuality in the second half of the 1930s. Almost exactly one year after his killing, on 28 June 1935, much stricter sentencing was introduced against homosexuals, vaguely justified with reference to 'bad experiences in the recent period . . .'. Under the new law, the definition of what constituted a punishable offence was greatly extended, from intercourse-like acts to any 'sex offence' between men, making it much easier for courts to prosecute homosexuals. Also, much harsher penalties were applied to particular types of offence, such as male prostitution and homosexual acts with persons under the age of 21 (§ 175a).[175] A number of jurists openly welcomed the legislation. According to one senior regional legal official, it was an 'indispensable measure to burn out such ulcers on the body of the nation'.[176] As legal sanctions against homosexuality were made more severe, the police also stepped up its assault on social outsiders (see Chapter 4). This entailed, not least, a crackdown on sexual deviance and any acts regarded as undermining Nazi population policy. Charges for 'criminal abortions', for example, increased substantially between 1936–37 and 1939.[177] But the police specifically targeted homosexuals. New police units were set up, and raids and operations against the homosexual subculture reached their peak. Male prostitutes were blackmailed into acting as police decoys and homosexual meeting places were put under close supervision. Numerous arrested suspects were maltreated and tortured by the police, who forced them to name other sexual partners.[178]

As a result, the number of men taken to court increased dramatically. Between 1936 and 1939, close to 30,000 men were convicted of homosexual offences in Germany.[179] Some courts were so overwhelmed by the number of defendants that they temporarily set up special chambers which dealt exclusively with homosexual offences.[180] The judges frequently resorted to Nazi ideology as justification for strict punishment. Again and again, the courts referred to the 'Röhm putsch'. As a Hamburg court put it in 1937: 'Neither the Röhm affair in 1934, nor the stricter legal regulations in 1935, have caused him [the defendant] to cease his activities.' [181] Anyone found guilty by the courts was virtually certain to be imprisoned (in the Weimar years, a significant minority of men had received fines). In addition, the length of imprisonment became much longer. Terms of one year or more – highly unusual in the Weimar period – were now common, with 30 per cent of all men sentenced to prison in 1936 receiving this sentence. Courts reserved the harshest penalties for men considered particularly depraved or dangerous, such as those described as male prostitutes.[182]

In short, in the prewar years, more and more homosexual men were sentenced to ever longer spells in penal institutions. Only during the Second World War did conviction rates by legal courts fall. According to official figures, convictions by criminal courts halved in the first year of the war, dropping from 7,614 (1939) to 3,773 (1940).[183] But this did not mean that terror directed against homosexual men as a whole declined sharply. Instead, the punishment of homosexuality by other agencies of the Nazi state now intensified, with many thousands of men being sentenced by military courts.[184]

Homosexuality was officially excluded from the provisions for forcible castration in the Habitual Criminals Law. 'The experiences of the castration of homosexuals are not positive,' the Reich Ministry of Justice had explained in late 1933, as in most of the cases the operation 'with the aim of healing their perverse drive has remained without effect.'[185] During the war, the views of leading legal officials changed. The Reich Ministry of Justice now proposed forcible castration of homosexuals, envisaged in the drafts for a law against community aliens. But the law was never implemented.[186]

Nevertheless, homosexuals still became victims of castration policy in the Third Reich. On 26 June 1935, the Sterilisation Law was amended to allow for the 'voluntary' castration of individual offenders, to 'liberate' them from their 'degenerate sex drive'. Given the escalating legal persecution of homosexuals at this time, it comes as little surprise that 'voluntary' castration was aimed not just at violent sex offenders and exhibitionists, but also at homosexuals.[187] There was no legal age limit for such operations, leading to the castration of men as young as 16.[188] Even though the judicial system maintained the façade that no one was coerced into 'voluntary' castration, in reality severe pressure was brought to bear on some men who came up for sentencing before the courts. As one homosexual man recalled after the war: 'The declaration of voluntariness has nothing to do with being voluntary. I had been advised to do this; I was told that I could [otherwise] possibly be met by the Gestapo and I had a good idea what that meant'.[189] This was no empty threat. In 1940, Heinrich Himmler ordered that all homosexual inmates in penal institutions who had 'tempted more than one partner' were to be taken into preventive police custody after the end of their sentence. In Berlin, some 40 per cent of men imprisoned for homosexual offences were arrested after the completion of their sentences. Among those exempted, according to the police guidelines, were men whose sex drive had supposedly died down after castration.[190] Others were apparently told by the prison authorities that, if they did not 'volunteer' for castration, they would eventually be taken into security confinement. Prison officials in security confinement institutions also encouraged inmates to sign up for castration, indicating that the officials would then support their release.[191] In this way, according to internal statistics in the Reich Ministry of Justice, some 174 men were 'voluntarily' castrated in penal institutions before the end of 1939.[192]

Looking at the treatment of homosexual prisoners in general, it is clear that they faced some official discrimination. It had long been a rule in German penal institutions that homosexuals were to be isolated, often by being held in single cells. But isolation was not always possible in Nazi prisons, as we have already seen. First of all, the massive overcrowding and the rapid increase in numbers of homosexual men – thanks to the zeal of the German courts – meant that strict segregation was increasingly difficult. In addition, the growing economic exploitation of prisoners resulted in increasing numbers of homosexual men being sent to prison camps, where inmates were kept in barracks. Some sticklers for regulations among the camp officials even tried to isolate them here. In the Ostmarkstraße camp, the authorities ordered the special construction of single cell barracks, into which homosexual inmates were bundled at night. The Reich Ministry of Justice opted for the smallest cells possible, which were 1.2 metres wide. Other prison camp officials pursued cheaper options to prevent the 'harmful influence' of homosexual prisoners. In Emsland and parts of Rodgau, homosexual prisoners were supposed to be disciplined by their fellow inmates. According to the Reich Ministry of Justice, homosexuals were divided among different barracks where they were 'confronted everywhere by a great majority of [prisoners who are] not sexually perverted, who keep both them as well as each other under control, on account of the healthy disgust against homosexuality which is very widespread among prisoners, too'. Brutal homophobia among inmates was thus actively encouraged by the authorities. Even though homosexuals did not wear a special sign on their uniform, as was mandatory in concentration camps, it was easy enough for other prisoners and staff to single them out. In the prison camps, for example, name tags on the bunks of inmates sentenced for offences against § 175 were supposed to be underlined in red.[193]

The increasing contact of homosexual prisoners with other inmates inside penal institutions strengthened the determination of prison officials in the Third Reich to prevent any sexual encounters among prisoners.[194] In the Weimar years, some prison officials had openly acknowledged that sexual activities between inmates were probably very common, especially in institutions with large community cells. But crucially, the primary concern in the Weimar years, it seems, was not the punishment of these prisoners. Instead the spotlight was on the 'corrupting' effects of incarceration on 'heterosexual' prisoners. This was a favourite theme of the heated Weimar debate about imprisonment and sexuality, raised most dramatically in the popular melodrama, *Sex in Chains* (1928). This film told the story of an engineer, convicted of homicide after he killed a man making improper advances to his wife. Behind bars, the man then starts a homosexual relationship with another inmate. Meanwhile, the engineer's wife also has an affair. When the two are finally reunited, both man and wife are so racked by guilt and revulsion about their behaviour that they commit suicide: 'two broken people die next to the gas valve', as one newspaper concluded its review of this 'deeply moving' film.[195] In Nazi Germany, the focus quickly shifted from the supposed danger of homosexual sex for 'straight' prisoners to the 'threat' of this activity to German society.

Punishment of homosexual sex in penal institutions became a greater priority in Nazi Germany. Prison authorities used different ways to detect sexual relations. In a number of cases, the authorities acted after tip-offs from other inmates. The motives of these denuncers varied. Homophobia was clearly widespread. In addition, the charge of homosexuality could be used to settle scores with unpopular prisoners. Also, some prisoners contacted the authorities because they saw themselves as victims of unwanted advances. Inmates found guilty of homosexual relations often received very harsh disciplinary punishment, in some cases even if no physical contact had taken place. For example, when the Aichach penitentiary authorities discovered a piece of paper with a loving message ('Open this paper a[nd] you find my heart') from a fellow prisoner in the cell of the inmate Frieda R., her rations were reduced for ten days to bread and water. Cases regarded as particularly serious by local prison officials were reported to the state prosecution service for further sentencing. For instance, when prisoner K. in the Emsland camp admitted to the authorities – alerted by another prisoner – that he had repeatedly tried to fondle a fellow inmate in the barracks at night, he was punished with 12 weeks in a punishment battalion. But his punishment did not end there. In addition, the prison authorities forwarded the case to the courts, demanding K.'s forcible castration. In the end, K. was not castrated, but sentenced to another nine months in prison. In these, as in many other cases, prison officials eagerly enforced racial policy against homosexual prisoners. Even so, not all homosexual inmates were hit equally hard. Neither did discrimination extend to all areas of prison life and some homosexual inmates even managed to attain coveted and privileged positions. In the final analysis, homosexuals were still better off in penal institutions than in concentration camps, a conclusion that also applies to the vast majority of other victims of Nazi terror (see Chapter 4).[196]

The Sterilisation of Prisoners

Life in the Nazi racial state was profoundly shaped by eugenic policies. Since the late nineteenth century, measures to improve the 'racial health' of the nation by social engineering had been put forward in Germany, as in many other states, by scientists, politicians, welfare workers, doctors and others. Often, their vision was driven by fear of a terminal decline in the 'racially valuable' members of the community. Advances in modern medicine and social policy, it was argued, had interfered with the natural elimination of 'degenerates', who procreated much faster than 'respectable' classes and now threatened to overwhelm them. Proposed remedies included measures to increase the birth rate of the 'racially valuable', as well as policies – such as sterilisation – to prevent the 'unfit' from reproducing. Support for racial hygiene increased in Germany during the years of social and political crisis after the First World War. In the 1920s, advocates of voluntary sterilisation set their sights on a heterogeneous group of individuals, including those suffering from schizophrenia and epilepsy, the feeble-minded, the physically disabled and other 'asocials'. There was a 'state of emergency', one psychiatrist warned in 1929, and the authorities needed to act in order not to 'suffocate in the swamp of degeneration'. Calls for voluntary sterilisation grew much louder with the collapse of the Weimar Republic. Faced with the breakdown of the welfare state, more and more observers saw sterilisation as the cheapest measure to fight 'degenerates', who were described as an unacceptable financial burden.

There were even plans for a sterilisation law. In July 1932, a draft law was worked out by the Prussian Health Council, which called for voluntary sterilisation of the severely mentally ill and epileptics, as well as other 'carriers of diseased genetic traits'.[197]

The Nazis had been vocal supporters of eugenic policy throughout the Weimar Republic and wasted no time after the 'seizure of power' to implement such measures. On 1 June 1933, the Marriage Loan scheme was introduced. Some six weeks later, on 14 July 1933, its negative mirror image, the Law for the Prevention of Offspring with Hereditary Diseases (Sterilisation Law) was passed. Both laws were central to Nazi racial thinking. The Marriage Loan scheme promoted the birth of healthy 'national comrades'; meanwhile, political opponents, 'asocials' and others seen as biological and social threats were excluded from the financial benefits for new parents. The Sterilisation Law aimed to prevent those suffering from 'hereditary diseases' from having children altogether. This would result in the gradual 'cleansing of the body of the *Volk*' and, according to Arthur Gütt, the Nazi activist in the Reich Ministry of the Interior who had drafted the law, it would also save the millions otherwise spent on the 'feeble-minded, slow-witted, mentally ill and asocials'.[198]

The illnesses listed in the Sterilisation Law included open-ended categories such as 'congenital feeble-mindedness', relying not so much on medical diagnosis as on the prejudices of the examining officials. In addition, there was 'chronic alcoholism', which even the law did not count as a hereditary illness. According to the law, the operations could be performed against the will of the individual – a fundamental change from the 1932 Prussian draft law. Applications for compulsory sterilisation could be made by the public health service, mental asylums and similar institutions.[199] The legal system was closely involved in the sterilisation procedure. Decisions about applications were made by one of the more than 200 Hereditary Health Courts set up all over the country. These courts, which consisted of one presiding judge and two doctors, were supposed to provide some semblance of legality for compulsory sterilisation. They also ensured that more and more legal officials participated in racial policy. By 1939, one in every 20 German judges and prosecutors had dealt with 'hereditary health' matters. The number of men and women they helped to condemn was immensely high. Overall, it is estimated that around 360,000 individuals became victims of the Sterilisation Law in Nazi Germany, the great majority of them before the outbreak of war.[200]

Sterilising Criminals?

One crucial question facing policy-makers in 1933 was whether the Sterilisation Law should also include certain criminals. This issue had been controversially debated for several decades in Germany. As early as 1899, the respected psychiatrist Paul Näcke had suggested the sterilisation of so-called habitual criminals, habitual sex offenders and some violent criminals. Similar proposals were advanced by other psychiatrists and legal professionals in the years before the outbreak of war.[201]

Interest in this issue increased significantly in the 1920s, during the general upsurge of popular support for racial hygiene. Among the most vocal champions of sterilisation in the 1920s was the Zwickau district health officer, Gerhard Boeters, also known as 'the sterilisation apostle'. In May 1923, he had sent a memorandum to the state government of Saxony, proposing the sterilisation of various social outsiders. This had included the demand for forcible sterilisation of some criminal offenders.[202] Boeter's fanatical support for sterilisation knew no limits and, over the next few years, he bombarded the Reichstag and no fewer than 13 state diets with versions of his Lex Zwickau. But there was as yet little support for compulsory measures, regarded by many as too extreme in the light of the uncertain laws of heredity.[203] At the same time, though, there was growing support among influential criminologists, psychiatrists and legal officials for the voluntary sterilisation of certain criminal offenders. These sentiments were echoed by prison officials, often informed by a rather crude biological understanding of criminality. Theodor Viernstein, the prominent Straubing prison doctor, exclaimed in 1926: 'Racial hygiene and criminal law belong together: both aim at selection by suppressing parasites of the race, enemies of society!'[204] This view was shared by other prison doctors. Viernstein's colleague in the Zweibrücken prison noted a few years later that: 'The fight against crime is not an educational but a biological problem. One ought to prevent the breeding of criminal dispositions by racial hygienic measures.'[205]

Weimar politicians, both left and right, had also made themselves heard on the issue of sterilising criminals. In particular, the topic was raised in the Reichstag committee which discussed the draft for a new criminal code. In a meeting on 30 October 1928, deputies from several bourgeois parties in the coalition government proposed that courts should be given the option to release 'dangerous habitual criminals' from security confinement, once it had become law, if these offenders had agreed to be sterilised. Despite some reservations, the SPD backed the measure. But there was opposition from the Communists and the Centre Party, as well as from the Reich Ministry of Justice, and in the end, the motion was passed on to a sub-committee which was never set up. Soon, the committee dealt with the issue again. In a meeting on 6 February 1931, the SPD members put forward a somewhat more moderate version of the 1928 proposal, calling for the voluntary sterilisation of 'habitual criminals dangerous to public safety'. Arguing that German society was in a state of emergency, the SPD deputy Wilhelm Hoegner, who after the Second World War served as the first Bavarian Prime Minister, warned that these offenders would otherwise burden society with ever more 'degenerates'. The response by the Reich Ministry of Justice was much more positive than previously. While the top legal officials had tried to derail eugenic proposals in 1928, they now envisaged forcible sterilisation as a possible option in the long term – a sign of the growing acceptability of eugenic ideas during the crisis of the early 1930s. The committee member most vocal in his approval was the Nazi deputy Hans Frank, who welcomed the proposal as a first step towards the compulsory sterilisation of all 'inferiors' – reflecting the biological view of criminality held by other leading Nazis. But there was also opposition, notably once more from the Communists and the Centre Party. Any decision on the issue was postponed and it soon slipped from the agenda in the political turmoil of the collapse of the Weimar Republic.[206] It did not disappear for long, however.

In early 1933, shortly after Hitler's appointment as Chancellor, the issue of sterilising criminals resurfaced, this time during discussions about the Sterilisation Law. Initially, it appeared likely that criminal offenders would be included in the law – hardly surprising, given the Nazis' previous support for such a policy. Preparing the draft law, Arthur Gütt in the Reich Ministry of the Interior apparently listed 'criminogenic traits' among the hereditary diseases to be eradicated. But this provoked opposition from the legal system. In a letter to the Ministry of the Interior on 6 July 1933, Reich Minister of Justice Gürtner demanded the 'separate treatment of criminals and the genetically ill'. Following this intervention, the provisions for criminals were dropped from the draft. But the issue was not yet off the agenda. It was brought up again by Hitler when the Sterilisation Law was presented to the cabinet on 14 July 1933. At the meeting, he asked Gürtner to draw up a law for the castration of sex offenders and the sterilisation of 'habitual criminals'.[207] As we have seen, castration was indeed added to the Habitual Criminals Law. But it did not introduce the sterilisation of 'habitual criminals', although this has been suggested by some historians.[208] Any plan for such a law was quietly dropped by the Reich Ministry of Justice. Clearly, the legal officials were still able to pursue their own policy objectives and were not entirely subservient to the Nazi leadership.

The Sterilisation Law of 14 July 1933 came as a great disappointment to all those prison officials and criminologists who had hoped for the inclusion of 'criminal traits'. From the day the law came into operation, it was attacked for not going far enough. Once more, prison doctors were particularly vocal. In 1935, for example, the Celle prison doctor complained that the law did not target truly dangerous 'hereditary criminals' and demanded a special law for the prevention of offspring of criminals.[209] These critics could count on the support of some Nazi officials and leading German psychiatrists such as Ernst Rüdin. In an expert commission for racial policy, Rüdin in March 1935 called for the sterilisation of the 'very large army of serious incorrigible endogenous criminals'. Three years later, he stressed the same point again in a paper delivered to the Criminology Congress in Rome.[210] But these persistent calls for the extension of the Sterilisation Law had no effect on legislation. Consequently, criminal behaviour was generally not recognised by the courts as sufficient reason for sterilisation.[211]

Why did the Reich Ministry of Justice oppose a law for the sterilisation of 'hereditary' criminals? In the first place, it appears that the officials were not fully convinced that criminology was clearly able to distinguish 'hereditary' criminals from all others. Indeed, while many criminologists agreed that hereditary factors played an important role in crime, further research carried out in the 1930s emphasised the complex causes of criminal behaviour, undermining demands to single out 'hereditary criminals' for sterilisation. A detailed survey of German criminological literature concluded in 1940: 'As the question of the hereditary character of criminal traits is still very unclear, the legislator was right not to include criminal dispositions in the Law for the Prevention of Offspring with Hereditary Diseases.'[212]

But this was not the whole story. Legal officials were also well aware that the courts in the Third Reich had a whole new range of other measures at their disposal which also prevented criminals suspected of hereditary defects from reproducing. Under the Habitual Criminals Law, offenders described as mentally ill were now sentenced to indefinite detention in asylums, the 'hereditary work-shy' were committed indefinitely to workhouses, 'degenerate' sex offenders were castrated, and 'dangerous habitual criminals' – often considered to be 'degenerate' as well – were locked up indefinitely in security confinement. Several commentators explicitly welcomed the eugenic benefits of these new measures, which made the sterilisation of criminals a less pressing issue. This opinion was shared by the top legal officials. Indeed, the Reich Ministry of Justice itself openly described the Habitual Criminals Law as protecting society from individuals who represent 'a danger for the national community, not only by their criminal activity, but also by burdening the community with inferior offspring'.[213]

Sterilising Prisoners

Of course, convicts were still sterilised. The mere exclusion of 'criminal traits' from the Sterilisation Law did not exempt prisoners from sterilisation under any of the other 'illnesses' listed in the law. The legal administration made sure that prisoners were among the first victims.[214] Once more, local prison officials participated in racial policy. It was the governors who formally applied for the sterilisation of prisoners. But this time, the key role was played by prison doctors, who had to support the governor's application (except in cases where the governor was a qualified doctor). The doctors had to contact the governor if they came across a prisoner whom they suspected of suffering from a 'hereditary illness'. Detection was not left to chance discoveries. Prison doctors were also asked to carry out special examinations of inmates they suspected of falling under the law.[215] In addition, expert reports by prison doctors were used by the Hereditary Health Courts. The 21-year-old servant Maria Schr. was committed to the Aichach prison in February 1934 for six months, convicted of abortion. Prison doctor Schemmel examined her after her arrival and suggested that she be sterilised as 'congenitally feeble-minded'. Apart from her having repeated two years in school, he pointed to her 'greatly diminished ability to concentrate and to make judgements'. The Passau Hereditary Health court followed his opinion, and explicitly noted that it regarded Maria Schr.'s feeble-mindedness as proven 'by the expert report of the prison doctor'.[216] Some prison doctors even joined Hereditary Health Courts as medical experts.[217]

So the fate of individual prisoners depended in large part on the willingness of local officials to denounce them for sterilisation to the courts. Many local prison officials proved keen supporters of Nazi racial policy: for example in 1934, the Zweibrücken prison authorities put forward around one in every 18 men for sterilisation.[218] Figures in Straubing were even higher (not least because the penitentiary included a special 'hospital for insane criminals'). Here the prison doctor Hans Trunk, like his predecessor Theodor Viernstein a fanatical believer in racial hygiene, initially assumed that he would propose for sterilisation between one-third and one-quarter of all inmates coming up for release. Trunk singled out more inmates than any other Bavarian prison doctor, but his zeal was dampened by the regional Hereditary Health Court, which rejected around 30 per cent of his applications. In 1935, Trunk calculated that, in the end, about 8 per cent of the inmates would actually be sterilised, a figure he regarded as far too low.[219]

Owing to the eugenic enthusiasm of local prison doctors in Germany, criminals were significantly more likely to be sterilised than the non-delinquent population.[220] In the first three years after the introduction of the Sterilisation Law, 3,394 prisoners became victims of the operation, about 2 per cent of all individuals sterilised in Germany in this period. In total, 5,397 prisoners (4,909 men and 488 women) had been sterilised by the end of December 1939.[221] Most of the male prisoners were forced to submit to a vasectomy in poorly equipped prison hospitals. The operations on women were more complicated, entailing the ligation of the fallopian tubes, and were generally carried out in state hospitals. A number of prisoners died during or after the operation.[222]

Sterilisation policy had a serious impact on life inside penal institutions. The involvement of local prison officials in its implementation increased the distrust and suspicion among inmates towards them.[223] And while only a rather small proportion of inmates was actually sterilised, many more were gripped by fear, especially in those institutions where extensive examinations of inmates took place. To subvert the examinations, the inmates circulated the answers to intelligence tests conducted by the doctors and learned them off by heart. Some of those singled out as mentally ill tried to resist the operations, terrified by the physical and mental effects. But appeals against the decisions by the Hereditary Health Courts were generally rejected and the operations went ahead. Prisoners who returned to penal institutions afterwards were often traumatised and also faced taunts from fellow inmates.[224]

On what grounds were prisoners sterilised? The number of inmates selected on the basis of what were regarded as purely medical symptoms (for example, schizophrenia or manic depression) was very low. This was almost inevitable, given that mentally ill offenders were generally not supposed to be held inside penal institutions. To start with, 'criminally insane' offenders were not to be sentenced to prison: they were to be sent by the courts straight to asylums (§ 42b). Many of those prisoners diagnosed as mentally ill only after they had begun a sentence of imprisonment were often taken to asylums as well. True, most prisoners exhibiting abnormal behaviour initially remained inside penal institutions. Since the late nineteenth century, special wings or buildings for the mentally ill had been set up in penal institutions all over Germany, part of the wider trend towards greater differentiation of offenders. In some states, such as Bavaria, inmates could be held there until the end of their sentence. But in Prussia, the inmates were to be observed and treated for no more than a few months and, if their condition had not improved, they often had their sentences suspended and were taken by the police to an asylum. In practice, prison doctors also used this policy to get rid of inmates they saw as particularly disruptive and subversive.[225]

Nearly all sterilised convicts were targeted because of their deviant social conduct on the outside, diagnosed in the great majority of cases as expressions of 'congenital feeble-mindedness'. In a sample of decisions by Hereditary Health Courts in Bavaria and Westphalia, around three out of four sterilised prisoners had been classified as 'congenitally feeble-minded', a significantly higher proportion compared to all the victims of sterilisation policy in Germany.[226] Initially, the courts had placed little importance on the social behaviour of these 'feeble-minded' offenders, focusing instead on their supposed intellectual defects. But increasingly, judges, with backing from the Reich Ministry of Justice, also referred to the individual's non-normative conduct – in particular when the offender's intellectual defects were regarded as minor. In such cases, the courts often listed behaviour associated with 'asociality' such as lack of cleanliness, as well as homelessness, unemployment and sexual deviance.[227] Other sterilised prisoners were generally singled out because of alcoholism. In a sample of 301 applications by Bavarian prison officials for the sterilisation of inmates, 53 cited alcoholism as the diagnosis, another judgement typically based on the individual's deviant social behaviour.[228] Alcoholics were brutally persecuted in the Third Reich by welfare authorities, municipal authorities, the police and the legal system as part of the work-shy and immoral sub-class of 'asocials'.[229]

The crucial importance of social criteria can be illustrated by a brief look at the women's institution in Aichach. The Aichach prison doctor Ludwig Schemmel was a supporter of racial hygiene, at times denouncing almost half the inmates he examined as possible candidates for sterilisation. As in other penal institutions, the great majority of Aichach inmates proposed for sterilisation were labelled as 'congenitally feeble minded'. This was the conclusion in all except one of the 54 applications made in 1934.[230] Applications constantly referred to the women's 'intellectual defects' and 'ethical defects'. Regarding the former, Aichach officials highlighted the prisoners' lack of intelligence, describing them as 'mentally inferior' and 'too stupid for words'. Such sweeping judgements were based on school records and performance in intelligence tests, which included general knowledge questions (such as 'Who discovered America?'), difficult to answer for the poorly educated prisoners. The officials also pointed to the inmates' 'asocial' lifestyle and 'amoral' character. Many of the sterilised women had one or more illegitimate children, so the prison officials labelled them 'sexually wayward' and 'morally unstable'. Criminal activity played a relatively subordinate role in the Aichach classifications. In a few cases, particularly those of multiple recidivists, the criminal record gained some importance. But a number of the sterilised women were first-time offenders or were given a positive 'social prognosis'.[231] The activism of local prison officials like those in Aichach ensured that the legal apparatus contributed to the Nazi racial state. The same was true for other aspects of legal terror, including the assault against German Jews.

German Jews and Legal Terror

Radical anti-Semitism had been a central element in Hitler's world-view from the very beginning of his political career and was shared by many other leading Nazi activists. Following Hitler's appointment as Chancellor, German Jews became the victims of waves of discrimination, public humiliation and physical violence. This culminated during the night of 9 to 10 November 1938, when an orgy of violence against Jews broke out all over Germany, instigated by the party leadership. During the pogrom, hundreds of Jews were brutally murdered or committed suicide, and thousands of synagogues and Jewish shops were destroyed or burned to the ground. Overnight, in line with Hitler's wishes, police orders went out for the arrest of some 20,000–30,000 Jewish men, most of whom were locked up temporarily in concentration camps.[232] By the time war broke out in September 1939, German Jews had been largely excluded from economic life, isolated from the rest of the population and officially designated second-class citizens, with the ultimate aim of driving them out of the country.

Laws and Courts

The legal system played an important part in enforcing Nazi policy against the Jews. Legal terror touched all aspects of their life, through the racial interpretation of existing legislation and the application of the 811 laws, directives and statutes directed against Jews, which had been published in the *Reichsgesetzblatt* by 1 September 1939. As the historian Michael Stolleis has put it: 'Until the gruesome final phase, in which disguise seemed superfluous, all discriminatory and disenfranchising measures were enacted within the forms of the law.'[233] No sphere of the law was free from discrimination. Many cases involving Jews came before industrial tribunals and civil courts, which often rubber-stamped anti-Semitic measures. In a number of cases judges approved the dismissal of Jews from their jobs, or the cancellation of contracts with Jews, purely on racial grounds.[234] Looking at criminal law, Jews arrested by the police and then sentenced by the courts in the first years of the Nazi dictatorship were still more likely to be persecuted for their political opposition to the regime, rather than as 'racial aliens'.[235] But soon Jews became the targets of legislation aimed specifically at criminalising their social and economic life.

The most notorious measure was the ban on sexual relations between Jews and non-Jews, one of the chief obsessions of racial anti-Semitism. In the Weimar Republic, Hitler himself had frequently expressed paranoia about such 'mixing' of 'alien blood'. In *Mein Kampf*, for example, he had fantasised that 'with satanic joy in his face, the black-haired Jewish youth lurks in waiting for the unsuspecting girl whom he defiles with his blood, thus stealing her from her people'.[236] Long before they came to power, the Nazis demanded brutal punishment for any such transgressions. In March 1930, just six months before the party's national electoral breakthrough, they had introduced a draft law in the Reichstag which proposed that those who contributed (or threatened to contribute) to the 'racial deterioration' of the German people by 'interbreeding with persons of Jewish blood or coloured races' should be convicted of 'betrayal of the race' and sentenced to imprisonment in a penitentiary – or, in particularly serious cases, to death.[237] This was not the first time the Nazis had made such a deadly threat. In 1922, Hitler had demanded, in one of his many public speeches, the death penalty for 'any Jew caught with a blond girl'.[238] All this fuelled the racial hatred felt by local Nazis, which exploded in the early years of the Third Reich. It was further inflamed by reports in the Nazi press which presented Jews as the personification of sexual lechery. Also, a number of the Nazi thugs felt that the party had betrayed its radical ideology after it had attained power, and had not gone far enough in its measures against the Jews. They decided to force the issue in the first half of 1935, brutally attacking individual Jews and non-Jews who were in relationships – part of another wave of anti-Semitic terror. In the summer of 1935, attempts were made at the top of the Third Reich to curb this terror from below by introducing anti-Semitic legislation outlawing 'betrayal of the race'. By July 1935, the Ministry of Interior and the Ministry of Justice were working on drafts to ban 'mixed marriages'. Soon, these plans became law.[239]

On 15 September 1935, Hitler announced the promulgation of the Law for the Protection of German Blood and German Honour, as part of the infamous Nuremberg Laws. Signed among others by Franz Gürtner, it outlawed future marriages and extra-marital sexual relations between Jews and non-Jews. Any man found guilty of 'race defilement' (*Rassenschande*) would be sentenced to prison or penitentiary. According to one Nazi jurist, 'race defilement' was the one offence which 'in its wickedness, comes close to the other great crimes against the body of the people – treason and high treason'.[240] Women were officially excluded from the law, presumably because of Hitler's conviction that they were passive partners in sexual activities. Nevertheless, some Jewish women were sentenced, too, convicted by the courts for lying to the authorities in order to protect their non-Jewish partners. Other women were punished directly by the Gestapo.[241]

Judges soon handed out very harsh sentences for 'race defilement'. Between 1936 and 1939, about 420 men were sentenced every year, often after denunciations by the general public, who played an important part in the execution of racial policy. More than two-thirds of those found guilty were Jews, who generally received longer sentences than convicted non-Jews. At first, courts had mainly handed out prison sentences of no more than one year. But following some pressure from the Gestapo and the Reich Ministry of Justice, and influential rulings by the Supreme Court, the courts increasingly resorted to lengthy penitentiary sentences, in some cases eight years and more. This move towards stricter sentencing can be illustrated by looking at individual courts. For example, in 1938 the Hamburg regional court (*Landgericht*) for the first time sent more men to penitentiaries than to prisons in cases of 'race defilement'. At the same time, German courts extended the definition of what constituted sexual relations, punishing even hugs and kisses between Jews and non-Jews.[242]

From late 1937 onwards, legal persecution intensified, as discrimination against Jews in Nazi Germany was stepped up. Several new measures designed to rob Jews of their assets were introduced. The aim of this policy was to drive Jews into poverty, ultimately forcing them to leave the country. Jews had to sell their possessions, art works and other valuables at throw-away prices. And when Jews emigrated, the possessions they could take with them were not allowed to exceed 1,000 Reichsmark in value. Some Jews, desperate to maintain some independent means, either to endure life in poverty in Germany or an uncertain future abroad, did not submit to this state-controlled theft. If denounced or found out by the police, they often faced trial. Sentences ranged from hefty fines to imprisonment for 30 months and more, often destroying their last hope of escaping Germany.[243]

Leading Nazis had long tried to construct a link between Jews and criminality, claiming that Jews played a dominant role in the criminal underworld. The legal system strongly supported this racist delusion and convictions of Jews were often used in anti-Semitic propaganda. Until 1938, state prosecutors were supposed to report every trial of a Jew to the press division of the Reich Ministry of Justice. Individual cases were then presented in degrading and salacious ways in the Nazi press, which was full of stories about Jewish 'sex offenders' and 'profiteers'.[244] In reality, the total number of Jews caught up in the criminal justice system remained rather small. German Jews made up a very small proportion of the population. In 1933, there were about 500,000 Jews living in Germany (0.76 per cent), and numbers declined throughout the prewar period, as many Jews fled the country. In addition, it seems that arrested Jews were more likely than others to be dealt with directly by the police, without the legal system being involved at all. For example, between 1933 and 1939, 33 per cent of all Gestapo cases in Krefeld against defendants linked to the KPD and SPD were ultimately decided by the courts. For Jews, the figure was only 16 per cent.[245] All this is reflected in the crime statistics. In 1939, a total of 4,623 Jews were sentenced by German courts (excluding special courts), making up some 1.5 per cent of all the recorded convictions. Jews were significantly over-represented in three areas, which were all linked directly to Nazi racial policy: 418 Jews were sentenced for so-called passport offences (12 per cent of all convictions), which included persons guilty of carrying passports which did not identify them as Jews; 227 Jews were sentenced for 'race defilement' (62 per cent of all convictions); and 494 Jews were sentenced for foreign currency offences (27 per cent of all convictions).[246] Summing up, the total number of Jews convicted by German courts remained relatively small, despite the avalanche of discriminatory legal regulations.

Inside Hitler's Prisons

Consequently, Jews were always a small minority inside penal institutions in the Third Reich. The only exception occurred in the days immediately following the November 1938 pogrom, when thousands of male Jews were briefly taken to penal institutions (see Chapter 4). Yet, even though the number of imprisoned Jews was rather small, the German prison administration was still preoccupied with their treatment – a reflection of the racial obsession of policy-makers in the Third Reich in general. The top legal officials made sure that the racial discrimination increasingly faced by Jews on the outside also shaped their life behind bars. Some directives were responses to wider measures taken against all Jews in the Third Reich. But some leading legal officials were also driven by their own anti-Semitic prejudice. Wilhelm Crohne, for example, insisted in 1933 that he had been 'brought up as an anti-Semite... and, as my personal files also show, remained an anti-Semite'.[247]

Jewish prisoners came under attack from the Reich Ministry of Justice from the mid-1930s. One of the first principles under threat was religious freedom. According to the Weimar prison regulations, Jews were allowed regular visits by representatives of their faith. Due to the small number of Jewish prisoners, rabbis had generally been employed on a part-time basis only. There were apparently only two full-time rabbis paid for by the German prison service. One of them was Dr Martin Joseph, who worked from 1928 in the Plötzensee prison in Berlin. There was no immediate change in this practice in 1933. The ministerial commission drafting a prison law in spring 1935 even included a provision that special rooms should be set aside for the religious services of Jewish prisoners. But soon the religious rights of imprisoned Jews were revoked. Following the Nuremberg Laws in September 1935, Dr Joseph was dismissed from his post (he died in 1943 in Auschwitz), and in the following year the Reich Ministry of Justice cut all aid for the religious support of imprisoned Jews. A month after the November 1938 pogrom, the Reich Ministry of Justice also barred Jewish organisations from providing religious assistance for Jewish prisoners.[248]

Special dietary rules for Jewish inmates were repealed centrally in February 1939. Even before this measure was passed, individual governors had denied Jewish inmates the right to receive unleavened bread during Passover. Curtailment and abolition of Jewish religious rights was accompanied by several other discriminatory measures. In 1935, all Jewish newspapers and magazines were banned from penal institutions, and in the following year, Jews were excluded from transport to the Emsland camp, presumably to limit their contacts with non-Jewish prisoners. In view of the brutal treatment of prisoners in this camp, this rule proved paradoxically beneficial for Jewish inmates.[249]

The most important measure introduced centrally against Jewish inmates in the prewar years was their isolation from other prisoners. In July 1937, Wilhelm Crohne instructed general state prosecutors that inmates who had 'vastly different kinds of blood' should not be brought together in small groups (which applied, for example, to sharing cells). Similar rules were applied to work outside penal institutions, once restrictions on the employment of Jewish prisoners on the outside were relaxed during the labour shortage of the late 1930s. As Crohne put it in May 1939, Jewish prisoners working outside had to be held 'completely separately' from other inmates.²⁵⁰ This was a crucial development. Just as Jews in German society were increasingly isolated from the rest of the population, so too were imprisoned Jews separated from other prison inmates. Initially, this did not necessarily worsen the position of Jews. Some prisoners welcomed the move from overcrowded community cells into single cells, and a number of inmates were presumably also relieved that they were now less at risk of being attacked or denounced by anti-Semitic inmates.²⁵¹

But in the long run, the isolation of Jews meant that local prison officials became more accustomed to treating Jewish inmates differently from others. It also made it easier for prison authorities to introduce ever more restrictive measures against Jews during the Second World War. To be sure, Jewish convicts figured somewhat less large in the minds of the prison officials during the war, as their numbers became ever smaller. Legal terror against 'racial aliens' now focused on Poles. Nevertheless, the prison authorities still made sure of introducing further discriminatory measures against Jews. For example, on 31 October 1941 State Secretary Freisler announced that Jewish prisoners had to wear the Star of David on their uniforms (two months after the same policy had been introduced for German Jews on the outside). Their pariah status was reinforced in January 1942, when Freisler informed officials that Jewish prisoners (as well as Poles) must never be addressed in a formal manner.²⁵²

The various directives from above set the tone for the treatment of Jews in penal institutions. But they still left much of the initiative to local officials. Looking at the actions of the prison warders, it is important not to see them as a homogenous group. Ian Kershaw has divided German attitudes in the Third Reich towards the Jews into three main groups, a distinction which generally holds true for officials in penal institutions as well.²⁵³ Firstly, a sizeable minority of the prison officials were radical haters of Jews. This was the case, for example, of some 'old fighters', the long-standing Nazi activists who had become prison warders in the Third Reich.²⁵⁴ A smaller group among the officials, possibly including a number who had previously supported the SPD, disapproved of the persecution of the Jews because of humanitarian or political motives.²⁵⁵ Additionally, the majority of local officials harboured anti-Semitic prejudices, without actively supporting brutal violence. Since the late nineteenth century, anti-Semitism had been a constitutive element of right-wing nationalism, and as such it was shared by many prison officials. Like most Germans in the pre-war years, these officials were probably not in favour of open, physical attacks against Jews. But at the same time they approved of legal restrictions, such as the 1935 Nuremberg racial laws. And it was the prison officials who were charged with punishing Jews prosecuted under these laws.²⁵⁶

A number of Jewish prisoners became victims of anti-Semitic officials, who bullied them, verbally abused them, beat them up or reported them for disciplinary punishment on trumped-up charges. Violent anti-Semitic outbursts by officials are documented in prisoner files throughout Germany. To pick one example of many, when Paul G. arrived in the Untermaßfeld penitentiary in early 1939, sentenced to two years for 'attempted race defilement', the governor noted in the prisoner's file that the inmate had attempted with the 'manners of a real Jew' to 'gloss over his offence in a disgusting, sycophantic way'.[257] Officials in other penal institutions were equally open in their anti-Semitism. The acting governor of the Wittlich prison described the engineer Eugen S., imprisoned for 'race defilement' in 1938, as an 'evil, typical Jew'. In the same prison, the 18-year-old Polish Jew Josef O., evidently unfamiliar with the strict censorship rules, complained in a letter to his mother on 17 June 1938: 'Also, I suffer very much because of the hatred of Jews. One official calls me Moses, even though he knows exactly what I am called ... Another one called me a damn Jewish swine this lunchtime.'[258]

Local prison officials' anti-Semitism manifested itself in many different ways. A number of Jewish inmates suffered abuse irrespective of their conduct. If they were found guilty of having broken the strict house rules, this infringement was explained by prison officials with reference to the inmate's supposed racial character: 'E. lied to me in typical Jewish fashion,' a senior Aichach official noted in 1935, 'and therefore deserves her sentence of detention.'[259] But good conduct could also be interpreted as characteristic of the 'devious' nature of Jews, 'typical of the racial character which understands [how] to conform even in a position of powerlessness', as another Aichach official wrote in 1939.[260] Those few Jews who had held privileged positions as trusties in the Weimar Republic soon lost these sought-after jobs, sometimes after complaints by the local Nazi party.[261] Jewish inmates in some institutions regularly received less food than other inmates.[262]

Disciplinary punishment was occasionally driven by racial hatred, as can be illustrated by the case of Betty O. Living in Coburg, she had planned to escape Germany in the late 1930s, together with her son and his wife. Preparing for emigration, she had tried to avoid the Nazi authorities' attempts to confiscate her belongings, not declaring all her valuables in her paperwork. But she was caught, and in August 1939 was sentenced to 15 months in a penitentiary. Betty O. was 62 years old and very frail when she arrived in September 1939 in the Aichach penal institution. She weighed only 40 kilos and had suffered for years from heart problems and other serious illnesses. The prison doctor Ludwig Schemmel, however, was not impressed. He dismissed her suffering as 'the whining bluster of this blabbering Jew'. In January 1940, Schemmel ensured that Betty O. had her rations reduced to bread and water for three days, after she had called three times during the night for a doctor, suffering from excruciating pain. Eventually, even Schemmel had to admit that her agony was real and at least prescribed additional milk for her malnourishment. But the prison governor was still not concerned. He ordered that Betty O. should not be allowed to apply for any special privileges, because she was an 'obstinate, impertinent Jew, a true representative of her race'.[263]

Another example of anti-Semitism leading to harsh disciplinary punishment involved Karel N. A Dutch Jew, sentenced in 1937 to two years in a penitentiary for 'race defilement', he was repeatedly singled out by the Untermaßfeld authorities and was severely punished for minimal transgressions of the rules. Once, he had a quick look during the daily exercise in the yard at a book he had just received from the library. The governor remarked about this incident that 'the Jew N. is an especially presumptuous impertinent lout, who breaks the house rules again and again' and ordered that Karel N. should receive no books for three months. Towards the end of his sentence he saw the prison teacher, who was responsible at that time for providing inmates with clothes for their release. When the teacher refused to give him any underwear, Karel N. complained. The teacher immediately notified his colleagues, claiming that the prisoner had started 'again and again to talk in a loutish way, in a real Jewish manner, despite repeated warnings'. As a punishment, Karel N.'s bed was removed for one week and he received only bread and water for four days.[264]

But not all local prison officials were driven by strong anti-Semitism. Many were rather indifferent and some even acted sympathetically towards Jews. One former Jewish inmate in the Freiendietz penitentiary noted that his treatment had been bearable 'because the old civil servants from the judicial administration, and not SS-men, were still working in the penitentiaries'.[265] Another former inmate even claimed, not entirely convincingly, that he had never been made to suffer because he was Jewish.[266] Many rights and privileges available to other inmates were also still open to a number of Jewish prisoners (at least German Jews), even in the early years of the war. These included visits from relatives, books from the prison library, consultations with the doctor, permission to keep flowers in their cells and extra pay for very productive labour. Occasionally, Jewish inmates also successfully applied for special benefits, such as longer visiting hours, toothpaste from home and special meetings with their lawyers. Some prisoners also received good references from warders. As late as June 1942, Ingeborg E. was characterised by an Aichach warder as 'friendly', 'good-natured', 'obedient', 'grateful' and 'patient'. Jewish prisoners sometimes escaped strict disciplinary punishment. In March 1938, Max H., who was serving a four-year penitentiary sentence in Brandenburg-Görden for receiving stolen goods for gain, admitted to the prison warders that he had secretly smoked and handed them his matchbox (he was scared that he would be denounced by fellow inmates). In the Weimar prison, smoking had often been punished severely, in some cases with several days in detention. But Max H. was only reprimanded.[267] On the whole, Jewish prisoners could expect much less brutal treatment than Jews in concentration camps, where conditions and treatment were significantly worse.

4   The Nazi Web of Terror

The legal apparatus, with its courts and prisons, had an important place in the Third Reich. But there was, of course, more to Nazi repression than legal terror. The police, too, fought against perceived threats to the Nazi 'national community'. Publicly, some leading officials at the time stressed that this shared purpose meant that the two agencies worked together harmoniously. For instance, on 29 November 1935, the senior police official Kurt Daluege claimed in a speech in the Reich Ministry of Justice that the activities of the legal apparatus and police in the fight against crime are 'directed at the same aim and therefore inevitably complement one another'.[1] But Daluege's listeners knew only too well that the reality was more complex. The police at times operated parallel to the legal system, with the concentration camp as its own place of confinement. This practice raises key questions about the relationship between the legal authorities and the police: was it characterised more by conflict or cooperation? To what extent was the legal apparatus overshadowed and overwhelmed by police terror? And how did internment in concentration camps compare to life inside penal institutions? To answer these questions, it is necessary first of all to chart the growth of police power after the Nazi takeover, and to look at the response of legal officials.

The Rise of the Police and the SS

The police were involved in Nazi repression from the very beginning. Police forces were under Nazi control in several German states including Prussia and the police approved or executed much of the early terror. Already in the first weeks after Hitler's appointment as Chancellor, the attention centred on political opponents of the new regime. SA and SS men carried out violent attacks on Communist supporters while the police stood idly by. In Prussia, such thugs were even employed as auxiliary policemen, following a decree by the new head of the Ministry of the Interior Hermann Göring on 22 February 1933. This meant that the same Nazi activists who only a few weeks previously had fought their political enemies on the street could now settle old scores as state officials. Looking at the police force in general, there was no large-scale purge in the Third Reich, some dismissals of senior officials notwithstanding. The vast majority of officials in the criminal and the political police departments kept their jobs and loyally served the new regime, finding much they could agree with.[2]

Police intimidation and assault on the left intensified dramatically after the Reichstag fire of 27 February 1933. Nazi leaders such as Hitler and Göring, in their blind hatred and fear of the left, saw the fire as the beginning of a Communist uprising. Even the fact that the culprit van der Lubbe was immediately caught, and confessed, could not shake Hitler's conviction that he faced a Communist revolt. After he arrived at the burning building, Hitler (according to Rudolf Diels, head of the Prussian political police) ranted hysterically: 'There will be no mercy now. Anyone who stands in our way will be cut down', before demanding that Communist officials be hanged or shot. By the following morning, 28 February, Hitler had recovered enough composure to decide on measures for the systematic repression of political opposition. At a meeting of the cabinet, the Decree for the Protection of People and State (Reichstag Fire Decree) was passed. This decree – the 'constitutional charter of the Third Reich', according to Ernst Fraenkel – suspended guarantees of personal liberty and served as the basis for the police arrest and incarceration of political opponents without trial, the euphemistically named 'protective custody' (*Schutzhaft*). Within days, up to 1,000 persons had been arrested by the police in Berlin alone.[3] Over the next months, many tens of thousands more political opponents were arrested, both Communists and other members of the organised working class.

At times, Hitler's jurists simply remained spectators. True, many police detainees were handed over for trial to the courts (see Chapter 3), but it was not unusual for others to stay in police custody, without any involvement of the judicial system. Many were held for only a few days or weeks, but on release their places were often taken by new arrivals. Even though numbers were falling by the summer, there were still almost 27,000 individuals in protective custody in Germany at the end of July 1933. In addition, tens of thousands more suspected political opponents were seized without such police authorisation in the spring and summer of 1933, in raids by local SA or SS units, who indulged in an orgy of violence leaving hundreds dead. Throughout most of that year the different detainees were tormented at hundreds of different sites all over Germany. These 'early camps' included police and SS jails, concentration camps, barracks, SA offices and cellars. They were not run by one central authority but by various police, SS and SA units. In Berlin alone, it is thought, the SA operated well over 100 sites where they tortured and sometimes murdered political opponents.[4]

With the assault on political opponents in full flow, the German police also extended its operation against suspected criminals and 'asocial' deviants. Of course, these individuals had been pursued by the police before the Nazis came to power, but it became clear in 1933 that police practice in the Third Reich would be quite different. First of all, the zeal of the police was greater, as is reflected in the numbers of arrested individuals. It has been estimated that in the course of a nation-wide police strike against the homeless and beggars in September 1933, accompanied by a propaganda campaign in the Nazi press, several tens of thousands of suspects were temporarily arrested – more than ever before in a single sweep by the German police. Secondly, the police stepped up their own 'preventive measures' against criminals. In the Weimar Republic, this term had often meant that suspected criminals were put under police supervision. But in the Third Reich, they were actually arrested even if they had *not* committed any new crimes, and remained in police custody. This measure was pioneered in Prussia. On 13 November 1933, the Prussian Ministry of the Interior introduced preventive police custody (*polizeiliche Vorbeugungshaft*) against 'professional criminals' and certain sex offenders (such as rapists and paedophiles) who had not committed any new offence.[5]

Various police activities during the 'seizure of power' clearly damaged legal authority. Indefinite detention without due judicial process was incompatible with the rule of law. But, on the whole, there were no loud complaints or protests from legal officials. On the contrary, they often even expressed sympathy and support for the police measures. How can this apparent paradox be explained? To start with, by no means every police action was seen as being in direct competition with the legal system. Many political opponents were arrested by the police for activities which had taken place before the Nazis had come to power. As they had not done anything considered illegal at the time, they could not really be persecuted by the legal authorities. The same was true of 'professional criminals' put in preventive police custody. The Prussian Ministry of Justice stated that it would not regard this as competing with the judicial security confinement of 'dangerous habitual criminals' in penal institutions. Instead, police confinement was seen as complementary. After all, judicial security confinement was applied only to individuals who had actually committed a new offence. Rather than wait until the remaining 'professional criminals' at large had committed new offences as well, it was argued, it would be better to take them into police confinement straight away.[6] These sentiments were apparently shared by many local police officials, who also saw their new powers as adding to rather than competing with legal sanctions.[7]

The response of leading judicial officials such as Reich Minister of Justice Gürtner was partly shaped by their long-standing conviction that the rule of law could not always apply during a state of emergency. As a result, Gürtner tolerated much of the terror which occurred during the Nazi takeover. Occasionally, he was even willing to play an active part in the undermining of the legal system, as became obvious in the aftermath of the Reichstag fire (see Chapter 2). He did not even stop short of covering for Nazi murders, if this was what Hitler wanted. This was plain to see after the notorious Night of the Long Knives in the summer of 1934. For obvious reasons, Hitler wanted to keep the regular courts from investigating the killings. Franz Gürtner obliged. In a cabinet meeting on 3 July 1934 he agreed to a law that legalised the killings as an exceptional measure of 'self-defence of the state' against 'treasonable attack'. Gürtner had accepted that Hitler was the law.[8] This reality was underlined ten days later by Hitler himself. In a dramatic speech in the Reichstag he justified the killings, for which he accepted personal responsibility, by claiming that they had saved Germany from a revolt. In this situation, Hitler added, he had been entitled to ignore the rule of law: 'Mutinies are broken according to eternal, iron laws. If I am reproached with not turning to the law-courts for sentence, I can only say: in this hour, I was responsible for the fate of the German nation and thereby the supreme judge of the German people.' The deputies and most Germans applauded Hitler – as did prominent jurists such as Carl Schmitt, the influential Professor of Constitutional Law and a Nazi sympathiser, who claimed that Hitler, as the supreme judge, 'defends the law'.[9]

Legal officials like Reich Minister Gürtner initially also supported the police detention of the left-wing opposition without trial, as a way to stabilise the new 'national' regime.[10] Such support was often hands-on. The legal authorities went so far as to provide room inside their penal institutions for arrested police prisoners. In the Weimar years, prisons had also sometimes held police detainees, but numbers had always been small. This changed radically during the 'seizure of power'. In the spring of 1933, with the SS camp system not yet developed, the police lacked space for arrested 'political enemies' and instead often used penal institutions. All over Germany, many thousands of police detainees (in protective custody) were taken to penal institutions, both small local jails and large prisons and penitentiaries such as Hamburg-Fuhlsbüttel, Remscheid-Lüttringhausen, Cologne, Gollnow, Chemnitz, Stuttgart and Waldheim. In some German districts there were well over three times more police detainees in penal institutions than were held by the police authorities themselves. Numbers were particularly high in Bavaria. On 3 April 1933, some

4,533 individuals in protective custody were held inside Bavarian penal institutions – making up around one-third of the maximum prisoner capacity of these institutions.[11] Some police detainees were held by the legal authorities for one year or more.[12] Occasionally, assistance to the police went even further than the provision of cells: individual prison officials actually participated in decisions about which police detainees held in their penal institution should be released.[13] In short, the legal system played its part in facilitating police terror during the 'seizure of power'. Had it not been for the prison system throwing open its doors to the police, it would have been impossible for the police to arrest as many political suspects as they did in 1933.

At the same time, Gürtner, like other officials in the traditional state bureaucracy, regarded the terror during the Nazi takeover as a temporary phenomenon that would disappear after the completion of the 'national revolution'. In the summer of 1934, many state officials believed that the Night of the Long Knives had been the final act in this drama. Now it was time for the re-establishment of the sole authority of the regular system of law and order, and the end to confinement in camps without legal procedure. Needless to say, the expectation of a return to 'normality' was based on a fatal misunderstanding of the true nature of Nazism. However, it did not seem completely illusory to the officials at the time. As early as July 1933, Hitler himself had declared that the revolution was over, and Göring had threatened SA men with serious sanctions if they continued to interfere with the jurisdiction of the state. Afterwards, numerous Nazi supporters were convicted of offences such as violence and corruption. In the same period, the number of individuals held in camps without trial began to fall sharply, following the decline in arbitrary terror. At the end of 1934, there were only around 3,000 prisoners left in concentration camps. Many of the early camps had been closed down, adding to the perception that such camps were on their way out. But this did not happen. Instead, the state of emergency became permanent.[14] This was closely linked to the rapid rise of SS leader Heinrich Himmler to the top of the German police. By April 1934, Himmler was already in charge of the political police in all the German states and on 17 June 1936 he was appointed by Hitler as Chief of German Police.

Himmler's rise went hand in hand with a change in the function of the police. By the mid-1930s, after most resistance to the Nazis had been destroyed, the police dramatically extended their mandate, once more encouraged and supported by Hitler. Their main ambition was 'racial general prevention': the cleansing of the German 'racial body' of all those written off as deviants and degenerates, with the ultimate aim of creating a totally homogenous society. Previously, the aim of the police had not been to intern all such individuals. For example, the criminal police had believed that the detention of a small number of 'professional criminals' – the 'usual suspects' with many previous convictions for organised crime – would serve as a deterrent to all others. Hence, the actual number of arrests had remained small, with around 300 people in preventive police custody in Prussia in the summer of 1934, according to the Nazi press. But this selected terror against the few was now replaced by an all-out assault on deviant behaviour.[15] Preventive police custody was extended to the whole of Germany on 14 December 1937. The targets were not just 'professional and habitual criminals', but everyone who 'endangers the public by his asocial behaviour'. This, Himmler's deputy Reinhard Heydrich explained on 4 April 1938, included 'beggars, tramps (Gypsies), whores, alcoholics' and the 'work-shy', among many others.[16] In several police raids in 1937 and 1938, many thousands of homeless people, beggars and others were arrested and sent straight to concentration camps. Inside these camps, political inmates were soon in a minority, outnumbered by supposed criminals and 'asocials'.[17] The late 1930s also saw the first mass arrests of German Jews, during and after the anti-Jewish pogrom of November 1938.

The result of this police terror was a sharp increase of inmates in concentration camps in the second half of the 1930s, reaching over 24,000 by early November 1938. In contrast to the 'early camps', these camps were now operated under the exclusive authority of the SS. They had been brought under the control of the SS from 1934, with Hitler's backing. At first, all the remaining camps had been reorganised along the lines of the 'model' concentration camp in Dachau – the first SS camp, set up in the spring of 1933 under orders from Heinrich Himmler during his brief tenure as head of the Munich police. But eventually, all the 'early camps' were abandoned by the SS, with the exception of Dachau. Instead, the SS built up a new structure, consisting of purpose-built concentration camps such as Sachsenhausen (1936), Buchenwald (1937) and Mauthausen (1938).[18] For most concentration camp inmates, Jews and non-Jews alike, life was characterised by the extreme violence and arbitrary terror of the SS guards, very poor living conditions and hard labour.

This development held obvious implications for the legal authorities. Police terror was here to stay, and like Hitler, the top police officials were open about the fact that they did not see themselves as bound by legal norms. In a speech to the Academy for German Law in October 1936, Himmler bluntly stated: 'Right from the start I took the view that it did not matter in the least if our actions were contrary to some clause in the law; in my work for the Führer and the nation, I do what my conscience and common sense tells me is right.'[19] Indeed, disregard of the letter of the law was seen as crucial to the defence of the national interest. The police styled itself the 'domestic army'. Just as the German army on the battlefield could not be subject to legal regulation, so too, it was claimed, the fight of the German police at home must not be constrained by the rule of law.[20] The same reasoning was applied to the concentration camps. The official 1934 camp guidelines even included the provision that 'agitators' could be hanged – openly challenging the judicial authority over the death penalty.[21] All this meant that the legal authorities had to come to a more permanent accommodation with the police.

Conflict and Compromise: the Law and the Police

The establishing of police terror created some areas of friction with the legal system. The Reich Ministry of Justice generally insisted that law-breakers, as far as was possible, had to be dealt with by the court system. Consequently, the legal officials objected to police measures which appeared to undermine legal monopoly of the punishment of criminal offenders. This included the relatively small number of cases where the police had failed to hand over to the legal system individuals arrested for specific criminal offences, taking them straight to concentration camps instead. Even more controversial were instances where the police simply arrested individuals who had been found not guilty in court. Such 'corrections' of sentences were regarded by legal officials as undermining the authority of the judges, above all when the police arrests were actually carried out inside the courtroom.

Legal authorities pursued two strategies to solve such conflicts over sentencing. Firstly, they tried to reach some compromises with the police. Thus, the police promised to refrain from arresting ex-defendants inside the courtroom and also from taking individuals into custody who had been found innocent by the courts. At the same time, the legal authorities accepted the police arrest of defendants set free because of lack of evidence. Sometimes, as we shall see, legal officials even actively supported this.[22] Secondly, the legal authorities pushed for ever harsher legal penalties. This was meant to combat police and SS claims that 'corrections' were necessary in the case of 'too lenient' court sentences. The assumption was that if sentences became harsher, the police would have no more excuse to 'correct' them. As State Secretary Roland Freisler explained to senior legal officials in 1937: 'We should not and must not create the impression anywhere, that we don't think that we're able to make and implement the final judgement of the state against the criminal.'[23] This approach influenced many aspects of penal policy. For example, in a meeting with the general state prosecutors in the following year, the Reich Ministry of Justice made it clear that the way to cut down on extra-legal police measures against 'habitual criminals' was for courts to decide on security confinement in all appropriate cases.[24] The judges quickly got the message. In 1939, 1,827 persons were sentenced to security confinement, more than twice as many as in 1937 (see Figure 9, pp. 400–1). It has been suggested that it was only intervention from above in 1938 – a response to police pressure – which perverted the practice of security confinement.[25] But this argument is unconvincing. After all, in 1934, the first year the Habitual Criminals Law was in operation, German judges had passed 3,723 sentences of security confinement – more than double the 1939 figure. Evidently, the German judges had their own reasons for cracking down on 'dangerous habitual criminals', independent of police activities.

Another sphere of potential conflict centred around life inside penal institutions. Legal officials strongly believed that defendants sentenced to imprisonment had to serve their time inside penal institutions, either until they had completed their sentence, or until they were released early in accordance with judicial procedures. From this viewpoint, there was no room for police interference in the discharge of sentences of imprisonment. This principle was even applied to police detainees held by the legal authorities.

Throughout the prewar years, prison authorities continued to provide the police with cells – or entire wings – in penal institutions. To be sure, the legal authorities were not keen to lock up police detainees. While it caused no extra costs (the police paid a fixed sum for each inmate), it did put added pressure on an already overstretched prison system. Still, the legal authorities saw it as their duty to assist the police, and numbers were smaller than during the 'seizure of power'. Between June 1935 and June 1937, on average only around 600 inmates in protective police custody were held inside larger prisons and penitentiaries per day (numbers in local jails were higher).[26] These figures increased sharply for a brief period after the pogrom on 9–10 November 1938, as the legal authorities quickly decided to assist the state-sponsored assault on the Jewish population. In the early hours of 10 November, the Reich Ministry of Justice instructed general state prosecutors all over Germany to make room in penal institutions for arrested Jews. Soon, prisons and penitentiaries temporarily filled up with thousands of Jews. In the Baden district alone, more than 1,000 Jews were taken into penal institutions after the pogrom.[27]

But the Reich Ministry of Justice made strict conditions for this internment of police detainees. In particular, it generally prevented any significant police interference in the treatment of these individuals inside penal institutions. Reich Minister Gürtner made this clear as early as 1935, arguing that for prisoners in protective custody 'only the rules of our prisons are valid, because we also carry the responsibility'.[28] The main motivation of the legal officials was not to protect these inmates from the police, but to maintain control over the penal institutions. As a result, police detainees in penal institutions were generally treated according to the rules for remand prisoners. This meant that they were not forced to work (until 1938), were allowed to write letters once a week, and could regularly receive packages of food from their relatives.[29] The Reich Ministry of Justice thwarted police attempts to ensure that these inmates were treated much more harshly than this. The legal authorities merely gave the police a say in minor issues, such as visiting rights and the surveillance of mail. Of course, this did not stop some individual governors from giving further powers, such as disciplinary punishments, to the police authorities of their own accord.[30] The Reich Ministry of Justice made one further condition: that police detainees should only be held for a short period in penal institutions. In most cases, the police obliged. If they failed to do so, the legal authorities sometimes contacted the police to ensure that the inmates were taken away, deliberately speeding up their transfer to concentration camps.[31]

Overall, the legal system successfully barred the police from exerting any significant influence over the prison system. Most importantly, legal officials resisted attempts by the police in the late 1930s to 'poach' prisoners before the end of their sentence and transfer them to concentration camps. In 1937 and 1938, the police leadership repeatedly tried to get their hands on certain prisoners (unemployed prisoners, inmates sentenced for treason and high treason, and security-confined inmates). Economic arguments were used to justify these initiatives. In reality, they probably owed more to the ambition of the police leadership to extend its power and undermine the authority of the legal system.[32] The Reich Ministry of Justice successfully subverted these efforts. Reich Minister Gürtner drily thanked Himmler for 'the interest which you, *Herr Reichsführer*, take in the deployment of labour of the prisoners', but the Reich Ministry of Justice made clear that the inmates were needed as labourers in the prison service.[33] No prisoners were handed over.

The police leadership was not deterred and in 1939 Himmler launched his most dogged attempt yet to gain control over some prisoners held by the legal authorities – the security confined. In spring, Himmler asked the head of the Chancellery of the Führer, Philipp Bouhler, for support. Following a conversation with Hitler, Bouhler undertook an investigation of the productivity of security-confined inmates which proved acutely embarrassing for the Reich Ministry of Justice. While the judicial authorities had claimed that the great majority of the inmates were engaged in essential work projects for the Four-Year Plan, Bouhler seized on the fact that in Brandenburg-Görden such projects included the painting of toy soldiers. On 8 August 1939, Gürtner was informed that, following a report by Bouhler, Hitler had decided that all expendable prisoners in security confinement should be handed over to Himmler.[34] The Reich Ministry of Justice was still not prepared to give up any of its prisoners, arguing that none of them was expendable. Gürtner also claimed that the painting of toy soldiers had netted foreign currency. In any case, he added, this line of work had been stopped and he needed the security confined for large projects of land cultivation and armament production.[35] This argument was largely spurious, as Gürtner knew that many of the security confined, on account of old age and illness, were unproductive and slow.

He was driven primarily by the desire to defend the authority of the legal system, and his ministry, against the police.

In the meantime, Bouhler had informed the police of Hitler's decision. The police leadership saw this as their best chance yet to gain control over some convicts. In a matter-of-fact letter, Heydrich informed the Reich Ministry of Justice in late August 1939 that the police demanded the transfer of all the security confined, not just the 'expendable' ones, to concentration camps as soon as possible.[36] Officials in the Reich Ministry of Justice decided not to respond to Heydrich and after the outbreak of war on 1 September 1939, the issue receded into the background. More important matters had to be dealt with.[37] It is not clear whether the Reich Ministry of Justice would otherwise have been successful in resisting the pressure from the SS in this instance. But the fact is that, by the outbreak of war, the Chief of Police and SS leader Heinrich Himmler had failed in his attempts to 'poach' prisoners.

The only time the police regularly got their hands on imprisoned offenders was during brief police interrogations. Prisoners could be taken for a short period to police headquarters. Others were interrogated inside penal institutions. Some prisoners returned from police custody badly bruised, as police officers did not hesitate to use brutal violence, beating, whipping and strangling their victims. Some regional legal officials as well as Reich Minister Gürtner initially objected to this police brutality. But the practice was backed by Hitler and Himmler, who described the methods as a way of 'opening the mouths' of enemies of the regime. Eventually, the legal system accepted police torture, but demanded that it be standardised. To this end, senior legal officials, led by Wilhelm Crohne, and police officials met in the Reich Ministry of Justice on 4 June 1937. After some discussion, it was agreed that police officials could be allowed to hit captives on the behind up to 25 times. The minutes of the meeting give a clear insight into the mind-set of the legal officials, who in their delusion saw their endorsement of police torture as a victory for the rule of law: 'A "regular cane" shall be designated to eliminate any arbitrariness.'[38]

In exceptional cases, police interrogation ended with the death of a convict. Ali Höhler, the man convicted of shooting the Nazi 'martyr' Horst Wessel in 1930, was murdered on 20 September 1933, on the way back to the Wohlau penal institution after a police interrogation in Berlin. According to an internal Gestapo report, the killing had been carried out by a group of SA men who had intercepted the police transport. Höhler's death was probably the first case of an individual, legally sentenced to imprisonment, being killed by Nazi activists. The first, but not the last. On 23 February 1934, Christian Heuck, a former KPD Reichstag deputy serving a prison sentence for attempted high treason, was killed in the Neumünster prison by a troop of SS men which had been admitted with the tacit agreement of the governor. The prison doctor played his part in the killing, too, obligingly classifying the prisoner's murder as 'suicide'. And a few months later, during the Night of the Long Knives, three more inmates – this time disgraced former SS men – serving prison sentences were taken out of their cells and shot.[39] But until the outbreak of war, such murderous 'correction' of a court sentence remained very rare.

Just as the police failed to gain any significant influence over the prison system, so, too, legal officials failed to assert any authority over the concentration camp system. The question of the torture and the killing of inmates by SS guards inside the camps generally proved to be beyond the reach of the judiciary. Attempts by Gürtner to remove executions and corporal punishment from the official concentration camp regulations were thwarted by Himmler. Other attempts to gain influence over the camps also failed. Until the war, the judiciary had on paper retained the authority to investigate and prosecute maltreatment and murder in the concentration camps, and the legal system was well informed about suspicious deaths of inmates, shot 'trying to resist' or 'escaping'. But judicial investigations were rare and generally unsuccessful. In part, this was due to sabotage by police and camp officials, but many legal officials themselves also quickly accepted that the killings in the concentration camps were, in practice, outside their brief. After the reorganisation and extension of the camp system in the mid-1930s, legal officials became used to concentration camps as regular instruments of terror. For example, in September 1937 the Jena general state prosecutor reported to the Reich Minister of Justice about killings in the new concentration camp in Buchenwald: 'In the first weeks, seven escaping inmates were shot by guards. The judicial proceedings [against the guards] have been set aside. Cooperation between the camp leadership and the state prosecution service has been good.'[40]

The legal system did win one significant concession from the police, however. Legal officials had insisted that if concentration camp inmates were sentenced by courts to imprisonment, then they had to be transferred to a penal institution to serve the sentence. Remarkably, until the war, SS and police officials generally agreed to this arrangement. When concentration camp inmates realised what was going on, some voluntarily confessed to real or invented criminal acts, hoping that they would then be tried and sentenced to regular imprisonment. In a number of cases, the inmates succeeded. But few could escape the concentration camps for good, as they were routinely taken straight back after their sentence. For example, in May 1939, Walter A., an Austrian Jew, was transported from the Buchenwald concentration camp to the Untermaßfeld penitentiary, convicted for thefts he had committed prior to his concentration camp confinement. At the end of his sentence, the prison governor sent Walter A. back to Buchenwald, as previously agreed, describing the prisoner as a 'typical Jew, who will always commit more crimes'.[41] But such transfers from concentration camps to penal institutions were probably rather uncommon. Much more regular were transports in the opposite direction, from prisons and penitentiaries to SS concentration camps.

Denouncing Prisoners to the Police

The police and the legal authorities regularly supplied each other with inmates for their respective places of confinement. That the legal authorities depended on the police to hand over arrested suspects to the court system is self-evident. What is much less well known is that, in turn, the legal authorities helped to supply the police and concentration camps with prisoners. Reporting scores of prisoners to the police, legal officials ensured that the camps received a steady stream of inmates – one more twist in the intertwining of prison service and other agencies of Nazi repression. Of course, such cooperation had some precedents in the pre-Nazi era. For example, in the nineteenth century prison officials were already reporting the release of individuals regarded as likely recidivists to the police, and also supported the continued imprisonment of some 'work-shy' ex-prisoners by the police in workhouses. But this practice escalated dramatically in the Third Reich, a prime example of the close cooperation between legal system and police. Because this policy of judicial denunciation has never been examined comprehensively – in great contrast to denunciations by the general public – it will be described in more depth here.

Individual remand prisoners were among the first victims of this policy. When state prosecutors decided not to charge a suspect, he or she was often handed over to the police for further confinement, rather than being set free. This practice had been pioneered in Prussia, where political suspects were targeted. On 6 May 1933, the Prussian Minister of Justice Kerrl complained that 'active pests of the people' were currently being released from remand prisons, if there was not sufficient evidence to try them. The result, Kerrl warned, was that these individuals 'could continue their seditious, subversive activity without interruption . . .'. To prevent this, the state prosecution service was asked to report such remand prisoners before their release to the police, who then decided on protective custody. After the coordination of the legal system, the Reich Ministry of Justice issued rather similar directives in 1935, targeting selected remand prisoners, such as foreigners, Sinti and Roma, and politically 'subversive' individuals.[42] Occasionally, legal officials went beyond simply reporting selected remand prisoners to the police and actively suggested that they be taken into police custody. For example, in January 1939, the Graz general state prosecutor reported that his office had asked the Gestapo in two recent cases to take remand prisoners into custody. One of them was described as a '13-year-old gangster', who could not be prosecuted because he was not legally responsible. The other was a priest whose use of force during a sex offence 'could not be clearly proven beyond doubt'. The courts were not able to discipline these individuals – but the police were.[43]

It has been argued that judges occasionally sentenced innocent defendants to imprisonment rather than set them free, as this would have led to their immediate arrest by the Gestapo. In this way, imprisonment in a penal institution protected defendants from the concentration camp.[44] While such cases did indeed occur, it should be added that the judges must have known that a spell in a prison or penitentiary often only meant a temporary reprieve for the defendants. As we shall see next, many prisoners were simply taken to the police *after* completing their sentences, with the full cooperation of the legal authorities. Police officials then decided whether the individual should be taken to a concentration camp.

Most judicial denunciations involved convicted prisoners who had come to the end of their sentences. Instead of being released, many thousands of them were arrested by the police, thanks in part to the administrative support of the legal system. The main targets were convicted political prisoners. Already in spring 1933, the Ministries of Justice in different German states were ordering prison governors to report the upcoming release of certain political inmates to the police. Probably the most extensive guidelines were introduced in mid-1933 in Bavaria. Here, the prison governors were asked to examine every inmate before release to decide 'whether protective custody should be proposed because of the great danger he poses to the state, in particular because of former active support for the Communist cause'.[45] Soon, this cooperation between legal officials and the police was regulated on a national level. On 18 December 1934, the Reich Ministry of Justice ordered that all inmates sentenced for treason should be reported to the police one month prior to their release. Regarding other political prisoners, a variety of arrangements between regional Gestapo and legal officials remained in place. In the Hamm district, for example, individual prison governors also reported inmates sentenced for high treason to the police before their release. In a directive issued on 18 January 1937, the Reich Ministry of Justice tried to systematise these practices. Penal institutions were now ordered to report all inmates sentenced for both treason and high treason to the police one month before their release.[46]

The decision by the police to take a released convict into custody was based in part on statements about the inmate written by the prison officials. To be sure, such statements were not decisive and in a number of cases released prisoners were arrested by the police despite a positive judgement by the prison authorities. But the police leadership still regarded the assessments as very valuable, a fact well known to both leading and local prison officials.[47] The reports were often written by the governors and were based on their own views as well as on information provided by other officials who had come into contact with the respective inmates. Officials also drew on letters the inmates had received from home and, at least in some cases, on brief interrogations of the prisoners. Occasionally, the local prison authorities even wrote to other state agencies and offices to collect more information about the prisoner.[48] Clearly, these reports by the prison officials to the police were indebted to the criminal-biological examinations introduced in the 1920s. Local prison officials were already practised at collecting information on the inmates and using it for sweeping judgements about their future behaviour.

In the Third Reich, prison governors showed great enthusiasm in denouncing prisoners to the police. An analysis of their reports shows that, in many cases, they welcomed subsequent police measures. In one sample of 364 statements written by Luckau officials up to August 1939, 160 were negative about the inmate, and 204 positive or undecided. In the end, 123 of the Luckau prisoners were transferred to the Gestapo for further 'examination' after their sentence, with another 11 being taken straight to a concentration camp.[49] A closer look at reports by the prison officials to the police shows that they can be divided into four broad categories.

To start with, a number of these reports made no detailed remarks about the inmate but merely stated briefly that he or she had not been politically conspicuous during the imprisonment. The police repeatedly criticised superficial statements and demanded more detailed reports.[50] Some of these short reports were probably designed to save prisoners from being arrested by the police. Other prison officials simply wanted to avoid paperwork. Secondly, many reports to the police were phrased positively, claiming that the inmate had been won over to Nazi ideology. In other cases, officials stressed the deterrent effect of punishment or the inmate's good behaviour. Such arguments were still put forward during the war. When the former Communist Willi B. in 1943 reached the end of a ten-year sentence for his involvement in the murder of two police officers, local officials in Untermaßfeld gave him a glowing reference: 'After his impeccable conduct in the institution, B. should be believed that he committed his offence because he had fallen into bad company back then. B. is a good craftsman, who is certainly in a position to get through life without offences.' The police were not impressed and arrested him anyway.[51]

Thirdly, in a number of cases the prison officials wrote negative reports. At times, they left no doubt that they supported the police arrest of the prisoner, without explicitly saying so. Hedwig S., a long-standing Communist activist, was transferred to the Aichach penitentiary in 1937 to serve the remainder of her three-year sentence for high treason. Anni Dimpfl, the right-wing Aichach prison teacher, was initially optimistic that S. could be turned into a Nazi. But she soon gave up, as Hedwig S. 'has revealed herself more and more to be a dogged Communist'. Shortly before the end of her sentence, the Aichach institution sent a negative report about Hedwig S. to the Gestapo, predicting that she was likely to continue her 'subversive' activities. Hedwig S. was duly transferred from Aichach to the Stuttgart Gestapo in October 1938.[52]

Finally, prison officials repeatedly demanded police measures against inmates after their release. Some of the prisoners singled out in this way were high-ranking left-wing officials, such as Karl Elgas, a former Communist deputy in the Reichstag, already encountered in the previous chapter. When his sentence came to an end in 1936, the Luckau governor suggested in a report to the Gestapo that he be transferred to police custody:

> The punishment does not appear to have impressed him in any significant way. Judging by the general impression of his personality, Elgas cannot give security that he will leave his seditious activities behind him in future. I therefore suggest that, following his penitentiary sentence, protective custody be imposed on Elgas.

The Gestapo agreed and on 15 August 1936, Karl Elgas was handed over to the Berlin police. Only in April 1939 was he finally released from Sachsenhausen concentration camp.[53]

Less prominent political prisoners were also targeted by the prison authorities. The printer Max K., a rank-and-file member of the Communist party, was sentenced in June 1934 to two years and three months in a penitentiary for his role in the underground movement. He was taken to the Untermaßfeld penitentiary. During his imprisonment, he kept his head down. But the prison officials collected information from various sources about his family, which was then used by the governor in his report to the Thuringian Gestapo on 5 May 1936, some 12 weeks before Max K.'s scheduled release:

> K. did not attract any special attention in the institution. But in view of his past life, I cannot believe that he has changed his mind and I believe that he has, just like most leading Communists, only kept out of trouble now through cunning calculation. In my view it is absolutely essential that this active, leading Communist is taken into protective custody after the end of his sentence.

The Gestapo subscribed to this assessment and when Max K. was released on 24 July 1936 he was taken to the Bad Sulza concentration camp.[54]

Some local prison officials singled out political prisoners with previous convictions for ordinary criminal offences. One such official was governor Dr Henning of the Kassel-Wehlheiden penal institution, who often recommended transfer to a concentration camp in such cases. In late 1937, when the prisoner Friedrich Z. came near to the end of his 11-month prison sentence for 'malicious' remarks he had made in a pub, the governor tried to ensure that the police would arrest him. The governor's official assessment of Friedrich Z. was clearly coloured by the prisoner's many previous convictions for fraud. For the governor, as for many other prison officials, criminality and political opposition merged into one:

> He is a completely asocial human being, who has become criminally recidivous again and again since 1919. There is a danger that he will continue his inflammatory political activity in the future. Therefore, it can only be useful if Z. is disciplined for some more time. Protective custody is therefore desirable.

But in this case, even the Gestapo concluded that the governor's demand went too far and decided that Friedrich Z. should be released.[55] Many other political prisoners were not so lucky. They were taken straight to the police after the completion of their sentences.

These prisoners were hit very hard when, after having longed for many months or years for the day of their release, they were told that they would not be set free after all. In a particularly cruel gesture, inmates were often not told by the prison officials about their imminent transfer to the police until the scheduled day of their release had arrived. As the former Communist prisoner Otto Oertel recalled after the war: 'Nobody can imagine how I felt. Until the last minute I had been given the impression . . . that I would be released today!' Instead, he spent six more years in SS concentration camps.[56] The families of the prisoners were also devastated. Having often waited for years for their release, they now faced an entirely uncertain future. There are several reports of wives of political prisoners trying to kill themselves when they discovered that their husbands would not be released after all.[57]

From the mid-1930s, as the scope of police persecution widened from political opponents to other social and racial outsiders, the policy of judicial denunciation was extended as well. On 13 April 1935, the Reich Ministry of Justice demanded that the police also be informed of the impending release from penal institutions of all Sinti and Roma, who were brutally persecuted in Nazi Germany. Two years later, on 2 July 1937, the same policy was applied to imprisoned Jehovah's Witnesses. And finally, on 8 March 1938 the Reich Ministry of Justice instructed officials to pass on the names of men serving sentences for 'race defilement' to the police six weeks prior to their scheduled release. These inmates were then routinely arrested by the police on the day of their release.[58]

In these cases, accompanying reports by prison officials broadly followed the pattern outlined above. Some reports remained neutral. Others stressed that no further police measures were regarded as necessary. For example, the Wittlich deputy prison governor informed the Cologne Gestapo in August 1939 that while the prisoner Richard B. would 'never give up his inner conviction, he has still become sensible enough not to be active any more as a Jehovah's

Witness. In my opinion, the punishment has cured him.'[59] Many other Jehovah's Witnesses were proposed for police detention. The thinking of local prison officials was explained in an article by the Eisenach governor Heinz Brandstätter, reflecting on his failure to brainwash these inmates: 'Those who have failed during imprisonment to come to an endorsement of the Third Reich, or at least to move away from the ideas of the Jehovah's Witnesses, belong in the concentration camp.'[60]

'Racial aliens' were also proposed to the police authorities for detention. In January 1939, the businessman Paul G. was sentenced to two years in a penitentiary for 'attempted racial defilement' and taken to Untermaßfeld. In a typically assiduous extension of the Nuremberg Laws, he had been convicted for allegedly asking a chambermaid in a hotel whether she wanted to sleep with him. When Paul G. came up for release, his impeccable conduct and good work performance cut no ice with the governor Gericke, who also served as a leading official of the local NSDAP and who had made no secret of his hatred of Paul G. from the start (see Chapter 3, p. 162). In his final report on the inmate, the governor once more displayed his rabid anti-Semitism:

> G. is a typical, smarmy Jew who tried to commit race defilement, even though he knew the Nuremberg Laws. He will probably try again in future to defile Aryan girls, if he thinks that he will not be caught, for his race has been inoculated through education and practice with this instinct for millennia. <u>In my opinion, he therefore belongs in protective custody</u>.

Following this report, the Dortmund Gestapo asked for G. to be transferred to their headquarters on the day of his release from the penitentiary.[61]

But why did the prison authorities denounce inmates to the police? There was certainly some police pressure on the Reich Ministry of Justice to do so.[62] However, it is wrong to suggest that the legal authorities ultimately disapproved of the incarceration in concentration camps of convicts after their release but were powerless to prevent it.[63] The reports by prison officials to the police tell a very different story, as we have just seen. Broadly speaking, the legal authorities supported police measures that were supposedly aimed at preventing future offences. In these cases, the police implemented measures which were regarded by legal officials as indispensable for the protection of the 'national community', but were seen at the same time as incompatible with the nature of the legal system. After all, legal officials could not continue to imprison individuals after their sentences ended, even if they were still regarded as dangers to the Nazi community. Officials at the very top of the legal apparatus put their endorsement of police measures on the record. Wilhelm Crohne acknowledged in 1935 that it was vital 'that persistent and unteachable enemies of the state continue to be kept in official confinement even after the end of their sentence'. Two years later, Reich Minister Gürtner himself assured the Gestapo that he generally supported police measures against Jehovah's Witnesses after they had served sentences of imprisonment.[64]

The support of local prison officials for 'preventive' police measures also extended to inmates imprisoned for 'ordinary' criminal offences. In the absence of clear instructions from above, the initiative in such cases was apparently left to individual prison governors and police officials. By the late 1930s, more and more prisoners sentenced for regular criminal offences were taken to the police, following completion of their sentences. Above all, it was suspected 'professional criminals' who often ended up in concentration camps.[65] One individual caught up in this escalation of 'preventive' police measures was the day-labourer Josef K., who had been committed to the Ebrach penitentiary in 1931, convicted of the manslaughter of his lover's brother. When the day of his release came near, the criminal police contacted the Ebrach prison authorities asking for a prognosis of Josef K.'s behaviour. The prison authorities were not obliged to reply, but in fact chose to write back almost immediately. While they acknowledged that Josef K. had been one of the most diligent prisoners and had been hit very hard by his sentence, they still concluded that he

> is a hot-blooded, brutal human being, whose asocial nature has been proven by his many serious previous convictions ... Thus, for reasons of education and as a serious and urgent warning, it is to be recommended that he be taken after his release from the penitentiary into preventive police custody for an appropriate period of time.

Following this devastating report, Josef K. was handed over to the criminal police on 28 May 1939, the day his penitentiary sentence came to an end.[66] In similar cases involving criminal offenders, it was sometimes the local prison officials themselves who had contacted the police, demanding that the inmate be taken straight to a concentration camp after release.[67]

Concern by legal officials about police activities, in so far as it was voiced at all, was restricted to the blanket transfer of entire categories of released prisoners into concentration camps, which occurred in some judicial districts. Acceptance of such a practice would have amounted to an acknowledgement that penal institutions were unable to prevent any individuals from reoffending. Applying the well-established division of inmates into 'reformable' and 'incorrigible', legal officials argued instead that some of those prisoners who had distanced themselves from their previous political or religious beliefs, as well as those who would be deterred from further offences by their punishment, should be allowed to return to the community after having served their sentence. The group of prisoners most likely to be arrested *in toto* by the police after release from penal institutions in the late 1930s were apparently Jehovah's Witnesses. However, this was clearly not a major issue for legal officials, not least because many of these individuals were quickly released by the police, once they had signed an agreement that they would terminate their activities as Jehovah's Witnesses. Increasingly, this agreement was presented to the prisoners while they were still inside penal institutions.[68]

The Reich Ministry of Justice eventually decided in 1939 that no explicit calls for police custody should be included in reports on prisoners sentenced for treason or high treason. Such suggestions were deemed 'not desirable on account of general considerations' – probably to demonstrate the supposed independence of the legal system from the police. This order is a good example of the hollow nature of the 'normative state' in this period. The prison administration made it easy for the police to take prisoners from penal institutions into custody by informing them of the dates of release. It even supplied information to the police about the prisoners' conduct, character, political views and family. But the actual decision on further police measures was to be left to the police. In any case, this ruling from Berlin did not deter local prison officials from continuing to make explicit demands for the transfer of prisoners to police custody after their sentence, and the Reich Ministry of Justice had to remind officials of the order in 1941.[69]

Judicial denunciation was not restricted to prisoners coming to the end of their term in a prison or penitentiary. Legal officials also occasionally reported to the police former prisoners who had already been set free and had dared to complain about prison conditions after their release. Such complaints could not be punished by law. But they could be punished by the police. In one such instance, the Jena general state prosecutor Wurmstich reported the Dutch Jew Karel N. to the Gestapo in early 1939 (for this prisoner, see Chapter 3, p. 163). Karel N., who had a child with a non-Jewish woman in Germany, had served a sentence for 'race defilement' in the Untermaßfeld penitentiary. After his release in early 1939, he warned the father of another inmate of the poor state of health of his son, who had been brutally mistreated by prison officials. When information about this reached general state prosecutor Werner Wurmstich, he contacted the Gestapo, clearly in order to protect, as he saw it, the reputation of the legal system. Karel N. was duly arrested on 15 February 1939 and subjected to interrogation. In the end he was released, after he had promised to leave Germany immediately. Karel N. also had to agree to keep his mouth shut about his treatment 'because after my interrogation today I realised,' he was forced to state in the Gestapo protocol which was sent to the legal authorities, 'that everything I would say in Holland would, in the country of my child, cause harm to it and its mother.'[70]

Prisons and Concentration Camps

Summing up, the relationship between legal system and police was characterised by compromise, cooperation and conflict, with the former two dominating the prewar period. Legal officials largely approved of police measures such as detention without trial in concentration camps as policies to cut down on crime. As a matter of fact, the attitude of legal officials often went beyond mere passive acceptance. In many cases, the legal system actually helped to facilitate police detention. Not only did legal officials agree to temporarily imprison police detainees, but they also enabled the police to take prisoners into custody *after* the end of their legal imprisonment by informing the police of their imminent release – at times even demanding that the inmate be taken to a concentration camp. In short, the legal officials often supported police measures against those individuals who were judged to be a future threat but were beyond the reach of legal terror.

All this is not to say that the legal system and the police coexisted harmoniously at all times. Punishment of criminal offences was still regarded as a matter for the legal system. And the legal authorities were determined to defend this monopoly of punishment. Therefore, they reacted angrily to the comparatively small number of police actions which appeared to be an alternative punishment of criminal offenders, substituting or correcting legal measures – especially in the second half of the 1930s, as the police extended their grasp and further encroached on judicial territory.

But the importance of these conflicts should not be overestimated. Often, they centred around individual cases, and the rather close working relationship between legal system and police meant that some problems were easily resolved. Also, conflict was largely the result of institutional rivalries and jealousies, arising from the desire of the legal apparatus to preserve its influence and the simultaneous attempt by the police to expand their powers. Criticism of police actions by legal officials was mainly motivated by resentment of police intrusion into their sphere, not by any deep ideological rifts. Individual instances of disagreement, criticism and pressure should not blind us to the fact that, by and large, the police and the legal system were loyal to the aims of the Nazi regime and united in the fight against its supposed enemies.

We have also seen that the legal system was not as weak as some historians have suggested. The legal authorities successfully defended several key areas under their influence against the police. Thus, the administration of the penal system largely remained a matter for the legal authorities. Despite SS and police criticism of the judiciary, there is not a single example in Reich Minister Gürtner's official diary of a judge being forcibly removed.[71] And police attempts to gain some influence over prison inmates came to very little. Efforts to poach prisoners *before* the end of their sentences failed. The treatment of inmates in penal institutions also remained a matter for the legal system – in most cases the police did not even gain a significant say in the handling of police detainees who were held in penal institutions.

Overall, the legal system remained the foremost agency in the punishment of criminal and political offences. The dominance of the legal system is clearly shown by the high number of prisoners in the prewar years, which dwarfed inmate numbers in SS concentration camps. In late 1936, for example, around 5,000 persons were held in the camps – 115,000 fewer than in penal institutions (see Figure 2, pp. 394–5). This gap between penal institutions and concentration camps narrowed in the late 1930s, as the police extended their mandate. But even when the concentration camp population reached its peak in the middle of November 1938 – with inmate numbers briefly rising to about 54,000 in the wake of the anti-Jewish pogrom – penal institutions still easily outstripped SS concentration camps in terms of numbers. What all this demonstrates beyond doubt is that the police handed over many more arrested individuals to the legal authorities for trial than were taken straight to concentration camps.[72]

Together, penal institutions and the SS concentration camps were part of a larger network of repression in the Third Reich. Once a 'community alien' was caught in this web of Nazi terror, it proved very hard to escape. One consequence was that, from the outside, there was a blurring of the lines between police and legal system. There was a busy traffic of inmates between penal institutions, the police and SS camps. In addition, a number of police detainees were held inside penal institutions. Matters were confused further by the fact that some penal institutions such as Sonnenburg and Zwickau were transformed into concentration camps in 1933 (and later passed back into the hands of the judiciary). The situation was particularly intricate in Hamburg. Here, police detainees were initially held in parts of the Fuhlsbüttel penal institution, run by the regular prison service. But after the Hamburg Gauleiter complained that the treatment here was too lax, the police inmates were taken in September 1933 to another part of the penal institution, the former women's prison, which was officially designated as the concentration camp Fuhlsbüttel, controlled by the SS. Still, the prison authorities continued to provide general maintenance and supply.[73] At the same time, former concentration camps in the Papenburg region were turned into a prison camp – one of several large scale camps run by the legal authorities, not the SS. The confusion did not end here. Indefinite detention was possible both inside concentration camps (protective custody and preventive police custody) and inside penal institutions (security confinement). Finally, a number of convicts were guarded by SS and SA officials who had joined the regular prison service as warders. Regarding all these developments, it is hardly surprising that some contemporary observers could no longer properly tell the difference between the police and legal systems. This even extended to some legal officials themselves, such as the Nuremberg state prosecutor, who once erroneously addressed the prison governor at Aichach as 'commander of the Aichach concentration camp'.[74]

So how did life inside penal institutions compare to concentration camps? In the prewar years, penal institutions and concentration camps were not entirely different worlds. They shared certain similarities. These included, for example, the rigid order of the inmates' days, centred around forced labour; the constant drill and military discipline; the official insistence on mindless order; the common disregard for the inmates' health; the strict rules limiting contact to the outside world; and the absence of rights protecting prisoners against their captors. The official functions of the two places of confinement also overlapped. Penal institutions and concentration camps both promised safe internment of dangerous individuals and deterrence of potential 'enemies of the regime', locking up a variety of racial, social and political outsiders. In addition, both stressed the 'rehabilitative' benefits of imprisonment. Attempts to brainwash inmates with Nazi propaganda played little part here. Instead, the authorities relied on strict treatment to 'educate' inmates. This had long served as an ideological justification for the prison. Similarly, reports in the Nazi media stressed the supposedly pedagogical effects of discipline and regular work in the concentration camps – thoughts which could not have been further from the minds of the SS guards, for whom education meant abuse and brutal forced labour. This work was largely inefficient, labour-intensive and exhausting, both in prisons and in camps, with moor cultivation one of the hardest types of labour in both places of confinement.

Still, there can be no doubt that even before the war conditions were better inside penal institutions, a point emphasised by former inmates who survived both forms of imprisonment. The Social Democrats in exile concluded in 1935 that 'the treatment of prisoners in the regular prison service is mostly more humane than in the police jails and concentration camps'. To start with, the mental pressure on camp inmates was often greater as they were held indefinitely, while most other prisoners knew when they were supposed to be released. As regards forced labour, concentration camp inmates who could not be properly occupied were at times forced to perform completely useless work, such as shovelling sand from one spot to another, and back again. Torture of this kind was more reminiscent of the treadmill in the nineteenth-century prison than of the 1930s prison. Rather than undertake useless work, in the aftermath of the great depression many prisoners remained without work. And those prisoners who were working at least received some payment, however small, in contrast to camp inmates who worked for nothing. The inmates of penal institutions often had at least a little time after work at their own disposal, to read novels and non-fiction books from the library, or (if they had gained permission) to write, draw or learn a foreign language. Sometimes they could also play board games with other inmates. In concentration camps, by contrast, distracting activities such as reading were greatly restricted by the harder claims made on the inmates by the camp authorities.

The most important difference, from the start, was the level of violence directed at the inmates. In the early concentration camps, inmates were regularly mistreated and tortured, with several hundred killed. Following the reorganisation of concentration camps under the control of the SS, written regulations were introduced. But this did not limit the violence. The regulations allowed for extreme punishment, including up to three months' strict detention in a dark cell with only water and bread, and corporal punishment. Unruly inmates were even threatened with hanging, as we have seen (though this was apparently not carried out in the early years). In any case, the importance of the myriad rules inside the concentration camps should not be exaggerated. SS guards often acted arbitrarily, with no regard to any rules whatsoever. Physical attacks were a constant feature of the camps, from the day the inmates arrived. And the terror increased significantly during the extension of the concentration camp system in the late 1930s. True, the camps only became sites of mass murder during the Second World War. Still, by 1939, on average, more than one prisoner died in each camp every day. The level of violence inside concentration camps had escalated even before the war broke out.

Treatment inside penal institutions was markedly different. Prison regulations did not allow for corporal punishment – four weeks' strict detention with bread and water being the harshest disciplinary penalty officially available in penitentiaries. The experienced prison warders took regulations rather more seriously than the often much younger SS guards took the camp rules. Many local prison officials, often after decades of service in the army and the prison, were drilled to enforce order and were less prone to attack inmates randomly than the SS camp guards. On a very basic level, prison regulations at least still limited arbitrary terror against inmates. Collective punishment, a common feature of the camps, was also relatively unusual in prisons and penitentiaries. This did not mean that rules were not regularly broken by officials and that prisoners were not assaulted. For example, prisoners who had tried to escape were often beaten up and brutally punished. But they were not likely to be killed, as were a number of concentration camp inmates who had fled. Overall, physical assaults were not yet everyday events in prisons and penitentiaries and the murder of prisoners remained highly exceptional. This was also linked to the fact that the *Kapo* system – a defining feature of concentration camp terror – did not exist in the same form inside prisons and penitentiaries. To be sure, some prisoners secured coveted positions in the prison infrastructure. But they gained limited power over their fellow inmates, very different from that of the *Kapos* in the camps.

The basic difference between concentration camps and prisons is particularly obvious in the treatment of Jews. In penal institutions, they were regularly discriminated against and at times abused, but often they enjoyed some of the privileges available to other prisoners, and Jewish prisoners were not at risk of being murdered before the war. All this was a far cry from the terror in the concentration camps. Arguably, the most savage treatment was reserved for the Jewish men taken to concentration camps in the aftermath of the pogrom in November 1938. Thousands of Jews were viciously assaulted and tortured, often for several weeks, before they were released, physically and mentally broken. Several hundred men were murdered or killed themselves in the days and weeks after their arrest.

The gap between legal imprisonment and the SS camps was least pronounced in the prison camps run by the legal authorities. By the late 1930s, there were five large prison camps where around 10,000 men were held. The largest was the Emsland camp and it was here that conditions came closest to those in concentration camps. Controlled in part by former SA guards who had been integrated into the prison service, life inside Emsland was characterised by brutal labour, random violence and sadistic torture. Prisoners were assaulted not only by the guards but also by fellow prisoners, who like the *Kapos* were chosen as supervisors by the authorities. Inmates were occasionally forced to perform utterly useless labour, designed as a punishment by the officials. Life in the Emsland camp was very far removed from the letter of the prison regulations. Even so, conditions were still better than in the SS concentration camps. In Dachau, for example, some 37 prisoners died in the years between 1934 and 1936 (not counting some 21 persons killed during the Night of the Long Knives), compared to 34 prisoners in the Emsland camp. Given that Emsland held maybe about twice as many prisoners at this time, it is clear that concentration camp inmates were at greater risk, even in this earlier period. This risk grew rapidly towards the end of the 1930s. In 1937 and 1938, when the Emsland camp still held more prisoners, some 439 inmates died in Dachau, compared to 48 in Emsland. Death had become common in concentration camps, a situation not found in the prison camps until the war, which brought with it a dramatic increase in legal terror.[75]

Part III Escalating Legal Terror, 1939–45

5 Law in Wartime

In the early hours of 1 September 1939, German troops invaded Poland, marking the beginning of the most destructive war in history. By the time the Germans capitulated in May 1945, tens of millions of civilians and soldiers had been killed or maimed, millions more were displaced from their homes, and countless cities in Europe lay in ruins. In 1955, ten years after the war ended, around half of the German population, reminiscing about the 'good years' they had enjoyed before 1939, still believed that Hitler would have been remembered as one of the greatest German statesmen, had it not been for the Second World War.[1] But war, aimed at the revision of Versailles and the conquest of 'living-space'(*Lebensraum*) had been at the core of Hitler's beliefs since the 1920s. After he came to power, the real question was not if, but when, war would begin.

It was during the war that Nazi terror against 'community aliens' escalated dramatically. The circle of 'dangerous' individuals was drawn wider and wider, and their treatment became ever more lethal. No longer content to segregate, discriminate and marginalise outsiders, the Nazi regime increasingly pursued murderous policies. Mass murder was already considered a legitimate policy during the occupation of Poland, before it was extended from 1941, with the extermination of European Jewry and other genocidal policies. This homicidal rage was not confined to occupied Europe. From the beginning of the war, murderous policies were also pursued inside Germany, starting with the 'euthanasia' programme, the extermination of the disabled, authorised by Hitler in 1939.

The legal system was in the thick of Nazi terror during the war. True, most genocidal policies were masterminded by the SS and police. But the legal apparatus also often participated in terror, especially on German soil. The war transformed penal policy. This was reflected, for instance, in the dramatic increase in prisoner numbers in penal institutions, from 108,685 (30 June 1939) to 196,700 (30 June 1944) (see Figure 1, pp. 392–3). At the same time, the make-up of the prison population changed significantly and became more heterogeneous than ever. German repeat offenders from the margins of society shared cells with previously socially integrated 'national comrades'. And these German prisoners now encountered inmates from all over Europe, as the regular legal system joined in the Nazi terror against foreigners. Treatment of these different prisoners will be discussed in the following chapters. Before that, it is necessary to sketch the general development of the legal system during the war, to explore the policies that resulted in the imprisonment of these different groups.

Terror on the Home Front, 1939–41

From the start of the war, Adolf Hitler envisaged the conflict as a battle on two fronts: a merciless struggle against 'alien races' and nations on the battlefield, and a ruthless fight against all internal enemies on the home front. As he told the leaders of the German military on 23 November 1939 in Berlin: 'Externally no capitulation, internally no revolution.'[2] His obsession with the home front dated right back to the German defeat of 1918 and the November Revolution. The impact of 1918 on Hitler can hardly be overstated. In *Mein Kampf*, he even claimed that on the day of the German defeat he had cried for the first time since his mother's funeral. Whatever one makes of this story, there can be no doubt that Hitler's thirst for revenge for the 'national humiliation' of 1918 was the driving force of his political career. Like many others on the nationalist right, he was convinced that Germany had not been beaten militarily in the First World War. Rather, Germany had been fatally undermined by defeatism, poor morale and political opposition on the home front, with subversives eventually stabbing the army in the back. He had learned the lessons, Hitler stated at the beginning of the Second World War, and this time there would be no surrender and no 'stab in the back' – a message he repeated again and again, both in private and in public, until his 'Thousand Year Reich' lay in ruins.[3]

Among Hitler's 'lessons' from the trauma of 1918 was the need to distinguish even more sharply between 'national comrades' and 'community aliens'. Regarding the former, he knew that excessive hardship for ordinary Germans had contributed to battle fatigue and unrest on the home front during the First World War. Hitler was anxious to avoid a repetition of such discontent. To be sure, mobilisation of the German economy meant that sacrifices were already being asked of the civilian population in the early years of the war, with consumer demand being further suppressed. But the regime was still sensitive about popular opinion and trod rather carefully. One of the key aims was to provide a basic standard of living for 'national comrades' at home, including an adequate and stable food supply. Just before the war began, the Nazis introduced an elaborate system of rations, designed to prevent the inadequate distribution and catastrophic shortages of goods which had been so damaging to morale in the First World War. The regime initially decided against the call up of German women for the war economy. Göring felt, reported one of his subordinates in 1940, that this would 'arouse too much concern among the population'. The significant labour shortages in the economy, following the call up of millions of German workers for the army, were partially made up by prisoners of war and foreign workers. At first, most of these workers were Poles. But after the end of the campaign in the west, French prisoners of war and workers from countries allied to Germany were also targeted. By late May 1941, over three million foreign workers and prisoners of war were already deployed in Nazi Germany.[4]

At the same time, Hitler demanded the ruthless repression of all internal 'enemies', in starker terms than ever. He railed against 'racial aliens', above all Jews, whom he had long seen as chiefly to blame for the German collapse in 1918. Between 1939 and 1941, the Nazi leadership searched for ever more radical 'solutions to the Jewish question', drawing up several plans of mass deportation, increasingly murderous in design. In the meantime, Jews were isolated and brutally repressed. In Poland, they were forced into ghettos, where thousands were soon dying from illness and starvation. Jews were not the only objects of Hitler's hatred. He also called for brutal measures against political opponents and ordinary criminals – claiming that most revolutionaries in 1918 had been criminal 'riff-raff' just released from prison.[5] Hitler left no doubt about his radical intentions. As early as October 1939, State Secretary Freisler told the top regional legal officials in graphic language that it was Hitler's view that every thief of handbags had to be put against the wall.[6] Early in the war, Hitler actually proposed strikingly similar measures against common criminals and 'racial aliens'. On 17 August 1940, at the same time as the Nazi leadership was seriously considering deporting millions of Jews to the island of Madagascar, Propaganda Minister Joseph Goebbels recorded Hitler's views on criminals:

> The Führer wants to deport the truly criminal elements to an island at some later stage. There, they should form a state of lawlessness. At home, they are being rendered harmless. Especially during the war, the death penalty must not be suspended – as happened during the [First] World War – one has to

intensify it. The asocial elements should not be conserved for a future revolution... Therefore: extirpate and create a healthy community for the people.[7]

Criminality, racial 'deviance' and political opposition were to merge even further in Hitler's mind during the course of the war.

The fight against all these 'enemies' inside Nazi Germany was largely in the hands of the two agencies of punishment, the court system and the police. There could be no doubt which agency Hitler favoured, given his support for the police in the prewar years. During the war, Hitler argued repeatedly that the police were best placed to realise his vision of a brutally disciplined home front, and he strongly supported the further extension of police powers. As soon as war had broken out, Hitler charged Heinrich Himmler with the maintenance of order in Germany 'at all costs'. Following these instructions, Himmler's deputy Reinhard Heydrich on the same day alerted the Gestapo that 'every attempt to undermine unity and the German people's will to fight' was to be suppressed 'ruthlessly'.[8] Before long, more and more individuals were persecuted. The police targeted Jews, deviant youths, property offenders, prostitutes, foreign workers, prisoners of war, the 'work-shy', 'professional criminals' and ex-convicts, among others. Police terror on the home front was coordinated by the Reich Security Head Office (RSHA), set up on 27 September 1939. Headed by Heydrich, the RSHA developed into the single most important agency of Nazi terror, merging the security police with the SD (security service).[9] The growing zeal of police officials was reflected in the increase of individuals sent to concentration camps. But this process was slower than many historians have assumed.[10] Overall, inmate numbers in concentration camps rose from about 21,000 (August 1939) to about 70,000–80,000 (spring 1942), excluding the newly constructed death camps in the east. This means that even at this late point, in the middle of the war, prisoners in penal institutions still easily outnumbered SS camp inmates (see Figure 2, pp. 394-5). Evidently, legal terror was still a crucial factor.

Laws and Sentencing

Like other agencies of the Nazi regime, the legal system changed during the war. To some extent, this was a result of the general escalation of Nazi violence from 1939, with legal officials more determined then ever to prove that they could implement the wishes of the Nazi leadership. However, the actions of legal officials during the war cannot be understood purely in these terms. Many legal officials had other reasons to call for more brutal punishment during the war. Like other members of the German ruling elite, they shared the view that the revolution of 1918 had proved that harsh discipline was required to prevent another collapse of the home front. Many senior legal officials, including Gürtner, Freisler and Wilhelm Crohne, had themselves fought on the front line during the First World War. They, too, were keen to learn the 'lessons' of 1918 and, from the start of the Second World War, made clear what they expected from their officials. Less than two weeks after the outbreak of war, on 12 September 1939, the Reich Ministry of Justice described judges as 'soldiers of the home front'. In other words, judges were to fight 'national pests', reverse the effects of the 'negative selection' of war (an argument that had been around in legal circles for decades) and protect Germany against another 'stab in the back'.[11] The memory of 1918 haunted many legal directives and communications. In early 1940, a Reich Ministry of Justice memorandum noted that 'during the war, the task of the legal system is the elimination of the demagogically and criminally inclined elements who, at a critical moment, might try to stab the fighting front from the back (e.g. the Workers' and Soldiers' councils of 1918)'.[12] This identification of the revolution with both political opponents and ordinary criminals was traditionally shared by many legal officials, as we have seen. In short, the determination of the legal apparatus during the Second World War to introduce ruthless measures was driven by various factors, including the desire to convince Hitler that the legal system was capable of defending the home front, the wish to contain the growing influence of the police, and the belief that brutal steps were justified to deter criminals and to prevent a repetition of 1918.

During the war, the scope of penal policy was greatly extended. The period between 1939 and 1941 saw an avalanche of new legal acts directed at all supposed threats to the German war effort. Several new measures were aimed at suppressing dissent and (real or imagined) threats of subversion. This included, for example, the Decree concerning Exceptional Measures relating to Radio (7 September 1939). Originally drafted by Goebbels, it was approved by Hitler despite strong objections from Reich Minister of Justice Gürtner. According to the decree, anyone found guilty of listening to foreign radio broadcasts could be sent to prison or penitentiary, as 'every word which the opponent broadcasts is of course a lie and intended to damage the German people'.[13] Another piece of legislation aimed at rooting out subversion was the Special Wartime Penal Code. The Reich Military Court and, from 1 June 1940, the legal courts were empowered to sentence to death both soldiers and civilians who were found guilty of 'undermining the war effort'.[14] Negative comments about the war and critical remarks about the Nazi leadership were now capital offences, further increasing legal uncertainty: dissent could be punished by almost any penal sanction, ranging from a small fine to death, depending largely on how the 'personality' of the offender was judged by the legal authorities.[15] A further measure introduced shortly after the outbreak of war was the Decree to Supplement the Penal Provisions for the Protection of the Military Strength of the German People (25 November 1939). At the centre of this piece of legislation stood the threat of prison or penitentiary for Germans found guilty of supposedly improper contact with prisoners of war (POWs). Typically for Nazi legislation, the decree referred in very general terms to conduct which constituted an affront to 'healthy popular feelings'.[16]

German judges were also given an arsenal of new weapons to fight ordinary crime. One crucial piece of legislation was the Decree against National Pests (5 September 1939), which specifically targeted three criminal 'types': the plunderer, the black-out exploiter and the anti-social saboteur. The decree gave German judges far-reaching powers to sentence property offenders to death, thanks to the vague definition of these different 'types'. State Secretary Freisler described the measure as an important weapon to 'exclude, and if necessary exterminate . . . the inner enemy'.[17] Further drastic measures against petty offenders were introduced in 1941, when all 'habitual criminals' were threatened with the death penalty 'if the protection of the racial community or the need for a just expiation demand it'.[18] The Nazi state also introduced new ways to fight the 'violent criminal' or 'gangster', whom Freisler blamed in part for the 'stab in the back'. They were targeted in the Decree against Violent Criminals (5 December 1939), which allowed the death penalty for all offenders who had used a weapon during violent crimes. Some judges soon interpreted the meaning of the term 'weapon' in the widest possible sense, sentencing offenders to death who had used brooms or their fists during robberies.[19] Following instructions by Hitler, the legal authorities also brought in harsher penalties for 'serious young criminal offenders' over the age of 16 (4 October 1939), who could now be punished as adults. This decree, realising a long-standing demand of German criminologists, was part of a wider crackdown on deviant youths to prevent a repetition of the rise in youth crime during the First World War.[20] In addition, several decrees criminalised actions regarded as offences against wartime rationing. The War Economy Decree (4 September 1939) and the Consumer Regulations Penal Decree (6 April 1940 and 26 November 1941) outlawed a large variety of such actions 'detrimental to the war'.[21]

Finally, there was the War Offenders Decree (11 June 1940) which allowed judges to label defendants whom they sent to a penitentiary as 'war offenders'. (The main targets were German men fit for military service, but Jews and Poles could also be singled out until late 1942.) This meant that the penitentiary sentence did not officially start until the end of the war. Until then, 'war offenders' were merely 'interned' in penal institutions, prolonging their original sentences. This measure had first been applied against German soldiers by army courts. The Reich Ministry of Justice argued that its extension to civilians was necessary to deter 'cowardly and dishonourable conscripts' from committing a criminal offence to save themselves from fighting in the war (penitentiary inmates were automatically disqualified from serving in the army after their imprisonment). Freisler later described this new decree as 'primitive'. In his mind, this was intended as a compliment.[22]

Not all of the draconian wartime legislation was drawn up with either the involvement or the approval of the top legal officials. But once it had been proclaimed, the legal system applied the new measures, often with great enthusiasm. In 1940, German judges inside the borders of the so-called Altreich (German borders pre-1938) had already convicted more than 8,800 defendants under the new legislation.[23] At the same time, judges also made eager use of the older legislation.

The result of all this was that sentencing by the German courts became significantly stricter. This was evident above all in the application of the death penalty, greatly extended in the wartime legislation. The number of death sentences passed by courts inside Germany increased significantly, first shooting up from 86 (1937) to 306 (1940), before increasing dramatically in the following year to 1,292 (1941) (see Figure 10, pp. 402–3). These sentences were often splashed across the Nazi press, intended above all as a stark reminder to the population not to step out of line. Deterrence remained a key part of Nazi penal policy. The courts also showed a growing preference for longer sentences of imprisonment.[24] Judges' enthusiasm for harsher custodial sentences was betrayed by their use of the War Offenders Decree. By 31 March 1941, there were already around 7,000 male 'war offenders' interned in penal institutions, after having been sentenced by legal courts.[25]

To ensure more brutal punishment, top legal officials championed the role of the special courts, set up in 1933. Already before the war, on 20 November 1938, their brief had been extended from political offences to include all crimes – mirroring the shift in police focus in the mid-1930s from political opposition to other social 'threats'. If the prosecution service declared an offence 'serious', then proceedings could now take place in front of a special court instead of a regular court. As soon as war had broken out, the leading legal officials stressed the crucial importance of the special courts in defending the home front. In a meeting in the Reich Ministry of Justice on 24 October 1939 with the chairmen of the special courts and regional state prosecution officials, the top brass spoke their minds. State Secretary Freisler described the special courts – in a telling military metaphor – as the 'tank corps of penal law', demanding that all those who 'stab the dagger in the people's back' had to be 'eradicated root and branch'. Reich Minister of Justice Franz Gürtner personally gave his blessing to these sentiments in his closing speech at the conference, confirming that a 'transvaluation of peace-values in criminal law' was now necessary.[26] Given such official appeals, it is hardly surprising that special courts in the following months and years imposed harsher penalties than before the war.

It has recently been argued that this wartime trend towards stricter punishment was substantially mitigated by the fact that the volume of special court cases declined significantly during the war.[27] In fact, the opposite is true. During the war, special courts dealt with a much larger number of offences, sentencing many more people than before. Figures increased in the early years of the war, only to climb even further later on. For example, the special courts in Frankfurt am Main, Braunschweig and Düsseldorf dealt with some 1,762 defendants in 1940–41, up from 910 in 1937–38 (see Figure 8, pp. 400–1). Another court which extended its sway in the early years of the war was the People's Court in Berlin. Headed by the committed Nazi, Otto-Georg Thierack, the number of individuals sentenced to imprisonment increased from 390 (1939) to 1,058 (1941) (see Figure 7, pp. 398–9).

Inmate numbers in penal institutions were on the rise. By June 1941, figures in all German penal institutions had increased by around 35,000, compared to two years earlier (see Figure 1, pp. 392–3). Looking at institutions in the Altreich, prisoner numbers initially declined, following an amnesty on 9 September 1939 for minor offences.[28] Inmate numbers increased once more in 1940, and soon outstripped the levels immediately before the war, reaching 110,729 on 30 June 1941. However, this still meant that numbers in the Altreich in the summer of 1941 were lower than they had been in the mid-1930s (see Figure 3, pp. 394–5). Given the stricter wartime penal policy, one might have expected a more significant increase after the outbreak of war.

So why did prisoner numbers in the Altreich not rise even further? Most importantly, the overall number of defendants before the legal courts had not yet risen sharply. This was linked, first of all, to the general level of criminality in this period. While it is difficult to make specific statements about common criminality in the first years of the Second World War, there was apparently no dramatic increase.[29] Furthermore, organised left-wing resistance inside Germany was probably weaker than ever before. Until the German attack on the Soviet Union in June 1941, the activities of German Communists apparently declined further, in part because their followers were still reeling from the shock of the non-aggression pact between Germany and the Soviet Union.[30] Most importantly, during the war a large section of the German population was removed from the grasp of the legal system. Millions of German men were conscripted into the army. As the sentencing of soldiers was in the hands of military courts, they were now generally outside the legal system – both as potential perpetrators and as potential victims of crime. Offences by full-time SS and police officials regarded as criminal were also increasingly removed from the jurisdiction of legal courts. Instead, they were tried by new SS and police courts, which were responsible for the execution of well over 1,000 individuals during the war.[31]

Legal and police officials inside the Altreich were also not yet acting indiscriminately. Nazi terror remained selective. Factors such as class, ethnicity, political affiliation, type of offence, previous criminal record and place of residence could still play a role in punishment. For example, various wartime offences by Germans were treated with comparative leniency. The police devoted few resources to enforcing the ban on listening to foreign radio, which was ignored by 'national comrades', including party and police officials, all over Germany. The relative restraint in these cases – and the apparent reluctance of the population to denounce those guilty of what was widely seen as a peccadillo – is reflected in the small number of offenders eventually brought to trial and convicted. In 1940, only 830 individuals were sentenced by German courts in the Altreich under the Radio Decree.[32] Of course, this is not to say that 'national comrades' always received more lenient punishment.[33] Still, they did often get off more lightly than others. Even if convicted, they did not always serve their full sentences, with thousands of prisoners being pardoned before or during their imprisonment (see Chapter 7).

Foreigners and Legal Terror

The fact that overall prisoner numbers were still increasing substantially in the first years of war was linked above all to the territorial extension of the legal apparatus. Before the war, a very small number of foreigners had ended up before German courts. In 1937, according to the official crime statistics, only 3.6 per cent of all criminal offenders were not German.[34] This changed from the late 1930s. As Nazi Germany swallowed up more and more of Europe, the number of individuals within reach of the German legal system also shot up.

The extension of the German legal apparatus beyond the German borders of 1937 had begun before the outbreak of war. Following the *Anschluss* of Austria in March 1938, this new German territory was divided into three judicial districts (in 1939 four: Graz, Innsbruck, Linz and Vienna). The judges continued to apply the Austrian criminal code, supplemented by the recent legal measures introduced in Nazi Germany. Sentences of imprisonment were largely served in penal institutions inside Austria, which were absorbed into the German prison administration. There were some 20 larger penal institutions in the former Austrian territory, where most of the 8,233 prisoners in this territory were held (figures for 30 June 1941). The next area incorporated into the German legal system had been the Sudetenland, the German-speaking Czech border region with Germany and Austria, which became part of the Third Reich after the Munich agreement of 30 September 1938. The German Criminal Code was introduced on 1 March 1939 and the new territory was administered as the Leitmeritz judicial district. Most of the population here were ethnic Germans, but the courts came down with particular force on those native Czechs living in the district. Defendants sentenced to imprisonment were often taken to one of the five (later six) larger penal institutions in the Leitmeritz district.[35]

Soon, German forces overran the remainder of the Czech territory. The troops invaded the country on 14 and 15 March 1939, and Hitler immediately designated the region as the Protektorat Böhmen und Mähren. Ultimately, the aim of the occupation was ruthless exploitation of the territory and its inhabitants for the German war effort. German legal officials also joined the occupation and in April 1939 the Prague legal district was set up. But the number of prisoners in this district remained rather small (1,587 on 30 June 1941). This was linked to the fact that the jurisdiction of the German courts was largely limited to ethnic Germans. Most ordinary criminal offences were still dealt with by the remaining Czech courts. The Gestapo often took the lead against the Czech resistance, especially after the appointment of Reinhard Heydrich as Deputy Reich Protector in September 1941: until 20 January 1942, newly created police courts sentenced at least 486 persons to death and another 2,242 to imprisonment in concentration camps – without any involvement of the legal authorities. Nevertheless, the German legal courts also participated in the repression of the Czech nationalists and Communists, who were often sentenced by the People's Court in Berlin. The massive influx of Czech defendants completely altered the focus of the People's Court. Before the war, it had largely targeted Germans accused of left-wing resistance. But in 1940–41, the majority of all individuals convicted by the People's Court (55 per cent) were Czechs. Among them was the Prime Minister of the Protektorat, General Eliáš, sentenced to death for attempted high treason in October 1941.[36]

In the Second World War, the German legal system extended its reach further. Following the German victory in the campaign in the west in the summer of 1940, Alsace-Lorraine and Luxemburg were brought under German civilian administration and closely integrated into the Third Reich. The German prison authorities took over eight penal institutions in these western territories (six in Alsace, one each in Luxemburg and Lorraine), which were administered from different legal districts inside Germany (Karlsruhe, Cologne and Zweibrücken). On 30 June 1941, a total of 2,220 prisoners were held in these western territories.[37]

Most important was the setting up of the legal apparatus in parts of occupied Poland. The eastward extension of the German legal system was swift. Following the invasion of Poland in September 1939, the German legal system was almost immediately established in the so-called incorporated territories, that is, the western part of Nazi-occupied Poland which was directly integrated into the Reich. The eastern part, the so-called General Government, was put under German administration, headed by Franz Gürtner's old adversary Hans Frank. Less than one week after the invasion had begun, German criminal law was made applicable in the incorporated territories. Special courts were operational almost instantly. The city of Bromberg, for example, had only been occupied by the Germans for a few days when a new special court passed its first sentences. Cases regarded as serious were brought before such courts. A vast number of trivial offences, rather than being dismissed, were dealt with by regular local courts (*Amtsgerichte*), in an attempt to crack down on any supposed transgressions by the population. The Polish court system was soon abolished and the German Criminal Code was officially introduced in the incorporated territories on 6 June 1940. The incorporated territories were divided into two judicial districts (three from 1941: Danzig, Kattowitz and Posen) and the German prison authorities absorbed a total of 23 additional larger penal institutions.[38]

German courts in the incorporated territories showed little restraint in the punishment of Poles, who made up the vast majority of defendants. From the beginning, the legal proceedings were perverted by racial ideology. Poles were generally treated more harshly than German offenders. Often, the Poles were maltreated, beaten up and tortured in the preliminary proceedings. During the trial, it was virtually impossible for them to get a fair hearing. They were deprived of almost all rights. Often, they had no access to lawyers and were unable to follow the proceedings, which were conducted in German. As the legal historian Ingo Müller has commented, trials by special courts in the east were often 'no more than a derisive mockery of an orderly criminal proceeding'. Judges at these courts also passed exorbitant sentences from the start. They applied the legal regulations loosely and made sure they interpreted the laws in the most extreme way. Among the most radical courts was the Posen special court, which passed death sentences in 49 of the 151 cases brought before it by the end of 1939. Other special courts applied the death penalty less frequently, and instead relied on very long sentences of imprisonment. Not surprisingly, the number of prisoners in the incorporated territories was high from early on (see Figure 4, pp. 396–7). The judges only turned a blind eye in cases which, they believed, did not touch on the interests of the 'national community', such as violent crimes where the victims were Poles. This approach was encouraged by State Secretary Freisler, who told his officials that the legal system had no interest in providing any special protection for 'alien people'.[39]

The brutal attitude of the German judges in the incorporated territories was influenced by a variety of factors. To some extent, they felt pressure to conform to the regime's violent occupation policy. Also, senior legal officials continued to remind judges of their duty to act without mercy. Individual judges in the incorporated territories, often ambitious to further their careers, knew that they were likely to be commended by their superiors for merciless sentencing of Poles. But the judges' own racist outlook was also crucial. Brutal treatment of Poles could build on the long-standing anti-Slavism in the wider German population. Poles had long been dismissed as degenerate, stupid and criminal, not least in German criminology. Such prejudices were radicalised after the Nazi invasion. In Nazi propaganda, the Poles were described as primitive and violent 'racial aliens', who were, at best, only fit to serve the Germans.[40] Many judges in the incorporated territories were ruthless supremacists who saw themselves as soldiers in the 'racial struggle' against the 'degenerates' in the east. As one judge wrote in a legal journal in 1940: 'If we are not careful here and do not rule the Pole with an iron hand, he will immediately become impertinent again. In view of the unfathomable malice, deceit and cruelty of the Pole, one cannot crack down hard enough.' Court judgments, too, were full of racist terminology, referring to 'Polish subhumans' or 'Polish rabble', language that was not commonly found in judgments in the Altreich.[41]

The repression of Poles was not restricted to the incorporated territories. More and more Poles also became victims of legal terror inside the old German territory. As previously noted, the Nazi leadership was determined to minimise the hardship of 'national comrades' during the war, particularly by ruthlessly exploiting foreign labour. By May 1940, there were already some 700,000 Polish foreign workers, making up the majority. Almost all of these Poles were put to work in German agriculture, to relieve shortages of labour and to secure a steady supply of food on the home front. Many had volunteered, deceived by Nazi propaganda which promised them an escape from poverty at home. Any hopes for a better life were soon crushed. The foreign workers were badly paid, inadequately fed, poorly housed, and excluded from society. Workers in Poland naturally became very reluctant to sign up. The German authorities responded by deporting Poles against their will, and by designating Polish POWs as foreign workers. The Poles working inside the Altreich were subjected to very rigid discipline. Breaches of the official regulations and the unspoken rules were to be strictly punished. Local Nazi leaders demanded that any Poles who were not sufficiently subservient to their German 'masters' or who dared to answer back were brutally disciplined. The German authorities were also determined that the Poles be worked as hard as possible. Any supposed 'slacking' was to be strictly punished. Finally, the authorities were obsessed with the desire to prevent social contact with the German population, above all else fearing sexual encounters with 'alien' races.[42]

The courts played their part in disciplining Poles inside the Altreich. Polish workers were sentenced for 'insubordination' or 'refusal to work', as well as for political resistance and property offences. Sentencing was often excessive. A number of judges agreed that Poles deserved harsher punishment than Germans because of their 'racial inferiority'. Just like their colleagues in the incorporated territories, they occasionally disregarded legal requirements altogether. Their desire to crack down on 'racial degenerates' was also evident in the use of the new wartime legislation, which was often applied much more harshly to Polish than to German offenders. Thus, in 1940–41, a greatly disproportionate number of death sentences by the special courts in the Altreich were passed against Poles. However, the same was not true for the ordinary courts. It was apparently still not unusual for local courts to apply the law without racial bias in minor cases, sentencing Poles and Germans to similar punishment for similar offences.[43]

The racial war waged against Poles by the legal system escalated further with the Criminal Law Decree for Poles and Jews of 4 December 1941. This decree targeted Poles who had lived in Poland before the Second World War, and it was applied both in the incorporated territories and in the Altreich (it also applied to Polish Jews, but as they were generally dealt with directly by the police, the decree had little impact on them). Such a measure had not been a foregone conclusion. In the first year of the Nazi occupation of Poland, the Reich Ministry of Justice had still opposed the idea of introducing a separate law code for Poles in the incorporated territories. Instead, judges relied on the German Criminal Code, augmented by special regulations targeting Poles. But the legal authorities were increasingly faced with demands from the Nazi leadership that Poles be treated fundamentally differently from Germans. The compliant Reich Ministry of Justice tried to realise these wishes and started to draw up a decree targeting Poles. In April 1941, State Secretary Schlegelberger – now acting Reich Minister of Justice, following Franz Gürtner's death in late January 1941 – sent a draft to the Reich Chancellery, which was suitably impressed, noting that the act aimed at a 'draconian special criminal law for Poles and Jews'.[44] The decree was eventually passed on 4 December 1941 and came into operation on 1 January 1942.

Few other legal decrees demonstrated more openly the willingness of leading legal officials to turn the law into a weapon of racial extermination. To be sure, many measures introduced in Nazi Germany blatantly ignored fundamental legal principles, but the Criminal Law Decree for Poles and Jews reached a new level of perversion. It occupies a special place in the history of the destruction of the rule of law in the Third Reich. Essentially, the decree opened the door for the unconditional execution of Poles and Jews, now deprived of any legal protection. At its centre stood a murderous threat to all 'racial aliens' seen as opposing the Germans. What this meant was left for the judges to decide. The application of legal norms had thus become totally arbitrary. According to the decree, Poles (and Polish Jews)

> are sentenced to death, or in less serious cases to imprisonment, if they demonstrate their anti-German mentality by spiteful or inflammatory

actions . . . or if they demean or damage the reputation or the well-being of the German Reich or the German people *by any other behaviour*.

State Secretary Freisler emphasised that this 'wonderful' blanket threat, as he called it, was specifically designed to enable judges to punish actions which were not formally illegal. For example, Freisler pointed out that any Pole 'guilty' of sexual intercourse with a German had to be punished, using the decree, as this 'runs counter to the Poles' duty to obey'.[45] The legal officials had finally declared open season on Poles and Polish Jews.

Police and the Legal System

In many respects, the legal system and the police continued to work together amicably, just as before the war. The police still handed over most suspected criminal offenders to the courts, and local jails and other penal institutions carried on temporarily holding police (and now also some SS) detainees on their way to police headquarters or to concentration camps. Legal officials also continued to denounce 'dangerous' prisoners to the police, enabling the police to arrest them *after* the completion of their sentences. Indeed, this practice was extended to more 'suspect' prisoners in the early years of the war. In this way, the legal system continued to provide the police with a steady supply of inmates for the concentration camps. Ex-convicts made up a large proportion of the individuals arrested by the police. In Duisburg, almost two out of every three orders of preventive custody by the criminal police (1940–44) concerned individuals just released from penal institutions. In a number of these cases, it had been the prison authorities themselves who had proposed police custody. Similar figures were reached elsewhere. In Cologne, over 70 per cent of all the property offenders taken into preventive custody by the criminal police in 1941 had just completed a term in a penal institution. The Cologne police focused especially on prisoners with multiple convictions, who had served fairly lengthy sentences. In short, the transfer of prisoners to the police, following completion of their sentences, had long become a routine procedure.[46] But the immense growth of the police as a parallel apparatus of punishment also caused a variety of conflicts with the legal system. The general relationship between the two agencies of punishment deteriorated in the early years of the war.

In no other area of Nazi terror was the competition between police and legal system more obvious than in the case of detained Poles, who were largely held in either penal institutions or SS concentration camps in the early years of the war. The police played a central role in the occupation of Poland, which was accompanied by widespread 'ethnic cleansing'. Between autumn 1939 and spring 1940, police officials were involved in countless terror attacks and raids. Tens of thousands of Poles were shot, including many who belonged to the nobility, clergy and the intelligentsia. Polish Jews and thousands of supposed criminal offenders were also among those killed. The police set up court-martials to give some semblance of procedural order to their terror campaign against Polish civilians. Under Nazi occupation, the surviving Polish population was subjected to a vast catalogue of repressive regulations, aimed at the destruction of Polish culture, the plunder of economic resources and the humiliation and degradation of the population. Again, the German police played a crucial role in the enforcement of this policy of expropriation and enslavement.[47]

The coexistence of the legal system and the German police in the incorporated territories was not always peaceful. In fact, there was considerable friction between the two agencies. The police officials wanted to secure primacy in the punishment of Poles, which they felt was being questioned by the operation of the legal system. Consequently, the police constantly criticised judges and tried to put pressure on sentencing. For their part, judges resented police interference and the fact that the police punished criminal offences which would otherwise have been dealt with by the courts. Judges repeatedly tried to assert their authority *vis-à-vis* the police. They actually competed to prove that they could run a more efficient apparatus of punishment that was able to enact swifter retribution than the police.[48]

Similar conflicts were played out at the same time inside Germany where the police had quickly claimed the leading role in disciplining Poles. This rested largely on Göring's instructions for the treatment of Polish foreign workers of 8 March 1940, introduced without the knowledge of the legal authorities. The guidelines contained stark threats to Polish foreign workers. To start with, Poles who had sex with Germans faced police execution. This was no empty threat. Throughout 1940 and 1941, such executions of Polish men took place all over Germany, often in front of hundreds of spectators. To prepare for the killings, local police officials in some regions had even travelled through the area and selected trees for hangings. The executions were very much in line with Hitler's wishes. In a meeting at the end of June 1940, he had approved Himmler's view that 'the racial alien, who seduces a German woman or a German girl, is doomed to be hanged'.[49] The scope of repressive police measures extended far beyond supposed sexual transgressions. The directives of 8 March 1940 claimed that Poles habitually exhibited 'disinclination to work, open insubordination, misuse of alcohol, unauthorised departure from work'. In such cases, the police were ordered to 'take appropriate, if necessary also the hardest state police measures'.[50] The police were soon devoting considerable effort to pursuing Poles and other foreign workers. For example, in June 1941, half of all individuals arrested by the Dortmund Gestapo were foreigners (mostly Poles). Among the most common charges by the Gestapo was 'refusal to work or shirking'. In the meantime, the criminal police prosecuted other supposed offences committed by destitute Polish workers, who were often forced by sheer hunger to commit theft or to deal on the black market. Many arrested Poles were tormented for several weeks or months in newly set up educational work camps (*Arbeitserziehungslager*) run by the police. Others were taken to a local police jail or straight to a concentration camp.[51] There can be no doubt that the number of suspected offenders taken to concentration camps without trial was on the rise, compared to the prewar years – another reason for the rather slow increase in prison inmates in the Altreich.

The duality of punishment of Poles inside Germany by police and legal system caused confusion and conflict. The Celle general state prosecutor complained in May 1942 that 'Gestapo and judiciary work next to and against one another' in the case of Poles. His colleague in Hamm had raised the same point more than a year earlier, warning that the result was a 'no longer bearable legal uncertainty'.[52] To be sure, the relationship between legal system and police was not static. For instance, the punishment of Poles for offences such as 'breach of contract' (a vague term covering a wide range of behaviour, from criticism of working conditions to escape) was increasingly considered a matter only for the police. The legal system limited itself to other, often more dramatic cases, such as alleged attacks by Poles on Germans where it continued to assert its position. On 22 June 1941, Heinrich Himmler met State Secretary Schlegelberger, to discuss the punishment of Poles. Himmler complained that court sentences against Polish foreign workers were not satisfactory, the common argument made by the police to justify extra-judicial measures. Schlegelberger promised that he would take action whenever Himmler regarded a court sentence as insufficient. But Schlegelberger also insisted that the legal system had to retain control of the punishment of illegal acts.[53]

Typically, Schlegelberger hoped to stifle future police criticism by pushing for even stricter sentencing of Poles. One month after meeting Himmler, he sent a letter to the general state prosecutors, claiming that some judges exhibited an 'incomprehensible, lenient attitude towards the . . . Polish people', despite repeated instructions to the contrary. Some Polish criminals had received completely inadequate prison sentences, 'causing a danger to the security of the German people and justifying the accusation that the administration of criminal justice fails to meet the necessities of war'. Serious criminals and sex offenders from Poland, Schlegelberger demanded, ordinarily should be sentenced to death.[54] His appeal apparently had an impact on some judges, who now passed even harsher sentences. But there was still no uniformity among the judiciary, with individual judges applying the law against Poles in very different ways.[55]

Another highly contentious measure was that of the so-called police 'corrections' of court sentences. In the prewar period, the legal system had managed to defend the principle that all offenders legally sentenced to imprisonment served their sentence in penal institutions. After war broke out, this position started to be undermined. True, the Reich Ministry of Justice initially continued to fend off renewed attempts by police officials to take large groups of prisoners to concentration camps before the end of their sentence.[56] But the police now executed a number of convicts, predominantly foreign labourers, often shortly after they had been sentenced by legal courts to imprisonment. Police executions were openly reported in the Nazi press. While some Germans welcomed these killings, the population regarded with scepticism the standard police claims that the offenders had been shot trying to resist or to escape. At least 25–30 such police 'corrections' in the first three years of the war had been initiated by Hitler personally. Before the war, demands by Hitler for the killing of individual prisoners (such as Marinus van der Lubbe) had been accommodated within the confines of the legal system itself. This now changed, and Hitler became even less willing to respect legal conventions and to rein in his murderous instincts. Ordinarily, he would order the execution of offenders after their trial had been reported in the Nazi press, intervening in cases involving bank robberies, sex offences, theft, fraud and arson. Court sentences in these cases had often been very strict, with terms of ten years' imprisonment and more. But this was still too lenient for Hitler.[57]

Among the most prominent victims of police 'corrections' were the Berlin brothers Erich and Franz Sass, probably the most famous 'professional criminals' in the Weimar Republic (see p. 57). They had been repeatedly charged by the Weimar police, but had managed time and again to escape punishment by the courts. After the Nazi takeover, the brothers had escaped to Denmark, where they were caught and convicted of theft and attempted theft in 1934. At the end of their sentence, they were handed over to the German authorities. For almost two years they were held under very strict conditions in remand. On 27 January 1940, they were finally sentenced by the Berlin district court for some of the crimes they were supposed to have committed in the Weimar years, including the spectacular break-in at the Disconto-Bank. They received sentences of 13 and 11 years in a penitentiary respectively, as well as security confinement. But these tough sentences did not satisfy Heinrich Himmler, who ordered the brothers' execution. On 27 March 1940, Erich and Franz Sass were taken from penal institutions to the Sachsenhausen concentration camp. Here, they were murdered by SS men under the command of Rudolf Höß, who recalled the execution after the war: 'They [the brothers] refused resolutely to stand against the post, and I had to let them be tied up. They resisted with all their strength. I was extremely relieved when I was able to give the order to shoot.' Their murder was promptly reported in the Nazi press.[58] This case demonstrates clearly the difference between punishment in the Weimar and the Nazi period. In the Weimar Republic, the two brothers had walked free because there was not sufficient evidence to convict them. In Nazi Germany, they were murdered, irrespective of legal regulations.

Regional legal officials were often highly critical of such police 'corrections'. The president of the Higher State Court in Hamm, for example, exclaimed in November 1940 that the police executions felt like a 'smack in the face for the judiciary'. Generally, such criticism was not motivated by humanitarian considerations for those killed. After all, most legal officials themselves supported brutal measures against serious criminals and 'asocials'. Rather, the officials were worried that the police invasion of judicial territory further undermined the reputation and the reach of the judiciary.[59] Such concern was echoed by leading officials in Berlin. Reich Minister Franz Gürtner complained to Hans-Heinrich Lammers, the head of the Reich Chancellery, about police 'corrections' as early as 28 September 1939, only to be told that Hitler would continue to order such executions in individual cases because the courts 'are not up to coping with the special circumstances of the war'.[60]

But the Reich Ministry of Justice did not readily give in. In March 1941, after Gürtner's death, State Secretary Schlegelberger approached Hitler once more. Schlegelberger pleaded with Hitler to inform the legal authorities (rather than the police) of any sentence 'which does not find your approval'. In such cases, a new trial could be ordered, virtually guaranteeing the outcome desired by Hitler.[61] Schlegelberger, like Gürtner a national-conservative civil servant, was eager to win the Nazis' support by submitting to Hitler's wishes. He was a willing collaborator in the war on Jews and Poles as well as German social outsiders. In part, Schlegelberger hoped that this would curb the growing influence of the police. But he also believed that it was right and proper for the legal system to act as the executor of the regime's wishes.[62] Schlegelberger encouraged judges to pass even stricter sentences, to prove to Hitler that the legal system was able, after all, to realise his call for strict punishment. Schlegelberger continued to remind legal officials that Hitler had demanded that those who undermined the home front had to die.[63] But this could not stop the police executions of individual prisoners on Hitler's orders. However lethal the legal system became, it could not dispel the mistrust of leading Nazis against the court system, which was to erupt spectacularly in 1942.

The Legal System under Attack, 1942

The Nazi policy of annihilation escalated dramatically from 1941. On 22 June the German army launched its attack on the Soviet Union, the greatest land invasion in modern times. Hitler had decided long before the invasion that this war would be very different from the one in the west. It would be a war of extermination. The invasion of the Soviet Union thus marked a further stage of terror in the Third Reich, removing any obstacles still in the way of genocide as state policy. During the attack, the German army wreaked terror on civilians and soldiers. Police and SS units, including the so-called task forces, followed the army into the occupied territory and started to murder the local Jewish population. Hundreds of thousands of Jews were killed in the first months. From autumn 1941, the regime prepared to extend genocide to Jews in Poland, Germany and elsewhere, and by summer in the following year, trains were rolling from all over Europe to extermination camps in the east. The Nazi leaders were well aware that war provided a cover for these genocidal policies. As Propaganda Minister Joseph Goebbels noted in his diary on 27 March 1942, after describing the murder of the European Jews: 'Thank God, during the war we now have a whole series of possibilities which were barred to us in peacetime. We must exploit them.'[64]

Nazi terror on the home front also intensified in the period after the invasion of the Soviet Union. The murderous Nazi policies against Jews, civilians and POWs in eastern Europe soon spilled back into Germany. Domestic policy was clearly shaped by the genocide. But it was also shaped by the spectre of 1918, which began to raise its head ever higher to haunt the Nazi leaders. Their thoughts returned again and again to the collapse of the home front in 1918. This was obviously linked to the changing fortunes of the war. The Nazis had hoped to defeat the Soviets before the winter and, at first, German troops advanced quickly. But the Nazi leadership had fatally underestimated the huge logistical difficulties of the campaign, and was surprised by the resistance put up by the Soviets. The advance soon slowed down and by late 1941 the German army was in serious trouble, facing a powerful counter-offensive around Moscow. At the same time, Germany's wider strategic position deteriorated after the declaration of war against the USA on 11 December 1941. Of course, the war was far from over at this point. The German army stabilised the eastern front, and in the first half of 1942, Hitler revelled in the destruction wreaked by the U-boats in the Atlantic and in Rommel's advance in Africa. He also planned for a new offensive in the east, which got under way on 28 June 1942. But the strategic advantage had already shifted away from Germany.[65]

The Nazi leaders were concerned about the impact of these developments on the morale of 'national comrades'. They were kept informed about popular opinion in regular digests prepared by the SD, and there can be no doubt that the public mood was deteriorating, after Hitler's standing had initially reached new heights during the rapid victories of the Germany army in 1939 and 1940. Indeed, in late 1941 and early 1942, the German public experienced its first serious shock of the war. The reversals on the eastern front and the regime's startling announcement of a collection of winter clothing for the soldiers raised serious doubts about the preparedness and the strength of the German army. The Soviet counter-attack and the US entry into the war brought home to the German population that they now faced a long and drawn-out conflict. Popular anxiety was exacerbated by the enormous losses sustained by the German army. More and more civilians lost friends and relatives at the front: by the end of 1941, the army in the east had suffered almost 750,000 casualties. In the following months, the public mood was punctured further by increased rationing and Allied air raids, with the first major British mass bombing raid on civilian targets hitting Lübeck on 28–29 March 1942.[66]

As popular support for the regime wavered, the Nazi leaders contemplated ever more brutal measures to rule out the possibility of an internal uprising. This was even more necessary, they believed, because of the supposed danger of 'negative selection' caused by the tremendous rate of casualties suffered by the army. Hitler argued that the extermination of hardened criminals, 'asocials' and political enemies at home was a necessity as 'the best' German men were dying at the front. During lunch with Heinrich Himmler on 5 November 1941, Hitler declaimed that:

> if I allow criminals to be kept alive, at a time when the best men die out there, then I shift the balance of the people... Degeneracy starts to triumph. If a nation now faces an emergency, then a handful of preserved criminals can deprive the fighters of the fruits of their sacrifice. We saw this happen in 1918.[67]

In the following months and years, Hitler returned obsessively to this point in private and public speeches, as well as in meetings with members of the Nazi elite and foreign leaders. For instance, he raised the issue again on 22 May 1942 at his lunch-table, as recorded by one of his loyal servants:

> If one permitted the filthy swine at home to be treated leniently and to be thus preserved, while a large number of idealists die at the front, then one would pave the way for a negative selection, demonstrating that one had not understood the lessons of the war years 1917–18... He [Hitler] was personally responsible for preventing the creation of a home front of villains as in 1918, while the heroes die in the war.[68]

One week later, Hitler echoed these thoughts in a meeting with Joseph Goebbels, adding that 'even in November 1918, something could still have been achieved, if a determined man had used brutal instruments of power'.[69]

Hitler was unambiguous about the solution he had in mind. In a time of national crisis, he repeated again and again, it was necessary to 'exterminate', 'eliminate', 'execute', 'beat to death', 'shoot' or 'liquidate' large numbers of 'scum', 'rats' and 'asocial vermin' on the home front.[70] On 23 May 1942, Hitler explained his murderous thoughts towards the end of a two-hour long, blazing speech to the Reichsleiter and Gauleiter, who had assembled in the

Reich Chancellery. If only the criminals had been shot dead in Germany in 1918, Hitler exclaimed (recorded by Goebbels), 'then there would have been no revolution; because this revolution only became dangerous when the prisons were opened. It is better to shoot the criminals, than to subject to their grasp a defenceless people, whose heroes are standing at the front or have fallen'.[71] While Hitler generally discussed the extermination of the Jews at his lunch and dinner table and in speeches to party officials only in rather broad terms, careful to keep some distance between himself and genocide, he never showed such reluctance in the case of criminal offenders. No doubt he was certain that his entourage and supporters completely supported his murderous views in this case.

Hitler was also open about his continued support for the police as his chosen weapon of repression on the home front. In his speech on 23 May 1942 in front of the Nazi top brass, Hitler explicitly ordered Heinrich Himmler to 'shoot the criminals in all concentration camps', if Germany faced a critical situation 'and there is a danger that the Reich will descend into chaos'.[72] Hitler openly demonstrated his reliance on police terror by appointing Himmler as Reich Minister of the Interior in August 1943, part of a general growth in influence of Nazi hard-liners during the last years of the war. A few months after his appointment, Himmler informed representatives of the German press that he was responsible 'for the welfare of the nation'. This meant, he promised, that he would not shy away from using the 'most brutal action' to prevent a repetition of 1918: 'For it is better that a hundred die somewhere, than for an entire people to pay with its life'.[73] Himmler saw the police as the unquestioning executor of Hitler's will. Nothing could stop the police in this mission. As Himmler explained to German army generals on 21 June 1944, he could not care less whether the actions were legal or not: 'what is necessary for Germany will be done, however horrifying it may be'.[74]

Himmler's ruthless determination, backed by Hitler, led to a further extension of police powers. The Gestapo cracked down with extreme brutality on all suspected subversives, with foreign workers the main target: 72 per cent of Gestapo arrests in the summer of 1943 were of foreigners. Foreign workers were simultaneously persecuted by the criminal police, which also stepped up its policy of 'crime prevention' from 1942. Increasing numbers of suspects (including ex-convicts, sex offenders and 'professional criminals') were rounded up and sent straight to concentration camps, rather than being handed over to the legal authorities.[75] Inmate numbers in the concentration camps exploded. Until the middle of the war, numbers in the camps had still been lower than in penal institutions. But the balance was reversed after 1942. By April 1943, about 200,000 inmates were held in concentration camps (excluding death camps), already some 10,000 more than in penal institutions. Just over a year later, in mid-August 1944, there were well over half a million concentration camp inmates, compared to about 200,000 prisoners. The concentration camps had finally replaced penal institutions as the main site of imprisonment in the Third Reich (see Figure 2, pp. 394-5).

Attacking the Legal System

While Hitler supported police terror as the best insurance against an internal uprising, his long-standing suspicion of the legal system grew even stronger, following the escalation of the Second World War. Despite the unprecedented legal terror, he continued to attack the legal apparatus as slow and formalistic, comparing it unfavourably with the unrestrained actions of the police. More than ever, it was the nightmare of 1918 that drove Hitler. In the autumn of 1941, he complained repeatedly in his private circle that the German judges passed too lenient sentences – with potentially dire consequences: 'The practice of our criminal jurisdiction leads to the criminals being preserved. As long as the nation is doing well, this is no danger. But when the foundations of the state are shaken by wars or famine, then this can lead to unimaginable catastrophes.' Hitler told his entourage that had he not pursued the 'correction' of court sentences – the brutal police murders of offenders legally sentenced to imprisonment – then Germany would already face disintegration. His wrath extended to prison officials as well. In May 1942, he complained to Goebbels that inmates could emerge from prison 'fresh and unused', ready to act once more against the state – a statement which showed Hitler's disregard for the brutal realities inside penal institutions. He had made a similar point a few months earlier to Himmler, telling him that criminals knew that inside penitentiaries 'everything is nice, hygienic, nobody will do one any harm, the Minister of Justice vouches for that'.[76]

Hitler's simmering hostility towards the legal system blew up in spectacular fashion in the spring of 1942. The spark was yet another supposedly lenient court sentence. On 14 March 1942, the district court in Oldenburg found the engineer Ewald Schlitt guilty of having abused his wife so badly that she eventually died. However, the judges decided that Schlitt had not acted in cold blood but was liable to sudden violent fits of temper. Rather than condemning him to death as a 'violent criminal', the court sentenced Schlitt to five years in a penitentiary. When Hitler heard about this case, he exploded with rage. Ignorant of the details, he demanded that Schlitt be executed and took the court's sentence as confirmation of the impotence of the judiciary. If there were any more such sentences, Hitler fumed in his private circle on Sunday 22 March 1942, he would 'send the Justice Ministry to hell through a Reichstag law'.[77] Hitler made no secret of his fury. On the very same day, he berated the acting Minister of Justice Schlegelberger on the telephone. Highly agitated, Hitler exclaimed that he could not understand why criminals were treated so leniently at a time when the 'best' German soldiers were dying at the front. Hitler threatened Schlegelberger with very serious consequences should the legal system fail to change.[78]

The Reich Ministry of Justice immediately engaged in damage limitation, following Hitler's outburst. Two days after his phone call, Schlegelberger wrote to Hitler to reassure him about the ruthlessness of the legal system: 'My Führer, I share your desire for the harshest punishment of criminal elements with the greatest conviction.' To prove his point, Schlegelberger informed Hitler that the Schlitt case would be taken up by the Reich Court.[79] The court duly delivered the desired result. On 31 March 1942, it quashed the original sentence against Schlitt and instead sentenced him to death, a decision which was immediately relayed to Hitler. Ewald Schlitt was guillotined two days later.[80] Schlegelberger did not let the case rest here. He was concerned enough to inform the general state prosecutors, in a meeting on the day of Schlitt's retrial, about Hitler's threats. In his speech, Schlegelberger used this case, as well as other supposedly lenient sentences, to renew his call for the 'total integration of the legal system into the national-socialist state' (he had already made the same plea one year earlier). Schlegelberger made absolutely clear what he expected: 'The desire of the Führer [for] the harshest punishment is an order which the judge has to follow.'[81]

In previous protests by Hitler against court sentences he considered too 'mild', the file had been closed after the execution of the offender. But not this time. One of the reasons why Hitler did not let matters rest was his growing concern about the home front. In March 1942, the Nazi leadership knew that rations would have to be cut and evidently feared a backlash among the population, following SD reports that widespread rumours about impending cuts were causing great anxiety and concern among the German public.[82] The Nazi leaders were convinced that the legal system would be unable to deal with any unrest. Thus, after Hitler had discussed the forthcoming cuts in rations with Goebbels on 19 March 1942, the two men went on to complain about the failures of the judiciary and to talk about the need for tougher measures on the home front. It was at this point that Hitler floated the idea of convening the Reichstag to give himself special powers against 'evil-doers', an idea he returned to after the Schlitt case.[83] The cut in rations, the most serious during the entire war, was finally introduced on 6 April 1942, and caused great disquiet.[84] Hitler's apparent concern about this was betrayed in an extraordinary outburst at dinner on the very next day. Inevitably, his thoughts circled around the 1918 revolution and, with unprecedented ferocity, he vented his homicidal determination to prevent another 'stab in the back':

> If a mutiny broke out somewhere in the Reich today, then he would answer it with immediate measures. To start with, he would:

a) have all leading men of an oppositional tendency . . . arrested at home and executed, on the day of the first report;
b) he would have all inmates in concentration camps shot dead within three days;
c) he would also have all criminal elements rounded up for execution within three days on the basis of the available lists, irrespective of whether they were in prison or at liberty at the time.
The shooting of this scum, which comprised a few hundred thousand people, would make other measures appear unnecessary, as the mutiny would break down by itself due to a lack of mutinous elements and fellow-travellers.[85]

Only two weeks later, Hitler rang Goebbels and instructed him to take the very unusual step of summoning the Reichstag.

On 26 April 1942, the Reichstag deputies assembled in Berlin, curious as to the purpose of the meeting. Hitler began his speech with a long and rambling account of the progress of the war, which included the obligatory reference to the German defeat in 1918 and was also brimming with anti-Semitic hatred. Then, he launched a brief but effective attack on the judiciary and the civil service. The legal system, Hitler warned, must have only one thought: German victory. It was high time, he continued, that the legal system realised that it did not exist for its own sake, but for the nation. As an illustration of the inane approach of the judiciary, Hitler pointed to the Schlitt case. Hitler's aim was to force judges to pass more brutal and less formal sentences. Otherwise, he threatened, he was 'going to intervene in such cases and relieve of their office judges who are obviously failing to recognise the requirements of the day' – openly breaking his 1933 promise that the judges were irremovable. The deputies cheered loudly, broke into chants of 'Heil' and then passed a resolution that explicitly exempted Hitler from 'existing statutes of law', giving him the right to remove from office and punish anyone 'failing their duties'. Hitler was officially above the law.[86]

Hitler's attack in the Reichstag on 26 April 1942 received a mixed reception from the German public. Many Germans, it seems, supported Hitler's views. But conservatives and members of the bourgeoisie started to voice some concerns about the threat to the rule of law. The German legal officials themselves were stunned. Hitler's attack carried all the more weight because his public speeches had become rare, this speech proving to be his last ever in the Reichstag. Senior officials in the regions reported that judges and other officials were dismayed and depressed by Hitler's public dressing-down. One senior judge exclaimed in private: 'Out of shame, each judge has to hide his face from the public.' The officials feared that the attack would destroy public confidence in the independence of the judiciary and provide further incentives for the police to interfere in the legal process.[87] To discuss measures which would increase Hitler's confidence in the judiciary, the Reich Ministry of Justice held two meetings with senior regional officials in early May 1942 in Berlin. The meeting on 6 May was chaired by State Secretary Freisler. Hitler's speech, he acknowledged, had hit the legal system like a 'thunderstorm'. Freisler reminded the officials of the lessons which needed to be drawn: the legal officials had to become harder, focusing even more on retribution.[88]

Following Hitler's speech, the acting Reich Minister of Justice Schlegelberger also intensified his attempts to win over the Nazi leadership. On 5 May, in a meeting of the presidents of the Higher State Courts, he cast himself in an almost messianic light: 'I will find a way to destroy the false views about the judiciary and its achievements. I will find a way to lead you out of darkness'.[89] On the following day, Schlegelberger proposed measures to Hitler which, he promised, would ensure that there could be no more complaints about the courts in the future.[90] But Hitler's mistrust of the judiciary was too deep-seated to be dispelled so easily. And Schlegelberger himself cut a most unlikely figure in his self-appointed role as saviour of the legal system. For Hitler made no secret about the fact that he had no time for him personally. An ageing career civil servant, he was the personification of all that Hitler detested about the judiciary, and Hitler continued to complain in private about the weakness of the legal system. On 22 July, for example, he once more ranted at length about the judiciary, concluding that nobody resembled the jurist more closely than the criminal.[91]

The Nazi leaders made sure that legal officials knew that Hitler was still unhappy. On the same day as Hitler's latest private outburst, on 22 July 1942, Goebbels made an explicit speech to the officials at the People's Court, outlining the Nazi leaders' criticism of the judiciary. Goebbels's comments had special significance because, as he informed his listeners, Hitler had personally approved them. Goebbels began by complaining that many judges still had the wrong attitude, derived in large measure from their legalistic training. After referring in detail to several 'unbearable' sentences, Goebbels made crystal clear what was required from the judiciary. During the war, it was not important whether a judgment was fair or unfair; rather, it had to protect the state by eradicating the 'inner enemies': 'The starting point is not the law, but the decision [that] this man has to disappear.' Such ruthlessness was vital at a time when, Goebbels concluded, the 'best part of the people' were sacrificing themselves at the front – raising Hitler's pet theme of 'negative selection'.[92]

The Shake-up of the Ministry of Justice

One month after Goebbels's speech, Hitler's discontent about the legal system resulted in further action. On 20 August 1942, he carried out a major reshuffle of the Reich Ministry of Justice: Schlegelberger, by now almost 66 years of age, received his retirement notice and a substantial pay-off. Otto-Georg Thierack, the president of the People's Court, was appointed as Reich Minister of Justice. This move had already been suggested to Hitler in March 1942 by Goebbels as a way of getting rid of the unpopular Schlegelberger.[93] The Nazi leadership regarded Thierack as the right man to bring the judiciary further into line with its genocidal thinking. A front-line soldier in the First World War, Thierack had worked as a state prosecutor in the Weimar Republic. In the Third Reich, he had a stellar career – thanks in part to his early support for the Nazis; he had joined the party on 1 August 1932. (Thierack was also a member of the SA, advancing to the rank of Gruppenführer by 1942.) In the months immediately preceding his appointment as Reich Minister of Justice, Thierack had overseen a massive rise in the number of death sentences handed out by the People's Court – demonstrating that he could be relied upon to dispense lethal justice.[94]

In the historical literature, the appointment of Thierack is often seen as the turning point when the law in Germany was finally perverted and unconditionally subordinated to the aims of the regime. There is no denying that Thierack did have a considerable impact. He clearly felt that he had a point to prove to the Nazi leadership, and Hitler was much more satisfied with Thierack than he had been with his predecessors. Of course, not even Thierack could completely erase Hitler's contempt for the legal profession. Still, Hitler was sufficiently impressed with his last Minister of Justice to order in his political testament, written in his bunker in Berlin the day before his suicide on 30 April 1945, that Thierack should retain his post in a new Nazi cabinet.[95] Yet Thierack was certainly not single-handedly responsible for legal terror. Presenting him as the evil spirit of law in the Third Reich – reminiscent of postwar attempts to shift the blame for all crimes onto a handful of devilish Nazis – effectively exonerates many of the other implicated legal officials. Also, the legal apparatus was already a loyal servant of the regime in the prewar years and once war broke out, the Reich Ministry of Justice consistently pushed for more brutal sentences and stricter punishment. The rule of law was progressively eroded and much of this had been accomplished with Gürtner and Schlegelberger at the helm. Thierack merely accelerated a process which was already well under way.

The shake-up of the Reich Ministry of Justice in the summer of 1942 did not stop at Schlegelberger. In autumn 1942, several high-ranking and experienced officials also left their desks. These included Wilhelm Crohne, the head of the department for the administration of criminal justice, who became vice-president of the People's Court. His new superior was also his old one, as State Secretary Roland Freisler took up Thierack's old position as president of the

People's Court, where he soon gained notoriety for his murderous sentences. Even Goebbels, noting that Freisler now behaved again like the 'radical nationalsocialist' he had been in the Weimar years, thought that Freisler went too far.[96] In Freisler's place, Hitler appointed the president of the Hamburg Higher State Court, Curt Rothenberger, as State Secretary. Hitler had taken notice of him in April 1942, when he read a memorandum by the highly ambitious Rothenberger on the need for a comprehensive reform of the legal system, based on the principle that judges had 'to judge "like the Führer"'. But Rothenberger was not a deeply committed Nazi like Thierack. He was an immoral careerist, who had become the undisputed ruler of the Hamburg judiciary thanks to his political opportunism and his ability to develop a remarkably close working relationship with the local Nazi party, police and SS leaders. Yet Rothenberger only remained near the top until the end of 1943. By then, his project to reform the legal system had failed and he had also fallen out with Thierack. He was replaced as State Secretary by Herbert Klemm, a close personal friend of Thierack, who had worked as his personal assistant in Saxony in 1933 and had later transferred to the Party Chancellery under Martin Bormann.[97]

On 20 August 1942, Thierack and Rothenberger were received at Hitler's Wehrwolf headquarters in the Ukraine. Hitler handed them their letters of appointment and, following the brief ceremony, he asked both men to lunch, where he spelt out what he expected from them. Repeating thoughts he had expressed many times over the previous months, Hitler set out his vision of the legal system in the Nazi state. During the war, 'the most barbaric means' were called for against those who had placed themselves outside the 'national community' through their crimes. Hitler complained that a prison sentence was no longer adequate punishment for many criminals; while 'the bravest' were killed at the front, the criminals survived in penal institutions:

> During this time, the total crook is cared for physically and mentally. Anyone who ever enters a prison knows with absolute certainty that nothing more is going to happen to him. If one imagines this going on for three or four years, then a gradual shift in the balance of the nation takes place ... If I decimate the good, while I preserve the bad, then what happened in 1918, when five or six hundred ruffians raped the entire nation, will happen again.

To avert such a catastrophe, Hitler concluded, one had to 'ruthlessly exterminate the vermin'. To enable Thierack to build a judiciary capable of carrying out this task, Hitler officially granted him express authority to 'disregard existing law'.[98] The speech made a great impression on Thierack. He arrived at his desk in Berlin determined to turn Hitler's vague if forcibly expressed views into reality.

Total War and Extermination, 1942–44

Legal terror was stepped up from 1942 onwards. Sentencing by the courts became harsher than ever and the number of convictions also increased. Repeatedly, judges overshot the mark and passed punishment regarded as too brutal even by the police.[99] Death sentences exploded from 1,292 (1941) to 4,457 (1942). In the next two years, the courts continued to use capital punishment as a weapon of racial warfare. In 1943 and 1944, some 9,600 death sentences were passed in the German Reich (see Figure 10, pp. 402–3). In these two years alone, more people were sentenced to death than in the entire 80-year period between 1861 and 1941.[100] Those who escaped the death penalty – still the great majority of defendants – often received lengthy sentences of imprisonment. By 1943, the number of custodial sentences for German offenders easily outweighed fines, reversing the balance from the prewar years. And these custodial sentences had become significantly longer. Prior to the outbreak of the Second World War, prison inmates had far outnumbered penitentiary inmates (who served much longer sentences). But by September 1944, there were three penitentiary inmates for every two prison inmates in the German penal institutions.[101]

The trend towards tougher sentencing was reflected in the still more prominent role of special courts in legal punishment. The number of cases which now came before these courts increased further (see Figure 8, pp. 400–1). In the prewar years, special courts had dealt with far fewer cases than regional courts (*Landgerichte*). In 1934, there were 2,767 special court sentences compared to 27,802 sentences by the regional courts. This balance changed during the war. In some judicial districts sentencing by the special courts actually outstripped the regional courts by 1943. To cope with the backlog of cases, a number of existing special courts were extended and several new courts were set up. Not only was the number of defendants up, but special courts also passed stricter sentences. The vast majority of convicted defendants received long custodial sentences, with three years being the average length of penitentiary sentence handed out by the Mannheim special court in 1943. The special courts also had few qualms about sending individuals to their deaths. The judges at the Hamburg special court were among the most bloodthirsty: in 1943, they applied the death penalty in 14.7 per cent of all their sentences.[102] The most lethal German court of all was the People's Court in Berlin, under its new president Roland Freisler. The homicidal rage of the judges here now reached its climax, and by 1943 death sentences surpassed sentences of imprisonment for the first time (see Figure 7, pp. 398–9).

The activities of the German courts contributed to a significant increase in the prison population in 1942. Inmate numbers in all penal institutions grew from 144,142 on 30 June 1941 to 181,137 on 30 June 1942 (see Figure 1, pp. 392–3). This increase was particularly strong inside the Altreich where, in the early years of the war, the prison population had only climbed rather slowly. This rise became much more pronounced from spring 1942. Between March and September alone, the inmate population in the Altreich shot up by almost 13 per cent (see Figure 3, pp. 394-5). In 1943 and 1944, this increase slowed down, despite the harsh sentences by the German courts. Inmate numbers in all penal institutions gradually rose to 196,700 by 30 June 1944 (see Figure 1, pp. 392-3). This figure would have been much higher still, had it not been for the simultaneous extension of the SS camps as well as a new approach to penal policy under Reich Minister Thierack, which ultimately left tens of thousands of prisoners and offenders to the police.

How can we explain the further increase in the severity of sentencing from 1942? After his appointment as Reich Minister of Justice, Thierack did not hesitate to revamp the legal system. To start with, he decided early on to put added pressure on individual judges. This was, of course, not an original idea. Under Gürtner, the Reich Ministry of Justice had already repeatedly tried to influence the judges. Thierack now intensified such efforts to 'guide' the judiciary. On 13 October 1942, the Reich Ministry of Justice ordered senior regional officials to conduct what became known as 'preliminary case reviews' and 'post-mortems' with judges and state prosecutors, a measure that further undermined the independence of the judiciary.[103] Only a few weeks earlier, Thierack had introduced so-called 'Judges' Letters'. On a monthly basis, state courts now received circulars with summaries of judgments regarded by the Reich Ministry of Justice as either laudable or misguided. The aim, Thierack explained on 7 September, was to 'illustrate how the judicial leadership envisages a national socialist application of the law . . .'.[104] Among other issues, Thierack used the 'Judges' Letters' to call for the 'extermination' of particularly 'dangerous' offenders, echoing Hitler's warnings about the threat of 'negative selection'. On 1 January 1943, he noted that

> criminal law today also has to fulfil a great national-hygienic task: protection of the national community through continual organic exclusion of the incorrigible asocial criminal. . . . We owe this ruthless severity against the incorrigible habitual criminal, which is demanded by the Führer, to our nation and its best sons who risk and sacrifice their lives for us.[105]

In the following months and years, Thierack repeated these warnings and continued to demand that 'traitors, saboteurs, national pests, violent criminals, and asocial criminals' be punished 'in the harshest possible way'.[106] Thierack's 'guidance' of judges certainly had some impact. However, its effect should not be exaggerated. The judges still retained a significant degree of independence and it was they who were ultimately responsible for the judgments.[107]

There were several other reasons for the rise in legal terror. Following Hitler's public attack on the legal system on 26 April 1942, many judges were more eager than ever to demonstrate their commitment to the Nazi cause. Shocked by Hitler's attack, they hoped to improve the standing of the legal system by handing out even stricter sentences. It was no coincidence that the number of death sentences passed by the legal authorities shot up in the immediate aftermath of Hitler's speech, with convictions rising from 129 (April 1942) to 233 (June 1942) – even Goebbels noted with approval that judges pushed for more brutal sentences following the speech.[108] The brutal crackdown by the courts also betrayed the growing paranoia about foreign workers, as the war turned against Germany and the number of these workers on German soil increased; by August 1944, there were almost six million, as well as two million POWs, labouring in Germany. Hitler himself at one point claimed that offences 'by asocial elements', such as thefts during air raids, were committed 'ninety-nine per cent by foreign workers'.[109]

Additionally, many judges felt that the progressive breakdown of morale in Germany after 1942 made brutal sentencing necessary, in order to protect the home front against another 'stab in the back'. The greatest shock for the German population in the entire war came with the surrender in early 1943 of the 6th Army, which had been encircled in Stalingrad since November 1942. The following years saw more and more losses for the retreating German forces, pushed back by the Allies. The German public was growing demoralised by the defeats, the wartime shortages and by the massive destruction wreaked by the Allied bombing raids, which made over seven million Germans homeless. Support for the regime evaporated steadily, and Hitler's popularity, a cornerstone of the regime, started to erode. The public mood turned so sharply that, in July 1944, Nazi leaders stopped the regular digests of popular opinion prepared by the SD. At that time, many Germans would already have been willing to surrender. The response of the regime, obsessed with the 'lessons of 1918', was the further escalation of terror against all 'subversives'.[110]

Legal officials saw their fears confirmed by the dramatic rise in property crime after 1942. Growing deprivation and anxiety about the war increased the willingness of the population to steal food and other goods, despite strict penalties. Rationing and the chaos following air raids created greater opportunities for committing such offences.[111] In some areas, the police responded by setting up special offices to deal with these economic offences.[112] And the German judiciary cracked down with force on those arrested for property crime, primarily hitting the lower classes.[113] The judges reserved particularly severe sanctions for offenders who had benefited from wartime circumstances, for instance, by stealing after air raids or during black-outs. In front of the courts, the theft of bars of chocolate, old clothes or bottles of wine could now be punished with several years in a penitentiary. Such brutal punishment of property offences was justified with reference to the supposedly grave threats these offences posed to discipline on the home front. Similar arguments were put forward by judges in cases where postal workers had stolen food, tobacco or soap from parcels meant for soldiers at the front. Not only did these thefts damage the trust of German citizens in the state and thus undermine the 'inner front', it was argued, but they also threatened soldiers' will to fight. Attempts by individuals to improve their lot by subverting wartime regulations were thus twisted into attacks on the German war effort by dangerous enemies which could lead to a revolution. Deterrence also played a crucial part in the minds of the judges. As many property offenders were never caught during the war, the legal authorities were determined to set a warning example in the case of convicted offenders. Bloody sentences for plunderers and thieves were splashed all over the newspapers and on posters in public places. The terror of the courts still often took place in broad daylight.[114]

Crucially, legal terror increasingly engulfed German 'national comrades'. Previously, the Nazi regime had not relied on terror alone in its attempt to control large sections of the German population. Propaganda and the 'Hitler myth' had also played a crucial role in mobilising Nazi society. Now, as the 'Hitler myth' began to disintegrate, terror became ever more important in disciplining the 'national comrades'. More and more Germans convicted during the war had not previously been in conflict with the legal authorities, often coming from sections of the population which had traditionally not been responsible for much criminal activity, such as women and youths. According to the sentencing statistics, women had made up only 14 per cent of all defendants convicted between 1933 and 1938. By contrast, in the first half of 1943 some 40 per cent of convicted Germans were female. The legal authorities were alarmed by this development. In fact, the rise in registered crime by women and young people was so sharp that as early as 1942 State Secretary Freisler ordered that crime statistics were no longer to be published. The German defendants were punished more harshly than ever before. To be sure, sentencing was not indiscriminate. Numerous Germans still received relatively lenient punishment, if their cases came to trial at all. Even so, by 1943, only about one-third of all Germans convicted of crimes and misdemeanours received fines, according to incomplete confidential sentencing statistics. Almost all others were handed custodial sentences.[115]

Most property offences were carried out by German 'national comrades'. Often, the defendants were sentenced under the specific wartime regulations. In the first half of 1943, convictions under the War Economy Decree and the Consumer Regulations Penal Decree – which covered offences such as the illegal slaughter of cattle, dealings on the black market and the forgery of ration cards – accounted for more than 10 per cent of all sentences against Germans. Only one in five of those found guilty of these offences had previous convictions, but offences against the economic wartime regulations were not taken lightly by the judges. Hundreds of Germans were sentenced to death, and lengthy custodial sentences were common.[116]

'National comrades' were also convicted of many other types of offences. For example, evidence from various special courts suggests that sentences for listening to enemy radio increased towards the end of the war. At the Kiel special court, the number of defendants jumped from zero (1940) to 51 (1944). Those found guilty in 1944 received, on average, a sentence of 16 months' imprisonment in a penitentiary.[117] Another growing 'crime' involved illegal contact with POWs. According to the confidential sentencing statistics, in the first half of 1943 alone, some 3,639 German women were convicted for contact with POWs from countries such as France or Belgium. (Relations with Poles, Russians and other 'Slavic people' were mainly punished by the police.) Courts were often strict, even though only a small number of the defendants had ever stood before a judge before. When sentencing these women, some judges fulminated about the women's 'degeneracy' and 'immorality'. One senior judge recommended the following yardstick to a subordinate: 'One buttered bread – 1 year in prison; one kiss – 2 years in prison; sexual intercourse – beheading.' In practice, women caught speaking to POWs or giving them a piece of bread were able to escape with minor punishment. By contrast, those found guilty of sexual contact largely received lengthy penitentiary sentences.[118]

The number of Germans accused of serious political crimes by the People's Court also quickly spiralled upwards in the last years of the war. After the judges had earlier dealt with more foreigners (especially Czechs), the focus now returned to the German population. The number of Germans in the dock rose from about 35 per cent of all defendants (1942) to almost 62 per cent (1944). Contrary to most people's presumptions, the men behind the 20 July 1944 plot on Hitler's life made up a minority among the Germans sentenced in the last year of the war. Communists, socialists and other members of the left-wing resistance were still much more likely to be sentenced by the People's Court than the national-conservative opponents of the Nazis. But the largest group of Germans now coming in front of the People's Court were not accused of any organised resistance against the regime at all. Instead, they were found guilty of undermining the home front, for example, by making 'defeatist comments'. Previously, critical comments about the regime had rarely been punished under the Special Wartime Penal Code. Even hard-line legal officials had not contemplated the use of this draconian measure, which could carry the death penalty. But faced with the growing demoralisation of the German population, trials of Germans for 'undermining the war effort' burgeoned and the People's Court was authorised in January 1943 to punish this offence. The judges showed no mercy. In the last year of war, around half of the convicted defendants were sentenced to death, often for no more than a single unguarded remark. Most others received penitentiary sentences of, on average, over five years.[119]

A New Role for the Legal System

Reich Minister Thierack called incessantly for stricter punishment. But he also believed that harsher sentencing alone was not enough to overcome the perceived crisis of the legal system in 1942. With Gürtner and Schlegelberger at the helm of the Reich Ministry of Justice, as we have seen, the general response to criticism by the Nazi leadership had been the tightening up of penal policy. While legal officials were very keen to accommodate the Nazi leadership, they were also eager to protect the judicial sphere of influence. In particular, they were determined that criminal offences should generally continue to be punished by the legal system, not by the police. By fulfilling the demands of the Nazi regime for brutal punishment, the legal officials hoped to preserve their authority against the invasion of the police. The historian Patrick Wagner has deftly characterised wartime punishment as resembling 'a kind of competition between police and legal system for the trophy of the most ruthless instrument of terror . . .'.[120]

Yet, as Thierack must have known, the legal system was always bound to lose this competition. Compared to Himmler's police and SS, the legal authorities were destined to be dismissed as overly legalistic. The legal monopoly of punishment was also increasingly being undermined by murderous Nazi policies, authorised by Hitler. Apart from the police 'correction' of court sentences, there was the 'euthanasia' programme, which had led to the murder of many asylum inmates who were still under legal jurisdiction. This was followed by the extermination of the Jews. From spring 1942 onwards, hundreds of Jewish prisoners were handed over to the police as part of the 'final solution', even though they had not yet completed their sentences (see Chapter 8).

It was against this background that Reich Minister Thierack aimed to find a new role for the legal apparatus within the Nazi dictatorship. Essentially, he proposed a division of labour between the state penal system and the police. As Thierack explained to the senior regional judicial officials in February 1943: 'one has to give the police what it is entitled to. One should be happy to leave to the police whatever the judiciary cannot do any more.'[121] In the long term, Thierack envisaged that the legal system would leave the internment of 'incorrigible' Germans and the punishment of 'racial aliens' to the police, and concentrate on the remaining offenders.

The fate of 'racial aliens' was discussed on 18 September 1942 during a meeting between Thierack and SS leader Heinrich Himmler in the latter's field headquarters in Zhitomir, west of Kiev. On the agenda were crucial issues regarding the relationship between judiciary and police. In discussions about the punishment of 'racial aliens', the two men agreed that, in future, criminal offences by Jews, Poles, Sinti and Roma, Russians and Ukrainians should no longer be pursued by the legal courts. Instead, they were to be 'dealt with by the Reichsführer SS'.[122] Thierack informed the legal hierarchy of this agreement during his first meeting with the senior regional judicial officials on 29 September 1942 in Berlin. After outlining various general points, Thierack swore the officials to secrecy for the key part of his speech. He told his listeners that the German people had to colonise the east in order to survive. The local population there had to be 'repressed', 'decimated' and 'exterminated'. 'These are also the thoughts of the Führer,' Thierack added, giving further weight to his remarks. He went on to say that this genocidal task could only be carried out by the police (and the army), not by the court system. After all, Thierack claimed, judges could not be asked to sentence every 'racial alien' to death. Addressing his audience directly, Thierack illustrated his point with an example:

> in the case of a Pole who used a swearword against some farmer on the field or raised the hand against him, you are already not inclined to apply the death penalty. However, it is quite right that the Pole who defies a German is removed and burnt out. But then this should be done by an agency which has nothing to do with the judiciary.

The punishment of 'racial aliens,' Thierack concluded, is 'none of my business, it's up to the police.' None of the leading legal officials criticised Thierack's views. On the contrary, a number of them, such as the Rostock general state prosecutor, agreed that the 'fight against these elements' – as he later put it – was better left to the police.[123] Thierack repeated his thoughts in a letter to Martin Bormann on 13 October 1942, arguing that the judiciary 'could only contribute on a small scale to the extermination of members of these races' (Poles, Russians, Sinti and Roma, and Jews). Handing 'racial aliens' over to the police would 'produce much better results'.[124] This view was shared by Hitler, who approved the agreement between Himmler and Thierack.[125]

But Thierack's decision to withdraw the legal apparatus from the war against 'racial aliens' was realised only in part. As planned, on 1 July 1943, it was publicly announced that 'criminal offences by Jews are punished by the police'. In practice, this did not lead to dramatic changes. True, the legal system had continued to play its part in the assault on Jews during the war. Legal discrimination had increased further, with more than 300 new laws, decrees and ordinances against Jews passed between late 1938 and early 1942. But the overall number of Jews in the Altreich was small and most of their alleged transgressions were already punished by the police. Therefore, Jews had rarely ended up in front of the courts in the early years of the war: in 1940, only 2,697 had been convicted by the courts in the Altreich (1 per cent of all convictions).[126]

Matters proved more complicated in the case of Poles. State and party officials in the incorporated territories in the east were concerned about possible unrest among the local population, if the police took sole charge. Thierack himself had second thoughts about his concession to Himmler. In a meeting with the top regional legal officials in February 1943, Thierack admitted that his earlier decision to leave all Poles to the police had been wrong, not least because the legal system had proved capable of passing extremely brutal sentences after all: 'Thank God, we now treat the Poles with total toughness. If a Pole working for a farmer is defiant and uses a fork or an axe, he has to be exterminated.'[127] The courts had indeed done their best to terrorise the Polish population. According to the incomplete sentencing statistics, some 63,273 individuals (including a small number of Jews) were convicted in 1942 under the new Criminal Law Decree for Poles, which had allowed ever more arbitrary and brutal sentences. The great majority of the convicted Poles received custodial sentences, served under particularly appalling conditions (see Chapter 7).[128]

In light of all this, Thierack now envisaged a sharing of responsibilities between police and legal system in the treatment of Poles. As he explained to the legal officials in February 1943, the judges would deal with serious criminal offences by Poles, such as sex crimes or attacks on Germans, while minor offences and the most dangerous crimes would be left to the police. Instantaneous and bloody police repression of the latter would be most fruitful, Thierack explained. He couldn't care less, he added, whether the police used court-martials or publicly hanged the Poles.[129]

But the police pressed ahead to establish its authority over the punishment of Poles. On 30 June 1943, the RSHA informed its officials that criminal offences by Poles and Russians would generally be dealt with by the police. Court cases would take place only if the police regarded this as desirable for tactical reasons. In such cases, it had to be ensured in advance that the judges would use the death penalty. The Reich Ministry of Justice informed regional officials of this decree two months later. Persecution of 'racial aliens' was now very much in the hands of the police.[130] But contrary to the arguments of many historians, it would be wrong to imply that hardly any Poles now appeared in front of the courts and that only a few were held in penal institutions anymore.[131] There continued to be ambiguity about the demarcation line between the police and the legal system. Regular German courts continued to convict Poles and as late as 30 September 1944, there were still more than 15,000 Poles inside German penal institutions.[132]

Thierack was also determined to rid the prison system of 'incorrigible' criminals. Here, he saw the Law against Community Aliens as the way forward. Such a law had first been conceived by the police in the late 1930s as a way to eradicate social outsiders, including certain criminal offenders. From 1939, the law went through many drafts. Initially, it was opposed by the Reich Ministry of Justice, keen to defend the role of the criminal courts. But after his appointment on 20 August 1942, Thierack championed the law in his discussions with Himmler. According to the Reich Ministry of Justice draft of 1 February 1943, the law was directed at 'asocials', including, among others, 'failures', 'dangerous addicts', 'parasites' and 'good-for-nothings'. The use of this terminology, which could be applied to all non-conformists, once more demonstrates the degree to which legal officials themselves were willing to pervert the principle of legal predictability. The law envisaged that 'asocials' who had committed an offence were to be sentenced by the courts – in line with Thierack's general demand that 'Germans, as soon as they are accused of a criminal offence, are left to the judiciary'. But a number of those convicted by the courts would not remain in the legal system for long. Judges were given different options. Criminals who were regarded as incorrigible were no longer sentenced to imprisonment. Either they were sentenced to death (executed by the legal system) or they were transferred to police confinement. Only offenders who were not yet judged incorrigible received indeterminate penitentiary sentences. If any of them were classified as incorrigible during their sentence, they were also handed over to the police. The explicit aim of the law was to adapt the 1933 Habitual Criminals Law to total war. 'Incorrigibles' were no longer to be 'preserved' (as Hitler had put it) in security confinement. Instead, they should be executed or transferred to the police. The Law against Community Aliens would have redefined the function of the prison system. In future, its sole two purposes would have been the imprisonment of 'reformable' offenders and the extermination of selected 'incorrigibles' using the death penalty.[133] This was never realised in this form, as the draft never became law. But the thinking behind it transformed prison policy from 1942, with thousands of supposedly 'asocial' prisoners being handed over to the police for 'annihilation through labour'.

6 Prison Conditions: from Bad to Worse

During the Second World War, the prison system was even more closely integrated into the Third Reich than before. Prison policy was supposed to contribute to Germany's victory in the war, and the authorities eagerly pursued a variety of measures to reach that goal, strengthening ties with other agencies of the Nazi dictatorship. Most importantly, productive labour moved to the centre of the prison. The use of prisoners for the war economy was relentlessly pursued, inside the already established penal institutions as well as in the expanding satellite camps and in two new prison camps in occupied Europe. For the prisoners, this had very serious consequences. Not only were some forms of prison labour extremely dangerous, but the growing exploitation of prisoners coincided with a significant deterioration in living conditions. Hunger, illness, overcrowding, neglect and violence were common. Consequently, penal institutions saw a sharp rise in the number of deaths in the last years of the war, often caused directly by prison policy and the brutal actions of local officials.

There has been some discussion among historians in recent years about the question of whether forced labour in concentration camps was used intentionally from 1942 to exterminate inmates. Were the camps governed by the primacy of economics or annihilation? In the end, it seems, no simple answer can do justice to the complex realities in the camps, where the two categories often overlapped.[1] Looking at prisoners in penal institutions, it is clear that the authorities used labour as a deliberate policy to exterminate selected groups among them, based on racial and political considerations. This policy of annihilation, pursued from 1942, will be explored in Chapter 8. For the bulk of prisoners, as will be seen in this chapter, death was certainly accepted by the authorities as a possible consequence of hard labour, violence and neglect. But it was not the result of a deliberate murderous strategy, and the large majority of convicts survived their imprisonment – in great contrast to concentration camp inmates.

Prisons as Penal Factories

Even before the Second World War, prison officials had been eager to trumpet the supposed importance of prison labour for the Nazi economy, hoping that this would assure Nazi leaders of the value of the prison service. This fanfare grew louder once war had broken out. The fighting was still in its very early stages when the Reich Ministry of Justice announced its resolve to exploit prisoners' labour power further. On 28 October 1939, less than two months after the Wehrmacht invaded Poland, State Secretary Freisler set much longer working hours for prisoners: inmates in penitentiaries and security confinement were expected to work 12 (previous maximum 10) hours per day and prison inmates 11 (previous maximum nine) hours per day: 'Any refusal to work, laziness and intentionally poor output is to be severely punished', Freisler added.[2]

There can be no doubt that this was primarily a propaganda exercise, designed to demonstrate the determination of the legal system to contribute to the war effort. Freisler himself knew that this measure would have little tangible economic benefit. Only one year earlier, he had himself argued against any increase in working time, as this would actually lower the inmates' relative output, presumably on account of their greater physical exhaustion.[3] The same point was made, to no avail, in late 1939 and 1940 by several general state prosecutors, who criticised Freisler's directive with unusual openness. Just as the general state prosecutors predicted, the measure could not be fully implemented and did little to increase the productivity of prison labour.[4] But this did not stop the top legal officials from publicly boasting about the important contribution of prison labour to the war effort. Thus, in 1940, State Secretary Freisler announced in an article that penal institutions had now been transformed into factories.[5]

In reality, the deployment of prison labour for the war was rather slow. A significant number of prisoners were simply too weak or ill to work productively. At the end of May 1940, more than one in ten prisoners in the Altreich (9,768) were classified as completely or partially 'incapable of work'. And of the 85,877 prisoners who were employed, many thousands continued to be occupied with traditional work such as making paper bags and brooms.

Only 14,746 of them were working directly for the army, largely repairing army uniforms, shoes and civilian clothing for the Wehrmacht. This compares rather unfavourably with the German economy as a whole, where half the industrial labour force was already working on the orders of the armed forces by 1940.[6] In part, the poor infrastructure inside prison workshops was to blame. Following the general reluctance to modernise prison labour over the previous decades, many workshops simply lacked adequate tools. During the war, it proved difficult to make up for this. As late as April 1941, the Reich Ministry of Justice official in charge of labour conceded that 'we have serious problems with the acquisition of machines'.[7] In addition, the army authorities were initially not always very eager to use prisoners, concerned that commercial contractors might lose out. The age-old prejudice against competition from prison labour was still alive and well.[8] Instead, prisoners often filled positions vacated by German workers drafted into the army. Just as in the late 1930s, state and municipal authorities competed with private companies to employ prisoners in a great variety of jobs, ranging from road building and agriculture to grave digging.[9]

But as the war went on, military production did become a top priority in prisons and penitentiaries. This was linked to a general shift in the German war economy as a whole. In the early years, production of armaments had actually stagnated, hampered by ineffective use of the available resources. This changed after the army got stuck in the Soviet Union in late 1941. Now, the rationalisation and expansion of the war economy was pursued with greater urgency. The key figure in this process was Hitler's favourite, Albert Speer, who was appointed Reich Minister of Armaments and Munitions in February 1942. Speer also played the leading role in the new Central Planning Board (part of Göring's Four-Year Plan Office), and oversaw a sharp increase in armaments production. At the same time, the Nazi regime pursued greater use of domestic labour, spearheaded by Fritz Sauckel, the new Plenipotentiary General for Labour Mobilisation.[10] Penal institutions were increasingly incorporated into the war industry. Leading prison officials in Berlin had discussions with Sauckel, Speer and top army officers about the deployment of inmates. There were also regular meetings on a regional and local level. The Reich Ministry of Justice promised to provide more skilled workers and thousands of prisoners were trained as metal-workers. A central index was established in Berlin to ensure that skilled inmates were occupied in their trade.[11]

By 1944, many tens of thousands of convicts were working hard for the German military, part of what Reich Minister of Justice Thierack described as the 'mobilisation' of prisoners.[12] The inmates were working in the production of tanks, aeroplanes, precision weapons, anti-aircraft guns, binoculars, ammunition and bombs. Often, they worked directly for leading German companies, who profited from the cheap labour. Prisoners toiled for firms such as Junkers,

Zeitz, Dornier, Klöcknerwerke, Messerschmidt, Arado, Agfa, Siemens and Bosch. Production for the war increasingly became the yardstick by which a governor's performance was measured. They were expected to exploit every inmate for armaments production. The Dresden general state prosecutor instructed the governors in his district on 3 February 1943, the day after the final surrender of the 6th Army in Stalingrad, to restructure prison labour: 'total war demands the concentration of all strength on achieving final victory'. Many of his colleagues echoed this sentiment. In the following year, the general state prosecutor in Hamm even went so far as to claim that 'today, every prison governor has to be, above all, a good works manager . . .'.[13]

There was constant pressure on prison officials to intensify war production. In February 1944, Albert Speer personally urged Thierack to ensure that prison labour focused almost exclusively on armaments. Speer acknowledged that this was already pursued to some extent. But, he added, 'much more can still be done'. This would help to offset the 'extraordinary lack of workers in the armaments production' and would result in 'great success'. One month later, the Reich Ministry of Justice instructed local officials to replace even more non-essential work with armaments production. Pressure on local officials was kept up in the following weeks. In May 1944, Thierack and Speer sent a joint letter to the general state prosecutors and the armaments inspectors, urging that further prisoners should be made available for armaments production by reducing or closing down less urgent lines of work.[14] This included the 485 inmates in the Kaisheim penitentiary who were still occupied in tailoring, making paper bags and envelopes, and recycling old goods.[15] But, on the whole, both the Nazi leadership and industry were positive about the contribution of the prisoners. Speer's ministry noted already in 1943 that employment of prisoners in the armaments industry had produced good results. And Speer himself valued the prisoners as 'mainly strong, largely trained and easily taught' – a claim which, at best, betrayed his ignorance of the conditions inside penal institutions.[16] Indeed, Speer regarded the contribution of prisoners as 'so good' that he proposed that certain trained inmates should be forced to remain in the factories they worked in even after their sentences ended. After some hesitation, the Reich Ministry of Justice agreed.[17]

The mobilisation of prison labour transformed individual penal institutions. It goes without saying that contemporary claims by prison officials about their supposed successes have to be treated with caution – after all, they continued to fiddle the statistics, designating inferior jobs as 'armaments production'. Still, case studies of individual institutions clearly show that prison labour changed. In March 1938, 170 (out of 400) prisoners in the Untermaßfeld penitentiary had been occupied in weaving mats and recycling old clothes, paper and technical appliances. By July 1944, hardly any Untermaßfeld prisoners were left in this line of work. At the same time, the number of

Untermaßfeld prisoners occupied in metalwork increased from four (March 1938) to 260 (July 1944). More and more inmates were working for companies in the armaments sector. In Untermaßfeld, four of every five prisoners were employed by private contractors in 1944.[18]

The transformation of prison labour did not exclude penal institutions for women. In the early years of the war, many women were still engaged in more traditional types of labour, including sewing, mending and knitting coats, hats and uniforms for soldiers. But towards the end of the war, more and more female prisoners became part of the armaments industry. On the whole, gender distinctions were now less strictly enforced, following demands by the Reich Ministry of Justice that female prisoners should be used in 'male work'.[19] What counted first and foremost was the total exploitation of male and female prisoners for the German war machine. This was also obvious in the Aichach women's penitentiary. In March 1943, 848 (out of 1,645) women were still knitting for the army. After a visit, the Munich general state prosecutor urged that this work had to be cut back. Instead, the women should be used in armaments production. Ten months later, only 250 women (out of 2,175) in Aichach were still knitting. Many of the others were now employed more directly in the war industry, both inside and outside the institution. Indeed, by late November 1944, just over half of the employed women in Aichach were held in satellite camps, working in armaments production.[20] The Reich Ministry of Justice was apparently satisfied with the results of the exploitation of women for the war economy. One official concluded in the summer of 1944 that 'it has been shown that the female prisoners gain the highest achievements also in those types of work, which one previously thought had to be restricted to men . . .'.[21]

The shift towards work in satellite camps was typical of prison labour during the war. Faced with the lack of industrial infrastructure inside penal institutions, it often proved easier for the authorities to set up camps near existing factories, than to move machinery inside penal institutions. During the war, such satellite prison camps mushroomed all over Germany. In the summer of 1938, only 4,042 prisoners (3.8 per cent of all inmates) in the Altreich had been held in such satellite camps. By June 1941, the figure had more than doubled, to 8,380 (7.6 per cent). Numbers continued to shoot up in the following years, reaching 22,890 (15 per cent) in the summer of 1944. By this time, almost twice as many inmates were held in satellite camps as in larger prison camps such as Emsland. Of course, by no means all prisoners in satellite camps worked in armaments factories. But they still worked for the regime, constructing roads, buildings, camps, railroad tracks, factories and air raid shelters. The shift towards satellite camps was especially pronounced among female prisoners. In the summer of 1938, only 147 women (1.6 per cent of all female prisoners) in the Altreich had been held in satellite camps. This figure had only increased to 314 (2.3 per cent) in June 1941. But three years later, it had rocketed to 9,381 (25.5 per cent). Given the rapid rise in female prisoners, the authorities were clearly using the satellite camps as one way of reducing the massive overcrowding inside penal institutions for women, all the more so because women were still excluded from all but one (Oberems) of the larger prison camps.[22]

Among the most dangerous types of work outside penal institutions was that of the bomb disposal squads. Hitler himself had ordered in October 1940 that concentration camp inmates and convicts should be used to neutralise Allied bombs which had not detonated. In July 1942, the Reich Ministry of Justice informed Hitler that the latter had already defused more than 3,000 bombs. Figures continued to rise in 1943, after the Allied air attacks intensified. Prisoners from penal institutions all over Germany were now deployed, supervised by air force and police officials. At first, most of them had officially volunteered, but as fatalities increased, prisoners were taken to bomb disposal units without their consent. Even the decisions of 'volunteers' generally had little to do with the exercise of free will. Many prisoners, both political and criminal offenders, felt that they had no choice. They were often serving lengthy penitentiary sentences and hoped that they might be pardoned for their services (apparently, this impression had been conveyed to them by the prison officials). Otherwise, they faced many more years inside the institutions and transfer to a concentration camp after their sentence, if they survived the imprisonment. But work in the bomb squads proved extremely dangerous for the largely untrained prisoners. Many were blown to pieces. Prisoners saw fellow convicts explode before their eyes and were left to wonder 'when it is our turn' to die, as one of them noted during the war. It is impossible to estimate how many were killed. According to the Reich Ministry of Justice, 27 were already dead by the summer of 1942. Fatalities were certainly much higher in the following years. Reich Ministry of Justice officials noted in 1944, after visiting the Remscheid-Lüttringhausen institution, that half the prisoners in bomb disposal units there were 'lost' each year.[23] Such treatment of convicts contrasts rather sharply with the First World War. From late 1916, prisoners had also been employed directly in the war economy, but the authorities had apparently not worked them much harder than civilians in the armaments industry.[24]

Productivity and Public Relations

The increasing emphasis on productive prison labour was not just a response to total war. It was also linked to the growing weakness of the legal system under the Nazi dictatorship. Following further expansion of the police and Hitler's public criticism of the judiciary in the Reichstag in April 1942, the

Reich Ministry of Justice was keener than ever to impress Nazi leaders with the supposed triumphs of prison labour. From mid-1942, the Ministry stepped up its public-relations offensive to present forced labour for the war as the *raison d'être* of prisons and penitentiaries. In early summer 1942, carefully stage-managed tours for journalists to penal institutions were set up, resulting in several glowing articles. One Berlin paper, for example, reported that an 'unbelievable amount of labour power' was activated by pushing inmates to their very limits. Nazi leaders and senior army officials, the prison administration decided, were also to be invited to visit prison workshops.[25]

Top legal officials developed an unprecedented interest in penal institutions. In recognition of its new-found importance, the prison administration was elevated in the summer of 1942 from a sub-section to an independent department in the Reich Ministry of Justice (section V). The new Minister of Justice Otto-Georg Thierack became personally involved in the organisation of prison labour, asking the ministerial official responsible, Siegmund Nörr, to report directly to him.[26] Thierack was apparently proud of the results. In an article sent to Goebbels's Ministry of Propaganda in 1944, he bragged about the contribution of prisoners to the armaments industry: 'From the smallest accessory to the finished missile – be it for the infantry, artillery, anti-aircraft defence or navy – everything is carried out by prisoners.'[27]

Prison labour dominated the only film known to have been shot inside Nazi prisons, *Work and Imprisonment in the Brandenburg-Görden Penitentiary* (1942). This film, which may have been intended for the recruitment or training of legal officials (it is unclear whether it was ever shown), was used as another opportunity to showcase prison labour. At the centre of imprisonment, according to the film, stood 'hard and long labour . . . an unpaid service for the national community'. Much of the film consists of shots of different prison workshops, with the narrator boasting about the amount of goods supposedly produced in each one. Prison labour was presented as highly efficient and productive, creating 'enormous revenue'. Beyond work, the film gives few glimpses of what happened to inmates, presenting life behind bars as well-ordered, with plenty of food, clean clothes and dedicated medical care. In 1942, this picture was of course largely fictitious.[28]

The main target of the campaign to spotlight prison labour was Hitler himself. From May 1942 onwards, immediately following Hitler's public attack on the judiciary, the Reich Ministry of Justice produced regular bulletins, so-called *Führer-Informations*, typeset by inmates in the print workshop in Tegel prison. In large typeface (in consideration of his poor eyesight), Hitler was updated on the reputed successes of the legal system.[29] Several of the bulletins highlighted the productivity of prison labour. Early on, the bulletins were especially keen to draw attention to the output of the security-confined prisoners, betraying the underlying anxiety of leading prison officials that the police might gain jurisdiction over these 'dangerous habitual criminals' if they were not seen to be working productively. For example, in June 1942, the Reich Ministry of Justice put together a *Führer-Information* detailing the work carried out by male prisoners in security confinement. The bulletin tried to impress Hitler by stressing that almost all the inmates were occupied with 'work important for the war effort' – more than half of them directly for the army. In the following month, Hitler was sent another bulletin, this time proudly announcing that more than 1,100 security-confined prisoners had been trained as metal-workers, to be employed in armaments factories.[30] These bulletins have to be read with some caution. Confidential ministerial statistics, on which the bulletins were based, reveal that the prison officials were not very candid with Hitler. To start with, the term 'work important for the war effort' in reality included activities which had little obvious relevance to the war at all. In addition, Hitler was not told that almost 10 per cent of the security-confined prisoners were officially classified as not fully fit for work, with another 5 per cent not working at all. In fact, these numbers were even higher, as the proportion of ill and frail inmates in security confinement continued to grow daily.[31]

The desire to impress Hitler with the achievements of prison labour continued almost until the end of the war. In 1943, the Reich Ministry of Justice decided to attract Hitler's attention with visual aids. In May and June 1943, the general state prosecutors were asked to assemble photographs of prisoners at work, in some cases in secret armaments production.[32] The photos were then collected and sent to Hitler, who apparently spent some time examining the pictures. During a meeting with general state prosecutors in October 1943, Thierack announced that he had spent five days in the 'Führer's' headquarters and that Hitler had even remembered what products were made in each penal institution.[33] The public-relations offensive by the legal system carried on in the following year. As late as November 1944, the Reich Ministry of Justice informed Hitler that the earnings of penal institutions had almost tripled between 1940 (53 million Reichsmark) and 1943 (153 million Reichsmark) thanks to the 'extensive deployment for work' of prisoners.[34]

Prison labour certainly became more profitable during the war. Thanks to the labour shortage inside Germany, prison authorities were paid more than previously for 'renting out' inmates to private industry. In 1939, one penal institution was already said to be operating with an overall profit, with several others supposedly close to reaching the same target by 1941.[35] Indeed, the inmates' meagre 'reward' for their labour also increased during the war, in individual cases by substantial margins. The prison authorities, keen to raise output, also paid bonuses to particularly productive inmates. But this money was not always of great use to the prisoners, as wartime shortages made it increasingly difficult to buy extra provisions. In addition, prisoners now often received no money for their labour at all. For example, the new national prison guidelines of 22 July 1940 had introduced the rule that all convicts had to be treated more strictly during the early period of their imprisonment. This meant, among other things, that penitentiary inmates were not paid for their work during the first six months of their sentence. (The same rule was applied to the first three months of each prison sentence.)[36]

The ideological approach to prison labour – the transformation of institutions into penal factories – may have enhanced the standing of the prison service, but it further subverted various elements of the prison regulations, much to the annoyance of some more traditionally minded officials. To start with, the rule that 'dangerous' inmates had to be isolated was incompatible with the desire to mobilise inmates for productive labour. This rule had already been undermined before the war, and this process now continued. What counted was often not so much how 'dangerous' the inmates were, but how hard they worked. As a result, individual inmates previously isolated in single cells, including some classified as 'active homosexuals' and 'spies', were now moved to large workshops or to outside labour. This policy was often encouraged from above. State Secretary Freisler himself ordered in 1941 that political prisoners should be employed in important work for the war effort.[37]

The growing focus on productive prison labour also created new opportunities for the prisoners. Communication between them became easier and inmates also came into closer contact with the outside world. Working in factories, it often proved impossible to keep them apart from other forced workers such as concentration camp inmates, prisoners of war and foreign workers. In the factories, convicts also encountered civilian employees, who were often their supervisors. At times, these employees were armed and acted no differently from brutal warders. But others helped the prisoners, some out of pity, others for bribes. Through these civilians, prisoners received information about the outside world, as well as newspapers and food. A number of employees agreed to take letters to the families of inmates. Prisoners also had more contact with the general population.[38] One member of a bomb squad noted that 'everywhere we go, once the people hear who we are, their sympathy is immediately on our side and the questions begin . . .'.[39]

Some political prisoners used their liberty to engage in isolated acts of resistance, taking astonishing risks. Walter Uhlmann, a former activist in a Communist splinter group, had been imprisoned in Brandenburg-Görden since 1937, sentenced by the People's Court to eight years' penitentiary. Towards the end of the war, Uhlmann became the orderly responsible for the maintenance of the prison truck. In this capacity, he was allowed to accompany the driver almost every week on trips to Berlin, driving to other penal institutions, suppliers and businesses. Uhlmann developed such a close relationship with the driver that the official apparently allowed him several times to get off on his own in town. As Uhlmann recalled after the war, he used these brief spells of freedom to visit his fiancée, giving her letters from other inmates to distribute. Once, he even met up with a former political associate, who handed him propaganda material to take back into the penitentiary.[40]

The growth of outside labour also inevitably resulted in more and more escapes, as work outside the walls of penal institutions presented inmates with greater opportunities to flee. The number of escapes had started to increase before the war. Now, facing the prospect of lengthy sentences under rapidly deteriorating conditions, many more took the risk. Their chances of success were helped by the increasing shortage of qualified warders (see also below).[41] In 1940, an average of 87 prisoners fled every month from penal institutions in the Altreich and Austria, causing senior legal officials privately to warn about this 'threat to public safety'.[42] And the longer the war lasted, the more prisoners escaped. This led to some disquiet among the German population, following reports of such escapes in the local press. In 1942, on average over 200 prisoners escaped every month, even though they knew that they risked their lives, for at least some prison officials pursued a shoot-to-kill policy.[43] Prisoners captured alive faced draconian punishment. Many were brutally beaten, even more so than before the war. One Dutch prisoner recalled that recaptured convicts in the Remscheid-Lüttringhausen penitentiary received 15 lashes with a rubber truncheon.[44] After these beatings, the inmates were taken for several weeks into strict detention, often in pitch-black and freezing cells.

Brutal as this punishment was, many inmates were still not deterred from escaping. On the contrary, the number of escapes continued to rise. By 1943–44, an average of almost 300 prisoners managed to escape each month, most of them from satellite and prison camps.[45] In response, in early 1944, the prison officials in Berlin decided to intimidate prisoners by introducing even more severe sanctions. It was envisaged that recaptured inmates would be taken to a special penal institution. Here, they would be subjected to harsher treatment than usual. They would be occupied with particularly heavy labour and warders would discharge their weapons at the slightest provocation.[46] In the following months, the Berlin officials considered a number of institutions as possible sites, all of them known for their dangerous working conditions and the high rate of injuries and fatalities. Following personal intervention by Thierack, angry that no decision had yet been reached, the officials in June 1944 hastily settled on the Ensisheim penitentiary in Alsace.[47] But only a few dozen prisoners had been taken to Ensisheim when the Reich Ministry of Justice stopped the transports in September 1944, following the rapid advances of Allied troops in the west. Individual governors were now told to introduce, in their own institutions, stricter treatment for recaptured prisoners, as well as for inmates sentenced for mutiny or attacking officials.[48] This was partially realised. In Brandenburg-Görden, for example, recaptured inmates had their heads shaven with a bald strip running from the forehead to the back of the head, received only half their normal rations, had to work even more than before and received no privileges or pay.[49] But prisoners continued to flee until the very last days of the war, desperate to escape the catastrophic living conditions.

Life and Death in Prisons

The exploitation of the inmates for the war effort caused great suffering. The work was hard and exhausting, making a mockery of the passage in the 1940 national prison guidelines, which stated that 'during work, damage to the health of prisoners should be avoided'.[50] Prisoners in some workshops were forced to work 12-hour shifts, day and night, to make full use of new machinery, and the daily work quota was often set so high that the prisoners had to suffer. Some were occupied with particularly dangerous work. Apart from the bomb disposal squads, this included, for example, work at the Rheika (Rheinische Kunstseide AG) silk factory in Krefeld-Linn, carried out by female prisoners from the Anrath penitentiary. At the end of 1941, the Anrath governor had effectively sold some of his prisoners to the factory. He signed a contract with the factory officials, who agreed to provide accommodation, food and clothing for the women. The factory also paid for the accommodation of warders who helped to guard the prisoners. The penitentiary received about 3.60 Reichsmark daily for each prisoner. In return, the women had to work about 60 hours each week, including Sundays. The factory was entitled to make them work even longer, at no extra charge.[51]

The prisoners at the Rheika factory, including political and non-German prisoners, were forced to operate one silk spinning machine each. The women were protected far less than German civilian workers in the same factory. They had no protective goggles, gloves or boots. As a result, they suffered severe burns from spilt acid. Florence P., one of the few British convicts in Nazi prisons, recalled the work at Rheika, after the war:

> The process of silkmaking used here was that the juice came up through the pumps and ran through a strong solution of nitric acid which had to be kept at a high temperature in order to cook it. Usually the fumes were cut off by glass but at the spinheads operated by prisoners the preventive glass was omitted. We had to stand over this steaming acid ten and more hours a day. The fumes caused our eyes to be blistering inside the lid of the eye and behind the eye causing a swelling and excruciating pains in the head and eyes. Water poured out of the eyes, nose and mouth causing

a suffocating sensation. The eyes themselves would swell up and eventually close.[52]

The female prisoners at Rheika were supervised by civilian foremen who routinely beat them. One foreman admitted after the war that he had attacked the prisoners. He claimed that his superiors had told him: 'If they do not obey, kick them in their behinds, hit them in their faces, and beat them in their mouths'.[53] Only when a prisoner was completely blinded by the fumes, or had collapsed, could she stop working. But after a few hours, she was forced back to the machine. Medical care was practically non-existent. A French prisoner, sentenced in 1942 for political resistance against the Germans, recalled after the war that a group of about 20 prisoners once tried to see the factory doctor. They waited,

> some with bleeding ulcers about six inches in diameter, others with boils caused by acid poisoning, some with bad eyes, others with burnt hands. It was like a group of medieval beggars. The doctor came out of the housekeeper's room, and exclaimed 'Oh my God!', pushed her way through the unfortunate women, chasing them with a 'ugh, ugh!' and walked downstairs.[54]

Conditions at Rheika were so bad that officials from the Reich Ministry of Justice, following an inspection of the factory, eventually asked for a medical report on the prisoners' health, only to be reassured by the Düsseldorf prison doctor that everything was fine.[55] The women at Rheika were not the only prisoners exposed to such hazardous work. Similar labour was carried out by convicts in other factories. There, too, many prisoners were severely poisoned or injured, some fatally.

Hunger, Illness, Overcrowding

While efforts to profit from prison labour intensified, rations were slashed. Inmates in carceral institutions were expected to subsist on lower rations than the rest of the German population, as was the case during the First World War, when provisions in workhouses, asylums and penal institutions had also been cut severely as resources were diverted to more 'deserving' parts of the population. In the Second World War, prisoners were officially entitled to no more provisions than concentration camp inmates. Rations for prisoners were fixed on 16 January 1940 by the Reich Ministry for Food and Agriculture. It decided that, despite the hard physical labour expected of them, they would receive significantly less meat, fat and flour than the general population. As the food supply inside Nazi Germany deteriorated, there were further cuts. By April 1944, the weekly prisoner ration of fat had been cut to 162 grams (from 200) and the meat allowance had been halved to 200 grams of horse and cheap meat. By contrast, civilians were eligible to receive 235 grams of fat and 362 grams of meat per week. In addition, civilians could of course further improve their food supply in shops or by barter on the black market.[56]

Prisoners often received even less food than they were entitled to. Much depended on the individual penal institution. Some places of confinement like Bernau, which owned sufficient agricultural land, were still able to provide inmates with the essentials, at least until the last years of the war.[57] But others were already experiencing severe shortages in 1940. Vegetables were particularly scarce. Peas and beans were often absent, and there were severe shortages of potatoes, which had traditionally played a central part in the prisoners' diet.[58] One female prisoner, held in the Anrath penitentiary, recalled the rations she had received for many months in 1941 and 1942:

> The food consisted of: for breakfast, one thin slice of bread and one cup of substitute coffee; for lunch, one litre of thinned soup; in the afternoons, one thin slice of bread and half a litre of substitute coffee; and for dinner, half a litre of thinned soup and one thin slice of bread ... During the entire time, I only once received a portion of potatoes. I remember the date, it was 1 November 1941.[59]

Nutrition inside German penal institutions was probably still better than during the First World War, when conditions had collapsed to catastrophic levels after the disastrous 'turnip winter' of 1916–17. This was linked to the comparatively better general food situation in Germany during the Second World War, not least due to the brutal Nazi plunder of resources in occupied Europe. Of course, rations were progressively cut, but the general supply remained reasonably stable until the end of 1944.[60] Even so, some prisoners were soon so hungry that they ate raw seeds, waste, animal fodder and mouldy carrots.[61] The former inmate Victor von Gostomski, who had worked in a bookbinding workshop, gave a vivid description shortly after the war of the conditions in 1943 in the Plötzensee prison:

> It was hunger that drove us to eat what we had cut off from the rollers of the printing presses. Hunger made us wolf down glue and dextrin. During the exercise, comrades grabbed leaves from the trees in the prison yard to cook a soup at their places of work. At the time, some wished that they could look after the guard dogs. The dog food in the prison was good: horse meat, potatoes, cereal. For us, these were unattainable delicacies.[62]

The impact of the strict forced labour and small rations on the prisoners' health was serious.

Throughout 1940, local officials reported weight losses among many inmates. In some cases, prisoners lost 20 kilos and more.[63] The Untermaßfeld prison doctor warned that malnourishment would lead to 'serious physical damage'.[64] Inmates were getting weaker and weaker. One female prisoner in the Cottbus penitentiary reported in May 1940 that 'one after the other collapses. This is not surprising, given the small rations . . . In the evening, I can hardly stand up. 12 hours' labour is a bit much. We are growing old and drained before our time.'[65] In the following years malnourishment became worse. In some institutions, the great majority of prisoners were emaciated. In Bochum prison in 1942, less than one in ten inmates were of normal weight. Two years later, the Zweibrücken prison doctor reported that well over half the inmates were underweight by more than 15 per cent.[66]

The security-confined prisoners, weaker and older than most other convicts, were hit particularly hard by the deteriorating living conditions in the early 1940s. Security confinement developed such a fearsome reputation that some offenders mutilated themselves in the expectation that this would save them from being sentenced to it.[67] The effective ban on release had a significant impact. From 1940, the Reich Ministry of Justice tried to ensure that the courts would reject the release of any inmates from security confinement – a measure designed in part to pre-empt accusations by the police that the legal authorities released dangerous criminals and thus failed to protect society from crime. Even critically ill inmates were now denied release.[68] In Brandenburg-Görden, inmates on the wing reserved for security confinement lost three times more weight in 1940 than penitentiary inmates in the same institution. One of them was the petty thief Karl Kakuschky (see p. 133). In April 1940, he wrote a desperate letter to his brother:

> In all likelihood, this will probably be my last letter; for I am now certain that I will not leave this house alive. [I] am nothing more than a wreck, compared to before. With my height of 1.68 m, I weigh only 51 kg, thus I am nothing more than skin and bones. [I] am totally malnourished.

Kakuschky added that two of his fellow inmates had died recently. The other inmates were 'teasing me that I am probably next in line'. He managed to survive for a few more years, but he grew weaker and weaker. In September 1942, he wrote another letter to his brother:

> My normal weight for my height is supposed to be 67 kilos, and now you will definitely be shocked; for at the moment I weigh exactly 43.3 kilos, that's 87 pounds. You can imagine what I look like. The only wish I have, is to once eat my fill; for I am always hungry . . . Hopefully, the war will be over soon, otherwise one will come to grief after all.

His brother never received these two letters. Both were held back by the prison authorities, who strictly forbade the prisoners to make any reference to weight loss.[69] There were so many frail inmates in security confinement that the Reich

Ministry of Justice from 1941 even designated the penal institution in Tapiau (East Prussia) for some particularly old and weak security-confined inmates. However, with room for only 155 inmates at maximum in Tapiau, many frail prisoners remained in their old institutions.[70]

Chronic deficiency caused many illnesses among the different prisoners. Thousands were suffering from famine oedema and open wounds all over their bodies. Others were covered with scabies and lice. Illness and epidemics spread quickly and raged in numerous prisons and penitentiaries. In 1943 alone, there were several outbreaks of typhus, scarlet fever and diphtheria in penal institutions all over Germany.[71] The spread of disease was accelerated by the often extreme overcrowding, once more prevalent during the war.

Inside the Altreich, female prisoners (and inmates in youth prisons) were hit hardest by the overcrowding, as more and more women were convicted by the courts.[72] The prison authorities had not been prepared for the sharp rise in female convicts, even though the same situation had occured during the First World War. As early as 30 June 1941, the 13,136 female prisoners in the Altreich already exceeded available places by about 2,400 – at a time when the number of male prisoners in the Altreich was still slightly below the maximum. (Many institutions for men were overcrowded nonetheless, as official capacity figures were often set at a very high level.)[73] This situation grew much worse over the following years, as convictions of women continued to increase. True, women were still less likely than men to receive custodial sentences. Even so, by June 1943, women in the Altreich already accounted for 23 per cent of prisoners – up from only 9 per cent in the summer of 1939. Penal institutions for women were bursting with inmates. By 30 June 1944, there were 19,466 women inside the larger regular penal institutions – exceeding their maximum capacity by about 8,600. This situation would have been even more critical had the prison authorities not decided to hold increasing numbers of female prisoners in satellite camps, as we have seen. In addition, the prison authorities had, over the previous years, designated more and more prisons and penitentiaries for women (some had previously been wings or entire penal institutions for men, others were former prisons attached to local courts). The total number of 'special penal institutions' reserved for women increased from six (1935) to 16 (1944), including youth prisons.[74]

The immediate consequence of overcrowding was very cramped and unhygienic conditions. In the Aichach women's institution, the prison population exceeded the regular capacity by around 250 as early as 1940. This meant that two or three inmates were often forced to share a single cell. As more and more women arrived in Aichach over the next few years, the prison authorities turned a chapel into four large makeshift community cells to provide extra space. As a result, maximum capacity increased to 828 (1943). But this was nowhere near enough to cope with the rise in prisoner numbers, with some 1,645 women in Aichach by 25 March 1943. By early 1945 the prisoner numbers in the main building (with a capacity for about 500 inmates) had risen even further, to over 2,000, with four or five prisoners now crammed into one single cell.[75]

Overcrowding led to massive problems, despite attempts by numerous local officials to maintain strict order and cleanliness. In the last years of the war, showers for inmates and clean clothes became rare. Inmates often had to wear the same clothes, encrusted with dirt and oil from the workshops and factories, for six months and more. Further pressures were created by the temporary imprisonment in prisons and penitentiaries of individuals from outside the regular court system, such as police prisoners in transit. For example, on the night of 16 June 1942, some 434 police detainees were held in the Klingelpütz prison in Cologne, many more than could be accommodated in the wing usually reserved for police use. The inmates had to be distributed throughout the entire institution, causing chaos and very poor conditions. According to the prison governor: 'The prisoners were lying on the bare floor, sat on school benches or stood upright for several days.'[76]

Most prisoners could not hope for proper medical treatment, with the exception of some more valued inmates (such as skilled workers). Long before the war, the treatment of ill prisoners had often been characterised by neglect and brutality. During the war, this became worse. There was less medication and fewer supplies, and doctors were absent more often than before, working instead for the army or the general population. Many prison doctors only visited for a few hours a week. It was not unusual for larger penal institutions to be temporarily without a prison doctor. If the inmates were lucky, they were seen instead by medical students, prison warders without qualification or imprisoned doctors.[77]

Once again, the situation was grave for the growing number of pregnant prisoners. Even basic supplies, including food, towels, soap and sterile cotton, were now lacking. With doctors often absent, women injured during birth sometimes had to wait for days before receiving proper care. Some women had arrived only a few days before giving birth. The heavily pregnant French prisoner Henriette C., for example, arrived in the Aichach institution on 10 April 1944, after more than three weeks on a prisoner transport. Her child, born on the very next day, only lived for a few months. In such cases, it was not unusual for the authorities to deduct the funeral costs from the prisoner's sparse earnings. Babies who survived were soon separated from their mothers and often put into children's homes. Some former prisoners searched for them in vain for years after the war.[78]

Violence and Punishment

Many prison officials were determined to work the inmates to the point of exhaustion, regardless of their state of health. Instead of medical treatment, many sick prisoners were disciplined when they failed to reach their quota. They were accused of being lazy and punished with food cuts or detention, as the political prisoner Erwin Köbrich, held in Brandenburg-Görden for treason, explained to his parents in 1942:

> Due to lack of sufficient food, I am in very bad shape a[nd] have no prospect of regaining what I have lost. Three months ago, my weight was 49 kilos (now, maybe only 46 or 47 kilos) . . . Naturally, this weakened condition has also affected my productivity. My situation was made even worse when my additional rations were cut because of [my] decline in output, which means that I physically deteriorate further . . . I fear the worst.[79]

Weakened by punishment, the prisoners were even less likely to work as hard as the authorities demanded. For a number of frail inmates, this vicious circle ended in death. One of them was the Czech prisoner Johann Pilnacek, who had been taken to Brandenburg-Görden in 1941, sentenced as a 'national pest' to four years' penitentiary. Pilnacek suffered from tuberculosis and his health deteriorated quickly. Still, he was forced from February 1943 to work in the Brennabor armaments factory. One year later, he was finally too weak to work at all. But the prison doctor did not believe him and demanded that he be punished for laziness. His rations were temporarily cut and in desperation, he tried to kill himself. Only in May 1944 did the authorities finally accept that he really was ill. Johann Pilnacek was taken to the prison hospital, where he died in early July 1944.[80] Cuts in food and detention were not the only punishment for 'lazy' prisoners. Prison officials and civilian workers did not hesitate to beat them during work.[81]

During the war, many ordinary Germans assumed that convicts were often beaten.[82] This was probably not true in the early years of the war. Available evidence suggests that in this period violence was only endemic in some institutions, above all in the Emsland prison camp (see below). Some warders from other penal institutions who visited this camp were shocked by the open brutality.[83] But, as the war continued, physical violence spread to other penal institutions. All over Germany, prisoners were now regularly punched and kicked by prison warders. Some governors were also involved. Outbursts were difficult to predict as almost any behaviour could serve as the pretext for a vicious beating. Inmates were beaten for reporting sick, for walking too slowly, for hiding potatoes or bread. In 1944, the prisoner Georg B., suffering from a high temperature, was beaten in a hospital ward until he bled because he was unable to salute properly. Afterwards, the warder shouted: 'if only you were already dead, then there would be another loafer less, and I will even get a medal for it'.[84]

How can the extent of this violence be explained? The growing pressure on officials working in penal institutions certainly played its part. Conditions were often difficult, exacerbated by the extreme shortage of prison personnel.

During the war, while inmate numbers continued to rise, the number of officials declined, after thousands of younger men had been drafted into the army. According to Reich Minister Thierack, the ratio of all personnel to inmates shifted from 1:6 (1939) to almost 1:14 (1944). Some 19,000 extra officials would have been needed in 1944 to reach the 1939 ratio.[85] The shortages put further pressure on the officials. Many could no longer cope and called in sick.[86] Others took out their frustration on the prisoners. Local prison officials were also brutalised by war in general, and the Nazi war against criminals in particular. With Hitler and Thierack referring to criminals as enemies who deserved to die, the officials probably felt free to lash out at offenders behind bars. Indeed, many of them witnessed the murderous crusade against offenders at first hand, as more than 30,000 inmates were executed inside penal institutions or transferred to be killed in concentration camps (see Chapter 8). Not surprisingly, violence by prison officials became widespread.

But by no means all officials raised their hand against prisoners. The fate of each prisoner still often depended on the individual warders they encountered. Different mentalities are obvious when looking at those officials newly appointed during the war. They included a number of party members, who signed up after the prison authorities had asked the SS, the Hitler Youth, the Reich Women's Leader and the SA for recruits. In the eyes of the Reich Ministry of Justice SA men were 'especially suited because of their ideologically reliable attitude and their habit of strict discipline'.[87] Some prisoners recalled that these party members were among the more brutal warders.[88] The reverse was true for many civilians employed as prison officials during the war. Having worked in jobs deemed not vital for the war effort, they had been conscripted to fill vacant positions as prison warders. They had no desire to serve in penal institutions and the Reich Ministry of Justice soon complained about their lack of responsibility, claiming that some were open to bribery. Berlin officials also worried that some of the civilians had a tendency 'to deal with the prisoners in an almost friendly way'.[89] Some new warders did indeed behave in an unorthodox manner. For example, the 23-year-old maid Maria U. was employed as a prison official in 1943. Working in a satellite prison camp, she apparently started a clandestine relationship with a male penitentiary inmate, to whom she got engaged soon after his release. Her superiors were apoplectic.[90]

A number of experienced warders were not violent towards the inmates either. Many of them had been in the prison service since the 1920s and had not been drafted into the army because of their advanced age. A few of these officials were motivated by compassion. In postwar accounts, former prisoners emphasised that individual officials had been 'quiet', 'very correct', 'pretty humane', 'popular' and 'clean'.[91] More commonly, the experienced warders were keen to adhere to the prison regulations, as they did in the pre-war period.

Instead of lashing out, they relied on the official catalogue of disciplinary punishment and reported 'disobedient' prisoners to the governor. Such disciplinary punishment became harsher than before the war. Strict detention, previously restricted to penitentiaries, was extended to all penal institutions and its maximum duration was extended from one to two weeks. The Reich Ministry of Justice also decreed that any time spent in detention for disciplinary offences no longer counted as part of the sentence: the more time prisoners spent in detention, the longer they had to spend in the penal institution.[92]

As the war went on, prison officials handed out extremely brutal disciplinary punishment even for the most trivial reasons. Prisoners were thrown into detention, often for several weeks, for transgressions such as keeping rosaries in their pocket, walking out of step, looking out of the window and losing a handkerchief.[93] For the inmates, already weak and exhausted, detention was a serious threat. Walter Hammer, a political prisoner, was punished harshly after being denounced for political comments he had made to fellow prisoners:

> Seven dark weeks in winter in the unheated hole in the cellar, including four weeks without a sip of warm coffee or tea, without a bite of warm food. In the mornings, I received 500 grams of bread for the whole day and a jug of cold, clear water. In the evenings, two woollen blankets were handed into the cell. There were also exceptions when I received none. Each night was a life-or-death struggle, because one had to lie on a block of stone, a brick platform, which continually drained strength and warmth from the abused body.[94]

Sometimes, prisoners were chained to the floor or the walls during detention, reviving a form of punishment common in German penal institutions in the nineteenth century.[95] In a number of cases, disciplinary punishment hastened the inmate's death.

Death

Thousands of prisoners died during the Second World War. Most succumbed to the meagre rations and the exhausting labour, which from 1942 proved a lethal combination. Typical causes of death included heart failure, pneumonia and tuberculosis. Obviously, the legal authorities cannot be blamed for every one of those deaths, which also have to be seen in the context of general wartime conditions and discrimination on the outside. Many convicts, especially non-Germans, arrived already in poor health, and food and other shortages were often out of the hands of senior prison officials. Most officials had no particular interest in deliberately starving prisoners to death, given that the use of forced labour had become the central justification for the prison service. The officials in the Reich Ministry of Justice even occasionally tried to improve the basic level of food inside penal institutions. In 1940, for example, the prison administration secured better rations for the minority of inmates working extra-long hours and nights.[96]

At the same time, though, the lives of many convicts clearly had no great value for the prison officials. Particularly weak inmates could contribute little to prison labour, and once they died, they were quickly replaced by new convicts, thanks to the zeal of the German judges. In addition, any interest in the prisoners' well-being was generally eclipsed by the desire for their brutal punishment and exploitation for the war effort. Many officials believed that prisoners deserved harsher treatment at a time when 'national comrades' faced more difficulties than before. Leading officials in the Reich Ministry of Justice were also extremely keen to demonstrate to the Nazi leadership that prisoners were not pampered. Deaths of prisoners were seen as regrettable, but largely unavoidable.

In reality, many deaths could have been prevented. The legal authorities had several options for improving the prisoners' lot. For example, they could have cut back on quotas and working hours; they could have stopped the most hazardous types of work; they could have banned the most brutal types of disciplinary punishment; and they could have allowed prisoners to receive food parcels from the outside. None of these options was taken. Instead, penal policy helped to create the lethal conditions. Even the shortages of provisions inside penal institutions were, in part, of prison officials' own making. Thus, keen as ever to demonstrate its allegiance to the Nazi cause, the Reich Ministry of Justice decided in the winter of 1941–42 to donate prison property to German soldiers in the Soviet Union. The collection yielded some 42,612 woollen blankets, 55,748 socks and 4,904 jumpers, leaving prisoners even more exposed than before.[97]

Although leading prison officials were clearly not greatly concerned about the inmates' fate, few could have been as openly cynical as the Jena official Dr Werner Wurmstich, the longest-serving general state prosecutor in Nazi Germany, in office since 1929. In late May 1944, Wurmstich participated in a seminar for leading legal officials at Castle Kochem. Over three days, the officials discussed various problems, including the fatalities in penal institutions. They also listened to a secret speech by Reichsführer SS Heinrich Himmler. After each of the sessions, the officials retired for lunch and dinner, which was served, in a strange twist, by selected convicts. Wurmstich was greatly offended by the sight of these badly dressed prisoners, which somewhat spoilt his enjoyment of the chamber music and the lavish meals at the conference. In a letter to Thierack, he complained that the prisoners' 'white uniforms were unclean. Their shoes were also badly polished. It was unpleasant that prisoners in patched blue uniforms carried the food from the kitchen, down the stairs, to the entrance of the dining room. They should also be dressed in white.' Dr Wurmstich also complained that the quality of the bottled beer served during the seminar was poor. 'Maybe,' he suggested helpfully, 'it would be sensible to open a small barrel of beer at lunch time and in the evening.' Dr Wurmstich was not just after beer. He was also unhappy that the discussions had lasted too long. Next time, he proposed, 'it would be nice in the afternoon to visit the famous wine sites at the Mosel . . .'.[98] It is not known whether this, or any other of Wurmstich's wishes, were satisfied at the next meeting in Kochem, three months later. What is clear, however, is that while Wurmstich was waiting for his answer, prisoners in his district were slowly starving to death.

A number of prisoners died during air raids on Germany, which were stepped up dramatically in the last years of the war. By late May 1944, more than 26 prison buildings had been seriously damaged, often leaving them for many weeks without running water, electricity or heating. Two prison camps and three other penal institutions, including one part of the Plötzensee prison, were almost or completely destroyed. At least 180 prisoners had died in the various attacks.[99] Many victims were opponents of the regime and had prayed for the Allies to win the war. Instead of being liberated, they were smashed by masonry or burned to death in their cells. Once again, the prison authorities bear much of the responsibility for these deaths. It would have been perfectly possible, in most prisons and penitentiaries, to take prisoners to cellars. Indeed, this had still occurred in many institutions in the early stages of Allied bombing. Later, however, the administration kept inmates locked in their cells during air raids although exceptions were made for female prisoners, whose screams of terror were thought to interfere with air raid protection measures. Once the alarm sounded, warders went into their bunkers; the prisoners were left to their fate.[100] Leading legal officials approved of this policy. Some, such as the Düsseldorf general state prosecutor, even claimed that prisoners should be thankful:

> Because there are no air raid shelters for prisoners, they remain in their cells during the alarms at night, so that they are not distracted by going to the cellars, taking along valuables and the emotional strain of looking after and calming the relatives, notably the children. The prisoners, who do not have to worry at all about clothes and food and the problems surrounding this at the moment, also enjoy on average a longer rest at night than the other national comrades.[101]

In reality, the 'emotional strain' on prisoners during the attacks was immense. One former inmate, the priest Josef Reuland, recalled one attack on the Münster penitentiary in 1944: 'As the whole building was swaying from side to side like a tree, in particular the fourth floor where my cell was, and I heard the shattering of the roof beams, thinking that it must collapse any moment and everything would be buried under the debris, I escaped into my psalms . . .'.[102]

The total number of deaths in penal institutions during the Second World War can only be guessed. It is possible that some 20,000 inmates died inside the larger prisons, penitentiaries and prison camps, not counting those who were executed after being sentenced to death. The vast majority of deaths of prisoners occurred in the last years of the war. In almost all penal institutions, fatalities increased enormously after 1941. In a sample of seven penal institutions, the average number of officially recorded deaths shot up from nine (1941) to 42 (1942), rising further to 56 deaths (1943). The growing threat to prisoners' lives is most obvious when the prewar years are taken into account: in the second half of the war, around 15 times more inmates died than before the war.[103] In the face of the growing death toll behind bars, the authorities decided to pass on some cheap advice to the prisoners. On 20 December 1942 the national prison newspaper, delivered to most inmates, featured an article entitled: 'How to draw up a will'.[104]

Torment in Prison Camps

The creation of large camps had been one of the major innovations in prison policy during the prewar years. They were retained during the war, when camps such as Rodgau, Oberems and Griebo continued to operate. The largest prison camp was still the Emsland camp, reserved for male prisoners. During the war, a great variety of men were taken to Emsland, including Poles, Jews, Belgians, and Germans in security confinement. But most inmates in the Emsland camp were Germans sentenced by military and civilian courts as so-called 'war offenders'. At the end of March 1941, 6,400 of the 8,100 prisoners in Emsland were 'war offenders', to be interned under 'aggravated conditions' until the war was over, and only then would their sentences of imprisonment officially begin.[105]

Inmates in the Emsland camp faced extreme conditions. Life was already very hard in the first years of the war, and conditions deteriorated rapidly thereafter. Inmates were forced to carry out extremely exhausting labour, while their rations became smaller and smaller. Many prisoners were so hungry that they ate grass, leaves, bones and potato peelings.[106] The consequence of the woefully inadequate rations, brutal treatment and hard labour in the Emsland camp was a dramatic increase in illness. In March 1941, the camp doctor reported that sometimes well over 10 per cent of inmates were so sick and weak that they could not work. The recorded cases of inmates taken to hospital with dysentery almost doubled between 1940 and 1941, and cases of tuberculosis were many times higher than before the war.[107] In late 1942, the completely overwhelmed prison doctors in the Emsland camp dealt with over 850 cases of ill, injured or exhausted prisoners each day. In one of the sub-camps, almost half of the inmates were judged not fully fit for work. Many more sick inmates did not report to the doctors because they knew that they might be beaten up if they did so.[108]

Brutality was endemic in the Emsland camp, more so than before the war. Warders casually beat prisoners with rubber truncheons, sticks, rifles, hoses or whatever else they could get their hands on. The camp authorities demonstrated their resolve to rely on physical violence from the very beginning of the war. Among the first victims were many of the 1,000 or so security-confined inmates held in late 1939 in the Esterwegen sub-camp. As might be expected, these prisoners were often unable to cope with the minimal rations and hard physical labour in the camp. A number of warders saw the inmates' failure to reach their work quotas as further proof of their 'work-shy' nature. This only heightened their aggression, which erupted shortly after the outbreak of war. On 7 November 1939, camp commander Werner Schäfer ordered a raid on the barracks of the security-confined inmates. He instructed warders to use their truncheons against 'particularly senseless and insubordinate big-mouths'. Many inmates were brutally beaten. More than 50 prisoners were picked out for special punishment four days later, and again brutally beaten up. This assault had a dramatic impact. Already overworked and weak, many of the security-confined inmates fell into despair. Previously, they had been attacked individually for real or alleged infractions of the rules. Now, they were collectively assaulted. Inmates took drastic actions to get out of Esterwegen. Many seriously injured themselves, hoping that this would lead to their transfer to another institution. According to official reports, no fewer than 62 security-confined prisoners in Esterwegen mutilated themselves between November 1939 and March 1940, hacking off fingers and toes, or swallowing forks, knives, nails and glass. But this only infuriated the prison officials further. Commander Schäfer suggested in a letter to the Reich Ministry of Justice on 2 January 1940 that these inmates deserved to die:

> It would be a crime against the German people if self-mutilators were left even one atom of hope that they would ever be included again in the national community. In my opinion, they should be eliminated [*ausgemerzt*] mercilessly. The only correct judgement appears to be the one with the most devastating impact. Disciplinary measures are not appropriate. A law should be created, according to which the offenders would either spend their entire life in a mental asylum or would be completely eliminated . . .

Even though some prison officials, such as one of the Emsland doctors, were sympathetic to Schäfer's demands, no such law was ever introduced. As we shall see later, no legal framework was needed to exterminate most of the security-confined prisoners.[109]

Only a few prisoners in the Emsland camp escaped the violence. A doctor who examined a large group of inmates in 1944 found that one-quarter of them showed visible signs of having been assaulted. The warders continued to demonstrate great enterprise in devising new ways to torture and humiliate the inmates. Thus, some starving prisoners who stole potatoes from the fields outside the moor were beaten senseless. Then they were forced to crawl all the way back to the camp, pushing the potatoes in front of them with their chin. Many prisoners, barely able to walk because of exhaustion, were battered for not working hard enough. Several prisoners who had collapsed during work were beaten to death by the warders.[110] Warders also increasingly encouraged individual inmates selected as barrack or work supervisors to punish their fellow prisoners. These supervisors regularly reported other inmates for political conversations or for having stolen food. They also assaulted the prisoners, using any available pretext. Most other prisoners kept their heads down, in order not to be picked out by warders or supervisors. But occasionally, inmates who had denounced fellow prisoners to the authorities were secretly beaten up.[111]

Leading prison officials in Berlin were well aware of the violence in the Emsland camp. Their response was complex, as it was before 1939. No doubt, a number continued to reject such random violence as it was not covered by the regulations. Repeatedly, they reminded local officials in the Emsland camp that illegal violence was not allowed.[112] However, this position was ambiguous. To start with, the officials in Berlin were not really motivated by concern for the inmates. Other factors, such as the desire to exploit inmates' labour power fully, were clearly more important.[113] Furthermore, the opposition to violence was not categorical. For example, the Reich Ministry of Justice allowed warders in the Emsland camp to use force against prisoners guilty of 'passive resistance'. Previously, prison warders had been officially allowed to hit inmates only if they were themselves attacked or directly threatened. Now, warders beat inmates who, for example, failed to fulfil the work quota, construing their physical exhaustion as 'passive resistance'.[114] In addition, there was a dramatic gap between the occasional official warnings against prisoner maltreatment, and the *de facto* acceptance of this violence in day-to-day operations. The few individual cases of beatings, torture and killings of prisoners which were actually investigated by the legal authorities (often triggered by complaints from brave inmates themselves), were routinely dismissed by the Emsland camp authorities. Such decisions were supported by the Reich Ministry of Justice, even in cases where the guilt of the warders could not have been more obvious.[115]

Only in exceptional circumstances were warders prosecuted and sentenced for violence. One such case involved the murder of the prisoner Wilhelm K., who had been taken to the Emsland camp in July 1942 for theft. A few days after his arrival, on 29 July 1942, he tried to escape. He was quickly discovered hiding behind a bush by another prisoner, who worked as a supervisor. Wilhelm K. was brutally beaten up by this prisoner, and then handed over to the warders, who assaulted him with sticks, rifles, truncheons and spades. Wilhelm K. was bleeding all over, and died from internal injuries only a few hours later.[116] This was by no means the only time an inmate was beaten to death by prison warders. So why did the legal authorities intervene in this case, but not in others? The main reason was that Wilhelm K.'s murder had been witnessed by civilians, who spread the story of his brutal killing among the local population. Legal officials were desperate to maintain the picture of a legitimate prison system, which had by this time become a façade behind which brutality was common. Officials were concerned about the public reputation of the legal system and worried that the assault on Wilhelm K. might 'discredit the prison service'.[117] The court sentence on the murderous warders demonstrates once more that the legal apparatus showed little real desire to punish violence against prisoners. The killers of Wilhelm K. received no more than a token punishment, between five and nine months' imprisonment. Warders could expect longer sentences for collaborating with inmates. For example, in 1943 the senior prison warder Richard L. was sentenced to two years' imprisonment in a penitentiary for secretly passing on letters to relatives of prisoners (the relatives paid him with tobbacco and food).[118] Evidently, helping prisoners was regarded as a more serious offence than killing them.

During the war, the death rate in the Emsland camp was very high. More and more inmates collapsed with colds, pneumonia, dropsy or general exhaustion. Given the combination of particularly exhausting labour and brutal violence, it comes as no surprise that more prisoners died in the Emsland camp than in any other German penal institution. Between 1940 and 1944, around 1,330 prisoners lost their lives there, according to the official figures. Crucially, the death rate increased sharply during the first years of the war, unlike in most other German penal institutions, where the death toll only shot up after 1941. Official statistics record that about 17 prisoners had died on average in the Emsland camp each year in the prewar period. In 1940, the annual figure had already risen to 59, even though inmate numbers were no higher than before. By 1941, there were some 176 dead registered in the Emsland camp. One year later, in 1942, the death toll reached its peak: some 472 prisoners lost their lives in the Emsland camp – almost 30 times more than in 1938 (see Figure 6, pp. 398–9).

New Prison Camps

Before the war, most Emsland inmates had toiled in moor cultivation. But the ideological significance of this type of work had already started to fade by the time war broke out, and in 1941 Hitler ordered that no new moor cultivation projects should be started in Germany. Following the conquest of forests and fields abroad, Hitler reasoned, this was no longer necessary.[119] The Emsland camp quickly lost part of its original purpose. Searching for alternative justifications for the camp, the authorities pursued two different paths. First, they tried to make a virtue out of the notoriously hard conditions, positioning Emsland as the destination for groups of prisoners who, in the eyes of the authorities, deserved especially harsh punishment. Secondly, the prison authorities changed the focus of work in the Emsland camp. Cultivation was cut back sharply and the convicts were now mainly employed on farms, construction sites and harbours, as well as directly for the armaments industry. By 1944, some 800 prisoners from the Esterwegen sub-camp were forced to produce hardware for BMW in a new factory set up just outside the camp.[120] But these changes could not prevent the Reich Ministry of Justice from moving thousands of Emsland prisoners elsewhere, to supposedly more productive work. Thus, in 1942 and 1943, two new prison camps were set up in occupied Europe, neither of which has, as yet, been examined in any detail by historians.

The first destination for prisoners from the Emsland camp was Norway, which was occupied by German forces in April 1940, primarily for strategic reasons. The German authorities lost no time in embarking upon vast building projects in order to incorporate Norway into the Nazi Empire, including new or extended military installations, power stations, roads and harbours. These projects were strongly supported by Hitler, who pressed, above all, for the urgent improvement of road and railway links to the Arctic lands, to supply the army in case of an Allied attack by sea. In the spring and summer of 1942, Hitler repeatedly warned that this project could determine the outcome of the war. The work in Norway was carried out by the Organisation Todt, officially led from 1943 by Albert Speer. Most of the workers were Norwegian civilians and Soviet prisoners of war.[121] But prisoners were also included in the plans. On 5 June 1942, the Reich Ministry of Justice informed Hitler that some 2,000 inmates had been earmarked for work in Norway, all from the Emsland camp.[122]

The prisoners departed for Norway on board two ships in August and September 1942. A large number of the convicts were former German soldiers, sentenced for offences such as desertion or 'sedition' (see Chapter 7). Most had apparently volunteered for Norway. Desperate to leave the Emsland camp, they had been tricked by the authorities, who had promised them better food, more lenient treatment and even possible early release. The prisoners quickly regretted their decision. Conditions on the ships were terrible. The inmates were crowded together below deck. Food was very scarce and almost inedible, and the hygienic conditions were appalling. Soon, a dysentery epidemic had broken out. One group of prisoners recalled that 'you literally slipped on the excrement of your neighbors . . . Half-dead, seriously ill people and the living were lying next to and above each other.' Most of the prisoners eventually disembarked at the harbours of Alta and Hammerfest, far north of the Arctic Circle. From here, they were taken to different locations in the Finnmark and Troms regions. In total, about 16 individual camps were set up, which together formed the prison camp North. At the end of 1942, some 1,877 prisoners were held here, guarded by warders from the Emsland camp and some other German penitentiaries.[123]

The Reich Ministry of Justice openly acknowledged that conditions in Norway were 'significantly harder' than inside regular penal institutions in Germany.[124] But this phrase conveys nothing of the terror which the prisoners faced. They were forced to perform extremely hard physical labour, and conditions during winter were particularly harsh. Many inmates had to shovel snow on the main road in the north of Norway, to keep it clear in case it was needed by the German army. The prisoners were working in the dark (there was no sunlight for about two months), facing snowstorms and temperatures as low as minus 40 degrees centigrade. Rations were poor and, to make matters worse, officials regularly stole provisions destined for the prisoners. The inmates' clothes were inadequate, offering little protection against the freezing cold. A number of them even lacked proper shoes, wearing wooden clogs instead. In the camps, prisoners slept in barracks or tents that were barely heated. Ice quickly formed on the walls, ceilings and floors. One inmate, serving a sentence for desertion, recalled the conditions:

> The cold penetrates our thin prison clothing and makes us numb. Movement and work generate warmth. But how can one work when hunger is nagging in the bowels? And no hope of a warm room and a hearty meal in the evening. The tent is waiting for us.[125]

Amputation of feet and hands was not uncommon. Violence was widespread. Warders frequently assaulted the prisoners, trying to force them to work even harder. Other inmates were viciously attacked for stealing food or for trying to escape. They were also set upon by fellow prisoners who had been selected by the authorities as supervisors, adopting the same *Kapo* system that was in force in the Emsland camp.

The death rate in camp North was very high, especially in the winter months. A group of former inmates estimated that about one in ten prisoners died in the first six months. This is broadly backed up by official figures, which show that more than 150 prisoners had died by late February 1943.[126] Several of the dirty, malnourished and exhausted prisoners froze to death – some after the warders forced them to strip to their underwear, tied them up and then poured water all over them. The warders used various other methods of torture. For example, when inmate T. could no longer keep up with the pace of work, he was beaten by one of the warders, then forced to carry a heavy rock on his back, until he collapsed under the weight. T. died later that same day.[127] A number of inmates were shot 'trying to escape' or hanged, if they were recaptured. Finally, several prisoners reported after the war that some sick inmates had been killed with lethal injections.

Other inmates were in such a poor physical state that the authorities in Norway sent them back to Germany. These transports soon became known among prisoners as 'crutch transports'. One of the transports, carrying 57 former prisoners in Norway, reached the Emsland camp on 27 October 1943. All but six of the convicts were suffering from great physical exhaustion and weakness.[128] The Speer ministry repeatedly urged the Reich Ministry of Justice to send replacements to Norway.[129] In 1943, the prison administration decided to put together a transport with inmates from penal institutions all over Germany (rather than just from the Emsland camp). The focus was on penitentiary inmates who had been sentenced by military courts. The Reich Ministry of Justice insisted that the selected prisoners should be in good health and properly equipped.[130] The transport left Germany in late June 1943, and these prisoners apparently fared little better than previous ones. A number succumbed to the bitter cold, hard labour, brutal treatment and malnourishment. Many others had to be transported back, sick and completely exhausted.[131] The gaps left by illness, injury and death were not filled quickly this time, and inmate numbers in camp North gradually declined throughout 1943 and 1944, until at the end of 1944, just over 1,000 prisoners were left in the camp.[132]

During 1944, more inmates were held in the other new prison camp, which was set up in occupied France. In October 1943, the first transport of prisoners from the Emsland camp had arrived in France. By the end of March 1944, some 2,474 inmates (largely sentenced by military courts) were held in various camps in northern France, including Calais, Arras and Cambrai. These camps, which were often moved, were part of the prison camp West (also known as Commando West and Commando X) and warders were again drawn from staff in the Emsland camp. The aim of camp West was the total exploitation of the prisoners for the war effort, supervised once more by Organisation Todt. Prisoners were forced to work on various secret military projects, geared towards strengthening Germany's defences in France. Together with other workers, they built military fortifications and railway lines as well as installations for artillery and rockets. The prisoners were forced to work harder than others, with warders and convicts appointed as supervisors abusing inmates accused of slacking. The warders also devised special rituals for punishment. In some cases, prisoners (carrying heavy bags of cement) were forced to run between two rows of warders, who kicked them and hit them with rifle butts. Given these brutal methods, it comes as little surprise that prisoners worked as hard as possible. Albert Speer's officials were not the only ones impressed with their output. Obviously, conditions during work were often very dangerous. The military installations the prisoners worked on were obvious targets for the Allies, and in November 1943 some 60 prisoners were killed during bombing raids. But the raids also had beneficial outcomes for some inmates, as many hundreds of them used the ensuing chaos to escape. The camps in France were closed down after little more than a year. In the face of rapid Allied advances, following the landing in June 1944, the prisoners in France were eventually transported to Lendringsen (Sauerland) in Germany in autumn 1944.[133]

Prisons and Concentration Camps

The Second World War transformed penal institutions and concentration camps. Overall, one can once more detect some similar trends in both places of confinement: a vastly increased prisoner population with a changing composition; a sharp rise in violence and murder; much worse living conditions, leading to a rapid spread of epidemics and illnesses, and more deaths; cuts in food provisions, with both concentration camp and prison inmates officially entitled to the same hunger rations; and finally, the greater exploitation of the inmates for the war effort, often in satellite camps, which grew all over Germany. In part, such parallels were the result of the wartime radicalism of the regime. But this was not the only reason. The legal authorities also increasingly looked to concentration camps for inspiration. This had already begun before the war, with the creation of prison camps like Emsland. And by the late 1930s, some legal officials were holding up concentration camps as models for penal institutions. Following a visit to Dachau in 1938, one senior official from the Reich Ministry of Justice praised the camp, concluding that such trips would benefit ministerial prison officials as well. State Secretary Freisler, keen to maintain superficial distance from the concentration camps, rejected pre-arranged official visits. However, he had no objections to occasional visits if the officials happened to be in the area.[134]

This approach changed during the war, especially under Thierack, when prison officials inspected numerous concentration camps. In June 1944, for example, a group of senior legal officials were given a tour of Auschwitz by a local SS official. In the internal report on the visit, the legal officials made constant references to prisons, comparing the rules concerning contact with the external world, hospital treatment, the separation of inmates, escapes and so on. With regard to forced labour, the visitors noted that the camp officials appeared to be much less 'thrifty' in the use of the labour force. Still the officials concluded with satisfaction that, apart from the use of large numbers of inmates for specific tasks, 'nothing was shown [to us] in the camp Auschwitz which surpasses prison labour in terms of intensity, rational work methods and productivity...'.[135] Thierack ultimately envisaged a prison service that would combine elements of the traditional prison with the concentration camps.[136] Given this intense interest in the camps, it is not surprising that aspects of the prison came to resemble the concentration camp system.

Still, during the war the conditions in concentration camps (even excluding the death camps) remained significantly worse than in penal institutions. The general shifts mentioned above were more extreme in the concentration camps: living conditions were much worse and inmate numbers increased much more sharply (with a higher proportion of non-German inmates). Most importantly, concentration camps became mass graves. From the early years of the war, the number of inmate deaths spiralled upwards. Inmates succumbed to the appalling living conditions created by the SS and to the violence, torture and killings in the camps. Concentration camps were also sites of systematic mass murder of selected groups, including Jews, Soviet POWs and ill inmates. Murder became the norm. Every day, scores of prisoners were killed. In the Dachau concentration camp, the annual inmate mortality shot up from 4 per cent (1938) to 36 per cent (1941). No penal institution ever reached similar depths of barbarity. For example, in the Emsland camp, where conditions were worse than in almost all other penal institutions, the overall annual mortality was around 7 per cent (1944) – many times higher than before the war, but still much lower than in concentration camps.[137]

Of course, conditions in both concentration camps and penal institutions were not the same for all inmates. Much depended on the classification of the prisoner, which determined inmates' place in the internal hierarchy. In turn, this had vital implications for their living conditions and their chances of survival. Historians of the concentration camps have stressed that this gap between different groups of inmates was often extremely wide, especially during the war. As the following chapters will show, there was a rather similar situation in penal institutions.

7 Privilege and Punishment

The different groups of prisoners were not equally affected by the illness, hunger, hard labour, violence and exhaustion which characterised life in penal institutions during the war. To start with, many thousands of convicts were not locked up until they had completed their sentences, but instead were transferred to special military formations at the front line. For prisoners remaining inside penal institutions, treatment often varied enormously – determined by criminological, racial and political considerations. For example, many Germans classified as 'national comrades' could expect comparatively lenient conditions. By contrast, foreign prisoners were often among the worst off. The war saw a rapid increase in inmates from different nations, and by spring 1943 more than one-third of the prison population was made up of foreigners.[1] These foreign prisoners were discriminated against in many ways. Often, they were prevented from sending or receiving letters. In other cases, local prison officials decided to allocate scarce supplies to certain German prisoners, depriving foreigners of food, blankets, covers, sheets, socks and other items. Many foreigners were also excluded from sought-after jobs in the prison economy, when the Reich Ministry of Justice barred 'alien races' from becoming prison trusties in responsible positions.[2] Finally, foreign prisoners were supposed to be separated from Germans as strictly as possible, even though this proved not always possible in practice.[3] But the experience of imprisonment was not identical for these foreign prisoners either, owing to the various prejudices and obsessions of Nazi leaders and prison officials.

'National Comrades' behind Bars

Among the most privileged convicts were undoubtedly German 'national comrades' – individuals who, in the eyes of the officials, had merely 'tripped up' and deserved a second chance. Long before the war, Nazi leaders and legal officials had agreed that these individuals were not yet lost to the 'national community', and special regulations for certain 'first offenders' – to 'win [them] back for the national community' – had been envisaged in the drafts for a prison law.[4] Such a provision was finally implemented as 'first imprisonment' (*Erstvollzug*) in the national prison guidelines of 22 July 1940. The official aim was to prevent certain adults in prisons (but not penitentiaries) from 'descending into criminality', protecting them from the supposedly corrupting influence of others by holding them separately. The regulations offered various benefits, partially reminiscent of the stages system during the Weimar years. According to the new rules, the selected inmates would all receive school lessons and be employed in work that would prove particularly useful after their release. The prisoners could also be awarded special privileges, such as keeping the light on in their cells for longer and meeting fellow inmates without supervision. Of course, only a minority of inmates were eligible for 'first imprisonment'. The authorities barred all those who were not of 'German or related blood', those who were 'criminal personalities' and prisoners regarded as unsuitable because of their offence. This included 'dangerous habitual criminals', individuals who had been sentenced in the past to imprisonment in a penitentiary and those who had served more than six months in prisons. In short, only future 'national comrades' were to receive beneficial treatment.[5]

The regulations for 'national comrades' behind bars were somewhat modified in 1942, following a private outburst by Hitler that year. Hitler declared that it was 'one of the worst sins of the past, that a person who had tripped up once, yet was thoroughly decent on the inside, should be put together with serious criminals, where he was now really corrupted'. From now on, one had to make a fundamental separation, Hitler added, repeating demands he had made earlier. Hitler's remarks were taken down and sent to the Reich Ministry of Justice by the office of Martin Bormann.[6] The prison officials in the Reich Ministry of Justice quickly responded. While they noted that the general rules for 'first imprisonment' already fulfilled Hitler's wishes, the officials agreed that the principle of separation had to be emphasised even more strongly. In December 1942, this resulted in several minor changes to the national prison guidelines. But, in essence, this new 'special imprisonment of the tripped up' was just another name for 'first imprisonment'.[7] The number of eligible prisoners no doubt increased further in the last years of the war, as more and more German 'national comrades' were locked up by the legal authorities (see Chapter 5). These 'tripped up' prisoners included a large proportion of female inmates, as many of these women were sentenced for first offences regarded as comparatively minor.[8]

In practice, the special treatment of 'national comrades' proved rather difficult to realise. Some local prison officials truly believed that inmates who had 'tripped up' could be reintegrated into Nazi society with the help of school lessons and other pedagogic intervention, as envisaged in the prison guidelines.[9] But the reality was often different. In the first place, the constant overcrowding meant that it was frequently impossible to separate these prisoners completely from others. Such separation was also hard to reconcile with the productive use of prisoners for the war industry. Often, economic considerations took precedence – at times with the explicit approval of the Reich Ministry of Justice – and many imprisoned 'national comrades' were forced to perform exhausting labour together with the other inmates.[10] In addition, school lessons for prisoners became rare during the war. The number of prison teachers had already been cut in the prewar years,[11] and wartime pressures meant that lessons were reduced further. Classes were cancelled because the prisoners were busy in workshops or factories, and because teachers were drafted into the army. In 1944, the general state prosecutors were finally told that any remaining lessons had to be cut completely.[12]

Religious measures to 'reform' prisoners were also cut back. Many local prison officials had long believed that religious instruction offered the best hope of redeeming prisoners. But the role of prison chaplains was gradually reduced during the war, not least because of the ideological hostility to the church felt by some leading prison officials. This development became obvious after Otto-Georg Thierack took over as Reich Minister of Justice in 1942.[13] In early 1943, the Protestant prison chaplain in Ichtershausen, an institution now reserved for 'tripped up' prisoners, complained that spiritual care for inmates was impossible 'because the files are no longer accessible to me [and] a visit to the cells is no longer possible . . .'[14] More obstacles were to come. In the autumn of 1943, the Reich Ministry of Justice ordered the removal of details of inmates' denomination from name tags outside their cells. Chaplains were only allowed to speak to prisoners who had explicitly asked to see them.[15] The most dramatic move was announced on 29 September 1944, when the Reich Ministry of Justice banned prison church services. Church leaders immediately responded with sharp criticism. Typically, the church authorities protested only against measures which threatened their narrow denominational interest, remaining silent about the various murderous Nazi legal policies.[16] The reflex action of the officials in the Reich Ministry of Justice was to hit back, effectively arguing that the church services wasted valuable resources at a time of total war: 'The support of the mental and spiritual needs of the prisoners has to come second to work deployment.'[17] In the end, though, the Reich Ministry of Justice sent out a somewhat more conciliatory decree on 12

December 1944, allowing church services to take place as long as this did not undermine security and war production in the penal institution.[18]

Nevertheless, the prison authorities made sure that many German 'national comrades' were better off than other inmates. Preferential treatment shaped a number of aspects of their lives, extending even to health care. This is evident, for example, in the authorities' policy towards inmates suffering from tuberculosis, which spread during the war. In the past, it had not been uncommon for different prisoners with TB to be temporarily taken for treatment to special wards, set up in institutions such as Hohenasperg (part of the Ludwigsburg penitentiary) and Glatz in Silesia. But in 1943, the Reich Ministry of Justice decided to bring this policy into line with its general discriminatory approach to penal policy. Male inmates infected with TB were divided into three groups (there were apparently no corresponding regulations for women). Those prisoners with 'German blood' could still receive treatment in Hohenasperg or Glatz – but only if they were regarded as 'worthy', a term primarily applied to young offenders and those who had 'tripped up'. The remaining German prisoners, such as those with many convictions, were no longer seen as deserving. Instead, they could be taken to a new 'isolation ward' in Lingen, or to the penal institutions in Brandenburg-Görden or Waldheim. Additionally, Polish and Czech prisoners with TB could be transported to the Mürau institution in the occupied Czech territory.[19]

There can be no doubt that the 'worthy' German prisoners with TB enjoyed the best of the bad conditions. Many were taken to the special ward in Hohenasperg, an old castle that had been used as a prison for weak or disabled prisoners since the late nineteenth century. Inmates from all over Germany arrived there in the last years of the Second World War, both property offenders and political prisoners. Even some prisoners sentenced for attempted high treason had been judged 'worthy' of treatment. Of course, life on the TB ward in Hohenasperg was harsh: disciplinary punishment was apparently handed out without much regard to the prisoners' health. In reality any 'treatment', one former prisoner recalled, was limited to a few helpings of cod liver oil. Not surprisingly, mortality was high. Between 1942 and April 1945, some 177 prisoners died of TB in Hohenasperg, with 53 deaths in 1944 alone (there were about 150 prisoners on the TB ward each day towards the end of the war). But while the prisoners received little medical attention, conditions could have been even worse. The prisoners do not appear to have been subjected to constant brutal violence, there was a rest hall modelled on tuberculosis sanatoriums and the prison doctor managed to obtain some extra rations for the inmates.[20]

This contrasts with the fate of German prisoners with TB classified as 'unworthy' of treatment, which included inmates described by local prison officials as 'morally weak, thoughtless and dangerous for the community'.[21] A number of them were transported to the Brandenburg-Görden penitentiary. Here, they were often taken to the TB barrack (about 140 inmates were held here towards the end of the war), where they suffered from lack of food and medical care. Even worse, they were exposed to physical violence. Many sick inmates were terrorised by a fellow prisoner, Robert H., who had been appointed by the prison officials as barrack supervisor. Robert H. brutally abused his position, as the authorities must have known. He and his friends maltreated other prisoners and also cheated them out of their already meagre rations. Gravely ill inmates were particularly vulnerable. They were sometimes thrown into wooden boxes in an adjacent, unheated room – bundled into their coffins while still alive. Hundreds of prisoners died of tuberculosis in Brandenburg-Görden in the Nazi period, with some 82 prisoners dying in the TB barrack in 1944 alone.[22]

Preferential treatment of German 'national comrades' was easiest to realise in those penal institutions entirely reserved for adults who had 'tripped up'. One such institution was the Wittlich prison for men in the Cologne district, which doubled up as a youth prison. Living conditions in Wittlich were better than in most other penal institutions. Here warders apparently acted less brutally and medical care by the prison doctor continued throughout the war. As a study of the Wittlich prison concluded, for prisoners who submitted to the strict military discipline, imprisonment was 'on the whole relatively bearable'. As a result, almost all the prisoners taken to Wittlich survived their imprisonment, with fewer prisoners dying during the war than before – another sign of the preferential treatment 'national comrades' received. This special treatment continued even at the end of their sentences. Hardly any prisoners were taken to the police or to concentration camps. Indeed, many Wittlich prisoners did not even have to serve their full sentence. Instead, they were released early and joined ordinary army units.[23]

Such early releases were always restricted to a rather small proportion of the prison population. The selected prisoners were often first offenders with a good disciplinary record, regarded as having 'tripped up'. But during the war, economic criteria also came to influence the decisions by the responsible legal authorities. Officials came under growing pressure to exempt workers regarded as crucial to the war effort, above all armaments and agricultural workers. The application procedure for their exemption was never properly streamlined and the legal authorities faced claims from a confusing range of agencies, such as the Reich Ministry of Food, the Reich Ministry for Armaments and Ammunition, the local and regional offices of the Reich Food Estate, the labour exchanges, the Four-Year Plan Office, the Gauleiter and individual private companies. The legal officials agreed to consider each application on its merits. Overall, they showed willingness to compromise in cases involving minor offenders who had received a short prison sentence. In such cases, they often pardoned the offenders, granted them temporary exemptions, released them on probation or replaced their prison sentence with a fine. Some peasants and farm workers were also allowed to serve their sentences in stages: they spent a few months during the winter in prison until they were released again to return to the fields, a practice criticised by some regional legal officials as undermining the effect of punishment. But despite the rather accommodating approach by the legal system, conflicts with other state and party agencies continued throughout the war. Officials in the Reich Ministry of Justice were particularly angry that these agencies sometimes tried to get more serious offenders off the hook when, in the minds of the legal officials, they had to be locked up to maintain discipline on the home front. The real victors of these conflicts were those prisoners who were released early and escaped the deteriorating conditions inside.[24] They were not the only prisoners who left the penal institutions before they had served their sentences, however. Thousands more were released early to fight in special military formations.

Soldiers as Prisoners – Prisoners as Soldiers

After the outbreak of war, it did not take long for the Nazi leadership to consider the use of convicts as soldiers. While German officials were still publically mocking the British army for supposedly recruiting 'professional criminals', senior Nazis were already making plans to deploy convicts themselves.[25] Once more, the initiative came directly from Hitler. In the early stages of the war, Hitler's thinking on this matter was not yet driven by military necessity. More decisive, no doubt, was his conviction that it was wrong to protect deviants from the killing at the front. On 21 December 1939, he noted in an army decree, in familiar language: 'When the best men must sacrifice their lives for the fatherland on the front, no one can understand that at the same time cowards and saboteurs are preserved in prisons.'[26] The first convicts chosen by Hitler for military duties, however, were not those he regarded as 'cowards' and 'saboteurs'.

In late March 1940, the Reich Ministry of Justice was informed that Hitler had decided that imprisoned 'respectable poachers' (*anständige Wilderer*) should be turned over to a special SS division. If they proved themselves, an amnesty would be provided. This order marked the birth of the notorious SS Special Formation Dirlewanger, which later committed murderous excesses against Jews and partisans in Poland, the USSR and Slovakia. In May and June 1940, some 88 poachers were transported from prisons and penitentiaries to the Sachsenhausen concentration camp, to be incorporated in the Formation Dirlewanger. In the following years, further prisoners were transferred. But these convicts were soon in a minority, as most other men were 'professional criminals' and 'asocials' from concentration camps. Overall, only a small number of convicts joined the Formation Dirlewanger. But their deployment was still significant. The Reich Ministry of Justice had agreed, with no apparent hesitation, to hand over prisoners to a special formation, long before their sentences were due to end. The legal authorities thus accepted that, in some cases, military and political considerations outweighed the demand that prisoners first complete their legally fixed punishment. Now that this precedent had been set, the door was open for many more prisoners to be drafted into the army. In addition, the SS authorities were impressed by the 'success' of the convicts during their missions in Nazi-occupied Poland. Given proper selection and strict discipline, it was argued, convicts could contribute to the Nazi war effort at the front line. These experiences shaped the views of the Nazi leadership. When more and more soldiers were needed at the front, the regime quickly decided to use thousands of prisoners.[27]

Military Justice and Probation Troop 500

A significant step towards the recruitment of large numbers of prisoners into the army was taken in late 1940, when Hitler announced that ex-soldiers sentenced by military courts could be sent to a special 'probation battalion'. This order directly affected the prison system, as thousands of these ex-soldiers were in fact held by the regular legal system, not by the military authorities. To understand this development fully, one must take a brief look at military justice in Germany.

As we have seen, the trauma of 1918 decisively shaped penal policy in the Nazi period. The same was true for the military justice system. In the Weimar years, the supposed leniency displayed by German court-martials during the First World War was widely attacked for having contributed to the 'stab in the back'. In *Mein Kampf*, Hitler claimed that the failure to use the death penalty 'had terrible consequences. An army of deserters, especially in 1918, poured into the reserve posts and the home towns, and helped to form that great criminal organisation, which, after 7 November 1918, we suddenly beheld as the maker of the revolution.' Once the Nazis were in power, two crucial steps were taken in the sphere of military justice to prevent another 'stab in the back'. First, the Army Law (*Wehrgesetz*) of 21 May 1935 introduced new guidelines to bar supposedly untrustworthy elements from entering the military service. These guidelines went far beyond previous regulations. Among those deemed 'unworthy of military service' were all those who had ever been sentenced to imprisonment in a penitentiary or security confinement, and those sentenced to prison for 'subversive activity'. Secondly, the authorities introduced draconian sentences to deter army personnel from illegal activities. This lay at the heart of the Special Wartime Penal Code, which was officially published on 26 August 1939, just days before the German attack of Poland. According to the historian Detlef Garbe, the Code was, in essence, 'nothing other than a military justice murder weapon'.[28]

During the war, German military courts used the murderous potential of the Military Penal Code to the full. There were probably over 1,000 military courts (not counting navy and air force courts), made up of one legal and two military officials. The courts operated at the front and in almost all the larger German cities. From the beginning, sentences were handed down fast and furiously. A comparison with Allied military courts reveals the extraordinary homicidal frenzy of German military justice. Fewer than 300 individuals were executed by the British, French and US authorities during the whole of the Second World War. By contrast, some 30,000 members of the German armed forces were sentenced to death by military courts (many thousands more civilians and POWs were also condemned by these courts). German military judges sent those suspected of undermining the Nazi war effort to their death, as execution became a regular punishment for desertion. In fact, it was desertion, not rape or murder, which was regarded as the worst possible crime for a German soldier. For many military officials, the trauma of the 'stab in the back' was decisive here. A number of judgments openly referred to 1918. As one navy judge put it: 'In determining the punishment I take into account whether the defendant could be considered a revolutionary type or not. I make sure that 1918 will not be repeated. I exterminate revolutionary types.' Other soldiers were sentenced by military courts to imprisonment in military institutions, ranging from special camps to army prisons. Penitentiary sentences were also a popular punishment among the military judges. Crucially, those sentenced to penitentiary did not remain inside army institutions.[29]

Soldiers sentenced to imprisonment in a penitentiary by German military courts were branded 'unworthy of military service', kicked out of the army and handed over as 'war offenders' to the prison service. (This practice only changed in autumn 1944, when these men were taken straight to new probation forces or to concentration camps.) This was not entirely without precedent: before the war, the legal authorities had occasionally locked up small numbers of army personnel after trials by military courts. But numbers were much higher in the war. By spring 1941, the army had already transferred some 3,500 men, sentenced to imprisonment in a penitentiary by military courts, to the legal system. According to army guidelines, these ex-soldiers had to receive especially harsh punishment. It did not take long for the legal authorities to decide that the Emsland camp best fitted the bill: the exhausting work, the violent disciplinary sanctions and the warders' brutality guaranteed that the imprisonment would be as painful as possible. Consequently, the vast majority of army offenders turned over to the prison service were taken to Emsland –

a total of more than 20,000 men throughout the entire war, according to one estimate. The majority had been convicted for offences against military discipline. Men sentenced for desertion, for being absent without leave and for 'sedition' made up well over half of the ex-soldiers taken to the Emsland camp.[30] The military authorities were clearly happy with the way these ex-soldiers were maltreated in Emsland. Imprisonment in this camp, the Navy High Command noted, seemed 'much more effective' than in other penal institutions.[31]

Initially, the former soldiers taken to the Emsland camp had little hope of getting out before the war was over. But this soon changed. Inspired by the deployment of criminal offenders in Formation Dirlewanger, in summer 1940 the military authorities started to discuss the possibility of drafting convicted soldiers into special formations. Finally, on 21 December 1940, Hitler announced that special 'probation troops' would be set up for army personnel who 'had failed once, but really were orderly'. This included selected soldiers sentenced to imprisonment in a penitentiary. While Hitler claimed that the new formation, soon known as probation troop 500, would not be a 'punishment battalion', he acknowledged that the men would be used for difficult missions.[32] Hitler's initiative has to be seen in the context of military planning for the invasion of the Soviet Union. The Nazi leadership was well aware that this campaign could lead to serious disciplinary issues among the troops, and probation troop 500 was created as an additional instrument of deterrence. Soldiers who wanted to escape front-line fighting now knew that the most likely outcome was either a death sentence, or a period of brutal imprisonment followed by a return to the front in a potentially even more exposed position.[33]

Regular prison officials in the Emsland camp played an important role in the creation of probation troop 500, as they were charged with examining potential candidates (sometimes named by the military authorities) among the imprisoned ex-soldiers. Only those men judged fit to return to the front were to be selected. Strict selection was considered vital to keep out trouble-makers and to prevent a repetition of 1918. The official requirements for an ex-soldier to be sent back to the army included that the inmate had behaved well, had only 'minor' convictions, had no 'serious deficiencies of character' and was physically and mentally fit for military service. According to the guidelines, the prisoner also had to volunteer (this rule was later relaxed). But in practice, some ex-soldiers were pressured from the start by the prison officials to put themselves forward. The fact that others really did volunteer is testament to the catastrophic conditions in the Emsland camp: the prisoners were so desperate to escape that they actually preferred front-line fighting.[34]

Reports about the ex-soldiers were sent by the prison officials to the military authorities. In a number of cases, prison officials insisted that further punishment was necessary before the inmate could be sent back to the front. For example, in the case of ex-soldier Herbert R., who had been sentenced by a military court in November 1943 to eight years' penitentiary for desertion, a senior official in the Emsland camp argued against his return to the army in August 1944: 'The impression made by R. is not exactly positive. He appears cunning and full of lies. Also, he has not been much impressed by his imprisonment up to now.' As a result, Herbert R. remained in the Emsland camp.[35] But if the prison officials sent in a positive report, and the military authorities agreed, then the ex-soldier was transferred to the army prison in Torgau. Overall, about 5,000 ex-soldiers were taken from the Emsland camp to Torgau. It appears that those sentenced for criminal offences such as theft and sex crimes were thought to make the best soldiers – they were significantly more likely to be transferred than those convicted of undermining military discipline. In Torgau, the prisoners were then 'tested' by the military for several weeks. If considered fit, they were classified as 'temporarily worthy of military service' and transferred to one of the companies in probation troop 500. The first soldiers saw combat in late June 1941, during the invasion of the Soviet Union. In the following years, the soldiers were used for various missions regarded as particularly dangerous and fatalities were extremely high. On average, each battalion was obliterated by death, injury and capture in the space of about six months.[36]

Probation Battalion 999

The military campaign against the Soviet Union also created the conditions for the drafting of prisoners sentenced by civilian courts (rather than military courts). Until 1942, they had not been considered as possible recruits. The only exceptions were those few convicts sent to Formation Dirlewanger, as well as a few hundred men from youth prisons. Following a suggestion by a local prison governor, State Secretary Freisler had contacted the army in May 1941, arguing that volunteers from youth prisons should be given the chance to 'prove themselves facing the enemy'. The agreement was finalised in October 1941.[37] But adults sentenced by civilian courts were not included. This changed only after the failure of the *Blitzkrieg* in the east and the immense casualties sustained by the German army. By late March 1942, German troops in the east had lost over one million men, a third of its total force. Over the previous months, the army leadership had already taken increasingly radical steps to increase its reserves, but the dramatic losses could not be fully replaced. More manpower was needed.[38]

The first sign that the policy of the military leadership relating to civilian offenders was changing came in spring 1942. The Supreme Army Command announced on 11 April 1942 that civilians 'unworthy of military service', who had been held in penitentiaries in the past, could now be drafted into the army under certain circumstances. This did not meet with universal support. Some officers feared that the reputation of the army might be sullied. And the police leadership worried that such ex-convicts, who included political offenders, could undermine army discipline. Police officials believed that many former penitentiary inmates should not be drafted, but rather be exterminated as dangers to the 'national community'. The spectre of 1918 loomed large, as we have seen, and the police in 1942 stepped up efforts to arrest ex-convicts. These police measures go some way to explain why only a small number of civilians were drafted following the April 1942 order.[39]

The decision to draft current penitentiary inmates sentenced by civilian courts was taken in autumn 1942. By then, the German summer offensive (*Operation Blau*), which had started on 28 June 1942, had suffered great losses. By mid-September 1942, more than a third of a million men had been lost.[40] At this point, the Army Command informed the Reich Ministry of Justice that it now considered calling up further men 'unworthy of military service'. They were to be collected in a special army formation, which became known as probation battalion 999. The decision to concentrate those 'unworthy of military service' in one special formation was supposed to prevent contact between such potential enemies of the Nazi state and ordinary soldiers. The details were discussed by army officials and civil servants from the Reich Ministry of Justice on 14 and 26 September 1942, when it was agreed that selected penitentiary inmates would be included in the battalion.[41]

The guidelines were published by the Supreme Army Command on 2 October 1942. From now on, penitentiary inmates who had been born in 1908 (or later) could be called up. In order to avoid calling up individuals considered to be potential revolutionaries, certain conditions were imposed. The main requirements were that the prisoners had received sentences of no more than three years, had served at least one year, had behaved well and were fit for military service. Prisoners convicted of treason or homosexual acts, and those sentenced to castration and security confinement were excluded. The army later added that those 'on the way to being professional criminals' should also be barred. Following the guidelines, the prison administration centrally compiled lists of eligible prisoners and sent them to the army, which was then free to call up the inmates.[42] In the following months and years, the army repeatedly relaxed the requirements regarding age and background of penitentiary inmates, desperate to get its hands on more recruits. By early 1944, those born in 1894 or later were judged eligible, including inmates with sentences of more than four years' penitentiary, if their offence was judged a 'one-off'.[43] The prison authorities generally cooperated willingly with the army. True, not all prison officials stuck to the guidelines. Some sensed an opportunity to get rid of unwanted inmates. Thus, they reported seriously ill and disabled inmates, as well as prisoners who were regarded as especially unruly.[44] By mid-December 1942, some 1,500 male prisoners had already been transferred to probation battalion 999 (they joined some 3,500 ex-convicts). By September 1944, the number of penitentiary inmates handed over had increased to about 10,000.[45]

According to oral testimony, the number of fatalities in probation battalion 999 was very high. The troops fought all over Nazi-occupied territory. Initially, the soldiers were deployed in Africa, in the wake of the British offensive in autumn 1942. Later, they fought in the Balkans and in the Soviet Union. But probation battalion 999 was never regarded as fully reliable by the military authorities, thanks to the subversive activities of former political prisoners. Many of these men tried to desert, others even prepared armed uprisings. The military authorities failed in their attempt to impose total discipline, despite extremely brutal punishment, including arrest, internment in a concentration camp and execution. This conduct of probation battalion 999 stands in some contrast to that of the ex-soldiers in probation troop 500 who were regarded by the military authorities, at least in the first years, as dependable and tough.[46]

The army was not alone in its desire to use prisoners for combat. At the beginning of September 1942, the Reich Ministry of Justice was informed that Hitler was once again considering the deployment of poachers in special companies to hunt down partisans.[47] This idea was followed up in more detail on 14 September by Hermann Göring. According to a report by Reich Ministry of Justice official Günther Joël, Göring was looking for 'daring lads who can be deployed in a special commando in the East', made up of prisoners who had 'failed once'. In particular, Göring, whose titles included that of Reich Master of the Hunt, was after poachers as well as members of smuggler gangs. The task of the special commando would be the destruction of the partisan leadership in the east. Operating behind enemy lines, the men would have licence to 'murder, burn [and] ravish', Joël noted.[48] The Reich Ministry of Justice was initially unable to fulfil Göring's wish: it could only locate a total of five eligible smugglers in all penal institutions, and all eligible poachers had already been handed over to the SS, following Hitler's earlier orders (on 17 September 1942 the latest transport of 100 prisoners described as 'poachers' had arrived with Formation Dirlewanger). But Göring was not deterred and more general guidelines were quickly agreed with the Reich Ministry of Justice. Around 8 or 9 October 1942, the general state prosecutors were given a couple of weeks to report the names of prisoners who volunteered for Göring's 'special commando in the East'. The requirements were that the prisoners should be between 18 and 45 years old, fit for service and sentenced for a 'not particularly dishonourable offence' to one year's imprisonment or more. Once again, 'racial aliens', prisoners convicted of treason or homosexual acts, and those sentenced to castration and security confinement were excluded.[49] Ignorant of the real mission of the 'special commando', many prisoners apparently saw this as a golden opportunity to get out of penal institutions. For example, some 42 prisoners in the Celle penitentiary volunteered, and 61 in the Hameln penitentiary.[50] However, it is unclear whether any of them were actually sent to the east. For according to the postwar testimony of a senior prison administrator, Göring's plan was never realised.[51]

The initiatives aimed at drafting prisoners into military formations reached a climax in the autumn of 1942. At exactly the same time, the legal authorities were also making preparations to remove other groups of inmates from the penal institutions before the end of their legally determined sentences. But these prisoners were not supposed to fight on the battlefield. Instead, they were selected for extermination (see Chapter 8). This included thousands of foreign prisoners, who had already endured very harsh conditions during their imprisonment over the previous years.

Foreign Political Prisoners

German courts cracked down with great force on suspected political subversives during the war, as we have seen. Not surprisingly, political prisoners continued to make up a sizeable group among the inmate population. On 31 March 1943, some 8,060 (7,591 men and 469 women) of the 57,724 (49,379 men and 8,345 women) inmates in penitentiaries had been convicted of treason and high treason.[52] But the political prisoners were often rather different from those imprisoned before the war. There were now far fewer German left-wing opponents of the regime, following the decline of the left-wing resistance. True, some activists, who had managed to escape abroad, were caught during the Nazi advance in Europe. For example, the former SPD Reichstag deputy Otto Buchwitz was arrested in April 1940 in Copenhagen, shortly after the Nazi occupation. Buchwitz, who was quickly taken to Germany and imprisoned until the end of the war, later remarked bitterly that the Danish police had carried out 'a hunt for the Gestapo', arresting a number of German emigrants.[53] But inside the German penal institutions, political prisoners such as Otto Buchwitz were increasingly outnumbered during the war by foreigners, as the legal apparatus extended its reach.

Czech Prisoners

Many of the foreign political prisoners were Czechs. At the end of March 1943, there were a total of 12,656 Czechs (11,823 men; 833 women) in German penal institutions, mostly inside the Altreich.[54] In some institutions close to the former Czechoslovakian border, such as Waldheim, there were more Czech than German prisoners.[55] Almost all Czechs were held for what the authorities described as political offences – in reality often no more than minor transgressions such as listening to foreign radio. Their treatment was partly determined by Nazi racial thinking. Thus, Czechs were treated better than Poles, but worse than most Germans. Unlike Poles, Czech prisoners were not subject to a whole set of discriminatory regulations and some inmates also gained coveted positions as trusties.[56] Nevertheless, Czechs were probably more likely to be beaten than Germans. The former prisoner Karel Reichel recalled that new inmates in Untermaßfeld were initially kept in solitary confinement:

> If you speak German, you have already won. Because in the morning and evening, you have to reel off the following sentence, in perfect military posture: 'Prisoner Reichel, serving three years penitentiary for radio [offences], date of release unknown' . . . Poor Czech tongues!

Some prisoners who failed in this task were beaten up. In some penal institutions, Czech prisoners were also deliberately put into colder and darker cells than Germans.[57]

Poor health did not stand in the way of brutal punishment. The Czech prisoner Ladislaus K., convicted of illegal possession of ammunition, was already weak when he arrived in Untermaßfeld in March 1943. Apparently, he did not receive enough clothes and was cold. One day, he made a fatal mistake. Occupied with mending clothes, he put on a pair of underpants designated for the army. The prison authorities discovered the 'theft' and punished him by cutting his meagre rations and withdrawing his mattress for two weeks. The punishment finished at the end of April 1943. Only one month later, Ladislaus K. was transferred to the tuberculosis ward, where he died on 11 June 1943.[58]

Hundreds of Czech prisoners died in German penal institutions. Some were simply worked to death. Bretislaus Krejsa, born in 1901, had been arrested in 1939, suspected of 'attempted high treason'. He was held for two years as a remand prisoner. When his wife visited him in 1941 in the Diez prison (district Frankfurt/Main), she was shocked to find that he had lost about 30 kilos. In early 1942, Krejsa was eventually tried by the People's Court in Berlin. Sentenced to ten years in a penitentiary, he was taken to Untermaßfeld in March 1942 (see Illustration 28). By this time, he had lost another 10 kilos and was already very weak. His poor health notwithstanding, he was forced to perform heavy manual labour as a metal-worker for the armaments industry. He died in March 1943 of 'heart failure'.[59]

Bretislaus Krejsa's fate was shared by other inmates in Untermaßfeld, where by 1943 about half of the prisoner population was Czech.[60] One of them was Josef Kopal. A teacher in a small Czech village, he was arrested in 1942 on suspicion of having listened to 'enemy radio'. He was taken to the remand prison in Prague, where he was interned until his trial. A fellow inmate described Kopal, who was in his early forties, as an intelligent and shy man who still made plans for the time after his release, hoping to get married. In February 1943 he was sentenced to three years and six months in a penitentiary, and taken to Bernau. It soon became clear that he was too weak to work in the moors around Bernau. On 13 March 1943, he was transported to Untermaßfeld. The prisoner photo (see Illustration 29) taken two weeks after his arrival shows a seriously malnourished man. Kopal, who was almost six feet tall, weighed only 55 kilograms and the prison doctor classified him as 'very weak'. Clearly, he belonged in a hospital. Instead, the prison authorities decided to make him work until he collapsed. He was forced to perform particularly strenuous work for the army in solitary confinement. Suffering from great hunger, his condition quickly deteriorated. On 11 May 1943, he was diagnosed with tuberculosis. Josef Kopal died one month later.[61]

A number of those Czech prisoners who survived until the end of their sentences were not freed, but instead died in SS concentration camps. To be sure, only in November 1944 was a formal agreement made between the police and the legal system to report all imprisoned Czechs before their scheduled release as 'enemies of the state'.[62] But this had not stopped local prison officials from denouncing some Czech inmates to the police prior to this agreement. In particular, some prison governors strictly opposed the release of Czechs sentenced for high treason and contacted the Gestapo to propose their transfer to police custody after the end of their sentence.[63] This practice sealed the fate of several prisoners. One was the 73-year-old Engelbert S., who had been sentenced in 1941 to 14 months in a penitentiary for 'attempted high treason', after he had cheered the Czech nation in a pub and made some critical comments about Germany. The judges were not alone in construing this as dangerous behaviour. The prison authorities in Untermaßfeld, where he served the end of his sentence, held the same view: 'S. is an old, impertinent fellow, a fanatical hater of Germans. For this enemy of the state, probably no punishment will have any lasting effect.' The prison officials were determined to ensure that S. would not be freed. When he came to the end of his sentence, the Untermaßfeld authorities reported him to the Gestapo. When there was no response, they contacted the Gestapo once more, asking whether the police intended to take him into protective custody. This time, the Gestapo replied and announced that the prisoner would indeed be arrested on the day of his release, 20 November 1942. Thanks to the vigour of the prison authorities, Engelbert S. was transported to Auschwitz.[64]

NN Prisoners

Czechs were, of course, not the only political prisoners from Nazi-occupied Europe. More and more civilians from western Europe were taken to German penal institutions. By late March 1943, some 12,013 prisoners came from western European states (10,804 men; 1,209 women).[65] Many were suspected or convicted of anti-Nazi resistance. They had started to arrive in 1941, when French, Belgian and Dutch civilians were first carried off to penal institutions inside Germany. They had not been sentenced by ordinary courts, but by military courts for offences against the German occupying forces. The military authorities felt unable to lock up all the offenders by themselves. Not only were local military prisons completely overcrowded, but the authorities also feared that resistance fighters might attempt to free inmates. Once more, the Reich Ministry of Justice stepped in and agreed to take some of the individuals to penal institutions. Presumably, it saw this as a way to strengthen the role of the prison system in the web of Nazi terror. In addition, the prison authorities made a modest profit. Military prisoners could be put to work by the legal authorities, while their living costs were charged to the military (at 1.5 Reichsmark per prisoner per day). These prisoners were transported to penal institutions in western Germany. In the Cologne district alone, there were already almost 400 such prisoners in early May 1941.[66]

From 1942, the ordinary court system inside Germany became more directly involved in the terror against west and north European civilians. This time, the initiative came from Hitler. Following the invasion of the Soviet Union, resistance to the German occupation in Europe had flared up. The Nazi leadership responded by stepping up the terror against the civilian opposition. In September 1941, Hitler ordered that arrested civilians, who could not be quickly sentenced to death, should no longer be tried by military courts. Instead, they should secretly be deported to Germany. They would disappear in 'night and fog' (*Nacht und Nebel*, or *NN*), and their family and friends would never hear from them again. The resulting uncertainty and fear, Hitler hoped, would have the desired deterrent effect. Military officials discussed Hitler's order in secret with State Secretary Freisler, who was keen for the legal apparatus, rather than the police, to realise it. Clearly, he regarded this as a good opportunity to cut out the police and to demonstrate the dedication of the legal authorities to fighting Germany's enemies. Freisler's discussions resulted in several decrees by the military and legal authorities, passed between December 1941 and April 1942, which transformed the treatment of many civilians arrested in western Europe. Those who could not be condemned to death by military courts within one week of their arrest could now be taken to penal institutions inside Germany. Here, they would await trial by the legal system, accused of political crimes such as producing anti-German propaganda, harbouring prisoners of war and sabotage (some were also suspected of 'ordinary' criminal offences, such as the illicit slaughter of animals). The prisoners came from all ages and backgrounds, including politicians, priests, judges, scientists, farmers, students and workers. Their trials could take place either before a special court or the People's Court. The first cases were heard in August 1942, but the wheels of 'justice' were grinding slowly, not least because of disruption by the war. The court procedures themselves were a travesty of regular judicial proceedings. Since they were conducted in secret, the defendants had no choice in their legal representation and were also generally denied the right to call their own witnesses. Sentences were often lethal. The desk officer dealing with *NN* cases in the Reich Ministry of Justice, Wilhelm von Ammon, estimated after the war that more than half of the defendants before the People's Court were sentenced to death. If there was not sufficient evidence to bring a case the prisoner was handed over by the legal authorities to the police, leading to a rise of *NN* prisoners inside concentration camps. This last measure had been implemented in autumn 1942 by the new Reich Minister of Justice Otto-Georg Thierack as part of his much wider plan to revise the relationship between legal system and police.[67]

By 1 November 1942, some 2,349 *NN* prisoners were in the hands of the legal authorities. Most of them had been taken to penal institutions in western Germany, in the Cologne, Essen and Kiel districts. But from 1943, following the intensification of Allied air raids on these areas, *NN* prisoners were transported to institutions all over central and eastern Germany.[68] Prisoner numbers continued to increase in the following months. At the end of April 1944, a total of 5,289 *NN* prisoners (4,460 men and 829 women) were held in German penal institutions.[69]

The life of *NN* prisoners was determined above all by the authorities' desire to keep their whereabouts secret. Reich Minister Thierack was apparently informed that Hitler wished these prisoners to remain completely isolated from the outside world. As a result, *NN* prisoners were forbidden to write or receive letters. They were also not allowed to have contact with other groups of prisoners, causing many practical problems. In the Bayreuth penitentiary, *NN* prisoners were isolated from others in the cells, the hospital, the exercise yard and even when they received their food. The governor, Hans Mayr, recalled that 'it was very tiring to keep them separate'. The prison authorities were also resolved to prevent escapes of *NN* prisoners at any cost. Consequently, the inmates were supposed to be excluded from labour outside the penal institution, and in penitentiaries such as Cottbus the female prisoners were handcuffed at all times, except when they washed. Many *NN* prisoners died inside the penal institutions. For example, 36 of 147 Norwegians held in 1943–44 in the Sonnenburg penitentiary perished. The cloak of secrecy over *NN* prisoners was not even lifted after their death. If they were executed or died in captivity, their relatives were not informed, their farewell letters were suppressed, and their bodies secretly buried by the Gestapo.[70]

Once again, particularly brutal treatment awaited prisoners transported to the Emsland camp. Between May 1943 and March 1944, about 1,800 NN prisoners were taken there (including some women), mainly civilians from Belgium. To guarantee that they would not come into contact with other prisoners, a special camp (Lager Süd) was set up inside the notorious Esterwegen sub-camp. Many prisoners arrived in a very poor state, after months of imprisonment elsewhere. According to an Emsland prison doctor, only 100 of some 300 NN prisoners who had come from the Bochum prison on 22 May 1943 were actually healthy. The inmates' condition quickly declined further. Prisoners were tortured by having to stand to attention in the cold, shivering and freezing for hours. Some warders beat up inmates on a daily basis. Exhausted, blind or disabled prisoners were not exempted. One warder specialised in hitting prisoners on the head to burst their eardrums. Another kicked a French inmate so hard in his kidneys and sexual organs that the prisoner was hospitalised for two months. Tuberculosis, diphtheria, scarlet fever, dysentery, pneumonia and other illnesses were rampant. Sick prisoners either had to leave the hospital ward before they were cured, or they died there. One warder told the prisoners: 'There are no sick [inmates], only the healthy and the dead.' The German hospital orderly nicknamed 'Le Fou' by the prisoners regularly refused to hand out available medication such as antidiphtheritic serum, causing the deaths of several inmates. At least the NN prisoners in Esterwegen were not forced to work, in contrast to NN prisoners in other penal institutions. However, this proved to be a mixed blessing, as it was used by the camp authorities as a justification for giving them less food than other inmates in the camp. One former prisoner recalled that 'for us, Esterwegen was a starvation camp'. On average, NN prisoners lost more than 15 kilos during their often brief time in Esterwegen. Mortality among them was high. In early 1944, half of all the fatalities in the Emsland camp were of NN prisoners.[71] Of course, the guards in Emsland were already used to meting out especially brutal punishment to foreign prisoners, having maltreated Polish prisoners in the camp for several years – just like German prison officers elsewhere.

Enforcing Racial Policy: Polish Prisoners

For most of the war, Poles made up by far the largest group of all non-German convicts. Most of them were held in penal institutions in the Polish territory incorporated into Germany in 1939, where conditions were very poor from the beginning of the Nazi occupation. Initially, this probably owed more to the brutality of German judges in the east, than to the local prison personnel. True, some German prison officials transferred from the Altreich abused Polish inmates right from the start. However, this situation was probably not yet pervasive. For, at least in the early years of the Nazi occupation, the legal system actually employed a large number of Polish warders in the incorporated territories. Given the severe shortages of prison personnel, the German authorities felt that they had no other choice.[72] More decisive for the experience of imprisonment in this period was the extreme overcrowding – a direct result of the blind assault of the German courts on the local Polish population (see Chapter 5).

Penal institutions in the east were soon packed with inmates, further exacerbating the unhygienic conditions and shortages of food and clothes. Some Nazi legal officials apparently believed that the way forward was the even greater use of the death penalty. In 1941, the Posen general state prosecutor Karl Drendel, who also held the rank of SS-Hauptsturmführer, argued in a legal journal that the frequent application of the death penalty prevented 'the undesirable and dangerous filling up of the eastern penal institutions with the mass of multiple recidivist serious Polish criminals'.[73] But judges were still far more likely to use sentences of imprisonment, and inmate numbers continued to rise. On 31 March 1941, there were already some 19,247 prisoners (mainly Poles) held in the incorporated territories – about 7,000 prisoners above the official maximum capacity.[74] At first, many Poles were serving sentences for alleged atrocities committed against Germans during the Nazi invasion. Others were sentenced for 'political offences', an extremely elastic term which covered a wide range of deviant behaviour, from active resistance to 'insubordination' towards German farmers. But most cases, undoubtedly, fell into the category of economic offences, which were widespread in the incorporated territories. The Polish population received significantly fewer rations than Germans, and many Poles had little choice but to break the law to try to secure their subsistence.[75]

Imprisonment in the incorporated territories was largely organised along the same lines as in the Altreich. But there were also some important differences, in particular in the early years of the occupation. Most importantly, penal institutions in the east were not yet geared to forced labour in the same way as the institutions inside the Altreich. For example, on 31 March 1941, less than 3 per cent of male prisoners in the incorporated territories were working in prison camps or permanent satellite camps, compared to 20 per cent inside the Altreich. Instead, about a quarter of the male prisoners in the incorporated territories were held in small jails, more then twice as many as in the Altreich. Traditionally, the prison authorities had failed to turn such small jails into productive entities. This task was made even more difficult in the east, due to overcrowding, the shortage of prison officials and the severe lack of raw materials. As a result, significant numbers of Polish prisoners were without work in the early stages of the Nazi occupation, much to the frustration of the officials in the Reich Ministry of Justice. Not only did numerous Polish prisoners escape from the heavy toil they deserved, in the eyes of the German authorities, but the labour shortage undermined the insistence by the legal system that all its prisoners be used productively for the war effort. Therefore, the ministerial officials decided that Polish prisoners judged capable of outside labour could be transported to the Altreich, just as Polish civilians were deported to work inside Germany as foreign workers.[76]

From 1940, thousands of Polish prisoners were transported to Germany. The state in which they arrived offers a glimpse into the dreadful conditions prevailing in penal institutions in occupied Poland: many inmates were starved, disease-ridden and covered in lice, and often had torn clothes. Some were too ill to work at all. The rest were put to hard labour, but many of them did not hold out for long. This can be illustrated by the fate of a group of 44 Polish penitentiary inmates, transported in early 1942 from the Schieratz (also Sieradsch) institution in the Posen district to the Remscheid-Lüttringhausen penitentiary. After working for less than three months in Remscheid, three of the prisoners were dead, two lay in the prison hospital, and ten totally drained inmates had been sent back to Schieratz. The Remscheid officials apparently suspected foul play, assuming that their colleagues in Schieratz had used the transport to get rid of their weakest prisoners. But this was strenuously denied by the Schieratz governor: 'The fact is, that all inmates in our local institution ... suffer from undernourishment and general physical weakness.'[77] To make sure that penal institutions in the Altreich could count on a continuous supply of outside workers, the Reich Ministry of Justice ordered that Polish prisoners who were sent back to the east could be replaced by other convicts from the incorporated territories. This movement of inmates between east and west, designed to exploit Polish prisoners to the utmost, only slowed down from late spring 1942, when the Reich Ministry of Justice apparently decided that the Polish prisoners could now be employed productively in the incorporated territories.[78]

Overall, the number of Polish prisoners inside the Altreich increased rapidly during the war. In summer 1940, the Jena general state prosecutor reported that in some institutions in his district the prison population was already one-quarter Pole.[79] Some of them, as we have just seen, had originally been sentenced in the incorporated territories and were temporarily taken west for forced labour. But others, generally foreign workers, had been arrested inside the Altreich itself. Often, they were now serving short sentences in local jails. From the beginning, these Polish prisoners in the Altreich were subject to brutal discrimination by local officials driven by racial prejudice. Disciplinary punishment was often severe, and some Poles were randomly beaten by warders. Once more, the prisoners' poor command of German was enough for warders to indulge in mindless violence. For example, in 1941 one inmate in the Untermaßfeld penitentiary observed two warders brutally beating a Polish prisoner with a rubber truncheon, with one warder yelling 'I will teach you to speak in German'.[80]

Physical violence against Polish prisoners was also routine in the Emsland camp. After the outbreak of war, the Reich Ministry of Justice had ordered that some Polish prisoners should be taken to Emsland, to be occupied with 'particularly hard and arduous work'.[81] The first large transport of Poles arrived in the Emsland camp in July 1940. They were taken to the sub-camp Neusustrum, which was soon reserved for Polish and a few Jewish prisoners. At the end of March 1941, some 1,600 Polish prisoners were held in Neusustrum.[82] The camp officials spoke no Polish and often relied on violence to make themselves understood. Individual prisoners, designated by the authorities as barrack supervisors, were equally brutal. Attacks on the Poles were extreme, even by the cruel standards of the Emsland camp. Inmates were assaulted on a daily basis and most of the Poles suffered from open wounds. There can be no doubt that they were treated worse than almost all other prisoners in the camp at that time. This is obvious in the official mortality statistics, which show that Poles in the Emsland camp were significantly more likely to die than Germans.[83]

Some Polish prisoners in the Altreich became the victims of vicious onslaughts. One of them was the welder Wladislaw Chlabicz, who had been sentenced to three years in a penitentiary for theft, which he served in the Luckau penitentiary, south of Berlin. On 27 August 1940, he managed to escape. But his luck soon ran out and he was re-arrested only six days later. Chlabicz now faced a vicious onslaught. For more than three months he was held in the cellar of the Luckau penitentiary, initially with the light kept on at all times. For months, his hands and feet were chained together so tightly that he developed ulcers. To dull his pain, he tore strips off a sheet and inserted them between the chains and his injured feet. When the warders found out that he had damaged prison property, they punished him with an additional two weeks' detention, this time in a completely dark cell. His ordeal continued after detention ended. On 5 February 1941, he was sentenced by a Cottbus court to ten years in a penitentiary and subsequent security confinement, convicted of six cases of theft committed during his brief escape. However, even this draconian sentence was not the end of the story, as now the police got involved. Apparently, they felt that Chlabicz should have been executed for his thefts: not long after his court sentence, they contacted the Reich Ministry of Justice and demanded that he be handed over. The legal officials put up no resistance. On the contrary, acting Reich Minister of Justice Schlegelberger himself agreed that Chlabicz's sentence was 'completely inadequate' and that he should have been sentenced to death. The Reich Ministry of Justice instructed the local prison officials to leave him to the police, putting its official stamp of approval on the 'police correction' of the court sentence.

On 28 July 1941, Wladislaw Chlabicz was handed over to police and SS officials. His fate is unknown, but he may well have been executed on the very same day.[84]

In the early stages of the Second World War, maltreatment of Polish prisoners was largely due to the initiative of local prison officials. The Reich Ministry of Justice made no serious attempt to introduce special rules discriminating against these inmates. But already in 1940, calls were growing for a more systematic policy of discrimination against Polish prisoners. The greatest pressure came from the police. At the end of August 1940, Bruno Streckenbach from the RSHA claimed in a letter to the Reich Ministry of Justice that Polish workers, who had been temporarily taken into protective custody in police jails for 'refusal to work', actually preferred their imprisonment to life outside because they now received better food and worked less hard. As a deterrent to these inmates, Streckenbach explained, the police authorities often cut their rations. Streckenbach suggested that similar measures should be applied to Polish police detainees held in jails run by the legal system.[85] Rather similar proposals were put forward at the same time by regional legal officials. The Stuttgart general state prosecutor Otto Wagner, an experienced official who had only joined the Nazi party in 1937, demanded that the rations of all Polish foreign workers serving short prison sentences in local jails should be cut, to make their imprisonment more unpleasant.[86] These calls did not fall on deaf ears in the Reich Ministry of Justice. In October 1940, State Secretary Freisler ordered that Poles sentenced for refusal to work or for insubordination had to be treated more strictly than others, because 'the ordinary prison service generally fails to achieve the desired result'. Up to three times a week, their rations at lunch would be reduced to bread and water and they would have to sleep on the stone floor at night. Previously, such sanctions had only been applied to prisoners found guilty of disciplinary offences. For many Polish prisoners, this exception now became the rule.[87] This was not the only measure introduced from the top against Polish inmates at the time. Just one month later, the Reich Ministry of Justice ordered that Polish prisoners had to be separated from Germans, following criticism (reported by the SD) that they shared facilities. Poles were now isolated in much the same way as Jewish prisoners.[88]

The official policy of racial discrimination against Polish prisoners escalated with the Prison Regulations for Poles (*Polenvollzugsordnung*) of 7 January 1942, which had been in the pipeline for several months. The Reich Ministry of Justice was busy from early 1941 drafting a separate criminal law for Poles (see p. 203), designed to step up the terror against 'racial aliens'. In this process, the legal officials also made plans to reorganise the imprisonment of Poles. In April 1941, State Secretary Schlegelberger presented a first draft of these new rules to the Reich Chancellery, together with the draft for a special criminal law. The difference from regular imprisonment was already obvious in the terminology: Poles were no longer to be sentenced to prison and penitentiary, but to 'punishment camp' and 'aggravated punishment camp'. This stricter treatment was necessary, Schlegelberger explained, because 'the Pole is less sensitive to regular sentences of imprisonment' – a view shared by leading Nazi officials such as Rudolf Heß, as Schlegelberger knew.[89] The pronouncement of the Criminal Law Decree for Poles and Jews on 4 December 1941 then paved the way for the Prison Regulations for Poles, introduced one month later.[90] These regulations applied to all Polish prisoners (including Polish Jews) who had lived in Poland before the Second World War, regardless of whether they had been sentenced in the former Polish territory or in Germany. These Polish prisoners were to be isolated from other inmates in selected penal institutions known as 'regular camps' (*Stammlager*), both inside Germany and in the incorporated territories. The rules left little doubt that the imprisoned Poles would be harmed, as they were to be subjected to 'unconditional discipline' and exhausting, unpaid labour. They were to be occupied with hard work for 13 hours each day, more than any other prisoners in penal institutions. Inmates sentenced to 'aggravated punishment camp' could even be forced to work for 14 hours a day. Disciplinary punishment for Poles was also harder than for German prisoners, including sanctions such as strict detention in a dark cell for up to two weeks.[91]

The new prison regulations exacerbated the deteriorating conditions for Polish prisoners in 1942. The situation was particularly grave in the incorporated territories. To start with, the food supply here was often insufficient. One survivor described the daily provision in the Krone institution (north of Bromberg) as follows: in the morning, half a litre of black coffee and a piece of bread; at noon, mostly soup, sometimes with a few potatoes; in the evenings, only coffee. At the same time, the hygienic conditions were worse than ever, for the prisoner numbers had continued to grow. On 30 September 1942, inmate numbers in the east peaked at 32,332 – an increase of more than 13,000 prisoners compared to spring 1941. The impact of this continual rise on individual institutions was dramatic. Within 18 months, the number of male and female inmates in the Sosnowitz institution (near Kattowitz) more than tripled, from 332 (30 June 1941) to 1,054 (31 December 1942). The story was similar elsewhere. By 1942, the Krone institution held four times more inmates than its official maximum capacity. Living conditions were compounded by the brutal approach of the local prison authorities. Forced labour was hard and disciplinary punishment often extremely severe. The Sosnowitz prison governor, for example, almost always opted for strict detention in a dark cell. Harsh punishment, exhausting labour, hunger rations and poor hygienic conditions all contributed to the spread of illness and epidemics. Most prisoners in the east were in a very bad physical condition. In the Rawitsch institution (north of Breslau) for men, some 190 prisoners (of the 1,177 inmates) were so ill in October 1942 that they could not work at all, despite the reluctance of most prison doctors to exempt inmates from work. Another 330 Rawitsch inmates were classified as only partially fit to work. Care for these sick prisoners was often completely inadequate. Even some local prison officials described the provisions as primitive.[92]

During the war, thousands of Polish convicts died in the incorporated territories. In some places, prisoner mortality shot up dramatically in 1942. In the Krone institution, 248 prisoners died in that year alone – compared to 27 deaths in 1941. According to official documents, most of these prisoners succumbed to tuberculosis, while others died of heart failure and general exhaustion (in part, this was the result of other penal institutions transferring prisoners suffering from TB to Krone). The racial penal policy pursued by the legal authorities meant that Polish prisoners in the east were far more likely than Germans to die in captivity. This becomes obvious when we look at the fate of German and Polish defendants sentenced to imprisonment by the Bromberg special court: one in every 40 German defendants died before they had completed their sentence. For Polish defendants, the figure was one in seven.[93]

Conditions for Polish prisoners in the Altreich were often not much better than in the east, on account of the official policy of racial discrimination. In a number of cases, Polish prisoners in the Altreich (who from late 1941 had to wear special insignia on their uniforms) were deliberately singled out by the authorities for particularly dangerous and harmful work, ahead of other prisoners. Justifying this policy, the Cologne general state prosecutor stated that 'experience has shown that Polish prisoners have greater powers of physical resistance'.[94] Given such views by senior legal officials, it is hardly surprising that the rate of illness and death among Polish prisoners inside the Altreich was also particularly high. Many were forced to work until they collapsed, as becomes clear when we examine the fate of the inmates in the Oberhausen-Holten camp. The camp, reserved for male Polish prisoners, had been set up in 1941 as a satellite camp of the Duisburg prison. It was built on the premises of the Ruhr-Chemie AG, and consisted of barracks, surrounded by a fence, barbed wire and guard dogs. Driven on by assistant warders and civilian workers, the prisoners were forced to perform heavy manual labour, such as digging earth and unloading goods. Many of the Polish prisoners, weak and emaciated, were unable to keep up. In the summer of 1942 it was not unusual for up to one-third of the 300–400 prisoners to be too sick to work at all. Some were gravely ill and the death rate was high. In May 1942 alone, 13 prisoners died, all of them because of physical exhaustion (the official cause of death was given as heart failure or circulatory collapse, caused by famine oedema).

In the end, the regional legal authorities decided to intervene in the Oberhausen-Holten camp. But this was not the result of concern about the well-being of the prisoners; it was a reaction to complaints by the Ruhr-Chemie AG about their poor performance. The industrialists had threatened that they would pay the legal authorities only half the sum agreed for the prisoners, because their output was so much lower than that of civilian workers. Eager to maintain its income, the office of the Düsseldorf general state prosecutor made proposals for increasing the inmates' output: prisoner rations were to be slightly improved and the inmates were to be divided into different work groups, depending on their physical strength. In practice, these measures did little to improve conditions, and large numbers of the Polish prisoners continued to collapse at work in the Oberhausen-Holten camp.[95]

From 1943, the total number of Polish convicts fell, as the police extended their role in the punishment of Poles and tried to push the legal apparatus further to the sidelines. By late March 1943, the overall number of Poles in all penal institutions had already declined by several thousand, to 36,148 (25,746 men; 10,402 women).[96] Numbers soon fell further (for the incorporated territories, see Figure 4, pp. 396–7). Even so, many thousands of Poles continued to be held in penal institutions. And they continued to face harsher conditions than most other inmates. After the war, a Dutch prisoner recalled seeing a group of Poles, who had been temporarily held in the Remscheid-Lüttringhausen penitentiary in autumn 1943. Covered in pustules, with oedematous legs and heads, they were 'human wrecks'. 'No,' the Dutch prisoner concluded, 'we were not yet that badly off . . . .'[97]

The sight of starving Poles was the norm in German penal institutions. The Amberg prison chaplain Benedikt Wein testified after the war that Polish prisoners had been in extremely poor health. And they were 'hungry like wolves. They also ate potato peelings. They also looked for scraps from the rubbish. This also led to cases of poisoning.'[98] Other Polish inmates became victims of the prison officials' unrelenting contempt, which manifested itself in so many different ways. In the Saarbrücken prison, for example, Polish (and Russian) prisoners were deliberately left in the otherwise empty fourth floor of the prison, which was most exposed to Allied air raids. Sure enough, when the prison was hit on 11 May 1944, this floor was partially destroyed and Poles and Russian prisoners suffered the greatest number of casualties.[99]

Disease continued to be rampant among Polish prisoners and treatment was often non-existent. Indeed, prison authorities at times hastened the death of sick prisoners. This was certainly true in the case of Poles suffering from tuberculosis, who were transported to the Mürau penal institution (Leitmeritz district) from 1943 onwards, on orders from the Reich Ministry of Justice. Mürau, reserved for Polish and Czech prisoners with TB, had originally been a medieval castle. With its thick stone walls and small windows, it was particularly unsuitable for the internment of individuals with tuberculosis. This did not trouble the prison authorities. After all, the official policy for Polish and Czech prisoners with TB was simply to segregate them. Isolation, not treatment, was the aim in Mürau, as the Reich Ministry of Justice announced in March 1943.[100] Health checks were perfunctory, conditions were primitive and food was scarce. The authorities did not even provide a trained doctor and the prison hospital had to be run by two fellow inmates. But the prisoners in Mürau were not merely left to die. Some were actually pushed into their graves. While a very large number were far too ill to be occupied with any kind of work, the authorities – keen to exploit the prisoners until the end – insisted that as many as possible had to work, with some of them forced to perform heavy manual labour in the woods or quarries outside the prison. The death rate in Mürau was extremely high, much higher than in TB wards reserved for German prisoners. In 1944 alone, some 302 prisoners died in Mürau (maximum capacity 500 prisoners), the great majority of them Poles.[101]

The differential treatment of prisoners with tuberculosis continued even if they survived their imprisonment. 'Worthy' German prisoners were, for the most part, released from prison, but the Polish (and Czech) prisoners held in Mürau were usually handed over to the police. After they had completed their sentences, they were left to the Gestapo, who then decided on their fate. For most prisoners, this meant that they were taken to Auschwitz. One such transport, with 15 former prisoners, left Mürau on 8 June 1943. All the prisoners on this transport were killed just one day after it reached Auschwitz.[102] But sometimes, local Gestapo officers refused to take over Polish convicts with tuberculosis, probably fearful of infection. In such cases, the prison authorities had little choice but to release the prisoners in question, much to the alarm of the police leadership in Berlin. On 17 January 1944, the RSHA insisted in a communication to regional police headquarters that 'infectious' Polish prisoners had to be arrested after their release. However, rather than taking these Poles on potentially lengthy transports to a concentration camp, they were instead to be 'proposed to the Reichsführer-SS for special treatment' – a common euphemism for extermination. German prison officials were informed of this policy in March 1944. None of them, it seems, raised any objections.[103]

A very large number of Polish convicts ended up in SS concentration camps. Prisoners with tuberculosis were by no means the only ones transferred after the end of their sentence. Many other Poles were also regularly handed over. As early as August 1940, the Reich Ministry of Justice, after prompting from the Reich Ministry of the Interior, asked regional legal officials to report to the police all prisoners from the incorporated territories who had either received penitentiary sentences of one year or more, or who offered 'no prospect of good behaviour in the future'. These prisoners could then be arrested by the police on the day of their release.[104] Later, this practice was further extended. On 21 April 1943, the Reich Ministry of Justice sent a secret directive to the general state prosecutors, informing them that new police guidelines had been passed. In keeping with these guidelines, the regional legal officials were now instructed to make sure that all Poles serving sentences of more than six months would be 'made available in time for collection' by the Gestapo, which would then transfer them from a penal institution to a concentration camp. All that was needed from the legal authorities was a completed standard document, sent to the police. In this way, the transfer of Polish prisoners to concentration camps after the end of their sentences became a routine procedure.[105]

Collaboration between prison and concentration camp authorities did not stop there. Crucially, the prison authorities also agreed to hand over certain Polish inmates *before* they had completed their sentence – breaking with another fundamental legal principle. At first, this practice was based not on central directives, but on case-by-case agreements between the regional police and legal authorities. The initiative in most cases presumably came from the police. But at times it was the local prison governors who set the ball rolling. For instance, on 5 February 1942 governor Ringk of the Teschen institution (Kattowitz district) wrote to the regional Gestapo concerning the Polish inmate Leopold T. This prisoner had already escaped once and the governor was certain that he would try again. Therefore, the governor proposed to leave the prisoner to the Gestapo for 'special use', with the full agreement of the state prosecution service. 'Asocial elements like that,' governor Ringk noted in a letter to the local court on 11 February 1942, 'are good for nothing.' Making plain his murderous intentions, the governor added that if the Gestapo took over Leopold T., 'he will have disappeared very soon, so that he will not have any more opportunities to commit further offences'. The police did not hesitate to get involved and T. was duly transferred to the Gestapo seven days later.[106] Such transfers of Polish prisoners to the police before the completion of their sentence were greatly extended and systematised in the autumn 1942, in an agreement between the Reich Ministry of Justice and the police. This was part of the 'annihilation through labour' programme, which occupies a central place in the transformation of the legal apparatus into an agency of mass murder.

8   Killing Prisoners

Many prisoners died during the Second World War. As we have seen, the prison authorities have to shoulder much of the responsibility for these deaths, which were often caused by neglect, forced labour, violence and terror. But the culpability of prison officials goes much further than that. This chapter will show that they were also involved in the systematic mass extermination of tens of thousands of prisoners. Prison officials helped to execute vast numbers of convicts on death row, condemned to die by German judges. But the prison authorities also participated in the mass murder of inmates who had not been sentenced to death. Among these murdered prisoners were thousands of 'incorrigible' German criminal offenders, Jews and many Poles, and political prisoners. Their fate was sealed by the racial and political obsessions of both legal officials and the Nazi leadership. In their case, annihilation was considered more important in the interests of the Nazi regime than their continued imprisonment and economic exploitation. The actual killings were largely left to the police and the SS, with the prisoners transferred from penal institutions to concentration camps. But over time, prison officials also became involved directly in the murder of 'asocial' and disabled inmates inside penal institutions.

'Annihilation through Labour': the View from Above

In the late summer of 1942, the new Reich Minister of Justice Otto-Georg Thierack arrived in Berlin determined to shake up the prison service. In the long run, Thierack envisaged that many 'racial aliens' and 'incorrigibles' would be left to the police (see Chapter 5). But what about those already inside penal institutions? In Thierack's eyes, this was an urgent question. After all, on the day of his appointment on 20 August 1942, Hitler had warned him against the dangers of 'preserving' the 'crooks', 'ruffians' and 'vermin' in prison, which would result in 'negative selection' and a repetition of the 1918 revolution. To make absolutely sure that Thierack had got this point, the Party Chancellery even sent him a typed copy of Hitler's table-talk of 20 August.[1]

Preparing for the Killings

Thierack lost no time in acting. In late August or early September 1942 he met with several leading prison officials in the Reich Ministry of Justice in Berlin. Thierack explained that it was wrong that the 'worst criminals' should be held inside penal institutions, while the 'most noble German blood' was flowing on the battlefield. He had spoken to Hitler, Thierack told the officials, and it was Hitler's opinion that the 'inferiors' had to be killed. Thierack added: 'Gentlemen, please do not think me a blood guzzler, certain things just have to be.' The prison officials in the Reich Ministry of Justice were soon referring to the plan as a way of 'balancing the biological scales'.[2] In the weeks following this meeting, Thierack determined which inmates were to be selected for annihilation and how these prisoners should be murdered. These questions were also debated between Thierack's deputy Curt Rothenberger and high-ranking SS officials. Thierack himself discussed the plans with leading members of the Nazi state such as Hans Heinrich Lammers, the head of the Reich Chancellery, and propaganda minister Joseph Goebbels, who applauded Thierack's 'national-socialist viewpoint' and made some important detailed proposals.[3]

The extermination programme was finalised at the meeting between Thierack and Himmler on 18 September 1942. Rothenberger was also present, as was his old acquaintance, SS-Gruppenführer Bruno Streckenbach, former head of the Hamburg Gestapo. According to the official minutes of the meeting, one of the key points of discussion was the 'transfer of asocial elements from the prison service to the Reichsführer SS for annihilation through labour'.[4] When deciding who exactly these 'asocial' prisoners were, Thierack and Himmler largely stuck to a draft which had been prepared shortly before the meeting.[5] The transfer was divided into two separate actions, which can be termed the 'general transfer' and the 'individual transfer'. The 'general transfer' meant that all Jews, Sinti and Roma, Russians and Ukrainians in penal institutions (and workhouses) were to be handed over to the police without exception. The same was agreed for all Polish prisoners with sentences of more than three years. Finally, individuals sentenced to security confinement were also to be transferred to the police. Their inclusion had important symbolic value. For years, the legal system had resisted police attempts to poach the security-confined prisoners. Thierack's decision to hand them over signalled an important U-turn, designed in part to demonstrate his resolve to the police and Nazi leadership.

The 'individual transfer' of prisoners was quite different. It included all German and Czech inmates with sentences of more than eight years' imprisonment in a penitentiary. They were not to be automatically transferred to the police. Rather, a commission of the Reich Ministry of Justice would examine them in order to determine their 'asociality'. Only if this commission concluded that the examined prisoners 'will forever be worthless for the national community', would they be turned over to the police. Following a suggestion by the Berlin general state prosecutor, Friedrich Jung, the Reich Ministry of Justice decided in early October 1942 that individual examination should be extended to some inmates in security confinement and those in penitentiaries who had been sentenced to security confinement after their imprisonment. If prison officials were 'convinced that because of their positive development they could be released in due time', probably after the end of the war, then such inmates were not to be automatically transferred to the police but should be examined by the commission of the Ministry of Justice, too.[6]

These exceptions clearly highlight the difference between 'criminal' and 'racial' categories in the Third Reich. While some German inmates could be classified as 'reformable' and escape from being transferred to the police, there were no exceptions for 'racial aliens' such as Jews. They were to be exterminated primarily on racial grounds, not as criminals. In their case, the paradigm of modern penal policy did not apply: Nazi ideology did not allow for any 'reform' of Jews. Similarly, the rules for transfer reflected the ranking of different groups in Nazi racial thinking. Jews and other prisoners at the very bottom of the Nazi hierarchy were to be killed without exception. But Poles, one step up, were to be handed over only if they were supposed to be serious criminal offenders, serving longer sentences.

This murderous programme serves as a good example of decision-making in Nazi Germany. The original initiative had come from Hitler, whose remarks at the lunchtime meeting on 20 August 1942 had been taken as an urgent order by Thierack. One month later, Thierack had agreed to hand over substantial numbers of prisoners for 'annihilation through labour' to the police. Himmler, for his part, was well aware that Hitler had been ranting for months about the danger of 'preserving' criminals inside prisons for a revolution. Himmler also knew that Hitler regarded lengthy legal imprisonment as pointless: 'After ten years' penitentiary,' Hitler had told Himmler on 8 February 1942, 'the [crook] is lost for the national community anyway. Who would still give him any work? Such a fellow should either be put into a concentration camp for life, or one should kill him. In the present time, the latter is more important: for deterrence.'[7] To be sure, Hitler's views had been expressed in rather general terms, and it was left to Thierack, Himmler and other officials to formulate a detailed policy. But Hitler's role was still decisive. This is demonstrated by the fact that both Himmler and Thierack quickly sought confirmation that their plans had Hitler's approval. On 22 September, just four days after his meeting with Thierack, Heinrich Himmler met Hitler at the Wehrwolf headquarters in the Ukraine. During a lengthy meeting, Himmler evidently raised his agreement with Thierack and received Hitler's consent.[8] A few days later, Thierack also received confirmation that Hitler had accepted the proposals for dealing with the 'asocial' prisoners.[9] Only after Thierack and Himmler got the go-ahead from Hitler did the transfer begin.

On 29 September 1942, Thierack personally told the leading regional judicial officials of the plans. He reported on his larger vision for 'our so well preserved asocials'. Without informing his listeners of the details, Thierack told them that Hitler had personally given him the green light for the extermination of 'asocials'. In this context, Thierack only mentioned individuals sentenced to imprisonment in a penitentiary for eight years or longer, and those sentenced to security confinement, whom he described as 'life unworthy of life in the highest degree' – the fact that the programme also included 'racial aliens' was not made explicit. The crucial influence of Hitler in the whole process becomes obvious once more when examining the reasons which Thierack set out in his speech for the programme of mass murder, where he repeated almost verbatim the points that Hitler had made to him on the day of his appointment. Thus, Thierack warned of the dangers of 'negative selection', which protected the 'asocials' in penal institutions for a possible revolution: 'something is not right here!' There was only one solution, Thierack concluded. The prisoners had to be 'annihilated'.

But how should this be done? One possibility, Thierack mused, would have been to let the prisoners freeze to death outside their cells during winter, just as German soldiers had died on the eastern front. But Thierack argued that this would have led to public outrage. While he did not explain this point in any detail, one can speculate that public disapproval of the centralised 'euthanasia' programme – halted by Hitler in August 1941 after the deaths of more than 70,000 people, in part in response to growing public disquiet about the murders – was one reason for avoiding such public mass killing of prisoners. In addition, Thierack presumably feared that if the judicial apparatus itself carried out the killing of persons legally sentenced to imprisonment, it would destroy any remaining belief the German public might still have had in the rule of law. Instead of letting the prisoners freeze to death, Thierack had decided upon what he called, perversely, a more 'ethical' solution: the 'asocials' would all be transferred elsewhere and occupied in such a way that they would 'perish'. Their destruction was not more than 'self-defence of the whole people', Thierack added, using the justification common in Nazi legal thinking about the death penalty.[10] In the debate following Thierack's speech, not one of the officials raised any objections. The judicial top brass closed ranks behind its new minister.

The General Transfer

The 'general transfer' started in late October 1942, when the Reich Ministry of Justice in Berlin received from penal institutions the first lists of names of those prisoners to be sent to the police.[11] The general transfer was organised by section V in the Ministry of Justice, the department responsible for the general running of the prison service, still led by the veteran Rudolf Marx. The official in charge of the day-to-day organisation of the general transfer was Robert Hecker, another long-serving ministerial official.[12] Hecker, an obedient and industrious bureaucrat, clearly had no scruples about his role. One of his former colleagues described him as a man who executed every order, regardless of its content, with great diligence: 'He was completely devoted to his work, he drowned in paper, and for him, the old Prussian sense of duty of the civil servant stood above everything.'[13]

Organisational details of the transfer were discussed in October 1942 in a meeting between Marx and Hecker and top officials from the RSHA, including Heinrich Müller, Arthur Nebe and Bruno Streckenbach. The agreed procedure was that Hecker would examine the lists of prisoners sent in by the penal institutions, checking whether the formal criteria for transfer were met. Then the lists would be passed on to the RSHA, which in turn would send the names of the prisoners to local police officials who organised the transport from penal institutions to a designated concentration camp.[14]

The general transfer was carried out with some urgency and was more or less completed by the summer of 1943. By February 1943, some 15,293 prisoners had already been reported by the Reich Ministry of Justice to the RSHA (13,839 men and 1,454 women). Two months later, on 24 April 1943, this figure had climbed to 16,830 prisoners (15,198 men and 1,632 women). The great majority had already been taken to concentration camps. These transports had started as early as November 1942, and by the end of April 1943 around 14,700 prisoners (13,100 men and 1,600 women) had been handed over to the police.[15] These figures can be broken down into various prisoner categories.

More than half of the prisoners handed over during the general transfer were Germans sentenced to security confinement. They were among the first inmates transported to concentration camps in November 1942. At this time, there were around 14,000 prisoners with sentences of security confinement (including prisoners in penitentiaries with sentences of subsequent security confinement). About two-thirds of them had been imprisoned since before the war.[16] Most posed no significant criminal threat. Instead, they were written off as 'asocial' and 'biologically inferior'. Richard F. was one of them. His father died in 1910, when Richard F. was four years old, and the boy had spent three years in a corrective state institution. After the First World War, he worked for several years as an unskilled labourer. He was frequently arrested and sentenced for minor thefts to a few weeks' or months' imprisonment, for the first time at the age of 20. From 1929, Richard F. was unemployed. In the following years, he travelled through Germany, seeking work and subsistence, and committed further small-time offences. In 1937, for example, he was sentenced to 15 months in a penitentiary for the theft of a garden hose. After his release, he tried to stay on the straight and narrow, but between late 1939 and spring 1940 he stole several chickens and rabbits. He probably knew that under the new draconian criminal law in wartime he might be sentenced to death, and while awaiting trial he tried to kill himself. In view of the economic hardship which had driven F. to his crime, the judge at the Jena special court decided to spare him the death penalty. But the sentence was still draconian: 15 years in a penitentiary with subsequent security confinement. After the agreement between Himmler and Thierack this became synonymous with a death sentence. On 29 November 1942, Richard F. was handed over as 'asocial' to the police, and transferred to Mauthausen concentration camp. Less than two months later, he was dead.[17]

The vast majority of the security confined were men. At first, the authorities had been undecided what to do with the small number of imprisoned women. They had not been part of the original agreement between Himmler and Thierack and as late as 9 October 1942, the Reich Ministry of Justice noted that their transfer was still 'doubtful' and would be raised with SS-Gruppenführer Bruno Streckenbach. In these discussions, it evidently did not take the officials long to decide that the women would be included in the transfer after all: the first transport of security-confined inmates from the Aichach women's institution to Auschwitz took place on 8 January 1943.[18]

The transfer continued at a great pace in the following months. By 24 April 1943, a total of 8,813 (8,323 men and 490 women) sentenced to security confinement had already been reported for transfer to the police. Most of the remaining prisoners soon followed.[19] At the end of 1943, virtually all of the individual security-confined prisoners encountered in the previous chapters – inmates such as Karl Kakuschky, Rosa S., Franziska K., Willy Leske and Magdalena S. – had been taken to concentration camps.

The other prisoners transferred to the police as part of the general transfer were the selected 'racial aliens'. In their case, there was never any question of exempting women – all prisoners were to be handed over. Most were Polish prisoners, whose transfer was organised with ruthless efficiency. In the Sosnowitz institution, for example, 93 eligible Polish prisoners were reported to the police between 1 November 1942 and 1 January 1943. By the end of February 1943, 81 had been taken to concentration camps. Of the remaining 12 inmates, 11 had died in Sosnowitz before they could be handed over.[20] In total, some 6,242 Polish prisoners (5,434 men and 808 women) had been reported to the police by 24 April 1943. The transfer of 'asocial' prisoners also accounted for the lives of Russian and Ukrainian inmates. However, their numbers inside German penal institutions had remained small, because of the virtual police monopoly of their persecution. By 24 April 1943, the Reich Ministry of Justice had reported a total of 451 Russians (409 men and 42 women) to the police for transfer.[21]

Racial fanaticism also influenced the decision to include the Sinti and Roma in the general transfer. Control and harassment of this small minority (around 26,000 in Germany in the 1930s) had been commonplace well before the Nazis came to power. But it soon intensified in the Third Reich. Of course, the legal system contributed to this process. In April 1935, Reich Minister Gürtner instructed state prosecutors to step up the fight against the 'Gypsy plague', as he called it. German courts passed strict sentences, and those convicted were treated harshly inside prisons and penitentiaries. Sinti and Roma were also, from early on, regularly handed over to the police after the end of their sentence. Legal officials clearly shared the popular prejudice against the 'criminal lifestyle' of the Sinti and Roma, an established theme in criminology for a long time. For example, in his 1926 book on the 'professional' criminal, Robert Heindl wrote that it was a well-known fact that 'every visit by Gypsies starts with begging and ends with theft'. In the Third Reich, such claims were increasingly mixed with racism, following the boom in 'Gypsy research', eagerly supported by the German police. For it was the police who played the leading role in the assault on the Sinti and Roma. Police persecution was extended and coordinated in the second half of 1930s, before the terror dramatically escalated during the war. Sinti and Roma in Germany and elsewhere in Nazi-controlled Europe became victims of the extermination policy, with 250,000 to 500,000 (estimates vary) murdered.[22] In all this, the legal apparatus played a rather peripheral role. Only few Sinti and Roma came before the courts, and they hardly figured in the discussions and plans of the prison officials, in contrast to the case of Jewish prisoners. Not surprisingly, there were only a small number of Sinti and Roma inside penal institutions by the autumn of 1942. Legal officials identified some 160 men and 86 women, who were duly reported for general transfer to the police.[23]

Finally, the general transfer included Jews inside German penal institutions, who had long been targeted by the police. Even before the war, Jewish men sentenced for 'race defilement' had been reported to the police prior to their release. Such reports were extended in 1941 to all Jewish prisoners coming to the end of their sentence.[24] The legal officials were well aware that, for Jews, prisons and penitentiaries were now mere stopping-places on the way to SS camps. In late October 1941, Adolf Eichmann, head of the 'Jewish department' in the RSHA, told the Reich Ministry of Justice that released Jewish prisoners would generally be 'taken into protective custody as asocial elements'.[25] Soon, as the genocidal programme was coordinated and systematised, Jewish prisoners were even handed to the police *before* the end of their sentence. On 17 March 1942, the Berlin Gestapo informed the regional general state prosecutor that it intended to 'evacuate' the Jewish prisoners in Berlin penal institutions. The Gestapo assumed that the prison officials would 'welcome the evacuation of these Jews'.[26] By that time, officials in the Reich Ministry of Justice knew that the regime had decided on the extermination of the Jews. State Secretary Freisler himself had taken part in the infamous Wannsee conference on 20 January 1942, and lower-ranking officials were present at follow-up conferences, discussing details of the 'final solution of the Jewish question'. So when officials in the Reich Ministry of Justice were informed of the request by the Berlin Gestapo, they quickly produced guidelines for the whole of Germany. On 16 April 1942, all regional legal authorities were instructed by State Secretary Freisler that the execution of sentences against Jews 'who should be evacuated, is to be discontinued after an official request by the state police authority'. In such a case, the prisoners were to be directly handed over to the Gestapo. The same principle was applied to Jewish remand prisoners, 'unless the death penalty is expected' – implying that 'evacuation' really meant extermination.[27] It is unclear how many Jewish prisoners were actually handed over, following the directive on 16 April 1942. The overall number of Jews in penal institutions at this time was even smaller than before, especially inside the Altreich. Fewer so-called offences by Jews reached the courts, as they were mainly dealt with directly by the police or SS. In Berlin, which traditionally had the highest density of Jews in Germany, there were only 89 Jewish inmates in prisons and penitentiaries in early 1942.[28] Still, the directive proved a death sentence for hundreds of Jewish prisoners. In mid-1942, a number of local penal institutions worked closely with the Gestapo to ensure that Jewish prisoners were handed over. In the Kattowitz district, for example, individual penal institutions sent monthly lists of names of Jewish prisoners and eligible remand prisoners to the regional Gestapo headquarters, which then picked up the inmates.[29]

Those Jews still remaining in penal institutions became victims of the general transfer from autumn 1942. They were promptly handed over to the police, with the last abuse from prison warders still ringing in their ears. The senior prison administrator Robert Hecker recalled after the war that 'pretty soon all Jews were taken out of the institutions', and by 24 April 1943, 1,078

Jewish prisoners (872 men and 206 women) had been reported to the police.[30] To ensure that those few Jewish prisoners who had not yet been handed over to the police by the time they reached the end of their legal sentence (presumably, this targeted mainly Jews sentenced after 31 October 1942, as the transfer only applied to individuals sentenced before that date) were not set free, the Reich Ministry of Justice reminded general state prosecutors on 21 April 1943 that all Jewish prisoners coming up to their release had to be left to the Gestapo. The Gestapo would then take them 'for life' to the Auschwitz concentration camp.[31] All roads for Jewish prisoners now led to Auschwitz.

The Individual Transfer

While the programme of general transfer was beginning to wind down by early summer 1943, the process of 'individual transfer' went on until almost the end of the war. The official put in charge of the individual examinations by Thierack was his close confidant Karl Engert. Born in 1877, Engert had joined the NSDAP in April 1921, and got to know Hitler personally. In 1932 he was elected as a Nazi member of the Bavarian State Parliament. Engert's political activism in Weimar paid dividends after 1933. A low-ranking regional judge in the 1920s, by 1938 he had risen to vice-president of the People's Court, where he was nicknamed 'the greatest bloodhound' by defence lawyers and passed numerous death sentences during the war. It was at this time that he became close friends with Thierack, then president of the People's Court. As a Nazi Reich speaker and SS-Oberführer on Himmler's staff, Engert also had close links to the party and SS. In 1940 he had even approached Himmler, whom he knew well, about a full-time job with the SS. In short, there was no doubt at all about Engert's Nazi credentials. In an article celebrating his 65th birthday, the *Völkischer Beobachter* on 24 October 1942 praised him as 'deeply steeped in national-socialist feeling, thinking and purpose'. Just one week later, he was officially appointed head of the newly created secret section XV of the Reich Ministry of Justice, which also included ambitious junior members of the Ministry (Albert Hupperschwiller and Friedrich Wilhelm Meyer, later also Otto Gündner).[32] Engert had been earmarked for this post several weeks earlier. Most likely, Thierack and Himmler had already agreed on 18 September 1942 that he would be the right man for this murderous job.[33]

The new secret section XV of the Reich Ministry of Justice dealt exclusively with the individual examinations of 'asocial' prisoners. Engert had Thierack's complete confidence and was made directly responsible to him. They worked closely together and in June 1943 Engert was, in addition, appointed head of the general prison administration (section V), again reporting directly to Thierack (rather than the State Secretary). Engert replaced Rudolf Marx, who was humiliated by being demoted to the brief for prison farming and security.

For the first time, a committed Nazi was now at the top of the German prison administration. Marx was not the only experienced senior official in the Ministry of Justice from the Weimar era who had to make way for new men under Thierack. But this change, significant as it was, should not be over-emphasised; after all, it was with Marx at the helm of the prison administration that most of the general transfer was realised.[34]

The prisoners included in the individual transfer were different in three respects from those transferred to the police as part of the general transfer. Firstly, many prisoners were serving very lengthy sentences for violent crimes, such as murder, homicide, rape and robbery, rather than petty property offences. In a number of penal institutions, these violent offenders made up the largest group among the inmates handed over in the individual transfer.[35] Secondly, the transports included no 'racial aliens' such as Poles and Jews, as they were handed over to the police as part of the general transfer. Thirdly, the individual transfer included a number of political prisoners, who had been largely absent from the general transfer.[36] About a third of all the prisoners to be examined by Engert's commission were serving sentences for treason and high treason. The great majority were German nationals who had been active Social Democrats or Communists.[37] To prepare for the examinations, political prisoners were handed special 'questionnaires for political offenders', apparently designed by Karl Engert himself. They included questions such as: 'Have your parents been Social Democrats?'; 'Since when have you been a member of a socialist party?' and 'Have you ever been to a training course in Moscow?' Inmates who gave false information risked being caught out by officials studying their files.[38]

From November 1942, officials from Engert's section XV travelled to penal institutions to carry out the examinations, sometimes alone, at other times together. Once, Albert Hupperschwiller even brought his wife along, presumably for her morbid entertainment. During such visits, the officials would check the files and papers concerning each prisoner. Generally, they would also personally examine the inmate. At least initially, Engert's officials only travelled to institutions reserved for male inmates. The legal authorities had apparently not yet decided what would happen to women with penitentiary sentences of over eight years (of whom there were few) and security-confined women judged as 'reformable' by the local officials. This issue was later settled and some female inmates were handed over to the police after examination as part of the individual transfer.[39]

At times, as in the case of some political prisoners, interrogations by Engert's commission took 30 minutes or more, with the officials asking the prisoners about their political convictions, how they felt about Hitler, and who they thought would win the war.[40] At other times, they lasted just a few minutes. Simon L., who had been sentenced in late 1933 to ten years in a penitentiary for manslaughter (while poaching, he had shot a forester), after the war recalled the perfunctory nature of his interrogation in spring 1943, carried out in the Kaisheim penitentiary by Albert Hupperschwiller from the Reich Ministry of Justice:

> There was not much talking. He briefly asked me about my offence and accused me of having committed a murder. I excused myself by pointing to my youth at the time. As far as I remember, he also said to me: 'you've also been a Communist' [L. had been a member of the Rotfrontkämpferbund]. Then he only made a movement with his hand, indicating that I should withdraw. The whole interrogation lasted at best two to three minutes.[41]

Shortly afterwards, Hupperschwiller told a Kaisheim warder, who had asked him to exempt Simon L. as a particularly hard-working prisoner, that he had decided to report L. as 'asocial'.[42] This meant that Hupperschwiller wrote his report on a red piece of paper, which signalled 'asocial' (a green sheet meant 'reformability', and a white paper 'unclear'). Karl Engert apparently insisted on personally re-examining some cases where his officials had decided on 'reformable' or 'unclear', probably because, as his former subordinate Robert Hecker recalled after the war, Engert was 'undoubtably extremely fanatical' in 'fighting these asocial elements'. If, on the other hand, the officials had decided on 'asocial' on their own accord, as in the case of Simon L., Engert would not be involved.[43] In such cases, the prisoner's name was transmitted to the police, which then organised the transfer. Only a few weeks after his interrogation, on 13 May 1943, Simon L. was taken by the police as an 'asocial' prisoner to Mauthausen concentration camp.

The term 'asocial' was popular in the Third Reich because it could be applied to all forms of non-normative behaviour. Its power lay precisely in the fact that it could not be clearly defined. It is possible nevertheless to isolate some criteria which influenced the commission of the Reich Ministry of Justice. In the case of political prisoners, Karl Engert insisted that the commission was to get rid of those who might participate in a revolution, echoing Hitler's obsession with preventing another 'stab in the back'. Engert was also interested in heredity and the 'character of the parents'. Apparently, he instructed his subordinates to judge whether the offender came from a 'degenerate' family. The officials had to determine, in Engert's words, 'whether the father was a drinker, the mother a whore'. A divorce, or lack of contact with the family on the outside, also counted as a minus point. Above all, the aim was to single out prisoners who were 'incorrigible'. Often, the decision was based in part on old criminal-biological examinations. Pioneered in the 1920s as a supposedly objective method of classifying criminals, these examinations now gave a semblance of scientific authority to the murderous decisions of Karl Engert and his henchmen.[44]

Still, the overall criteria for the classification of prisoners as 'asocial' remained rather vague. Herbert Peter, who had joined Engert's commission in 1943, complained after the war: 'I never received any hint about what was to be understood by the term "asocial"; I had to work it out by myself.' Peter focused on left-wing activists, recalling that 'the prisoners I judged as asocial were mostly Communists'.[45] They included the Austrian Franz L., whom Herbert Peter examined at the beginning of April 1943 in the Untermaßfeld penitentiary. Franz L. had been sentenced by the People's Court to 15 years' penitentiary, having been active in the Austrian Communist Party, producing flyers and donating money for the families of imprisoned political activists. His political views had already outraged the Untermaßfeld prison authorities when he arrived in 1941: 'Dyed-in-the-wool Communist . . . Here only solitary confinement. Will continue to agitate. Heavy labour,' a prison official noted. Herbert Peter also judged the inmate to be a dangerous political opponent of the Nazi regime. On 11 June 1943, Franz L. was transported as an 'asocial' prisoner to the Buchenwald concentration camp. This is where his trail disappears.[46]

Karl Engert was aware that some prisoners were due to be released before they had been examined by his commission. To prevent this, he ordered that they should be held until a decision had been reached.[47] For some inmates, this order was a death sentence. The worker Rudolf Larm was committed to the Untermaßfeld penitentiary at the age of 24 in 1928. He had been sentenced for robbery to 15 years' imprisonment, a very harsh sentence possibly influenced by the fact that he was a locally well known Communist. Larm was due for release on 12 January 1943. However, after instructions from the Reich Ministry of Justice, he was held until his case could be dealt with by Engert's commission. The prisoner was deeply distressed. On 17 January 1943, he wrote to his brother, in a letter kept back by the authorities: 'Until now, I have endured all torment, I said to myself, one day all this will be over, you still have half a life in front of you – now everything hangs in the balance. This life for me has neither purpose nor meaning!' Engert's commission finally classified Larm as 'asocial', and more than four months after the date originally scheduled for his release, he was transported to Buchenwald concentration camp. Within three weeks, he was dead.[48]

The individual transfer went on for about two years, with significant organisational effort. By 23 February 1944, the members of Engert's commission had examined some 5,959 inmates in 46 different penal institutions all over Germany. Another 1,300 inmates were still to be investigated. Of all the inmates already examined, only 998 prisoners were judged 'reformable' and remained in the penal institutions. A further 437 were reported for service in a special military formation for criminal offenders. By contrast, more than 40 per cent of examined inmates (2,464) were handed over as 'asocial' to the police. Another 105 'asocial' Czech prisoners were recommended by Engert's commission to the responsible Reichsprotektor Wilhelm Frick for transfer to the police. For a further 1,250 inmates, a decision by the commission had been postponed for economic reasons. These inmates were skilled labourers (mainly Communists and Czechs) employed in armaments factories. Their fate depended on Germany's military fortune. If it deteriorated and the inmates became a security risk, then they too would be handed over. Such economic considerations also temporarily saved another 705 of the examined inmates from transfer to the police. Although they had already been classified by the commission as 'asocial', they still remained in penal institutions for the time being, for reasons of economic productivity.[49] As we shall see, being judged as an indispensable labourer offered the best hope for supposedly 'asocial' prisoners to escape transfer to the police.

Murder in the Camps

Overall, more than 20,000 prisoners were handed over as part of the 'annihilation through labour' agreement between Himmler and Thierack.[50] In the concentration camps, they were systematically killed. Probably about half of them were dead within three months of their arrival.[51] 'Annihilation through labour' was clearly an intentional policy of extermination of individuals previously held in penal institutions. At a very conservative estimate, around two-thirds of them died in concentration camps; the real total was probably higher.[52] Legal officials were well aware of this. The Reich Ministry of Justice was officially informed by the concentration camp administration about the scale of the deaths.[53] Leading prison officials may even have witnessed some killings themselves. Karl Engert, for example, travelled to as many concentration camps as he could, visiting several camps where transferred prisoners were murdered.[54]

The prisoners were taken to concentration camps all over Nazi-controlled Europe. All Jewish prisoners ended up in Auschwitz, at around the same time as other Jews were deported there from concentration camps inside Germany.[55] One Jewish prisoner was the 34-year-old Therese N. from Vienna. Convicted for sharing some food with prisoners of war, she had been sentenced to one year in a penitentiary. Her act of kindness sealed her fate. She arrived in the Aichach institution on 6 July 1942, and six months later, on 8 December 1942, she was handed over to the police. On the same transport from Aichach was Gabriele M., a 61-year-old woman, also from Vienna, who had served half of her four-year sentence for listening to 'enemy radio'.[56] On arrival in Auschwitz, former Jewish prison inmates were apparently dealt with in the same murderous way as all other Jews. Some were picked out as slave labourers by the SS. The others were immediately gassed. 'We never saw those not fit for work again,' recalled the former prisoner Samuel S., who had been taken to Auschwitz from the Celle penitentiary. Most of the Jewish prisoners who were not killed on arrival died within the next few weeks and months.[57]

The majority of the transferred Polish prisoners were taken to Auschwitz and Mauthausen. Mieczyslaw W., who had been sentenced to ten years' penitentiary for breach of the public peace in 1940, was one of the prisoners taken to Mauthausen in early 1943. After the war, he described his treatment: 'The living conditions in the camps were terrible: exhausting labour and catastrophic provisions led the prisoners to their deaths.'[58] Most transferred Polish prisoners died in the camps. One of them was Johann K., who had been sentenced by the People's Court for treason and attempted high treason in November 1941 to six years' imprisonment. On 15 January 1943, he was taken by the police from the Schieratz institution to the Auschwitz concentration camp, some 200 kilometres further south. Within one month, Johann K. was dead.[59]

'Asocial' German prisoners were largely taken to concentration camps inside the Altreich and Austria (some female prisoners were also taken to Auschwitz). Women were often transported to the concentration camp in Ravensbrück, while a number of male prisoners were taken to camps in Buchenwald and Neuengamme. But most men ended up in the Mauthausen camp, which was personally inspected by both Reich Minister of Justice Thierack and State Secretary Rothenberger in late 1942.[60] Former prison inmates were savagely beaten on arrival at the train station in Mauthausen; some prisoners were dead before they had reached the camp. Once inside the camp, the torture continued. The security-confined prisoner Josef B. recalled that 'we immediately had to undress. SS people walked along the rows and completely arbitrarily beat up people so that they were left dead'.[61] The SS also selected old, weak or ill prisoners for extermination. Many of those inmates who survived the beatings and shootings of the first weeks faced 'annihilation through labour' at the notorious quarry of the main camp in Mauthausen (Wiener Graben). The Wiesbaden state prosecutor described this torture in 1949, based on several prisoner testimonies:

> In a completely mindless way, without any obvious economic use for the war effort, the inmates there had to perform the hard labour of cutting big blocks of stone, weighing up to 50 kilograms, which they had to carry up and down 186 steps. In all cases, this had to be performed at a running pace. Weakened by insufficient nutrition, inmates often broke down under the weight of the stones they had to carry and plunged with their load into the quarry. If they did not die instantly, they were shot by SS guards or beaten to death by *Kapos*. Many inmates were simply thrown down into the quarry from a height of 30 to 40 metres. Also, inmates at the top of the site were

often forced to empty their trucks of stones, thus striking dead many prisoners working beneath them in the quarry. A great number of prisoners also voluntarily jumped down into the quarry to put an end to the agony, which they had to endure again and again.[62]

In Buchenwald, too, the transferred prisoners were systematically murdered. They were also forced to work in a quarry, and regularly broke down or were beaten by SS officials and *Kapos*.[63] In the Neuengamme camp not a day went by during a period in the spring of 1943 without at least one of the transferred prisoners being brutally killed. 'I had the impression,' one survivor recalled after the war, 'that we were supposed to be exterminated in the concentration camp.'[64]

Among the transferred non-Jewish German prisoners, the security confined were most likely to become victims of murderous violence in the concentration camps in late 1942 and early 1943. Forced to wear a special sign, distinct from both the green triangle of the so-called 'professional criminals' and the black triangle worn by other 'asocials' in the camps, they could be immediately identified by the SS guards.[65] The security-confined prisoners were practically at the bottom of the concentration camp hierarchy. Those in Buchenwald in 1943 were far more likely than any other group of inmates to be killed. In this year, their average monthly mortality rate was 14 per cent, compared to about 1 per cent for the other inmate categories. Conditions for them were even more lethal in Mauthausen, which according to the SS guidelines was reserved for the most dangerous inmates, in particular those with 'previous criminal convictions' and 'asocials'. At the end of 1942, the monthly mortality rate among the security-confined prisoners in Mauthausen was 35 per cent, far exceeding the death rate of all other inmate groups except Jews. By comparison, the mortality rate of other 'deviant' Mauthausen inmates, classified as 'professional criminals' and as 'asocials', was 1 per cent or less per month.[66]

Why were the security-confined prisoners systematically killed while other 'deviant' concentration camp inmates were not? The growing focus of the SS on productive labour may have condemned those security-confined prisoners to death who were barely able to work on account of their old age, illness or malnourishment. Yet, even those who could still work were often quickly and brutally exterminated. Ideological factors clearly played an important role, too. After all, most security-confined prisoners had been classified as biologically 'incorrigible' and Hitler had repeatedly demanded that all such potential threats to the 'national community' be ruthlessly eliminated. The SS guards did their best to realise this aim and only a small number of security-confined inmates handed over to the police are known to have survived the camps.[67]

'Annihilation through Labour': the View from Below

Many policies against prisoners introduced in the Third Reich depended on the cooperation and initiative of local prison officials. This was also true of the 'annihilation through labour' programme. All governors of penal institutions whom the Reich Ministry of Justice envisaged would be involved in the programme were personally initiated on 19 and 20 October 1942 in the ministry in Berlin. Written guidelines followed on 22 October.[68] Most local officials supported the transfer – even though they often knew exactly what happened to the transferred prisoners in the concentration camps, as did their superiors in Berlin. For instance, of 23 inmates transported from the Untermaßfeld penitentiary to the Buchenwald concentration camp on 18 April 1943, the penitentiary administration was informed that 14 had died within three weeks of their arrival in Buchenwald.[69] True, some local officials privately criticised the transfer as illegal. In exceptional cases, they even tried to save individual inmates from being transferred. But on the whole, even these officials soon got used to handing over prisoners to the police.[70]

Economics and Extermination

The most controversial aspect of the transfer, in the eyes of local prison officials, was the potential threat it posed to the smooth running of their penal 'factories'. Reich Minister of Justice Thierack had been adamant that the killing of 'asocials' was more important than any economic gain that could be derived from their labour power. In his speech to the leading judicial officials on 29 September 1942 in Berlin, Thierack had tackled this issue head-on: 'Now there will be people who think: there is a wonderful factory in Werl; there is supposed to be a downright exemplary armaments factory! I am sorry, but the thoughts I have presented go much further.'[71] It was no coincidence that Thierack explicitly referred to the security confinement institution in Werl. Since the late 1930s, Werl had gained a reputation as a model institution under its new governor August Faber. An ambitious man, Faber made up for his very poor qualifications by the relentless exploitation of inmates for the Nazi economy. During the war, Faber's single-minded approach won him promotion, military decorations, cash rewards, as well as supporters in high places, including Albert Speer. At one point, Speer even suggested that Faber should be given a special mission to increase war production inside other penal institutions. This request was turned down by Reich Minister Thierack, who was suspicious of Faber's attempts to 'draw attention to himself'. Still, even Thierack acknowledged Faber's skill in exploiting prison labour.[72] Thanks to its privileged status, Werl had apparently even been allowed to offload sick and weak prisoners on to other penal institutions, probably another reason for its comparatively high output.[73] For Werl made more revenue from prison labour than any other security confinement institution, and it was one of the first penal institutions in Germany to focus on armaments production. By 1942, the security-confined prisoners in Werl already produced motor parts for Junkers aeroplanes, cables for tanks and submarines, gas mask filters and detonators.[74]

Not surprisingly, Faber and some of his colleagues disagreed with Thierack's plans to hand over all the prisoners eligible for transfer to the police. Asked by the Reich Ministry to provide details about the anticipated impact of the transfer on armaments production, a number of governors in late October 1942 warned of short-term shortages of skilled labour. This response could not have come as a revelation to the prison administrators in Berlin. After all, they knew very well that some institutions stood to lose large numbers of inmates. The Ebrach governor, for example, expected to hand over around 260 of his 684 inmates, most of whom were working in jobs classified as directly relevant to the war effort. Several governors argued that they would only be able to hand over prisoners if they were replaced by other skilled ones, who would also need to be trained first. Without such replacements, the governor of the Kaisheim penitentiary claimed, the transfer could have 'catastrophic consequences' for war production.[75]

The Reich Ministry of Justice decided to settle for a compromise between economics and extermination. While the 'transfer' began without delay, causing some disruption to the production process, penal institutions were instructed at first to report only prisoners employed in less productive lines of work. Skilled labourers in vital industries were temporarily exempted. This special provision did not apply to Jews, Poles or Sinti and Roma. Just as these prisoners could not be classified as 'reformable', their economic skills were also regarded as irrelevant. For them, no escape was possible in the Nazi racial state and all were transferred to the police.[76] Regarding those prisoners spared for the time being, the Reich Ministry of Justice initially insisted that their transfer could only be delayed for as long as it took to train a replacement.[77] Until the end of the war, Engert's team continued to check whether any 'asocial' prisoners who had not yet been transferred for economic reasons could now be handed over. However, by 1944 the ministry was more inclined to accept a request by local officials to prevent any transferral of skilled, 'asocial' prisoners.[78]

For a number of inmates, exemption from the transfer on economic grounds made the difference between life and death. By April 1943, 3,068 'asocial' prisoners, who would otherwise have been transferred to the police, had been temporarily spared.[79] This probably included most of the security-confined prisoners in Werl. The Werl governor August Faber had been one of the strongest critics of the initial plans to hand over prisoners irrespective of economic performance. Faber had clearly been concerned that this would severely damage output in Werl and undermine his position. Well-connected as he was, he contacted officials in the armaments industry, who intervened on his behalf. As a result, only about 250 of the well over 1,000 Werl prisoners were taken to concentration camps between December 1942 and January 1943. Elsewhere, it was a rather different story. In Straubing, where labour was geared less towards armaments, 803 inmates of the around 1,100 prisoners were handed to the police between 26 November 1942 and 7 January 1943.[80] The exempted prisoners worked to survive in Werl and hundreds of them were still alive in the last months of the war. By 31 December 1944, no fewer than 925 security-confined prisoners were still held in Werl (including some sentenced by the courts after 1942).[81] It seems that the determination of governor Faber to turn Werl into an armaments factory may inadvertently have saved hundreds of prisoners.

It would have frequently been possible for governors to claim inmates as irreplaceable workers – not for economic reasons but to save them from being handed over to the police. However, it seems that local prison officials only employed this strategy in exceptional cases. The best-documented case is that of the Remscheid-Lüttringhausen governor Dr Karl Engelhardt. Initially a supporter of the Nazi regime, by the time he was appointed governor of the penitentiary in 1939 he had already distanced himself from it and the local Nazi party openly opposed his appointment. During the war, Engelhardt was shocked when he started to realise that some of his former prisoners were killed in concentration camps. He responded by trying to subvert the transfer of political prisoners to the police (he showed no such consideration for criminal offenders). Engelhardt pursued different strategies. Some political prisoners were simply held as 'indispensable' workers in armaments factories, even after their sentences had ended. Other men were sent to army 'probation battalions', or were told to 'volunteer' for bomb-clearance commandos. Dangerous as these positions were, they often still offered better chances of survival than the camps. The Gestapo was angry about Engelhardt's tactics and complained in January 1944: 'Various penal institutions have in the past transferred to our office inmates who have been sentenced to long terms in penitentiaries for attempted high treason. It is conspicuous that until now no such prisoners, apart from two Jews, have been transferred from Lüttringhausen.'[82] Engelhardt's case shows that local prison officials were able to save at least some prisoners from transfer to the police. But only a few others, it seems, followed his example.

The general support of most local prison officials for the transfer was obvious in many ways. To start with, the governors assisted Engert's commission by filling in general questionnaires about the prisoners who were part of the individual transfer. In these forms, they commented on the labour power of each prisoner, the state of health and the supposed eugenic value ('Has the offender a bad hereditary disposition?'), and in conclusion had to answer the question: 'Is his inner being asocial?'[83] As the governors had little detailed knowledge of most inmates, they drew on specially written reports by other local officials, such as the prison doctor, the chaplain and senior warders. No doubt, the final statements by the governors were often explicit, as in the case of the Untermaßfeld prisoner Otto A., who had been sentenced to 15 years in a penitentiary for attempted murder in 1928 (he had attacked a family of three who had surprised him during a burglary). While he had conducted himself well during his imprisonment, the Untermaßfeld governor was in no doubt that Otto A. should be transferred to the police. He reported the prisoner 'as asocial, as a thug who is lost to the national community, who would commit any murder and who is no longer reformable'.[84] It was apparently easy for local prison officials to write off inmates as 'asocial'. After all, the officials had long been used to characterising offenders as 'incorrigible' in the criminal-biological examinations. They now drew on this experience, viewing classification of prisoners for the individual transfer as the continuation of a well-established practice.[85]

The governors' backing for the transfer can be demonstrated most clearly by examining the fate of inmates sentenced to security confinement. It was the governor's responsibility to divide up these inmates into 'asocials' and 'reformables'. The former were transferred directly to the police (unless a temporary exemption was granted on economic grounds) as part of the general transfer, while the latter were examined by the commission of the Reich Ministry of Justice for individual transfer, thus giving the inmates the chance of escaping the concentration camps. So if governors wanted to try and save prisoners from the grasp of the police, they could have classified a large number of these inmates as 'reformable'. In late 1942, the German prison governors reported the results of their first examinations to the Ministry of Justice. Of an estimated 14,000 inmates with sentences of security confinement, they reported only about 600 as 'reformable'. Most others were left to the police as 'asocial'.[86]

Ideology and Expediency

How can we explain this support for 'annihilation through labour' by the local officials? To start with, many officials believed that, in 'total war', it was right that certain offenders were killed. Typical of these officials was the Brandenburg-Görden prison doctor Werner Eberhard. Before the war, Eberhard had been somewhat concerned about the poor health of inmates in

19. During his speech in the Reichstag on 26 April 1942, Hitler launches an attack on the German legal system, with far-reaching consequences.

20. On the day of their appointment, Hitler meets with his new State Secretary Curt Rothenberger (right) and Reich Minister of Justice Otto-Georg Thierack (centre), 20 August 1942.

21. Transition of power inside the Reich Ministry of Justice. From the right: Curt Rothenberger and Otto-Georg Thierack, the new men in charge, take over from former State Secretaries Franz Schlegelberger and Roland Freisler, 26 August 1942.

22. Roland Freisler in his new position as president of the People's Court, c. 1944. Between 1942 and 1945 the court passed some 5,000 death sentences.

23. Karl Engert, a key legal official in the 'annihiliation through labour' of prison inmates. In 1943 Engert was promoted to head of the German prison service.

24. Inside the Brandenburg-Görden penitentiary, c. 1930–40. For some time the biggest Nazi penal institution, its modern design with glazed roof was a legacy from the Weimar Republic.

25. Prisoners producing army uniforms at the tailor's workshop in Brandenburg-Görden, c. 1942.

26. Inmates from the Duisburg-Hamborn prison sorting coal at a nearby pit, summer 1943. Photos such as this were taken to impress Hitler with the productivity of prison labour.

27. Two Brandenburg-Görden prisoners in security confinement sorting buttons for army uniforms, c. 1942. Not long after this picture was taken, most inmates in security confinement were killed.

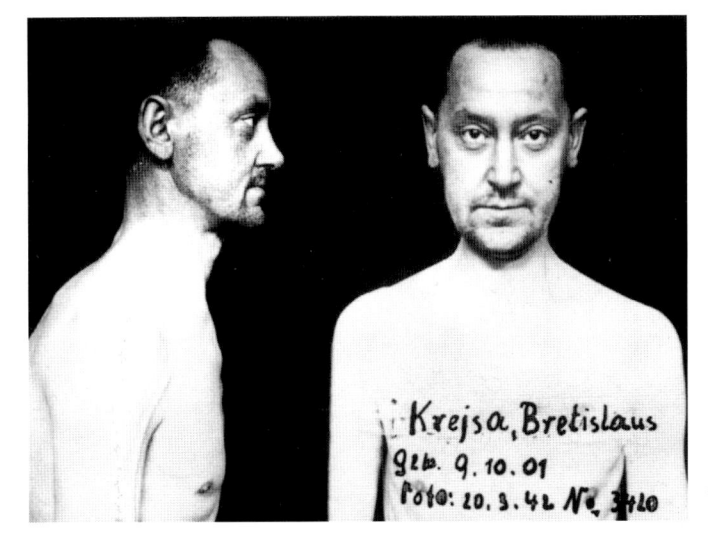

28. The Czech political prisoner Bretislaus Krejsa, imprisoned since 1939, soon after his arrival in the Untermaßfeld penitentiary in early March 1942. Krejsa was forced into hard labour and died one year later.

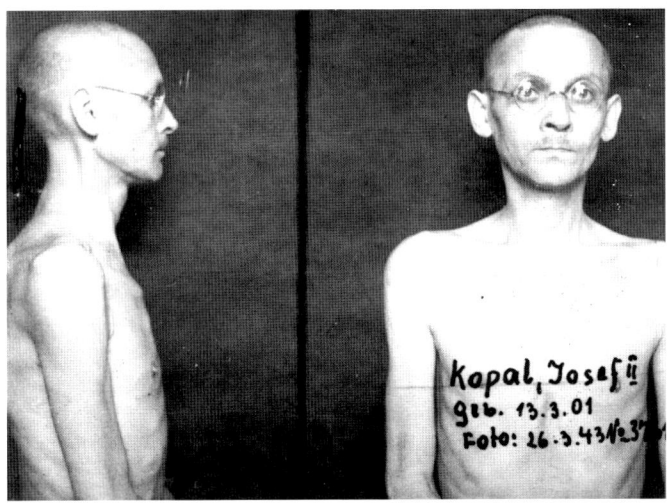

29. This picture was taken two weeks after the Czech prisoner Josef Kopal, sentenced for listening to 'enemy radio', arrived in Untermaßfeld in mid March 1943. Kopal, who had already been held as a remand prisoner in Prague, died less than three months later.

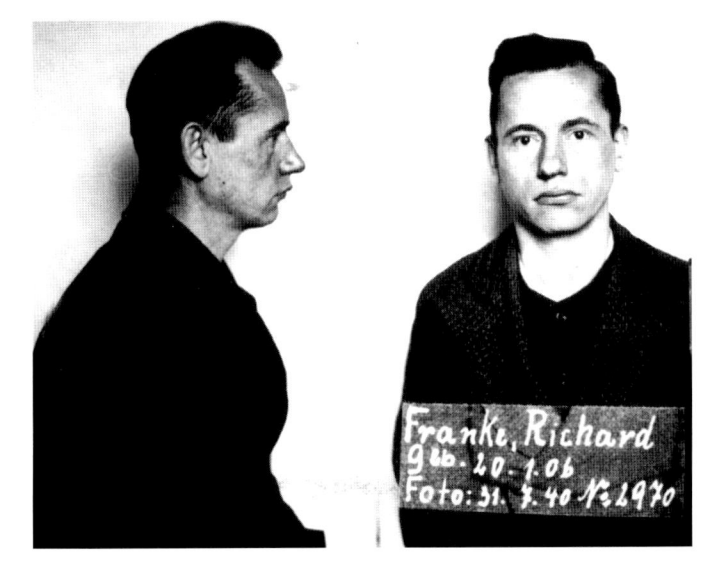

30. The petty criminal Richard Franke shortly after he was sentenced to security confinement in early July 1940. In January 1943, Franke became a victim of 'annihilation through labour'.

31. SS photo of inmates carrying stones up the 'stairs of death' at the Wiener Graben quarry (Mauthausen concentration camp), 1942. Many former prison inmates died here.

32. The Sonnenburg penitentiary after the massacre of inmates: over 800 prisoners were murdered here on 30–31 January 1945.

33. An Allied officer talks to three liberated prisoners at the Werl penitentiary, 11 April 1945.

34. Officials from the Werl penitentiary hand over their keys, 11 April 1945.

35. The guillotine at the Plötzensee prison, May 1945. German legal courts passed around 16,000 death sentences during the Second World War, which were usually carried out in penal institutions.

36. Former legal officials on trial, Nuremberg 1947. First row, fourth from right: Karl Engert. Second row, first from right: Franz Schlegelberger, second from right: Curt Rothenberger.

security confinement, but by 1942 he argued that 'habitual criminals' had no right to live. Writing in the most respected German criminological journal, Eberhard demanded that 'all those, who have been positively diagnosed as habitual criminals, should be extirpated through the death penalty'.[87] The local prison officials also knew that this was what Hitler evidently expected. Only a few days after he had given his consent to the agreement between Thierack and Himmler, Hitler used the occasion of a speech he made in the Berlin Sport Palace on 30 September 1942 and broadcast by radio, to make public his views on the treatment of persistent and dangerous offenders during the war:

> At a time when the best of our people have to be deployed at the front and are answerable there with their lives, at this time there is no room for criminals and for good-for-nothings, who destroy the nation! . . . Most importantly, no habitual criminal should be under the illusion that he can save himself until the end of the war by a new crime. We will ensure that not only the decent one may die at the front, but that the criminal and the indecent one at home will under no circumstances survive this time! . . . We will exterminate these criminals, and we have exterminated them![88]

The Reich Ministry of Justice made sure that Hitler's jurists remembered this passage in the speech, repeating it in several communications.[89] Inevitably, Hitler's speech left a mark on local legal officials, and many judges referred to the speech when passing bloody sentences.[90]

Prison officials were also influenced by the views of their superiors, which were repeatedly publicly broadcast. The top legal officials saw no reason to hide their murderous sentiments, assuming that the general public was behind them. In late autumn 1942, State Secretary Rothenberger declared in a public speech in Vienna that, at a time when the most valuable Germans were killed at the front, it was wrong to protect 'asocial elements' in penal institutions.[91] On 17 February 1943, he repeated this point in Lüneburg, warning that if measures were not now taken to 'ruthlessly annihilate the asocials, the inferiors, then we preserve these people for years, and at the end of the war they may be superior in numbers to the others'.[92] Most influential was a speech by Thierack at a mass propaganda meeting in Breslau on 5 January 1943. In parts, the speech repeated the script of the talk he had given to the general state prosecutors on 29 September 1942. Thierack once more invoked the danger of 'negative selection'. This had become a 'burning' issue, Thierack claimed: 'It is not right, my national comrades. It is not right that the idealist dies outside and the inferior scum is preserved inside.' But he reassured his listeners that this 'problem of the asocials' had been solved, making it clear that thousands of penitentiary inmates were now employed in such a way that they would die. This passage in Thierack's speech was summarised succinctly three days later in the

Völkischer Beobachter, which carried a long article about the speech, reporting that Thierack had demanded nothing less than the 'ruthless extermination and extirpation of incorrigible criminals'.[93] The same message was repeated to local prison officials by the members of Karl Engert's commission during visits to the individual institutions.[94]

Also, local prison officials had long got used to handing over 'dangerous' prisoners to the police. Since 1933, tens of thousands of prisoners had been taken to the police after their sentence. After the outbreak of war, this had also happened to inmates who had not yet completed their sentence. Some of them had been shot by the police in order to 'correct' supposedly lenient prison sentences. Others, including individual Poles and hundreds of Jewish prisoners, had been transferred to the police authorities before the autumn of 1942 in full cooperation with the prison authorities.

But there were additional, more practical concerns, which help to explain local officials' support for the transfer. To start with, some governors apparently welcomed it as a way of reducing overcrowding.[95] Other officials saw the transfer as a golden opportunity to get rid of prisoners they regarded as a nuisance. These included inmates who complained about conditions, their treatment or their sentences, as well as prisoners who had found out about corruption among the ranks of the officials. In a number of cases, the local officials reported such inmates as 'asocial' to Berlin. As Karl Engert recalled after the war: 'Some prison governors had been irritated a couple of times by inmates and wanted to get rid of these people.'[96] Finally, at a time when economic output had become the overriding goal of penal policy, prison officials were keen to rid their institutions of prisoners who stood in the way of higher productivity. These included older security-confined prisoners, weak and physically disabled inmates in penitentiaries, and some Polish and political prisoners excluded for security reasons from armaments production and outside labour. Some governors had complained in the past that such inmates were a great burden for the work process. The governors' desire to remove these prisoners was shared by the top officials in the Reich Ministry of Justice, who decided from the start that ill prisoners should be included in the transfer to the police, as long as they were 'transportable'. Robert Hecker explained such thinking with brutal honesty after the war: 'the legal system did not want to be saddled with the ill waste'.[97] Presumably, this had not been cleared with the police. For in spring 1943, the head of the SS concentration camp system, Oswald Pohl, complained that the prison authorities had used the transfer to 'get rid of inmates afflicted with every imaginable illness'.[98] In the case of these sick and weak prisoners, the phrase 'annihilation through labour' as another word for murder could scarcely be clearer. After all, many of the prisoners found it difficult to work at all because of old age, illness or disability.

Prisoners and their Relatives

The transfer caused unrest and fear among some prisoners, even before it had started. On 18 October 1942, the national prisoner newspaper reprinted Hitler's Sport Palace speech of 30 September on its front page, for all the inmates to read. Hitler's murderous threat to criminals was put into bold print. Reading this article must have greatly increased some prisoners' concern about their future treatment.[99] Very soon after, as knowledge of the impending transfer spread among local prison officials, the rumour mill among inmates started turning further. True, many prisoners were completely surprised when told that they would be taken elsewhere. But others had already learned that something was up. Sometimes, the officials gave broad hints. In the Kaisheim penitentiary, the prison chaplain darkly hinted that some prisoners would be taken away to a place where they would face great hardship. But the true destination of the transfer remained unclear to many prisoners. Some officials apparently told inmates that they would be taken to Poland for building and agricultural work. Not all prisoners believed this. In Brandenburg-Görden, for example, prisoners were sure that 'habitual' and 'professional' criminals would be liquidated in concentration camps.[100] Some prisoners were so concerned that they took desperate steps to escape the transfer. The Jewish journalist Dagobert Lubinski, a Communist who served a ten-year sentence in the Remscheid-Lüttringhausen penitentiary for attempted high treason, succeeded in alerting his wife. In a letter smuggled out of the institution by a fellow prisoner, Lubinski pleaded with his wife (who was not Jewish) to step in: 'It appears to be an evacuation to the East, in the immediate future. Intervention is urgently required . . . intervention of course also, if I should already be gone.' His wife immediately travelled to the penitentiary, arriving unannounced on 18 January 1943. But her husband was already on a transport to Auschwitz, where he was killed one month later.[101]

On the day of their transfer, the prisoners were dressed in their old civilian clothes. Some particularly cruel prison officials used these last moments to taunt the prisoners, telling them that they were on their way to a place 'from where nobody returns'.[102] Then the prisoners were picked up by police officials, who informed the local prison authorities which concentration camp their former inmates would be taken to.[103] During the transport on trains or lorries, guarded by the police officials, the prisoners worried about their fate. One prisoner, who had been held in security confinement for theft, recalled after the war that 'we talked a lot during the journey about where we would end up, but nobody knew anything about it'.[104]

Parents and spouses of prison inmates were left in the dark about the transfer. Generally, they only heard about it weeks or even months later. Some received the news after they wrote to the prison authorities to inquire why their children, husbands or wives had not been in touch. For example, in late April 1943, the mother of Arnold W. wrote to the Untermaßfeld authorities because she had received no news about him recently, 'which causes me great distress'. The reason he had not written was that Arnold W., a Czech Jew serving a three-and-a-half-year sentence for attempted high treason, had already been handed over to the police. As the prison authorities swiftly replied to his mother: 'Your son – the inmate Arnold Israel W. – was transferred on 25 Mar. 1943 to the work and education camp Auschwitz (east Upper-Silesia) on orders from above.'[105] Other parents heard about the transfer only when they were told that their child had died in a concentration camp. A number of distraught and agitated spouses and parents wrote to the prison authorities to find out what had happened. One mother, whose son had been taken from Straubing to Mauthausen, demanded to know 'why he got there, to have to die, was he mentally ill, or did he not behave himself [?]'. Other parents cast doubt on the official cause of death.[106] In their curt replies, the prison authorities kept silent about the real reasons for the transfer, claiming that inmates had been moved to the camps 'purely for administrative reasons' or for an 'important work assignment'.[107] Many parents probably never found out that their children had been murdered.

Extending the Killings: 'Asocials' and the Disabled

The decision by the Reich Ministry of Justice in 1942 to hand over prisoners for 'annihilation through labour' paved the way for the killing of other inmates. After it was accepted that particularly 'dangerous' prisoners could be taken to concentration camps and killed, even though they had not been sentenced to death, further groups of inmates were soon targeted as well. Above all, more 'asocial' prisoners were singled out to be worked to death – this time inside penal institutions, rather than in concentration camps.

'Asocial' Prisoners

According to the September 1942 agreement between Thierack and Himmler, only certain categories of prisoners were subject to 'annihilation through labour'. But from the very beginning, the officials in the Reich Ministry of Justice envisaged that other 'asocials' should also be singled out. In their eyes, this need was confirmed during visits to individual penal institutions. According to Karl Engert, writing in 1944, it became clear that there were very many inmates not eligible for 'transfer' because of their shorter sentences who were as 'worthless and intolerable for the national community' as the inmates already handed over. Their inclusion in the examinations was also demanded by various prison governors – not for the first time, pressure for radical measures came from below. As a consequence, the Reich Ministry of Justice ordered in late 1942/early 1943 that 'asocials' in penitentiaries with sentences of less than eight years, as well as 'asocials' in prisons, were to be reported by the governors as well. Many of those targeted were offenders with comparatively minor sentences, who had accumulated a number of previous convictions and fitted the criminological type of the 'incorrigible offender'. Others were vaguely described by Engert as 'alien to the community for other reasons', a term applied to numerous political offenders.[108]

Once again, the governors played a crucial role. By spring 1943 they had already reported 1,350 such 'asocial' inmates to section XV in Berlin. Some of them were examined by Engert's commission. In about three out of four cases, they agreed with the governors' judgement. This apparently convinced Engert of the urgency of this project, and by early 1944 a much wider and more extensive examination of inmates with sentences of less than eight years was under way. One official estimated that a total of 4,000 such inmates were reported by the governors to Engert's commission.[109] After the 'asocials' among them had been selected, the officials in the Reich Ministry of Justice had to decide what to do with them. The officials instructed the regional legal authorities to report the 'asocial' prisoners to the police, so that they could be arrested after they had served their sentence. But until their release, the prisoners would remain in selected penal institutions where they would be 'occupied with work which is exceptionally tough, harmful to their health or dangerous'.[110]

In effect, the prison administration tried to introduce its own programme of 'annihilation through labour'. The officials' thinking is illuminated by an article in a bulletin prepared by the Reich Ministry of Justice in June 1944 for former prison officials who now served in the army. Under the heading 'Special Treatment of Asocials', Albert Hupperschwiller, a key member of Engert's team, made it clear that many 'asocial' prisoners were now being killed – another example of the striking openness with which legal officials acknowledged these murders. Claiming that 'asocials' always represented 'an unworthiness, a danger and a burden' to society, Hupperschwiller justified their deaths in familiar fashion by pointing to the deaths of German soldiers at the front:

> The asocial does not belong in the normal prison service! . . . In war, which costs so much blood of our most valuable ones at the front and at home every day, it is even less acceptable than in peace to spare him. Therefore, the judicial administration endeavours to remove asocial elements from the normal penal institutions and to lead them to special tasks.

These tasks, Hupperschwiller added, consisted of work which pushed inmates to the 'final boundary of their physical fitness', as well as 'life-threatening' duties.[111]

But where were these selected 'asocial' prisoners to be taken? In their deliberations, prison officials once again focused on male convicts, who were expected to make up the great majority of 'asocial' inmates. One obvious destination for these men, chosen by Karl Engert, was the lethal prison camp North. But it would not have been practical to transport all 'asocial' men to Norway. So, in order to select penal institutions in Germany with particularly atrocious working conditions, in late January 1944 Engert dispatched another member of his commission, Otto Gündner, to visit three institutions for male prisoners. All three were chosen by Engert one month later. The first was the Siegburg penitentiary, where inmates were forced to pack explosives into detonators and cartridges for Dynamit-A.G. Conditions there were exceptionally dangerous, Engert (who had himself visited the factory on 4 January 1944) noted with approval, because accidents and explosions were frequent. The second was the Ensisheim penitentiary in Alsace, where prisoners were used in the mining and transport of potash salts. Working up to 1,100 metres underground, in very cramped conditions and extreme heat, was especially exhausting. Gündner recommended that the 120 penitentiary prisoners employed there at that time could be replaced with more than twice as many 'asocials', presumably in order to create more lethal conditions for the workers. Similarly exhausting was the work carried out by prisoners in the quarry of the Rottenburg prison, the third destination. After the war, one former inmate described the conditions in Rottenburg in 1944: the mortality rate of workers in the quarry was high, due to the brutal working conditions, malnourishment and constant beatings by most warders. One warder was only happy when a 'prisoner was lying on the ground, bleeding'.[112] In addition to these destinations for male prisoners, Engert decided that female prisoners labelled 'asocial' should be taken to a nitrogen factory at the Griebo prison camp.

It is not known how many 'asocial' prisoners were transported to these selected institutions, and how many of them died there. The murderous intention behind the policy was clear enough, however. As Karl Engert remarked casually in February 1944: 'Those physically not fully fit will probably perish after a short while . . .'. As he knew only too well, hardly any prisoners were still 'fully fit' at that time.[113]

The 'Criminally Insane'

'Asocial' prisoners were not alone in being targeted for extermination. German legal officials also set their sights on several other groups of offenders, such as the disabled. During the planning for the 'annihilation through labour' programme in autumn 1942, legal officials raised the possibility of transferring mentally ill offenders to the police. This included those individuals who had been referred as 'criminally insane' by courts to mental asylums. Their fate, the Reich Ministry of Justice officials decided on 9 October 1942, would be discussed with SS-Gruppenführer Streckenbach.[114] This was not the first time that the 'criminally insane' were singled out for murder in the Third Reich. To put the events from 1942 onwards into context, we must briefly examine the earlier treatment of these outsiders.

Before the Nazis came to power, the 'criminally insane' had remained outside the jurisdiction of German courts. If a court had found an offender not responsible because of insanity, it automatically lost its authority over the defendant. It was then left to the police to take the individual to a mental asylum. This changed with the Habitual Criminals Law of 24 November 1933 (§ 42b). Now, judges sent 'criminally insane' offenders indefinitely to a mental asylum. Nevertheless, although these people were no longer imprisoned within the legal system, the courts still had ultimate authority over them. The same was true for offenders with diminished responsibility, who were sent to asylums. This category was newly introduced in the Habitual Criminals Law, realising a demand which had been made by German criminologists and legal professionals since the turn of the century. Offenders with diminished responsibility got the worst of both worlds if they were seen as a risk to public safety. Like offenders judged legally responsible, they were sentenced to regular punishment, for example, in a prison or a penitentiary. But like offenders judged not responsible at all, they were later sent to a mental institution as soon as the original sentence had been served.[115]

German judges sent large numbers of 'criminally insane' offenders to mental asylums. In all, some 5,142 sentences were passed by the courts under § 42b between 1934 and 1939 (see Figure 9, pp. 400–1). Nazi publications often presented the 'criminally insane' as particularly dangerous because of their supposed dual threat of insanity and criminality. In newspaper articles about asylums they were portrayed in lurid language as brutal killers. And in the 1936 Nazi propaganda film *Erbkrank* ('Hereditary Ill'), a personal favourite of Hitler's, a succession of inmates in mental asylums – paraded before the camera by doctors in white coats – were identified in crude captions as 'robber murderer', 'murderer', 'sexual murderer' and so on. In reality, many of the inmates held under § 42b were not violent at all. Instead, they had been committed for homosexuality, petty theft, arson, exhibitionism, fraud and political offences, such as derogatory remarks about the Nazi regime. Initially, these individuals were probably better off in asylums than in penitentiaries. But only a relatively small minority of them were ever released.[116]

In 1940 and 1941, several thousand 'criminally insane' offenders in mental asylums became victims of the Nazi 'euthanasia' programme.[117] Already before the Second World War, Hitler had approved a programme of killing disabled children. Shortly after the invasion of Poland, he signed an authorisation extending the programme to adults. Code-named 'Aktion T4', it was masterminded by the Chancellery of the Führer and the Reich Ministry of the Interior. Following perfunctory examinations of their files by 'expert' doctors, the victims were transferred to several asylum-cum-killing centres set up inside Germany.[118] From the beginning, the T4 doctors targeted 'criminally insane' offenders committed by the courts. Indeed, their murder was regarded as a matter of urgency. As early as February and March 1940, six transports with a total of 141 men committed by the courts (under § 42b) left the Waldheim mental asylum for the killing centre in Brandenburg-Havel, a former penitentiary. Such transports were welcomed by some asylum directors, who had long resented the presence of criminal offenders in their institutions, because they regarded them as unruly and dangerous. The asylum director at Egelfing-Haar, for example, had claimed in November 1939 that it was 'the criminally inclined, anti-social elements, the majority committed on grounds of public safety, who are increasingly silting up and burdening the asylum in ways which are intolerable'.[119]

It was the disappearance from asylums of individuals who had remained under the jurisdiction of local courts that had alerted the Reich Ministry of Justice to the 'euthanasia' programme. The legal officials, sticklers for the rules, complained that the killings caused serious administrative problems. Also, as knowledge of the killings spread throughout the German population, there was concern among the legal officials that the mass murders undermined the rule of law and public trust in the judiciary. Initially, the then Reich Minister of Justice Gürtner hoped that this could be prevented if an official 'euthanasia' law was introduced. Otherwise, he argued, the whole programme would have to be stopped. But once Gürtner had seen a copy of Hitler's commission for the 'euthanasia' programme, in late August 1940, he dropped his objections. After all, as Gürtner later lectured an opponent of the programme of mass murder, the 'will of the Führer' was the 'source of law'. In the following months, several general state prosecutors were also informed of the details. The remaining top legal officials were initiated on 23 and 24 April 1941 in Berlin by two leading T4 officials, Viktor Brack and Werner Heyde. Introduced by State Secretary Schlegelberger as the officials who would clarify the programme for the 'annihilation of life unworthy of life', they explained the details of the killings and passed around selected photographs of severely disabled patients. The legal officials were even shown a copy of Hitler's authorisation, which Schlegelberger described as 'a legally valid decree of the Führer'.[120]

The 'euthanasia' action was the first systematic programme of mass extermination in the Third Reich and it clearly influenced the 'annihilation through labour' of prisoners in 1942, just as it proved crucial for the genesis of the Holocaust. There were some striking similarities between the transfer of 'asocial' prisoners to the police and the 'euthanasia' programme. Here, too, forms were sent out to individual institutions, asking about inmates' state of health and ability to work. These forms were then processed by 'experts', who marked them with a red cross if the patients were to die. Others were selected to live, or classified as doubtful. Karl Engert himself had been present at the meeting in April 1941 in Berlin, when the leading members of the judiciary were informed about the 'euthanasia' programme. The murder of the disabled no doubt informed his later designs for exterminating 'asocial' prisoners.[121] Apart from organisational similarities, there were also personal connections. The Chancellery of the Führer of the NSDAP, a party organisation, played a central role in the 'euthanasia' programme. In a highly unusual move, Engert asked a senior member of this agency, Kurt Giese, to join his team in the examination of prisoners. Giese responded enthusiastically to Engert's proposal. As he recalled after the war, 'I was very keen to get personally involved. I have time and again been inspired by high idealism . . .'. Thus, members of the judicial system and the Chancellery of the Führer worked hand in hand in the selection of 'asocials' to be exterminated.[122]

The murder of asylum patients continued in a less public and more decentralised way, once the first stage of the 'euthanasia' programme was halted by Hitler in August 1941. Many thousands more were killed by lethal drugs and methodical starvation.[123] These included numerous 'criminally insane' patients in mental asylums. And this time, the legal authorities tried to play an active part in their murder. In the autumn of 1942, the Reich Ministry of Justice quickly reached an agreement with Himmler's officials about the fate of 'criminally insane' individuals in asylums. As a result, two doctors from the 'euthanasia' programme, Kurt Borm and Curd Runckel, travelled to mental asylums all over Germany – Borm estimated after the war that he had visited 25 to 30 asylums. Their job was the registration of 'criminally insane' patients for transport to concentration camps. In particular, the two doctors singled out those patients who were fit for work but no longer 'required institutionalisation'. They reported their conclusions to the Reich Ministry of Justice, which put together lists of all the selected patients. In March 1943, these lists were then sent to the individual directors of mental asylums. The police would take the inmates to concentration camps.[124] But several asylum officials raised objections. While they continued to see the 'criminally insane' as particularly dangerous, these fears were now often overridden by economic considerations. For some officials regarded the inmates as 'the best and most useful workers' and were unwilling to let them go.[125] This led to further discussions between the Ministry of Justice, the Ministry of the Interior and the police, and in July 1943 the guidelines for transfer were changed. Asylum directors were now allowed to keep those patients who were occupied in important work.[126]

Much depended on the ability of the 'criminally insane' asylum inmates to work. But this was not enough to ensure survival. The 'criminally insane' also needed to remain inconspicuous. For even some hard-working inmates were liable to be taken away, if they proved to be 'unruly elements' or 'psychopaths' who 'harm the running of the mental institutions', in the words of the Ministry of the Interior official responsible for the state asylums.[127] Throughout 1944, German asylums sent such 'criminally insane' inmates to concentration camps in Mauthausen, Buchenwald, Auschwitz and Dachau, as well as to killing centres such as the asylum in Hadamar. Others were killed in the asylums they were held in.[128]

At the end of September 1944, some 3,346 'criminally insane' offenders (2,855 men, 491 women) were still alive in the asylums.[129] A significant number of them presumably died before the war was finally over. In the Wittenau asylum, some 25 per cent of the inmates committed after September 1943 by the penal authorities died before the war was out – often, apparently, after being poisoned by the medical staff. Another 25 per cent of the Wittenau inmates were taken to the killing asylum Obrawalde. One of them was 56-year-old Frau B., who had suffered acute psychological distress since the death of her son. She was finally committed to Wittenau asylum as 'criminally insane', after she had tried to burn down her apartment. In early March 1944, the asylum authorities described her as very stubborn and proposed that she be transferred. On 27 March 1944 Frau B. was taken to Obrawalde asylum. Two days later she was dead.[130]

Frail and Physically Disabled Prisoners

After the legal officials had opened the door to killing the 'criminally insane' in mental asylums, it was only a question of time before they also set upon disabled prisoners inside penal institutions. As early as autumn of 1942, the officials in the Reich Ministry of Justice talked about handing over supposedly insane prisoners to the police. Once again, it was decided that the matter would be discussed with the SS.[131] The result of these talks is unknown, even though there is some sketchy evidence to suggest that a number of selected inmates were indeed handed over to the police, just like 'asocial' prisoners.[132]

The legal authorities clearly condoned and actively supported the killing of frail and disabled prisoners. This became obvious in December 1943, when the Reich Ministry of Justice designated the workhouse in Vaihingen for inmates who were partially or completely unable to work. Transfer to Vaihingen, a former castle near Ludwigsburg, was limited to male penitentiary inmates who were not blind and did not require constant care. Individual penal institutions reported prisoners they wanted to get rid of to the Reich Ministry of Justice, which then coordinated the transport.[133] For many prisoners, transfer to Vaihingen was a death sentence. Conditions were atrocious. Rations were even smaller than elsewhere and punishment was extremely brutal. Corporal punishment was introduced in 1943, even though it was officially still outlawed. In detention cells, the heating was deliberately turned off at night. Prisoners were constantly beaten, with the warders using knives, forks, broken bottles and other instruments to torture them.[134]

One of the victims was the inmate P., originally sentenced to imprisonment for arson. Shortly after his arrival in Vaihingen on 2 March 1944, he started to scream and tear off all his clothes. It is not clear whether this fit was linked in any way to his epilepsy. The warders certainly did not think so and punished him for insubordination. After the prisoner had been beaten up several times, he was thrown into the so-called 'lion cage', a dark hole in the cellar, with stone walls and one tiny window. The prisoner was completely naked and received no blankets; he had to lie on the stone floor. He was hardly able to move at all, as his hands were tied behind his back and his right leg was chained to the window bars. Water and bread were allowed only at irregular intervals and he was also beaten up by the warders. One freezing cold day in early March 1944, P. was dragged into the prison yard, where the other inmates had assembled. A few hours earlier, another prisoner, who had tried to escape, had been shot dead. The governor displayed the corpse to the prisoners, warning that the same fate awaited them should they try to flee. P., still naked and in a terrible state, was also paraded in front of the inmates as a deterrent. The postwar trial of the governor established what happened next:

> P. had to stand next to the corpse for at least eight to ten minutes, trembling with cold, until he was taken back to the lion cage after the defendant had finished his address. In the following days, the prisoner lost further weight and a severe state of physical and mental exhaustion set in. The chains around his hands, pulled tightly, had now entered into his flesh, and on his right foot he had heavily blood-encrusted chafing wounds from the leg chains.

He died on 15 March 1944, less than two weeks after his arrival in Vaihingen. His death was no exception. At least 225 prisoners died in Vaihingen as a result of hunger, systematic neglect and violence. Their places were taken by other ill and infirm prisoners, who were seen as obstructing the work process in their penal institutions.[135]

Disabled prisoners were not safe, even if they were not taken to Vaihingen. In July 1944, one member of Engert's commission, Albert Hupperschwiller, examined prisoners in the Werl penal institution; he later described them as repulsive and 'cretinous'.[136] His visit to Werl was apparently part of a larger plan. For a few months later, on 16 November 1944, the Reich Ministry of Justice informed the general state prosecutors that it was looking at the nationwide extermination of disabled inmates:

Time and again during different visits to penal institutions, inmates are being noticed who on account of their physical build do not deserve to be called human; they look like monstrosities straight out of hell. The submission of photographs of such prisoners is desirable. Getting rid of these inmates, too, is being considered. Type of offence or length of sentence is immaterial.[137]

This threat to inmates' lives, it seems, was real. After the war, a former inmate in Werl testified that some infirm, mentally and physically disabled prisoners selected by Hupperschwiller were taken away shortly after his visit.[138] This attack on disabled inmates was one more step in the extension of murderous policies to more and more prisoners.

Capital Punishment

At the same time that German prison officials were organising the murder of inmates legally sentenced to imprisonment, they also participated in the mass killing of defendants sentenced to death. Penal institutions had traditionally been the sites of capital punishment, and judicial executions in Germany had increased sharply after the Nazis gained power, rising from an annual average of 13 in the Weimar years (1919–32) to 88 (in 1933–38). But this was insignificant compared to the dramatic increase in the war years. More offences were made punishable by death and senior legal officials constantly urged the judges to apply the death penalty more often, at the expense of lengthy terms of imprisonment. State Secretary Roland Freisler had made his views known in an article as early as 1939: 'If the community needs to be securely protected against the criminal personality for years on end, why not snuff it out and thereby ensure perfect protection at one blow?'[139] The judges had to recognise, Freisler's subordinate Wilhelm Crohne urged in the same year, that it was their duty 'to exterminate the traitors and saboteurs of the inner front'.[140] As we have seen, German judges in the following years passed a vast number of death sentences, especially after 1941. In all, they handed down some 14,000 death sentences between 1942 and 1944 (see Figure 10, pp. 402–3).

Who were these condemned prisoners? Most fell into one of three groups. To start with, a large number of prisoners, in particular in 1942, were Poles sentenced as 'racial aliens' under the Criminal Law Decree for Poles and Jews. Convicted Poles were many times more likely than Germans to receive the death penalty. In the first half of 1942, almost half of all the death sentences passed by German courts were handed out against Poles, often for the most trivial offences. According to the Reich Ministry of Justice, those sentenced to death included 45 Poles convicted of 'illegal possession of weapons', 20 guilty of 'illegal slaughter of animals', 14 convicted of 'disobedience against their German masters' and 10 sentenced for 'damage to the well-being of the German people (including sexual intercourse with German women)'. The number of death penalties against Poles further increased in the following months, as the assault by the courts intensified.[141]

Many others sentenced to death were Germans and others found guilty of property offences. In 1943 alone, some 1,621 individuals received the death penalty for property offences, well over one-third of all the death sentences pronounced that year (excluding those in the incorporated Polish territories).[142] These included hundreds of defendants sentenced as 'national pests' – doomed because of their supposed criminal personality, even though their actual offences had often been trivial.[143] Among them was the 69-year-old stateless Kasimir P., who had lived in Germany since his youth. During an air raid on Essen on 5 March 1943, his flat had been destroyed, and when three days later he passed a bombed shop he took three cheap tin cups, which he wanted to use for eating his food in. He was caught by a policeman, and sentenced to death on the very same day by the Essen special court, which wanted to set an example and deter other 'plunderers'. Kasimir P. was executed by a police firing squad at 9.20 the following morning.[144]

Alleged political enemies of the Nazi regime made up another large group among the condemned prisoners. The People's Court in Berlin passed an extraordinary 4,876 death sentences between 1942 and 1944 (see Figure 7, pp. 398–9). According to one study, almost 60 per cent of all defendants found guilty by the People's Court in the period between June 1942 and February 1944 were sentenced to death (compared to about one in ten defendants in the immediately preceding years). Many of those condemned in this period were foreigners. Czechs, in particular, suffered the full force of the judges' fury. In the early years of the war, death sentences against Czechs had been very unusual, as the German authorities tried to limit open confrontation with the Czech population. But this later changed, especially after the death of the Deputy Reich Protector Reinhard Heydrich on 4 June 1942, assassinated by Czech resistance fighters. As the People's Court noted in a judgment only one week after Heydrich's death, the strictest penalties were necessary as a deterrent because of the 'political obstinacy of certain sections of the Czech people'. As a part of the great wave of Nazi terror against Czech opposition, the judges now habitually sentenced Czech defendants to death, often irrespective of the extent of their involvement in resistance activities.[145]

The torrent of judicial death sentences turned some penal institutions into killing factories. The practice of capital punishment was quickly transformed. As the numbers of prisoners on death row grew and Hitler became more impatient with the delay between sentence and execution, the Reich Ministry of Justice introduced measures to speed up the killings. Thus, more and more prisons and penitentiaries were designated as sites for capital punishment. The number of such institutions almost doubled from 11 (1937) to 21 (1945).[146] Rituals of state executions were increasingly discarded. The executions were now allowed to take place at any time, not just at dawn. And the guillotine, the traditional instrument of killing, was starting to be replaced by other methods of killing such as hanging and shooting. In November 1942, Hitler personally ordered that inmates could also be shot by police and army units – another example of the growing cooperation between legal system and police in the extermination of 'community aliens'.[147] The Reich Ministry of Justice considered the introduction of further execution methods. Not long after Karl Engert visited Auschwitz in June 1944 – at around the time when more Jews were gassed in the camp than ever before – he even toyed with the idea of building 'gas cells' to kill prisoners.[148]

But the number of prisoners on death row continued to grow, thanks to the murderous determination of the judiciary. Prisons and penitentiaries were crowded with men and women sentenced to death. In Brandenburg-Görden, up to 150 condemned individuals were imprisoned at any one time. They came from different social backgrounds, nationalities and age groups. The oldest prisoner executed in Brandenburg-Görden was 72 years old. The youngest was only 15.[149] In some other institutions there were even more inmates on death row. In Plötzensee prison, there were probably more than 300 condemned inmates when the prison and execution facilities were partially destroyed during a British air raid on the night of 3–4 September 1943. In order to prevent escapes, Thierack personally ordered the mass execution of the Plötzensee inmates on death row. Thierack's decision was applauded by the Nazi leadership. 'That is the last thing we need,' Goebbels had noted in his diary, 'that after the air raids a few hundred [prisoners] condemned to death would be let loose on the population in the Reich capital.' On 7 September 1943, the first night of the mass killings in Plötzensee, a total of 186 condemned prisoners were hanged. In their haste to kill as many prisoners as possible, the officials also executed six other inmates 'by accident'. 'Only in the morning,' the Protestant prison chaplain Poelchau recalled, 'did the exhausted executioners cease their activity . . .' According to one estimate, about twice as many people were executed on this one night in September 1943 than during the entire First World War in Germany.[150]

The corpses of the prisoners hanged in Plötzensee in September 1943 were handed over to the local Berlin anatomical institute. Such medical use of the bodies of executed prisoners had been customary for a long time. However, during the last years of the Weimar Republic the practice had almost disappeared, due to the virtual suspension of executions. From 1927 until 1932, only 16 death sentences were carried out in Germany. The return of state executions under the Nazis was welcomed by German doctors. The head of the Halle anatomical institute recalled that for most of the Weimar years he had received 'no corpses of executed individuals . . . For the realisation of scientific projects, this was a great deficit.' But during the war, with the vast increase in executions, some medical institutions now received more dead bodies than they had ever wanted. In September 1943, the Jena anatomical institute informed the judicial authorities that it refused to take any more 'supplies' because of the 'total overcrowding of our storage facilities'.[151] Other scientists, by contrast, were still keen to get their hands on the corpses of executed prisoners. Among them was the gynaecologist Professor Hermann Stieve, who was obsessed with the effect of mortal terror on the sexual glands of humans. The legal authorities gave him free rein to violate the bodies of prisoners, allowing Stieve to examine condemned women immediately after their execution, when he removed their wombs. He published his conclusions in academic journals, both during and after the war.[152] In isolated cases, prisoners on death row were also used as human guinea pigs in experiments with poisoned gas.[153]

At least one penal institution even allowed the blood of executed prisoners to be collected. In 1944, Dr Rudolf Bimler, deputy director of the Brandenburg-Havel hospital and an SS member, contacted the nearby Brandenburg-Görden penitentiary. He was concerned, he said, by the general shortage of blood supplies. What about the blood of executed prisoners, which, as he later put it, 'flows off without use'? The prison authorities gave him the go-ahead. Every two weeks, Dr Bimler and the Brandenburg-Görden prison doctor drew a blood sample from new convicts on death row. One day before each round of executions, Dr Bimler received a list of the persons to be killed. He chose five or six, based on the results of the earlier blood tests. The next day, he attended their execution. Once one of the pre-selected prisoners had been guillotined, Bimler's assistant recalled, 'Dr Bimler pulled him to the side, so that the bloodstream from the neck did not splash against the blade. I held the receptacle and caught the blood.' The assistant received extra pay for his services. The blood was temporarily preserved by adding sodium citricium and then used for transfusions in the local hospital. After the war, Dr Bimler estimated that during his 25 visits to the execution chamber he had gained enough blood for about 1,500 transfusions.[154]

The assembly-line executions in numerous prisons and penitentiaries, and the casual way in which prisoners' corpses were violated after their death, inevitably struck fear into the hearts of the other inmates. At the same time, the killings brutalised the warders. The warders supervised the condemned men and women, who were often held for months before they were executed. During this period, the inmates were shackled at their hands, and sometimes their feet at almost all times, even during air raids. Despite their chains, they were often still forced by the warders to work until the day they were killed. At night, many prisoners were only allowed to wear their shirts and underpants. All other clothes had to be given to the officials.[155] Individual warders were at hand to ensure the smooth operation of the execution. As the Plötzensee chaplain recalled, during the mass executions on 7 September 1943, one condemned prisoner began 'to scream and threw himself to the floor. He resisted with hands and feet. But to no avail. Four strong officials jumped on him and dragged him away.'[156]

Apparently, there was never a shortage of collaborators among the warders. In 1942, the Reich Ministry of Justice ordered that they were to be rewarded with cigarettes for their services during executions. The amount of cigarettes due to each prison or penitentiary was determined by the Reich Ministry of Justice, presumably based on calculations of the average number of executions in each institution. The Cologne prison Klingelpütz, for example, received 200 cigarettes each month for those warders willing to participate in the killings. Some warders increased their bloody loot by stealing tobacco from the cells of executed prisoners. In their minds, every executed prisoner equalled a few cigarettes more.[157] Mass execution of condemned inmates continued until the very end of the war, when the prison service collapsed in one last orgy of violence.

9   Final Defeat

Terror in the Third Reich showed no sign of waning as the Allies closed in. On the contrary, the more the German army was overwhelmed on the battlefield, the more repression seemed to escalate inside Nazi Germany.[1] This last phase of the Nazi dictatorship has been described by historians as a period of almost random violence on the part of the regime against the German population, which had so far widely been spared.[2] It is certainly true that the regime now struck further sections of the German population, even though we should be careful not to overplay this point. The last months of the Third Reich also saw a final escalation of violence inside penal institutions. As the German prison system disintegrated, thousands of inmates lost their lives, during exhausting evacuation marches, due to hunger and illness inside penal institutions, and at the hands of German officials who murdered prisoners until the last days of the war.

The Last Stand of Nazi Terror

The terror in defeat was linked to the further erosion of popular support for the regime. Alienation of large sections of the German population from their leaders, which had grown since 1942, gathered momentum in early 1945. The military successes of the Allies, with the dramatic offensive on the eastern front in January and the crossing of the Rhine in March, finally brought home to most Germans that the war was well and truly lost. Any remaining hopes for a reversal of their fortunes with the help of secret weapons, which had been promised by Nazi propaganda for some time, were dashed. Most Germans were exhausted and resigned to defeat, unwilling to sacrifice their property and their lives. But the Nazi leadership was determined to stamp out defeatism, as well as any efforts to surrender or damage army defences. For example, as late as 3 April 1945, Himmler ordered that 'where a white flag appears all the male persons of the house concerned are to be shot'. Hundreds of Germans, who had tried to act against the regime, were killed even in the last moments before liberation, in a wave of wild shootings and hangings. As the 'Hitler myth' disintegrated, the regime relied ever more on terror to discipline the German population.[3]

Himmler's men held centre stage. All over Germany, police and SS officials executed men and women. Some were killed in secrecy in forests or police jails, others were publicly hanged. Many more died in concentration camps. Conditions in the remaining concentration camps inside Germany were infernal, worse than ever before. Epidemics spread rapidly, not least because the camps were seriously overcrowded, following the arrival of inmates from other SS camps further east (Auschwitz, Stutthof, Groß-Rosen), which had been abandoned in the face of the advancing Red Army. Tens of thousands of inmates had died during these marches. Many of the survivors perished in the camps shortly afterwards. In concentration camps such as Flossenbürg and Mauthausen, inmates were dying faster than the officials could cremate their corpses.[4]

The police were not always indiscriminate. To be sure, some police and concentration camp officials, accepting the inevitable defeat in the war, were filled with the murderous desire to take as many others as possible with them into their graves and killed randomly. But other officials were still blindly driven by ideological conviction, aiming at the murderous repression of all those who threatened to 'stab the army in the back'. They focused on those groups who had been singled out for years, even though criteria for membership of these groups now became even more open-ended. The targets of the police included any real and suspected political enemies of the regime, in particular Communists. The police also continued to crack down with extreme force on common criminals, including the armed criminal gangs which had formed in German cities, using the chaos and confusion towards the end of the war for organised theft and black-marketeering. Finally, local police officials were given free rein to murder 'racial aliens', in particular foreign workers from eastern Europe. On 4 November 1944, Himmler authorised regional Gestapo offices to take 'measures of retribution' against foreign workers for 'terror and sabotage activities', even if these workers were not suspected of any offences themselves. Three months later, regional Gestapo leaders were given the green light to organise, on their own initiative, the 'special treatment' of 'eastern workers' who had committed 'crimes worthy of death'. Officials were encouraged to interpret this last term 'widely'.[5]

SS terror in concentration camps was not always arbitrary, either. From early 1945, the authorities in the remaining concentration camps started to murder selected groups of inmates. Apart from those who were weak and ill, the officials singled out those considered to be a potential threat, once the Allied troops had closed in on the camp. This included German political opponents, often prominent ones. For example, on 9 April 1945, several well-known members of the German resistance, including Pastor Dietrich Bonhoeffer, were hanged in Flossenbürg camp. Jewish prisoners and inmates from eastern Europe also had little hope of surviving the violence in the concentration camps in the last months. By contrast, some German camp inmates considered less dangerous were actually released and joined the forces at the front. Others were given privileged positions inside the camps.[6] Clearly, racial, social and political criteria still influenced police and SS terror, even in the last months. The same was true for the legal system.

The legal authorities did not leave the final battle on the home front entirely to the police. Many legal officials were eager to make a last stand. Reich Minister of Justice Thierack led from the top, still relying on a combination of new legislation and pressure on judges to drive legal terror. He was personally involved in countless decisions, unrelentingly pushing for ruthless sentences, the execution of 'enemies of the people' and the exploitation of prisoners for the war effort. To this end, Thierack visited several judicial districts, courts and penal institutions in the last phase of Nazi rule, sometimes turning up unannounced.[7] Other senior legal officials also still kept an eye on the application of the law by the regional courts. On 1 March 1945, State Secretary Klemm put further pressure on some regional judges to pass even stricter sentences.[8] Another senior official who made his voice heard was the president of the People's Court, Roland Freisler, who urged his colleagues on 30 January 1945 – the anniversary of Hitler's appointment as Chancellor – to fight until the end: 'Now the message is: All hands on deck! Employ the last reserves! Everything is now at stake.'[9] This proved to be Freisler's last battle-cry. On 3 February 1945, during a trial of three men involved in the July 1944 bomb plot, the People's Court was hit during a US air raid. Freisler, hiding in the cellar, was crushed to death by a falling beam.[10]

Disruption of the legal system by air raids, already evident in the previous years, was now common. All over Germany, the court system was slowly breaking down towards the end of the war. Court buildings were damaged, with crucial documents lost or destroyed. Many courts were deserted in the face of the advancing Allied troops. Before evacuating the buildings, the retreating legal officials often destroyed further documents. There was also a growing shortage of legal personnel, as more and more officials were drafted into the German forces. The destruction and ensuing chaos often made regular judicial business impossible. But many German judges were not put off, determined to carry on until the very end. Thousands of defendants were brought before the courts in 1945, facing very harsh punishment. While the overall number of cases dealt with by most special courts was much lower than in previous years (see Figure 8, pp. 400–1), due to the gradual collapse of the court system, in these last months of the war some judges passed proportionally more death sentences than ever before.[11] Legal officials continued to justify their brutal sentencing by claiming that this would prevent another 'stab in the back'. For example, the Hamm general state prosecutor Günther Joël, who also held the rank of Obersturmbannführer in the SS, stressed as late as 6 February 1945 that the long-term results of too lenient sentences 'could be no different than 1918'.[12]

Similar sentiments were expressed by judges, as is highlighted by the example of the coal worker Max Schlichting. On 16 January 1945, Schlichting was sentenced to death by the Hamburg Higher State Court for 'undermining the war effort' and 'helping the enemy'. Schlichting's offence was, on the face of it, trivial. Standing in a public toilet in Hamburg, he had expressed to a soldier his well-founded doubts about the German prospects of winning the war. His words were overheard by an undercover Gestapo officer, on the lookout for Communist resistance fighters. Schlichting was quickly condemned to death, and executed on 24 March 1945. His sentence highlights both the ruthlessness of some judges at the end of the war, and the fact that punishment by the legal system was not yet meted out completely arbitrarily. For in the eyes of the judges, what made Schlichting's comment a mortal crime, was his past: he had briefly been a member of the Communist party in the Weimar Republic and was also accused of having led an 'asocial' lifestyle. 'There can be no doubt,' the judges noted, 'that the accused would immediately participate actively on the side of the revolution in the case of domestic unrest or a civil war, and that, judging from his outward appearance, he would show no mercy at all.'[13] Other individuals, who had fitted better into Nazi society, might not have paid with their lives for a comment similar to Schlichting's. Penal policy against 'national comrades' could, at times, still be more lenient. Some offenders, who were thought to have merely 'tripped up', even had a chance of escaping punishment altogether, for on 20 December 1944 the Reich Ministry of Justice ordered that short prison sentences under three months should only be served in exceptional circumstances.[14] At the same time, however, it should be stressed that it was often impossible for many German defendants to predict how an individual judge might classify them – as 'national comrade' or as 'community alien' – a distinction that could make the difference between a lenient sentence and the death penalty.

One crowning moment in the history of the perversion of penal policy in the Third Reich came at the very end. On 15 February 1945, Reich Minister of Justice Thierack announced the setting up of civilian drumhead courts martial, on Hitler's orders. These courts were chaired by a professional judge, and included two assessors: one Nazi party official, and one officer from the army, Waffen SS or the police – another instance of the growing merger of legal system, party and police. The courts were given total power over defendants, virtually free from procedural or legislative shackles. They were authorised to sentence to death anyone who avoided 'duties to the community... [and] jeopardize[d] German combat strength or determination'.[15] Of course, such loose terminology could be applied to almost any behaviour, which had been the intention of the Nazi leadership.

Martin Bormann praised the new courts as 'a weapon for the annihilation of all parasites of the people'. The reign of the drumhead courts martial was indeed particularly bloody. True, some judges, now with one eye on their postwar career, passed rather lenient sentences or tried to excuse themselves from serving on the courts altogether. But others were determined to eradicate anyone suspected of defeatism. In fanatical pursuit of this goal, officials were scouring the country, often disregarding any remaining legal requirements. For example, in some cases the courts were wrongly constituted, with the mandatory legal official missing altogether. In the words of a postwar court, judgments of the drumhead courts martial were often little more than 'orders for murder'.[16] The defendants were not the only victims of the legal apparatus in the last stages of the war, however. Many thousands more prisoners died or were killed in this period.

Prison Evacuations

The looming defeat of Nazi Germany had a dramatic impact on penal institutions. Following the advances by Allied troops in the west and the east, after the Normandy landings on 6 June and the start of the Soviet offensive on 22 June, German prison officials from the summer of 1944 faced the possibility of penal institutions being captured by the Allies. What should be done with the inmates?

By this time, the prison administration had already gained some experience of evacuations. In the wake of Allied bombing raids, several institutions had to be closed and the inmates moved elsewhere. In most cases, this was apparently accomplished without serious incidents. One exception had occurred in Hamburg at the end of July 1943, when the prison authorities simply released large numbers of remand prisoners and inmates with lengthy sentences (including many political prisoners) after local prisons and penitentiaries had been severely damaged. This prompted Reich Minister of Justice Thierack to send a stern warning to all general state prosecutors, emphasising that inmates could only ever be released in exceptional circumstances, and only when 'the prisoner was no longer a public risk'; this explicitly barred political prisoners. Thierack added that the responsible officials in Hamburg would be severely punished for their actions. The Hamburg general state prosecutor was eventually sentenced to four months in prison.[17]

In the second half of 1944, preliminary plans were made for the evacuation of inmates from prisons and penitentiaries near the front line. Initially, it seems, only inmates regarded as 'particularly dangerous' were moved from threatened districts. But soon, entire institutions were emptied. At the end of November 1944, for example, Thierack ordered the withdrawal from penal institutions on the left bank of the Rhine. By early December 1944, Hitler was informed that some 8,000 prisoners had already been moved out of judicial districts in the west (Cologne, Karlsruhe) and the east (Königsberg, Posen). The evacuated prisoners were taken to penal institutions in central Germany.[18]

Once the Allied forces moved even closer to Germany, the judicial officials in Berlin drew up general guidelines for the evacuation of penal institutions. These secret instructions were intended as general 'pointers' for the regional and local legal officials, who were authorised to improvise, working together with the local state and party officials who were in overall charge of evacuations in the regions.[19] It seems likely that these guidelines were drawn up after an agreement between leading members of the police and the legal apparatus, maybe even between Himmler and Thierack personally.[20] Once the guidelines had been agreed, possibly in late 1944, they were evidently transmitted from January 1945 onwards to all those judicial districts faced with being overrun by the Allies.[21]

According to the prison evacuation guidelines, inmates were not to be treated equally. Prison policy remained selective. Until the very end, the fate of prisoners was decided in part by racial, political and criminological labels. Prison officials were asked to divide the inmates into three groups. The first group included prisoners regarded as ready to return to society, provided that they had no more than nine months left to serve, or that they had only once 'slipped up' (the authorities were thinking of acts of criminal negligence, crimes of passion, offences against the War Economy Decree). All these inmates qualified for early release. The second group of prisoners contained inmates who could be handed over to another state agency: for example those originally sentenced by military courts, who only had short sentences left to serve, could be sent to join army formations. And police detainees in penal institutions, of which there were about 7,000 every day in late 1944/early 1945, were to be handed back to the police authorities. Finally, there was the third group of prisoners. They were not to be set free under any circumstances whatsoever. This included so-called racial aliens (any remaining Jews, 'half-Jews', Sinti and Roma, and most Poles), 'politically dangerous prisoners' (including most Czechs) and supposedly serious criminal offenders ('habitual criminals' and 'serious psychopaths'). If evacuation of these inmates proved impossible, the Reich Ministry of Justice ordered that they must not fall into enemy hands. Instead, 'particularly asocial subversive prisoners' had to be killed. This official licence for murder was made crystal clear in the guidelines: the prisoners should be 'transferred to the police for removal or, if this is also impossible, be neutralised by shooting them dead. The evidence of neutralisation is to be carefully cleared up.'[22]

Asked after the war about the thinking behind these murderous orders, the former head of the prison service, Karl Engert, argued that he had wanted to protect German civilians from the threat of dangerous criminals. Once more, he looked to 1918 to justify his actions. After the German defeat in the First World War, Engert claimed, 'many people were beaten to death in Bavaria by former penitentiary inmates. I wanted to prevent a repetition.'[23] How this – fictitious – precedent could justify the killing of priests, Poles, German political prisoners, foreign resistance fighters and small-time criminals was left unanswered by Engert. It should be added that the Reich Ministry of Justice was not alone in ordering the execution of prisoners in the face of the advancing Allies. Similar orders had been going out to regional police officials in occupied Europe for months. As early as July 1944, the commander of the security police and the SD in the General Government had ordered that if inmates in police jails could not be evacuated, then they 'should be liquidated'.[24] This order had been quickly implemented. One of the first massacres took place on 2 August 1944, when an SS commando slaughtered at least 250 Polish inmates in the Warsaw prison.[25]

The mass evacuation of penal institutions in the east started in late January and early February 1945. The Soviet winter offensive had begun on 12 January, and made very swift progress. By the end of January, Soviet troops had already crossed the Oder near Breslau, encircled Posen, occupied Bromberg and gained ground in East Prussia.[26] Many German prison officials were caught up in the advance, as the Red Army rapidly penetrated six different German judicial districts in the east. The legal officials in these districts quickly had to decide what to do with the approximately 35,000 prisoners who were held in 75 large penal institutions and many hundreds of small jails.[27] Most of these prisoners, it seems, were forced to leave their institutions, often in chaotic circumstances. Orderly evacuations proved almost impossible, owing to lack of supplies and means of transport, contradictory information about the Soviet advances, and the reluctance of some civil authorities to prepare properly for the evacuation (so as not to spread panic among the population). Even so, by late January 1945, many thousands of prisoners were on their way from penal institutions in the east towards central Germany. They formed part of a massive wave of men, women and children fleeing before the advancing Red Army.

The great majority of these prisoners had to march on foot; only a few were fortunate enough to be transported by train. They were forced to walk very long distances, in extreme cold and icy winds. Sometimes the snowstorms were so bad that treks lost all sense of direction. One governor described the march of inmates assembled at the Preußisch Stargard prison (south of Danzig) to the west in late January and February 1945:

> The weather conditions were disastrous. The progress of the trek was hindered by the heavy snowfall, the cold, the mass of refugee and army vehicles as well as the flooding back of masses of troops, prisoners of war etc. Every road was jammed, so that the treks sometimes had to wait for hours on one spot, just to move a few hundred metres forward.[28]

The prisoners had to march for 17 days along the Baltic coast, covering more than 400 kilometres between Preußisch Stargard and Bützow (near Rostock). Many of the inmates were extremely poorly equipped, arriving in Bützow without shoes and proper clothes.[29]

Not only did the evacuated prisoners lack adequate clothing, but most received minimal rations on the way. Many treks ran out of food completely. Prisoners from the Wronke penal institution (Posen district), for example, who had already marched for days, covered some 120 kilometres in five days to the Luckau penitentiary. During this period, they received two small helpings of potatoes, five helpings of thin soup and a small piece of bread. The Wronke governor described the last day in his official diary:

> 4.2.45 Breakfast for the prisoners: soup out of the last remaining potatoes and porridge. Marching off 9 o'clock to Luckau[.] 32 km mostly through forest. On the way, about 25 prisoners left lying behind due to exhaustion, in part handed over to local police authorities[,] some of them brought to Luckau later. No bread and no lunch for the prisoners. One prisoner escaping through the undergrowth is shot dead. At 18h arrival in Luckau... general exhaustion. Condition of the feet in parts very bad (several days in snow water).

Only 465 of the 1,128 prisoners who had set out on foot from Wronke in January actually arrived in Luckau. But they were only allowed to rest there for two days. On 7 February, they were forced to march further, covering another 93 kilometres over the next three days.[30]

Fatalities were particularly high among female inmates. As the Breslau general state prosecutor stated bluntly: 'The women were less resistant to the winter conditions.'[31] Among the many victims were inmates from the women's penitentiary in Fordon (near Bromberg), which was evacuated early on 21 January 1945. After marching for the entire day, covering 36 kilometres, the trek finally reached the Krone prison late at night. Only 40 of the 565 Fordon inmates had made it. As the Fordon governor reported:

> It was about minus 12 degrees [centigrade] and it was very icy. As a result, the prisoners as well as the warders fell over all the time... During the march, I observed numerous prisoners who were left behind, struggling to drag themselves forward. Many were sitting or lying by the side of the road, and nothing could move them to get up again.[32]

Overall, a significant number of prisoners in the east died of exhaustion, cold and hunger. Weak prisoners were sometimes pulled on sledges by other inmates; others just collapsed and froze to death. Hundreds who were too sick or frail to continue with the march, as well as inmates regarded as 'dangerous', were handed over by prison officials to the police along the way. Many of them were shot. Some weak inmates were also killed during the marches by prison warders or SS officers, who had been drafted in to guard the treks. The chaos on the roads in the east, littered with corpses and burnt-out vehicles, and overflowing with fleeing civilians, soldiers, SS men and prisoners of war, held further dangers for the prisoners: one group of inmates from the Krone prison was mown down by retreating SS officers with machine-guns, while some female prisoners were snatched by retreating German soldiers and raped. In addition, a number of inmates were killed or captured by Soviet troops.[33]

Nevertheless, the death rate during these marches was significantly lower than in simultaneous death marches from concentration camps. Prison inmates were not subjected to the same levels of violence. Hundreds of convicts with short periods left to serve were released during the march. And a number of other prisoners saved their lives by running away, despite the shoot-to-kill policy of the prison and police officers guarding the marches. Some were intimidated by the corpses of escaped prisoners from earlier transports lying along the roads, but many others took the risk, and their initial chances of getting away were good. Escaped convicts in the east, who were mostly Polish, could sometimes count on the sympathy of the native population, who gave them shelter and protected them from the retreating warders. For German officials, chaotic conditions made the control of the prisoners difficult. Some officials also complained that they lacked sufficient weaponry to shoot escaping inmates. In addition, a number of warders failed to enforce strict discipline against the prisoners as they were now concerned primarily with their own welfare (and that of their wives and children, who in some cases accompanied the treks). Some warders simply ran away to save their own skin. Given these circumstances, it is not surprising that on some marches, maybe about a third of all prisoners managed to flee.[34] How many of them survived in the freezing conditions is unknown.

The prisoners from the east generally headed for penal institutions further west. One exception were *NN* prisoners, many of whom were taken to concentration camps instead. In a meeting on 9 September 1944 in Berlin, state and party representatives had agreed that these prisoners should be left to the police – except in cases where the legal authorities had already ordered the discharge of a death sentence, indicating that *NN* prisoners were not expected to live for long inside concentration camps. Following this meeting, the Reich Ministry of Justice informed the regional legal authorities that *NN* prisoners should be handed over from penal institutions to the local Gestapo. General state prosecutors were told that this transfer should be implemented 'quickly and smoothly' to create room for prisoners arriving from penal institutions evacuated in the face of the advancing Allies. Consequently, from late 1944, several thousand *NN* prisoners were transported to the camps. For example, about 1,600 French, Belgian and Dutch prisoners from penal institutions in Brieg, Breslau, Groß-Strehlitz (which had held many *NN* prisoners previously in Emsland) and Schweidnitz were taken to the Groß-Rosen concentration camp in Lower Silesia from October 1944 onwards. They were soon joined by other *NN* prisoners. The inmates arrived in a very weakened state and by the time Groß-Rosen was evacuated in early 1945, a large number of them were reportedly dead.[35]

But the transfer of *NN* prisoners to the concentration camps did not proceed as 'smoothly' as the prison administration had hoped. Some local prison officials were in no hurry to implement the deportation orders, probably anxious to get no more blood on their hands after the war was effectively lost. Concentration camp officials also sometimes proved uncooperative. This was obvious in the case of 446 *NN* prisoners, who had left a prison camp in the Kattowitz district on 22 January 1945 on foot, heading for Groß-Rosen. Conditions during the march had been appalling. After six days, more than one-third of the men had been lost: some had escaped, others had died of exhaustion or had been shot by the Gestapo. When the remainder finally reached Groß-Rosen, they were turned away because the camp was already overcrowded. The legal authorities now tried to redirect the trek to Buchenwald.[36] Faced with such obstacles, the Reich Ministry of Justice urged both the general state prosecutors and the RSHA to speed up the transfer of *NN* prisoners to concentration camps.[37] Some inmates were transferred as late as April 1945.[38] Even a few weeks before the end of the war, prison officials still sent foreign political prisoners to the concentration camps.

Inside Germany, the evacuation of prisoners was increasingly under way. From February 1945 onwards, with the Allies advancing further, many penal institutions in the Altreich were evacuated, while others were closed down after they had been partially destroyed in air raids. In the Düsseldorf district, all remaining penal institutions on the left bank of the Rhine were empty by early March 1945.[39] A large number of prisoners in Berlin were also moved, after parts of the Red Army had advanced to only about 80 kilometres outside the German capital by 1 February 1945. Among the first to leave were political prisoners scheduled to be tried by the People's Court. To ensure that the People's Court would keep up its murderous work, following the partial destruction of the court building on 3 February 1945, Hitler ordered two days later that parts of the court should be moved from Berlin to Bayreuth, together with selected remand prisoners.[40] The Reich Ministry of Justice quickly sprang into action. On the following day about 220 male prisoners suspected of treason and high treason left for Bayreuth. Presumably because no trains were available at such short notice, the first stage of the transport was carried out by boat.[41] For about a week the prisoners were forced into the coal bunkers of barges heading along the Havel and the Elbe to Magdeburg, and then further to Coswig. Conditions were very poor. The political prisoners, unsure of their fate, suffered from the cold and the lack of food and drink. In Coswig they were forced into overcrowded trains, which finally took them to Bayreuth. Numerous prisoners fell ill and several died during the transports. But many of those who reached Bayreuth probably survived the war, as the People's Court never came into operation there after all.[42]

The prison authorities also desperately tried to transport more inmates from outside Nazi Germany back to the Reich. For example, the evacuation of the prison camp North in Norway to Germany had been planned since late 1944. The aim was to deploy many of the inmates in special army formations at the front, but due to the shortage of available ships, many prisoners were stuck in freezing conditions for months. Two groups of inmates finally left Norway in March and April 1945. Several hundred prisoners were left behind, concentrated in one camp near Harstad.[43] After the German capitulation, the prison camp was initially run by the German army, which continued to enforce brutal discipline. On 9 May 1945, for example, prisoner S., who had tried unsuccessfully to escape, was sentenced to death and executed, following a perfunctory trial by a court-martial. Only in mid-May did the first British officers enter the camp.[44]

In the chaos of the last months, with the Allied advances and the destruction of further penal institutions, prison inmates were constantly on the move. One of them was the priest Josef Reuland. Originally, Reuland had been held in the Münster prison. After the prison was damaged in a bombing raid in October 1944, he was transferred to Essen. Only two months later, the Essen prison was completely destroyed by Allied bombs, apparently killing more than 200 prisoners. He survived once more, with concussion and bruises. This time, he was taken to the nearby penal institution in Bochum. Reuland, by now in very bad health, did not stay there for long. With US troops quickly closing in on Bochum, the order was given on 27 March 1945 to take the inmates by train to Hanover. However, the train was almost immediately hit by Allied bombers, killing and wounding numerous prisoners. The survivors were taken back to Bochum. Two days later, half of the prisoners were forced to leave again, this time to march on foot to Celle. Reuland was too weak to march, suffering from malnourishment and illness, and he collapsed repeatedly with exhaustion. On each occasion, he was forced to get up again by prison warders, who kicked and beat him. Eventually, the warder Hans Brodowski, an invalid ex-soldier who had fought on the eastern front, announced to a colleague: 'This is one of those black brothers [i.e. a priest], I know him. He has to disappear. I'll take him to St Peter. Go and report; "Shot while trying to escape".' Warder Brodowski dragged Reuland to an open field, shot him in the neck and left him for dead. Miraculously, Reuland survived once more and dragged himself to a nearby home for the elderly. Here, he was denounced to the police and transported back to Bochum prison. Half paralysed, Reuland clung on to life until the prison was liberated by US troops on 8 April 1945.[45]

Prisoner evacuations continued until the last weeks of the war, even though the officials were fast running out of options: roads were cut off and it was often not clear where the prisoners could be taken, as many penal institutions were already abandoned or seriously overcrowded. Some local authorities pressurised the prison officials to kill the prisoners to solve the problem. After the war, one former governor recalled the response he had received, when he arrived with about 70 evacuated prisoners in the town of Spittal (Carinthia) in the spring of 1945:

> ... everywhere I asked for shelter or food for the prisoners – I was thinking especially about empty barracks of the labour service or the like – I got the same answer: 'What? Convicts? Criminals? Why must they, of all people, be taken to safety? We have our hands full with decent refugees. Just put these people against the wall, just take a hand grenade!'[46]

Still the evacuation of prisoners continued. One of the very last attempts was made by officials from the Straubing penitentiary. On 25 April 1945, three days before US troops captured Straubing, more than 3,000 prisoners had to leave the institution. The destination was Dachau concentration camp. During the march, the prisoners were brutally beaten and suffered from great hunger. In several villages, local inhabitants tried to give bread to the prisoners. But some warders beat up prisoners for accepting the food and pushed back civilians, threatening them with machine-guns. (Similar scenes took place during the death marches from some concentration camps.) After several days of marching, the exhausted Straubing prisoners reached the town of Freising, where the governor apparently heard that Dachau had already been liberated by the US army. He now ordered the prisoners to turn back to Straubing, but US troops soon caught up with the trek and set them free.[47]

Evacuations were a crucial feature of imprisonment in the last phase of the Third Reich. Many prisoners died during marches and transports, collapsing with exhaustion or murdered by police and prison officials.[48] But by no means all inmates of abandoned penal institutions were forced on the marches.

Following the ministerial guidelines, prisoners were divided into different groups. 'Dangerous' prisoners were singled out and put on the transports. During their selection, the prison authorities could often draw on 'lists of dangerous prisoners', which had apparently been routinely kept in penal institutions for some time.[49] Many thousands of 'reformable' inmates were released prior to the evacuations. Typically, these were prisoners described by the legal officials as 'decent' and 'orderly', similar to those labelled as having only 'tripped up'. Most of these prisoners had received shorter sentences (often up to one year) or had only a few months left to serve (this included some Polish prisoners). Some other inmates were spared, too. For example, the Königsberg general state prosecutor was authorised by the Reich Ministry of Justice to release more female prisoners, after he had argued that they were unlikely to survive the marches westwards. It is impossible to say how many prisoners were released before the evacuations. Much depended on the attitudes of the individual governors, the local police and party officials. What is clear is that the numbers were high. In some institutions, about a third of all the inmates were released. In one case, a governor panicked and released all inmates, escaping on his own.[50]

In February 1945, the policy of releasing 'reformable' prisoners was extended by the Reich Ministry of Justice to penal institutions not yet under immediate threat of being overrun. In several decrees, regional legal officials were encouraged to set free temporarily those prisoners not regarded as particularly dangerous, such as selected inmates who had less than six months left to serve. The ministerial officials pursued two aims. First, they hoped that releases would diminish overcrowding in individual institutions. Secondly, the released prisoners could immediately be used to build defences against the advancing Allies or as soldiers. Even selected penitentiary inmates, the Reich Ministry of Justice announced on 7 February 1945, should be 'given the opportunity' to 'prove themselves with a weapon in their hand before the enemy' in a special formation of the Waffen SS. This was described by the officials as an 'honour', from which non-Germans, 'asocials', 'habitual criminals', Jews, homosexuals and supposedly dangerous political offenders were excluded.[51] In reality, this 'honour' often meant death. The ex-prisoners were used as cannon-fodder by the poorly equipped German forces, which were overpowered on the battlefield. Meanwhile, many of their former fellow inmates, who had not been released, died as well.

Chaos, Murder, Liberation

In the last months of the war, several thousand prisoners judged 'dangerous' were murdered all over Germany. Some executions had apparently not been planned. For example, on 6 April 1945 a total of 391 prisoners from the Stein penitentiary in Austria were shot dead after a 'rebellion' by the inmates, according to regional legal officials. But in most cases, the killings were premeditated days or weeks in advance, in the context of the evacuations of penal institutions. Local legal officials first discussed the fate of individual prisoners with party and police officials, in line with the official evacuation guidelines. Often, the legal officials also asked for approval from their superiors in the Reich Ministry of Justice. In the end, the police picked up the selected inmates from penal institutions, and then often shot them elsewhere. The police officials had their own reasons for getting involved. Apparently, they had received independent instructions from the RSHA that certain inmates, including political offenders, should not fall into the hands of the Allies.[52]

The largest single massacre took place in the penitentiary in Sonnenburg, a small town about 100 kilometres east of Berlin. In January 1945, during the rapid Russian advance, there had been several preliminary discussions about the future of the penal institutions east of Berlin, involving the regional general state prosecutor Kurt-Walter Hanssen, SS and police officials, and Reich Defence Commissioner, Gauleiter Emil Stürtz (responsible for civil defence in the region). On 30 January 1945, Hanssen was informed that Soviet troops were getting dangerously close to Sonnenburg. Hanssen, a young, ruthless and ambitious jurist who had worked between 1937 and 1942 as personal assistant to Martin Bormann, ordered that the majority of inmates in Sonnenburg were to be handed over to the Gestapo, while the remaining 'useful elements' were to be marched westwards. This course of action had evidently been agreed upon in earlier discussions with the other state and party officials. It had also been cleared with the Reich Ministry of Justice.

Later on 30 January 1945, a commando consisting of police and SS officials from Frankfurt an der Oder arrived in Sonnenburg, with orders to execute the prisoners. The Sonnenburg prison officials had apparently already made a pre-selection among the inmates during the previous days. This now formed the basis for the division of the prisoner population into 'useful' inmates and the rest, which was made by the governor Theodor Knops (in agreement with the leader of the Gestapo commando). Those prisoners chosen to be killed included both criminal offenders and political prisoners. Sick prisoners, unable to march, were also singled out. By deciding which inmates were to be killed, the local prison officials played a key role in the mass murder. Many of them were willing participants. Some had already taken part in the killing of prisoners over the previous years, during the 'annihilation through labour' programme. Others were motivated by their fear of the revenge of those prisoners whom they had treated worst.

The murders in Sonnenburg began in the late evening of 30 January. The inmates were forced to run in groups of ten to a secluded part of the penitentiary, driven on by prison officials. Here, they were ordered by the SS men to kneel down. Then they were shot in the neck. Prisoners too sick to walk were executed in their beds. When the shooting stopped hours later, over 800 prisoners had been murdered. Most of them were foreigners, including Belgian, French, Dutch, Norwegian, Polish and Russian inmates. Soon after, the remaining 150 inmates, who had been classified as 'useful' by the prison officials, began their march to Berlin. The police and SS killers returned to their headquarters. The first thing they did on arrival was to wash their blood-stained uniforms.[53]

Many other 'dangerous' prisoners earmarked for extermination towards the end of the war were spared, for various reasons. In some cases the legal authorities had done their best to facilitate their extermination, only to find that the local police officials refused to kill the prisoners.[54] At other times, local officials ignored the murderous orders. Even in the last months of the Nazi dictatorship, there were few acts of open sabotage. Nevertheless, unprecedented acts of disobedience now took place in many walks of life.[55] One such incident occurred in the Gollnow penitentiary (Stettin district). On 3 February 1945, Reich Minister of Justice Thierack had personally ordered that the Gollnow inmates, in line with the evacuation guidelines, should be divided into 'dangerous' and 'harmless'. The latter could be released in due course, while the 'politically important and dangerous prisoners' were to be taken away immediately. Those 'dangerous prisoners' who could not be moved in time were to be 'transferred to the police'.[56] The officials in Stettin lost no time in implementing Thierack's order. After consultations with representatives of the regional Higher SS- and Police Leader and the Reich Defence Commissioner, the general state prosecutor in Stettin, Otto Stäcker, ordered on 5 February 1945 that prisoners in Gollnow who were expected to 'behave well' could be released. Also, a first transport of selected other prisoners left Gollnow. The rest were kept in captivity. They included foreigners, remand prisoners, prisoners with many previous convictions, inmates who had more than one year left to serve and 'asocials'. Stäcker and the regional Higher SS- and Police leader discussed which of these 'dangerous prisoners' should be transferred to the police 'for liquidation'. In the end, it was decided that some 37 Gollnow prisoners should be killed, a plan approved by the Reich Defence Commissioner.[57] But the Gollnow governor subverted this plan. To save the inmates from execution, the governor included them in a second transport of selected political prisoners, which left Gollnow on 11 February. This shows that it was possible for local officials, during the chaos of the last months of the war, to disobey murderous orders from above. Such actions did not necessarily have grave consequences for them personally. While the general state prosecutor and the Reich Defence Commissioner were furious, the Gollnow governor got away with a reprimand.[58] But few governors took similar steps to prevent the killing of their prisoners.

Meanwhile, living conditions in those penal institutions not yet destroyed or abandoned were worse than ever. Here, inmates suffered from an extreme shortage of supplies. Food allocation in Germany as a whole declined dramatically in the last months of the war, and, once again, inmates in penal institutions were among those hit hardest.[59] Some inmates had to survive the last months of the war on a starvation diet of watery soup. Prison officials in Ebrach, for example, only handed out soup and carrots, deliberately holding back other goods. The Ebrach inmate Johannes E., who served a sentence for listening to foreign radio, recalled after the war: 'Every single day, at noon and in the evenings, one only got carrots, carrots, carrots, every single week, every single month.'[60] Many other basics were also lacking: there were severe shortages of clothing, medication and other essentials. There were not even enough bags of straw for prisoners to sleep on. And, due to fuel shortages, many cells were no longer heated. Sometimes the temperature barely climbed above freezing point.[61]

The inmates were subjected to brutal violence inside penal institutions. True, some warders started to treat prisoners – above all political prisoners – better than before. Conscious that the war was lost, these officials were positioning themselves for the time after the war. Other warders, however, acted with unprecedented brutality. Violent excesses took place in penal institutions all over Germany. Some attacks were committed by new officials, who had recently joined the prison administration after serving in the army. Returning from the eastern front, they had become accustomed to using excessive violence against 'enemies of the people'. But long-serving prison officials were also guilty. Hans D., a senior prison officer in Straubing who had worked in the Bavarian prison service since 1918, was sentenced in 1949 for 40 proven attacks on inmates (there may have been many more), committed in the final year of the war. Hans D. regularly hit inmates with his fists and feet, as well as with keys, clubs, brooms and spades. His fury could be unleashed by any behaviour. Individual prisoners in Straubing were attacked for talking to other inmates, for collapsing at work, for walking too slowly, for giving a piece of food to others and for swapping a wedding ring for a bit of bread and tobacco.[62]

The arrival of prisoners from evacuated institutions created further pressures inside prisons and penitentiaries. With fewer and fewer institutions in use, numbers inside reached new heights. At the end of the war, the four Bavarian penal institutions in Ebrach, Straubing, Aichach and Kaisheim together peaked at over 11,000 inmates per day – around 8,000 prisoners more than their official maximum capacity.[63] This meant that food and other supplies became even more scarce. The new inmates also often arrived in a catastrophic condition. After days or weeks of exhausting marches and transports, they were dressed in rags, disease-ridden and starving. The Untermaßfeld governor described one group of 87 prisoners, who had arrived in March 1945 from the Waldheim penitentiary, as 'again completely covered in lice'. Only 53 of the men had been wearing shoes or slippers, and only 17 had socks. Many of the men weighed less than 50 kilos.[64] Some died within a few days of their arrival. According to the prisoner Rudolf Kriß, many of the exhausted new arrivals in the Straubing penitentiary 'did not even make it to the hospital ward, but died in the corridors'.[65] The local prison authorities were often at a loss as to what to do with the new arrivals. Court documents about them had been destroyed or lost and the officials knew only the names of the new inmates, no more. In such cases, the officials relied on their instinct when determining the prisoners' treatment.[66]

Prison labour was severely disrupted in the last months of the war. True, many inmates were still forced to work very hard. In late January/February 1945, over 17,000 prisoners were still held in satellite camps.[67] Some were toiling underground in mines, in thin and dirt-encrusted clothes, exposed to freezing temperatures. Others had to build anti-tank barriers, clear up after bomb damage and remove debris and rubble from railway lines. Prison officials were also anxious to redeploy inmates from evacuated institutions. Some prisoners were employed in the same workshops they had worked in before, as entire barracks, machines and other equipment from abandoned institutions had been dismantled and then set up in central Germany. Evacuated inmates were forced to work as soon as possible after their arrival. When the exhausted inmates from the Wronke prison finally arrived at the Straguth prison camp (north of Dessau) in February 1945, after an arduous march of about 400 kilometres in total, they were immediately forced to work at the Zerbst airport. It seems that many inmates in the camp died, due to exhaustion and maltreatment.[68] Still, it proved increasingly difficult to find employment for prisoners. German war production as a whole was collapsing by early 1945, following damage to the infrastructure and shortages of raw material caused by the bombing and the advances of Allied troops. As a result, production in armaments factories and workshops in many penal institutions was scaled back or abandoned.[69]

The consequences of overcrowding, malnourishment, brutal treatment and lack of medical care were disease and death among the prisoners. In the Ebrach penitentiary, 61 inmates died between January and May 1945 – as many as in the previous five years together.[70] In other penal institutions, one inmate or more died every day.[71] Many succumbed to infectious diseases which spread quickly in the overcrowded cells. According to the Leipzig prison governor, inmates suffered from 'dysentery, erysipelas of face and extremities (complicated by abscesses), scabies, lice almost everywhere in the institution, tuberculosis of the lung, many cases of flu . . .'.[72] One of the worst epidemics broke out in the Siegburg penal institution. At the end of 1944, Siegburg held some 2,600 prisoners, three times more than its official maximum capacity.

For months, the inmates – jammed together into single cells – had hardly been allowed to wash or change their clothes. Lice had multiplied, with prison officials making few attempts to get rid of them. Presumably, this was the main cause of the rapid spread of the typhus epidemic that broke out in December 1944, infecting about half the inmate population. The prison doctor failed to spot the outbreak for two months and well over 200 inmates died.[73] Hundreds more prisoners died during bombing raids in the last months of the war. The closer these prisoners came to being liberated, the more likely they often were to die.

For many prisoners, the last days before the Allies arrived were almost unbearably tense. Some had longed for many years for the day of their liberation, and freedom was now within their grasp. But the danger was far from over and the prisoners were holding their breath. They were still locked in their cells, completely exposed to bombing raids and artillery fire. In addition, many inmates, including political prisoners, lived in constant fear that they would be taken away by the police or the SS at the last minute. As one prisoner put it after the war, their thoughts circled around questions such as: 'Execution or not? Liberation or liquidation?'[74] Such fears were not unfounded.

Legal executions inside penal institutions continued until the end of the war. Of course, they were disrupted by the growing chaos and breakdown of the lines of communication. But, whatever the obstacle, the legal authorities were determined to kill as many of the condemned prisoners as possible. Once the failure of executioners to get to prisons and penitentiaries threatened to delay killings, Reich Minister of Justice Thierack ordered that the condemned inmates could be shot by prison officials instead.[75] The executions stopped only when the penal institutions were evacuated or liberated by the Allies. In the Halle penitentiary, for example, four inmates convicted of property offences were killed by the executioner on 10 April 1945, just one day before the institution was evacuated.[76] Similar last-minute executions took place in other penal institutions. In the Brandenburg-Görden penitentiary, the last execution, of some 33 inmates, took place on 20 April 1945. In the Third Reich, no executions had previously been allowed to be scheduled on 20 April, Hitler's birthday, in a truly perverse show of reverence for the 'Führer'. But by 1945 legal officials were in such a hurry to kill prisoners on death row that they had no time for such conventions. Thierack himself had insisted on 19 April that no time should be lost and that the executions in Brandenburg-Görden had to go ahead on the very next day. As no regular executioner was available, the killings were perpetrated by several prison warders. For their bloody deeds, they were rewarded with money and cigarettes by the governor. Only one week after this last mass execution, the Red Army liberated the Brandenburg-Görden penitentiary.[77]

Until the end, prisoners were considered fair game. Police and SS officials appeared in penal institutions to pick up inmates, who were then either taken to another prison or murdered.[78] Sometimes, the initiative for such killings came from the army. Shortly after US forces had encircled German territory in the Ruhr, the commander of the German troops in the cut-off area, Field Marshal Walter Model, ordered on 7 April 1945 that penitentiary inmates should be handed over for 'examination' to the police. The same applied to remand prisoners held for political offences or for offences which carried a penitentiary or death sentence. Following Model's orders, which had presumably been cleared with the regional general state prosecutor Günther Joël, over 200 prisoners were executed in the area. These included 71 'dangerous' inmates from Wuppertal prisons and from the Remscheid-Lüttringhausen penitentiary, who were executed by the police on 13 April outside Solingen. The dead were Russian and Polish inmates, prominent German political prisoners and criminal offenders, all of whom had been selected with the help of local prison officials.[79] In the homicidal atmosphere of final defeat, any high-ranking figure could try to claim authority over the prisoners' lives. For example, on 11 April 1945 a 21-year-old apprentice chimney sweep arrived in the Aschendorfermoor camp (a sub-camp of the Emsland camp), wearing the uniform of an army captain he had found. The impostor ordered the execution of dozens of prisoners in the camp. Several warders followed his orders, and in the following days they, together with a group of soldiers, executed more than 100 prisoners, mainly inmates with a poor disciplinary record and those who had at one time tried to escape.[80]

The fears of prisoners lasted until they were finally freed. The final hours before liberation were characterised by confusion, panic and rumours among the inmates. This atmosphere of terror was captured after the war by the political prisoner Curt Letsche, who had been held with others in a detention cell below ground when the Kaisheim penitentiary was liberated by US troops:

> It was dark, one could hear the sound of motors, detonations, shots. One or two hours passed, we forgot the cramped conditions and the difficulty of breathing due to the fear that the SS would commit a terrible blood-bath with a few hand grenades, feeling our powerlessness and helplessness more than ever. Finally, the door was unlocked, we saw machine-guns directed at us, at the front they shouted 'the SS' – then the heavy detention door was slammed shut. Minutes passed, until one [of us] carefully peeked at the corridor. One heard noise – warders were not to be seen. Some dared to go as far as the stairs and there the door was also no longer locked. This is how we experienced the liberation.[81]

In the following weeks and months, tens of thousands of prisoners in penal institutions were freed by the Allies. The Soviet authorities indiscriminately released inmates from many prisons and penitentiaries. US troops, too, initially released almost all inmates, assuming them to be racial and political prisoners, victims of Nazi ideology. Other prisoners used the chaotic conditions to escape, sometimes taking prison property and equipment with them. By the summer of 1945, the inmate population in the US zone had fallen to 20 per cent of its total capacity.[82] A few of the new prisoners behind bars in the summer of 1945 knew their cells extremely well. They were former prison officials, now held captive in the same institutions they had ruled during the Third Reich.

Part IV Aftermath

10   The Nazi Prison in Perspective

Hitler's prisons ceased to exist in the spring of 1945. After Hitler's suicide and the German capitulation, the Nazi legal system was no more and its penal institutions had either been abandoned, destroyed or liberated. But Hitler's prisons left a legacy for many years to come, as will be seen in this chapter, which explores different aspects of the prison system and the legal apparatus after the war, looking at both East and West Germany. The Nazi prison is then placed in an international context. A brief comparison with other countries provides new insights, for studying Hitler's prisons in complete isolation inevitably runs the risk of portraying them as more unusual than they might have been. After all, the prison itself was not a German invention. And Nazi Germany was not the only country at the time which saw a rapid rise in political prisoners – in some ways, this trend was rather typical of authoritarian regimes in interwar Europe as a whole.[1] So how different were Hitler's prisons from penal institutions elsewhere at the time? Before this question is addressed, the aftermath of Nazi legal terror in postwar Germany is assessed, starting with the German judges themselves.

Bloody Hands, Clean Conscience: Nazi Jurists and Postwar Justice

Many German jurists emerged from the ruins of the Third Reich with blood on their hands. Political, racial and social outsiders had been imprisoned, exploited, abused and killed by legal officials. After the German capitulation, the Allies were determined that these crimes should not go unpunished and resolved to bring some senior officials to justice. At Nuremberg, they delivered a crushing indictment of the German legal system under the Nazis.

The trial of representatives of the German legal system – later fictionalised in the Hollywood drama *Judgment at Nuremberg* – was one of the 12 'successor' trials of the original Nuremberg trial of major war criminals. It opened in front of US judges in March 1947 (Justice Case). Several of the most senior German jurists could no longer be charged. Franz Gürtner and Roland Freisler had died in January 1941 and February 1945, respectively. Gürtner's old adversary, Hans Frank, had been sentenced to death and executed in 1946 for his murderous reign as governor of parts of Nazi-occupied Poland. And some other legal officials had committed suicide. During the final days of the Third Reich, probably several thousand Germans killed themselves, Nazi leaders as well as lower party, SS, army and state officials. One of them was the president of the Supreme Court, Erwin Bumke, who killed himself on 20 April 1945, Hitler's birthday. He was not the only top legal official to escape punishment in this manner. The last Reich Minister of Justice, Otto-Georg Thierack had been arrested after the war, but committed suicide in 1946 in a British prisoner camp near Paderborn.

Accused at Nuremberg were 16 defendants, who represented a cross-section of German jurists. Most were former civil servants from the Reich Ministry of Justice, led by the three surviving State Secretaries Franz Schlegelberger, Curt Rothenberger and Herbert Klemm. Another ministerial official in the dock was Karl Engert, the last head of the German prison service. The remaining defendants were officials from the People's Court and special courts, as well as one former general state prosecutor. The Nazi jurists on trial were accused of war crimes and crimes against humanity, among other charges. The daily proceedings went into considerable detail. For months, the judges patiently heard the defendants and their lawyers, examined 2,093 exhibits, questioned 138 witnesses and read hundreds of statutory declarations. The judges gained a deep insight into many aspects of the legal system in the Third Reich. They studied the racial legislation against 'community aliens', such as the Nuremberg Laws and the Criminal Law Decree for Poles and Jews, and also explored how these laws had been applied by the courts. The judges also considered aspects of Nazi prison policy. Thus, the court heard about the fate of *NN* prisoners; the malnourishment, abuse and murder of inmates inside penal institutions; the transfer of prisoners to the police after the end of their sentence; the 'annihilation through labour of asocial prisoners'; and the murder of inmates in the last stage of the war.

In December 1947, the Nuremberg court finally passed judgment. In the immediate postwar years, German critics liked to caricature Allied trials as corrupt 'victor justice', in a blatant attempt to discredit the findings of the courts. Nothing could be further from the truth. The proceedings were conducted meticulously and the judgment was balanced and differentiated. To start with, the court did not condemn all German judges, but acknowledged that a number of them had in fact 'administered justice with a measure of impartiality and moderation'. Indeed, if anything, the judgment erred on the side of caution. For the court excluded from its considerations much of the Nazi legislation primarily directed at German nationals, such as 'habitual criminals', 'wartime plunderers' and those found guilty of 'undermining the war effort'. In addition, the Nuremberg judges found four of the defendants not guilty because of insufficient evidence (three members of the People's Court and one special court judge). Karl Engert also managed to get away with murder. The architect of the individual transfer of 'asocial' prisoners to the police attended on just two days of the trial and the prosecution against him was eventually dropped because of his supposed poor health. He died early in 1952.

The balanced approach by the Nuremberg judges made their general conclusions about the justice system in Nazi Germany all the more devastating. The court found that the German legal apparatus had played an important part in the extermination policy of party and state, sometimes even breaking criminal Nazi laws to participate more fully in the atrocities. As the judges memorably put it, 'the dagger of the assassin was concealed beneath the robe of the jurist'. The court considered in some detail two justifications given by the defendants for their murderous actions, excuses which were to be used at an inflationary rate by Nazi jurists over the next decades. First of all, the claim that the officials had been ignorant of the crimes committed by the police and in the concentration camps was exposed by the court as the feeble lie it was: 'This Tribunal is not so gullible as to believe these defendants so stupid that they did not know what was going on.' Secondly, the Nuremberg judges forcefully rejected the claim, made by Schlegelberger among others, that the officials had only remained in their posts to protect the administration of justice from falling into the hands of lawless forces such as the SS. The judges' opinion is worth citing at some length:

> Upon analysis this plausible claim of the defense squares neither with the truth, logic, or the circumstances. The evidence conclusively shows that in order to maintain the Ministry of Justice in the good graces of Hitler and to prevent its utter defeat by Himmler's police, Schlegelberger and the other defendants who joined in this claim of justification took over the dirty work which the leaders of the State demanded, and employed the Ministry of Justice as a means for exterminating the Jewish and Polish populations, terrorizing the inhabitants of occupied countries, and wiping out political

opposition at home. That their program of racial extermination under the guise of law failed to attain the proportions which were reached by the pogroms, deportations, and mass murders by the police is cold comfort to the survivors of the 'judicial' process and constitutes a poor excuse before this Tribunal. The prostitution of a judicial system for the accomplishment of criminal ends involves an element of evil to the State which is not found in frank atrocities which do not sully judicial robes.

Schlegelberger, Klemm and two special court judges were given life sentences. The rest received prison sentences ranging between five and ten years, with Rothenberger sentenced to seven years. The leading Nazi jurists had been convicted as criminals.[2]

The Nuremberg judges must have thought that their judgment would spark off many more judicial investigations of the Nazi legal system. But any such hopes were quickly disappointed. Nuremberg proved to be not so much the starting point as the high point of all the postwar attempts to bring Nazi jurists to justice. This tale of the deeply flawed de-Nazification of the German legal system will be told here briefly, focusing on western Germany.

In the occupied German territory, the Allies had initially ordered the temporary closure of German courts. The Allies set up military courts, like the one in Nuremberg, all over the Western zones to bring Nazi criminals to justice. In total, US, British and French military courts tried well over 8,000 Germans during the following years, both inside Germany and abroad. But German courts were soon involved, too, after they were gradually reopened from late summer and autumn 1945 onwards, with the Allies keen to offload some of the administrative burden of enforcing justice. The German courts were allowed to try most civil and criminal cases, including Nazi crimes against German nationals. (Crimes against citizens from the Allied nations were dealt with by the Allied military courts until 1950.) But the German judiciary showed no great desire to tackle the Nazi past. True, the number of cases briefly increased from 1948. But the total number of Nazi criminals prosecuted by German courts remained rather low. Even in the early years after the war (1945–50), the courts in the territory that became West Germany convicted only 5,228 defendants of Nazi crimes, almost all of them sentenced to temporary imprisonment. But this number was high compared to the following years (1951–55), when it dropped to a paltry 638. And over the next 25 years (1956–81), only about 24 individuals were convicted on average each year. A vast number of criminal acts went unpunished.[3] To understand this fully, the development of the German legal system after the war needs to be discussed in more detail.

The de-Nazification of German jurists in the west was an abject failure. At first, the Allies had pursued a hard line and in the summer of 1945, around 90 per cent of all German legal officials were removed. In some areas, there were hardly any officials left. For example, in the Bamberg district, only seven judges and prosecutors returned to their office in August 1945 – the other 295 had been removed as former Nazi party members. The Allies quickly concluded that such a radical policy would make the rebuilding of the legal system difficult, to say the least, and decided that former Nazis could, after all, be re-employed. The fate of the former officials soon rested in the hands of de-Nazification tribunals, which were set up in the Western zones in 1946. The German jurists did their best to protest their innocence, giving all manner of excuses for having joined the Nazi party. In addition, like most other Germans, they solicited reports from untainted colleagues or respected members of society, testifying to their supposed 'inner rejection' of Nazism – soon known among the population as 'Persil certificates' because they thoroughly cleansed the suspects from any guilt. The tribunals had a range of options for classifying an individual, ranging from 'exonerated' to 'main offender'. At first, classifications had been quite stringent. But soon the tribunals operated leniently and routinely let almost all suspects off the hook. The vast majority of German judges received a more or less clean political bill of health, and quickly re-joined the bench. There was a striking continuity with the Third Reich, with about 80 per cent of former officials re-employed. Familiar faces included many former ministerial officials who had moved from their old desks in Berlin to new ones in the Justice Ministry in Bonn. Even former members of the most lethal Nazi court – the People's Court – continued their legal career in postwar Germany. In total, some 72 former judges and prosecutors from the People's Court were re-employed by the West German state, some of them serving until the 1970s.[4]

In view of this continuity, it is hardly surprising that not a single Nazi judge or prosecutor was convicted by his colleagues in West Germany (the exception was the case of a few members of the civilian drumhead courts martial, who got away with very lenient sentences). The legal system proved utterly incapable of facing its own Nazi past. Thus, it decided that only the intentional perversion of legal codes would count as a criminal offence. All that the former Nazi judges had to do to be acquitted, therefore, was to argue that they had believed themselves to be acting in accordance with the law at the time. In allowing for this unique defence plea, the West German judiciary virtually gave all Nazi judges and prosecutors an amnesty. Of course, it was rarely necessary for this legal construction to be applied in practice. By 1968, only four criminal proceedings had been initiated against regular members of the judiciary for illegal death sentences in the Third Reich. This passivity brought the West German judiciary into sharp conflict with the conclusions of the 1947 Nuremberg Justice Case. But that did not matter to most German judges, as the 'inconvenient' Nuremberg judgment was quickly brushed under the carpet and forgotten. The text of the judgment itself was barely accessible in Germany for decades. In 1948, it was published in a very small print run and made available only to selected senior officials. The version open to other jurists and the general public, by contrast, contained just the general part. The crucial sections about the crimes committed by the individual defendants were missing – supposedly due to 'paper shortage'. Only in 1996, almost 50 years after the original trial, was the whole judgment finally published in Germany.[5]

Amnesia, whitewash and rehabilitation were the main trends in the postwar judiciary. They were also typical of West Germany in the 1950s as a whole. As soon as the federal parliament of the new West German state was opened, there was cross-party support for a revision of earlier de-Nazification attempts. This policy of official exculpation, based on a broad social and political consensus, should be understood not least as an assertion of German independence and nationalism – a symbolic break with the occupation period. The policy-makers quickly erased the guilt of many Nazi criminals with generous amnesties. At the same time as these offenders were let off, former officials were eased back into respectable society. Most Nazi judges, as we have seen, were already back at work by 1949. Similar leniency was applied to almost all other former civil servants, including many major perpetrators in the police force. This exoneration of virtually all Germans went hand in hand with the portrayal of Nazi crimes as committed by a few madmen around Hitler, who had misled and betrayed the rest of the population. In 1950s West Germany, the former members of the Nazi 'national community' saw themselves as victims – both of a criminal Nazi regime and of Soviet atrocities in the east. In this atmosphere, many Nazi war criminals who had been sentenced by the Allies were quickly released, often after serving only a fraction of their sentences. Those freed in the early 1950s included all three most senior surviving legal officials, Schlegelberger, Rothenberger and Klemm, who could now draw their generous pensions.[6]

Signs of a more critical approach by sections of the German judiciary towards its own past began to emerge from the late 1950s onwards. In part, this was brought on by East German propaganda, which aimed to undermine West Germany by portraying it as the reincarnation of the Third Reich. The judiciary was one of the focal points in this propaganda battle during the Cold War. At a press conference in 1957, the East German authorities presented a document with the names of 118 Nazi jurists now allegedly working in the West German judiciary. Two years later, this list had grown to 800 'blood judges'. East Germany (GDR) kept up the pressure in the following years, singling out prominent West German jurists and publishing damaging documents in so-called 'Brown Books'. This barrage of accusations, which had an echo abroad, triggered widespread and heated debates in West Germany. At the same time, several high profile trials, such as the 1958 task force trial in Ulm and the trial of Adolf Eichmann in Jerusalem in 1961, made plain that many Nazi criminals were still unpunished. Some of these trials were discussed in unprecedented detail and depth in the German media, part of a growing engagement with Nazi crimes in the West German public sphere as a whole. Also, a younger generation of jurists gradually emerged, some of whom began to ask critical questions. A few of these officials eventually came to work for the new coordinating agency for the investigation of Nazi crimes, the Central Agency for the Solution of National-Socialist Crimes, which had been set up in late 1958. But despite all this, by the 1960s and 1970s, successful prosecution of Nazi jurists appeared even more unlikely. The advancing age of the suspects would have made it easy for them to avoid trial on medical grounds. And, in any case, most crimes had long come under the statute of limitations.[7]

The failure of the de-Nazification of the German judiciary has been publicly acknowledged by the German state in recent years. In 1985, the West German parliament declared the People's Court an 'instrument of terror' of the Nazi state. This was followed by an exhibition put together by the Federal Ministry of Justice, which detailed the contribution of the German judiciary to the Nazi regime. The exhibition catalogue concluded that the legal system had to admit its failure to deal with its past. In 1998, the German parliament declared a vast number of sentences handed down in the Third Reich null and void, including sentences against 'deserters', 'national pests' and those found guilty of 'undermining the war effort'. Additionally, in 2002 sentences by hereditary health courts and military courts were repealed as well. Despite the important symbolic value of these gestures, they ultimately proved to be a rather painless way of dealing with the past. After all, they no longer threatened serious conflict with the judiciary, as all the guilty Nazi officials had long since died or retired.[8]

Back to Work: Prison Officials in West Germany

The virtual amnesty of former Nazi legal officials was extended to the great majority of Nazi prison officials in the western parts of Germany. But, in contrast to the judges, not all of them proved untouchable by the law. To be sure, only a small minority were ever taken to court. The German legal system made no real attempts to investigate what conditions in penal institutions had been like. Instead, proceedings were generally initiated only after complaints by former inmates. In some of these cases, the abuse had been so blatant that it simply could not be ignored by the courts. Thus, in the early years after the war, several former local prison officials, including a few governors, were tried and convicted. A number of them were very experienced officials who had been working in the prison service for decades, even before the Nazi takeover.

Several other trials took place in front of Allied military courts, which sometimes handed out severe punishment. In 1947, a British military court tried some prison officials from the Esterwegen sub-camp (part of Emsland prison camp), who were blamed for the high number of deaths among the NN prisoners there. The judges handed out tough punishment, including two death sentences and two sentences of 15 years' hard labour. But the Allied courts were not uniformly harsh. In 1948, for example, a different British military court sentenced the former governor of the Anrath women's prison, who had forced inmates to work in the atrocious conditions of the Rheika silk factory, to only 18 months' imprisonment, eliciting protests by some of the former prisoners.[9]

Most cases against former prison officials were dealt with by German civilian courts. It was the Emsland camp that came under the closest judicial scrutiny. Between August 1948 and June 1950 alone, the Oldenburg district court passed 41 sentences in 15 separate trials against former officials from this camp. More often than not, it seems, the judges showed considerable leniency. A conviction for causing bodily harm typically carried no more than one or two months in prison. Some sentences were scandalously mild. The brutal former commander of the Emsland camp, Werner Schäfer, was sentenced by the Osnabrück district court in 1951 to just four years in prison. On appeal, his sentence was further reduced in 1953 to two years and six months. In other cases, convictions were completely overturned on appeal. The former head of the Börgermoor sub-camp had originally been sentenced in 1950 to 15 years in a penitentiary for abusing and killing inmates. But this sentence was quashed in 1959 and the governor was found innocent.[10]

The reasons behind the often lenient treatment of former prison officials become clear when looking at the conduct of the trials. To start with, many judges were clearly suspicious of the testimony of former inmates. Because of their 'criminal past', courts often had little time for these convicts. Above all, judges were very reluctant to believe offenders who had served time for common criminal offences. As one court put it, their previous convictions 'reveal character defects', which meant that their testimony had to be treated with 'caution'. This rule was even applied to individuals who had committed no offences for more than a decade, as the following extract from a judgment by the Oldenburg district court in 1949 reveals:

> Because of his many convictions – he has 15 convictions for begging and vagrancy – the witness Fu. is not a witness of flawless character. Despite the fact that he was sentenced for the last time in 1935 and seems to have turned his back on his earlier work-shy life, the testimony of this witness has to be judged with particular caution because of his previous convictions.

By contrast, many judges showed great sympathy for the accused prison officials. In a way, these officials were like colleagues to them. After all, they had served together in the legal system in the Third Reich. And as the judges maintained that this system had acted, on the whole, honourably, some claimed that imprisonment could not have been all that bad either. In this vein, the Regensburg district court, in a trial of five warders of the Straubing penitentiary in 1949, referred to the 'well-known fact' that conditions of imprisonment in penal institutions in Nazi Germany had been 'strict, but lawful and ordered...'. Judges often tried hard to find mitigating circumstances for the accused prison officials. The fact that they had no previous convictions counted in their favour – evidence of what the courts saw as good character – as did the supportive statements by friends and former colleagues who testified on their behalf. One judge even tried to explain away the brutal violence of one defendant as a sign of 'youthful exuberance'. Finally, courts often pointed out that prison officials had faced a very tough task, confronted as they were with 'difficult-to-educate criminals'. Not a few judges expressed their belief in the need for a 'strict' prison service and openly voiced support for the use of physical force against disobedient prisoners.[11]

Probably the darkest chapter among the attempts in West Germany to bring former prison officials to justice was the 1951–52 trial of the men responsible for organising the transfer of 'asocial' prisoners to the police for 'annihilation through labour'. This trial offered the best opportunity for a German court to punish the most senior former prison officials for their part in mass murder. In the dock were all except one of the surviving officials involved in running the transfer: Rudolf Marx, Albert Hupperschwiller, Friedrich Wilhelm Meyer and Otto Gündner from the Reich Ministry of Justice, as well as Kurt Giese from the Chancellery of the Führer. Robert Hecker had died in January 1951.[12] In preparation for the trial, dedicated state prosecuton officials interviewed scores of eyewitnesses, including local prison officials and prisoners who had survived deportation to the concentration camps. They also put together a dossier of revealing documents, even though key ministerial files were not available to them, having been burned on Thierack's orders by Otto Gündner in February 1945 – proof that the officials themselves had been only too aware that their activities were criminal.[13]

Immediately after the war, some of the ex-ministerial officials had still been unsure how best to justify the 'annihilation through labour' programme. This is obvious in the early interrogations by the Allies in preparation for the 1947 Nuremberg Justice Case. The most brazen tactic was employed by Rudolf Marx, the long-time head of the national prison administration (from 1942: section V), who had continued his career after the war as head of the Schleswig-Holstein prison service. Initially, Marx decided simply to deny any knowledge of the programme – rather audacious, given that he had overseen the general transfer of more than 17,300 'asocial' prisoners to the police. At the beginning of his interrogation in Nuremberg on 25 March 1947, Marx feigned ignorance when asked about the role of his department in the transfer: 'We have not handed over any people ... I am not aware that Jews, Poles and Gypsies were handed over.' But this tactic was doomed to failure, as Marx came to realise only a few minutes later. For his direct subordinate Robert Hecker had already disclosed aspects of the transfer. Faced with this incriminating testimony, Marx now demanded that he be brought face to face with Hecker. The interrogator was happy to oblige, and brought in Hecker.

> *Interrogator:* Herr Hecker, what tales have you told me?
> *Hecker:* About what?
> *Interrogator:* About the transfer of Jews, Poles and Gypsies by section V.
> *Hecker:* Why?
> *Interrogator:* Herr Marx knows nothing about the matter.
> *Marx:* This was done by section XV ... After all, we did not make any transfers.
> *Hecker:* But we did make them.
> *Marx:* When did that start?
> *Hecker:* 1942.
> *Marx:* Did you work on this?
> *Hecker:* Yes. You know, the lists were regularly presented and processed.
> *Marx:* I have never seen a list.
> *Hecker:* These lists were presented every month.
> *Marx:* Who signed them?
> *Hecker:* You as head of department, I presume.
> *Marx:* I am horrified [...]
> *Hecker:* It was like this: each institution regularly presented the lists of the Jews, Poles and Gypsies to be transferred. They went through your hands.
> *Marx:* Then I have to say that I must have a serious loss of memory.

Marx became increasingly agitated as he was confronted with still more details, which made his own supposed loss of memory – an 'affliction' which affected so many German professionals after the war – seem ever more absurd. Finally, Marx admitted: 'Now I remember.' But he still refused to shed any light on his own involvement, protesting, two days later: 'I couldn't even hurt a fly.'[14]

By the time Rudolf Marx, together with his former colleagues, stood trial in Wiesbaden, he had regained his composure. He now admitted to participation in the deportations. In the face of the evidence presented by the prosecution, he really had no other choice. But Marx claimed that he had not known that the inmates would be killed in the concentration camps. He had believed, he testified, that the prisoners would merely be used for hard labour. This story, also put forward by his co-defendants, was clearly untrue. The top prison officials had been aware from the start that the motive for the transfer was not economic. Thierack had talked openly about the murderous aims of the transfer, and for their part, the senior prison officials had decided that even sick prisoners should be included on the transports to the concentration camps. In addition, details about the mass deaths of prisoners in the camps had soon reached the Reich Ministry of Justice. Before his death, Robert Hecker admitted as much, conceding that he had been aware that the transferred prisoners were killed in the camps. Another former official from the Reich Ministry of Justice also testified that he had known about the deaths of many 'asocial' prisoners transported to Mauthausen. But at trial, the defendants stubbornly maintained that they had been ignorant. Some were openly defiant. Hupperschwiller, for example, used his time in the dock to wax lyrical about the 'positive' aspects of Nazi justice, which had supposedly made the streets safe for women at night.[15] He was not alone in his views.

The Wiesbaden judges gladly swallowed the lies of the men accused of participation in mass murder. To start with, the judges themselves expressed some sympathy for Nazi policy, stating that during the war the German state had faced a 'fight for survival' which justified the internment of 'criminal elements' in camps. Therefore, the court found, the deportation of prisoners from penal institutions to concentration camps from 1942 onwards was lawful. In the judges' eyes, this applied not only to German criminal offenders, but to Poles, Russians, Ukrainians as well as Sinti and Roma. Even for Jewish prisoners, the judges concluded, transfer to the camps 'was objectively not illegal'. The court also accepted that the accused had not known what fate awaited the prisoners in the concentration camps. To reach this conclusion, they had to keep their eyes and ears firmly shut and ignore all evidence to the contrary. Even the fact that Albert Hupperschwiller actually admitted that he had read a letter, by Martin Bormann to Thierack about the extermination of prisoners was not enough. The judges ruled that the 'observation of the word "extermination" alone . . . does not represent a sufficient basis for determining the defendant's knowledge or presentiment about the killings'. In the end, all the accused left the court as free men.[16] Not surprisingly, no other prison or police officials were convicted for their part in the deportations.

Continuity and Change

The bias of the West German judiciary contributed to considerable continuity among the prison personnel. Broadly speaking, the cycle of de-Nazification and re-employment followed the same pattern as described above for judges. At first, until the end of 1945, the Allies dismissed most former party members among the prison officials. In exceptional cases, their places were taken by reform-minded officials who had been removed by the Nazis, such as the Untermaßfeld governor Albert Krebs who served as head of the prison service in Hesse from 1945. The number of dismissed prison officials was high in 1945, albeit lower than among judges. In Baden-Württemberg, the Americans removed some 25 per cent of all prison officials, while in Bavaria, about half of all the officials in the larger penal institutions were discharged, including 17 of the 20 governors. But there was soon pressure on the authorities to fill these posts again. Following the increase in the prisoner population from 1946 – a result of the postwar crime wave, consisting largely of non-violent offences such as black-marketeering and vagrancy – penal institutions all over Germany reported serious staff shortages. Many of the vacant places were filled with former Wehrmacht soldiers and others who had no previous experience in the prison service. In some German states, these new recruits initially made up the majority of all prison staff. But many prison officials, who had only just been dismissed for their Nazi connections, also quickly returned, facilitated by the generous policy of the de-Nazification tribunals, which spared almost all former prison officials. Such a benign approach was encouraged by some of the top German legal officials. In January 1948, for example, the Justice Minister of Rhineland-Palatinate informed a tribunal that the lack of prison officials was causing enormous problems: 'To remedy this shortage, it would be desirable if quite a lot of dismissed warders could be returned quite soon to the service.' The door was soon wide open for the sacked officials. As early as mid-1948, 27 per cent of the former Bavarian prison officials were back in their posts. In Baden-Württemberg, the equivalent figure was a staggering 96 per cent.[17]

Many West German prison officials were familiar figures from the Nazi period. They included a few former ministerial officials from Berlin such as Johannes Eichler (desk officer between 1935–45), who by 1947 was running the prison service in the Celle district. The continuities were particularly striking on the local level, among the governors, doctors, chaplains, teachers and warders. It will suffice to name just a few of the officials we have encountered previously. Theodor Knops, who had been involved as governor in the 1945 massacre of prisoners at Sonnenburg, served for years as governor of the Aachen penal institution. August Faber, the Werl governor who had done his utmost to exploit prisoners as forced labourers for the war industry, still held his position in Werl in the 1950s. And the Brandenburg-Görden prison doctor Werner Eberhard, who had demanded in 1942 that 'habitual criminals' should be 'extirpated', now worked in the Lingen prison.[18]

The ease with which local prison officials continued their careers after 1945 can best be illustrated with a brief case study of an individual institution, the women's prison in Aichach. Following the liberation of the institution by US forces, almost all the senior Aichach officials were quickly removed: governor Hermann von Reitzenstein, prison doctor Ludwig Schemmel, prison teacher Anni Dimpfl and the Protestant prison chaplain Ernst Stark (who had worked in the Niederschönenfeld youth prison from 1941) were all dismissed because of their Nazi party membership. These four officials knew each other very well, as they had served in Aichach for many years. The governor had joined the penal institution in 1933 and the others had already worked there in the Weimar Republic. The most senior Aichach official to hang on to his post in 1945–46 was the Catholic prison chaplain Martin Kraus, another experienced official (he had joined the institution in 1929). Chaplain Kraus had certainly not been an opponent of the Nazi regime. He had joined various Nazi organisations and, as late as 1944, had been praised by governor Reitzenstein for his support for the 'measures taken by state and party during the war'. But, crucially, Kraus had never joined the Nazi party and was therefore allowed to remain in his post after the German defeat.[19]

Before long, the other former senior local officials were also working again in Aichach. The only exception was the 64-year-old former governor Reitzenstein, who was granted early retirement. Chaplain Kraus, as a member of the board of Aichach prison officials, played a central role in the rehabilitation of his ex-colleagues, handing out one 'Persil certificate' after another. The first went to prison teacher Anni Dimpfl. In the Third Reich, Dimpfl had made sure that inmates in prison school were indoctrinated with Nazi propaganda. In addition, she had written negative reports about inmates, including political prisoners, which had probably contributed to their being handed over to the police. But this did not stand in the way of her postwar career. Chaplain Kraus, with whom she had a close relationship, supported her case and she was back in Aichach in mid-1947 (she finally retired in 1959).[20]

Next up was the former Aichach prison doctor, Ludwig Schemmel. In several previous chapters, examples of Schemmel's conduct in the Third Reich have been outlined. He neglected and abused prisoners, resulting in a string of complaints by inmates and even some local warders. Governor Reitzenstein himself, not known for treating prisoners with kid gloves, noted in 1943 that Dr Schemmel was 'easily agitated' and 'at times too rough'. Equally damaging, one would have thought, was Schemmel's involvement in the forcible sterilisation of Aichach inmates. But he was another recipient of absolution by prison chaplain Kraus, who declared that Schemmel had acted impeccably and had never reported any inmate for sterilisation on his own initiative. In October 1947, Schemmel was re-employed in the prison service, and was soon back in Aichach. Promoted in 1953, he also became a pillar of the local community in Aichach, serving for many years as a city councillor. Dr Schemmel apparently found it hard to shake off his old habits, though, for there were fresh allegations of abuse of prisoners in the 1950s. But he remained in the Aichach institution until his retirement in 1962.[21]

The last to be brought back into the fold was chaplain Ernst Stark, who had been the most committed Nazi member among the senior Aichach officials.

He had joined the party in 1933 and served as its local representative in the institution, trying to make sure that the other officials toed the party line. Stark, known for his strict treatment of prisoners, had even used his religious services for Nazi propaganda. But his Nazi past did not have serious repercussions after 1945. In 1948, a de-Nazification tribunal classified him as a 'fellow-traveller' and his former Aichach colleagues, above all chaplain Kraus, also put in a good word for him. Only one year later, Stark was back in the prison service, first in Straubing and from 1953, after a promotion, back in Aichach until his retirement in 1960.[22] In short, by the mid-1950s, the Aichach penal institution was again firmly in the hands of the old guard – just like many other prisons and penitentiaries in West Germany.

In view of these continuities among jurists and prison officials in West Germany, it is not surprising that there was no complete overhaul of penal and prison policy. In legislation, there were crucial changes after the Second World War. The Allies repealed a number of laws introduced in Nazi Germany, such as the Law against Malicious Attacks and the Nuremberg racial laws, and the death penalty was abolished in the Basic Law of 1949. But many legal changes introduced in the Third Reich were retained in West Germany, often unchanged or only cosmetically altered. This practice was defended by German jurists, who argued that these had not been Nazi perversions of the law but acceptable and effective weapons in the fight against crime. With this justification, the Nazi versions of the law against homosexuality and abortion were kept on the books until 1969 and 1976 respectively. The Habitual Criminals Law of 1933 was also kept in its original form after the war (only the provision for the castration of sex offenders was dropped). To be sure, security confinement was applied much less frequently than in the Third Reich. But German judges still continued to send to potentially lifelong imprisonment individual offenders who were anything but serious threats to society. This only really changed after 1970, when much more restrictive regulations were finally introduced. As a result, the number of individuals sent to security confinement by the courts has dropped sharply, from 199 (1960) to just 27 (1993).[23]

As regards the postwar prison regulations, it must be emphasised from the outset that imprisonment in West Germany was very far removed from the violent reality of the Nazi period. There were no more sterilisations and prisoners were no longer worked to death, to make just two obvious points. But at the same time, the postwar prison regulations themselves did not mark a clear break with the Third Reich, retaining the general emphasis on retribution and strict discipline. Indeed, the regulations in many German states were based for years on the national prison guidelines of 1940, cleansed of a few passages. In an effort to coordinate the practice of imprisonment in Germany, the different states agreed on new federal prison regulations, which came into force in 1962. But even these regulations did little to change the official face of the German prison service. The rules were still largely similar to the Nazi regulations of 1934 and 1940, despite the fact that disciplinary punishments such as food cuts – still allowed under the new regulations – were now in fact unconstitutional. The aim of imprisonment was defined in the 1962 regulations as the protection of society and the exacting of retribution. Rehabilitation was mentioned last, almost as an afterthought. All this changed only from the late 1960s onwards, a development reflected most clearly in the Prison Law, which came into force in 1977 and declared resocialisation to be the aim of imprisonment. It had taken many years after the war for the rehabilitative spirit of the Weimar prison guidelines to resurface in West Germany.[24]

The treatment of prisoners in the immediate postwar years is also instructive in this context. To start with, a number of inmates continued to be held inside penal institutions long after the fall of the Third Reich. While those sentenced as political prisoners or on purely racial grounds were released and their sentences quickly quashed, some prisoners had to stay behind bars. By no means all of them were particularly dangerous. Still, the authorities were unwilling to set them free. In Hamburg, the judicial authorities simply cut the length of sentences against criminal offenders by half, at least acknowledging the excessive punishment in the Nazi period. But this still meant that many sentences remained disproportionate to the original offence. This was true, not least, for many prisoners in security confinement. Having escaped the 'annihilation through labour' programme because they were used as forced labourers in penal institutions, a number were initially kept inside after the end of the war. The fact that many had already been imprisoned for ten years or more for petty property offences did not move the authorities. In a sample of 60 inmates who had been held in security confinement in the Rendsburg institution in 1945, 35 were still locked up in the same penal institution in early 1947.[25]

In a number of cases, the authorities even rearrested prisoners originally released by the Allies, to ensure that they served the rest of their sentences. One such case involved the 68-year-old road maintenance worker S., who had originally been sentenced to death by the Kiel special court in January 1945 for the theft of two bottles of wine and two pieces of bacon after an air raid. In the chaos of the last months of the war, his sentence was not implemented and he was eventually released by Russian forces from the Dreibergen-Bützow penitentiary. S., not unreasonably, thought that 'the matter was now closed', as he later put it. But he had not reckoned on the zealousness of the new head of the Kiel state prosecution service, himself a former special court official, who reopened the proceedings. In the end, S.'s sentence was converted to three years in a penitentiary which he had to serve from February 1946 onwards. (He was released in October 1946 because of ill health and died a few months later.)[26] In other cases, former inmates were quickly recommitted after further offences. These included some former political prisoners, above all Communists, who were soon sentenced in West Germany during the Cold War. In such trials, it was not unheard of for judges to point to previous sentences in the Third Reich as a sign of the defendant's 'incorrigibility'. One judge told a Communist activist: 'You have learned nothing from your imprisonment in the years 1933 to 1945.'[27]

While virtually all former Nazi jurists continued their careers or drew their pensions as if nothing had happened, many victims of Nazi penal policy never even received compensation. Until the 1980s, individuals brutally persecuted for non-normative social behaviour, such as homosexuals, were not eligible for compensation from the federal German authorities. Since then, some social outsiders, whose punishment was judged excessive or unjust in retrospect, have received a certain amount of financial help. The same is true for prisoners who were forcibly sterilised. Finally, the newly created foundation 'Memory, Responsibility and Future' is currently distributing funds provided by the German government and German businesses to former forced labourers, including scores of ex-prisoners. Unfortunately, this has come too late for many victims of Nazi terror. Only as more and more of them have died have benefits been made available to a greater number of victims. And the rules still do not apply to all victims of Nazi legal terror. Supposedly 'incorrigible' criminals, for example, who spent many years under extremely poor conditions in security confinement for utterly trivial offences before being taken to concentration camps, are still not eligible for any compensation today.[28]

The only individuals recognised as Nazi victims from a relatively early stage were Germans and foreigners persecuted on political, racial or religious grounds. But even here, there were, at least at first, numerous exceptions. For example, ex-prisoners who had not been politically organised were often excluded from benefits, as were those Communists who did not quickly recant their beliefs after 1945.[29] Of course, these former Communist prisoners were at the same time hailed as martyrs and heroes in East Germany, which took a rather different route in dealing with the Nazi past.

East Germany and the Perversion of the Law

In the Soviet zone, efforts to remove former Nazi officials from positions of power were more sweeping and sustained than in the west. This was true, in particular, of the legal sphere, which was systematically purged in the first years after the war. A number of Nazi measures were removed from the Criminal Code and virtually all former legal officials were dismissed. In contrast to the west, they were generally not allowed to re-join. Of around 1,000 East German judges in 1950, only one had been a member of the NSDAP. To fill the gaping holes left by the mass dismissal of Nazi officials, the authorities in the east trained so-called people's judges in crash courses initially lasting six months. All this amounted to a decisive break with the national-conservative professionals, who had traditionally dominated the German judiciary and were already on their way back into office in the Western Zones.[30] Naturally, the purge of the legal system in the Soviet zone also included the prison service. At the end of 1945, all the old prison governors had been removed, and by late 1948 a total of 1,694 former prison officials had been dismissed. Virtually no Nazi officials remained. Only 3 per cent of all 1,732 prison officials in September 1947 had been members of the NSDAP or its organisations.[31]

Numerous prison officials in the Eastern Zone not only lost their jobs, but also their freedom and sometimes their lives. Some were killed by Soviet troops immediately after the occupation of their penal institution. Others were transported to the USSR, following Soviet orders in April 1945 that prison personnel – together with SS and concentration camp officials – were to be taken to prisoner of war camps run by the NKVD (People's Commissariat of Internal Affairs), where they were held under appalling conditions. Those lucky enough to survive only returned after several years.[32] A number of former prison officials were tried by Soviet military tribunals, and later also increasingly by German courts in the east. By late 1948, the German authorities reported, some 126 prison officials had been convicted in the Soviet zone. These figures may have included 16 officials from the Halle penitentiary, convicted in November 1945 after a summary trial by a Soviet military tribunal. Ten of the Halle officials, including the governor, his deputy and several warders, were sentenced to death and executed. The remaining six officials, including the prison doctor and the Protestant chaplain, received lengthy sentences of forced labour.[33]

Finally, some former prison officials ended up in so-called special camps in the Soviet zone. As the Allies conquered Germany in 1945, internment camps were set up, to isolate individuals regarded as potential threats. For this purpose, the Allies took over various German prisons and former concentration camps, such as Dachau (in the US zone) and Buchenwald (in the Soviet zone). In the west, the internment camps were soon also used to filter out individuals guilty of war crimes. Other inmates were gradually released. The approach was very different in the Soviet zone. Here, far fewer of the inmates in the special camps were leading perpetrators of Nazi terror. Instead, most were ordinary party members or local functionaries. They were largely ignored by the Soviet authorities, who made no efforts to assess their individual guilt. Indifference – coupled with bureaucratic chaos, ineptitude and postwar shortages – resulted in truly dreadful conditions: great hunger, deprivation, cold, dirt and illness prevailed, and at least one in every three German inmates died in the special camps in the Soviet zone. Only in the summer of 1948 did the

Soviet authorities decide to release some 28,000 inmates, closing down most, but not all of the special camps.[34]

In the first years after the war, the Soviet authorities were supported in the administration of their zone by German officials. Regarding law and order, the Soviets concentrated on removing Nazi officials and on fighting real or imagined opponents of the new order. Beyond this, there was some leeway for the newly appointed central and regional German officials. Crucially, German Communist functionaries initially played no great part here, focusing instead on gaining control over the police. This left Social Democrats and liberals to take the initiative in rebuilding the legal apparatus. In June 1945, the Soviet military administration had created the central German Judicial Administration (DJV), staffed with German officials. Designed as an agency of occupation policy, the DJV also developed its own policies. Until 1948, its president was Eugen Schiffer, a prominent liberal politician who had briefly served in the Weimar period as Reich Minister of Justice. Schiffer and most of his officials aimed at a fundamental reform of the German legal system, to be based on the rule of law. To achieve this goal, some officials were determined to pick up reform initiatives from the Weimar years that had been buried under the ruins of the Third Reich.[35]

This was also the position adopted by Dr Werner Gentz, head of the prisoner service in the DJV. It is not surprising that Gentz was looking back to the Weimar years. After all, he had served in the Prussian prison administration until his removal by the Nazis in 1933. After the war, Gentz advocated a complete break with the Nazi prison system, and a revival of the ideals of the Weimar reform movement. In October 1945, the DJV issued general guidelines for the prison service in the Soviet zone, written by Gentz, which were deeply indebted to the vision and terminology of prison reform formulated decades earlier. The aim of imprisonment, according to Gentz, was rehabilitation. The prison had to be run not by military command but by humane treatment, group pedagogy and a progressive stages system that would allow prisoners increasing freedom and responsibility. Gentz could initially count on the support from the new Socialist Unity Party (SED), and even the Soviet authorities were not opposed to his plans in principle. Thanks to his enthusiasm and activism, some polices aimed at the social reintegration of prisoners were actually introduced.[36]

But all this made precious little difference to life inside prisons in the East, where conditions in the immediate postwar period were even worse than in the West. Penal institutions were overcrowded, on account of the postwar crime wave and the lack of adequate buildings (some had been damaged or destroyed, others were occupied by the Soviets). In addition, there was a great shortage of clothes, bedding and other equipment, after much prison property had been looted in 1945 by Soviet troops, former inmates and the local population. Food and medical care were in very short supply, too, and were poorly distributed by the newly recruited prison officials, who often turned out to be incompetent administrators.[37] By the time these conditions had eased somewhat, the moderate reformers were being pushed aside by fervent Communists, who now took control of the legal apparatus. Gentz's vision of the prison was quickly consigned to oblivion once more.

After the Cold War began and the iron curtain descended in the late 1940s, the Soviet zone was quickly turned into a dictatorship inspired by the example of the 'friends' – as they were officially called – in the USSR. The East German state, founded in 1949, was ruled by hard-line Communists in the SED, who took over leading positions in the economy and the state. The population was to be controlled by propaganda and repression, and the judiciary was expected to punish those singled out as opponents of the regime. To fulfil this role, the legal apparatus was transformed between 1947/48 and 1952/53. It was coordinated and centralised in the hands of the SED, and there was another purge of legal officials, with positions now filled by conformists loyal to the new regime, graduates of the increasingly politicised 'people's judges' courses. Judges suspected of deviating from the party line were disciplined, transferred, dismissed or, in extreme cases, imprisoned. Already in the early 1950s, the regime was in direct control of the judiciary, more so than the Nazis had ever been.[38]

The first major test of the Soviet-inspired justice system in East Germany came in 1950. Early that year, the remaining three Soviet special camps in East Germany were dissolved. Half of the almost 29,000 inmates were to be finally released, while 10,500 individuals, already convicted by Soviet military tribunals, were handed over to the Germans for further imprisonment. Most of the remaining prisoners were tried from April 1950 onwards, accused of serious Nazi crimes. In June 1950, the East German authorities held ten show trials in Waldheim, designed both to exhibit the anti-Fascist credentials of the new regime and to demonstrate the formal legality of judicial proceedings. In reality, these trials had been fixed in advance, a front for over 3,300 cases conducted in secret. These summary trials lasted only 30 to 60 minutes each, with no defence counsel and no examination of evidence. Many of the defendants had not committed any crimes and were tried simply for having been members of Nazi organisations. But this made no difference. The judges had often been hand-picked by the SED, which directed the trials and instructed the judges to convict defendants even if there was no evidence of personal guilt. The judges complied, finding all but four defendants guilty. Punishment was extremely harsh, with over half the defendants sentenced to 15 years' imprisonment or more (most prisoners were released in 1956). The East German legal authorities had passed their test of total compliance and soon took over the handling of all political trials from the Soviets. The methods pioneered in Waldheim to stamp the will of the party on legal proceedings shaped the East German justice system for years to come. True, judges were not always exactly sure how their political masters wanted them to apply or break the law, confused by the SED's oscillation between more liberal and more repressive policies. Still, the legal apparatus functioned as a reliable tool of the political leadership.[39]

The prison system clearly had an important function in the new regime. While East Germany retained the death penalty, the courts used it not as a weapon of mass extermination, but as a symbolic deterrent.[40] The judges' weapon of choice against political suspects and others was imprisonment, and penal institutions were mostly overcrowded, except in periods immediately after the periodical amnesties. In total, the proportion of prisoners in East Germany was about twice as high as in West Germany, reaching similar levels to prewar Nazi Germany.[41] Life inside was often hard. Soon after the foundation of East Germany, the entire prison system fell into the hands of the police, the most unscrupulous enforcers of the new regime, which had controlled a number of prisons from early on. But this had not been enough for the new police force, determined to grab more. Arguing that the legal authorities were unable to prevent escapes from penal institutions – a spurious allegation supported by the Soviet authorities – the police and the new East German Ministry of the Interior advanced their claim to the prison service. The campaign quickly ended in total victory for the police. The first penal institutions were handed over by legal authorities in 1950, with the rest following in 1952. The loss of judicial authority over the prison system, the nightmare of legal officials in the Third Reich, had become a fact.[42]

Prison policy in East Germany was turned around sharply, as soon as the police had gained control. Some officials continued to pay lip-service to the immediate postwar ideals. But the reality was very different. The reform programme was attacked and measures such as inmate councils and prisoner leave were quickly abolished. The arguments for this reversal could have been lifted straight out of the articles and books of the critics of the Weimar prison, written many years earlier. Even some of the language was similar, with East German officials railing against 'sentimental humanitarianism' in the prisons. The attitude of the new guard was summed up in 1950 by the incoming governor of Brandenburg-Görden, police officer Heinz Marquardt: 'We have to learn to hate the prisoners. We want to turn this house back from a sanatorium into a penitentiary.' Prison governors such as Marquardt reintroduced a strict military tone, and local prison officials were either replaced or instructed to change their ways. The prison service in East Germany was characterised by military discipline, harsh punishment and, at times, brutal physical abuse. The Ministry of the Interior also put great emphasis on the exploitation of prison labour. Right from the start, officials were determined to deploy inmates' labour power in the interests of the state. The prison service became one of the largest providers of labour in the GDR and was fully integrated into the planned economy. A number of prisoners worked outside the prison walls, in factories or mines, and were held in prison camps.[43]

Certain aspects – the humiliation, exploitation and repression of individual inmates – were reminiscent of the prison service in the Third Reich. But one should not lose sight of the many differences with the Nazi period. Overall, the East German prison was far removed from the murderous and racist Nazi prison – just as legal repression in East Germany and the Third Reich was ultimately very different.[44] The roots of the GDR prison system extend well beyond the Third Reich. Thus, strict military discipline had already been a feature of imprisonment in the Weimar Republic. Another obvious influence was the Soviet penal system. After all, the USSR served as the organisational model for the East German regime. And while penal practice remained different in the two states (especially in the early 1950s), East German officials still copied Soviet ideas, structures and policies.[45] Most obviously, the exploitation of prison labour for the planned economy – so prominent in East Germany – had been advanced in the Soviet Union for decades.

Special Path? A Comparative View

It would be easy to claim that the entire Nazi prison system was a barbaric aberration, completely different from prison systems in other states at the time. Such a view would certainly fit into the general argument – put forward under different guises for a long time – for the peculiarity of modern German history: that it followed a special path culminating almost inevitably in the crimes of the Third Reich. Admittedly, it is impossible within the confines of this book to undertake a detailed comparative study of penal practice outside Nazi Germany. Still, a brief glance at the international context will reveal some preliminary findings about the singularity, or otherwise, of Hitler's prisons.

Punishment and the Prison in Soviet Russia

One obvious starting point for an international comparison is Stalin's Soviet Union in the 1930s and 1940s – the only regime that could, at the time, compete with the Third Reich for the title of bloodiest dictatorship. But, as has recently been observed, despite the heated political debate since the end of the Cold War over the comparative criminality of the USSR and Nazi Germany, there have been surprisingly few detailed historical comparisons of terror in these two states.[46] Regarding the legal system, it is clear that it served – at least in part – a similar purpose in both dictatorships. The existence of criminal codes and regular courts was supposed to demonstrate the lawfulness and legitimacy of the regimes, both domestically and internationally. But behind this façade the law was often used for the political ends of the regime – controlling, repressing, persecuting, imprisoning and killing suspected 'enemies'. Criminal justice was perverted, with basic principles undermined and the rules of fairness and transparency ignored. Hitler and Stalin were personally involved in this process, from very general matters to specific decisions about the killing of individual prisoners. At the same time, action from below was crucial in escalating penal policy in both dictatorships, because of the initiative of local officials eager to realise their own ideological obsessions and what they assumed to be the will of the political leadership. There were also similarities in sentencing. Stalin, like Hitler, felt that retribution and deterrence were more important than rehabilitation. And in the 1930s, court sentences in both countries became harsher and imprisonment more frequent and more lengthy. This was true not only for political offences but also for ordinary crimes, which were increasingly politicised.[47]

One can also detect some broad parallels in the practice of imprisonment. Stalin's prisons were notoriously overcrowded and conditions were often even worse than in Germany. The growing economic exploitation of inmates for large-scale work projects in Nazi Germany actually mirrored the Soviet example. From the late 1920s onwards, the Soviet regime had begun to exploit the inmates in state projects and by 1933 prisoner output was part of the Five-Year-Plan in all the provinces. Prisoners were felling trees, working in coal and gold mines, constructing houses and building canals, often in remote and isolated corners of the Soviet Empire. Life was extremely harsh. Some inmates were forced to work for months without a day's rest, suffering from hunger and disease. The authorities' disregard for the inmates was reflected in the very high mortality.[48]

Like their German counterparts, the Soviet authorities showed no scruples about murdering individuals legally sentenced to imprisonment. This policy was enforced, for example, in many Soviet prisons in the first weeks after the German attack in June 1941 – eerily foreshadowing the gruesome scenes in some German prisons in 1944–45. In case of an invasion, Soviet plans had envisaged the evacuation of prisons. But orderly withdrawal often proved impossible, because of organisational chaos and the speed of the German advance. Some prison officials in regions threatened with being overrun by the German army simply fled, leaving prisoners in their cells. Elsewhere, inmates on criminal charges were freed, while those that remained were marched eastwards on foot under appalling conditions, which left thousands dead. In addition, several tens of thousands of prisoners were executed by Soviet officials, which had been sanctioned by the Soviet leadership. On 24 June 1941, the head of the NKVD, Lavrenty Beria, secretly ordered regional officials to execute supposedly dangerous prison inmates, including those held for 'anti-Soviet activities' and 'economic sabotage'. One of the bloodiest massacres took place in Lvov, where around 3,000 prisoners were murdered in late June 1941.[49]

But these broad parallels should not blind us to the manifest differences between Stalin's Russia and Hitler's Germany. For the structure, position and practice of the judicial apparatus were in some ways strikingly different. There was no real tradition of abstract law in Tsarist Russia, and attempts to establish an independent legal order did not really take root. Legal consciousness was poorly developed among the population, and the Tsarist courts never reached a majority of the people. After the revolution of 1917, the bloody and arbitrary justice of the Bolsheviks did nothing to increase respect for legality. As for the Soviet legal officials, they were untrained and poorly educated party members, who often served only for brief periods as judges or prosecutors. For most of the 1930s and 1940s, the central legal authorities had no firm hold over these amateur jurists, who were in practice subordinated to local party leaders. The jurists showed little or no regard for norms and freely participated in state terror. One reason for their excesses was fear of reprisals by the security police and political leaders. Anyone suspected of leniency towards 'enemies of the people' was at real risk of dismissal and punishment, not least because untrained officials could easily be replaced. During Stalin's Great Terror in 1937–38, almost half the judges lost their position, with many of them also being arrested. Most importantly, many sentences in the USSR were not pronounced by legal courts at all, but by police courts and panels, active against supposed political enemies and 'socially harmful' individuals (including beggars, vagrants and ex-convicts). The Soviet police took the lead during the Great Terror, and afterwards regular courts were virtually excluded from political cases. The legal apparatus even lost control of its own places of confinement. By the end of 1934, all prisons, camps and forced labour colonies were controlled by the NKVD. And within this system, prisons played a subordinate role: they held remand prisoners, inmates in transit, and those with shorter custodial sentences. In terms of numbers, prisons were far outstripped by the camps in the late 1930s and early 1940s. For example, on 15 January 1939, there were 350,000 inmates in Soviet prisons, while around 1,300,000 persons were held in the camps.[50]

The contrast is obvious. In Germany the legal system was a firmly established part of the fabric of society. Legal officials were career civil servants, highly trained professionals with a strong sense of their own social status. Judges had to complete many years of state-controlled training, first at university then as legal assistants and assistant judges, before they could hope for a permanent position. This did not change in the Third Reich. True, a number of jurists were promoted above their station for ideological reasons, but legal training and professional qualifications remained the basis for a career in the

Nazi legal system. And despite Hitler's violent dislike of jurists, German judges retained considerable independence and there were no mass purges of legal personnel. All this meant that the legal system in Nazi Germany was much more firmly entrenched than in the Soviet Union. While the Soviet system relied more widely on the police, the German legal apparatus played a key role in Nazi terror, sentencing political and other outsiders and maintaining a large network of penal institutions under its jurisdiction.

The existence of a traditional legal apparatus in Germany did not prevent the perversion of the law. To be sure, legal officials in the Third Reich acted less arbitrarily than their Soviet counterparts, being somewhat more concerned to remain within what they interpreted, broadly, as the boundaries of the law. But they still lent their hand to brutal repression and murder. This shows that the total subordination of the legal apparatus to the political leadership and the police, or far-reaching purges of legal officials, are not necessary preconditions for turning an ostensibly sophisticated legal system into a weapon against political, social and racial outsiders. In other words, an established legal system and a professional body of trained jurists provide no secure barrier against a descent into terror.

Punishment and the Prison in the West

The tradition of a legal apparatus discharging the state monopoly of punishment put Germany in the mainstream of western countries. There were many parallels in penal policy between Germany before 1933, and liberal, western states where the legal system in the nineteenth and early twentieth century had developed along rather similar lines. This was no coincidence. Penal policy and criminology were truly international fields, with officials often looking abroad for inspiration and innovation. Ministerial officials, criminologists and prison personnel were corresponding across state borders and regularly met at international congresses. They also went on many study trips abroad. The influential Hamburg Professor for Criminal Law, Moritz Liepmann, visited almost 50 penal institutions and reformatories in the USA in 1926. Just one year later, his Frankfurt colleague, Berthold Freudenthal, made a similar journey to the USA and to England.[51] A brief look at western states such as Britain (the focus below is on England) and the USA will help to establish the extent to which the Third Reich broke with this shared tradition.

Looking at penal policy and imprisonment during the Second World War, the vast disparity between Nazi Germany and liberal states is glaringly obvious. In Germany, the legal system participated in the ferocious assault on internal and foreign 'enemies'. Between 1941 and 1944, for example, German courts passed 15,349 death sentences. In the same period, English courts passed 84 death sentences.[52] The ruthlessness of the German legal system was also reflected in incarceration rates in penal institutions, which jumped from 108,685 (30 June 1939) to 196,700 (30 June 1944), with hundreds of thousands more held in concentration camps. In the same period, the average daily population in English prisons increased very modestly, from about 11,000 (1939) to 12,915 (1944). This great gulf was also evident inside the prison. To start with, the brutality and murderous violence against convicts in Nazi Germany, with the prison authorities colluding in the mass extermination of inmates, was obviously not matched elsewhere. But even more traditional elements, such as prison labour, operated in a strikingly different way. To be sure, prison labour in England and the USA was also influenced by the war: the demand for production increased, and numerous workshops produced some forms of military equipment. But this development proceeded along lines very different to those of Nazi Germany. Prison labour was apparently quite marginal in the thinking of the Allied decision-makers. In the USA, war contracts were actually terminated in 1944, bringing production in many prisons to a standstill and putting an end to the era of the 'productive prison'. And those prisoners who were working for the war industry were never exploited in the same way as in Nazi Germany, where a significant number of inmates, suffering from starvation rations, were worked to death, with official working hours for Polish prisoners as high as 14 hours per day. By contrast, the daily period of employment in English prisons fell well below eight hours, and the prisoners' rations were in accordance with those handed out to civilians.[53]

This picture becomes somewhat more complex when we look at the years before the war. Broadly speaking, the development in western, liberal states in the early twentieth century was towards comparatively fewer prison sentences. Penal policy was widely influenced by the conception of punishment as social defence, advocated by the modern school of criminal law. Punishment was to be adapted to the personality of each offender. In the case of certain defendants, courts in Europe and the USA began to turn away from the prison towards non-custodial alternatives, such as suspended sentencing, early release on parole, and fines.[54] This broad shift in penal policy had also taken place in Germany before the Nazis. But imprisonment made a comeback in the Third Reich, not least because of the courts' participation in breaking down political resistance and dissent. The imprisonment of many tens of thousands of political opponents marks one of the key differences from liberal states at the time. And the fact that prisoner numbers shot up, despite the gradual economic recovery, also increasingly set Germany apart. In Nazi Germany, the prisoner number stood at 176 per 100,000 inhabitants on 30 November 1936 (183 including concentration camps). This meant not just a dramatic increase over the later Weimar period (97 prisoners in 1927), but a striking contrast to many European states, where prisoner numbers in 1936 hovered around 80 (Belgium), 60 (Holland), 40 (France) and 25 (England). Even so, incarceration rates in Nazi

Germany before the war were not a total aberration. In the USA, there were 158 convicted prisoners (excluding remand prisoners) per 100,000 of the population (1933). In Switzerland, this figure was around 165 (1936), and in Finland it even reached around 200 (1936) – exceeding numbers in Nazi Germany.[55]

How did the everyday life of German prisoners in the mid-1930s compare to that of inmates in other western states? On the whole, the trend in many western states in the interwar years was towards slightly more lenient prison conditions, influenced in part by the vision of the prison as a more therapeutic institution. Concerts, prison bands, radio broadcasts, prison theatre and sport became increasingly widespread in England and America, where inmates were also allowed to communicate more freely with each other and with their relatives on the outside, relaxing the monotonous and harsh prison life. Similar measures had been pioneered in Weimar Germany, but were often cut back again in the Third Reich. However, this did not mean that prison life in Nazi Germany was harsher in every respect. Compared to England, German prison buildings were in a somewhat better general condition and the medical equipment was also often superior. Disciplinary punishment in the prewar Nazi prison was probably not notably excessive in an international comparison, at least on paper. Many sanctions common in German penal institutions, such as solitary detention and the reduction of rations to bread and water, were well known to English prison officials. And corporal punishment was still allowed in England until 1967, though it was rarely used. In Germany, it had been officially abolished in the late nineteenth and early twentieth century, though of course this did not stop individual German prison officials from beating up inmates. Corporal punishment was also still on the statute book in at least 26 US prisons in 1937. US prison officials also deployed other forms of physical punishment. For example, some inmates were held in solitary confinement in dark cells underground or were shackled for 12 hours per day to the door of their cell.[56]

Looking at prison labour, there were also some parallels. Dreary and repetitive work remained the staple of most prisons. Many prisoners could not be trained because their sentences were too short, and there was also persistent opposition from trade unions and manufacturers to competition from prison labour. The most important development in prewar Nazi Germany was the creation of large prison camps, where treatment was especially violent. There were no corresponding developments in places such as England. But some liberal states did practise brutal and exhausting outside labour. In the 1920s, all US states allowed the employment of convicts outside the prison, on farms, roadwork camps and other construction sites. This was seen both as a convenient solution to overcrowding, which blighted many American prisons, and as a way to improve prisoner productivity and the state's infrastructure. Of course, conditions during outside labour varied greatly across the different states, and could at times be better than inside. Worst off were prisoners in the notorious chain gangs in the south, which built on a long tradition of inmate maltreatment and exploitation. For several decades after the Civil War, the southern states in the USA had contracted offenders to private businessmen for forced labour on plantations, mines, brickyards, farms and the like. The vast majority of these prisoners were African-Americans, betraying the roots of convict leasing in slavery. This brutal abuse of prisoners was only abandoned in the late nineteenth and early twentieth century (Alabama was the last state to abolish such treatment, in the mid-1920s).[57] But this did not necessarily improve the inmates' conditions. For convict leasing was effectively replaced in the south with roadwork by chain gangs. Although it was promoted as a humanitarian and rehabilitative measure, life on the chain gangs was dominated by dirt, neglect, foul food and violence. Prisoners had to perform hard physical labour, driven on by the warders' clubs and whips. Inmates were chained at their ankles, even at night, when they were often forced into small wheeled cages. Minor disciplinary infraction could result in brutal punishment, including detention in a 'sweat box' in the glaring sun. In Mississippi, discipline was even enforced by brutal fellow prisoners, elevated to supervisors by the authorities. The chain gang proved resilient and remained a fixed feature of the southern penal system for decades. It still existed in the 1920s and 1930s and only slowly disappeared from the roads thereafter.[58]

Nor was Nazi Germany alone in its crusade against 'degenerate', 'habitual' and 'incorrigible' offenders before the war. There was widespread consensus in Europe, the USA and elsewhere that certain dangerous and hardened criminals had to be incapacitated with the help of protective measures. In outline, these measures – reflecting the repressive side of modern penal policy – often resembled those of the German prison regime. This was true, above all, of policies against 'habitual criminals'. New South Wales in Australia and New Zealand had already introduced indefinite confinement at the start of the twentieth century, much to the envy of some German criminologists, and in the following years similar legislation was introduced in different guises around the globe. A number of states introduced indefinite, potentially lifelong, detention for 'habitual criminals', to be served either after an initial term of imprisonment as in Nazi Germany (for example, the Norwegian Criminal Code of 1929) or in place of it (for instance, the Swiss Criminal Code of 1937). In other countries, the term of preventive detention had a statutory limit. For example the Prevention of Crime Act (1908) in England provided that 'habitual criminals' sentenced to penal servitude could be ordered to serve an additional period of detention, ranging from five to ten years. The English detainees were taken to the newly built Camp Hill Preventive Detention Prison, where the social background of the inmate population at the beginning to some extent resembled that in German security confinement. Many of the inmates turned out not to be highly dangerous criminals, but small-time petty offenders, convicted for the theft of food and the like.[59]

Several states also experimented with medical measures to fight crime. To start with, castration of sex offenders was on the international agenda. Denmark was the first European state to introduce voluntary castration (1929), with Norway (1934), Holland (1938) and Sweden (1944) soon to follow suit. Other countries, including Finland (1935) and some states in the USA, even allowed compulsory castration of sex offenders. Not surprisingly, there was some backing in these countries for the German policies. For example, the *Eugenic News*, published by prominent US eugenics societies, in 1934 expressed support for the castration of sex offenders in Nazi Germany.[60] Some countries also began to sterilise selected criminal offenders. The first such sterilisations were probably carried out in the Jeffersonville state prison in Indiana. This practice fed into the first eugenic sterilisation laws, adopted in Indiana in 1907, which targeted persons classified as mentally ill and criminally insane. At the end of the 1920s, similar laws had been introduced in 28 US states. By this time, around 15,000 individuals had already been sterilised – including, according to one observer, over 3,000 'habitual criminals'. There was considerable popular support in the USA for the compulsory sterilisation of certain criminal offenders. The US practice was repeatedly cited in the Weimar Republic as an example of the backwardness in the fight against crime in Germany, which had as yet failed to implement such policies. Even when sterilisation was introduced in the Third Reich, however, classification as an 'habitual criminal' did not result in the operation.[61] Scandinavian countries also saw a surge of support for eugenic policies, culminating in the 1930s in the passing of sterilisation laws with some compulsory element in Denmark, Sweden, Norway and Finland. But, as in Germany, criminal behaviour played little part in the decision for sterilisation; instead the mentally ill and 'feeble minded' were targeted.[62]

Ultimately, what was different about the prewar German approach to 'habitual' and 'incorrigible' offenders was not so much the policies themselves, as their application. Sentencing in Nazi Germany put all other countries in the shade. In the statistical year 1929–30, there were only some 50 inmates in indeterminate detention in Australia. In England, there were around 124 persons in preventive detention in the mid-1930s. By contrast, there were almost 5,000 inmates in security confinement in Nazi Germany at the end of 1939. This outstripped incarceration rates even in other dictatorships. Italy, for example, held only around 500 'habitual criminals' in indeterminate confinement between 1934 and 1937. The same difference between Germany and other states is evident in the implementation of castration. In Finland, a total of 54 sex offenders were castrated between 1935 and 1950. By contrast, more than 1,800 men were sentenced to forcible castration between 1934 and 1939 in Germany.[63] In short, German pre-war measures such as indefinite confinement and castration were an extremely radical expression of 'preventive' modern penal policy, as practised in many other states.

German penal policy between 1933 and 1939 – with its politicisation of the legal system, stress on strict punishment, sharp rise in the prison population and excessive measures against 'habitual' criminals – began to set the Third Reich apart from a number of western countries. At the same time, though, Germany had not yet taken a completely separate path. The somewhat ambivalent attitude of international observers towards Nazi penal policy before the war was exposed at the XI International Prison and Penitentiary Congress, held in Berlin in August 1935.

The 1935 Prison and Penitentiary Congress

The German authorities were determined to exploit this prestigious congress as a showcase for the Third Reich and its penal policy, and as an opportunity to refute publicly charges that opponents of the regime were unfairly treated in its prisons and camps. (Berlin had been chosen as the venue for this congress long before the Nazis came to power.) The regime was well aware of the propaganda potential of the congress and Reich Minister of Justice Franz Gürtner did his best to realise it. In April 1935, he informed the regional legal officials that the congress offered a 'unique opportunity to enlighten foreign legal elements who are dismissive and hostile towards the new Germany'.[64] The penal institutions chosen as sites for visits by foreign officials had been meticulously prepared to appear in the best possible light. Entire buildings were renovated, and corridors and cells were cleaned from top to bottom. In Brandenburg-Görden, inmates were even put into model cells in a specially selected wing, mocked as the 'Potemkin wing' by the prisoners.[65] The German delegates were hand-picked and included criminologists, prison administrators and governors, as well as representatives from other state agencies such as Theodor Eicke, the inspector of the SS concentration camps. To ensure the unanimity of the German delegates, they were instructed how to vote on the resolutions discussed at the congress. In addition, they were supervised by police officers during the proceedings. One British delegate later recalled, according to *The Times*, that 'members of the secret police sat insolently at the back of committee rooms, smoking cigarettes and chattering while speeches were being made'.[66] Nothing was to be left to chance. The Propaganda Ministry even proposed that the delegates should be instructed on how to answer potentially difficult questions, for example about the treatment of Jews.[67]

Foreign opinion in the run-up to the Berlin congress proved more difficult to control. A few weeks before it opened, the Social Democrats in exile published a 15-page report on the Nazi prison and concentration camp system, with details of harsh regulations, brutal quotes from leading Nazi officials and descriptions of life inside. The authors concluded that the German prison aimed at 'vengeance and extermination'. This report was sent to some foreign delegates and was also quickly picked up by several foreign newspapers, which used it to attack the forthcoming congress.[68] The respected Howard League for Penal Reform in Britain announced that it would boycott the congress, above all because it had been told that its chairman would not be allowed to speak. Lack of freedom of speech, the League concluded, meant that the proceedings would be 'doomed to complete futility and sterility'.[69]

But such concerns could not deter around 300 officials from over 50 countries (including Britain, France and the USA) from travelling to Berlin. Here, the scene was set for an exhibition of Nazi propaganda. The congress opened under a bust of Hitler and the Nazi flag on 18 August 1935 in the Kroll Opera House, the building where the Reichstag deputies had passed the Enabling Act some two years earlier. On the opening day, the delegates elected Franz Gürtner as honorary president and Erwin Bumke as president of the congress. Some foreign delegates even joined Bumke in his cries of 'Heil Hitler'. Franz Gürtner, Hans Frank, Roland Freisler and Joseph Goebbels had been lined up as the main speakers, and they all used the opportunity to present Nazi policy in its best light. Goebbels, for example, spelled out some of the core values of Nazism, such as *völkisch* nationalism, in his speech on 23 August. He also seized the opportunity to defend the imprisonment of thousands of 'enemies' in concentration camps, claiming that this had saved Germany from anarchy. Goebbels added that the camp inmates were being turned into useful members of the community.[70] The Nazi press exploited the presence of the foreign officials, presenting it as an endorsement of the Third Reich. Some of the delegates themselves soon suspected that they were bestowing legitimacy on the Nazi regime. One British delegate noted that the German authorities could now confront any internal critics of its penal policy 'with a multitude of photographs of distinguished foreign officials, criminologists and reformers cheering the monstrous proposals put forward by Dr Gürtner and by Dr Frank'.[71]

Still, the congress did not proceed quite as smoothly as the German hosts had hoped. In one session, a French lawyer spoke out against the repression of inmates in concentration camps, provoking an indignant German delegate to counter that it was well known that the camps were mere 'educational institutions'.[72] On the very next day, the German authorities came under pressure during an organised visit to Moabit prison, when some foreign delegates asked to see the imprisoned Communist leader Ernst Thälmann. After some prevarication, the prison officials allowed the delegates to catch a distant glimpse of Thälmann during his exercise in the yard. But they could not speak to him, the delegates were told, because Thälmann had received too many visits of late and objected – a lie so brazen as to further increase the suspicions of some delegates.[73]

The main controversy came in a debate about the question of whether privileges and lenient treatment could help the education and reform of prisoners. Not surprisingly, the German delegates, led in the debate by Professor Georg Dahm and by Edgar Schmidt from the Reich Ministry of Justice, were sceptical, backed by delegates from Fascist Italy. Representatives from Britain, the USA, Belgium and other countries, however, supported a more humanitarian amendment, much to the annoyance of the German authorities. One German prison official afterwards complained that these foreign officials had obviously not 'come to terms with the realities of the prison service in the new Germany'. When the issue came to a vote, the German position initially won – hardly surprising, given the fact that the Germans made up the majority of delegates. But in a rather heated discussion, some foreign delegates now demanded a second vote by nation, and this time the German position was narrowly defeated. This proved a considerable embarrassment for the German organisers, even though it still demonstrated that Nazi Germany was by no means alone in its pursuit of a stern penal policy.[74] The German attempts to manipulate the proceedings, as well as the constant Nazi propaganda, resulted in a negative echo in the UK, the USA and elsewhere. The US delegates were presumably also angered by German newspaper reports published towards the end of the congress about the treatment of African-American prisoners in the USA, which had been printed on the express orders of the Propaganda Ministry.[75]

However, while the Berlin congress was not an unmitigated triumph for Nazi penal policy, the extent of the disagreements with other countries should not be overstated either. Relations between many delegates remained cordial. Some German and English delegates, for example, knew each other well from exchange visits between German and English penal institutions in June and October 1934. The official British delegate and prison commissioner, Alexander Paterson, wrote to *The Times* just days after the congress had ended, to defend his 'friend and colleague' Erwin Bumke against any criticism, applauding his 'fairness and impartiality'.[76] A number of votes at the congress were carried unanimously, and some contentious issues, such as the compulsory castration of certain criminal offenders, were supported not just by the German delegates, but also by some representatives from liberal states. Some foreign delegates were also clearly impressed by the harsh discipline inside those German penal institutions they visited, accompanied by Gürtner, Freisler and Bumke. Support for such strict treatment of prisoners could be found not only in Mussolini's Italy, but also in other countries. A Swiss governor enthused after a trip to the Emsland prison camp, the most brutal of all places of judicial confinement, that the warders were 'young and bright people who all make a good impression'.[77] Clearly, Germany was not yet isolated in the field of penal policy. This did not happen until the dramatic intensification of German policy in the war.

Conclusion

The Third Reich did not become an all-out police state. Of course, Hitler strongly supported the transformation of the police into an independent apparatus of repression, with concentration camps as its places of confinement. Led by Himmler, the police system was designed as the instrument to realise the 'will of the Führer', removed from outside interference. At the same time, Hitler and his closest allies regarded the legal system as rather feeble, bureaucratic, slow and soft on criminals. The courts were clearly not their first weapons of choice against 'community aliens'. So why did the Nazi leadership not simply abolish the traditional legal apparatus and its prisons? Why was the legal system retained until the very end of the Third Reich?

To start with, the dismantling of the legal apparatus would have required a far more radical assault on the core structures of German society than the Nazis were prepared, or able, to undertake. Instead, just like many other areas of the dictatorship, Nazi terror was based on a combination of existing and newly created agencies, which at times pursued rather similar goals.[1] In addition, the legal system made a convenient scapegoat for some of the most obvious failures of the regime. For example, the picture of the Third Reich as a crime-free society, so popular in postwar Germany, was no more than crude Nazi propaganda. It was opportune, therefore, for the Nazi leadership to shift the blame for deviance and crime partly on to the traditional courts and penal institutions, rather than the police, which was much more closely associated with Hitler personally. Furthermore, the Nazi leaders presumably saw the continued operation of the legal system as a way to secure the support of many

Germans, who had long placed a great deal of importance on the maintenance of law and order. The promise to restore order had been a key part of the Nazis' electoral appeal in the chaos at the end of the Weimar Republic. While many Germans accepted that this goal might, at times, only be achieved by actually breaking the law, most of them also wanted to retain the traditional legal structures, not least in their own interest. In other words, had the Nazi regime relied solely on the police and the concentration camps, it would have destroyed the semblance of the rule of law vital for its popular support. Instead, the continued operation of the legal bureaucracy helped to mask the terrorist nature of the Nazi regime. This was reinforced by press reports about prisons and penitentiaries, which often painted an idealised picture of strict discipline and productive labour, drawing a veil over the hunger, illness, overcrowding, violence, death and murder. In this way, the legal system became indispensable to the image of the Third Reich. It provided the regime with a 'veneer of legality' and a vital counter-balance to the terror of the police and concentration camps.[2]

But the legal apparatus had one more crucial role. The courts and penal institutions were more than leftovers from the pre-Nazi era or smokescreens for police terror. They actually played a central part in the criminalisation of political dissent and the politicisation of common crime. The legal apparatus took part in the Nazi assault on social, political and racial outcasts, including Communists, foreign resistance fighters, Jehovah's Witnesses, Jews, homosexuals, 'dangerous habitual criminals' and others. Despite the repeated attacks by Hitler and other Nazi leaders on the supposed incompetence of the legal system, it demonstrated again and again that it was, in fact, willing to crack down hard on 'enemies of the people'. Not only did the legal system actively participate in Nazi terror, but it served to deter others from stepping out of line. Legal terror also helped to legitimise the parallel, more radical police measures, branding 'community aliens' as lawbreakers who deserved to be punished – either by the police or by the legal authorities.[3]

Clearly, then, the legal apparatus fulfilled several vital functions in the Third Reich: it preserved a degree of legal stability in some areas, it could be blamed for the failure of the homogenous 'national community' to materialise, it legitimised the regime, and it helped in the brutal repression of 'community aliens'. For all the misgivings of the Nazi leaders, the legal apparatus was a fundamental pillar of the Nazi dictatorship and the prisons were very much Hitler's prisons. Of course, the role of the legal system in the Nazi dictatorship changed over time. But it always remained important for the operation of the regime. If this contribution of the legal apparatus is overlooked, the view of Nazi terror inside Germany will inevitably be lopsided.

Conclusion

Legal Terror and Imprisonment before the War

In the prewar years, the significance of the legal apparatus was evident in the sheer number of inmates held inside penal institutions. Of course, many of these prisoners were 'ordinary' criminals, who would also have been imprisoned had the Nazis not come to power. But a large proportion of inmates was held as a direct result of changes in penal policy in the Third Reich. After the 'seizure of power', prisoner numbers shot up due to more arrests, stricter sentences and new laws. Penal institutions were the main sites of imprisonment in Nazi Germany before the war, eclipsing SS concentration camps, at times by an inmate ratio as high as 25:1. These conclusions clearly contradict recent views that the 'law was overshadowed by the extra-judicial powers of the police', as the regular penal system in the Third Reich was 'too rule-bound to be an effective form of terror'.[4] On the contrary, the legal system was central to Nazi terror against 'community aliens' in the prewar years. This becomes even clearer when we look at legal terror in more detail.

First of all, the regular courts played a crucial part in the repression of – real or imagined – political opposition. In the prewar years political suspects were more likely to end up in a prison or penitentiary than in a concentration camp. At the end of June 1935, the legal authorities classified a massive 22,955 of all 107,162 inmates in penal institutions as political prisoners. This figure includes those suspected of active resistance to the regime, such as Communists and Jehovah's Witnesses. Judges also punished other forms of non-conformity. Until 1939, they sentenced tens of thousands for criticising or grumbling about the regime. Prison sentences in these cases were often much shorter than those handed out to supposed active opponents of the regime. But the number of convictions is still evidence for the willingness of many legal officials to enforce the total claim of Nazism over society.

The legal apparatus also moved against racial and social outsiders. The overall number of Jews taken to penal institutions remained rather small. In their case, the SS concentration camps became more important in enforcing terror. Still, the legal system played its part in the Nazi anti-Jewish crusade. The courts applied new legislation that criminalised many aspects of the life of Jews, such as the ban on sexual relations with non-Jews, introduced in the notorious 1935 Nuremberg Laws. Jews were not the only victims of judges prying inside the bedroom to enforce racial policy. Homosexuality had been punishable long before the Nazis came to power. But in the second half of the 1930s much harsher sentences were introduced, and the number of defendants increased dramatically, with some 24,500 men convicted of homosexual offences in the years between 1937 and 1939. Overall, many more homosexual men were taken to a regular prison or penitentiary than to a concentration camp.

It would, of course, be wrong to see Nazi legal terror as the negation of Weimar penal policy, with no links to the past. Not only did the great majority of Weimar legal officials remain in their posts, but much of German criminal law actually remained unchanged as the Nazis failed to implement a new criminal code.[5] The sense of continuity is most obvious in the case of common crime, which largely continued to be punished by the legal authorities. Even new measures introduced under the Nazis were often indebted to the years before 1933. The most important piece of new legislation was the Habitual Criminals Law of 24 November 1933, which introduced stricter sentences and indefinite security confinement (among other sanctions). But this law was not a product of Nazi ideology. From the late nineteenth century, the modern school of criminal law had demanded that 'incorrigible' criminals and others be permanently removed from society. By the 1920s, there was broad support for their potentially lifelong internment, a measure that was included in all the Weimar drafts of a criminal code. Indeed, the 1933 law was largely based on a draft law of 1927. All this helps to explain the ease with which the measure was introduced in the Third Reich, and then eagerly applied by the courts. This sense of continuity is also obvious when looking at the individuals sentenced to security confinement, who were rather similar to those often singled out as 'incorrigible' in the Weimar Republic: recidivist petty property offenders, whose deviant lifestyle was pathologised by the authorities as degenerate.

Turning to penal institutions, life inside became harder in Nazi Germany than it had been in the immediately preceding years. Of course, some prisoners in Nazi Germany suffered more than others: inmates classified as 'community aliens' faced a range of discriminatory measures as well as abusive behaviour from local officials. But prison life became more severe for many other inmates as well. New regulations ensured stricter general treatment, the cutting back of privileges and the right to complain, and the introduction of harder disciplinary punishment. Inmates were apparently more likely to be physically assaulted, not least because of the employment of many hundreds of Nazi activists as prison warders. Living conditions also deteriorated. Rations were cut and sanitary conditions became worse, thanks to the massive overcrowding. Illness and hunger spread, often made worse by negligent and sometimes violent prison doctors. Prisoners could no longer hope to improve their treatment by appealing to the outside world: this was impossible in the tightly controlled Nazi public sphere. And some progressive measures pioneered in the 1920s were abolished soon after the Nazi takeover. The Weimar prison system had been a contested field and some officials and criminologists had aimed to turn it into a more rehabilitative institution. Their ideas had shaped life in some penal institutions, including Untermaßfeld in Thuringia which had seen new initiatives such as the employment of social workers – quickly abandoned under the Nazis.

But the Nazi prison did not completely break with the past. Life inside the Weimar prison system had often been hard as well. Especially in the early years, living conditions had been very poor: provisions were scarce, cells were massively overcrowded, and disciplinary punishment was harsh. While this had changed somewhat by the late 1920s, conditions began to deteriorate once more during the depression in the early 1930s. In addition, in most institutions progressive reforms had been introduced only slowly and cautiously in the 1920s. Most officials had continued to put their trust in the traditional methods of strict discipline and military order. In the last years of the Weimar Republic, they had joined in the loud attacks against 'sentimental humanitarianism' and had demanded the stricter treatment of prisoners. The harsher measures inside Nazi prisons were thus in line with the wishes of many local prison officials. No wonder, then, that the great majority of them remained in their posts in 1933. Finally, one has to differentiate between the official picture of the Nazi prison and the reality of prison life. State Secretary Freisler's vision of the penal institution as a 'house of horror' was not true for every prisoner, not only because the Nazis strictly differentiated between offenders, but also because self-imposed pressures such as the serious overcrowding often hindered the enforcement of ideals such as total military discipline.

Legal Terror and Imprisonment During the War

During the war, the legal apparatus continued to play a prominent role in Nazi terror inside Germany. New laws and regulations allowed for much stricter punishment and created many additional offences. The new courts set up before the war, the special courts and the People's Court, now extended their role in punishment. To be sure, not every German judge abandoned all sense of balance and reason. But a significant number of them whipped themselves up into a frenzy, which led to the inflationary use of the death penalty in the second half of the war. Capital punishment was still carried out inside penal institutions, and the prison officials there soon got used to mass killings. But sentences of imprisonment remained much more common than death sentences, with terms becoming longer than before the war. Combined with the territorial expansion of the German legal system, this contributed to a sharp increase in the number of prisoners, with inmate numbers virtually doubling during the war. This meant that penal institutions continued to hold more inmates than the SS concentration camps (excluding the death camps). Only in the last years of the war, when the concentration camp system expanded dramatically, was this balance finally reversed.

The composition of inmates in penal institutions changed substantially after 1939. Firstly, while political prisoners still made up a sizeable group, they were quite different to those held previously. In the prewar years, a very large proportion of political prisoners had belonged to the left-wing German opposition. Now, more and more foreign political prisoners arrived, as the legal apparatus participated in the repression of the civilian opposition in parts of Nazi-occupied Europe. Secondly, many judges went on the rampage against property offenders, with sentences often bearing no relation to the crime. Those convicted included a growing number of German 'national comrades' with no previous criminal record. Thirdly, the number of prisoners discriminated against as 'racial aliens' increased sharply after 1939, as the legal system now brutally suppressed Poles, both inside Germany and in incorporated Poland. It seems likely that, at least until 1942, there were still more Poles held in penal institutions than in SS concentration camps. Poles generally received stricter sentences than Germans, and by spring 1943, close to one in every five prisoners was Polish, suffering savage discrimination and abuse. Numbers declined in the following years, after the new Reich Minister of Justice Thierack agreed that punishment of 'racial aliens' should be left to the police. But this was never fully implemented, and in 1944 the German courts still sentenced tens of thousands of Poles. Right until the end of the war, the legal system remained a part of the racial state.

In part, penal institutions were assigned a similar role during the war as before 1939. They were still supposed to ensure deterrence and retribution through strict treatment of the inmates. Overall, life inside prisons and penitentiaries became much harder in wartime. Living conditions deteriorated, disease was rampant and many inmates were starving. This situation was not entirely of the legal officials' own making. However, they did much to make conditions more inhumane: arduous forced labour, deliberate neglect of prisoners, overcrowding, brutal disciplinary punishment – all this heightened the inmates' suffering. The situation was particularly poor in the prison camps, such as the Emsland camp and the new camp North in Norway, where inmates were especially likely to suffer physical assaults. As the war progressed, such violent excesses increasingly took place in other penal institutions as well. In total, perhaps 20,000 prisoners died during the war in penal institutions (excluding executions). In the Emsland camp alone, more than 360 prisoners died each year between 1942 and 1944 – 22 times more than the annual mortality in the camp before the war.[6]

The function of penal institutions underwent significant changes in the war so that they were integrated even more closely with the Nazi regime. To start with, prisoners were increasingly exploited for the Nazi war effort, inside prisons and penitentiaries, in large prison camps, and in smaller satellite camps which sprang up all over Germany. Productive labour, previously largely ignored, was now considered to be the main function of imprisonment.

Ironically, this had also been an ideal of liberal prison reformers in the past, who had hoped that it would facilitate the inmates' reintegration into society after their release. But this was not on the minds of the Nazi officials, who simply wanted to extract as much labour from the prisoners as possible. Many prisoners never returned to society. Work was extremely exhausting and sometimes very dangerous, and many thousands of inmates were worked to death.

The Nazi prison also became subject to greater political, economic and military imperatives. Often, this had lethal results. Before the war, most prisoners had been held until the end of their legally pronounced sentences. This became less likely during the war, as other considerations often took precedence. Thousands of offenders were released early, or spared imprisonment altogether for economic reasons, as their contribution on the outside was considered more vital to the war economy than their work inside prison. Thousands more were released early to fight in special army formations at the front, where fatalities were very high. Most importantly, many prisoners legally sentenced to incarceration – and no more – were exterminated. Some of them were killed as part of larger genocidal programmes, such as the 'euthanasia' action and the Holocaust. Other murderous schemes focused specifically on prisoners. Starting in November 1942, more than 20,000 'asocial' prisoners were taken to concentration camps for 'annihilation through labour'. Soon after, selected 'asocial' prisoners were killed inside penal institutions without police or SS involvement. The murder of inmates continued until the end of the war, with thousands of 'dangerous' prisoners, both Germans and foreigners, killed during the prison evacuations in the last months.

Still, most inmates in penal institutions continued to have much greater hopes of survival than concentration camp inmates, just as before the war. Conditions in the concentration camps were generally worse and the number of deaths in the camps dwarfed those inside penal institutions. Of course, not every concentration camp inmate was worse off than every convict. Certain privileged camp inmates were in a better position, at least temporarily, than individual convicts singled out for especially brutal treatment. This was the case, for example, for some foreign political prisoners. Out of 147 Norwegians held in the Sonnenburg penitentiary between 1943 and 1944, some 36 died behind bars. The survivors were taken in November 1944 to the Sachsenhausen concentration camp, where their condition initially improved significantly.[7] But these were, on the whole, exceptions and most prisoners were better off than concentration camp inmates. This was true, above all, for Jews, who were exposed to instant murderous violence in the concentration camps, something they did not encounter in prisons and penitentiaries. Even so, Jewish prisoners, as well as many other imprisoned 'community aliens', still ended up in concentration camps. It was only a question of time before they were taken from penal institutions to the camps – often with the support of the legal authorities themselves.

Police and Legal Apparatus: a Dual State?

Many historians of Nazi Germany have described the Third Reich as a Dual State, inspired by Ernst Fraenkel's book of the same title. Fraenkel's work is one of the most cited works on the structure of the Third Reich, a key text used to investigate the nature of Nazi dictatorship. Legal historians, in particular, have used Fraenkel's analysis to describe the system of parallel punishment in Nazi Germany. Some have argued that the Third Reich was characterised by a deeply antagonistic relationship between the 'normative' legal state and the 'prerogative' police and SS state, which operated outside the constraints of legal regulations, relying instead on organised extra-normative force (see the Introduction). But how useful is this model for understanding the relationship between legal authorities and police?

Clearly, the two agencies did not operate in an identical fashion. The legal system was, by its very nature, unable to go as far as the police. The abandonment of all legal rules was simply not an option as it would have made the legal profession superfluous. While legal officials got used to applying the law 'loosely', as one senior official put it, they were still bound by some of its remnants.[8] For example, while court proceedings had been perverted, with the rights of defendants at times virtually non-existent and with frequent collusion between prosecution and judges, trials were still necessary to sentence individuals. And even though many prison officials became used to treating inmates with great brutality, they often still showed at least minimal regard for some of the rules, which helps to account for the fact that conditions in penal institutions remained better than in the concentration camps.

The police force was not constrained in the same way, locking up or killing individuals without formal trial. The police became consciously different from traditional bureaucratic institutions, driven by increasingly unrestrained radicalism, not just in their organisational structure but also in practical policy.[9] Himmler himself repeatedly held up disregard for the statutes as a virtue, if it served the ultimate interests of the regime. This remained his creed until the end. In May 1944, Himmler proudly told German generals in a secret speech that, in his fight against crime, he had done 'many things – I admit this very openly – which are not possible according to the written laws, but which were called for according to the laws of reason and common sense'.[10] The police force was destined to encroach on territory traditionally occupied by the legal authorities, leading to the conflict, rivalry, overlapping authority and administrative confusion typical of the 'polycracy' in Nazi Germany. But this development did not weaken the overall force of Nazi terror. On the contrary, it helped to make the legal system more radical, with its officials keen not to be outdone by the police. Yet, however brutal the legal system was, it could always be surpassed in ruthlessness by the police.

But the Dual State as pictured by some historians still fails to convince as a descriptive model. To start with, it is problematic to conceptualise the legal apparatus as a normative entity generally dedicated to upholding the rule of law. For, in truth, how normative was the Normative State? Clearly, many legal regulations enforced in Nazi Germany were fundamentally unjust, inspired by open contempt for the principles of fairness and equality. Even observers who subscribe to a value-free understanding of the law – defined as acts conforming to certain formal standards – cannot subscribe to the notion of an entirely normative Nazi legal state.[11] For long before the outbreak of war in 1939, legal officials actively pursued policies which undermined the rule of law. Firstly, numerous regulations were deliberately framed in such a way as to compromise predictability. This arbitrariness was already evident in 1933, both in political and in common criminal cases. Soon, judges could even convict individuals who had not broken any law but had simply offended against 'healthy popular feeling'.[12] Secondly, existing and new legal norms were repeatedly stretched by judges to undermine legal certainty, with some courts, for example, punishing Jews and non-Jews for 'race defilement' even if they had not consummated sexual relations. Thirdly, the legal authorities repeatedly ignored the regulations altogether. Reich Minister Gürtner accepted that the rule of law could be overridden by supposedly vital national interests. Gürtner openly demonstrated this in the aftermath of the Reichstag fire, the 'Röhm putsch' and the pogrom of November 1938. Many other norms were also ignored. For example, the rule in the national prison regulations that 'unnecessary hardship' was to be avoided in the treatment of prisoners was habitually disregarded by prison officials. Finally, aspects of the cooperation between legal apparatus and police also undermined fundamental legal principles. In short, certain aspects of the operation of the legal apparatus became so inconsistent that it is misleading to label it – as a whole – as normative.[13]

An even greater problem with this interpretation of the Dual State is the portrayal of the legal system and the police as two entirely separate entities with opposing agendas, engaged in permanent battle. While there were important differences and conflicts, this picture obscures the cooperation of the two agencies. Often, they complemented one another and worked closely together. Police and legal system were not two different states, but separate yet enmeshed agencies of repression that served the same regime. Ultimately, they pursued one and the same goal: the fight against 'community aliens' in the Third Reich.

In no small measure, the police and the legal system actually depended on one another. Most importantly, they provided each other with inmates for their respective sites of imprisonment. Looking at prisons and penitentiaries, the vast majority of inmates had originally been arrested by the police, before being transferred to the legal authorities for trial (in addition, the penal institutions held many thousands of police detainees without trial). This raises a point of fundamental importance. Even though the police could have taken all those arrested straight to concentration camps, they did not do so. True, in the course of the war, the police transported more individuals straight to the camps or killed them, without judicial involvement. But even then, judging from the large number of court proceedings, the police still transferred a large proportion of persons arrested on criminal charges to the legal authorities.

The traffic of inmates was not all one-way. For the SS camp system, in turn, secured a significant number of its prisoners from the legal authorities. This included defendants who had not been tried due to lack of evidence or had been found not guilty by the courts, prisoners who had completed their legal sentence, and later even prisoners who had not yet finished their sentence. Numbers were high. In a sample of defendants before the Frankfurt am Main special court, the Gestapo later arrested 7 per cent of those defendants whose cases had been dismissed, 13.5 per cent of those who had been found not guilty by the judges, and 28.6 per cent of those who had completed their prison or penitentiary sentence.[14] In most such cases (except when defendants had been found not guilty), the legal authorities did not generally object to the 'preventive' police measures. Contrary to the claim that these measures were forced on the legal officials, they often actively supported them.[15] In the case of certain political prisoners, criminal offenders and 'racial aliens' coming to the end of their sentences, many legal officials believed that the inmates still needed to be locked up to protect the 'national community', even though this was no longer legally possible. Further police detention without trial was regarded as an essential complementary measure to legal imprisonment.

To sum up, the picture of the police and legal system as two antagonistic and competing agencies of the Nazi state, subscribed to by numerous historians, is not particularly persuasive. Not only does this picture fail to encapsulate fully the complicity of the legal authorities in Nazi terror, it also rather misreads the work of Ernst Fraenkel, on which it purports to rest. His book *The Dual State* has often been simplified, misunderstood and shorn of its more radical conclusions, at times until it conformed to the popular, rather charitable image of the legal system in the Third Reich. But this was not Fraenkel's view. Fraenkel, who had worked as a lawyer in Nazi Germany until he emigrated in 1938, argued that the rule of law in Nazi Germany had been replaced by the Dual State. The Prerogative State maintained the Nazi dictatorship by controlling the political sphere, unlimited by constitutional restraints. And as all matters could be defined as political in the Third Reich, the Prerogative State was free to intervene in all spheres of life. In the economic sphere, it came up against the Normative State, based on existing or newly enacted law. Its main function was the protection of the economic order against complete arbitrariness, securing the necessary minimum of predictability. Of course, such protection was only extended to those individuals judged by the political authorities to be 'constructive forces'; all others, such as Jews in the second half of the 1930s, were completely subjected to the Prerogative State.

So where did Fraenkel place the police and the courts? The Gestapo, according to Fraenkel, was the main agency of the Prerogative State. But the classification of the legal courts was more complicated. Contrary to the impression given by some of his followers, Fraenkel did not simply equate the Normative State with the legal system. True, Fraenkel did see many courts – especially in civil law – as part of the Normative State, 'responsible for seeing that the principles of the capitalist order are maintained'. Repeatedly, such courts came into conflict with the Prerogative State, which for political reasons intervened and corrected court decisions through the agency of the police. In this sense, Fraenkel concluded, 'the police power controls the courts in the interests of political expediency'. However, Fraenkel made clear that other courts actually gave explicit backing to the actions of the Prerogative State, suspending legal rights. These courts, which based their decisions on political considerations, therefore belonged to the Prerogative State themselves. This was true, according to Fraenkel, of the special courts and the People's Court ('the creation of the Prerogative State'), as well as of a number of other traditional courts. For example, Fraenkel concluded that a particular judgment of the Munich Higher State Court had 'degraded its status to that of an instrument of the Prerogative State'. Fraenkel's views would surely have been even more damning had he had access to political cases and to documents from the period after 1938.[16]

Understood in this way, Fraenkel's work can still offer a stimulating approach to Nazi legal terror. Following Fraenkel, it is clear that the legal apparatus combined elements of the Normative and the Prerogative State. It maintained some degree of social and economic order for the majority of the population, preventing the Third Reich from descending into complete anarchy. Even the Nazi leadership regarded an element of legal predictability as necessary for the functioning of the dictatorship, to guarantee, as Hitler's right-hand man Martin Bormann put it, the 'order of the life of the people' – not counting 'community aliens', of course, who were deprived of their rights.[17] But simultaneously, the instruments of the legal system also – to a lesser or greater extent – operated as political agencies of the regime, as part of the Prerogative State. Over time, the remaining normative elements within the legal apparatus became weaker, as more and more matters were defined as political. The Dual State gradually disappeared.

Of course, there was more to terror in Nazi Germany than the police and the legal apparatus. While they stood at the centre of the Nazi web of terror, there were many other parts, including various state and party agencies, municipal and welfare offices, the army and members of the general public. They all contributed, in one way or another, to the same broad aim: the eradication of 'community aliens' from Nazi society. Once caught, it proved difficult for them to escape. Crucially, the web of terror was not static, but constantly evolved and adapted. This applied, above all, to the relationship between police/SS and legal system, intertwined by competition and cooperation, on both central and local levels. Before the war, there was still a fairly clear division of labour between the police, charged with preventing suspected enemies from committing crimes in the future, and the legal authorities, who generally punished offences that had already taken place. This began to change in the war, as the police increased their dominance and meted out punishment to more suspected offenders without involving the legal authorities. Steadily, the police moved into the centre of the web of terror, with the legal system gradually pushed further towards the sidelines.

Nazi Terror and the Germans

In recent years, important works have been published on the relationship between Nazi terror and the German population, offering significant new insights (see the Introduction). Some of these conclusions have been confirmed in this study. But this book has also touched on areas where further discussion will prove fruitful. The picture of a highly selective terror apparatus, which only at the very end collapsed into complete arbitrariness, needs some revision. Clearly, Nazi terror was often selective, and the authorities were determined to single out all supposedly dangerous political, racial and social outsiders for especially harsh punishment. But crucially, this pattern of selectivity never disappeared completely – not even during the breakdown of the Nazi dictatorship. At the very end, the prison authorities were still guided, at least to some extent, by the separation of inmates into 'national comrades' and 'community aliens'. For example, during the evacuation of the prisons and penitentiaries in the last months of the war, the legal authorities laid down general guidelines, dividing inmates into two groups: those judged as harmless were set free, while the others were forced on to brutal evacuation marches or killed.

However, Nazi terror always contained arbitrary aspects, right from the very beginning. For the boundary between 'national comrade' and 'community alien' was always fluid. Both concepts were nebulous and could, by their very nature, not be comprehensively defined. Therefore, the classification of offenders depended at least to some extent on the personal views and prejudices of the individual judges, prison personnel and other legal officials, introducing an element of arbitrariness into the legal sphere which clearly had a deterrent function. One wrong word or unthinking gesture could turn even an exemplary 'national comrade' into a 'community alien'. This did not happen in all cases: far from it. But it was a possibility, as these 'national comrades' – in the eyes of some judges – had betrayed the trust of the community and deserved hard punishment. In short, Nazi terror at all times combined elements of both selectivity and arbitrariness.

Nor did selectivity mean that 'German-on-German terror' became very common only towards the very end of the war. To start with, a large number of 'community aliens' were, of course, themselves German. In the prewar years, many hundreds of thousands of Germans were imprisoned at one time or another, most of them in prisons and penitentiaries. All the way through the Third Reich, Germans made up the majority of inmates in penal institutions. Many served sentences for 'ordinary', sometimes appalling, crimes, and they cannot be described straightforwardly as victims of Nazi terror. But this term can be applied without question to many other prisoners: political and religious opponents of the regime, 'grumblers', German Jews and other 'racial outsiders', homosexuals, and also those petty criminals who received exorbitant punishment. During the war Nazi terror engulfed more and more 'ordinary' Germans, that is, those Germans who had previously not figured large among those persecuted. It is this phenomenon which historians mean when they argue that terror against Germans escalated at the end of the war. However, this development was clearly not confined to the last months of the war. It had already emerged in the middle of the war, with many very harsh sentences for 'ordinary' Germans found guilty of economic offences, dissent and illegal contacts with prisoners of war. One obvious manifestation of this was the rapid increase in the number of German women behind bars, who had previously made up only a small proportion of the prison population. Life for these female inmates changed, too. For example, gender distinctions now played a lesser role in prison labour, as more and more women were forced into hard manual labour for the war.

Turning to the public face of Nazi repression, the operation of the terror apparatus, including the legal system, was never completely hidden – or intended to be so – from the general population. The popular perception of legal terror was shaped in part by rumours and experiences of friends and acquaintances. Also, owing to the growing exploitation of prison labour for the war effort – with the deployment of prisoners in satellite camps, bomb disposal squads and armaments factories, among other places – imprisonment became more visible to the public. The most important part was played by information released by the Nazi authorities themselves. National and regional newspapers were full of reports of court cases, covering a variety of alleged offences and crimes. For example, in the autumn of 1942 hardly a day went by without an article in the *Völkischer Beobachter* about stiff sentences against 'national pests'. Newspapers were not the only medium used by the authorities. During the war, death and prison sentences were also often announced on posters in the area where the supposed crime had been committed. All this raises the question about the intentions of the regime: what were the ultimate aims of open legal terror?

There is certainly some truth in the argument that the Nazis successfully used these reports to gain support among the German people. There can be little doubt that the crackdown on 'community aliens' was popular. As we have seen, the campaign against 'dangerous habitual criminals' could build on widespread prejudices which long predated the Nazi takeover. The same was true for other groups persecuted in Nazi Germany, as the historian Jeremy Noakes, among others, has stressed convincingly:

> A crucial element in popular consent to the regime was the fact that Nazism embodied, albeit in an extreme form, many of the basic attitudes of a very large section of the German people . . . Such people also approved of the regime's hostility towards unpopular minorities, not just Jews but also gypsies, and of its harsh attitude towards deviant groups – homosexuals, tramps, habitual criminals, the so-called asocials and the 'work-shy' . . . In short, the regime confirmed and enforced the values and prejudices of a substantial section of the population, giving them official status as 'sound popular feelings'.[18]

One should be careful, however, not to push this point too far, as some other historians have done. It is self-evident that Nazi terror against some social groups gained more popular support than against others. Thus, millions of German workers did not applaud the destruction of the organised left. Also, the Nazi assault on outsiders was only one of many determinants of public opinion in the Third Reich, and it was not among the most important. For example, notwithstanding the public terror against the left and 'professional criminals', the Nazi regime still faced widespread dissatisfaction and criticism in the spring of 1934, brought about by economic crisis and disillusionment with the Nazi 'revolution'.[19]

The regime was not publicising terror merely to court the public. An excessive emphasis on this aspect downplays another, ultimately more important, public role of Nazi terror: deterrence. This had long been regarded as a key part of punishment, and in the Third Reich, this traditional method of control was increasingly harnessed as a weapon of repression. Reports about Nazi terror always carried a warning to the rest of the population. At times, this was made absolutely plain, with posters announcing death sentences with the threat: 'Let this punishment be a warning to you.' The overall result was an atmosphere of menace. No doubt, the threat posed by the Gestapo and the concentration camps was foremost in people's minds, while courts and penal institutions were probably regarded as less arbitrary and dangerous. But the legal apparatus still helped to intimidate the population. This was true, in particular, of the People's Court and the special courts, presented in the Nazi press as swift and ruthless instruments of punishment. State Secretary Freisler noted with approval that the belief 'Woe betide those who come before the special court!' was deeply held among the German population.[20] Of course, this did not mean that all Germans were living in terror. Nor were they deterred from breaking the law. Especially during the later stages of the war, even the threat of murderous punishment could not stop many Germans from stealing or looting to improve their lot. Even so, anxiety among the population was widespread.

This raises another fundamental point about Nazi terror. This book has focused mainly on the reality of this terror, as far as it can be reconstructed. But this was, of course, not identical to the picture projected by the regime. The popular image of legal terror, disseminated in the public sphere, was in large part a propaganda construct. The Nazi authorities tried hard to mould the public perception of law and terror, for example, by strictly controlling reports about court cases.[21] Certain cases were picked out and highlighted, while others were downplayed or ignored. The often considerable gap between legal terror and its public image can be illustrated by an analysis of the sentences of the People's Court and their representation in the Nazi media, focusing on the period between September 1939 and February 1944. In this time, over 70 per cent of the articles in the *Völkischer Beobachter* about defendants sentenced by the People's Court featured Germans born inside the Altreich – even though they made up less than 20 per cent of those actually sentenced. The discrepancy between representation and reality is equally evident when looking at the charges made against these German defendants. Half of them were convicted of left-wing resistance, but only 4 per cent of the newspaper articles dealt with these types of offence – a clear sign that the regime was no longer overly concerned with deterrence against the left. Instead, some 32 per cent of the articles dealt with cases of 'undermining the war effort', exceeding the proportion of defendants actually punished for this offence by more than half. Finally, while around half of all defendants were sentenced to death at the height of the judges' murderous rage (1942–4), all except one of the cases reported in the *Völkischer Beobachter* during the war had resulted in a death sentence.[22] The conclusion is clear: media reports about the People's Court were used to heighten the terrorist pressure on the general population, suggesting that dissent was frequently uncovered and punished with death. All this made it more difficult for the German population accurately to gauge the threat they faced if they did step out of line.

Finally, denunciations require a very brief look. Some recent work on Nazi terror has stressed that the police tended to be reactive, acting on information from the outside, above all from 'ordinary Germans'. Voluntary denunciations by private citizens were indeed an important aspect of terror throughout the Third Reich. Such denunciations proved crucial in the enforcement of various rules regulating private lives. Contacts between Germans and Jews or foreign workers, listening to foreign radio and grumbling about the regime – persecution of all these 'offences' inevitably relied to a significant extent on private denunciations. But this does not apply to other aspects of Nazi terror. For example, civilian denunciations were often peripheral in cases against the organised left-wing resistance, Jehovah's Witnesses, 'professional criminals', homosexuals and many 'asocials'. Here, the German police took a proactive role, surveying suspects, raiding premises, arresting suspects and beating confessions out of them.[23] In sum, the relative importance of private denunciations varied greatly, depending on the type of 'offence' and 'offender'. This is also illustrated by court cases. At the People's Court, only about 20 per cent of cases against the organised German resistance had been initiated by private individuals, as opposed to more than 75 per cent of cases against defendants guilty of making 'defeatist' remarks.[24]

It should also be stressed that most Germans were not willing denouncers. Some recent literature comes rather close to replacing the myth of the ever-present Gestapo with the myth of the ever-present denouncer. But the total number of denouncers made up only a rather small section of the German population. Millions of potential offences – which would have resulted in arrest, trial, prison, camp and execution – were never reported by 'ordinary Germans'. A determined minority of willing denouncers was enough to maintain pressure on the population as a whole. The picture of a self-policing society also tends to underestimate the role played by the state apparatus in Nazi terror. After all, it was only when the state made its 'offer of denunciation', that essentially trivial talk became a basis for state terror.[25] Speaking more broadly, we need to remind ourselves that Hitler and the Nazi leadership, the police and legal officials, alongside other state and party bureaucrats, were ultimately much more important in the creation and perpetuation of Nazi terror than the general population.

Hitler and the Legal Officials

Hitler was a vital force in shaping terror inside Germany. This was true, above all, of the police and SS apparatus. Hitler backed them throughout the Third Reich, and he remained in close contact with Himmler about questions of repression inside Germany.[26] Naturally, given his antipathy to the legal 'bureaucracy' and his support for Himmler, his relationship to the legal system was more fraught. But this did not stop him from exercising a crucial role in legal terror, too. Hitler's influence was felt in many different ways. Several of his actions and pronouncements gave broad indications of his vision for the legal system. From the start, Hitler made it clear that he expected the brutal punishment of all 'enemies' of the Nazi state. And during the war, he hammered home the message that rigid discipline had to be maintained on the home front to prevent another revolution like that of 1918. The trauma of 1918, central to Hitler's thinking, justified the most ruthless measures in his eyes. Regarding imprisonment, Hitler favoured harsh treatment, except for offenders who had merely 'tripped up'. He also showed an interest in exploiting prison labour for the ideological aims of the regime and gave public support to the notoriously brutal Emsland prison camp. Hitler's actions and public statements set the general parameters for the activities of the legal officials. All over Germany, they turned into concrete policy what they saw as Hitler's 'will', taking it as a guideline for penal policy and sentencing. The result was the intensification of legal terror. All this was clearly a case of what historians have called 'working towards the Führer' or 'anticipated obedience'.[27] The essence of this concept was already well understood at the time. As Hans Frank exclaimed at a 1936 mass congress for German jurists: 'Ask yourself with every decision you take: how would the Führer decide in my place?'[28]

This dynamic can be seen at work in the aftermath of Hitler's criticism of the legal system in the Reichstag on 26 April 1942. Hitler's attack itself had been brief and rather general. But its impact was considerable. Legal officials everywhere sprang into action, frantically searching for ways to overcome the 'crisis of the judiciary' and to remove, once and for all, the stigma of bureaucratic inefficiency and weakness. The Reich Ministry of Justice and regional legal authorities looked for different measures to ensure even stricter punishment, and also tried to convince Hitler of the economic importance of prison labour. Meanwhile, German judges started to apply the death penalty more often than ever before. There can be no doubt that this was exactly what Hitler had intended, at a time when he felt that repression on the home front had to become more vigorous. In this, as in a number of other cases, Hitler deliberately encouraged others to work towards him. After all, his threat in the Reichstag had not been a sudden outburst but was planned in advance. It was one way for him personally to 'guide' the legal officials.

At other times, Hitler went further than merely giving broad indications of his wishes and obsessions. Typically, he would demand a certain policy in different degrees of detail, leaving his subordinates to work out the practicalities, before giving his final stamp of approval. This pattern resulted in several new pieces of legislation, including the Nuremberg Laws. In prison policy, too, some initiatives originated from Hitler, as we have seen. A good example of this is the 'annihilation through labour' of 'asocial' prisoners. Hitler's personal involvement began with his decision to appoint the reliable Nazi Otto-Georg Thierack as the new Reich Minister of Justice, who was expected to pursue a radical line. Then, on the day of Thierack's appointment, Hitler told him in no uncertain terms that the current 'preservation' of 'total crook[s]' inside penal institutions would have catastrophic consequences. Of course, this still left much to the initiative of others, with Thierack and Himmler working out the details. Crucially, though, their agreement then went back to Hitler. Only after he had given the green light – confirming that the proposed mass extermination of 'asocial' prisoners was indeed in line with his wishes – could the killing begin. Hitler remained the ultimate arbiter.

Finally, Hitler made a significant number of direct and detailed interventions in the legal sphere, becoming involved in individual court proceedings and prison matters. He had the power to pardon political prisoners sentenced for treason, and he also used his authority to ensure the early release of numerous Nazi activists behind bars. Even while he was directing the German army on the battlefields across Europe, he repeatedly took time to ensure that individual criminal offenders, who he felt had received too lenient court sentences, were executed. Of course, the impact of these direct interventions went far beyond the individual cases Hitler chose to become involved in. Hitler's actions also intensified the determination of the legal officials to anticipate his 'will' better in future. This dual function was obvious in the Schlitt case in 1942 (see Chapter 5). Not only did Hitler's furious intervention prompt the legal authorities to change one particular sentence from imprisonment to death, but it also intensified attempts to push for harsher sentences in general, as we have just seen. Clearly, then, Hitler was a crucial factor in legal terror.

But narrowing our vision to Hitler alone would produce a completely unbalanced picture. Legal terror amounted to more than the realisation of Hitler's demands. The initiative of legal officials themselves, both in Berlin and the regions, was also of great importance. True, by no means all of the German legal officials were involved in this terror. But many thousands were. After the war, much was made of the positivist tradition in German jurisprudence, which had supposedly made it impossible for judges and other legal personnel to resist Nazi injustice. Used to slavishly following the letter of law, whatever it might be, they had merely done what they had been trained to do. While this claim has been accepted by some historians, the active support of legal officials for many different aspects of repression – at times in actual breach of the law – shows that the 'positivism tale' was largely designed to excuse the involvement of legal officials in Nazi crimes.[29] The legal officials were allowed considerable room for their own initiative, not least because Hitler's interventions often remained too unsystematic and vague to provide detailed guidance. While actively interpreting Hitler's 'will', they also pushed their own policies.

Officials in the Reich Ministry of Justice in Berlin played a key role in shaping legal terror, drafting legislation, appointing officials, monitoring court decisions, sending out instructions to general state prosecutors, and so on. The prison department in the ministry was also buzzing with activity, laying down and enforcing a vast array of rules and guidelines for life inside penal institutions. Some of these activities were responses to pressures from Hitler or agencies such as the police. However, the ministerial officials were also proactive, pursuing their own objectives. In a few instances, at least before the war, they even went against Hitler's wishes, burying his call for the sterilisation of criminals and ignoring his decision that certain security-confined prisoners should be left to the police. Regional and local legal officials were also fuelling the escalation of legal repression. Despite growing attempts by the Reich Ministry of Justice to direct individual judges, they continued to possess significant power – not least because the wording of the new legislation was often opaque, leaving much discretion to the judges. Inevitably, sentences did not always conform to the wishes of the top brass in Berlin. Some courts were seen as not being radical enough, triggering renewed demands from above for more brutal sentences. But at other times, individual judges used their powers to push the law considerably further than the officials in Berlin had anticipated. For example, the German courts passed close to 10,000 sentences of security confinement between 1934 and 1939 – ten times the figure envisaged by Reich Minister Franz Gürtner when the measure was first introduced.

In penal institutions, the power exercised by local governors, doctors, teachers, chaplains and warders was striking. The general guidelines by the prison administration left much room for their enterprise. The treatment of individual groups of inmates was shaped to a significant extent by the whims of local officials, but their influence extended far beyond the mere confinement of inmates. Local prison officials reported inmates to the courts for sterilisation and for retrospective sentencing to security confinement and castration. In several cases, the prison officials also denounced prisoners for having made anti-Nazi remarks, ensuring further sentences. In addition, local prison officials passed on details about the inmates to the police, sometimes openly recommending their transfer to police custody after their judicial imprisonment. During the war, the power of the local officials increased still further. Most importantly, many came to play a prominent role in the mass murder of prisoners. Local prison officials were closely involved in turning penal institutions into sites for assembly-line executions of individuals sentenced to death by the legal courts. At the same time, the prison officials took an active part in designating other convicts for extermination. Without their eagerness, many thousands of inmates would have survived the war.

The activity of legal officials – judges, prosecutors, prison officials and others – was pivotal for the enforcement of terror in the Third Reich. It should be stressed again that many were not die-hard Nazi activists, but experienced practitioners who had already been working in the legal service in the Weimar years. Clearly, it was not necessary to be a fanatical Nazi to push for the brutal punishment of Communists, Jews or 'asocials'. The same was true, of course, for many other German officials, including scores of policemen, doctors, social workers, army officers and others who helped to hold together the Nazi web of terror.

So why did so many legal officials become involved in repression, ignoring basic tenets of justice and helping to demolish the rule of law? There was no one single cause. Certainly, pressures by other agencies of the Nazi dictatorship played their part. Hitler was a strong influence, as were the escalating police actions. Equally important was the brutalisation caused by the policy of extermination directed at Jews and the mentally ill in particular. But legal terror was not simply a response to such developments. Many legal officials genuinely believed that the ruthless punishment of 'community aliens' was imperative, and were keen to make use of the new powers available to them in the Nazi era. In a way, the regime freed these officials from earlier constraints and opened the door to more radical initiatives. Before the war, there was already a considerable overlap in the field of law enforcement between the broad aims of the Nazi leadership and those of the largely national-conservative legal officials. Both agreed, for instance, on the authoritarian approach to 'habitual criminals' and the need for the destruction of the left. During the war, many legal officials felt that it was only right that punishment should become even more merciless. Often, they were veterans of the First World War, desperate to make a contribution to the German war effort. As two historians have recently concluded, the officials 'wanted to fight at home with legal articles as weapons'.[30] Ministerial civil servants, judges, prosecutors and prison officials shared Hitler's view that brutal measures were necessary to prevent another 'stab in the back' on the home front. The spectre of 1918 provided a focal point for a wide range of racial, political and social prejudices and anxieties, around which even those legal officials who had never become unconditional supporters of the regime could rally. As the war slowly turned against Germany, these officials saw more and more signs which magnified their fears of another revolution: public morale deteriorated markedly, for instance, and property crime shot up. This only heightened the determination of many officials to enforce ruthless discipline on the home front. The legal system continued to enforce terror to the end, propping up the Nazi regime until its final collapse.

Figures

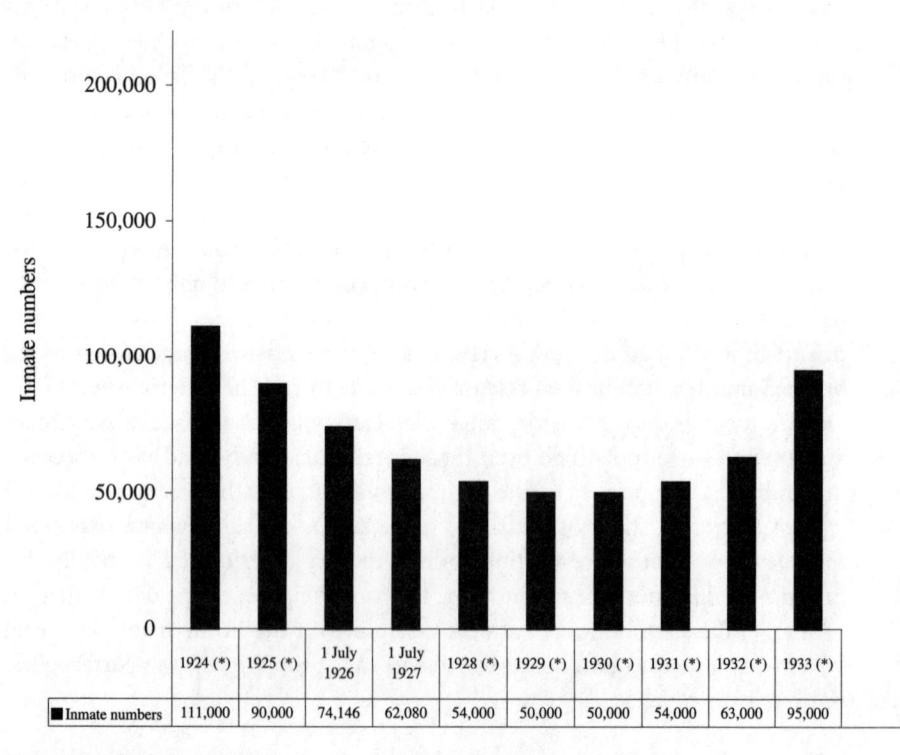

	1924 (*)	1925 (*)	1 July 1926	1 July 1927	1928 (*)	1929 (*)	1930 (*)	1931 (*)	1932 (*)	1933 (*)
■ Inmate numbers	111,000	90,000	74,146	62,080	54,000	50,000	50,000	54,000	63,000	95,000

Figure 1. Inmate numbers in German penal institutions, 1924–44

Sources: 'Statistik des Gefängniswesens im Deutschen Reich'; BA Berlin, R 3001/9882; ibid., R 3001/9920/2; ibid., R 3001/alt R 22/1417; ibid., R 3001/alt R 22/897.
(*) = estimated annual daily figure, based on the average number of inmates inside Prussian penal institutions; see *Statistik über die Gefangenenanstalten in Preußen 1924, 1928–9*; Edgar Schmidt, 'Statistik'; idem, 'Kosten'.

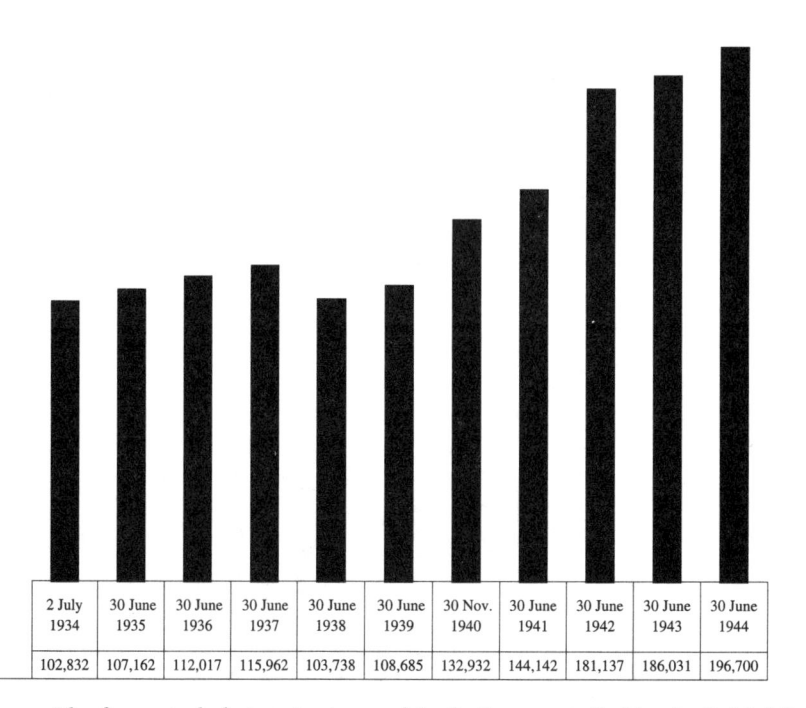

2 July 1934	30 June 1935	30 June 1936	30 June 1937	30 June 1938	30 June 1939	30 Nov. 1940	30 June 1941	30 June 1942	30 June 1943	30 June 1944
102,832	107,162	112,017	115,962	103,738	108,685	132,932	144,142	181,137	186,031	196,700

The figures include inmates in penal institutions controlled by the Reich Ministry of Justice. From 1939, the figures include inmates in Austria (judicial districts Graz, Innsbruck, Linz and Vienna), the Sudetenland (Leitmeritz district) and the Memel area. From 1940, they include inmates in Eastern European territory incorporated into Nazi Germany (largely in the new Danzig, Kattowitz and Posen judicial districts). From 1941, they include inmates in Prague, as well as Alsace-Lorraine and Luxemburg. From 1943, they include inmates in the camp North in Norway. For 1944, they include inmates in camp West in France.

Figures

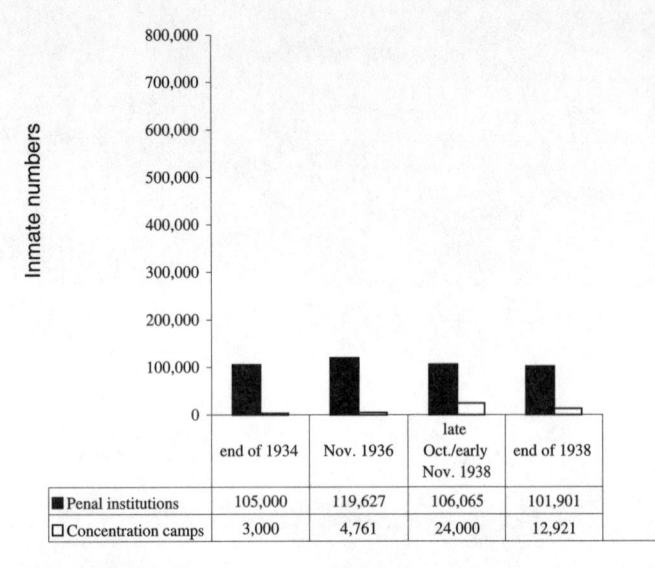

Figure 2. Inmate numbers (per day) in German penal institutions and SS concentration camps, 1934–45 (selected dates)

	end of 1934	Nov. 1936	late Oct./early Nov. 1938	end of 1938
Penal institutions	105,000	119,627	106,065	101,901
Concentration camps	3,000	4,761	24,000	12,921

Sources: BA Berlin, R 3001/9882; ibid., R 3001/9920/2; ibid., R 3001/alt R 22/897; Orth, *System*, 32, 51, 53, 97, 192, 222.

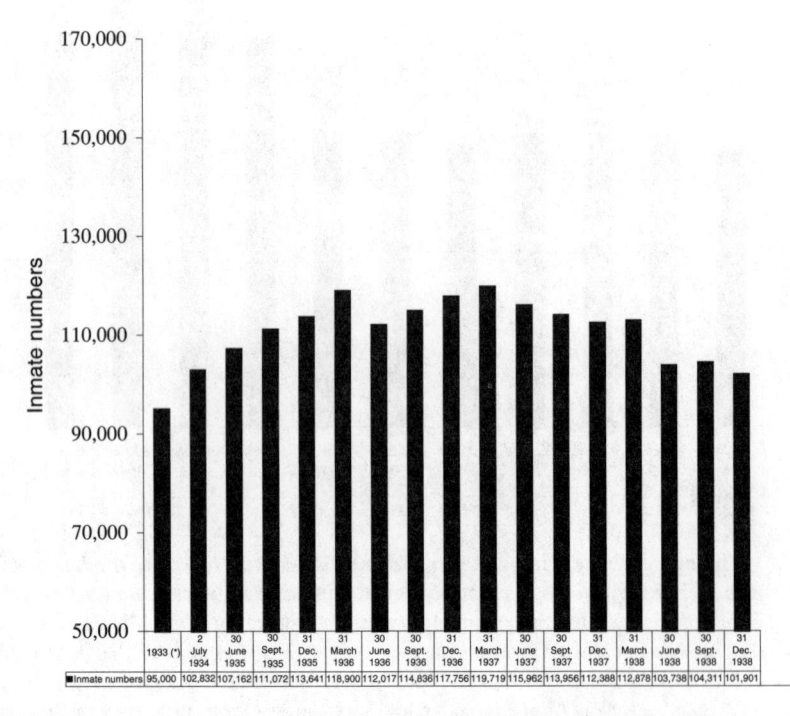

Figure 3. Inmate numbers in penal institutions in the Altreich, 1933–44

Date	Inmate numbers
1933 (*)	95,000
2 July 1934	102,832
30 June 1935	107,162
30 Sept. 1935	111,072
31 Dec. 1935	113,641
31 March 1936	118,900
30 June 1936	112,017
30 Sept. 1936	114,836
31 Dec. 1936	117,756
31 March 1937	119,719
30 June 1937	115,962
30 Sept. 1937	113,956
31 Dec. 1937	112,388
31 March 1938	112,878
30 June 1938	103,738
30 Sept. 1938	104,311
31 Dec. 1938	101,901

Sources: BA Berlin, R 3001/9882; ibid., R 3001/9920/2; ibid., R 3001/alt 22/1417; ibid., R 3001/alt 22/897.
(*) = estimate.

Figures 395

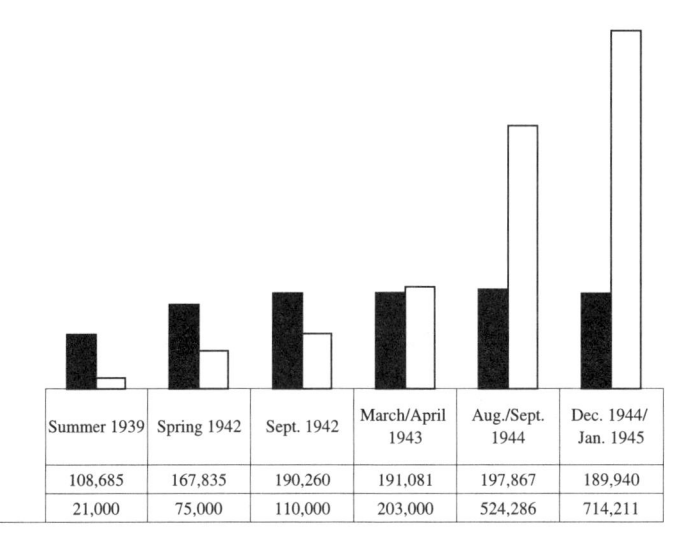

Summer 1939	Spring 1942	Sept. 1942	March/April 1943	Aug./Sept. 1944	Dec. 1944/ Jan. 1945
108,685	167,835	190,260	191,081	197,867	189,940
21,000	75,000	110,000	203,000	524,286	714,211

The figures for the camps include only those camps under the SS Inspection of the Concentration Camps (IKL). The figure for spring 1942 is an estimate. The figures for penal institutions refer to the following dates: 30 Nov. 1936, 31 Oct. 1938, 31 Dec. 1938, 30 June 1939, 31 March 1942, 30 Sept. 1942, 31 March 1943, 30 Sept. 1943, 30 Sept. 1944, 30 Dec. 1944. The figure for the end of 1934 is an estimate.

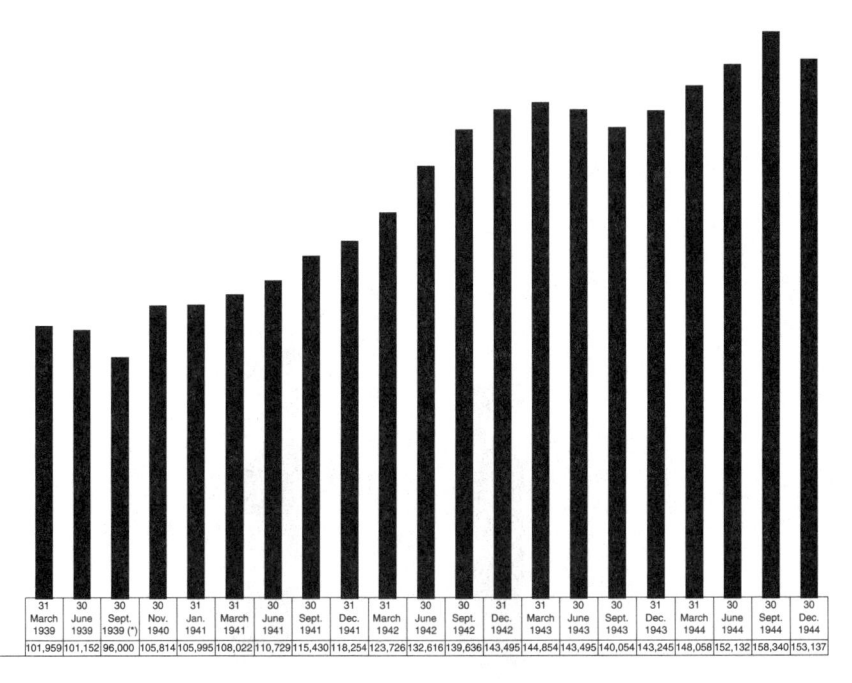

31 March 1939	30 June 1939	30 Sept. 1939 (*)	30 Nov. 1940	31 Jan. 1941	31 March 1941	30 June 1941	30 Sept. 1941	31 Dec. 1941	31 March 1942	30 June 1942	30 Sept. 1942	31 Dec. 1942	31 March 1943	30 June 1943	30 Sept. 1943	31 Dec. 1943	31 March 1944	30 June 1944	30 Sept. 1944	30 Dec. 1944
101,959	101,152	96,000	105,814	105,995	108,022	110,729	115,430	118,254	123,726	132,616	139,636	143,495	144,854	143,495	140,054	143,245	148,058	152,132	158,340	153,137

The figures include inmates in penal institutions controlled by the Reich Ministry of Justice inside the German borders up to 1937, plus the Leitmeritz district (from June 1939) and parts of the Danzig and Kattowitz districts (from March 1943). During the war, three former Polish penal institutions were added to the Königsberg judicial district.

Figures

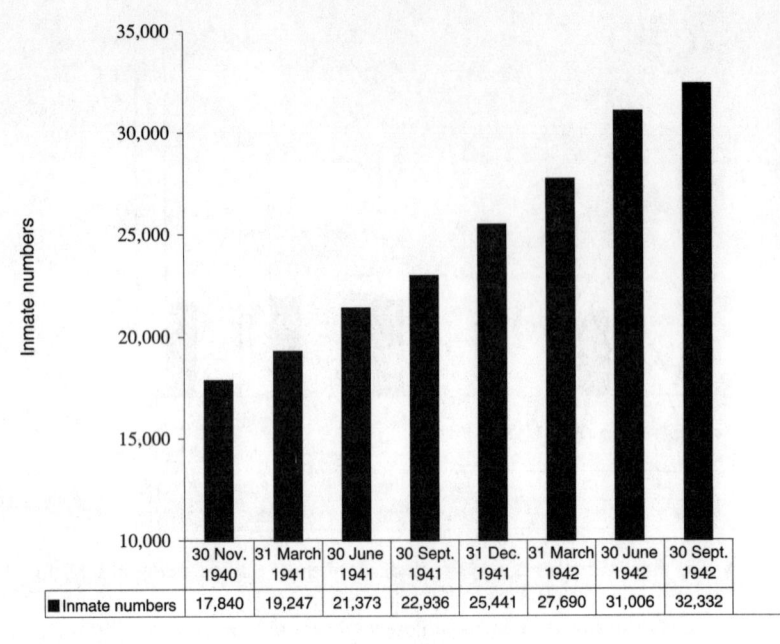

Date	Inmate numbers
30 Nov. 1940	17,840
31 March 1941	19,247
30 June 1941	21,373
30 Sept. 1941	22,936
31 Dec. 1941	25,441
31 March 1942	27,690
30 June 1942	31,006
30 Sept. 1942	32,332

Figure 4. Inmate numbers in penal institutions in the incorporated territory in Eastern Europe, 1940–44

Sources: BA Berlin, R 3001/alt R 22/1417; ibid., R 3001/alt R 22/897.

Figures include inmates held in penal institutions controlled by the Reich Ministry of Justice in the Danzig, Kattowitz, Posen and Königsberg (East) districts. The judicial districts

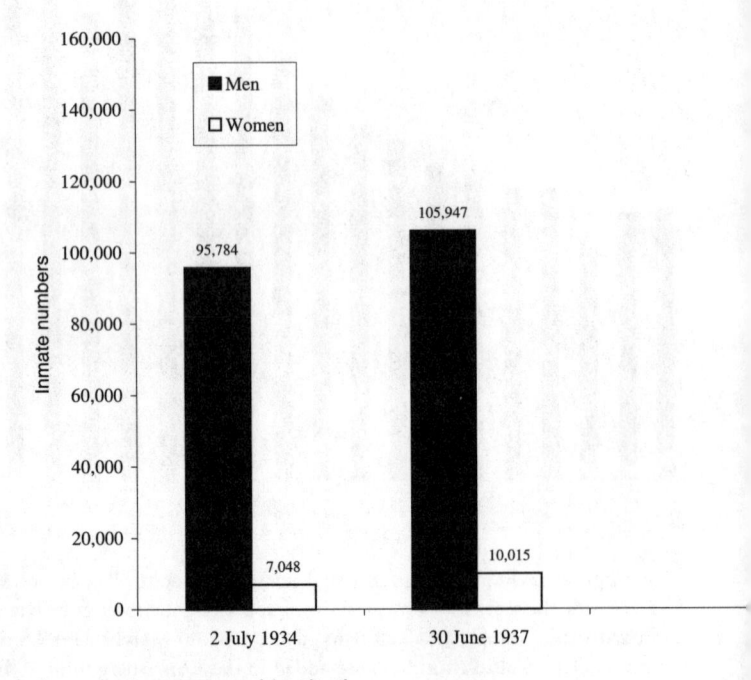

Date	Men	Women
2 July 1934	95,784	7,048
30 June 1937	105,947	10,015

Figure 5. Gender balance in German penal institutions, 1934–43

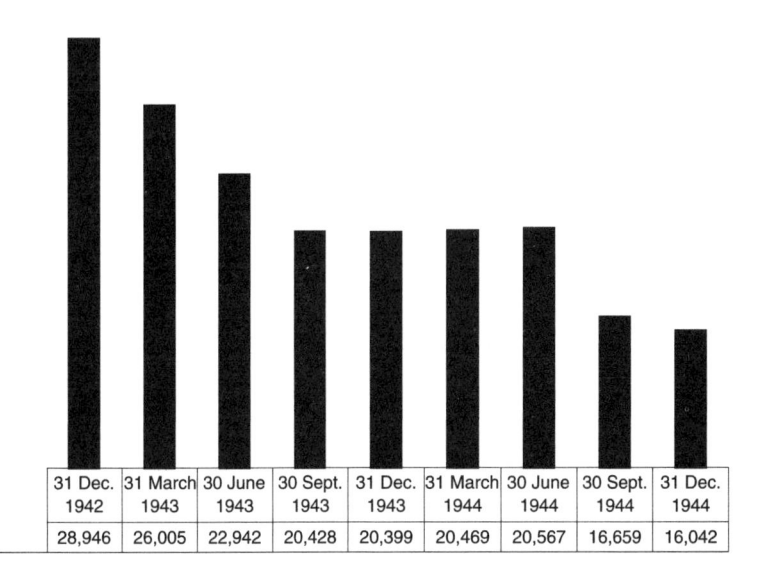

31 Dec. 1942	31 March 1943	30 June 1943	30 Sept. 1943	31 Dec. 1943	31 March 1944	30 June 1944	30 Sept. 1944	31 Dec. 1944
28,946	26,005	22,942	20,428	20,399	20,469	20,567	16,659	16,042

in the incorporated territories did not completely overlap with the old border. For example, the Kattowitz judicial district included six penal institutions previously administered in the Breslau (Altreich) district. And from 31 March 1943, the figures not longer include several thousand prisoners in parts of the Danzig and Kattowitz judicial district.

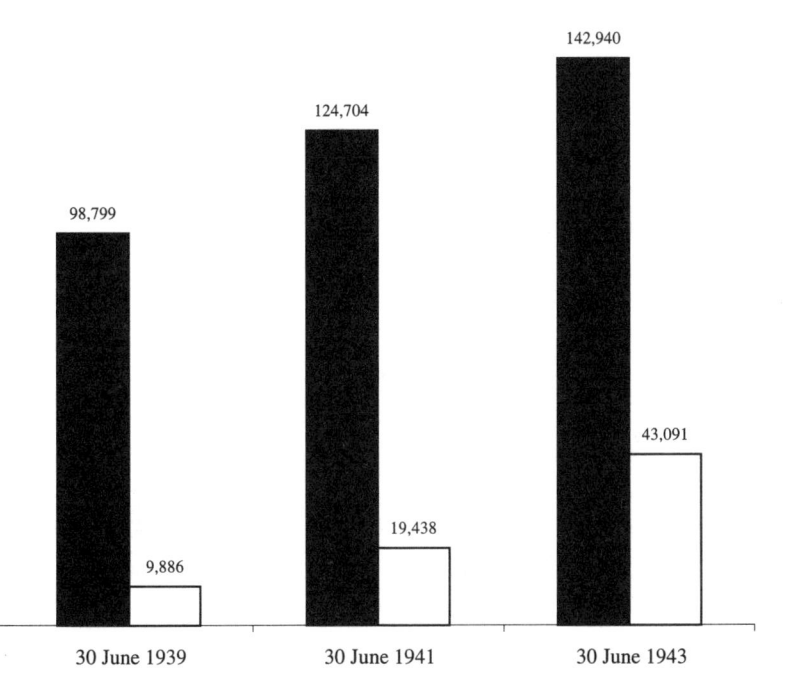

	30 June 1939	30 June 1941	30 June 1943
	98,799	124,704	142,940
	9,886	19,438	43,091

Sources: BA Berlin, R 3001/9882; ibid., R 3001/alt 22/1417; ibid., R 3001/alt 22/897.

398 Figures

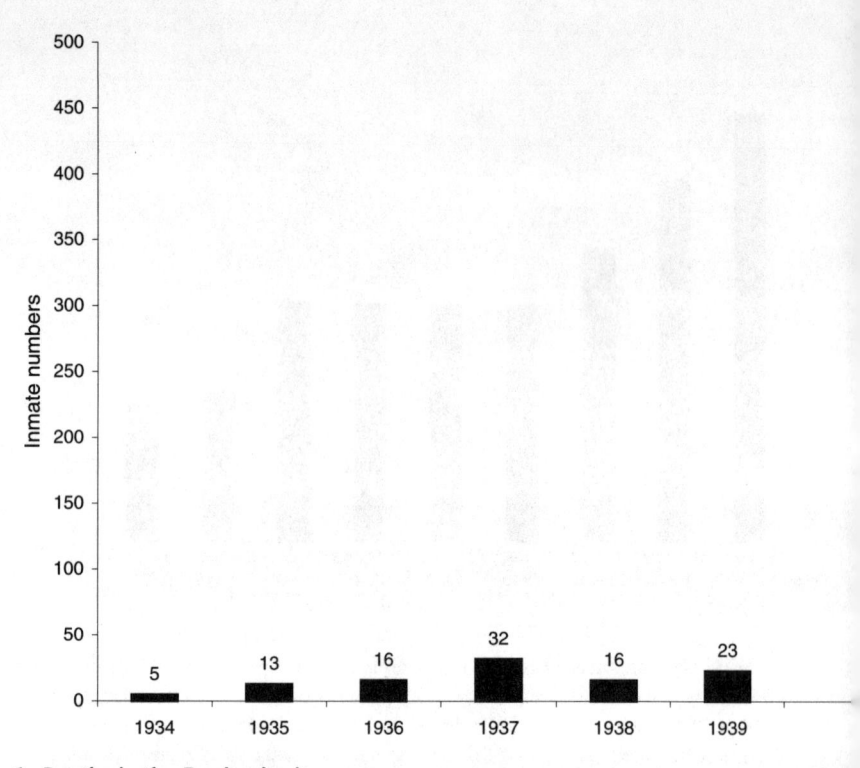

Figure 6. Deaths in the Emsland prison camp, 1934–45

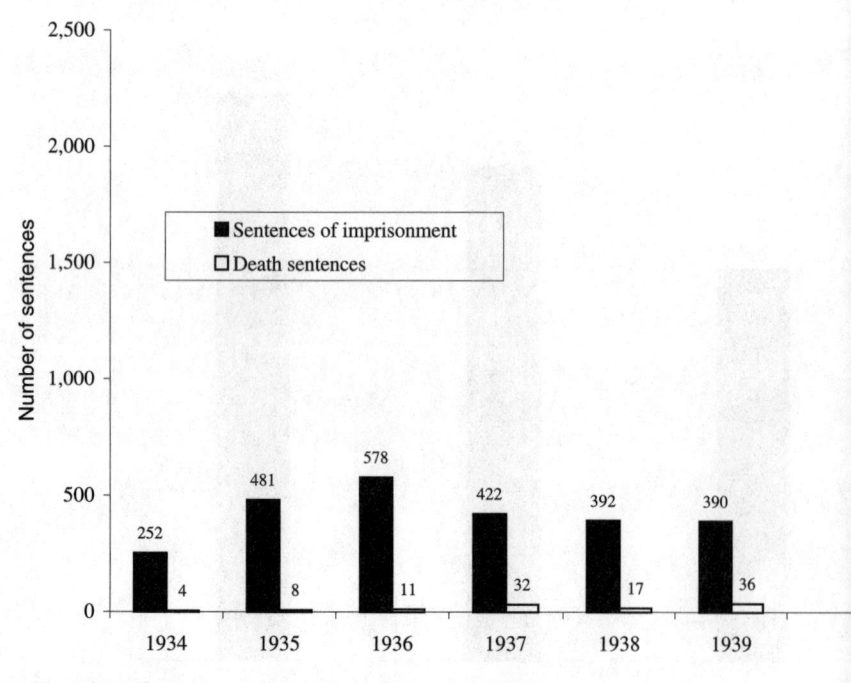

Year	Inmate numbers
1934	5
1935	13
1936	16
1937	32
1938	16
1939	23

Figure 7. Number of sentences by the People's Court, 1934–45

Year	Sentences of imprisonment	Death sentences
1934	252	4
1935	481	8
1936	578	11
1937	422	32
1938	392	17
1939	390	36

Source: Schlüter, *Urteilspraxis,* 38.

Figures 399

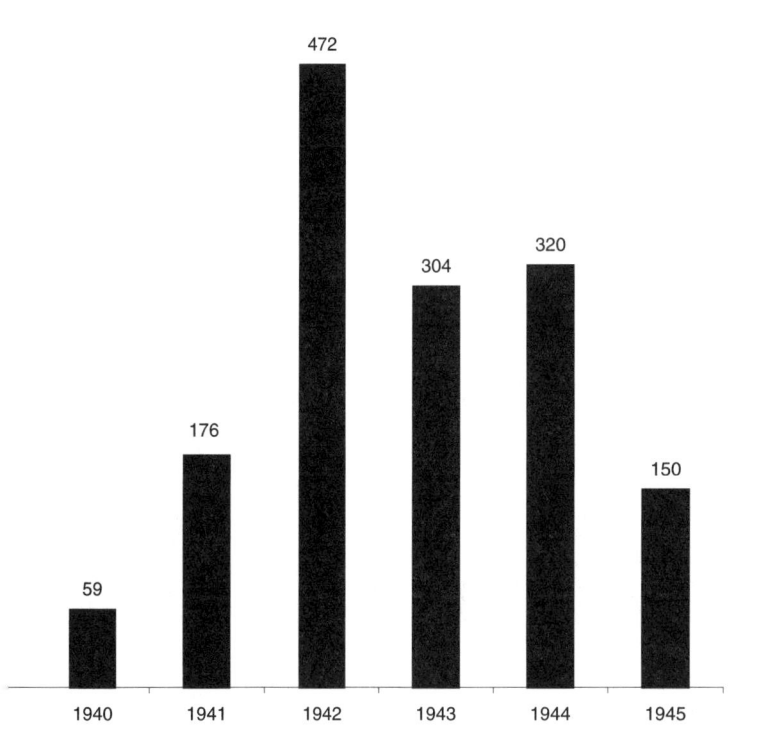

Source: Kosthorst, Walter (eds), *Strafgefangenenlager*, vol. 3, 3552.

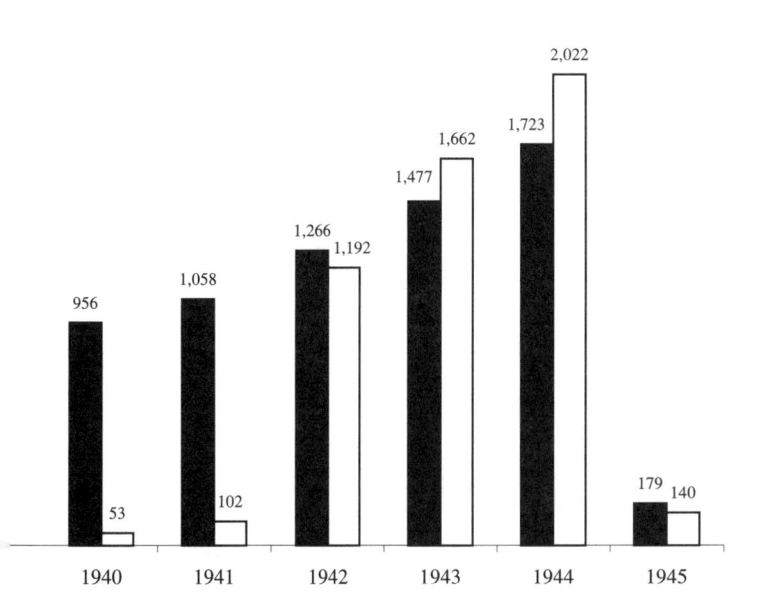

The figures cover sentences by the trial court, excluding decisions by the Special Senate. The figures for 1934–36 and 1945 are based on postwar results from the research project on the People's Court, and are given as the minimum number of sentences possible.

400 Figures

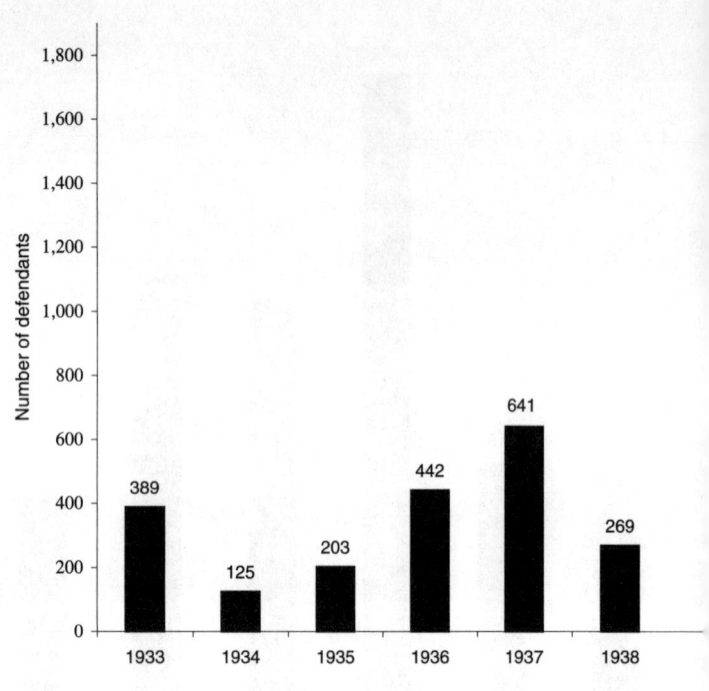

Figure 8. Number of defendants before the special courts in Frankfurt am Main, Braunschweig and Düsseldorf, 1933–45

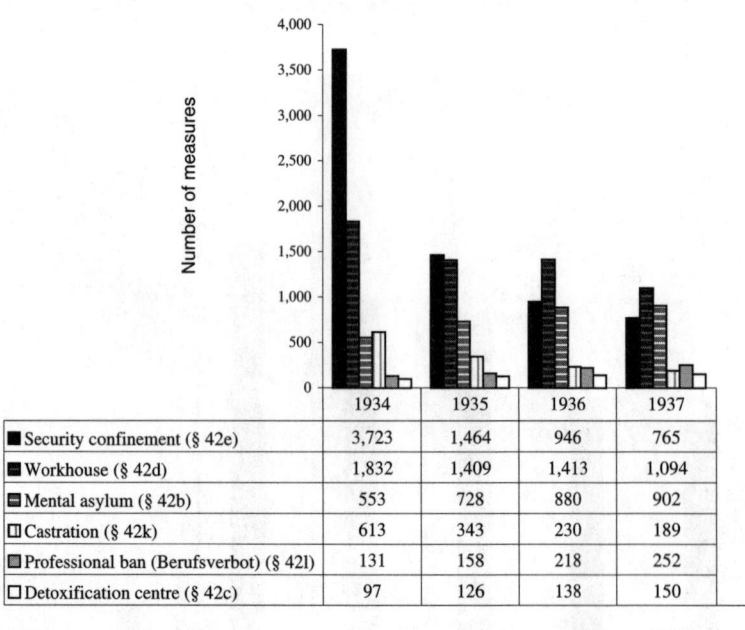

	1934	1935	1936	1937
■ Security confinement (§ 42e)	3,723	1,464	946	765
■ Workhouse (§ 42d)	1,832	1,409	1,413	1,094
■ Mental asylum (§ 42b)	553	728	880	902
☐ Castration (§ 42k)	613	343	230	189
■ Professional ban (Berufsverbot) (§ 42l)	131	158	218	252
☐ Detoxification centre (§ 42c)	97	126	138	150

Figure 9. 'Preventive and rehabilitative measures' (based on the Habitual Criminals Law) ordered by German courts, 1934–43

Sources: Kriminalstatistik 1935 und 1936, 18, 26, 34; BA Berlin, R 3001/alt R 22/1160, Bl. 25–66: Statistisches Reichsamt, Entwicklung der Kriminalität.

Figures 401

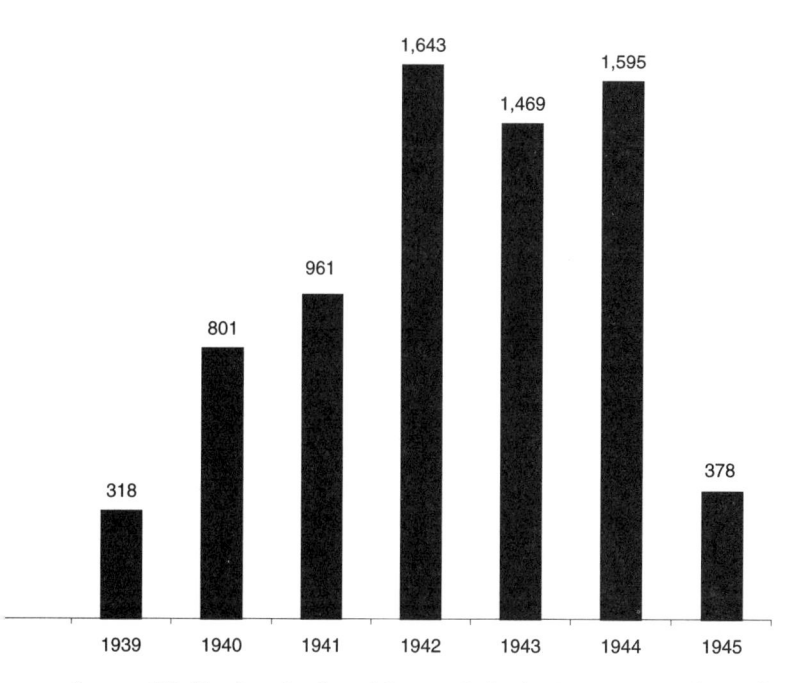

	1939	1940	1941	1942	1943	1944	1945
	318	801	961	1,643	1,469	1,595	378

Sources: Weckbecker, *Sondergerichte*, 65; Ludewig, Kuessner, *Sondergericht Braunschweig*, 38–9; Schmidt, *Oberlandesgerichtsbezirk Düsseldorf*, 152.

The figures are based on the documentation still available in the archives today. Naturally, the number of undocumented cases is unknown.

1938	1939	1940	1941	1942	1943
964	1,827	1,929	1,658	1,423	1,130
1,026	729	528	414	400	400
992	1,087	1,048	917	912	900
195	238	198	153	152	120
269	294	263	340	298	260
148	226	171	158	91	40

The figures for 1934–39 miss out the extremely small number of sentences by the People's Court. Apparently, they also miss out the few sentences by the special courts (Müller, *Gewohnheitsverbrechergesetz*, 53), which may also be true for the wartime figures. The 1942 figures exclude Czechs, as well as Poles and Jews sentenced under the Criminal Law Decree of 4 December 1941. The 1943 figures are estimates based on the statistics for the first half of the year only. They are also incomplete and only include German defendants.

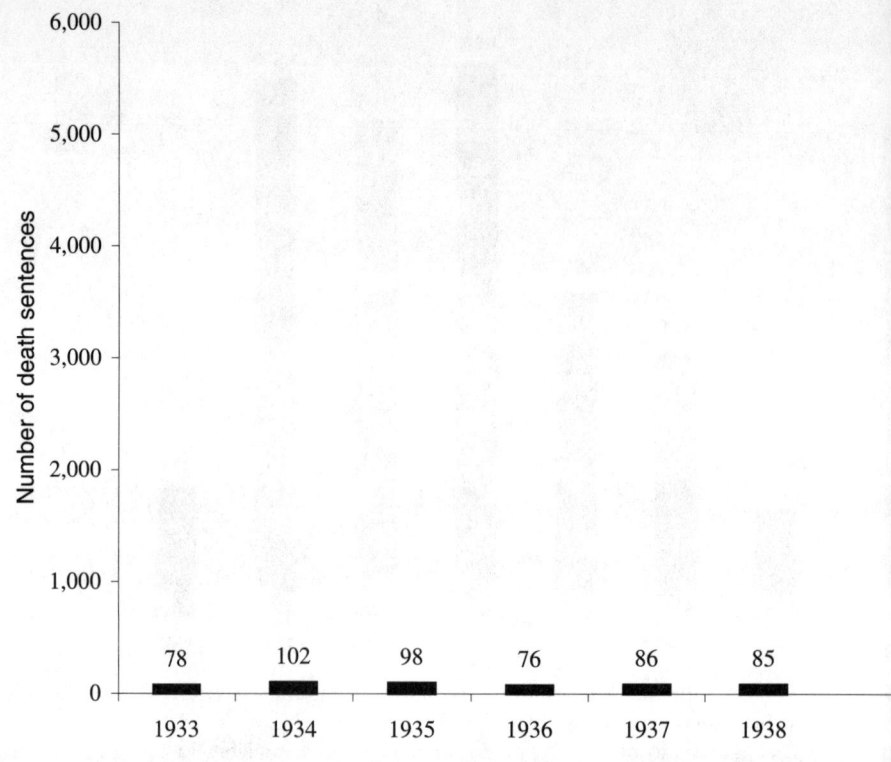

Figure 10. Number of death sentences by judicial courts in the territory of the Third Reich, 1933–45

1933	1934	1935	1936	1937	1938
78	102	98	76	86	85

Source: Düsing, *Abschaffung*, 209–20; BA Berlin, R 3001/alt R 22/1160, Bl. 48.

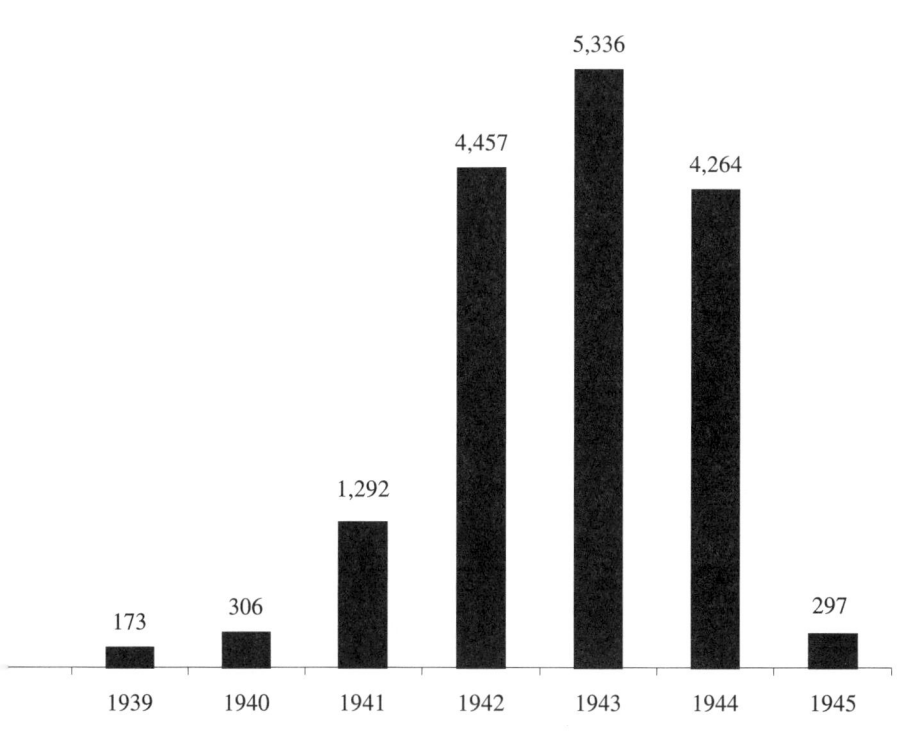

Year	Count
1939	173
1940	306
1941	1,292
1942	4,457
1943	5,336
1944	4,264
1945	297

The figures for 1933–40 are taken from the official criminal statistics, and include death sentences by the People's Court. The figures for 1941 and 1943 are based on information drawn up by Reich Minister of Justice Thierack in 1944. The figures for 1942, 1944 and 1945 are estimates based on the number of executions carried out by Johann Reichhart, one of the three established German executioners at the time.

Notes

Introduction

1. The exclusive control by the legal system over the prison did not have a long tradition in some German states. For example, control over Prussian penal institutions had been divided until 1 April 1918 between the Ministry of Justice and the Ministry of the Interior; Schwandner, 'Das Ende des Dualismus im preußischen Gefängniswesen', *BlGefK* 52 (1918), 47–60.
2. In this text, generic terms such as 'prison', 'prisoners', 'convicts' and 'prison officials' mostly refer to penal institutions in general (in other words to prisons, penitentiaries and prison camps). Exceptions are marked in the text. Prisoners under the authority of agencies other than the legal apparatus are clearly differentiated, for example, by terms such as 'police detainees' or 'concentration camp inmates'. For the basic legal regulations, see *Strafgesetzbuch für das Deutsche Reich*, 31st edition (Leipzig, 1926). For a brief introduction to sentencing in Germany, see G. Wilke, 'The German Criminal Law', in H.C.B. Scott (ed.), *German Prisons in 1934* (Maidstone, 1936), 11–13. For the statistics, see *Kriminalstatistik 1935 und 1936* (Berlin, 1942), 16.
3. Most of the remaining inmates were remand prisoners (24,607). See BA Berlin, R 3001/9920/2, Bl. 1–2.
4. The figure for the number of inmates has been calculated without the Emsland prison camp. All statistics are based on the figures in Reichsjustizministerium (ed.), *Das Gefängniswesen in Deutschland* (Berlin, 1935), 35–42. Of the 167 'special institutions', 77 were combined prisons and remand prisons, 37 prisons, 22 penitentiaries (eight with additional wings for security confinement), with another 31 mixed institutions of one kind or another. Some, like Fuhlsbüttel in Hamburg, held prisoners, penitentiary inmates, remand prisoners and security-confined inmates, all at the same time. In addition to the 'special institutions', there were

another 982 smaller penal institutions, generally county jails attached to local courts. None of them had a full-time governor, because of their small size (almost 90 per cent were built to hold fewer than 50 prisoners).
5. See E. Goffman, *Asylums. Essays on the Social Situation of Mental Patients and Other Inmates* (Chicago, 1961).
6. E. Fraenkel, *The Dual State. A Contribution to the Theory of Dictatorship* (New York, 1969; first published 1941).
7. L. Gruchmann, *Justiz im Dritten Reich. Anpassung und Unterwerfung in der Ära Gürtner*, 2nd edition (Munich, 1990), *passim*, quotes on 535, 1124. For a brief summary of his views, see idem, 'Rechtssystem und nationalsozialistische Justizpolitik', in M. Broszat, H. Möller (eds), *Das Dritte Reich* (Munich, 1986), 83–103; idem, 'Die "rechtsprechende Gewalt" im nationalsozialistischen Herrschaftssystem', in W. Benz, H. Buchheim, H. Mommsen (eds), *Der Nationalsozialismus. Studien zur Ideologie und Herrschaft* (Frankfurt am Main, 1993), 78–103.
8. See, for example, E. Crankshaw, *Gestapo. Instrument of Tyranny* (London, 1956); J. Delarue, *Geschichte der Gestapo* (Düsseldorf, 1964).
9. R. Gellately, *Backing Hitler. Consent and Coercion in Nazi Germany* (Oxford, 2001), quotations on vii, 192, 231, 262. See also R. Gellately, *The Gestapo and German Society* (Oxford, 1991); idem, 'Allwissend und allgegenwärtig? Entstehung, Funktion und Wandel des Gestapo-Mythos', in G. Paul, K.-M. Mallmann (eds), *Die Gestapo. Mythos und Realität* (Darmstadt, 1995), 47–72; idem, 'Denunciations in Twentieth-Century Germany: Aspects of Self-Policing in the Third Reich and the German Democratic Republic', *Journal of Modern History* 68 (1996), 931–67.
10. For the most recent general contribution to this debate, see P. Panayi (ed.), *Weimar and Nazi Germany. Continuities and Discontinuities* (Harlow, 2001).
11. This chapter expands on my recent article 'Between Reform and Repression: Imprisonment in Weimar Germany', *The Historical Journal* 45 (2002), 411–32.
12. See, for example, I. Müller, *Furchtbare Juristen. Die unbewältigte Vergangenheit unserer Justiz* (Munich, 1989), 93–7.
13. Some material on sentencing and imprisonment was included in works published before and during the war by German émigrés. See, for example, G. Rusche, O. Kirchheimer, *Sozialstruktur und Strafvollzug* (Frankfurt am Main, 1981), first published in English in 1939.
14. See, for example, H.D. Quedenfeld, *Der Strafvollzug in der Gesetzgebung des Reiches, des Bundes und der Länder* (Tübingen, 1971); H. Schattke, *Die Geschichte der Progression im Strafvollzug und der damit zusammenhängenden Vollzugsziele in Deutschland* (Frankfurt am Main, 1979).
15. E. Kosthorst, B. Walter (eds), *Konzentrations- und Strafgefangenenlager im Dritten Reich: Beispiel Emsland*, 3 vols (Düsseldorf, 1983); E. Suhr, *Die Emslandlager. Die politische und wirtschaftliche Bedeutung der emsländischen Konzentrations- und Strafgefangenenlager 1933–1945* (Bremen, 1985).
16. See, for example, M. Habicht, *Zuchthaus Waldheim 1933–45. Haftbedingungen und antifaschistischer Kampf* (East Berlin, 1988).
17. For one example, see M. Frenzel, W. Thiele, A. Mannbar, *Gesprengte Fesseln* (East Berlin, 1975).
18. W. Sarodnick, ' "Dieses Haus muß ein Haus des Schreckens werden . . .". Strafvollzug in Hamburg 1933 bis 1945', in Justizbehörde Hamburg (ed.), *'Für Führer, Volk und Vaterland . . .'. Hamburger Justiz im Nationalsozialismus* (Hamburg, 1992), 332–81; K. Drobisch, 'Alltag im Zuchthaus Luckau 1933 bis 1939', in D. Eichholtz (ed.),

Brandenburg in der NS-Zeit (Berlin, 1993), 247–72; F. Maier, 'Strafvollzug im Gebiet des nördlichen Teiles von Rheinland-Pfalz im Dritten Reich', in Ministerium der Justiz Rheinland-Pfalz (ed.), *Justiz im Dritten Reich*, 2 vols (Frankfurt am Main, 1995), vol. 2, 851–945, 970–1006; E. Scharf, 'Strafvollzug in der Pfalz unter besonderer Berücksichtigung der JVA Zweibrücken', ibid., 757–849; K. Fricke, *Die Justizvollzugsanstalt 'Roter Ochse' Halle/Saale 1933–1945. Eine Dokumentation* (Magdeburg, 1997).

19. C. Dörner, *Erziehung durch Strafe. Die Geschichte des Jugendstrafvollzugs von 1871–1945* (Weinheim, 1991); B. Oleschinski, '"Ein letzter stärkender Gottesdienst . . .". Die deutsche Gefängnisseelsorge zwischen Republik und Diktatur 1918–1945' (Ph.D., Free University Berlin, 1993).

20. R. Möhler, 'Strafvollzug im "Dritten Reich": Nationale Politik und regionale Ausprägung am Beispiel des Saarlandes', in H. Jung, H. Müller-Dietz (eds), *Strafvollzug im 'Dritten Reich'. Am Beispiel des Saarlandes* (Baden-Baden, 1996), 9–301. For a much briefer overview, see C. Hottes, 'Grauen und Normalität. Zum Strafvollzug im Dritten Reich', in Oberstadtdirektor der Stadt Hamm (ed.), *Ortstermin Hamm. Zur Justiz im Dritten Reich* (Hamm, 1991), 63–70. See also the documentary collection Justizakademie des Landes Nordrhein-Westfalen (ed.), *Zum Strafvollzug 1933–1945 und seiner Vorgeschichte in der Weimarer Republik* (Recklinghausen, no date).

21. M. Broszat, 'Nationalsozialistische Konzentrationslager 1933–1945', in H. Buchheim et al. (eds), *Anatomie des SS-Staates* (Munich, 1994), 323–445, here 323.

22. For an overview of some of the literature, see U. Herbert et al. (eds), *Die nationalsozialistischen Konzentrationslager* (Göttingen, 1998), 2 vols. General studies include F. Pingel, *Häftlinge unter SS-Herrschaft* (Hamburg, 1978); J. Tuchel, *Konzentrationslager. Organisationsgeschichte und Funktion der 'Inspektion der Konzentrationslager' 1934–1938* (Boppard, 1991); W. Sofsky, *Die Ordnung des Terrors: Das Konzentrationslager* (Frankfurt am Main, 1997); K. Orth, *Das System der nationalsozialistischen Konzentrationslager* (Hamburg, 1999).

23. Quoted in J. Muntau, *Strafvollzug und Gefangenenfürsorge im Wandel der Zeit* (Bonn, 1962), 74.

24. One of the few historians to deal with criminals and the criminal police is Patrick Wagner. See his examplary study *Volksgemeinschaft ohne Verbrecher. Konzeptionen und Praxis der Kriminalpolizei in der Zeit der Weimarer Republik und des Nationalsozialismus* (Hamburg, 1996). For an effective local study of the criminal police in Cologne, see T. Roth, 'Die Kölner Kriminalpolizei', in H. Buhlan, W. Jung (eds), *Wessen Freund und wessen Helfer?: die Kölner Polizei im Nationalsozialismus* (Cologne, 2000), 299–366.

25. See, for example, T. Berger, *Die konstante Repression. Zur Geschichte des Strafvollzugs in Preußen nach 1850* (Frankfurt am Main, 1974); F. Mecklenburg, *Die Ordnung der Gefängnisse: Grundlinien der Gefängnisreform und Gefängniswissenschaft in der ersten Hälfte des 19. Jahrhunderts in Deutschland* (Berlin, 1983); T. Nutz, *Strafanstalt als Besserungsmaschine. Reformdiskurs und Gefängniswissenschaft 1775–1848* (Munich, 2001). For the discussion of the term 'rebirth', see N. Finzsch, 'Elias, Foucault, Oestreich: on a Historical Theory of Confinement', in idem, R. Jütte (eds), *Institutions of Confinement* (Cambridge, 1996), 3–16, esp. 8–13.

26. Good introductions to the history of punishment and the prison include P. Spierenburg, 'Four Centuries of Prison History', in Finzsch, Jütte (eds), *Institutions*, 17–38; N. Morris, D.J. Rothman (eds), *The Oxford History of the Prison* (New York, 1995).

27. M. Foucault, *Discipline and Punish. The Birth of the Prison* (London, 1991). Other important studies include M. Ignatieff, *A Just Measure of Pain. The Penitentiary in the Industrial Revolution 1750–1850* (London, 1978); D.J. Rothman, *The Discovery of the Asylum. Social Order and Disorder in the New Republic* (Boston, 1971).
28. See, for example, M. Broszat, 'Zur Perversion der Strafjustiz im Dritten Reich', *VfZ* 6 (1958), 390–443; I. Staff (ed.), *Justiz im Dritten Reich. Eine Dokumentation* (Frankfurt am Main, 1964); W. Johe, *Die gleichgeschaltete Justiz* (Frankfurt am Main, 1967).
29. H. Weinkauff, *Die deutsche Justiz und der Nationalsozialismus* (Stuttgart, 1968), 170. See also H. Schorn, *Der Richter im Dritten Reich. Geschichte und Dokumente* (Frankfurt am Main, 1959).
30. R. Angermund, *Deutsche Richterschaft 1919–1945* (Frankfurt am Main, 1990).
31. See, for example, Justizbehörde Hamburg (ed.), *'Für Führer, Volk und Vaterland...'*; Justizministerium des Landes NRW (ed.), *Justiz und Nationalsozialismus* (Düsseldorf, 1993); Ministerium der Justiz Rheinland-Pfalz (ed.), *Justiz im Dritten Reich* (Frankfurt am Main, 1995), 2 vols.
32. For the People's Court, see in particular K. Marxen, *Das Volk und sein Gerichtshof* (Frankfurt am Main, 1994); H. Schlüter, *Die Urteilspraxis des nationalsozialistischen Volksgerichtshofs* (Berlin, 1995). For regional districts, see above all H.-E. Niermann, *Die Durchsetzung politischer und politisierter Strafjustiz im Dritten Reich* (Düsseldorf, 1995). For some of the recent literature on special courts and related publications, see J. Zarusky, 'Gerichte des Unrechtsstaates', *Zeitschrift für neuere Rechtsgeschichte* 22 (2000), 503–18.
33. For example C. Müller, *Das Gewohnheitsverbrechergesetz vom 24. November 1933* (Baden-Baden, 1997); B. Dörner, *'Heimtücke'. Das Gesetz als Waffe: Kontrolle, Abschreckung und Verfolgung in Deutschland 1933–1945* (Paderborn, 1998). See also F. Kebbedies, *Außer Kontrolle. Jugendkriminalität in der NS-Zeit und der frühen Nachkriegszeit* (Essen, 2001).
34. Books first published in German include I. Müller, *Hitler's Justice* (London, 1991); H.W. Koch, *In the Name of the Volk. Political Justice in Hitler's Germany* (London, 1997); M. Stolleis, *The Law under the Swastika* (Chicago, 1998).
35. Among the most widely read is M. Burleigh, *The Third Reich. A New History* (London, 2000). See also the important documents and discussion in J. Noakes, G. Pridham (eds), *Nazism*, vol. 2 (Exeter, 1984), 471–89; J. Noakes (ed.), *Nazism*, vol. 4 (Exeter, 1998), 121–61.
36. These works include R.J. Evans, *Rituals of Retribution. Capital Punishment in Germany, 1600–1987* (London, 1997); R.F. Wetzell, *Inventing the Criminal. A History of German Criminology, 1880–1945* (Chapel Hill, 2000).
37. See, for example, Gellately, *Gestapo*; G. Browder, *Hitler's Enforcers. The Gestapo and the SS Security Service in the Nazi Revolution* (Oxford, 1996); E. Johnson, *The Nazi Terror. Gestapo, Jews & Ordinary Germans* (London, 2000). For a survey of the German literature on the Gestapo, see G. Paul, K.-M. Mallmann (eds), *Die Gestapo – Mythos und Realität* (Darmstadt, 1995); idem (eds), *Die Gestapo im Zweiten Weltkrieg* (Darmstadt, 2000).
38. For some of this literature, see B. Faralisch, '"Begreifen Sie erst jetzt, daß wir rechtlos sind?". Zeitzeugenberichte über den Strafvollzug im "Dritten Reich"', in H. Jung, H. Müller-Dietz (eds), *Strafvollzug im 'Dritten Reich'. Am Beispiel des Saarlandes* (Baden-Baden, 1996), 303–79.
39. For a good snapshot of the institution in English, see 'Strafanstalt Brandenburg', in Scott (ed.), *German Prisons*, 79–85. For files on its construction, see GStA PK, I. HA Rep. 84a Justizministerium Nr. 17608 (M).

40. M. Reuß, *Der Strafvollzug an Frauen* (Munich, 1927), 4. For the imprisonment of women in Germany before the First World War, see S. Leukel, 'Reformvorstellungen zum Frauenstrafvollzug im deutschen Kaiserreich', paper delivered at the workshop 'Crime and Criminal Justice in Modern Germany', May 2001, German Historical Institute (Washington, DC).
41. The importance of a gendered approach has been highlighted by individual studies of women's prisons in the US and elsewhere. See, for example, N.H. Rafter, *Partial Justice. Women in State Prisons, 1800–1935* (Boston, 1985).
42. StAMü, GStA bei dem OLG München Nr. 49, Gefangenenanstalt Aichach to GStA Munich, 16 Aug. 1937. For Aichach in general, see F. Schroeder, 'Die Landesfrauenstrafanstalt Aichach', *Das Bayernland* 37 (1926), 184–6; BayHStA, MJu 22535, 'In einem modernen Frauengefängnis', *Münchner Zeitung*, 7 July 1926. In the case of correspondence addressed to two or more recipients, the footnotes in this book have generally been restricted to one of the recipients only.
43. Kosthorst, Walter (eds), *Strafgefangenenlager*.
44. *Sopade – Deutschland-Berichte der Sozialdemokratischen Partei Deutschlands 1934–1940*, 7 vols (Salzhausen, 1980).

Chapter 1

1. O. Thierack, 'Der Strafvollzug im Dienste der Volksgemeinschaft', *MGGE* 11 (1936), 209–15, quotations on 212.
2. Janus, 'Rückblick – Ausblick', *Der Strafvollzug* 23 (1933), reprinted in Justizakademie NRW (ed.), *Zum Strafvollzug 1933–1945*, source 13. *Der Strafvollzug* was the journal of the *Inspektionsbeamten*, the senior administrative officials in penal institutions.
3. For Peukert's influence, see, for example, Wagner, *Kriminalpolizei*; E.R. Dickinson, *The Politics of German Child Welfare from the Empire to the Federal Republic* (Cambridge, Massachusetts, 1996); Y.-S. Hong, *Welfare, Modernity and the Weimar State, 1919–1933* (Princeton, 1998); D.F. Crew, *Germans on Welfare: from Weimar to Hitler* (New York, 1998).
4. For this view, see also G. Eley, 'German History and the Contradictions of Modernity: The Bourgeoisie, the State, and the Mastery of Reform', in idem (ed.), *Society, Culture, and the State in Germany, 1870–1930* (Ann Arbor, 1996), 67–103; idem, 'What Produces Fascism: Preindustrial Traditions or a Crisis of the Capitalist State?', *Politics and Society* 12 (1983), 53–82.
5. Quoted in D.J.K. Peukert, *The Weimar Republic* (London, 1993), 276, 282; idem, *Grenzen der Sozialdisziplinierung: Aufstieg und Krise der deutschen Jugendfürsorge von 1878 bis 1932* (Cologne, 1986), 259; idem, 'The Genesis of the "Final Solution" from the Spirit of Science', in D.F. Crew (ed.), *Nazism and German Society* (London, 1994), 275–99, here 285, 289.
6. For the general background, see Evans, *Rituals*, 534–41; idem, *The Coming of the Third Reich* (London, 2003), chapter 2; H.-H. Liang, *Die Berliner Polizei in der Weimarer Republik* (Berlin, 1977), 129–33. See also B. Kreutzahler, *Das Bild des Verbrechers in Romanen der Weimarer Republik* (Frankfurt am Main, 1987); I. Classen, *Darstellung von Kriminalität in der deutschen Literatur, Presse und Wissenschaft 1900 bis 1930* (Frankfurt am Main, 1988).

7. Cited in R. Bessel, *Germany after the First World War* (Oxford, 1995), 243. See also ibid., 242–4; Evans, *Rituals*, 524.
8. M. Liepmann, *Krieg und Kriminalität in Deutschland* (Berlin, 1930), 73–4. For the figures, see Bessel, *Germany*, 242, table 31.
9. BA Berlin, R 3001/5606, 'Das Elend der Strafgefangenen', *Vorwärts*, 17 Apr. 1923.
10. BayHStA, MJu 22663. See also BayHStA, MF 67427, Staatsministerium der Justiz to Staatsministerium der Finanzen, 20 Apr. 1920; BA Berlin, 61 Re 1/1527, Bl. 176–7: 'Überfüllung der Berliner Gefängnisse', *Berliner Tageblatt*, 18 Jan. 1921.
11. Bessel, *Germany*, 220–53.
12. For these developments, see Peukert, *Weimar*, 129–44, 263–73; Dörner, *Erziehung*, 59–73; Hong, *Welfare*, 12–36, 243–50.
13. Eberhard Schmidt, *Einführung in die Geschichte der deutschen Strafrechtspflege*, 3rd edition (Göttingen, 1965), 232–46, 314–21; idem, *Zuchthäuser und Gefängnisse* (Göttingen, no date), 20–3; R.F. Wetzell, 'Criminal Law Reform in Imperial Germany' (Ph.D., Stanford University, 1991), 10–32, 41–2.
14. E. Kräepelin, 'Das Verbrechen als soziale Krankheit', in idem, *Vergeltungsstrafe, Rechtsstrafe, Schutzstrafe. Vier Vorträge* (Heidelberg, 1906), 22–44, here 35. This essay has now been reprinted in W. Burgmair et al. (eds), *Emil Kraepelin. Kriminologische und forensische Schriften* (Munich, 2001). For the general development of criminology in this period, see Wetzell, *Inventing, passim*; M.J. Wiener, *Reconstructing the Criminal. Culture, Law and Policy in England, 1830–1914* (Cambridge, 1990), esp. 337–81.
15. F. von Liszt, 'Der Zweckgedanke im Strafrecht', in idem, *Strafrechtliche Aufsätze und Vorträge*, vol. 1 (Berlin, 1905), 126–79, quotations on 166, 169, 173. For deportations, see R.J. Evans, *Szenen aus der deutschen Unterwelt* (Reinbek, 1997), 26–140; J.H. Voigt, 'Die Deportation – ein Thema der deutschen Rechtswissenschaft und Politik im 19. und frühen 20. Jahrhundert', in A. Gestrich et al. (eds), *Ausweisung und Deportation* (Stuttgart, 1995), 83–101.
16. For Liszt and his influence, see Wetzell, *Inventing*, 33–8, 75–90; W. Naucke, 'Die Kriminalpolitik des Marburger Programms 1882', *ZStW* 94 (1982), 525–64.
17. For the US, see D. Rothman, 'Perfecting the Prison: United States, 1789–1865', in idem, N. Morris (eds), *The Oxford History of the Prison* (New York, 1995), 111–29. For England, see R. McGowen, 'The Well-Ordered Prison: England, 1780–1865', ibid., 79–109. For Germany, see Nutz, *Strafanstalt*, 310–33; Mecklenburg, *Ordnung, passim*; S. Scheerer, 'Beyond Confinement? Notes on the History and Possible Future of Solitary Confinement in Germany', in Finzsch, Jütte (eds), *Institutions*, 349–61; *Vorentwurf zu einem Deutschen Strafgesetzbuch* (Berlin, 1909), 76, note 2. See also the forthcoming Ph.D. by Andreas Fleiter, 'Straf- und Gefängnisreformen in Deutschland und den USA: Preußen und Maryland, 1870–1935' (University of Bochum).
18. K. Krohne, *Lehrbuch der Gefängniskunde* (Stuttgart, 1889), 357, note 15; Berger, *Repression*, 99; Schwandner, 'Die Tuberkulosenfrage in den Strafanstalten', *BlGfK* 45 (1911), 153–72. Corporal punishment in Prussian penitentiaries for men was officially abolished only in December 1918. But it had hardly been used in the previous years. In 1913, for example, only four cases of corporal punishment were recorded in the penitentiaries administered by the Prussian Ministry of the Interior; *Statistik der zum Preußischen Ministerium des Inneren gehörenden Strafanstalten 1913* (Berlin, 1915).
19. Foucault, *Discipline and Punish*, 135–69.

20. See, for example, H. Herrmann, 'Militärische Achtungsbezeugungen von Strafgefangenen im Verkehr mit den Gefängnisbehörden', *BlGefK* 50 (1916), 70; Radusch, 'Achtungsbezeugung von Strafgefangenen', ibid., 51 (1917), 70–3; Michaëlis, ' "Audiatur et altera pars!" ', ibid., 74–9.

21. Krohne, *Lehrbuch*, 522. For Krohne, see G. Stammer, 'Krohne und sein Einfluss auf die Fortentwicklung des Gefängniswesens', *BlGefK* 46 (1912), 7–13. For female warders, see E. Ellering, 'Der Strafvollzug an Frauen', in Bumke (ed.), *Gefängniswesen*, 353–62, here esp. 361. See also the files of female prison officials in Aichach, collected in the StAMü.

22. A. Paterson, *A Report of Visits to some German Prisons and Reformatories in August 1922* (Maidstone, 1923), 5.

23. Dienstanweisung für Aufseher vom Ministerium des Inneren, 19 Dec. 1902, cit. in Hornig, 'Die Bedeutung des Aufsichtsbeamten im Strafvollzuge', in Preußisches Justizministerium (ed.), *Strafvollzug in Preußen* (Mannheim, 1928), 201–10, here 202.

24. Cited in K. Wilmanns, *Die sogenannte verminderte Zurechnungsfähigkeit als zentrales Problem der Entwürfe zu einem deutschen Strafgesetzbuch* (Berlin, 1927), 93.

25. G. Radbruch, 'Die Psychologie der Gefangenschaft', *ZStW* 32 (1911), 339–54.

26. S. Oerter, *Acht Jahre Zuchthaus* (Berlin, 1908), 102. See ibid., 81–111; H. Leuss, *Aus dem Zuchthause* (Berlin, 1903), esp. 87–92, 158–60, 184–88.

27. O. Zirker, *Der Gefangene. Neuland der Erziehung in der Strafanstalt* (Werther, 1924), 66.

28. M. Grünhut, *The Development of the German Penal System 1920–1932*, English Studies in Criminal Science, vol. 8 (1944), 12; Liang, *Polizei*, 134–5. See also Liepmann, *Krieg*, 164.

29. A. Behrle, *Die Stellung der deutschen Sozialisten zum Strafvollzug von 1870 bis zur Gegenwart* (Berlin, 1931), 22–3, 156–7.

30. 'Grundsätze für den Vollzug von Freiheitsstrafen vom 7. Juni 1923', *Reichsgesetzblatt*, part II; Schattke, *Geschichte*, 150–7. For the most recent account of the introduction of the guidelines, see C. Schenk, *Bestrebungen zur einheitlichen Regelung des Strafvollzugs in Deutschland von 1870 bis 1923* (Frankfurt am Main, 2001), 99–113. For experiments with the stages system before the First World War, see R. Plischke, 'Historische Rückblicke ins 18. und 19. Jahrhundert zum Stufenstrafvollzug', *MSchriftKrim* 19 (1928), 417–29; A. Krebs, 'Von den Anfängen des Progressivsystems und den Vorschlägen Carl August Zellers', in H. Kaufmann *et al.* (eds), *Erinnerungsgabe für Max Grünhut* (Marburg an der Lahn, 1965), 93–110. For the SPD and the early postwar reforms, see Behrle, *Stellung*, 22–48, 157.

31. For the Study Group, see O. Zirker, 'Erste Tagung der Arbeitsgemeinschaft für Reform des Strafvollzugs', *MSchriftKrim* 15 (1924), 102–5; 'Arbeitsgemeinschaft für Reform des Strafvollzugs', *BlGefK* 56 (1924–25), 121–5; R. Sieverts, 'Die Arbeitsgemeinschaft für die Reform des Strafvollzuges. Tagungen 1929 und 1930', *ZStW* 51 (1931), 255–68.

32. For Untermaßfeld, see the files of the Thuringian Ministry of Justice in the ThHStAW. Printed material includes the chapters by H. Gieseler, E. Hapke, A. Krebs and F. Rösch in *Gefängnisse in Thüringen. Berichte über die Reform des Strafvollzugs* (Weimar, 1930); A. Krebs, 'Die Selbstverwaltung Gefangener in der Strafanstalt', *MSchriftKrim* 19 (1928), 152–64; idem, 'Die GmbH als Betriebsform der Arbeit in der Strafanstalt', in H. Müller-Dietz (ed.), *Freiheitsentzug: Entwicklung von Praxis und Theorie seit der Aufklärung* (Berlin, 1978), 498–508; L. Frede, 'Der Strafvollzug in Stufen', in idem, M. Grünhut (eds), *Reform des Strafvollzuges* (Berlin, 1927), 102–36;

idem, 'Der Strafvollzug in Stufen in Thüringen', *ZStW* 46 (1925), 233–48. Sources also include two of the very few studies of Weimar penal institutions: U. Sagaster, *Die thüringische Landesstrafanstalt Untermaßfeld in den Jahren 1923–1933* (Frankfurt am Main, 1980); K. Witter, 'Funktion und Organisation der Zuchthäuser im kapitalistischen Deutschland, dargelegt am Beispiel des Zuchthauses Untermaßfeld, 1813–1945' (Diplomarbeit, Humboldt University, East Berlin, 1982).

33. ThHStAW, Justizministerium Nr. 423, Bl. 45–6: Landesverband der Gefängnisaufsichtsbeamten Großthüringens to Justizministerium, 16 Apr. 1928.
34. Ibid., Bl. 4–5: Landesverband der Gefängnisaufsichtsbeamten Großthüringens to Staatsregierung, 14 Feb. 1925. See also ibid., Nr. 397, Bl. 65–6: Strafanstalt Untermaßfeld to Justizministerium, 9 Nov. 1922; ibid., Bl. 103: Strafanstalt Untermaßfeld to Justizministerium, 27 Oct. 1923; ibid., Personalakten Justizministerium, Julius Mentzner, Bl. 91–3: Beschluss des Staatsministeriums, 8 Aug. 1923; ibid., Personalakten Justizministerium, Dr Albert Krebs, Bl. 264–75: Strafanstalt Untermaßfeld to Justizministerium, 7 June 1933.
35. For an overview, see M. Ignatieff, 'State, Civil Society and Total Institutions: A Critique of Recent Social Histories of Punishment', in S. Cohen, A. Scull (eds), *Social Control and the State* (Oxford, 1983), 75–105.
36. Peukert, *Weimar*, 275–6.
37. BayHStA, MJu 22504, Staatsministerium der Justiz to Strafanstalten, 16 Apr. 1921.
38. The intentions of the senior Prussian prison officials are evident in the 1929 prison regulations, which were never properly put into practice. See R. Sieverts, 'Die preußische Verordnung über den Strafvollzug in Stufen vom 7. Juni 1929', *MSchriftKrim*, Beiheft 3 (Heidelberg, 1930), 129–51; B. Koch, 'Das System des Stufenstrafvollzuges in Deutschland unter besonderer Berücksichtigung seiner Entwicklungsgeschichte' (Ph.D., Freiburg University, 1972), 63–71. For the prison service offices, see A. Hasse, 'Die Gefangenenanstalten in Deutschland und die Organisation ihrer Verwaltung', in Bumke (ed.), *Gefängniswesen*, 33–70, here especially 38. For the number of penal institutions, see 'Statistik des Gefängniswesens im Deutschen Reich', *Stenographische Berichte über die Verhandlungen des deutschen Reichstags*, IV. Wahlperiode (1928), vol. 434, supplement 814, table 1.
39. Quoted in ThHStAW, Justizministerium Nr. 1781, Bl. 52: Justizministerium to Landesgefängnis Ichtershausen, 6 Feb. 1926. See also ibid., Bl. 53–6: Landesgefängnis Ichtershausen to Justizministerium, 17 Feb. 1926; ibid., Nr. 1339, Bl. 88–92: Landesgefängnis Ichtershausen to Justizministerium, 29 Jan. 1926; ibid., Nr. 1398, Bl. 7: Arresthausstrafen in Ichtershausen, 1923–1930; ibid., Bl. 9: Arresthausstrafen in Untermaßfeld, 1923–1930; ibid., Personalakten Justizministerium, Max Vollrath.
40. 'Statistik des Gefängniswesens', table 8.
41. Krohne, *Lehrbuch*, 536.
42. This term was used in an obituary to describe Albert Poller, governor of the Waldheim penal institution; 'Nachruf auf Albert Poller', *BlGefK* 64 (1933), 344–8, here 346.
43. JVA Straubing (ed.), *100 Jahre Justizvollzugsanstalt Straubing* (Straubing, 2001), 71.
44. Cited in JVA Straubing, Autobiography by Hermann D.
45. See, for example, BA Berlin, R 3001/5606, Verein der deutschen Strafanstaltsbeamten, Beschlüsse der 18. Mitgliederversammlung vom 30. und 31. August 1923; E. Bumke,

'Die Freiheitsstrafe als Problem der Gesetzgebung', in idem (ed.), *Gefängniswesen*, 16–32, here 28, note 1. See also the correspondence in BayHStA, MJu 13143.
46. 'Stenographischer Bericht', *BlGefK* 58 (1927), Sonderheft zur Augsburger Tagung des Vereins der deutschen Strafanstaltsbeamten, 118–389, here 213–15. Founded in 1864, the Association of German Prison Officials was the central organisation of higher ranking local prison officials. Members also included other officials, administrators and criminologists.
47. 'Die Preußentagung des Vereins der deutschen Strafanstaltsbeamten', *BlGefK* 62 (1931), 1–329, here 306–7. See also C. Bondy, 'Moritz Liepmann', *BlGefK* 61 (1930), 279–81.
48. For the quotation, see BayHStA, MJu 22498, M. Scherübl, 'Erziehung und Unterricht im Strafvollzug', 1922. See also idem, 'Die Gefängnisschule', *Das Bayernland* 37 (1926), 176–9; BayHStA, MJu 22694, Anonyme Eingabe von Gefangenen aus Amberg, no date [1925]; E.J. Gumbel, 'Strafvollzugsstatistik', *Die Justiz* 5 (1929–30), 690–703, here 702.
49. See Oleschinski, 'Gefängnisseelsorge', 67, 88–9, 154; E. Eichholz, 'Gefangenenseelsorge und nationalsozialistischer "Strafernst"', *Kirchliche Zeitgeschichte* 12 (1999), 172–88, here 181. For religious welfare organisations in Weimar, see Crew, *Welfare*, 16–31.
50. ThHStAW, GStA bei dem OLG Jena Nr. 197, Bl. 36–7: Landesgefängnis Ichtershausen, Liste der Beamten, Angestellten, 20 May 1927. See also Bund der Gefängnis-, Straf- und Erziehungsbeamten und -Beamtinnen Deutschlands (ed.), *Probleme der Strafvollzugsreform* (Berlin, 1930), 54, 76–7.
51. BA Berlin, R 3001/5631, Bl. 111: 'Fortschrittlich – aber nur auf dem Papier', *Vossische Zeitung*, 13 Feb. 1929.
52. H. Stapenhorst, *Die Entwicklung des Verhältnisses von Geldstrafe zu Freiheitsstrafe seit 1882* (Berlin, 1993), 42, 54–7; H. von Hentig, 'Die Anpassung des Verbrechens an die Deflation', *MSchriftKrim* 18 (1927), 51–2.
53. Gebert, 'Umfang der in Preußen geschlossenen Gefangenenanstalten', *MSchriftKrim* 23 (1932), 754–5. The total number of jails with room for less than 50 inmates declined from 1,418 (1927) to 865 (1935). See 'Statistik des Gefängniswesens', table 1; Reichsjustizministerium (ed.), *Gefängniswesen in Deutschland*, 43.
54. See *Statistik über die Gefangenenanstalten in Preußen 1924*; *Statistik über die Gefangenenanstalten in Preußen 1929*; ThHStAW, Justizministerium Nr. 1339, Bl. 68: 'Die Reform der thüring. Strafanstalten', *Das Volk*, 5 Dec. 1925. For one example of changes to the prisoner diet, see BayHStA, MJu 22686, Besichtigung der Strafanstalt Aichach vom 27.11.1923, appendix; StAMü, GStA bei dem OLG München Nr. 49, Strafanstalt Aichach, Gefangenenkost vom 16. mit 31. Juli 1929.
55. JVA Straubing (ed.), *100 Jahre*, 31.
56. ThHStAW, Justizministerium Nr. 1683, Bl. 30–5: Strafanstalt Untermaßfeld to Justizministerium, 20 Nov. 1924. For the rest of Germany, see BA Berlin, R 3001/5611, E.J. Gumbel, 'Gedanken zum Strafvollzug', *Dresdener Volkszeitung*, 16 Nov. 1929. Very few larger penal institutions were built in the Weimar period (Lübeck-Lauerhof, Brandenburg-Görden, Hamm).
57. It should be recalled that only criminal offenders with longer sentences of imprisonment qualified for the stages system. The Bavarian practice is detailed by C. Müller, 'Verbrechensbekämpfung im Anstaltsstaat. Psychiatrie, Kriminologie und Strafrechtsreform in Deutschland 1871–1933' (Ph.D., University of Essen, 2002), 253–9, who sees the aims of the Bavarian prison administration as almost diametrically opposed to those of the modern school of criminal law inspired by Liszt. For the regulations of Bavarian penitentiaries, see Ministerialentschließung, 17

Apr. 1924, reprinted in Bayerisches Staatsministerium der Justiz (ed.), *Der Stufenstrafvollzug und die kriminalbiologischen Untersuchungen der Gefangenen in den bayerischen Strafanstalten*, 3 vols (Munich, 1926, 1928, 1929), vol. 1, 42–6, here 44.

58. BayHStA, MJu 22504, Strafanstalt Aichach to Staatsministerium der Justiz, 24 Feb. 1923; ibid., Zuchthaus Straubing to Staatsministerium der Justiz, 5 Mar. 1923; ibid., MJu 22507, Zuchthaus Straubing to Staatsministerium der Justiz, 15 Jan. 1926, appendix.
59. E. von Salomon, *Die Geächteten* (Berlin, 1931), 439. See also, for example, H. Ellger, 'Der Strafvollzug in Stufen', *BlGefK* 57 (1926), 189–233, here 233.
60. For the last point, see Starke, 'Die Behandlung von Gefangenen', in Bumke (ed.), *Gefängniswesen*, 147–77.
61. A. Fleiter, 'Strafen auf dem Weg zum Sozialismus. Sozialistische Standpunkte zu Kriminalität und Strafe vor dem Ersten Weltkrieg', *Mitteilungsblatt des Instituts für soziale Bewegungen* 26 (2001), 105–38, here 115. See also Behrle, *Stellung*, 9–24.
62. For individual accounts, see HStAD-Kalkum, Gerichte Rep. 22/343; ibid., Rep. 321/340. (For the polite soldiers, see Bl. 123: Staatsanwalt M.–Gladbach to Oberstaatsanwalt Düsseldorf, 9 Nov. 1918.) For the reference to Lenin, see S. Haffner, *Die deutsche Revolution 1918/19* (Munich, 1979), 64.
63. BayHStA, MJu 7149, Zuchthaus Straubing to Staatsministerium der Justiz, letters of 7 Jan. 1919, 10 Jan. 1919, 25 Jan. 1919; ibid., Vermerk, no date [Feb. 1919].
64. B. Weisbrod, 'Gewalt in der Politik. Zur politischen Kultur in Deutschland zwischen den beiden Weltkriegen', *Geschichte in Wissenschaft und Unterricht* 43 (1992), 391–404, quote on 392.
65. For the German judiciary, see H. Hannover, E. Drück-Hannover, *Politische Justiz, 1918–1933* (Frankfurt am Main, 1966); G. Jasper, 'Justiz und Politik in der Weimarer Republik', *VfZ* 30 (1982), 167–205.
66. I. Kershaw, *Hitler. 1889–1936: Hubris* (London, 1998), 175–6; JVA Straubing, Autobiography Hermann D.
67. Kershaw, *Hitler. 1889–1936*, 211–42.
68. BLHA, Pr. Br. Rep. 29 Zuchthaus Brandenburg Nr. 691; M. Broszat (ed.), *Kommandant in Auschwitz. Autobiographische Aufzeichnungen des Rudolf Höß* (Munich, 1963), 51–3, 64–5, 71–4. For the role of Bormann (who got away with a one-year prison sentence) in the killing, see J. von Lang, *The Secretary* (New York, 1979), 28–35.
69. For teachers, see T. Just, 'Rheinisch-Westfälische Gefängnis-Gesellschaft', *BlGefK* 44 (1910), 189–94. For chaplains, see Oleschinski, 'Gefängnisseelsorge', 154, 350–54.
70. BayHStA, MJu 7149, Zuchthaus Straubing to Staatsministerium der Justiz, 16 May 1919. See also ibid., Zuchthaus Straubing to Staatsministerium der Justiz, 4 July 1919; Evans, *Szenen*, 119, 123.
71. E. Rosenhaft, *Beating the Fascists? The German Communists and Political Violence 1929–1933* (Cambridge, 1983), esp. 16–17, 134, 202.
72. M.M. Weber, *Ernst Rüdin. Eine kritische Biographie* (Berlin, 1993), 89–90; B. Walter, *Psychiatrie und Gesellschaft in der Moderne* (Paderborn, 1996), 284–5; BayHStA, MJu 22616, Zuchthaus Straubing to Staatsministerium der Justiz, 26 Jan. 1925.
73. 'Statistik des Gefängniswesens', table 6.
74. Bund der Gefängnis-, Straf- und Erziehungsbeamten und -Beamtinnen Deutschlands (ed.), *Der Aufsichtsbeamte im Strafvollzuge* (no place, no date, around 1927), 32–4. In 1921 alone, 649 prisoners were sentenced to further imprisonment of three months or more for their participation in riots; *Kriminalstatistik 1921*.

75. BA Berlin, 61 Re 1/1527, Bl. 163: 'Revolte im Zuchthaus', *Berliner Tageblatt*, 29 Mar. 1920. For the quotation, see ibid., Bl. 167: 'Das Schwurgericht im Zuchthaus', *Berliner Tageblatt*, 19 June 1920.
76. F. Fechenbach, *Im Haus der Freudlosen. Bilder aus dem Zuchthaus* (Berlin, 1925), passim. See also BayHStA, MJu 22504, 'Fechenbach auf der Folter', *Berliner Volkszeitung*, 2 Jan. 1923.
77. K. Großmann, 'Strafvollzug', in Deutsche Liga für Menschenrechte (ed.), *Acht Jahre Politische Justiz* (Berlin, 1927), 99–101, here 99. For the League, see Evans, *Rituals*, 513–15.
78. For the political exploitation of trials, see Evans, *Third Reich*, chapter 2.
79. *Stenographische Berichte über die Verhandlungen des deutschen Reichstags*, 147. Sitzung, 19 Nov. 1921, 5123–4; ibid., Mündlicher Bericht des 37. Ausschusses, 17 Dec. 1921, 5359–61; BA Berlin, 61 Re 1/1528, Bl. 3: 'Lichtenburger Genossen harren aus!', *Rote Fahne*, 21 Nov. 1921; ibid., Bl. 6: 'Lichtenburg', *Deutsche Allgemeine Zeitung*, 22 Nov. 1921. For other examples, see BA Berlin, R 3001/6709.
80. For one such publication, see Zentralvorstand der Roten Hilfe Deutschland (ed.), *Gefangen. Dreissig politische Juli-amnestierte berichten über ihre Erlebnisse in deutschen Zuchthäusern* (Berlin, 1928). For the general background, see BayHStA, MJu 22617, Nachrichtensammelstelle im Reichsministerium des Inneren to Nachrichtenstellen der Länder, 11 May 1932, appendix; H. Weber, *Die Wandlung des deutschen Kommunismus*, vol. 2 (Frankfurt am Main, 1969), 219; H. Sommer, *Literatur der Roten Hilfe in Deutschland* (Berlin, 1991), 7–12.
81. See BA Berlin, R 3001/5658, Bl. 134: 'Die Reform des Strafvollzuges', *Berliner Tageblatt*, 2 Feb. 1926; Oleschinski, 'Gefängnisseelsorge', 91–4; Behrle, *Stellung*, 58–60, 71.
82. One such incident was the death on 20 April 1925 of the former German Minister for the Postal Service, Dr Höfle in the Moabit remand prison. The case was critically reported in the national press, leading to an investigation by a commission of the Prussian state diet; see various articles in BA Berlin, 61 Re 1/1528.
83. Fechenbach, *Haus*, preface.
84. E.E. Kisch (ed.), *Max Hoelz. Briefe aus dem Zuchthaus* (Berlin, 1927).
85. M. Hoelz, *Vom 'Weißen Kreuz' zur roten Fahne* (Frankfurt am Main, 1969; first published 1929). See also R. Müller, 'Der Fall Max Hoelz', *Mittelweg* 36 8 (1999), 78–94.
86. K. Plättner, *Eros im Zuchthaus* (Berlin, 1929). For Plättner and his book, see V. Ullrich, *Der ruhelose Rebell. Karl Plättner 1893–1945* (Munich, 2000), passim.
87. See, for example, G.F. von Cleric, 'Das Sexualproblem im Strafvollzug', *MSchriftKrim* 20 (1929), 621–7; W. Gentz, 'Das Sexualproblem im Strafvollzuge', *ZStW* 50 (1929), 406–27. For the broader debate, see Peukert, *Sozialdisziplinierung*, 235.
88. For example L. von Koerber, *Menschen im Zuchthaus* (Frankfurt am Main, 1930).
89. Novels include Lion Feuchtwanger's *Erfolg* (1930) and Gustav Regler's *Wasser, Brot und blaue Bohnen* (1932). The most famous novel about the Weimar penal system, Hans Fallada's *Wer einmal aus dem Blechnapf frisst*, was not published until 1934.
90. J. Willett, *The New Sobriety. Art and Politics in the Weimar Period 1917–1933* (London, 1982), 154–5; Peukert, *Sozialdisziplinierung*, 230–41; K. Petersen, *Literatur und Justiz in der Weimarer Republik* (Stuttgart, 1988), 183.
91. For his personal file, see BLHA, Pr. Br. Rep. 4 A, Kammergericht, Personalia Nr. 396.
92. BayHStA, MJu 22507, K.M. Finkelnburg, 'Amnestie', *Vorwärts*, 1 Feb. 1930.
93. BA Berlin, R 3001/5631, Bl. 173: 'Aktuelles Theater in der Volksbühne', *Vorwärts*, 20 Jan. 1930. See also Petersen, *Literatur*, 186; Kreutzahler, *Bild*, 187.
94. For one such example, see BLHA, Pr. Br. Rep. 29 Zuchthaus Brandenburg Nr. 1010, Stefan M. to Dr Knipp and Dr Kroemer, 6 July 1924.

95. See, for example, Zentralvorstand (ed.), *Gefangen*, 7; BayHStA, MJu 22616, Zuchthaus Straubing to Staatsministerium der Justiz, 26 Jan. 1925.
96. BayHStA, MJu 22617, Nachrichtensammelstelle im Reichsministerium des Inneren to Nachrichtenstellen der Länder, 11 May 1932, appendix.
97. Hoelz, *Vom 'Weißen Kreuz'*, 480.
98. 'Bericht über die XVII. Versammlung zugleich Fünfzigjährige Jubiläumsfeier des Vereins der deutschen Strafanstaltsbeamten e.V. in Hamburg vom 25.–29. Mai 1914', *BlGefK* 48 (1914), 291–526, here 438. See also B. Freudenthal, 'Die rechtliche Stellung der Gefangenen', in Bumke (ed.), *Gefängniswesen*, 141–6.
99. For the Breslau case, see E.J. Gumbel, 'Strafvollzugsstatistik', *Die Justiz* 6 (1930–31), 21–42, here 30.
100. BA Berlin, R 3001/5631, Bl. 68: K. Grossmann, 'Der Strafvollzug in Theorie und Praxis', *Berliner Tageblatt*, 7 Dec. 1927; BayHStA, MJu 22471, Oberstaatsanwalt Bamberg to Zuchthaus Ebrach, 14 Dec. 1925; ibid., MJu 22472, Staatsministerium der Justiz to Strafanstalten, 31 May 1929. See also various examples in ThHStAW, Justizministerium Nr. 1716.
101. See, for example, Peukert, *Sozialdisziplinierung*, 245.
102. ThHStAW, Justizministerium Nr. 1712, 'Das fidele Zuchthaus Untermaßfeld', *Meininger Tageblatt*, 18 Mar. 1924; ibid., Nr. 1339, Bl. 151: ' "Genesungsheim" Untermaßfeld', *Eisenacher Zeitung*, 4 Sept. 1928.
103. See, for example, BayHStA, MJu 22866, 'Das Zuchthaus als Erholungsheim', *Oberfränkische Zeitung*, 29 Dec. 1928; BA Berlin, R 3001/5659, Bl. 133: 'Wie leben die Strafgefangenen?', *Deutsche Zeitung*, 25 May 1929.
104. BA Berlin, 62 DAF 3/1787, Bl. 101: 'Der Kampf gegen die Feinde des Menschentums', *Kreuzzeitung*, 7 Oct. 1927.
105. See, for example, B. Freudenthal, 'Maßregeln der Sicherung und Besserung', in P.F. Aschrott, E. Kohlrausch (eds), *Reform des Strafrechts* (Berlin, 1926), 153–72; C. Bondy, 'Zur Frage der Erziehbarkeit', *ZStW* 48 (1928), 329–34.
106. H. von Hentig, *Strafrecht und Auslese* (Berlin, 1914), 68, note 1; G. Aschaffenburg, *Das Verbrechen und seine Bekämpfung*, 3rd edition (Heidelberg, 1923), 224.
107. For the apparent rise in recidivism, and some of the reasons behind it, see Müller, 'Verbrechensbekämpfung', 186–7.
108. Quoted in J.A. Davis, *Conflict and Control. Law and Order in Nineteenth-Century Italy* (London, 1988), 330. See also M.E. Wolfgang, 'Cesare Lombroso', in H. Mannheim (ed.), *Pioneers in Criminology* (London, 1960), 168–227.
109. JVA Straubing, Fortbildungsschule für Aufsichtsbeamte der Gefangenenanstalt Landsberg 1921–22, 'Verbrechens-Ursachen in der Person des Täters'.
110. M. Gadebusch Bondio, *Die Rezeption der kriminalanthropologischen Theorien von Cesare Lombroso in Deutschland von 1880–1914* (Husum, 1995).
111. F. von Liszt, 'Kriminalpolitische Aufgaben', in idem, *Strafrechtliche Aufsätze und Vorträge*, vol. 1 (Berlin, 1905), 290–467, here 311; idem, 'Zweckgedanke', 167. See also D. Pick, *Faces of Degeneration. A European Disorder, c.1848–c.1918* (Cambridge, 1989), 44–59; Gadebusch, *Lombroso*, 94–6; Wetzell, 'Criminal Law Reform', 160–2; S.F. Weiss, *Race Hygiene and National Efficiency. The Eugenics of Wilhelm Schallmayer* (Berkeley, 1987), 9–11.
112. K. Schneider, *Die psychopathischen Persönlichkeiten*, 2nd edition (Leipzig, 1928), esp. 3, 13, 16. For Schneider, see also Wetzell, *Inventing*, 146–9. For the use of the term in England, see W.J. Forsythe, *Penal Discipline, Reformatory Projects and the English Prison Commission, 1895–1939* (Exeter, 1990), 159.

113. M. Schwartz, '"Proletarier" und "Lumpen". Sozialistische Ursprünge eugenischen Denkens', *VfZ* 42 (1994), 537–70, quotation on 559. See also idem, 'Kriminalbiologie und Strafrechtsreform. Die "erbkranken Gewohnheitsverbrecher" im Visier der Weimarer Sozialdemokratie', in Justizministerium NRW (ed.), *Kriminalbiologie* (Düsseldorf, 1997), 13–68, here esp. 28–43; Fleiter, 'Strafen', *passim*.

114. W. Gentz, 'Berufsverbrecher', in Bumke (ed.), *Gefängniswesen*, 334–52, quote on 349. See also Liszt, 'Zweckgedanke', 167; G. Aschaffenburg, 'Einheitlichkeit der Sicherungsmaßnahmen', *MSchriftKrim* 22 (1931), 257–65.

115. R. Heindl, *Der Berufsverbrecher* (Berlin, 1926), quote on 156.

116. Wagner, *Kriminalpolizei*, 155–64.

117. The draft was nevertheless influenced by the demand for stricter measures against 'habitual offenders', introducing harsher sentences for recidivists; *Vorentwurf*, 82–7, 94, 359–66. See also Wetzell, 'Criminal Law Reform', 281–5; Reichardt, 'Der Vorentwurf zu einem deutschen Strafgesetzbuch von 1909', *BlGefK* 44 (1910), 5–50.

118. See, for example, G. Aschaffenburg, 'Die Stellung des Psychiaters zur Strafrechtsreform', *MSchriftKrim* 16 (1925), 145–66, here 156–7.

119. Only the German Communists opposed security confinement consistently, primarily because they feared that it could be used against political offenders. Of course, this opposition to indefinite confinement was restricted to capitalist states. See Müller, 'Verbrechensbekämpfung', 209–18, 319, quote on 215.

120. See Grüllich, 'Der Gewohnheitsverbrecher nach dem Entwurfe des neuen Strafgesetzbuchs', *MSchriftKrim* 18 (1927), 671–8, here 675–6; Heindl, *Berufsverbrecher*, 383–6; J. Eichler, 'Neuzeitlicher Strafvollzug', *ZStW* 48 (1928), 171–94, here 177; F. Exner, 'Der Vollzug der bessernden und sichernden Maßnahmen', in Frede, Grünhut (eds), *Reform*, 244–60, here 256–7.

121. Ministerialentschließung, 3 Nov. 1921, reprinted in Bayerisches Staatsministerium der Justiz (ed.), *Stufenstrafvollzug*, vol. 1, 10–18, here 15.

122. Ministerialentschließung, 7 July 1923, reprinted ibid., 26–38. For the origin of the term, see O. Liang, 'Criminal-biological Theory, Discourse, and Practice in Germany, 1918–1945' (Ph.D., Johns Hopkins University, Baltimore, 1999), 10.

123. A 'criminal-biological' questionnaire is reprinted in Bayerisches Staatsministerium der Justiz (ed.), *Stufenstrafvollzug*, vol. 1, 86–92.

124. Foucault, *Discipline and Punish*, 249. For criminal-biology in Bavaria, see W. Burgmair, N. Wachsmann, M.M. Weber, '"Die soziale Prognose wird damit sehr trübe . . .": Theodor Viernstein und die Kriminalbiologische Sammelstelle in Bayern', in M. Farin (ed.), *Polizeireport München* (Munich, 1999), 250–87; Wetzell, *Inventing*, 128–37.

125. Ministerialentschließung, 14 Dec. 1927, reprinted in Bayerisches Staatsministerium der Justiz (ed.), *Stufenstrafvollzug*, vol. 2, 26–50.

126. BayHStA, MJu 22507, Gutachten Dr Viernstein, Dr Trunk, 4 Feb. 1930, appendix.

127. See, for example, BayHStA MJu 22509, Zuchthaus Ebrach to GStA Bamberg, 13 Jan. 1933, appendix.

128. See, in particular, W. Petrzilka, *Persönlichkeitsforschung und Differenzierung im Strafvollzug* (Hamburg, 1930), esp. 39–61.

129. 'Stenographischer Bericht', 378. See also O. Weissenrieder, 'Zur Geschichte des Besserungsgedankens im Vollzug der neuzeitlichen Freiheitsstrafe', *BlGefK* 56 (1924–25), 5–43 here esp. 42–3.

130. For Saxony and Hamburg, see R. Fetscher, 'Die Organisation der erbbiologischen Erforschung der Strafgefangenen in Sachsen', *BlGefK* 57 (1926), 69–75; C. Rothmaler,

' "Prognose: Zweifelhaft". Die kriminalbiologische Untersuchungs- und Sammelstelle der Hamburgischen Gefangenenanstalten 1926–1945', in Justizministerium NRW (ed.), *Kriminalbiologie* (Düsseldorf, 1997), 107–50, here 119–20, 137.
131. For the general background, see Sieverts, 'Die preußische Verordnung'.
132. BA Berlin, R 3001/5631, Bl. 139: K. Finkelnburg, 'Die einschneidenste Gefängnisreform West-Europas', *Berliner Tageblatt*, 11 July 1929.
133. I have examined the investigations carried out in Moabit between 1 May 1930 and 29 Dec. 1930, collected in the LaB, Rep 5 Acc 2863, Nr. 97 (for the quotation, see Bl. 5: Vorgutachten über den Gefangenen Albert M., 3 May 1930). For examinations in Bavaria, see Liang, 'Criminal-biological Theory', 141–57. See also T. Viernstein, 'Über Typen des verbesserlichen und unverbesserlichen Verbrechers', *MKG* 2 (1929), 26–54.
134. Quoted in W. Luz, *Ursachen und Bekämpfung des Verbrechens im Urteil des Verbrechers* (Heidelberg, 1928), 194, 251.
135. See, for example, Bayerisches Obsorge Amt (ed.), *Die Gefangenenobsorge* (Lichtenau, 1928).
136. P. Becker, 'Randgruppen im Blickfeld der Polizei. Ein Versuch über die Perspektivität des "praktischen Blicks"', *Archiv für Sozialgeschichte* 32 (1992), 283–304; A. Lüdtke, 'Gemeinwohl', Polizei und 'Festungspraxis'. Staatliche Gewaltsamkeit und innere Verwaltung in Preußen, 1815–1850 (Göttingen, 1982), 233–7; Luz, *Ursachen*, 243–6; Wagner, *Kriminalpolizei*, 146–8.
137. BayHStA, MInn 71579, Gesetz zur Bekämpfung von Zigeunern, Landfahrern und Arbeitsscheuen; ibid., Ministerialentschließung zur Ausführung des Zigeuner- und Arbeitsscheuengesetzes.
138. Ibid., MJu 22525, Staatsministerium der Justiz to Strafanstalten, 16 Feb. 1927.
139. BayHStA, MInn 71560, Zuchthaus Straubing to Polizeidirektion Munich, 24 May 1929. See also ibid., Staatsministerium des Inneren to Regierung von Oberbayern, 16 July 1929.
140. For the unemployment figures, see V. Berghahn, *Modern Germany*, 2nd edition (Cambridge, 1987), 284, table 18.
141. *Kriminalstatistik 1929* (Berlin, 1932); *Kriminalstatistik 1932* (Berlin, 1935). For the general background, see R. Bessel, *Political Violence and the Rise of Nazism* (New Haven, 1984); Rosenhaft, *Beating the Fascists?*
142. StAMü, Justizvollzugsanstalten Nr. 1820, Lebenslauf Maria B., 22 Aug. 1930. See also Wagner, *Kriminalpolizei*, 215, table 6; P. Martell, 'Zum Problem der Vorbestraften', *MdRfW* 7 (1932), 10–13. The proportion of recidivists among male convicts in Germany increased from 34.8 per cent (1928) to 45.1 per cent (1932); *Kriminalstatistik 1932*, 18.
143. Evans, *Rituals*, 591–610, 915.
144. One of the most frequently cited works was J. Lange, *Verbrechen als Schicksal. Studien an kriminellen Zwillingen* (Leipzig, 1929). For a detailed discussion of Lange's study, see Wetzell, *Inventing*, 161–8.
145. 'Die Preußentagung', 261–71; T. Viernstein, 'Die kriminalbiologischen Untersuchungen der Strafgefangenen in Bayern', *MKG* 3 (1931), 30–8; idem, 'Referat auf der Augsburger Tagung vom 3. Juni 1927', special print in the possession of the author; BayHStA, MJu 22507, Gutachten Dr Viernstein, Dr Trunk, 4 Feb. 1930, appendix. For the impact, see ibid., 'Bankrott des modernen Strafvollzuges', *Deutsche Zeitung*, 7 Nov. 1930; R. Sieverts, 'Gedanken über Methoden, Ergebnisse und kriminalpolitische Folgen der kriminal-biologischen Untersuchungen im bayrischen Strafvollzug', *MSchriftKrim* 23 (1932), 588–601.

146. For this and the preceding paragraph, see Wagner, *Kriminalpolizei*, 164–79. For the Sass brothers, see also E. Schwerk, *Die Meisterdiebe von Berlin* (Berlin, 2001).
147. Cited in Evans, *Rituals*, 625. See also ibid., 626–7; point 18 of the NSDAP party programme, reprinted and translated in J. Noakes, G. Pridham (eds), *Nazism*, vol. 1 (Exeter, 1983), 14–16.
148. K. Marxen, *Der Kampf gegen das liberale Strafrecht* (Berlin, 1975). See also BA Berlin, 62 DAF 3/1787, Bl. 25: 'Streit um das neue Strafrecht', *Vossische Zeitung*, 14 Sept. 1932.
149. For students in Weimar, see M. Grüttner, *Studenten im Dritten Reich* (Paderborn, 1995), 31–42.
150. F. Exner, *Studien über die Strafzumessungspraxis der deutschen Gerichte* (Leipzig, 1931), esp. 20–30.
151. Cited in H. Seyfarth, 'Durchhalten!', *MdRfW* 7 (1932), 130–1.
152. Stapenhorst, *Entwicklung*, 42.
153. Wagner, *Kriminalpolizei*, 188–9.
154. BayHStA, MJu 22493, Entschliessung des Reichsverbandes der katholischen Strafanstaltslehrer, 23 May 1932.
155. Walter, *Psychiatrie*, 369–408; Peukert, *Sozialdisziplinierung*, 253–60.
156. G. Dahm, F. Schaffstein, *Liberales oder autoritäres Strafrecht?* (Hamburg, 1933), quotations on 19, 48.
157. Janus, 'Rückblick – Ausblick', *Der Strafrollzug* 22 (1932) 169–75.
158. See, for example, *Stenographische Berichte über die Verhandlungen des deutschen Reichstags*, 26. Sitzung, 14 Feb. 1931, 1036; 'Gegen tendenziöse Fehlberichte über Strafvollzug', *Dortmunder Generalanzeiger*, 10 Oct. 1930, reprinted in Justizakademie NRW (ed.), *Zum Strafvollzug 1933–1945*, source 8b.
159. ThHStAW, Justizministerium Nr. 1340, Bl. 2: 'Das Klavier im Zuchthaus', *Meininger Tageblatt*, 2 Jan. 1932; ibid., Bl. 3: Strafanstalt Untermaßfeld to *Meininger Tageblatt*, 12 Jan. 1932; ibid., Bl. 19: Landtagsfraktion der Reichspartei des deutschen Mittelstandes to Justizministerium, 8 Feb. 1932.
160. E. Siefert, *Neupreußischer Strafvollzug. Politisierung und Verfall* (Halle an der Saale, 1933), quotations on 5, 11, 17. The brochure was written before the Nazi 'seizure of power'. For the dating, see also Hottes, 'Strafvollzug im Dritten Reich', 175, note 45.
161. 'Anregungen der Vereinigung der Preußischen Staatsanwälte zu Ersparnissen auf dem Gebiet der Justizverwaltung und Rechtsprechung', *Juristische Wochenschrift* 61 (1932), 917–18. See also 'Ersparnisvorschläge des Preußischen Richtervereins', ibid., 916–17.
162. H. Seyfarth, 'Der Humanitätsgedanke im Strafvollzug', *MdRfW* 5 (1930), 67–82, quotations on 72, 74. For Seyfarth, see O. Weissenrieder, 'Pastor Dr Phil Seyfarth', *BlGefK* 60 (1929), 145–8. Seyfarth was General Secretary of the Deutscher Reichszusammenschluß für Gerichtshilfe, Gefangenen- und Entlassenenfürsorge.
163. K. Echternacht, 'Modernes Strafrecht, Strafvollzug und öffentliches Gewissen', *MdRfW* 7 (1932), 18–25, quotation on 24; BA Berlin, R 3001/5630, Bl. 32–7: Bund der Gefängnis-, Straf- und Erziehungsbeamten und -Beamtinnen Deutschlands, Tagesordnung zum XVII. ordentlichen Bundestage am 11.–13.6.1931.
164. ThHStAW, Justizministerium Nr. 1337, Besprechung der Strafvollzugsreferenten am 18.1.1930.
165. See, for example, various articles in BA Berlin, R 3001/5632; H. Brandstätter, 'Verpflegung der Strafgefangenen', *MSchriftKrim* 23 (1932), 111–13; Eberhard Schmidt, 'Kritisches zur Kritik am modernen Strafvollzuge', *MSchriftKrim* 22 (1931) 193–207.

166. Sieverts, 'Gedanken über Methoden', 600.
167. Bondy, 'Moritz Liepmann'; idem, 'Fortschritte und Hemmungen in der Strafvollzugsreform', in *MSchriftKrim*, Beiheft 3 (Heidelberg, 1930), 90–102, here 95–8; Brandstätter, 'Zur Situation der Strafvollzugsreform', *MSchriftKrim* 23 (1932), 431–2.
168. For instance, see ThHStAW, Justizministerium Nr. 1339, Bl. 185: 'Hinter verschlossenen Türen', *Thüringer Tageszeitung*, 26 Apr. 1932; Bondy, 'Fortschritte', 92.
169. Sarodnick, '"Dieses Haus"', 359; Edgar Schmidt, 'Haushalt der Strafanstaltsverwaltung 1933', *Der Strafvollzug* 23 (1933), 164–72; idem, 'Aus der Statistik der preußischen Gefangenenanstalten', *Deutsche Justiz* 96 (1934), 1023–6; idem, 'Die Kosten des Strafvollzuges', ibid., 1346–7. For the welfare state, see Crew, *Welfare, passim*.
170. The figures for the progressive stages are based on a sample of five Bavarian penal institutions; BayHStA, MJu 22509, Gefangenenanstalt Aichach to GStA Munich, 14 Jan. 1933; ibid., Gefangenenanstalt Amberg to Staatsministerium der Justiz, 9 Jan. 1933; ibid., Gefangenenanstalt Bernau to Oberstaatsanwalt Munich, 30 Dec. 1932; ibid., Zuchthaus Kaisheim to GStA Munich, 3 Jan. 1933; ibid., Zuchthaus Straubing to GStA Nuremberg, 30 Dec. 1932.
171. Sarodnick, '"Dieses Haus"', 340. For pressure by the Communists on the Bavarian prison administration, see BayHStA, MJu 22470, F. Gürtner, Behandlung der Überzeugungstäter, 7 Jan. 1932.
172. Gruchmann, *Justiz*, 325, note 21. The amnesty also applied to some criminal offences commited due to 'economic hardship'.
173. W. Ayaß, *Das Arbeitshaus Breitenau* (Kassel, 1992), 253–8; M. Burleigh, *Death and Deliverance: 'Euthanasia' in Germany 1900–1945* (Cambridge, 1994), 33–4.
174. B. Post, 'Vorgezogene Machtübernahme 1932: Die Regierung Sauckel', in D. Heiden, G. Mai (eds), *Thüringen auf dem Weg ins 'Dritte Reich'* (Erfurt, no date), 147–82. This was not the first time the Nazi party participated in the Thuringian administration: in 1930–31, Wilhelm Frick had served as Minister of the Interior and Education.
175. ThHStAW, Personalakten Justizministerium, Dr Albert Krebs; H. Müller-Dietz, 'Albert Krebs. Annäherungen an Leben und Werk', *ZfStrVo* 42 (1993), 69–76.
176. ThHStAW, Justizministerium Nr. 1707, Bl. 1–9: Karl Rompel to Dr Weber, 30 Oct. 1932; ibid., Bl. 32–5: Karl Rompel to Dr Weber, 13 Nov. 1932.
177. Albert Krebs was offered the post of governor at the Eisenach Youth Prison. But he never took it up. In late 1933, he was formally dismissed from the prison service under the Law for the Restoration of the Professional Civil Service. See ThHStAW, Personalakten Justizministerium, Dr Albert Krebs.
178. See ThHStAW, Justizministerium Nr. 1683. For Gericke, see BA Berlin, R 3001/alt R 22/Pers. 57132.
179. Bondy, who was Jewish, was imprisoned temporarily in Buchenwald in 1938 and later emigrated to the US. For Bondy, see Rothmaler, '"Prognose: Zweifelhaft"', 123; E. Harvey, *Youth and the Welfare State in Weimar Germany* (Oxford, 1993), 262.
180. ThHStAW, Justizministerium Nr. 1707, Bl. 64: 'Thüringer Plauderei', *Meininger Tageblatt*, 14 Jan. 1933.

Chapter 2

1. BA Berlin, R 3001/alt R 22/4085, Bl. 18–21: Rede vor dem preußischen Landtag, 18 May 1933, here Bl. 20.

2. Zweite Sitzung des Reichstags, 23 Mar. 1933, transcript partially reprinted in M. Hirsch *et al.* (eds), *Recht, Verwaltung und Justiz im Nationalsozialismus. Ausgewählte Schriften, Gesetze und Gerichtsentscheidungen von 1933 bis 1945* (Cologne, 1984), 93–108, here 97.
3. For a study of the picture of the Weimar legal apparatus as painted by the Nazi party press, see M. Krohn, *Die deutsche Justiz im Urteil der Nationalsozialisten 1920–1933* (Frankfurt am Main, 1991).
4. For details of the campaign by *Das schwarze Korps*, see Gruchmann, *Justiz*, 663–75.
5. BA Berlin, R 3001/alt R 22/4085, Bl. 23–5: 'Rede vor den preußischen Staatsanwälten', *Berliner Börsen-Zeitung*, 13 July 1934, here Bl. 24. See also ibid., Bl. 22: 'Rede vor dem Staatsrat', *Berliner Lokal-Anzeiger*, 19 June 1934; Zweite Sitzung des Reichstags, 23 Mar. 1933, transcript partially reprinted in Hirsch *et al.* (eds), *Recht*, 93–108, here 97.
6. Gellately, *Backing Hitler*, passim.
7. See Wagner, *Kriminalpolizei*, 214; D.J.K. Peukert, 'Alltag und Barbarei. Zur Normalität des Dritten Reiches', in D. Diner (ed.), *Ist der Nationalsozialismus Geschichte?* (Frankfurt am Main, 1987), 51–61, here 56.
8. For example, the types of offence dealt with by the People's Court were excluded after 1933; J. Zarusky, 'Politischer Widerstand und Justiz im Dritten Reich', *Jahrbuch der Juristischen Zeitgeschichte* 1 (1999/2000), 36–87, here 74.
9. The amnesties in 1934 and 1936 applied to certain cases where a fine or a short prison sentence (less than six months in 1934, less than one month in 1936) had been expected. Not all of these cases included offences which would have been counted in the criminal statistics. For the figures, see BA Berlin, R 3001/alt R 22/1157, Bl. 29–35: Über die Entwicklung der Kriminalität in den letzten Jahren, 16 Feb. 1939.
10. For the pogrom and the judiciary, see Gruchmann, *Justiz*, 484–96.
11. For this view, see Gellately, *Backing Hitler*, 88.
12. Statistics about property offences reported to the police show that such reports had fallen by the mid-1930s (following the social crisis in the early 1930s) to a level comparable with 1927, before declining further in the late 1930s. While these figures are no unambiguous guide to common crime in Nazi Germany, they still suggest that property offences, on the whole, may have declined before the war. See Wagner, *Kriminalpolizei*, 214–18, 297–8.
13. For Prussia, see Schmidt, 'Aus der Statistik'; idem, 'Kosten'. For Hamburg, see Sarodnick, '"Dieses Haus"', 352.
14. BA Berlin, R 3001/9920/2, Bl. 2.
15. On 1 January 1927, there were 69,176 prisoners in Germany, more then 50,000 less than on 28 February 1937. The level of ordinary criminality was presumably rather similar in 1937 and 1927. (General economic conditions, which always have a crucial bearing on crime, were slightly better in 1937 than in 1927; and the number of property offences reported to the Prussian police in the mid-1930s was comparable to 1927. For these statistics, see Berghahn, *Germany*, 284, 290, tables 18 and 25; Wagner, *Kriminalpolizei*, 216.) Therefore one can assume that the excess in prisoners was largely due to the changes in the legal system after the Nazis took power.
16. There were different reasons for this fall in prisoner numbers, including the simultaneous extension of the police mandate; the amnesty of 30 April 1938, after the *Anschluss* of Austria; the significant fall in conviction rates for political offences, after most organised resistance had been destroyed.
17. Jasper, 'Justiz', 198–9; H. Wrobel, *Verurteilt zur Demokratie. Justiz und Justizpolitik in Deutschland 1945–1949* (Heidelberg, 1989), 20–2; Angermund, *Richterschaft*, 66–7.

18. The most detailed, if occasionally rather charitable, account of Gürtner's career can be found in Gruchmann, *Justiz*, 9–83, on which I have drawn in the following paragraphs. For a brief summary of Gruchmann's views, see idem, 'Franz Gürtner – Justizminister unter Hitler', in R. Smelser *et al.* (eds), *Die braune Elite*, vol. 2 (Darmstadt, 1993), 128–36. In the preface to the third edition of his *Justiz im Dritten Reich* (Munich, 2001), Gruchmann briefly responds to criticism that his picture of Gürtner is apologetic. For Gürtner's personal files, see BA Berlin, R 3001/alt R 22/Pers. 58396–58400.
19. For a detailed account of Hitler's appointment, see H.A. Turner, *Hitler's Thirty Days to Power: January 1933* (London, 1997).
20. Gruchmann, *Justiz*, 825–31, quotations on 829, 830.
21. Gesetz zur Änderung des Strafgesetzbuchs, 18 June 1935, reprinted in Hirsch *et al.* (eds), *Recht*, 455–6.
22. Gesamtergebnis der Durchführung des Gesetzes zur Wiederherstellung des Berufsbeamtentums vom 7.4.1933, reprinted in Bundesminister der Justiz (ed.), *Justiz und Nationalsozialismus* (Cologne, 1989), 78–9; Angermund, *Richterschaft*, 50–6; Gruchmann, *Justiz*, 1117. Jewish war veterans were officially exempted from dismissal until 1935.
23. For a detailed description, see N. Frei, *National Socialist Rule in Germany. The Führer State 1933–1945* (Oxford, 1993), 39–43.
24. A. Plett, 'Von Peine aus: Hanns Kerrl, eine Karriere im 1000-jährigen Reich', *Heimatkalender Peiner Land* 31 (2001), 59–68.
25. BA Berlin, R 3001/alt R 22/Pers. 56247; Gruchmann, *Justiz*, 100. There are two biographies of Freisler: G. Buchheit, *Richter in roter Robe* (Munich, 1968); H. Ortner, *Der Hinrichter. Roland Freisler – Mörder im Dienste Hitlers* (Vienna, 1993).
26. BA Berlin, R 3001/5660, R. Freisler, 'Gedanken zum Strafvollzuge', *General-Anzeiger Dortmund*, 8 Aug. 1933. For Freisler's views on criminal law, see J. Telp, *Ausmerzung und Verrat: zur Diskussion um Strafzwecke und Verbrechensbegriffe im Dritten Reich* (Frankfurt am Main, 1999), 105–32.
27. Quoted in Gruchmann, *Justiz*, 233; idem, 'Die "rechtsprechende Gewalt"', 92; H. Frank, 'Der Sinn der Strafe', *BlGefK* 66 (1935), 191–2, here 192. For Frank, see C. Kleßmann, 'Hans Frank – Parteijurist und Generalgouverneur in Polen', in R. Smelser *et al.* (eds), *Die Braune Elite*, vol. 1, 4th edition (Darmstadt, 1999), 41–51; Bundesminister der Justiz (ed.), *Justiz*, 146–7.
28. Gruchmann, *Justiz*, 92–123, 243–7; M. Broszat, *Der Staat Hitlers* (Munich, 1992), 154; Angermund, *Richterschaft*, 58–9. For Schlegelberger, see M. Förster, *Jurist im Dienst des Unrechts. Leben und Werk des ehemaligen Staatssekretärs im Reichsjustizministerium, Franz Schlegelberger* (Baden-Baden, 1995).
29. BA Berlin, R 3001/5606, Bayerisches Staatsministerium der Justiz to Staatsministerium des Äußeren, 10 Apr. 1923.
30. BayHStA, MJu 22507, RJM to Landesjustizverwaltungen, 24 Feb. 1930, appendix.
31. Quoted in Dörner, *Erziehung*, 190; Möhler, 'Strafvollzug', 27.
32. Cited in Sarodnick, '"Dieses Haus"', 347.
33. 'Die für den Strafvollzugsbeamten wichtigen, seit dem 30. Januar 1933 erlassenen Bestimmungen', *BlGefK* 66 (1935), Beilage zu Heft 3, 1–15, here 10.
34. BA Berlin, R 3001/alt R 22/Pers. 53758; ibid., R 2/Pers. SG (ex-BDC), Wilhelm Crohne; I. Müller, 'Der Weltbühnenprozeß von 1931', in S. Berkholz (ed.), *Carl von Ossietzky. 227 Tage im Gefängnis* (Darmstadt, 1988), 13–28, Ossietzky quote on 20;

Möhler, 'Strafvollzug', here 17 for the reference to 'elimination'; Angermund, *Richterschaft*, 42–3, note 129.
35. BA Berlin, Film 44840, Interrogation of Rudolf Marx, 25 Mar. 1947. See also ibid., R 3001/alt R 22/Pers. 67687; ibid., R 2/Pers. SG (ex. BDC), Rudolf Marx. The other two officials from the Prussian Ministry of Justice were Ludger Weddige and Robert Hecker. Siegmund Nörr and Johannes Eichler had joined, respectively, from Bavaria and Saxony; see ibid., R 3001/alt R 22/Pers. 59371; Gruchmann, *Justiz*, 244 (note 21), 259 (note 94), 261 (note 104).
36. BA Berlin, R 3001/alt R 22/Pers. Edgar Schmidt.
37. Gruchmann, *Justiz*, 226, 288–9, 1211–14. The figure for 1933 includes the general state prosecutor at the Berlin Kammergericht, but not the one at the Berlin district court. For most of the Weimar Republic, the regional prison administration in Prussia had been in the hands of the regional prison offices (*Strafvollzugsämter*), dissolved in 1933.
38. Edgar Schmidt, 'Der neue Strafvollzug', *Deutsche Justiz* 95 (1933), 638–40, here 638; idem, 'Treatment of Prisoners and of Habitual Offenders Sentenced to Preventive Detention', in Scott (ed.), *German Prisons*, 25–8, here 25. See also Möhler, 'Strafvollzug', 20–1.
39. 'General observations', in Scott (ed.), *German Prisons*, 106–14, here 112.
40. 'Die Wende im Strafvollzug!', *Der Strafvollzug* 23 (1933), 153–64, quotation on 154.
41. A meeting of the Study Group planned for April 1933 was cancelled, and there is no record of any meetings after this date in the Third Reich; ThHStAW, Justizministerium Nr. 1364, Bl. 30: Arbeitsgemeinschaft to Justizministerium, 31 Mar. 1933. The Study Group was re-formed after the war, meeting for the first time in 1948; A. Krebs, 'Tagung der "Arbeitsgemeinschaft für Reform des Strafvollzugs"', *ZfStrVo* 1 (1950), Nr. 6, 57.
42. Sarodnick, '"Dieses Haus"', 341–2.
43. BA Berlin, R 3001/alt R 22/Pers. 57079, Bl. 104: Gentz to Preußisches Justizministerium, 1 Apr. 1933. Gentz acknowledged his pacifism but denied the other claims, adding courageously that he would not be ashamed of being either a Jew or a member of the SPD paramilitary organisation. For the removal of the other two officials, Richard Preuss and Ludwig Bürger, see Möhler, 'Strafvollzug', 34.
44. Möhler, 'Strafvollzug', 39–42.
45. BayHStA, MJu 22509, Gefangenenanstalt Zweibrücken to GStA Zweibrücken, 12 July 1933.
46. Cited in Liang, 'Criminal-biological Theory', 241.
47. BayHStA, MJu 22470, Gefangenenanstalt St Georgen-Bayreuth to Oberregierungsrat Resch, 28 Sept. 1933.
48. E. Leißling, 'Die Anstaltsdisziplin', *BlGefK* 64 (1933), 320–9. This phrase had already been cited by Karl Krohne in the late nineteenth century; Krohne, *Lehrbuch*, 361.
49. Janus, 'Rückblick – Ausblick', reprinted in Justizakademie NRW (ed.), *Zum Strafvollzug 1933–1945*, source 13.
50. O. Weissenrieder, 'Vorwort', *BlGefK* 64 (1933), 113–17, here 116.
51. BayHStA, MJu 22508, Betreff Nr.2 der Tagesordnung für die Zusammenkunft der Landesjustizminister am 6. Mai 1933. See also Gruchmann, *Justiz*, 230–2.
52. P. Heinke, 'Der Strafvollzug in Sachsen nach dem 5. März 1933', *BlGefK* 65 (1934), 140–65.
53. BayHStA, MJu 22473, Preußisches Strafvollstreckungs- und Gnadenrecht, 1 Aug. 1933; Schmidt, 'Der neue Strafvollzug'.

54. BA Berlin, R 3001/5660, 'Der Strafvollzug', *Berliner Tageblatt*, 3 Aug. 1933; ibid., 'Was wir dazu sagen', *Der Angriff*, 3 Aug. 1933; ibid., R 3001/5659, Bl. 200: 'Das Ende des Dreiklassen-Strafvollzuges', *Völkischer Beobachter*, 27 Apr. 1933.
55. BA Berlin, R 3001/9803/64, Bl. 2–19: Niederschrift über die Konferenz vom 5/6. 10. 1933.
56. This was the first step towards the centralisation of the German prison service. Unlike the 1923 basic principles, the 14 May 1934 directive was legally binding for the different states. For a detailed discussion of the legal implications of the 14 May 1934 directive, see Quedenfeld, *Strafvollzug*, 24–32.
57. BA Berlin, R 3001/9803/64, Bl. 2–19: Niederschrift über die Konferenz vom 5./6.10.1933; 'Verordnung über den Vollzug von Freiheitsstrafen und von Maßregeln der Sicherung und Besserung die mit Freiheitsentziehung verbunden sind', *BlGefK* 65 (1934), Erstes Sonderheft, 1–21.
58. BA Berlin, R 3001/alt R 22/1292, Bl. 359–74: Vorstand der SPD, Entwicklungstendenzen im Deutschen Strafvollzug, 1935, here Bl. 362. See also Union für Recht und Freiheit (ed.), *Der Strafvollzug im III. Reich. Denkschrift und Materialsammlung* (Prague, 1936), 64–5.
59. BA Berlin, R 3001/alt R 22/5055, Bl. 1–33: Niederschrift über die Eröffnungssitzung der Kommission am 28.1.1935, quotation on Bl. 19.
60. A. Schoetensack et al., *Grundzüge eines deutschen Strafvollstreckungsrechts* (Berlin, 1935), 86–7; H. Finke, 'Der zukünftige Strafvollzug', *MSchriftKrim* 26 (1935), 537–40.
61. ThHStAW, Justizministerium Nr. 1573, Bl. 35: Strafanstalt Gräfentonna to GStA Jena, 23 Feb. 1935.
62. BA Berlin, R 3001/alt R 22/5055, Bl. 1–33: Niederschrift über die Eröffnungssitzung der Kommission am 28.1.1935.
63. Krohne, *Lehrbuch*, 353–62.
64. For a detailed account, see Gruchmann, *Justiz*, 753–822. See also Broszat, 'Perversion', 393.
65. BayHStA, MJu 22472, Staatsministerium der Justiz to Reichs- und Preußischer Justizminister, 6 Dec. 1934.
66. ThHStAW, Justizministerium Nr. 414, Bl. 62–3: Strafanstalt Ichtershausen, Beamtenbesprechung, 15 June 1936.
67. BA Berlin, R 3001/5660, 'Der neue Strafvollzug', *Vossische Zeitung*, 14 Oct. 1933.
68. See Union für Recht und Freiheit (ed.), *Strafvollzug*, 68–9; *Sopade*, vol. 2, 822–3; Maier, 'Strafvollzug', 927.
69. BA Berlin, R 3001/alt R 22/1300, Bl. 224: 'Achtungsbezeugungen der Strafgefangenen im Verkehr mit den Strafanstaltsbeamten', *Der Deutsche Justizbeamte*, 8 Sept. 1935.
70. W. Haensel, 'Militärische Formen im Strafvollzuge', *BlGefK* 67 (1936), 166–70, here 168.
71. E. Voigtländer, 'Über den Strafvollzug an Frauen', *BlGefK* 68 (1937), 268–78, here 269.
72. G. Begemann, 'Strafvollzug an Frauen', *BlGefK* 69 (1938–39), 202–6, here 202.
73. For some of these aspects, see Sarodnick, '"Dieses Haus"', 364; BA Berlin, R 3001/9939, Bl. 68–87: Strafanstalt St Georgen-Bayreuth, Dienstvorschriften, 1937; StAMü, Justizvollzugsanstalten Nr. 13822, Schießübung der Strafanstaltsbeamten, 6 July 1939.
74. BA Berlin, R 3001/9993, Bl. 207–10: Oberstrafanstaltsdirektor Brandenburg-Görden, 9 Oct. 1934. See also ibid., Bl. 205: Angaben zur Kenntnis des Geschäftsumfangs, no date. For the figure of 1,100, see Scott (ed.), *German Prisons*, 80.

75. ThHStAW, GStA bei dem OLG Jena Nr. 754, Bl. 7–16: Strafanstalt Untermaßfeld to GStA Jena, no date [summer 1936].

76. For this point, see K. Naumann, 'Die Justizvollzugsverwaltung im Institutionengefüge des NS-Staats. Das Beispiel Kassel-Wehlheiden', *Hessisches Jahrbuch für Landesgeschichte* 52 (2002), 115–44, here 120.

77. BA Berlin, R 3001/9819; ibid., R 3001/9820; ibid., R 3001/9821.

78. Ordinarily, most such positions had been reserved for ex-soldiers. But after pressure from the Nazi leadership, the Reich Ministry of Justice reserved many hundreds of warder positions between 1934 and 1938 for 'old fighters'. For an overview, see BA Berlin, R 3001/9820, Dr Schmidt, 'Die Ausbildung der Strafanstalts-Beamten', *Nationalsozialistische Beamtenzeitung*, 30 Oct. 1938.

79. ThHStAW, Justizministerium Nr. 414, Bl. 36: Beamtenbesprechung, 12 June 1935. For some other examples, see ibid., Nr. 421, Bl. 122–3: Strafanstalt Untermaßfeld to GStA Jena, 23 Apr. 1935; BA Berlin, R 3001/9993, Bl. 71: Wirtschaftsinspektor der Strafanstalt Brandenburg, 20 May 1933.

80. The upward mobility of new recruits was restricted by the rules governing promotion. For example, the 21 most senior warders in the Untermaßfeld penitentiary in 1937 had all been employed since at least 1929. See ThHStAW, GStA bei dem OLG Jena Nr. 229, Bl. 59–60: Beamte und Angestellte des Zuchthauses Untermaßfeld, 3 July 1937.

81. BA Berlin, R 3001/9993, Bl. 64–6: W. Kupfer to Kerrl, 3 May 1933; ibid., Bl. 67–8: A. Grutzeck to Göring, no date; ibid., Bl. 61–3: Bemerkungen zu den Angaben Kupfer und Genossen, 27 May 1933, quote on Bl. 62; ibid., Bl. 46–8: Präsident des Strafvollzugsamts Berlin to Preußischer Justizminister, 17 Aug. 1933; ibid., R 3001/alt R 22/Pers. Dr Rudolf Schwertdfeger; ibid., R 3001/alt R 22/721, Bl. 68: official diary Gürtner, 4 May 1937. For rather similar examples elsewhere, see GStA Düsseldorf, Vermerk, 8 June 1937, reprinted in Justizakademie NRW (ed.), *Zum Strafvollzug 1933–1945*, source 29c; Maier, 'Strafvollzug', 874–5, 972–6, 1000–1.

82. The *Bund der Gefängnis-, Straf- und Erziehungsanstaltsbeamten und -Beamtinnen* and the *Fachverband der deutschen Gefängnis- und Strafanstaltsoberbeamten und -Beamtinnen*, voluntarily dissolved themselves. The *Verein der deutschen Strafanstaltsbeamten* joined the BNSDJ. The *Verein* soon changed its name to *Deutsche Gesellschaft für Gefängniskunde* and in 1935 Frank became its leader; BA Berlin, R 3001/5659, Bl. 205: 'Aufgelöste Beamtenverbände', *Vossische Zeitung*, 21 June 1933; 'Verein der Deutschen Strafanstaltsbeamten, Protokoll über die Mitgliederversammlung vom 20.12.1933', *BlGefK* 65 (1934), 42–5; O. Weissenrieder, 'Mitteilungen der Schriftleitung', *BlGefK* 66 (1935), 302–4.

83. For example BA Berlin, R 3001/alt R 22/4273, Bl. 36: GStA Nuremberg to RJM, 10 Mar. 1937; ThHStAW, GStA bei dem OLG Jena Nr. 230, Bl. 297: Zuchthaus Untermaßfeld to GStA Jena, 21 July 1945. The Aichach governor Reitzenstein was only promoted after he received his party membership in 1940, following repeated conflicts with the local NSDAP; BA Berlin, R 3001/alt R 22/Pers. Dr von Reitzenstein.

84. ThHStAW, Justizministerium Nr. 421, Bl. 70–4: A. B. to Oberregierungsrat Regis, 17 Aug. 1934. For this case, see also ibid., Bl. 63–6: Beschwerden der alten Kämpfer, no date [1934].

85. *Sopade*, vol. 2, 370.

86. ThHStAW, Justizministerium Nr. 1718, Bl. 1–2: Beschwerde des Gefangenen O., 3 June 1935.

87. Cited in Sarodnick, '"Dieses Haus"', 365.

88. For some examples, see Oerter, *Zuchthaus*, 125–6; Leuss, *Zuchthause*, 218; Witter, 'Funktion und Organisation', 80. For the legal regulations, see Naumann, 'Justizverwaltung', 140. The court could only charge prisoners who had used force or damaged property during their escape attempt.
89. Drobisch, 'Alltag', 260–4.
90. See, for instance, *Sopade*, vol. 3, 47, 1021.
91. For the figures, see BA Berlin, R 3001/9908.
92. *Statistik über die Gefangenenanstalten in Preußen 1929*. See also, for example, BayHStA, MJu 22489, Staatsministerium des Inneren to Staatsministerium der Justiz, 24 Nov. 1924; G. Fuchs, *Wir Zuchthäusler. Erinnerungen des Zellengefangenen Nr. 2911 im Zuchthaus geschrieben* (Munich, 1931), 69; H. Völker, 'Das System der Hausstrafen im modernen Strafvollzug' (Ph.D., University of Leipzig, 1931), 68; BA Berlin, R 3001/5611, E.J. Gumbel, 'Gedanken zum Strafvollzug', *Dresdener Volkszeitung*, 16 Nov. 1929.
93. Cited in Möhler, 'Strafvollzug', 26.
94. O. Weissenrieder, 'Der Wachtmeisterkurs im Oberlandesgerichtsbezirk Stuttgart', *BlGefK* 67 (1936), 12–33, here 27–8.
95. BayHStA, MJu 22496, Jahresbericht des Anstaltsgeistlichen in Zweibrücken, 23 June 1934; ibid., MJu 22510, Gefangenenanstalt St Georgen-Bayreuth to GStA Bamberg, 14 July 1934. For Prussia, see Schmidt, 'Der neue Strafvollzug'. For some time, Saxony apparently retained more privileges on the higher stages than most other German states; *Sopade*, vol. 4, 1549; vol. 5, 880, 884; Union für Recht und Freiheit (ed.), *Strafvollzug*, 66.
96. See, for example, BayHStA, MJu 22496, Verzeichnis der besonderen Veranstaltungen vom 1.7.1933 mit 1.7.1934; ibid., MJu 22499, Vollzugsanzeigen zur Entschließung vom 26.6.1933; G. Joerger, *Die deutsche Gefängnispresse in Vergangenheit und Gegenwart* (Stuttgart, 1971), 35–7.
97. BA Berlin, R 3001/9803/78, Bl. 7–18: Geheime Staatspolizei to Reichsführer SS und Chef der deutschen Polizei, 12 July 1938.
98. See BayHStA, MJu 22556, Anstaltslehrer Burkel to Staatsministerium der Justiz, 8 June 1934; *Sopade*, vol. 3, 54; StAMü, GStA bei dem OLG München Nr. 49, Lehrplan 1938/9 der Frauenstrafanstalt Aichach.
99. ThHStAW, GStA bei dem OLG Jena Nr. 754, Bl. 21–3: Strafanstalt Untermaßfeld to GStA Jena, 4 Nov. 1936.
100. I. Kershaw, *The 'Hitler Myth'. Image and Reality in the Third Reich* (Oxford, 1989), *passim*.
101. BayHStA, MJu 22620, Sächsisches Ministerium der Justiz to Gefangenenanstalten, 9 Aug. 1933.
102. Ibid., Staatsministerium der Justiz to Badischer Minister für Kultus, Unterricht und Justiz, 7 Aug. 1933.
103. See, for example, BA Berlin, R 3001/alt R 22/131, Bl. 87: official diary Gürtner, 17 Dec. 1934; ibid., 3001/alt R 22/706, Bl. 128–9: official diary Gürtner, 26 Feb. 1937.
104. See Oleschinski, 'Gefängnisseelsorge', 177–8, 187; Maier, 'Strafvollzug', 935; *Sopade*, vol. 3, 48; BA Berlin, R 3001/5603, *Zentralblatt für das deutsche Reich*, 31 Dec. 1920.
105. M. Schumacher (ed.), *M.d.R.. Die Reichstagsabgeordneten der Weimarer Republik in der Zeit des Nationalsozialismus* (Düsseldorf, 1991), 331. For Muntau's fanaticism, see BA Berlin, R 3001/5611, 'Beinahe Revolte im Zuchthaus', *Vorwärts*, 3 Jan. 1931.
106. For example *Sopade*, vol. 2, 818; ThHStAW, GStA bei dem OLG Jena Nr. 755, Bl. 49–55: Niederschrift über die Besprechung der Direktoren, 26 Oct. 1937.

107. BA Berlin, R 3001/alt R 22/1292, Bl. 359–74: Vorstand der SPD, Entwicklungstendenzen im Deutschen Strafvollzug, 1935. According to official statements, the expenditure on food in Prussian penal institutions was cut by over 10 per cent in real terms in 1933; Edgar Schmidt, 'Kosten', 1346–7.
108. U. Thoms, '"Eingeschlossen/Ausgeschlossen". Die Ernährung in Gefängnissen vom 18. bis 20. Jahrhundert', in U. Spickermann (ed.), *Ernährung in Grenzsituationen* (Berlin, 2002), 45–69, here 53–6.
109. BA Berlin, R 3001/alt R 22/1438, Bl. 330: GStA Naumburg to RJM, 20 Feb. 1937.
110. BayHStA, MJu 22473, Preußisches Strafvollstreckungs- und Gnadenrecht, 1 Aug. 1933. See also BA Berlin, R 3001/5660, 'Was wir dazu sagen', *Der Angriff*, 3 Aug. 1933.
111. See D.J.K. Peukert, *Inside Nazi Germany. Conformity, Opposition and Racism in Everyday Life* (London, 1993), 50, 55; Noakes, Pridham (eds), *Nazism*, vol. 2, 325; K. Eden, 'Prison Economy', in Scott (ed.), *German Prisons*, 47–53.
112. *Sopade*, vol. 3, 1025.
113. Ibid., 1019. See also ibid., 46, 48, 53, 1004; ibid., vol. 4, 715.
114. See, for example, Strafanstaltsdirektor Herford, Betrifft Medizinalrat Dr Ulrich, 14 Nov. 1936, reprinted in Justizakademie NRW (ed.), *Zum Strafvollzug 1933–1945*, source 23a; ThHStAW, GStA bei dem OLG Jena Nr. 1069, Bl. 35–6: Gesundheitszustand, Zuchthaus Untermaßfeld, 11 Jan. 1938.
115. BA Berlin, R 3001/alt R 22/1439, Bl. 105: Vermerk, March 1938.
116. Ibid., Bl. 114–15: RJM to Generalstaatsanwälte, 25 Apr. 1938.
117. BA Berlin, R 3001/alt R 22/1439, Bl. 166–7: GStA Oldenburg to RJM, 25 June 1938. See also ibid., Bl. 239: Gefangenenbeköstigung, no date [November 1938].
118. Union für Recht und Freiheit (ed.), *Strafvollzug*, 73–5, 91.
119. See, for instance, BA Berlin, R 3001/alt R 22/1292, Bl. 359–74: Vorstand der SPD, Entwicklungstendenzen im Deutschen Strafvollzug, 1935; *Sopade*, vol. 4, 717. See also Möhler, 'Strafvollzug', 89.
120. StAMü, GStA bei dem OLG München Nr. 49, GStA Munich to Staatsministerium der Justiz, 31 Mar. 1934.
121. Union für Recht und Freiheit (ed.), *Strafvollzug*, 75.
122. Strafanstaltsdirektor Remscheid-Lüttringhausen to GStA Düsseldorf, 11 July 1935, reprinted in Justizakademie NRW (ed.), *Zum Strafvollzug 1933–1945*, source 21.
123. For inmate figures, see BA Berlin, R 3001/9882 (the figures do not include female inmates in workhouses and youth prisons). The official maximum capacity was probably around 6,000; RJM (ed.), *Gefängniswesen*, 35–42.
124. Krohne, *Lehrbuch*, 360 (note 2), 448.
125. E.J. Gumbel, 'Strafvollzugsstatistik', *Die Justiz* 5 (1929–1930), 738–58, here 750–1; 'Grundsätze für den Vollzug von Freiheitsstrafen', § 11.
126. For one example, see StAMü, Justizvollzugsanstalten Nr. 13789, Zuchthaus Aichach to Staatsministerium der Justiz, 7 Jan. 1929; BayHStA, MJu 22686, Staatsministerium der Justiz to Zuchthaus Aichach, 25 Nov. 1929.
127. C. von Gélieu, *Frauen in Haft* (Berlin, 1994), 68–70; StAMü, GStA bei dem OLG München Nr. 49, Gefangenenanstalt Aichach to GStA Munich, 7 Sept. 1937.
128. StAMü, GStA bei dem OLG München Nr. 49, Nachschau in Aichach, 14 Feb. 1936; Union für Recht und Freiheit (ed.), *Strafvollzug*, 99.
129. The remaining 69 institutions were reserved for men only; RJM (ed.), *Gefängniswesen*, 35–42.
130. For the Weimar period, see Ellering, 'Strafvollzug', 355.

131. See BayHStA, MJu 22675, Gefangenenanstalt Aichach to Staatsministerium der Justiz, 15 June 1931; F.-W. Kersting, *Anstaltsärzte zwischen Kaiserreich und Bundesrepublik* (Paderborn, 1996), 368.
132. StAMü, Justizvollzugsanstalten Nr. 13807, Personalbogen Ludwig Schemmel, no date; ibid., Nr. 6051, Bl. 54: Anstaltsarzt to Direktion, 10 Mar. 1936.
133. Ibid., Nr. 5258, Bl. 23: Appolonia J. to Direktion, 3 Nov. 1940. See also ibid., Nr. 13807, Oberstaatsanwalt Munich to Frauenstraf- und Verwahrungsanstalt Aichach, 11 Oct. 1938.
134. Ibid., GStA bei dem OLG München Nr. 49, Anstaltsbeamte der Strafanstalt Aichach to GStA Munich, no date [March 1938]; ibid., Beamtinnen der Strafanstalt Aichach to GStA Munich, 31 Jan. 1937.
135. For one example, see ThHStAW, GStA bei dem OLG Jena Nr. 754, Bl. 7–16: Strafanstalt Untermaßfeld to GStA Jena, no date [summer, 1936]. Such costs did not arise in cases where a prisoner was classified as so ill that the sentence was officially suspended.
136. Eden, 'Prison Economy', 49.
137. ThHStAW, GStA bei dem OLG Jena Nr. 856, Bl. 55–7: Staatspolizeileitstelle Weimar, Befragung des Karel N., 16 Feb. 1939.
138. Niederschrift über die Vorsteherbesprechung am 16.11.1934, reprinted in Justizakademie NRW (ed.), *Zum Strafvollzug 1933–1945*, source 19.
139. E. Wutzdorff, 'Die Arbeit der Gefangenen', in Bumke (ed.), *Gefängniswesen*, 178–97; Gumbel, 'Strafvollzugsstatistik', 30–2. See also 'Statistik des Gefängniswesens', table 9.
140. Schmidt, 'Aus der Statistik'. In 1932, 37 per cent of the male penitentiary inmates in Prussia were unemployed. For women, the figure was 25 per cent.
141. Frei, *National Socialist Rule*, 71–2. For the Nazi economy in general, see R. Overy, *The Nazi Economic Recovery 1932–1938* (Cambridge, 1996).
142. BA Berlin, R 3001/9882, Bl. 6.
143. BA Berlin, R 3001/9957, Dr Crohne, Vermerk, 6 Nov. 1934.
144. *Sopade*, vol. 2, 824.
145. F. Schlotterbeck, *Je dunkler die Nacht, desto heller die Sterne* (Berlin, 1948), 62.
146. BA Berlin, R 3001/9803/64, Bl. 2–19: Niederschrift über die Konferenz vom 5/6.10.1933; ibid., R 3001/alt R 22/1395, Bl. 17: Preußischer Justizminister to Strafvollzugsämter, 5 Apr. 1933; ibid., R 3001/9957, Dr Crohne, Vermerk, 6 Nov. 1934.
147. Ibid., R 3001/9957, Preußischer Justizminister to Finanzminister, 1 Dec. 1933.
148. BA Berlin, R 3001/alt R 22/1263, Bl. 90–9: Zusammenkunft der Oberreichsanwälte und Generalstaatsanwälte, 23 Jan. 1939.
149. BA Berlin, R 3001/alt R 22/1437, Bl. 440: Übersicht über den Arbeitseinsatz der Gefangenen.
150. *Sopade*, vol. 4, 1546.
151. Hitler memorandum, translated and reprinted in Noakes, Pridham (eds), *Nazism*, vol. 2, 281–7. For the general background, see R. Overy, *War and Economy in the Third Reich* (Oxford, 1994), passim. See also L. Herbst, *Das nationalsozialistische Deutschland 1933–1945* (Frankfurt am Main, 1996), 160–77.
152. Wilmanns, *Zurechnungsfähigkeit*, 96. See also Krohne, *Lehrbuch*, 388–407.
153. BA Berlin, 62 DAF 3/1786, Bl. 53: 'Besserung durch Strafe', *Frankfurter Zeitung*, 15 Nov. 1924; GStA PK, I. HA Rep. 84a Justizministerium Nr. 17962 (M), Bl. 45–175: Nachweisung über die gesundheitlichen Verhältnisse, no date; P. Borchers, 'Die Gefangenenarbeit in den deutschen Strafanstalten', *BlGefK* 54 (1921), 7–146, here 43;

F. Rinke, 'Die Gefängnisarbeit als Problem des Strafvollzugs und der Gewerbepolitik' (Ph.D., University of Cologne, 1926), 9–25.
154. M. Polenz, 'Gefängnisarbeit', in Preußisches Justizministerium (ed.), *Strafvollzug*, 214–23.
155. 'Die Strafanstalten in Deutschland'. County jails are not included in these figures. See also ThHStAW, Justizministerium Nr. 1339, Bl. 28: 'Der moderne Strafvollzug', *Leipziger Tageblatt*, 3 June 1924.
156. K. Uhl, 'Das "verbrecherische Weib" im Diskurs der Humanwissenschaften vom Kaiserreich bis zum "Dritten Reich"' (M.A. diss., Hamburg University, 1997), *passim*; Reuß, *Strafvollzug*, 20. See also Ellering, 'Strafvollzug', 356.
157. BayHStA, MJu 22495, A. Dimpfl to Staatsministerium der Justiz, 1 May 1928.
158. A. Neuhaus, 'Die Frau im Gefängnis', in Preußisches Justizministerium (ed.), *Strafvollzug*, 114–33, here 116; Reuß, *Strafvollzug*, 18–20.
159. BA Berlin, R 3001/alt R 22/1437, Bl. 443: Zahl der in den Arbeitsbetrieben im Werktagsdurchschnitt des zweiten Viertels des RJ 1937 beschäftigten Gefangenen. For the English and US practice, see M. Grünhut, *Penal Reform* (Oxford, 1948), 205–6.
160. Langenhan, 'Der Vierjahresplan und die Gefangenenarbeit', *BlGefK* 68 (1937), 294–6; IfZ, Ms 361, W. Schwerdtfeger, 'Zuchthausjahre 1935–1945', 97–104. For the quotation, see BA Berlin, R 3001/5659, Bl. 142: 'Pensum', *Vorwärts*, 6 Aug. 1929.
161. SPD officials in the Weimar period had generally been skilled workers and artisans; H. Grebing, *Geschichte der deutschen Arbeiterbewegung* (Munich, 1970), 166.
162. BA Berlin, R 3001/alt R 22/1429, Bl. 76–9: R. Freisler, 'Arbeitseinsatz des Strafvollzuges im Dienste des Vierjahresplanes', *Deutsche Justiz* 100 (1938). See also *Sopade*, vol. 5, 882.
163. See, for example, Leiter der Reichsstelle für Raumordnung, Vermerk, 13 Feb. 1939, reprinted in Kosthorst, Walter (eds), *Strafgefangenenlager*, vol. 1, 822–3.
164. See, for example, BA Berlin, R 3001/alt R 22/1437, Bl. 153: RJM to Reichsführer SS und Chef der deutschen Polizei, 14 July 1938 (handwritten draft).
165. Ibid., R 3001/alt R 22/1429, Bl. 67–9: RJM to Reichsanstalt für Arbeitsvermittlung, 22 Mar. 1938. See also ibid., R 3001/alt R 22/1261, Bl. 106: Tätigkeitsbericht über das Gefangenenarbeitswesen, 17 Dec. 1938.
166. ThHStAW, GStA bei dem OLG Jena Nr. 430, Bl. 30–9: Besprechung am 12.4.1938; BA Berlin, R 3001/alt R 22/1429, Bl. 67–9: RJM to Reichsanstalt für Arbeitsvermittlung, 22 Mar. 1938.
167. BA Berlin, R 3001/alt R 22/1429, Bl. 76–9: R. Freisler, 'Arbeitseinsatz des Strafvollzuges im Dienste des Vierjahresplanes', *Deutsche Justiz* 100 (1938). See also ibid., R 3001/alt R 22/1263, Bl. 36–53: Arbeitstagung der Generalstaatsanwälte am 14.11.1936; ibid., R 3001/alt R 22/1395, Bl. 103: RJM to Generalstaatsanwälte, 22 Mar. 1938; ibid., R 3001/9863, Bl. 40: RJM to Generalstaatsanwälte, 11 Aug. 1939.
168. BA Berlin, R 3001/alt R 22/5087, Bl. 90–2: GStA Jena to RJM, 30 June 1937; ThHStAW, GStA bei dem OLG Jena Nr. 430, Bl. 30–9: Besprechung am 12.4.1938; ibid., Bl. 57–70: Arbeitstagung am 6. und 7.2.1939.
169. BA Berlin, R 3001/alt R 22/1263, Bl. 90–9: Zusammenkunft der Oberreichsanwälte und Generalstaatsanwälte, 23 Jan. 1939.
170. Ibid., R 3001/alt R 22/1395, Bl. 143: Gesamtübersicht über die Auswirkungen des Runderlaßes vom 18.5.1938, no date [Dec. 1938].
171. BA Berlin, R 3001/alt R 22/1437, Bl. 436–7: Vermerk, Stand vom 31.5.1938; ibid., Bl. 440: Übersicht über den Arbeitseinsatz, no date [1938]; Drobisch, 'Alltag', 257.
172. G. Schwarz, *Die nationalsozialistischen Lager* (Frankfurt am Main, 1996).

173. For the complex early years of the camps in the Emsland, see Tuchel, *Konzentrationslager*, 65–91. See also Suhr, *Emslandlager*, 27–43; Kosthorst, Walter (eds), *Strafgefangenenlager*, vol. 1, 527–41.
174. Kosthorst, Walter (eds), *Strafgefangenenlager*, vol. 2, 1806.
175. Cited in Suhr, *Emslandlager*, 212.
176. Michaëlis, 'Harrende Aufgaben', *BlGefK* 52 (1918), 68–71, here 70. For Prussia, see Berger, *Repression*, 134.
177. *Statistik über die Gefangenenanstalten in Preußen 1926*; 'Die Strafanstalten in Deutschland', 35; Behrle, *Stellung*, 128.
178. JVA Straubing (ed.), *100 Jahre*, 73–7.
179. At that time, the Emsland camp included the camps Börgermoor, Neusustrum, Aschendorfermoor, Brual-Rhede, Oberlangen, Walchum and Esterwegen. See D. Lüerßen, '"Moorsoldaten" in Esterwegen, Börgermoor, Neusustrum', in W. Benz, B. Distel (eds), *Frühe Konzentrationslager 1933–39* (Berlin, 2002), 157–210, here 207. For the inmate figures, see Kosthorst, Walter (eds), *Strafgefangenenlager*, vol. 2, 1777.
180. BA Berlin, R 3001/alt R 22/1437, Bl. 166: Beauftragter für den Vierjahresplan to RJM, 14 June 1938. For the importance of the Four-Year Plan office, see G. Aly, S. Heim, *Vordenker der Vernichtung* (Frankfurt am Main, 1993), 49–52.
181. BA Berlin, R 43 II/1537, Bl. 46: Reichskanzlei, Vermerk, 13 Jan. 1936; ibid., Bl. 101: Reichskanzlei, Vermerk, 10 Feb. 1937.
182. BA Berlin, R 3001/alt R 22/1263, Bl. 36–53: Arbeitstagung der Generalstaatsanwälte am 14.11.1936, here Bl. 41.
183. ThHStAW, GStA bei dem OLG Jena Nr. 997/1, Bl. 109–11: RJM to Reichsminister des Inneren, 9 Feb. 1939; BA Berlin, R 3001/alt R 22/1261, Bl. 100–1: Tätigkeitsbericht, 19 Dec. 1938; ibid., R 3001/alt R 22/1437, Bl. 440: Übersicht über den Arbeitseinsatz, no date [1938].
184. H. Semler, 'Strafvollzug in festen Anstalten und in Lagern', *BlGefK* 70 (1939), 3–14, here 3, 8–9.
185. The other camps were Wohnschiff Biber, Schleusendurchstich, Elbebogen and Saaledurchstich. See HStAD-Kalkum, Gerichte Rep. 321/1030, Bl. 42: GStA Naumburg to GStA Cologne, 17 Nov. 1936; ibid., Bl. 68: GStA Naumburg to GStA Cologne, 30 June 1937; Möhler, 'Strafvollzug', 86; Fricke, *Justizvollzugsanstalt*, 32.
186. BA Berlin, R 3001/alt R 22/1395, Bl. 123–4: RJM to Generalstaatsanwälte, 14 July 1938.
187. See ibid.; Kosthorst, Walter (eds), *Strafgefangenenlager*, vol. 1, 541–8; ibid., vol. 2, 1777; Suhr, *Emslandlager*, 194–8; BA Berlin, R 3001/alt R 22/1437, Bl. 306–8: Vermerk über die Besprechung in der Reichsstelle für Raumordnung vom 22.2.1939.
188. So-called 'Hossbach memorandum', reprinted and translated in Noakes, Pridham (eds), *Nazism*, vol. 3 (Exeter, 1988), 680–7.
189. Order for 'Operation Green', reprinted and translated ibid., 712.
190. Ollmann, 'Der Einsatz der Strafgefangenen beim Bau der Ostmarkstraße', *BlGefK* 72 (1941–42), 53–61; W. Nerdinger (ed.), *Bauen im Nationalsozialismus. Bayern 1933–1945* (Munich, 1993), 79; K. Drobisch, 'Konzentrationslager und Justizhaft. Versuch einer Zusammenschau', in H. Grabitz *et al.* (eds), *Die Normalität des Verbrechens* (Berlin, 1994), 280–97, here 287.
191. W. Dreßen, 'Westwall', in W. Benz *et al.* (eds), *Enzyklopädie des Nationalsozialismus* (Munich, 1997), 806.
192. RJM to Preußischer Finanzminister, 14 Sept. 1938, reprinted in Kosthorst, Walter (eds), *Strafgefangenenlager*, vol. 1, 783–5; Staatshochbauamt Lingen to Preußischer

Finanzminister, 20 Sept. 1938, reprinted ibid., 787–8; BA Berlin, R 3001/9859, Bl. 16: Vermerk zur Besichtigungsreise vom 6–8.7.1941; ibid., R 3001/alt R 22/1437, Bl. 194: Höherer SS- und Polizeiführer-Westgrenze to Ministerialdirektor Crohne, 7 Sept. 1938; Möhler, 'Strafvollzug', 87.
193. See Nerdinger (ed.), *Bauen*, 80; Ollmann, 'Einsatz', 53–7. The camp Bayerische Ostmark included the following camps: Grassersdorf, Oberviechtach, Zeinried-Süd, Zeinried-Nord, Bischofsgrün and Prackenbach.
194. Ollmann, 'Einsatz', 58.
195. BayHStA, MInn 71571, Auszug aus dem Monatsbericht des Bezirksamts Oberviechtach, 30 Sept. 1938.
196. BLHA, Ld. Br. Rep. 214 Forschungsstelle Zuchthaus Brandenburg Nr. 2, Bl. 248–51: curriculum vitae Walter N., no date.
197. Ibid, BLHA, Pr. Br. Rep. 29 Zuchthaus Luckau Nr. 122, Willi B. to his wife, 4 Sept. 1938.
198. Letter of inmate M., 15 Sept. 1937, reprinted in Kosthorst, Walter (eds), *Strafgefangenenlager*, vol. 3, 2411. See also Schwurgerichts-Anklage gegen W. Schäfer vor dem Landgericht Oldenburg, 22 July 1950, reprinted ibid., 2506–50, here 2527–8; Suhr, *Emslandlager*, 115–16.
199. Urteil Schwurgericht Oldenburg, 9 ks 1/49, reprinted ibid., 1985–2035. See also BA Berlin, R 3001/9820, RJM to Generalstaatsanwälte, 21 Mar. 1938.
200. For Schäfer, see Schwurgerichts-Anklage gegen W. Schäfer vor dem Landgericht Oldenburg, 22 July 1950, reprinted in Kosthorst, Walter (eds), *Strafgefangenenlager*, vol. 3, 2506–50, here 2508–9.
201. See, for example, Urteil Schwurgericht Oldenburg, 9 ks 1/49, reprinted in Kosthorst, Walter (eds), *Strafgefangenenlager*, vol. 2, 1985–2035, quotation on 1997; Aussage Gefangener M., reprinted ibid., vol. 3, 2411–12; Suhr, *Emslandlager*, 141–3. For one of several postwar accounts by former prisoners, see K. Schröder, 'Die letzte Station', in F. Ausländer (ed.), *Die letzte Station* (Bremen, 1995), 34–137.
202. BA Berlin, R 3001/alt R 22/945, Bl. 149–59: official diary Gürtner, 15 Feb. 1939.
203. Aussage Gefangener P., reprinted in Kosthorst, Walter (eds), *Strafgefangenenlager*, vol. 3, 2414.
204. Aussage Gefangener Z., reprinted ibid., 2417.
205. Suhr, *Emslandlager*, 138–9; Kosthorst, Walter (eds), *Strafgefangenenlager*, vol. 3, 3549; Aussage Gefangener F., reprinted ibid., 2411; Urteil Schwurgericht Oldenburg, 9 ks 1/49, reprinted ibid., vol. 2, 1985–2035, here 1995; BA Berlin, R 3001/alt R 22/945, Bl. 104–5: official diary Gürtner, 29 Jan. 1939.
206. Kosthorst, Walter (eds), *Strafgefangenenlager*, vol. 3, 2326.
207. Ibid., 2324–7, 2524; 'Fünf Jahre Moor-SA', *Ems-Zeitung*, 28 Nov. 1938, extract reprinted ibid., vol. 1, 1089–92.
208. Ibid., vol. 2, 1910. See also Suhr, *Emslandlager*, 223–5.
209. Cited in Fricke, *Justizvollzugsanstalt*, 32. See also BA Berlin, R 3001/9862, Bl. 30: Befehl Nr. 7, 21 Jan. 1939; Ayaß, *Arbeitshaus*, 297.
210. BA Berlin, R 3001/9862, Bl. 74–5: Befehl Nr. 32, 3 Nov. 1938.
211. BLHA, Ld. Br. Rep. 214 Forschungsstelle Zuchthaus Brandenburg Nr. 2, Bl. 248–51: curriculum vitae Walter N., no date; Ollmann, 'Einsatz', 60.
212. BA Berlin, R 3001/alt R 22/734, Bl. 23–6: official diary Gürtner, 9 Sept. 1937; ibid., R 3001/alt R 22/945, Bl. 42–6: official diary Gürtner, 18 Jan. 1938. For Semler, see H.-E. Niermann, 'Strafjustiz und Nationalsozialismus im OLG-Bezirk Hamm, 1933–1945',

in Oberstadtdirektor der Stadt Hamm (ed.), *Ortstermin Hamm. Zur Justiz im Dritten Reich* (Hamm, 1991), 17–45, here 22–3.
213. Semler, 'Strafvollzug', 11–12; Ollmann, 'Einsatz', 58–9; BA Berlin, R 3001/9862, Bl. 19–23: Befehl Nr. 4, 17 Jan. 1939.
214. BA Berlin, R 3001/alt R 22/245, Arbeitstagung am 23. und 24.4.1941, here Bl. 185.
215. BLHA, Ld. Br. Rep. 214 Forschungsstelle Zuchthaus Brandenburg Nr. 2, Bl. 248–51: curriculum vitae Walter N., no date. According to the Regensburg police, some 90 penitentiary inmates escaped between June and November 1938; BayHStA, MInn 71571, Staatsministerium des Inneren to GStA Nuremberg, 15 Dec. 1938.
216. BA Berlin, R 3001/9862, Bl. 43–6: Befehl Nr. 11, 2 May 1939; ibid., Bl. 78–9: Befehl Nr. 29, 31 Oct. 1938; BayHStA, MInn 71571, GStA Nuremberg to Staatsministerium des Inneren, 15 Nov. 1938; Ollmann, 'Einsatz', 58–60.
217. ThHStAW, GStA bei dem OLG Jena Nr. 430, Bl. 57–70: Arbeitstagung am 6. und 7.2.1939, quotation on Bl. 68. See also Dübbers, 'Vierjahresplan und Außenarbeit der Gefangenen', *BlGefK* 68 (1937), 365–9.

Chapter 3

1. Cited in Broszat, 'Konzentrationslager', 328. For Nazi attacks on the left-wing parties, see also T. Klepsch, *Nationalsozialistische Ideologie. Beschreibung ihrer Struktur vor 1933* (Münster, 1990), esp. 197–200.
2. BA Berlin, R 3001/9920/2.
3. I. Kershaw, *Popular Opinion & Political Dissent in the Third Reich* (Oxford, 1983), 94–5, 109, quote on 374; idem, *'Hitler Myth'*, 65, 71, 86–7, 126–8; Noakes, Pridham (eds), *Nazism*, vol. 2, 351–3, 373–4. For the long-standing debates about the definition of resistance in Nazi Germany, see, for example, I. Kershaw, *The Nazi Dictatorship. Problems and Perspectives of Interpretation*, 3rd edition (London, 1993), 151–79; D.C. Large (ed.), *Contending with Hitler. Varieties of German Resistance in the Third Reich* (Cambridge, 1995).
4. The decree and the law are reprinted in Hirsch *et al.* (eds), *Recht*, 90–1, 286–8. For the general background see Dörner, *'Heimtücke'*, 17–25, Schlegelberger quotation on 18.
5. For this and the preceding paragraph, see Decree for the Formation of Special Courts, partially reprinted Hirsch *et al.* (eds), *Recht*, 470–1; P. Hüttenberger, 'Heimtückefälle vor dem Sondergericht München 1933–1939', in M. Broszat *et al.* (eds), *Bayern in der NS-Zeit*, vol. 4 (Munich, 1981), 435–526, esp. 443, 455, 476; G. Weckbecker, *Zwischen Freispruch und Todesstrafe. Die Rechtsprechung der nationalsozialistischen Sondergerichte Frankfurt/Main und Bromberg* (Baden-Baden, 1998), 77, 388, 779, 800; Dörner, *'Heimtücke'*, 69–70, 78–9, 87–93, 169, for the quotation see 313; K. Bästlein, 'Sondergerichte in Norddeutschland als Verfolgungsinstanz', in F. Bajohr (ed.), *Norddeutschland im Nationalsozialismus* (Hamburg, 1993), 218–38, here 221–2, 227; H.-U. Ludewig, D. Kuessner, *'Es sei also jeder gewarnt'. Das Sondergericht Braunschweig 1933–1945* (Braunschweig, 2000), 303; M. Zeidler, *Das Sondergericht Freiberg. Zu Justiz und Repression in Sachsen 1933–1940* (Dresden, 1998), 33, 58; C. Oehler, *Die Rechtsprechung des Sondergerichts Mannheim 1933–1945* (Berlin, 1997), 243–4; Broszat, *Staat Hitlers*, 408; Angermund, *Richterschaft*, 133–45.

6. D.J.K. Peukert, *Die KPD im Widerstand* (Wuppertal, 1980), 98–250; idem, 'Working-class Resistance', in Large (ed.), *Contending with Hitler*, 35–48; H. Mehringer, 'Sozialdemokratischer und sozialistischer Widerstand', in P. Steinbach, J. Tuchel (eds), *Widerstand gegen den Nationalsozialismus* (Bonn, 1994), 126–43; M. Stolle, *Die Geheime Staatspolizei in Baden* (Konstanz, 2001), 224–5.
7. Zarusky, 'Politischer Widerstand', 56–7; A. Knobelsdorf, 'Das Bielefelder Landgericht 1933–1945', in Justizministerium des Landes NRW (ed.), *Justiz und Nationalsozialismus* (Düsseldorf, 1993), 47–101, here 68–9.
8. Niermann, *Strafjustiz*, 217.
9. Gruchmann, *Justiz*, 823–4, 844–7; Zarusky, 'Politischer Widerstand', 42–9, 80. The 28 February 1933 decree should not be confused with the Reichstag Fire Decree of the same date.
10. 'Die für den Strafvollzugsbeamten wichtigen Bestimmungen', 4; Gruchmann, *Justiz*, 776, n. 7.
11. *Kriminalstatistik 1932*, 106–7; *Kriminalstatistik 1933*, 162–3.
12. D. Pohl, *Justiz in Brandenburg 1945–1955. Gleichschaltung und Anpassung* (Munich, 2001), 322.
13. Mehringer, 'Widerstand', 130, note 6.
14. C. Schiller, *Das Oberlandesgericht Karlsruhe im Dritten Reich* (Berlin, 1997), 430.
15. For the quotations, see Stolleis, *Law*, 2; W. Wagner, *Der Volksgerichtshof im nationalsozialistischen Staat* (Stuttgart, 1974), 863.
16. For this and the preceding paragraph, see Marxen, *Volk*, 34, 42, 57–61, 79–87; Schlüter, *Urteilspraxis*, 37, 140–55; Gruchmann, *Justiz*, 956–68. The sentences of the People's Court in some 1,743 trials are available on microfiche in the edition *Widerstand als 'Hochverrat' 1933–1945* by the Institute for Contemporary History, Munich.
17. Knobelsdorf, 'Bielefelder Landgericht', 70. The figures actually cover the periods Oct. 1935 to Oct. 1936, and Oct. 1936 to Oct. 1937.
18. The quotation is from K.-M. Mallmann, 'Kommunistischer Widerstand 1933–1945', in P. Steinbach, J. Tuchel (eds), *Widerstand gegen den Nationalsozialismus* (Bonn, 1994), 113–25, here 123. See also Peukert, *KPD*, 251–324.
19. N. Frei, 'Zwischen Terror und Integration. Zur Funktion der politischen Polizei im Nationalsozialismus', in C. Dipper *et al.* (eds), *Faschismus und Faschismen im Vergleich* (Cologne, 1998), 217–28, here 226.
20. BA Berlin, R 3001/alt R 22/1160, Bl. 25–66: Statistisches Reichsamt, *Die Entwicklung der Kriminalität im Deutschen Reich vom Kriegsbeginn bis Mitte 1943* (Berlin, 1944).
21. BA Berlin, R 3001/9920/2, Bl. 1–2. Of course, the amnesty of 30 April 1938 also played some part in this decline, with the total number of political prisoners falling from 16,181 at the end of March 1938 to 13,383 at the end of June 1938.
22. Ibid., R 3001/9803/78, Bl. 27–8: Crohne to Freisler, 9 Sept. 1938; Liang, 'Criminal-biological Theory', 159.
23. BA Berlin, R 3001/alt R 22/1259, Bl. 25: RJM to Generalstaatsanwälte, 5 June 1936. See also ibid., R 3001/9803/78, Bl. 44: Vermerk, no date [1938]; BayHStA, MJu 22509, Zuchthaus Straubing to GStA Nuremberg, 8 July 1933.
24. *Sopade*, vol. 4, 1549. Thälmann had been taken as a remand prisoner to Moabit in May 1933. In November 1935, his classification as a remand prisoner was lifted, after plans for a show trial were evidently dropped. But he was not released. Instead, he was now officially held in protective police custody. However, Thälmann was not taken to a concentration camp, but remained for almost nine years in penal institutions, first in Moabit, later in Hanover and Bautzen. In August 1944, he was

taken to the Buchenwald concentration camp and killed; see E. Thälmann, *Zwischen Erinnerung und Erwartung* (Frankfurt am Main, 1977), 82–90.
25. For the details of the killing, see Rosenhaft, *Beating the Fascists?*, 22–3.
26. BLHA, Pr. Br. Rep. 29 Zuchthaus Brandenburg Nr. 775; ibid., Nr. 776. Kandulski was handed over to the police for 'annihilation through labour' on 26 November 1942.
27. Möhler, 'Strafvollzug', 125–6; *Sopade*, vol. 5, 880–1; Drobisch, 'Alltag', 254; Habicht, *Zuchthaus Waldheim*, 66, 130–1; BA Berlin, R 3001/9949, Gestapo Berlin to RJM, 1 June 1937; Schlotterbeck, *Nacht*, 64–8.
28. Strafanstalt Remscheid-Lüttringhausen to GStA Düsseldorf, 11 July 1935, reprinted in Justizakademie NRW (ed.), *Zum Strafvollzug 1933–1945*, source 21. See also BA Berlin, R 3001/9923, Zuchthaus Amberg to GStA Nuremberg, 7 July 1936; *Sopade*, vol. 2, 821; ibid., vol. 3, 1019–20; E. Fox to his wife, 10 Mar. 1935, in Brandenburgische Landeszentrale für politische Bildung (ed.), *Was bleibt, ist die Hoffnung. Eine Briefdokumentation aus Brandenburger Konzentrationslagern, Zuchthäusern und Gefängnissen der NS-Zeit 1933–1945* (Potsdam, 1994), 44–5.
29. BA Berlin, R 3001/9803/78, Bl. 7–18: Gestapo to Reichsführer SS und Chef der deutschen Polizei, 12 July 1938.
30. For one such example, see StAMü, Justizvollzugsanstalten Nr. 13704, Nachbericht, 12 Jan. 1939.
31. Drobisch, 'Alltag', 265. See also Habicht, *Zuchthaus Waldheim*, 46, 97.
32. E. Niekisch, *Erinnerungen eines deutschen Revolutionärs*, vol. 1 (Cologne, 1974), 343–4.
33. ThSTA Mgn., Zuchthaus Untermaßfeld Nr. 663, Aufnahmebogen, 18 July 1934.
34. BA Berlin, R 3001/alt R 22/4552, Bl. 42–3: Einberufung für die Justizwachtmeisterlaufbahn, 23 Jan. 1935; ibid., Bl. 45–156: Verzeichnis der Personen, die für die Einberufung in Frage kommen.
35. See, for example, *Sopade*, vol. 4, 715, 1546–8.
36. Of all the women taken to the Aichach penitentiary in 1935 after a sentence of high treason, 15 stayed long enough to qualify for the progressive stages system. Eight of the women remained on stage one, while seven were given added privileges on a special section on stage one (*Führungsklasse*). This compares favourably with the Aichach inmates in general; StAMü, Justizvollzugsanstalten Nr. 12338.
37. BLHA, Pr. Br. Rep. 29 Zuchthaus Luckau Nr. 414.
38. Cited in Drobisch, 'Alltag', 265. See also H.J. Nicke, *In Ketten durch die Klosterstraße. Leben und Kampf eingekerkerter Antifaschisten im Zuchthaus Luckau* (East Berlin, 1986), 27; Habicht, *Zuchthaus Waldheim*, 59; BLHA, Ld. Br. Rep. 214 Forschungsstelle Zuchthaus Brandenburg Nr. 2, Bl. 248–51: curriculum vitae Walter N., no date; ibid., Nr. 32, Bl. 24–5: W. Hammer to Staatsanwaltschaft Brandenburg, 25 Aug. 1949.
39. Frenzel *et al.*, *Gesprengte Fesseln*, 29, 38, 45, 106–10, 136.
40. IfZ, Ms 361, W. Schwerdtfeger, 'Zuchthausjahre 1935–1945', 175–95, quotation on 185.
41. Cited in Habicht, *Zuchthaus Waldheim*, 119. See also, for the war period, J. Kammler *et al.* (eds), *Volksgemeinschaft und Volksfeinde. Kassel 1933–1945* (Fuldabrück, 1984), 349. For Communists in the camps, see L. Niethammer (ed.), *Der 'gesäuberte' Antifaschismus. Die SED und die roten Kapos von Buchenwald* (Berlin, 1994).
42. Quoted in B. Gerstenberg, 'Der gläserne Sarg. Erinnerungen an das Zuchthaus Brandenburg in den Jahren 1938–1940', *aus politik und zeitgeschichte* 18 (3 May 1980), 19–32, here 20; Faralisch, 'Zeitzeugenberichte', 359.
43. BA Berlin, R 3001/9803/78, Bl. 7–18: Gestapo to Reichsführer SS und Chef der deutschen Polizei, 12 July 1938; BayHStA, MJu 22484, Staatsministerium der Justiz to

GStA Nuremberg, 12 Sept. 1933. For some general background, see Peukert, 'Working-class Resistance'.
44. BA Berlin, R 58/2235, Bl. 1: Preußisches Geheimes Staatspolizeiamt to GStA Berlin, 2 July 1936.
45. Cited in C. Friedrich, *'Sie wollten uns brechen und brachen uns nicht . . .'. Zur Lage und zum antifaschistischen Widerstandskampf weiblicher Häftlinge im Frauenzuchthaus Cottbus 1938–1945* (Cottbus, 1986), 14. See also Gerstenberg, 'Der gläserne Sarg', 26.
46. F. Selbmann, *Alternative-Bilanz-Credo* (Halle, 1969), 293–4.
47. See, for example, BA Berlin, R 3001/9803/78, Bl. 19: Reichsführer SS und Chef der deutschen Polizei to RJM, 8 Aug. 1938.
48. Frenzel et al., *Gesprengte Fesseln*, 9, 197, 228.
49. A. Schaefer, 'Die Widerstandskämpfer im Zuchthaus Brandenburg-Görden 1933–1945', *aus politik und zeitgeschichte* 18 (3 May 1980), 3–6.
50. *Sopade*, vol. 5, 876–7.
51. W. Hirsch, *Hinter Stacheldraht und Gitter. Erlebnisse und Erfahrungen in den Konzentrationslagern und Gefängnissen Hitlerdeutschlands* (Zurich, 1934), 27.
52. BA Berlin, R 58/2235, Bl. 1: Preußisches Geheimes Staatspolizeiamt to GStA Berlin, 2 July 1936; ibid., Bl. 2–4: Staatspolizeileitstelle Frankfurt/Oder to Geheimes Staatspolizeiamt Berlin, 29 Aug. 1936; ibid., Bl. 21–4: Staatspolizeileitstelle Hamburg to Geheimes Staatspolizeiamt Berlin, 25 Mar. 1937; ibid., R 3001/alt R 22/4371, Bl. 24: RJM to Generalstaatsanwälte, 13 Nov. 1937; ibid., R 3001/9803/78, Bl. 7–18: Gestapo to Reichsführer SS und Chef der deutschen Polizei, 12 July 1938; BLHA, Pr. Br. Rep. 29 Zuchthaus Brandenburg Nr. 1210, Vermerk, 14 July 1937.
53. Gestapo Düsseldorf report, 1937, translated and reprinted in Noakes, Pridham (eds), *Nazism*, vol. 2, 591–3; BA Berlin, R 3001/9803/78, Bl. 7–18: Gestapo to Reichsführer SS und Chef der deutschen Polizei, 12 July 1938; BA Berlin, R 58/2235, Bl. 8: Auszug aus den Tagesmeldungen, 1936; ibid., Bl. 64: Vermerk, Gestapo, 18 Aug. 1937.
54. BA Berlin, R 58/2235, Bl. 73: Staatsfeindliche Demonstration von Zuchthäuslern, 2 July 1935; ibid., R 3001/alt R 22/706, Bl. 122–5: official diary Gürtner, 25 Feb. 1937.
55. For two examples, see IfZ, Sp. 1.13., Spruchkammer Nord-Württemberg, Verfahren gegen Max K., 21 Dec. 1949; ibid., ED 106/86, Bl. 131–5: E. Wald to Oberstaatsanwalt Hanover, 15 May 1948.
56. G. Paul, 'Private Konfliktregulierung, gesellschaftliche Selbstüberwachung, politische Teilhabe? Neuere Forschungen zur Denunziation im Dritten Reich', *Archiv für Sozialgeschichte* 42 (2002), 380–402, here 388.
57. For denunciations in prison camps, see C. von Bülow, 'Verurteilt nach Paragraph 175', *DIZ Nachrichten* 20 (1998), 42–8, here 45.
58. BA Berlin, R 3001/alt R 22/721, Bl. 63–5: official diary Gürtner, 3 May 1937; ibid., SAPMO, RY 1/I 2/3/163, Bl. 123: Betreff: Anfrage vom 25.7.1950; ibid., R 58/2235, Bl. 5: Preußische Geheime Staatspolizei, Vermerk, 9 Sept. 1936.
59. IfZ, Ms 361, W. Schwerdtfeger, 'Zuchthausjahre 1935–1945', 110. See also Union für Recht und Freiheit (ed.), *Strafvollzug*, 82–5, 119; *Sopade*, vol. 3, 48; ibid., vol. 4, 1547–8; Frenzel et al., *Gesprengte Fesseln*, 27; Faralisch, 'Zeitzeugenberichte', 362.
60. BA Berlin, SAPMO, DY 55/V 278/6/592, Bl. 77–81: W. Hammer, 'Mußte das sein?', no date. For other examples, see *Sopade*, vol. 5, 880; Gerstenberg, 'Der gläserne Sarg', 20.
61. Cited in N. Krüger, '"Wenn Sie nicht ins KZ wollen . . .". Häftlinge in Bombenräumkommandos', *aus politik und zeitgeschichte* 16 (23 Apr. 1977), 25–37, here 34.

62. Angermund, *Richterschaft*, 145–51, 155–6; Johnson, *Nazi Terror*, 225–7. The strong Catholic milieu in regions such as Bavaria and the Rhineland also militated against excessive sentences for Catholic priests there. The same applied to Protestant priests in Schleswig-Holstein.
63. For this and the preceding paragraph, see D. Garbe, *Zwischen Widerstand und Martyrium. Die Zeugen Jehovas im 'Dritten Reich'* (Munich, 1993), *passim*, estimate on 483; M.H. Kater, 'Die ernsten Bibelforscher im Dritten Reich', *VfZ* 17 (1969), 181–218; Angermund, *Richterschaft*, 151–6, 174; Niermann, *Strafjustiz*, 295–306; Weckbecker, *Sondergerichte*, 165–71; Zeidler, *Sondergericht Freiberg*, 49–55; H. Schmidt, *'Beabsichtige ich die Todesstrafe zu beantragen'. Die nationalsozialistische Sondergerichtsbarkeit im Oberlandesgerichtsbezirk Düsseldorf 1933 bis 1945* (Essen, 1998), 105–7; BA Berlin, R 3001/alt R 22/4277, Bl. 149–91: Besprechung am 18.6.1937, quotation on Bl. 182. According to Michael Kater, there were some 19,268 Jehovah's Witnesses in Germany in April 1933; Kater, 'Die ernsten Bibelforscher', 181.
64. BA Berlin, R 3001/alt R 22/4277, Bl. 149–91: Besprechung am 18.6.1937. See also Garbe, *Widerstand*, 264–5.
65. For the quotation, see ThHStAW, GStA bei dem OLG Jena Nr. 604, Bl. 9: Gefängnis Eisenach to GStA Jena, 13 May 1938. See also H. Brandstätter, 'Erfahrungen im Strafvollzug an Gefangenen, die wegen Verstoßes gegen das Verbot der Internationalen Bibelforscher bestraft worden sind', *BlGefK* 70 (1939), 48–55.
66. Cited in Garbe, *Widerstand*, 282. See also ibid., 279.
67. See Anstaltslehrer Mayer to GStA Zweibrücken, 5 Nov. 1937, reprinted in Scharf, 'Strafvollzug', 832–3.
68. ThHStAW, Justizministerium Nr. 1765, Bl. 224: Strafanstalt Ichtershausen to GStA Jena, 23 Mar. 1936.
69. Ludewig, Kuessner, *Sondergericht Braunschweig*, 89–90.
70. For the background, see BA Berlin, R 3001/5982, Bl. 89–99: Kommissarische Beratung vom 11.10.1933; *Akten der Reichskanzlei. Die Regierung Hitler 1933–1938*, part 1, vol. 2 (Boppard, 1983), 946–7; Müller, *Gewohnheitsverbrechergesetz*, 36–41. Christian Müller also discusses the differences between the Weimar drafts and the 1933 law.
71. For the quotations, see R. von Hippel, 'Zum Reichsgesetz vom 24. November 1933', *BlGefK* 65 (1934), 1–16, here 1; R. Schwerdtfeger, 'Gedanken über die Sicherungsverwahrung', *MGGE* 10 (1934–35), 81–6, here 81; Möhler, 'Strafvollzug', 63. For chaplains, see Oleschinski, 'Gefängnisseelsorge', 272–3.
72. 'Auszug aus dem Gesetz gegen gefährliche Gewohnheitsverbrecher und über Maßregeln der Sicherung und Besserung', in *Gesetz zur Verhütung erbkranken Nachwuchses vom 14. Juli 1933. Bearbeitet und erläutert von A. Gütt, E. Rüdin, F. Ruttke*, 1st edition (Munich, 1934), 179–82.
73. O. Rietzsch, 'Die Anordnung der Sicherungsverwahrung', in R. Freisler, F. Schlegelberger (eds), *Dringende Fragen der Sicherungsverwahrung* (Berlin, 1938), 25–67, here 47.
74. BayHStA, MJu 22512, Frank to Landesjustizverwaltungen, 15 Aug. 1933, Anlage, Dr Viernstein, 'Kriminalbiologie und Erneuerung der Rechtsordnung'. For Viernstein's role in the Third Reich, see Burgmair et al., '"Die soziale Prognose"', 277–83.
75. BLHA, Pr. Br. Rep. 12 A Landgericht Berlin Nr. 171, AV des RJM, 30 Nov. 1937; Edgar Schmidt, 'Der kriminalbiologische Dienst im deutschen Strafvollzug', *BlGefK* 69 (1938–39), 164–77; F. Neureiter, 'Die Organisation des kriminalbiologischen Dienstes in Deutschland', *MKG* 5 (1938), 21–8. The history of criminal-biology in the Third Reich has now been examined in some detail. See Liang, 'Criminal-biological Theory', 232–309; Wetzell, *Inventing*, 179–231; J. Simon, 'Kriminalbiologie –

theoretische Konzepte und praktische Durchführung eines Ansatzes zur Erfassung von Kriminalität', in Justizministerium des Landes NRW (ed.), *Kriminalbiologie* (Düsseldorf, 1997), 69–105.

76. See Rothmaler, '"Prognose: Zweifelhaft"', 130; BA Berlin, R 3001/9923, Anstaltsarzt Straubing, Bericht über den Stufenstrafvollzug, 16 June 1934; Möhler, 'Strafvollzug', 131.
77. Other measures in the Habitual Criminals Law not discussed in this book included an occupational ban on offenders who had abused their professional position (§ 42l), and a provision for deporting certain foreign offenders (§ 42m).
78. Ayaß, *Arbeitshaus*, 30–3, 266–75, 306–13; idem, 'Die "korrektionelle Nachhaft". Zur Geschichte der strafrechtlichen Arbeitshausunterbringung in Deutschland', *Zeitschrift für Neuere Rechtsgeschichte* 15 (1993), 184–201; 'Auszug aus dem Gesetz gegen gefährliche Gewohnheitsverbrecher', 185–8.
79. For these claims, see, for example, M. Burleigh, W. Wippermann, *The Racial State* (Cambridge, 1991), 172; G. Lewy, *The Nazi Persecution of the Gypsies* (Oxford, 2000), 24.
80. 'Auszug aus dem Gesetz gegen gefährliche Gewohnheitsverbrecher', 187.
81. Müller, 'Verbrechensbekämpfung', 316.
82. Heindl, *Berufsverbrecher*, 191–5.
83. BA Berlin, R 3001/alt R 22/Pers. 58398, Bl. 25: 'Schutz der Gemeinschaft', *Berliner Tageblatt*, 17 Nov. 1933; ibid., Bl. 27: Dr Gürtner, 'Sicherung des Volkes!', *Schlesische Zeitung*, 25 Nov. 1933.
84. Liszt, 'Zweckgedanke', 168–70; J. Schurich, *Lebensläufe vielfach rückfälliger Verbrecher* (Leipzig, 1930), 158–9; Grüllich, 'Gewohnheitsverbrecher', 672; Aschaffenburg, 'Die Stellung des Psychiaters', 157; Viernstein, 'Typen', 44–5; 'Statistik des Gefängniswesens', table 6.
85. BayHStA, MJu 22523, Dr Dürr to Staatsministerium der Justiz, 13 Oct. 1933; BA Berlin, R 3001/5982, Bl. 89–99: Kommissarische Beratung vom 11.10.1933; ibid., R 3001/alt R 22/1453, Bl. 4–5: Preußischer Justizminister to Generalstaatsanwälte, 29 Nov. 1933.
86. BayHStA, MJu 22510, Zuchthaus Straubing to GStA Nuremberg, 18 June 1934; Schwerdtfeger, 'Gedanken', 83; *Kriminalstatistik 1934*, 26.
87. BayHStA, MJu 22472, Staatsministerium der Justiz to RJM, 6 Dec. 1934. See also ibid., MJu 22515, Gefangenenanstalt Zweibrücken to GStA Zweibrücken, 30 July 1934; ibid., MJu 22510, Bericht des Anstaltsgeistlichen in Amberg über den Zeitraum 1.7.1933–1.7.1934.
88. J. Wüllner, 'Das Verhalten der Gefangenen angesichts der zu erwartenden Sicherungsverwahrung und Unfruchtbarmachung', *MGGE* 10 (1934–35), 236–40.
89. Quoted in Müller, *Gewohnheitsverbrechergesetz*, 74–5.
90. Reichsjustizministerium (ed.), *Gefängniswesen*, 35–42; Möhler, 'Strafvollzug', 71; BA Berlin, R 3001/9920/2, Bl. 1.
91. See, for example, BA Berlin, R 3001/alt R 22/1277, Bl. 131–2: Eggensperger to Eichler, 15 Oct. 1940; H. Möller, *Die Entwicklung und Lebensverhältnisse von 135 Gewohnheitsverbrechern* (Leipzig, 1939), 74.
92. Edgar Schmidt, 'Sicherungsverwahrung in Zahlen', in Freisler, Schlegelberger (eds), *Fragen*, 105–13, here 112.
93. For contemporary and postwar examinations of the background of the security-confined, studies which have to be treated with some caution, see J. Hellmer, *Der Gewohnheitsverbrecher und die Sicherungsverwahrung 1934–1945* (Berlin, 1961), here

41–50, 59–61, 209–47, 261–6, 285 (Hellmer examined the files of 250 security-confined male prisoners from different German regions); Möller, *Entwicklung*, 30, 43, 53, 56 (Möller examined the files of 135 male and female inmates sentenced retrospectively); L. Lotz, *Der gefährliche Gewohnheitsverbrecher* (Leipzig, 1939), 66–88 (Lotz's sample consisted of 200 male and female prisoners in Straubing and Aichach). See also Peukert, *Sozialdisziplinierung*, 166–7; H. Mayr, 'Die Sicherungsverwahrung in Süddeutschland', *MSchriftKrim* 27 (1936), 209–15; F. Weber, 'Erfahrungen in der Sicherungsanstalt', *BlGefK* 68 (1937), 429–48; BA Berlin, R 3001/alt R 22/1334, Bl. 39–41: GStA Berlin to RJM, 4 Apr. 1935; StAMü, Justizvollzugsanstalten Nr. 12019, Rosina W.'s mother to Frauenverwahrungsanstalt Aichach, 2 Jan. 1941.

94. BLHA, Pr. Br. Rep. 29 Zuchthaus Brandenburg Nr. 6425. For the quotation, see Sicherungsanstalt Brandenburg-Görden to GStA Berlin, 6 June 1939.
95. The last point is also stressed in Müller, 'Verbrechensbekämpfung', 319.
96. Schmidt, 'Sicherungsverwahrung', 105, 112; Lotz, *Gewohnheitsverbrecher*, 62–4.
97. StAMü, Justizvollzugsanstalten Nr. 13693, Anklage der Staatsanwaltschaft Freiburg, 3 Nov. 1934; ibid., Nr. 12340, Krankenakte Rosa S., IQ-test, 1936. For some background on prostitution in Germany, see L. Abrams, 'Prostitutes in Imperial Germany, 1870–1918: Working Girls or Social Outcasts?', in R.J. Evans (ed.), *The German Underworld. Deviants and Outcasts in German History* (London, 1988), 189–209.
98. Cited in Naucke, 'Kriminalpolitik', 548.
99. Exner, 'Vollzug', 251–7.
100. BA Berlin, R 3001/9803/64, Bl. 2–19: Niederschrift über die Konferenz vom 5/6. Oktober 1933.
101. 'Auszug aus dem Gesetz gegen gefährliche Gewohnheitsverbrecher', 187.
102. 'Verordnung über den Vollzug von Freiheitsstrafen', 19–20.
103. Visits were allowed every six weeks in prisons, every two months in security confinement and every three months in a penitentiary. Letters were allowed every four weeks in prisons and security confinement, every two months in a penitentiary.
104. BayHStA, MJu 22522, Staatsminister der Justiz to Generalstaatsanwälte, 20 Dec. 1933; A. Wingler, '1. Tagung der Gesellschaft für Deutsches Strafrecht, München 27.–29. Oktober 1938', *BlGefK* 69 (1938–39), 305–12, here 309.
105. ThHStAW, GStA bei dem OLG Jena Nr. 690, Bl. 2–16: Bericht über Beobachtungen und Erfahrungen in Gräfentonna, 15 Oct. 1937.
106. BA Berlin, R 3001/9908.
107. See, for example, ibid., R 3001/alt R 22/1247, Bl. 45–9: Vermerk über Besichtigung in Straubing, 16 Oct. 1937; K. Schiefer, 'Der Verwahrungsvollzug in der Sicherungsanstalt Waldheim', *BlGefK* 68 (1937), 448–65.
108. BA Berlin, R 3001/alt R 22/1437, Bl. 282: RJM, Vermerk, 14 Mar. 1939; ibid., R 3001/alt R 22/1277, Bl. 120: RJM to Generalstaatsanwälte, 21 Mar. 1939.
109. BA Berlin, R 3001/alt R 22/1429, Bl. 106–21: Niederschrift über die Besprechung am 14.8.1939. For Aichach, see StAMü, GStA bei dem OLG München Nr. 51, Nachschau in Aichach, 30 Sept. 1940.
110. BA Berlin, R 3001/alt R 22/1429, Bl. 128–30: Gürtner to Chef der Reichskanzlei, 22 Aug. 1939.
111. BLHA, Pr. Br. Rep. 29 Zuchthaus Brandenburg Nr. 8152, Willy Leske to his wife, Oct. 1939. See also W. Eberhard, 'Vergleich der Gewichtsverhältnisse bei Gefangenen des Zuchthauses und der Sicherungsanstalt in Brandenburg (Havel)-Görden', *BlGefK* 68 (1937), 470–5; BA Berlin, R 3001/9852, Bl. 196–7: Frauenstrafanstalt Lübeck-Lauerhof to GStA Kiel, 25 May 1938; Weber, 'Erfahrungen', 442–3.

112. StAMü, Justizvollzugsanstalten Nr. 5470, Franziska K. to her parents and siblings, 6 Dec. 1936, underlined in the original.
113. For one example, see StAMü, Justizvollzugsanstalten Nr. 8223, Karl F. to Gertrud P., 12 Jan. 1939.
114. Ibid., Justizvollzugsanstalten Nr. 10514. For the quotation, see Strafen, 24 Sept. 1938. Magdalena S. survived in Aichach until early January 1943, when she was handed over as an 'asocial' prisoner to the police for 'annihilation through labour'.
115. 'Auszug aus dem Gesetz gegen gefährliche Gewohnheitsverbrecher', 188–9.
116. BA Berlin, R 3001/alt R 22/1263, Bl. 36–53: Niederschrift über die Erörterung von Strafvollzugsfragen, 14 Nov. 1936.
117. StAMü, Justizvollzugsanstalten Nr. 461, Hedwig J. to her sister, 7 Mar. 1937, 14 Mar. 1937.
118. BA Berlin, R 3001/9852, Bl. 280–6: Beamtenkonferenz mit dem GStA Werl, 15 Sept. 1937.
119. Ibid., Bl. 294–320: Die Entlassung aus der Sicherungsverwahrung, no date.
120. R. Freisler, 'Ein Querschnitt durch die Fragen der Sicherungsverwahrung', in idem, Schlegelberger (eds), *Fragen*, 7–14, quote on 14.
121. BA Berlin, R 58/473, Bl. 82–3: AV über Strafsachen gegen gefährliche Gewohnheitsverbrecher, 3 Mar. 1938.
122. Wingler, '1. Tagung', 307–9.
123. ThHStAW, GStA bei dem OLG Jena Nr. 690, Bl. 20–34: Bericht über Beobachtungen und Erfahrungen in Gräfentonna, 15 Feb. 1938; StAMü, Justizvollzugsanstalten Nr. 5470, Verwahrungsanstalt Aichach to Staatsanwaltschaft Munich, 17 Feb. 1939; ibid., Beschluß des Amtsgerichts Munich, 10 Mar. 1939; BA Berlin, R 3001/9852, Bl. 280–6: Beamtenkonferenz mit dem GStA Werl, 15 Sept. 1937.
124. See, for example, Wingler, '1. Tagung', 309–10.
125. Stolzenburg, 'Die Entlassung aus der Sicherungsverwahrung', in Freisler, Schlegelberger (eds), *Fragen*, 83–94, here 85.
126. StAMü, Justizvollzugsanstalten Nr. 461, Beschluß des Amtsgerichts Berlin, 19 Jan. 1940.
127. ThHStAW, GStA bei dem OLG Jena Nr. 701, Oberstaatsanwalt Meiningen to RJM, 10 July 1939; ibid., Oberstaatsanwalt Weimar to RJM, 25 Mar. 1938; BLHA, Pr. Br. Rep. 29 Zuchthaus Brandenburg Nr. 5117, Sicherungsanstalt Brandenburg-Görden to Strafentlassenenhilfe Berlin, 12 Apr. 1938.
128. Cited in H. Fickert, *Rassenhygienische Verbrechensbekämpfung* (Leipzig, 1938), 65–6. See also Gesetz zum Schutze der Erbgesundheit des deutschen Volkes, 18 Oct. 1935, reprinted in Hirsch *et al.* (eds), *Recht*, 357; ThHStAW, GStA bei dem OLG Jena Nr. 701, Amt für Volkswohlfahrt to GStA Jena, 17 June 1939.
129. For some initial release figures, see Wingler, '1. Tagung', 310.
130. In Hellmer's sample of 250 security-confined inmates, 15 of the 25 released inmates were readmitted even before the outbreak of the war in 1939; Hellmer, *Gewohnheitsverbrecher*, 366–70.
131. BLHA, Pr. Br. Rep. 29 Zuchthaus Brandenburg Nr. 8152.
132. Lotz, *Gewohnheitsverbrecher*, 92; StAMü, Justizvollzugsanstalten Nr. 9000.
133. H. Rodenfels, 'Sittenstrolche und Verbrecher', *Neues Volk* 7 (1939), Nr. 4, 19–25, quotation on 22.
134. See, for example, ThHStAW, Justizministerium Nr. 1779.
135. A. Langelüddeke, *Die Entmannung von Sittlichkeitsverbrechern* (Berlin, 1963), 28–31, 118.

136. In 1932, the German section of the International Union of Penal Law (IKV) called for the compulsory castration of dangerous sex offenders; Brenner, 'Internationale Kriminalistische Vereinigung', *Deutsche Richterzeitung* 24 (1932), 306–8. For the influence of the Kürten case on the debate in general, see BA Berlin, R 3001/6094.
137. BA Berlin, R 3001/6094, Bl. 320–4: Landeshauptmann von Niederschlesien to RJM, 6 June 1933. See also 'Diskussion', *MKG* 4 (1933), 267–76.
138. In addition, sex killers could also be castrated, irrespective of whether they had any previous convictions. See 'Auszug aus dem Gesetz gegen gefährliche Gewohnheitsverbrecher', 191; C. Müller, 'Das Gewohnheitsverbrechergesetz vom 24. November 1933', *Zeitschrift für Geschichtswissenschaft* 47 (1999), 965–79, here especially 970–1. Quotations in idem, *Gewohnheitsverbrechergesetz*, 34, 38. For the discussions about the minimum age at which castration should be allowed, see ibid., 36–40.
139. Statistics based on figures in BA Berlin, R 3001/9945, Bl. 116, 123, 128, 139, 142, 151, 197, 225.
140. *Akten der Reichskanzlei*, 947.
141. Cited in F. Sparing, 'Zwangskastrationen im Nationalsozialismus. Das Beispiel der Kriminalbiologischen Sammelstelle Köln', in Justizministerium des Landes NRW (ed.), *Kriminalbiologie* (Düsseldorf, 1997), 169–212, here 210.
142. *Kriminalstatistik 1934*, 26.
143. See, for example, HStAD-Kalkum, Gerichte Rep. 321/878, Bl. 8: Strafanstaltsoberdirektion Cologne to GStA Cologne, 1 Aug. 1936.
144. *Kriminalstatistik 1934*, 175; *Kriminalstatistik 1935 und 1936*, 101, 255; Rothmaler, '"Prognose: Zweifelhaft"', 145.
145. ThSTA Mgn., Zuchthaus Untermaßfeld Nr. 1569, Bl. 35: Dr Gericke to Oberstaatsanwalt Gera, 8 Feb. 1934.
146. *Kriminalstatistik 1934*, 175; *Kriminalstatistik 1935 und 1936*, 101, 255.
147. Sparing, 'Zwangskastrationen', 207; Möhler, 'Strafvollzug', 77; BA Berlin, 62 DAF 3/1808, Bl. 9–10: Frommer, 'Zusammenstellung der Untersuchungsergebnisse von 100 Entmannten', *Deutsche Justiz* 27 (8 July 1938).
148. BayHStA, MJu 22522, Referat 11, Materialien für die Ausführungsvorschriften zum Gesetz gegen gefährliche Gewohnheitsverbrecher, no date [1934].
149. BA Berlin, R 3001/alt R 22/1334, Bl. 8–30: Übersicht über den Vollzug der Maßregeln der Sicherung und Besserung, no date; ibid., R 3001/alt R 22/1453, Bl. 36–7: RJM to Generalstaatsanwälte, 15 Apr. 1936.
150. Cited in G. Giles, '"The Most Unkindest Cut of All": Castration, Homosexuality and Nazi Justice', *Journal of Contemporary History* 27 (1992), 41–61, here 46. See also E. Lexer, 'Die Eingriffe zur Unfruchtbarmachung des Mannes und zur Entmannung', in *Gesetz zur Verhütung erbkranken Nachwuchses*, 319–26, here 324.
151. Lexer, 'Eingriffe', 325–6. In the 1930s, general anaesthetic was still medically and technically difficult to administer and was avoided by doctors as much as possible. I wish to thank Dr Matthias M. Weber for this information.
152. LaB, Rep. 5 Acc. 2863, Nr. 129, Bericht des Facharztes für Chirurgie bei den Hamburger Gefangenenanstalten, 25 Nov. 1935.
153. 'Auszug aus dem Gesetz gegen gefährliche Gewohnheitsverbrecher', 192.
154. BA Berlin, R 3001/alt R 22/1453, Bl. 22–3: RJM to Generalstaatsanwälte, 9 May 1935.
155. Cited in Rothmaler, '"Prognose: Zweifelhaft"', 142.
156. LaB, Rep. 5 Acc. 2863, Nr. 98, Auszug aus einem internistischen Versorgungszeugnis, 15 Mar. 1955; ibid., Nr. 129, Strafanstalt Rendsburg, Beobachtung an entmannten Gefangenen, 1 July 1936; ibid., Dr Riffel to Kriminalbiologische Sammelstelle, 24 Jan.

1936; BA Berlin, R 3001/alt R 22/1247, Bl. 12–13: Vermerk über Besichtigung in Kaisheim, 16 Oct. 1937; Langelüddeke, *Entmannung*, 38, 85–98; G. Grau (ed.), *Hidden Holocaust? Gay and Lesbian Persecution in Germany 1933–45* (London, 1995), 247–8.
157. See, for example, N. Jensch, *Untersuchungen an entmannten Sittlichkeitsverbrechern* (Leipzig, 1944).
158. Langelüddeke, *Entmannung*, 40.
159. Cited in Sparing, 'Zwangskastrationen', 200. See also LaB, Rep. 5 Acc. 2863, Nr. 129, Landesgefängnis Rottenburg, Bericht über die entmannten Gefangenen, 20 Nov. 1935; ibid., Anstalt Rheinbach to Kriminalbiologische Sammelstelle, 4 Dec. 1935.
160. For one example, see B. Hansen, 'Something Rotten in the State of Denmark: Eugenics and the Ascent of the Welfare State', in G. Broberg, N. Roll-Hansen (eds), *Eugenics and the Welfare State. Sterilization Policy in Denmark, Sweden, Norway, and Finland* (East Lansing, 1996), 9–76, here 14.
161. See, for instance, LaB, Rep. 5 Acc. 2863, Nr. 129, Bericht des Abteilungsarztes bei den Hamburger Gefangenenanstalten, 22 Nov. 1935.
162. J. Lange, 'In welchem Falle und nach welchen Grundsätzen empfiehlt sich im modernen Strafsystem die Anwendung der Sterilisation durch Kastration oder durch Vasectomie oder Salpingectomie?', *ZStW* 55 (1936), 291–306, here 297.
163. Cited in HStAD-Kalkum, Gerichte Rep. 321/975, Bl. 46–9: Kriminalbiologische Sammelstelle to RJM, 13 May 1938.
164. Sparing, 'Zwangskastrationen', 199.
165. G. Aschaffenburg, 'Gleichzeitige Anordnung der Entmannung und der Sicherungsverwahrung', *MSchriftKrim* 26 (1935), 385–8.
166. See, for example, ThHStAW, Justizministerium Nr. 1573, Bl. 37–8: Strafanstalt Ichtershausen to GStA Jena, 21 June 1935; Sparing, 'Zwangskastrationen', 191–2.
167. Peukert, *Weimar*, 8–9, 102; idem, *Inside Nazi Germany*, 219.
168. Cited in Burleigh, Wippermann, *Racial State*, 192–3.
169. B. Jellonnek, 'Staatspolizeiliche Fahndungs- und Ermittlungsmethoden gegen Homosexuelle', in idem, R. Lautmann (eds), *Nationalsozialistischer Terror gegen Homosexuelle* (Paderborn, 2002), 149–61, here 160.
170. Cited in Grau (ed.), *Hidden Holocaust?* 65.
171. H.G. Stümke, 'The Persecution of Homosexuals in Nazi Germany', in M. Burleigh (ed.), *Confronting the Nazi Past* (London, 1996), 154–67, here 154–7.
172. B. Jellonnek, *Homosexuelle unter dem Hakenkreuz. Die Verfolgung von Homosexuellen im Dritten Reich* (Paderborn, 1990), 82; Jürgen Müller, '"Bekämpfung der Homosexualität als politische Aufgabe!" Die Praxis der Kölner Kriminalpolizei bei der Verfolgung der Homosexuellen', in H. Buhlan, W. Jung (eds), *Wessen Freund und wessen Helfer?: die Kölner Polizei im Nationalsozialismus* (Cologne, 2000), 492–517, here 496–500.
173. *Kriminalstatistik 1932; Kriminalstatistik 1933; Kriminalstatistik 1934*.
174. Kershaw, *Hitler. 1889–1936*, 499–520.
175. Cited in Grau (ed.), *Hidden Holocaust?* 66. See ibid., 64–7. Lesbian women were not included in § 175. But their sexuality was, in some cases, criminalised by their being prosecuted for other offences; see C. Schoppmann, *Nationalsozialistische Sexualpolitik und weibliche Homosexualität* (Pfaffenweiler, 1991), 77–95.
176. Cited in Knobelsdorf, 'Bielefelder Landgericht', 83.
177. For abortions, see G. Czarnowski, 'Women's Crimes, State Crimes: Abortion in Nazi Germany', in M.L. Arnot, C. Usborne (eds), *Gender and Crime in Modern Europe* (London, 1999), 238–56.

178. For a detailed description of police practices in Cologne, see Müller, 'Praxis', 495–6, 500–5. For the general background, see also Jellonnek, 'Staatspolizeiliche', 159–60.
179. According to the official statistics, some 29,767 individuals were sentenced under the different provisions of § 175 between 1936 and 1939. This figure includes a small number of cases of bestiality; *Statistisches Jahrbuch 1937*; *Statistisches Jahrbuch 1938*; *Statistisches Jahrbuch 1939/40*; *Statistisches Jahrbuch 1941/42*.
180. Knobelsdorf, 'Bielefelder Landgericht', 83–4.
181. Cited in H.-C. Lassen, 'Der Kampf gegen Homosexualität, Abtreibung und "Rassenschande". Sexualdelikte vor Gericht in Hamburg 1933 bis 1945', in Justizbehörde Hamburg (ed.), *'Für Führer, Volk und Vaterland . . .'*, 216–89, here 239. The article offers a good overview of the legal terror against homosexuals in Hamburg.
182. *Kriminalstatistik 1936*.
183. *Statistisches Jahrbuch 1941/42*.
184. Grau (ed.), *Hidden Holocaust?* 162–5.
185. 'Auszug aus dem Gesetz gegen gefährliche Gewohnheitsverbrecher', 193.
186. Entwurf für ein Gesetz über die Behandlung Asozialer, 1 Feb. 1943, reprinted in W. Ayaß (ed.), *'Gemeinschaftsfremde'. Quellen zur Verfolgung von 'Asozialen' 1933–1945* (Koblenz, 1998), 323–5.
187. Gesetz zur Änderung des Gesetzes zur Verhütung erbkranken Nachwuchses, 26 June 1935, *Reichsgesetzblatt*, part I, 773.
188. Sparing, 'Zwangskastrationen', 174.
189. Cited in Langelüddeke, *Entmannung*, 176.
190. Cited in Jellonnek, 'Staatspolizeiliche', 154. See also G. Grau, ' "Unschuldige" Täter. Mediziner als Vollstrecker der nationalsozialistischen Homosexuellenpolitik', in B. Jellonnek, R. Lautmann (eds), *Nationalsozialistischer Terror gegen Homosexuelle* (Paderborn, 2002), 209–35, here 216; A. Pretzel, V. Kruber, 'Jeder 100. Berliner. Statistiken zur Strafverfolgung Homosexueller in Berlin', in A. Pretzel, G. Roßbach (eds), *Homosexuellenverfolgung in Berlin 1933–1945* (Berlin, 2000), 169–85, here 171.
191. LaB, Rep. 5 Acc. 2863, Nr. 98, Fragebogen betr. Entmannung des Jakob H., 7 Aug. 1935; BA Berlin, R 3001/alt R 22/1247, Bl. 45–9: Vermerk über Besichtigung in Straubing, 16 Oct. 1937.
192. BA Berlin, R 3001/9945.
193. BA Berlin, R 3001/alt R 22/1261, Bl. 154–6: RJM to Reichsführer SS und Chef der deutschen Polizei, 15 Dec. 1939, quotation on Bl. 155. See also ibid., R 3001/alt R 22/1437, Bl. 206: RJM to GStA Berlin, 20 Sept. 1938; ibid., R 3001/9862, Bl. 19–23: Befehl Nr. 4, 17 Jan. 1939.
194. See, for example, BA Berlin, R 3001/9862, Bl. 5–6: Befehl Nr. 2, 5 Jan. 1939.
195. BA Berlin, R 3001/5631, Bl. 87: 'Geschlecht in Fesseln', *Die Welt am Abend*, 25 Oct. 1928. See also C. Bondy, ' "Geschlecht in Fesseln" ', *MSchriftKrim* 20 (1929), 166–8.
196. Bülow, 'Verurteilt', *passim*; StAMü, Justizvollzugsanstalten Nr. 13685, Niederschrift, 2 Dec. 1940. For another example, see ThHStAW, GStA bei dem OLG Jena Nr. 855, Bl. 5: Oberstaatsanwalt Meiningen to Amtsgericht Meiningen, 17 Feb. 1938.
197. Entwurf und Begründung eines Sterilisationsgesetzes, 30 July 1932, reprinted in J.-C. Kaiser *et al.* (eds), *Eugenik, Sterilisation, 'Euthanasie'. Politische Biologie in Deutschland 1895–1945* (Berlin, 1992), 100–2. Good accounts of racial hygiene in Germany before 1933 include Walter, *Psychiatrie*, 370–414; P. Weindling, *Health, Race and German Politics between National Unification and Nazism, 1870–1945* (Cambridge, 1989), *passim*; Burleigh, Wippermann, *Racial State*, 23–34. For the 1929

quotations, see O. Kankeleit, *Die Unfruchtbarmachung aus rassenhygienischen und sozialen Gründen* (Munich, 1929), 5, 32.
198. Begründung zum Gesetz zur Verhütung erbkranken Nachwuchses, 26 July 1933, reprinted in Ayaß (ed.), *'Gemeinschaftsfremde'*, 18–21. For the Marriage Loans, see Noakes, Pridham (eds), *Nazism*, vol. 2, 451–6.
199. 'Gesetz zur Verhütung erbkranken Nachwuchses', 14 July 1933, in *Gesetz zur Verhütung erbkranken Nachwuchses*, 56–9.
200. G. Bock, *Zwangssterilisation im Nationalsozialismus* (Opladen, 1986). For the figures, see ibid., 198, 237–8, referring to the German borders of 1937.
201. Wetzell, *Inventing*, 100–5.
202. Dr Boeters to Sächsische Staatsregierung, reprinted in Kaiser *et al.* (eds), *Eugenik*, 95–6.
203. Joachim Müller, *Sterilisation und Gesetzgebung bis 1933* (Husum, 1985), 62–71.
204. Viernstein, 'Der kriminalbiologische Dienst in bayerischen Strafanstalten', *MSchriftKrim* 17 (1926), 1–21, here 5. For Viernstein's support of the sterilisation of criminals at this time, see idem, 'Entwicklung und Aufbau eines kriminalbiologischen Dienstes im bayerischen Strafvollzug', in Bayerisches Staatsministerium der Justiz (ed.), *Stufenstrafvollzug*, vol. 1, 68–85. For a contemporary survey of the medical and criminological literature, see E.P. Hellstern, 'Bekämpfung des Verbrechertums. Sicherungsverwahrung, nichtbegrenzte Strafzeit und Sterilisation', *Archiv für Psychiatrie und Nervenkrankheiten* 78 (1926), 705–30.
205. BayHStA, MJu 22509, Bericht des Anstaltsarztes in Zweibrücken, 6 Jan. 1933.
206. Müller, *Sterilisation*, 76–7; M. Schwartz, *Sozialistische Eugenik. Eugenische Sozialtechnologien in Debatten und Politik der deutschen Sozialdemokratie 1890–1933* (Bonn, 1995), 293–311; Müller, 'Verbrechensbekämpfung', 219–34.
207. Quoted in Müller, *Gewohnheitsverbrechergesetz*, 34; Wetzell, *Inventing*, 257.
208. See, for example, Gellately, *Backing Hitler*, 93.
209. BA Berlin, R 3001/9945, Bl. 65–8: Strafanstaltsmedizinalrat in Celle, 'Zur Unfruchtbarmachung erbkranker Verbrecher', 3 Apr. 1935. See also, for example, ThHStAW, GStA bei dem OLG Jena Nr. 1071, Bl. 13–17: Strafanstalt Untermaßfeld to Justizministerium, 23 Jan. 1934.
210. Cited in Walter, *Psychiatrie*, 570. See also MPIP-HA, GDA 39, E. Rüdin, 'Die Bedeutung rassenhygienischer Massnahmen für die Vorbeugung des Verbrechens', 1938.
211. E. Mezger, 'Inwieweit werden durch Sterilisationsmaßnahmen Asoziale erfaßt?', *MKG* 5 (1938), 81–98.
212. A. Hoffmann, *Unfruchtbarmachung und Kriminalität* (Leipzig, 1940), 49. For the wider argument, see Wetzell, *Inventing*, 276–80, 301–2.
213. BA Berlin, R 3001/6094, Bl. 384: RJM to Landesjustizverwaltungen, 15 Dec. 1933.
214. Ibid. In Bremen, a similar directive went out ten days earlier; N. Schmacke, H.-G. Güse, *Zwangssterilisiert, verleugnet – vergessen. Zur Geschichte der nationalsozialistischen Rassenhygiene am Beispiel Bremen* (Bremen, 1984), 66.
215. BA Berlin, R 3001/alt R 22/1451, Bl. 43–5: Preußischer Justizminister to Generalstaatsanwälte, 23 Mar. 1934; *Gesetz zur Verhütung erbkranken Nachwuchses*, 56, 136.
216. StAMü, Justizvollzugsanstalten Nr. 12333, Ärztliches Gutachten, 4 May 1934; ibid., Beschluß des Erbgesundheitsgerichts Passau, 26 July 1934.
217. Scharf, 'Strafvollzug', 810.
218. Liang, 'Criminal-biological Theory', 287.

219. BayHStA, MJu 22847, Anstaltsarzt to Direktion des Zuchthauses Straubing, 17 May 1934; BA Berlin, R 3001/9923, Zuchthaus Straubing, Anstaltsärztlicher Bericht, 14 June 1935; G. Leuthold, 'Veröffentlichungen des medizinischen Schrifttums in den Jahren 1933–1945 zum Thema: "Gesetz zur Verhütung erbkranken Nachwuchses vom 14. Juli 1933"' (Ph.D., University Erlangen-Nuremberg, 1975), 122–4. For the Straubing hospital, see JVA Straubing (ed.), *100 Jahre*, 51–2.
220. Wetzell, *Inventing*, 269–71.
221. BA Berlin, R 3001/9945, Bl. 116, 123, 128, 139, 142, 151, 197. For slightly different figures, see Möhler, 'Strafvollzug', 134. For the number of all sterilised individuals in Germany, see H. Friedlander, *The Origins of Nazi Genocide. From Euthanasia to the Final Solution* (Chapel Hill, 1995), 28.
222. See Burleigh, *Death and Deliverance*, 56. For one death among prisoners, see ThHStAW, Justizministerium Nr. 1820, Bl. 22–3: Gesundheitszustand im Gefängnis Ichtershausen, 15 Jan. 1935.
223. See, for instance, BayHStA, MJu 22496, Jahresbericht des katholischen Anstaltsgeistlichen in Zweibrücken, 23 June 1934.
224. See, for example, Wüllner, 'Verhalten', 239–40; BA Berlin, R 3001/alt R 22/1247, Bl. 12–13: Vermerk über Besichtigung in Kaisheim, 16 Oct. 1937.
225. F. Leppmann, 'Geisteskranke und geistig Minderwertige', in Bumke (ed.), *Gefängniswesen*, 233–55; Müller, 'Verbrechensbekämpfung', *passim*. See also Walter, *Psychiatrie*, 499.
226. Leuthold, 'Veröffentlichungen', 124; Walter, *Psychiatrie*, 888. In 1934, 52.9 per cent of all those sterilised in Germany were classified as 'feeble-minded'; Friedlander, *Nazi Genocide*, 29.
227. Walter, *Psychiatrie*, 568–75; F. Dubitscher, 'Asozialität und Unfruchtbarmachung', *MKG* 5 (1938), 99–110, here 104–5. For a detailed analysis, see Wetzell, *Inventing*, 260–71.
228. Mezger, 'Inwieweit', 81–6.
229. For the treatment of alcoholics, see Ayaß (ed.), '*Gemeinschaftsfremde*', *passim*; G. Giles, 'Drink and Crime in Modern Germany', paper delivered at the symposium 'The Criminal and his Scientists', Florence, 15–18 October 1998.
230. StAMü, Justizvollzugsanstalten Nr. 13807, Dr Schemmel to Bezirksamt Aichach, 15 Jan. 1935; ibid., GStA bei dem OLG München Nr. 49, Anstaltsarzt Aichach to Direktion, 4 June 1936.
231. For this section on the Aichach penal institution, see numerous files of sterilised inmates in StAMü, Justizvollzugsanstalten Nr. 12333; ibid., Justizvollzugsanstalten Nr. 12334.
232. For the police orders, see H. Müller to Stapostellen, 9 Nov. 1938, reprinted in *IMT*, 42 vols (Nuremberg, 1947–49), vol. 25, 377–8.
233. Stolleis, *Law*, 14. See also H.-C. Lassen, 'Zum Urteil gegen Jacobsohn', in Justizbehörde Hamburg (ed.), '*Von Gewohnheitsverbrechern, Volksschädlingen und Asozialen . . .'. Hamburger Strafurteile im Nationalsozialismus* (Hamburg, 1995), 177–84, here 177, note 1.
234. For industrial tribunals and civil courts see, for example, E. Noam, W.-A. Kropat, *Justiz und Judenverfolgung*, 2 vols (Wiesbaden, 1975), vol. 1, 29–33, 81–4.
235. Johnson, *Nazi Terror*, 96–8, 175.
236. A. Hitler, *Mein Kampf* (London, 1992), trans. R. Manheim, 295.
237. Cited in Gruchmann, *Justiz*, 864.
238. Cited in P. Longerich, *The Unwritten Order* (Stroud, 2001), 22.

239. P. Longerich, *Politik der Vernichtung* (Munich, 1998), 70–111; Gruchmann, *Justiz*, 873–5. Longerich and other historians have made a persuasive case against the supposedly *ad hoc* origin of the laws, which had been emphasised in much of the older literature. The most detailed account of the genesis of the Nuremberg Laws has recently been provided by C. Essner, *Die 'Nürnberger Gesetze' oder die Verwaltung des Rassenwahns 1933–1945* (Paderborn, 2002).
240. R. Leppin, 'Der Schutz des deutschen Blutes und der deutschen Ehre', *Juristische Wochenschrift* 66 (1937), cit. in Noam, Kropat, *Justiz*, vol. 1, 109. The law itself is translated and reprinted in Noakes, Pridham (eds), *Nazism*, vol. 2, 535–6.
241. Gruchmann, *Justiz*, 881–6; Johnson, *Nazi Terror*, 105, 111.
242. Noam, Kropat, *Justiz*, vol. 1, 109–68; Gellately, *Gestapo*, 160–4; Gruchmann, *Justiz*, 879–80; Angermund, *Richterschaft*, 125–32; BA Berlin, R 3001/alt R 22/1160, Bl. 25–66: Statistisches Reichsamt, *Die Entwicklung der Kriminalität im Deutschen Reich vom Kriegsbeginn bis Mitte 1943* (Berlin, 1944).
243. See, for example, Landgericht Hamburg, Urteil vom 24.7.1939, reprinted in Justizbehörde Hamburg (ed.), *'Von Gewohnheitsverbrechern'*, 170–7; S. Friedländer, *Nazi Germany & the Jews. The Years of Persecution 1933–39* (London, 1997), 62, 284. For other examples, see Noam, Kropat, *Justiz*, vol. 1, 213–39.
244. Gellately, *Backing Hitler*, 49; Friedländer, *Nazi Germany*, 254. For Nazi propaganda about Jewish criminality, see also BA Berlin, Film 14769, K. Daluege, 'Der Jude in der Kriminalstatistik!', 20 July 1935.
245. Johnson, *Nazi Terror*, 356; Noakes, Pridham (eds), *Nazism*, vol. 2, 522, 549.
246. BA Berlin, R 3001/alt R 22/1160, Bl. 25–66: Statistisches Reichsamt, *Die Entwicklung der Kriminalität im Deutschen Reich vom Kriegsbeginn bis Mitte 1943* (Berlin, 1944).
247. BA Berlin, R 3001/alt R 22/Pers. 53759, Bl. 7: Breuer to Goebbels, 6 May 1933, note by Crohne in the margin.
248. Oleschinski, 'Gefängnisseelsorge', 335–8. For the various directives, see BA Berlin, R 3001/alt R 22/4371. In the mid-1920s, there was also a full-time rabbi employed in the Hamburg penal institutions; 'Die Strafanstalten in Deutschland', 15.
249. Möhler, 'Strafvollzug', 141, 248; ThHStAW, GStA bei dem OLG Jena Nr. 1086, Bl. 80: Strafgefängnis Ichtershausen to Dr Freund, 10 Mar. 1938.
250. BA Berlin, R 3001/alt R 22/1277, Bl. 80: RJM to Generalstaatsanwälte, 9 July 1937; ibid., R 3001/alt R 22/1437, Bl. 326: RJM to GStA Berlin, 23 May 1939.
251. See, for example, BLHA, Pr. Br. Rep. 29 Zuchthaus Brandenburg Nr. 826, Ernst K. to his parents and sister, 18 June 1939.
252. BA Berlin, R 3001/alt R 22/1422, Bl. 105: RJM to Generalstaatsanwälte, 31 Oct. 1941; ibid., R 3001/alt R 22/1338, Bl. 117: RJM to Generalstaatsanwälte, 10 Jan. 1942.
253. I. Kershaw, 'The Persecution of the Jews and German Popular Opinion in the Third Reich', *Leo Baeck Institute Yearbook* 26 (1981), 261–89.
254. It might well be true that a majority of the Nazi 'old fighters' originally joined the movement less because of its anti-Semitism than because of its anti-Marxism, as Peter Merkl's study suggests. But once they were part of the movement, they were exposed to virulent anti-Semitic propaganda; P.H. Merkl, *Political Violence under the Swastika* (Princeton, 1975), 522; Kershaw, *Hitler. 1889–1936*, 410–11.
255. For anti-Semitism and the labour movement, see R.J. Evans, 'Anti-Semitism: Ordinary Germans and the "longest hatred"', in idem, *Rereading German History* (London, 1997), 149–86, here 158–9.

256. For the history of anti-Semitism in Germany, see S. Volkov, 'Kontinuität und Diskontinuität im deutschen Antisemitismus, 1878–1945', *VfZ* 33 (1985), 221–43. The issue of public opinion toward the Jews in Nazi Germany has occupied scholars for many years. For a brief summary, see Friedländer, *Nazi Germany*, 163–4, 324–5.
257. ThSTA Mgn., Zuchthaus Untermaßfeld Nr. 347, Strafantrittsmitteilung, 3 Feb. 1939.
258. Cited in Maier, 'Strafvollzug', 937–8.
259. StAMü, Justizvollzugsanstalten Nr. 252, Bl. 16: Äußerung Regierungsrat Häge, 30 Dec. 1935.
260. Ibid., Justizvollzugsanstalten Nr. 412, Bl. 144: Frauenstrafanstalt Aichach to Staatsanwaltschaft Mannheim, 25 July 1939.
261. Sarodnick, '"Dieses Haus"', 363; WL, Reel EW 8, Bl. 8574–80: P. Wolff, 'Bericht eines "Rückwanderers" über Sachsenburg', no date [summer 1936].
262. BLHA, Pr. Br. Rep. 29 Zuchthaus Brandenburg Nr. 826, Ernst K. to his parents, 26 Feb. 1939; ibid., Ld. Br. Rep. 214 Forschungsstelle Zuchthaus Brandenburg Nr. 2, Bl. 248–51: curriculum vitae Walter N., no date.
263. For the quotations, see StAMü, Justizvollzugsanstalten Nr. 699, Bl. 49: Anstaltsarzt Aichach to Vorstand, 16 Jan. 1940; ibid., Bl. 96, Führungsbogen, 22 July 1940.
264. ThSTA Mgn., Zuchthaus Untermaßfeld Nr. 1018, Meldung, 9 Mar. 1938, 26 Jan. 1939; ThHStAW, GStA bei dem OLG Jena Nr. 856, Bl. 55–7: Staatspolizeileitstelle Weimar, Befragung des Karel N., 16 Feb. 1939.
265. WL, Reel EW 8, Bl. 8582–91: F. Schnapper, 'Forging banknotes in Sachsenhausen', no date.
266. WL, Reel EW 6, Bl. 6797–824: A.J. Bruck, 'Brandenburg 1940', September 1948. Bruck's testimony is curious for a number of reasons, not least his claim that he had never been made to suffer. This is contradicted by one episode where he recalls being abused as a 'lazy Jew' by a senior warder.
267. BLHA, Pr. Br. Rep. 29 Zuchthaus Brandenburg Nr. 5652, Anzeigen, 30 Mar. 1938. For the other examples, see StAMü, Justizvollzugsanstalten Nr. 412; ibid., Nr. 2950 (here Bl. 48: Führungsbogen Ingeborg E., 25 June 1942), Nr. 6051, Nr. 6234, Nr. 9053, Nr. 9953, Nr. 11660, Nr. 12338 (here Krankenakte Emma E.); BLHA, Pr. Br. Rep. 29 Zuchthaus Brandenburg Nr. 723; ThSTA Mgn., Zuchthaus Untermaßfeld Nr. 1589.

Chapter 4

1. BA Berlin, Film 14769, K. Daluege, 'Staatsanwaltschaft und Polizei in der Verbrechensbekämpfung', 29 Nov. 1935.
2. Broszat, *Staat Hitlers*, 93–5; W.S. Allen, *The Nazi Seizure of Power*, 2nd edition (London, 1989), 157–8; Gellately, *Backing Hitler*, 17–18.
3. For the Reichstag fire and the historical debate surrounding it, see Kershaw, *Hitler. 1889–1936*, 456–60, 731–2. The recollections of Diels are reprinted and translated in Noakes, Pridham (eds), *Nazism*, vol. 1, 139–41. The Reichstag Fire Decree is reprinted in Hirsch *et al.* (eds), *Recht*, 89–90. For the Nazi terror immediately after 27 February 1933, see Tuchel, *Konzentrationslager*, 97–100. For the Fraenkel quotation see his *Dual State*, 3.
4. Tuchel, *Konzentrationslager*, 103; Broszat, 'Konzentrationslager', 332–7; P. Longerich, *Die braunen Bataillone. Geschichte der SA* (Munich, 1989), 165–79; Orth, *System*, 23–6.

5. W. Ayaß, *'Asoziale' im Nationalsozialismus* (Stuttgart, 1995), 20–40; BA Berlin, R 3001/alt R 22/1469, Bl. 6–9: Erlaß des Preußischen Ministers des Inneren, 13 Nov. 1933.
6. K.-L. Terhorst, *Polizeiliche planmäßige Überwachung und polizeiliche Vorbeugungshaft im Dritten Reich* (Heidelberg, 1985), 72–85.
7. See, for example, Roth, 'Kriminalpolizei', 333.
8. Gruchmann, *Justiz*, 324, 433–84, quote on 450. Only in one of the various cases where individuals had used the cover of the 'Röhm putsch' to settle personal scores, did a regular court try to sentence the perpetrators.
9. Hitler quotation in Kershaw, *Hitler. 1889–1936*, 519; see also ibid., 519–21. For the Schmitt quote, see C. Schmitt, 'Der Führer schützt das Recht', *Deutsche Juristen Zeitung* 39 (1934), 946–8.
10. Gruchmann, *Justiz*, 545.
11. K. Drobisch, G. Wieland, *System der NS-Konzentrationslager: 1933–1939* (Berlin, 1993), 43–5; Peukert, *KPD*, 92.
12. See, for example, StAMü, Justizvollzugsanstalten Nr. 24, 30, 40.
13. See StAMü, Justizvollzugsanstalten Nr. 27, Aktennotiz, 11 Dec. 1933; ibid., Nr. 29, Gefangenanstalt Aichach to Politische Polizei Nuremberg, 29 Mar. 1934.
14. Hitler speech to the Reich Governors, 6 July 1933, reprinted and translated in Noakes, Pridham (eds), *Nazism*, vol. 1, 170–1; Angermund, *Richterschaft*, 63–9; U. Herbert, 'Von der Gegnerbekämpfung zur "rassischen Generalprävention"', in idem et al. (eds), *Die nationalsozialistischen Konzentrationslager*, vol. 1, 60–86, here 60–1; Orth, *System*, 32.
15. For this development, see U. Herbert, *Best. Biographische Studien über Radikalismus, Weltanschauung und Vernunft* (Bonn, 1996), 168–77; idem, 'Gegnerbekämpfung', *passim*; P. Wagner, '"Vernichtung der Berufsverbrecher". Die vorbeugende Verbrechensbekämpfung der Kriminalpolizei bis 1937', in Herbert et al. (eds), *Die nationalsozialistischen Konzentrationslager*, vol. 1, 87–110; Roth, 'Kriminalpolizei', 332; BayHStA, MJu 22522, '300 Berufsverbrecher unschädlich', *Völkischer Beobachter*, 5 June 1934.
16. BA Berlin, R 58/473, Bl. 46–9: Vorbeugende Verbrechensbekämpfung durch die Polizei, 14 Dec. 1937; ibid., Bl. 63–72: Richtlinien zum Erlaß 'Vorbeugende Verbrechensbekämpfung durch die Polizei', 4 Apr. 1938.
17. Herbert, 'Gegnerbekämpfung', 80–1.
18. Orth, *System*, 26–38, 51. For Hitler's role, see also Tuchel, *Konzentrationslager*, 353–9.
19. Himmler's speech translated and reprinted in Noakes, Pridham (eds), *Nazism*, vol. 2, 505–6.
20. For the self-image of the police, see Herbert, 'Gegnerbekämpfung', 67–8; idem, *Best*, 163–8.
21. The camp regulations are translated and reprinted in Noakes, Pridham (eds), *Nazism*, vol. 2.
22. For the above, see Gruchmann, *Justiz*, 584–603.
23. BA Berlin, R 3001/alt R 22/4277, Bl. 149–91: Besprechung am 18.6.1937, here Bl. 191.
24. Johe, *Justiz*, 142–3.
25. Gruchmann, *Justiz*, 1128.
26. BA Berlin, R 3001/alt R 22/1278, Bl. 115: In den Vollzugsanstalten untergebrachte Schutzhaftgefangene, no date. It is unclear how many individuals in preventive police custody were held in penal institutions in the late 1930s.

27. R. Heydrich to Staatspolizeileit- und Staatspolizeistellen, 10 Nov. 1938, reprinted in *IMT*, vol. 31, 518–19; HStAD-Kalkum, Gerichte Rep. 321/571, GStA Düsseldorf, Vermerk, 10 Nov. 1938; Möhler, 'Strafvollzug', 149, note 570.
28. Cited in Gruchmann, *Justiz*, 577.
29. For one local example, see the treatment of police prisoners in the Aichach penal institution, StaMü, Justizvollzugsanstalt Aichach Nr. 13; ibid., Nr. 27, Nr. 38, Nr. 40, Nr. 47.
30. BA Berlin, R 3001/9919, Bl. 1: RJM to Geheimes Staatspolizeiamt Berlin, 19 Nov. 1935; ibid., R 3001/alt R 22/1278, Bl. 152: RJM to Generalstaatsanwälte, 7 July 1939; ibid., R 3001/alt R 22/1089, Bl. 24–7: offical diary Gürtner, 25 Oct. 1935; Gruchmann, *Justiz*, 576–83; Naumann, 'Justizverwaltung', 128, 131.
31. BA Berlin, R 3001/alt R 22/1278, Bl. 113–14: Besprechung vom 16.8.1937; ibid., Bl. 146: RJM to Reichsführer SS und Chef der deutschen Polizei, 27 July 1939.
32. Ibid., R 3001/alt R 22/1437, Bl. 60–1: RJM, Vermerk, 15 Feb. 1937; ibid., Bl. 152: Heydrich to RJM, 28 June 1938; ibid., R 3001/9803/78, Bl. 19: Himmler to Gürtner, 8 Aug. 1938.
33. Ibid., R 3001/alt R 22/1437, Bl. 65–6: Gürtner to Himmler, 17 Feb. 1937. See also ibid., Bl. 153: RJM to Reichsführer SS und Chef der deutschen Polizei, 14 July 1938.
34. Ibid., R 3001/alt R 22/1429, Bl. 123–5: Bouhler to Lammers, 26 July 1939; ibid., Bl. 122: Lammers to Gürtner, 8 Aug. 1939. For the painting of toy soldiers in the penitentiary, see also Faralisch, 'Zeitzeugenberichte', 353–4.
35. BA Berlin, R 3001/alt R 22/1429, Bl. 128–30: Gürtner to Lammers, 22 Aug. 1939.
36. Ibid., Bl. 133: Heydrich to RJM, 26 Aug. 1939.
37. Ibid., Bl. 134: RJM, Vermerk, 7 Sept. 1939. Gürtner did contact Lammers, however, and requested clarification of Hitler's views; ibid., Bl. 135: Gürtner to Lammers, 8 Sept. 1939.
38. Besprechung im Reichsjustizministerium am 4.6.1937, reprinted in Bundesminister der Justiz (ed.), *Justiz*, 160–1; Gruchmann, *Justiz*, 703–19, Himmler quotation on 711. See also HStAD-Kalkum, Gerichte Rep. 321/682, Bl. 1: GStA Düsseldorf to Staatspolizeistelle Düsseldorf, 8 Aug. 1935; ibid., Bl. 19–20: RJM to Generaltstaatsanwälte, 13 May 1937.
39. Schumacher (ed.), *M.d.R.*, 280–1; Gruchmann, *Justiz*, 352, 675. For Heuck's trial, see Zarusky, 'Politischer Widerstand', 53–4.
40. BA Berlin, R 3001/alt R 22/5087, Bl. 96–9: GStA Jena to RJM, 30 Sept. 1937. For the general background, see Gruchmann, *Justiz*, 345–67, 564–73, 632–58; Tuchel, *Konzentrationslager*, 339–40.
41. ThSTA Mgn., Zuchthaus Untermaßfeld Nr. 2, Entlassungsanzeige, 5 Oct. 1939. For the general background, see Gruchmann, *Justiz*, 610–11. See also A. Pretzel, 'Vorfälle im Konzentrationslager Sachsenhausen vor Gericht in Berlin', in idem, G. Roßbach (eds), *Homosexuellenverfolgung in Berlin 1933–1945* (Berlin, 2000), 119–68, here 128–9.
42. Gruchmann, *Justiz*, 587–9, quotation on 587.
43. BA Berlin, R 3001/alt R 22/1467, Bl. 314–17: Besprechung mit den Generalstaatsanwälten am 23.1.1939.
44. This argument has been put forward, among others, by Martin Broszat, in *Staat Hitlers*, 414–15.
45. BayHStA, MJu 22525, Staatsministerium der Justiz to Generalstaatsanwälte, 31 May 1933. See also Johe, *Justiz*, 138; Gruchmann, *Justiz*, 612.
46. Niermann, *Strafjustiz*, 120–1; Gruchmann, *Justiz*, 613, 618–20.
47. BA Berlin, R 3001/9803/78, Bl. 7–18: Gestapo to Reichsführer SS und Chef der deutschen Polizei, 12 July 1938; Habicht, *Zuchthaus Waldheim*, 64.

48. Union für Recht und Freiheit (ed.), *Strafvollzug*, 13; ThSTA Mgn., Zuchthaus Untermaßfeld Nr. 663.
49. Drobisch, 'Alltag', 270.
50. See, for example, BA Berlin, R 3001/9803/78, Bl. 7–18: Gestapo to Reichsführer SS und Chef der deutschen Polizei, 12 July 1938.
51. ThSTA Mgn., Zuchthaus Untermaßfeld Nr. 44, Bl. 183: Entlassungsverhandlung, 5 Aug. 1943.
52. StAMü, Justizvollzugsanstalten Nr. 13704, Psychologisch-soziologischer Befundbogen, 3 Aug. 1937; ibid., Nachbericht, 12 Jan. 1939; ibid., Frauenstrafanstalt Aichach to Staatspolizeileitstelle Stuttgart, 26 Sept. 1938.
53. BLHA, Pr. Br. Rep. 29 Zuchthaus Luckau Nr. 414, Strafanstalt Luckau to Geheimes Staatspolizeiamt Berlin, 9 July 1936; Schumacher (ed.), *M.d.R.*, 283–4. Elgas survived the war and served as a SPD deputy in Berlin between 1959 and 1967.
54. ThSTA Mgn., Zuchthaus Untermaßfeld Nr. 663, Aufnahmebogen, 18 July 1934; ibid., Strafanstalt Untermaßfeld to Thüringisches Geheimes Staatspolizeiamt, 5 May 1936; ibid., Thüringisches Geheimes Staatspolizeiamt to Strafanstalt Untermaßfeld, 7 May 1936.
55. Cited in Naumann, 'Justizverwaltung', 129. I am grateful to Kai Naumann for sending me some more details on this case.
56. O. Oertel, *Als Gefangener der SS* (Oldenburg, 1990), 75.
57. See, for example, *Sopade*, vol. 5, 854.
58. AV des RJM, 13 Apr. 1935, reprinted in Ayaß (ed.), *'Gemeinschaftsfremde'*, 59–61; BA Berlin, R 3001/alt R 22/1337, Bl. 319: RJM to Generalstaatsanwälte, 2 July 1937; ibid., Bl. 330: RJM to Generalstaatsanwälte, 8 Mar. 1938.
59. Cited in Maier, 'Strafvollzug', 983.
60. Brandstätter, 'Erfahrungen', 55.
61. ThSTA Mgn., Zuchthaus Untermaßfeld Nr. 347, Schlussbericht, 6 Oct. 1940, underlined in the original. For Gericke, see BA Berlin, R 3001/alt R 22/Pers. 57132, GStA Jena to RJM, 4 May 1937.
62. This was true, for example, in the case of 'race defilers'; see BA Berlin, 99 US 2 FC 588, Mikrofilm 22942, Bl. 153: Chef der Sicherheitspolizei to Staatspolizeileitstellen, 12 June 1937.
63. For this view, see Gruchmann, *Justiz*, 623–6.
64. BA Berlin, R 3001/alt R 22/1467, Bl. 37–41: RJM to GStA Karlsruhe, 19 June 1935; Geheimes Staatspolizeiamt Berlin to Staatspolizeileit- und Staatspolizeistellen, 5 Aug. 1937, reprinted in Fricke, *Justizvollzugsanstalt*, 66.
65. Roth, 'Kriminalpolizei', 339.
66. ThSTA Mgn., Zuchthaus Untermaßfeld Nr. 644, Bl. 65: Strafgefängnis Ebrach to Kriminalpolizei Ludwigshafen, 16 May 1939.
67. For one such example, see Scharf, 'Strafvollzug', 811–12.
68. For the Jehovah's Witnesses, see Garbe, *Widerstand*, 286–309. For some general background, see BA Berlin, R 3001/alt R 22/1467, Bl. 312–13: Besprechung mit den Chefpräsidenten am 24.1.1939; ibid., Bl. 314–17: Besprechung mit den Generalstaatsanwälten am 23.1.1939.
69. GStA Hamm to GStA Düsseldorf, 16 June 1939, reprinted in Justizakademie NRW (ed.), *Zum Strafvollzug 1933–1945*, source 32c; Gruchmann, *Justiz*, 619.
70. ThHStAW, GStA bei dem OLG Jena Nr. 856, Bl. 55–7: Staatspolizeileitstelle Weimar, Befragung des Karel N., 16 Feb. 1939.

71. The diary covers the period between 1934 and 1938. See M. Löffler, *Das Diensttagebuch des Reichsjustizministers Gürtner 1934 bis 1938* (Frankfurt am Main, 1997), 156–7. The originals of the diary are kept in the Federal Archive in Berlin.
72. For the camp figures in mid-November 1938, see Orth, *System*, 52.
73. Sarodnick, '"Dieses Haus"', 353–6; Drobisch, 'Konzentrationslager', 282.
74. StAMü, Justizvollzugsanstalten Nr. 61. See also Union für Recht und Freiheit (ed.), *Strafvollzug*; BA Berlin, R 3001/alt R 22/1292, Bl. 359–74: Vorstand der SPD, Entwicklungstendenzen im Deutschen Strafvollzug, August 1935.
75. This whole section is particularly indebted to Drobisch, 'Konzentrationslager' and Pingel, *Häftlinge* (for the Dachau figures, see 50, 81). Other sources include Orth, *System*, 25–30, 52; Tuchel, 'Planung und Realität des Systems der Konzentrationslager 1934–1938', in U. Herbert *et al.* (eds), *Die nationalsozialistischen Konzentrationslager. Entwicklung und Struktur*, vol. 1 (Göttingen, 1998), 43–59, here esp. 56; Sofsky, *Konzentrationslager*, 246–55; Gellately, *Backing Hitler*, 51–7; Noakes, Pridham (eds), *Nazism*, vol. 2, 502–4; E. Kogon, *Der SS-Staat* (Munich, 1995), 150–6; Longerich, *Politik*, 203–6. For the SPD quotation, see *Sopade*, vol. 2, 820–1. For the Emsland figures, see Kosthorst, Walter (eds), *Strafgefangenenlager*, vol. 2, 1777, 3552. Looking at the mortality statistics for the Emsland camp, the real figures were probably somewhat higher. First of all, the statistics are not complete. Also, sick inmates were often transported from the Emsland camp back to a prison or penitentiary, with some soon dying there.

Chapter 5

1. M. Fulbrook, *German National Identity after the Holocaust* (Cambridge, 1999), 169.
2. Cited in M. Domarus (ed.), *Hitler. Reden und Proklamationen 1932–1945*, 4 vols, vol. II/1 (Wiesbaden, 1973), 1427.
3. Hitler, *Mein Kampf*, 183, 185–6; I. Kershaw, *Hitler. 1936–45: Nemesis* (London, 2000), 609, 747, 754; idem, *Hitler. 1889–1936*, 104.
4. Quoted in Marotzke to Kritzinger, 4 June 1940, reprinted and translated in Noakes (ed.), *Nazism*, vol. 4, 316. See also ibid., 188–95, 321–5, 510–20; T. Mason, 'The Legacy of 1918 for National Socialism', in A. Nicholls, E. Matthias (eds), *German Democracy and the Triumph of Hitler* (London, 1971), 215–39; Overy, *War*, 259–314; Herbst, *Deutschland*, 262–6.
5. See H. Picker (ed.), *Hitlers Tischgespräche im Führerhauptquartier* (Berlin, 1997), 282, 617.
6. Niermann, *Strafjustiz*, 364.
7. E. Fröhlich (ed.), *Die Tagebücher von Joseph Goebbels* (Munich), part I: 1924–41, 4 vols (Munich, 1987), vol. 4, entry for 17 Aug. 1940, 284.
8. Cited in Gruchmann, *Justiz*, 676.
9. The SD was the central SS organisation dedicated to the systematic surveillance of Nazi opponents and German society. The security police included the criminal and the political police. For the RSHA, see M. Wildt, *Generation des Unbedingten. Das Führungskorps des Reichssicherheitshauptamtes* (Hamburg, 2002).
10. Orth, *System*, 109.
11. Cited in Angermund, *Richterschaft*, 201. See also Gruchmann, *Justiz*, 901, 1103, 1131. For references to 'negative selection' before 1933, see, for example, Viernstein, 'Stufenstrafvollzug', 4.

12. Cited in Gruchmann, *Justiz*, 921.
13. Decree concerning Exceptional Measures relating to Radio, reprinted and translated in Noakes (ed.), *Nazism*, vol. 4, 126. For the background, see Gruchmann, *Justiz*, 902–4.
14. Special Wartime Penal Code, reprinted and translated in Noakes, Pridham (eds), *Nazism*, vol. 4, 124. See also Gruchmann, *Justiz*, 901.
15. Dissent could be dealt with as 'disorderly conduct' by local courts, as a 'malicious attack' by special courts, as 'treason' by the Higher State Courts or as 'undermining the war effort' by the People's Court; F. Anders-Baudisch, 'Aus der "Rechts"-Praxis Nationalsozialistischer Sondergerichte im "Reichsgau Sudetenland" 1940–1945', *Bohemia* 40 (1999), 331–66, here 342, 366.
16. Verordung zur Ergänzung der Strafvorschriften zum Schutz der Wehrkraft des Deutschen Volkes, 25 Nov. 1939, reprinted in Kosthorst, Walter (eds), *Strafgefangenenlager*, vol. 2, 1523–4.
17. Cited in Gruchmann, *Justiz*, 909. See also Noakes (ed.), *Nazism*, vol. 4, 129–30.
18. Cited in Evans, *Rituals*, 690.
19. Gruchmann, *Justiz*, 913–14. Freisler quote ibid., 916.
20. Wagner, *Kriminalpolizei*, 311; Gruchmann, *Justiz*, 910–11; Dörner, *Erziehung*, 201.
21. Kriegswirtschaftsverordnung and Verbrauchsregelungs-Strafverordnung, both reprinted in Hirsch *et al.* (eds), *Recht*, 466–8.
22. Verordung über die Vollstreckung von Freiheitsstrafen wegen einer während des Krieges begangenen Tat, 11 June 1940, reprinted in Kosthorst, Walter (eds), *Strafgefangenenlager*, vol. 2, 1536–7; RJM to Generalstaatsanwälte, 27 Jan. 1943, reprinted ibid., 1373–4. For the Freisler quote, see BA Berlin, R 3001/alt R 22/245, Arbeitstagung am 23. und 24.4.1941, here Bl. 177.
23. Figures excluding those sentenced for 'undermining the war effort', but including the Leitmeritz district; BA Berlin, R 3001/alt R 22/1160, Bl. 25–66: Statistisches Reichsamt, *Die Entwicklung der Kriminalität im Deutschen Reich vom Kriegsbeginn bis Mitte 1943* (Berlin, 1944). This document includes the confidential sentencing statistics for the period 1937–43, compiled in 1944 by the Reich Office for Statistics. According to the statisticians, the figures include those individuals convicted of crimes and misdemeanours against Reich laws, including those sentenced by the People's Court. But it is obvious that the figures for 1942–43 are not complete. To what extent this is true of the earlier figures is unclear. For the methodical limitations of these statistics, see also B. Blau, 'Die Kriminalität in Deutschland während des zweiten Weltkriegs', *Zeitschrift für die gesamte Strafrechtswissenschaft* 64 (1952), 31–81, here 35–42.
24. Compared to 1937, judges in the Altreich in 1940 handed out proportionally longer prison and penitentiary sentences. They also resorted less to fines than previously. See BA Berlin, R 3001/alt R 22/1160, Bl. 25–66: Statistisches Reichsamt, *Die Entwicklung der Kriminalität im Deutschen Reich vom Kriegsbeginn bis Mitte 1943* (Berlin, 1944).
25. BA Berlin, R 3001/alt R 22/897, Bl. 9–10.
26. Quoted in Gruchmann, *Justiz*, 1103; Dörner, '*Heimtücke*', 42–3; Bästlein, 'Sondergerichte', 225. See also ibid., 223.
27. Johnson, *Nazi Terror*, 318.
28. For the initial fall in prisoner numbers, see BA Berlin R 3001/9920/2, Bl. 2–3. The amnesty was for predicted and already pronounced prison sentences of less than three months. Offenders who had previously been sentenced to more than six months' imprisonment in total were not eligible; Stapenhorst, *Entwicklung*, 70;

Weckbecker, *Sondergerichte*, 380. This echoed an amnesty at the beginning of the First World War, which had also resulted in the release of numerous prisoners with short sentences; C. Birkigt, 'Die Wirkung der bei Kriegsausbruch erlassenen allgemeinen Amnestie', *BlGefK* 49 (1915), 161–6.
29. See, for example, BA Berlin, R 3001/alt R 22/1158, Bl. 241–50: Die Kriminalität im Deutschen Reich im 1. und 2. Vierteljahr 1941.
30. Noakes (ed.), *Nazism*, vol. 4, 584–5.
31. See Blau, 'Kriminalität', 36, 43; F. Wilhelm, *Die Polizei im NS-Staat. Die Geschichte ihrer Organisation im Überblick* (Paderborn, 1997), 126–30.
32. Johnson, *Nazi Terror*, 322–33; M.P. Hensle, '"Rundfunkverbrechen" vor NS-Sondergerichten', *Rundfunk und Geschichte* 26 (2000), 111–26; BA Berlin, R 3001/alt R 22/1160, Bl. 25–66: Statistisches Reichsamt, *Die Entwicklung der Kriminalität im Deutschen Reich vom Kriegsbeginn bis Mitte 1943* (Berlin, 1944).
33. Oehler, *Rechtsprechung*, 254; Weckbecker, *Sondergerichte*, 771.
34. *Kriminalstatistik 1935 und 1936*, 23.
35. BA Berlin, R 3001/alt R 22/897, Bl. 14–16; 'Die selbstständigen Vollzugsanstalten der Reichsjustizverwaltung', *BlGefK* 71 (1940), 338–54; Gruchmann, *Justiz*, 277–8; Anders-Baudisch, 'Sondergerichte', 336–7, 347–9. The first territory added to the German legal administration in the Third Reich had been the Saarland, reintegrated into Germany in March 1935. See Möhler, 'Strafvollzug', 198–202.
36. O. Sládek, 'Standrecht und Standgericht. Die Gestapo in Böhmen und Mähren', in Paul, Mallmann (eds), *Die Gestapo im Zweiten Weltkrieg*, 317–39, esp. 331; M. Kárný, 'Protektorat Böhmen und Mähren', in W. Benz et al. (eds), *Enzyklopädie des Nationalsozialismus* (Munich, 1998), 656–7; BA Berlin, R 3001/alt R 22/897, Bl. 15–16; Gruchmann, *Justiz*, 279; Marxen, *Volk*, 36–8, 42. For Eliáš, see H. Heiber, 'Zur Justiz im Dritten Reich: Der Fall Eliáš', *VfZ* 3 (1955), 275–96. Eliáš was actually sentenced in Prague, where the First Senate of the People's Court had briefly travelled to conduct this case. I follow Klaus Marxen in calling 'Czech' those prisoners who were classified by the Nazis as *Protektoratsangehörige*.
37. 'Die selbstständigen Vollzugsanstalten'; BA Berlin, R 3001/alt R 22/897, Bl. 14–15.
38. E. Zarzycki, *Besatzungsjustiz in Polen. Sondergerichte im Dienste deutscher Unterwerfungsstrategie* (Berlin, 1990), 10–11; Weckbecker, *Sondergerichte*, 446, 768, 799 (n. 1); D. Majer, *'Fremdvölkische' im Dritten Reich* (Boppard, 1981), 766, 777; 'Die selbstständigen Vollzugsanstalten'. The judicial districts in the incorporated territories did not completely overlap with the old border. For example, the Kattowitz judicial district included six penal institutions previously administered in the Breslau (Altreich) district, while three Polish penal institutions were added to the Königsberg (Altreich) judicial district. It should be noted that, in this book, the names of German-occupied places are generally given in German.
39. For the Müller quote, see his *Furchtbare Juristen*, 172. See also Zarzycki, *Besatzungsjustiz*, 13–14; Majer, *'Fremdvölkische'*, 720, 775–81; Weckbecker, *Sondergerichte*, 443, 456, 777; BA Berlin, R 3001/alt R 22/4162, Arbeitstagungen der OLG Präsidenten und Generalstaatsanwälte, Vortrag Dr Freisler, no date [31 Mar. 1942].
40. U. Herbert, *Fremdarbeiter. Politik und Praxis des 'Ausländer-Einsatzes' in der Kriegswirtschaft des Dritten Reiches* (Berlin, 1986), 74; K.-H. Keldungs, *Das Duisburger Sondergericht 1942–1945* (Baden-Baden, 1998), 93. For anti-Slav sentiments in German criminology, see P. Becker, 'Der Verbrecher als "monstruoser

Typus"', in M. Hagner (ed.), *Der falsche Körper. Beiträge zu einer Geschichte der Monstrositäten* (Göttingen, 1995), 147–73, here 163–5.
41. Cited in Wrobel, *Justiz*, 73; Zarzycki, *Besatzungsjustiz*, 15; Zarusky, 'Gerichte', 514. For the motivation of the judges, see also Majer, 'Fremdvölkische', 775.
42. Gellately, *Gestapo*, 218–19; Herbert, *Fremdarbeiter* 70–88; Noakes, Pridham (eds), *Nazism*, vol. 3, 983–5; Noakes (ed.), *Nazism*, vol. 4, 241.
43. Majer, 'Fremdvölkische', 608–19; Niermann, *Strafjustiz*, 352–3.
44. BA Berlin, R 43 II/1549, Bl. 54: RJM to Chef der Reichskanzlei, 20 Nov. 1940; ibid., Bl. 55: Chef der Sicherheitspolizei und des SD to RJM, 9 Oct. 1940; ibid., Bl. 61–3: Schlegelberger to Chef der Reichskanzlei, 17 Apr. 1941; ibid., Bl. 70: Reichskanzlei, Vermerk, 22 Apr. 1941.
45. Verordnung über die Strafrechtspflege gegen Polen und Juden in den eingegliederten Ostgebieten, 4 Dec. 1941, reprinted in Hirsch *et al.* (eds), *Recht*, 496–8, my italics; R. Freisler, 'Das deutsche Polenstrafrecht', reprinted ibid., 498–500; Majer, 'Fremdvölkische', 744–59, first Freisler quotation on 753. The decree did not apply to Poles singled out by the authorities for 'Germanisation'.
46. For Duisburg, see Wagner, *Kriminalpolizei*, 344–61. For Cologne, see Roth, 'Kriminalpolizei', 339.
47. Longerich, *Politik*, 243–81; Majer, 'Fremdvölkische', 796–9.
48. Majer, 'Fremdvölkische', 793–9; Wrobel, *Justiz*, 85.
49. Cited in Niermann, *Strafjustiz*, 347. See also Herbert, *Fremdarbeiter*, 76–82; Gellately, *Gestapo*, 232–44; G. Wysocki, 'Lizenz zum Töten. Die "Sonderbehandlungspraxis" der Stapo-Stelle Braunschweig', in Paul, Mallmann (eds), *Gestapo im Zweiten Weltkrieg*, 237–54; Stolle, *Geheime Staatspolizei*, 247–8.
50. Cited in Herbert, *Fremdarbeiter*, 77.
51. G. Paul, A. Primavesi, 'Die Verfolgung der "Fremdvölkischen"', in Paul, Mallmann (eds), *Gestapo – Mythos und Realität*, 388–401, here 390; Gellately, *Gestapo*, 226–7; Wagner, *Kriminalpolizei*, 326–8; G. Lotfi, 'Stätten des Terrors. Die "Arbeitserziehungslager" der Gestapo', in Paul, Mallmann (eds), *Gestapo im Zweiten Weltkrieg*, 255–69.
52. Cited in H. Michelberger, *Berichte aus der Justiz des Dritten Reiches* (Pfaffenweiler, 1989), 392, 349.
53. Gruchmann, *Justiz*, 693, 1088–9; Herbert, *Fremdarbeiter*, 116.
54. BA Berlin, 99 US 57991, Schlegelberger to Generalstaatsanwälte, 24 July 1941.
55. Niermann, *Strafjustiz*, 356–7.
56. RJM, Vermerk, 29 Apr. 1940, reprinted in Kosthorst, Walter (eds), *Strafgefangenenlager*, vol. 2, 1341.
57. Broszat, 'Perversion', 400; ibid., documents 6, 11; Gruchmann, *Justiz*, 682–8; H. Boberach (ed.), *Meldungen aus dem Reich, 1938–1945*, 17 vols (Herrsching, 1984), vol. 2, 376.
58. Broszat (ed.), *Kommandant*, 115–16, quotation on 116. See also Wagner, *Kriminalpolizei*, 219, 332; Schwerk, *Meisterdiebe*, 89–92.
59. Cited in Niermann, *Strafjustiz*, 350. See also BA Berlin, 99 US 2 FC 588, Mikrofilm 22941, Bl. 46–8: GStA Berlin to RJM, 31 Mar. 1942; Angermund, *Richterschaft*, 190–3.
60. Cited in Michelberger, *Berichte*, 367.
61. Schlegelberger to Hitler, 10 Mar. 1941, reprinted in Broszat, 'Perversion', 417–18.
62. Förster, *Jurist*, 55–6.
63. BA Berlin, 99 US 57991, RJM to Generalstaatsanwälte, 15 Dec. 1941.

64. E. Fröhlich (ed.), *Die Tagebücher von Joseph Goebbels* (Munich), part II: 1941–45, 15 vols (Munich, 1993–96), vol. 3, entry for 27 March 1942, 561. For the general background, see U. Herbert (ed.), *Nationalsozialistische Vernichtungspolitik 1939–1945* (Frankfurt am Main, 1998).
65. Kershaw, *Hitler. 1936–45, passim*; Noakes, Pridham (eds), *Nazism*, vol. 3, 812–45.
66. Kershaw, '*Hitler Myth*', 169–77; Noakes (ed.), *Nazism*, vol. 4, 509–39, 552–4; O. Bartov, *Hitler's Army* (Oxford, 1992), 38–9.
67. W. Jochmann (ed.), *Adolf Hitler. Monologe im Führerhauptquartier 1941–1944* (Hamburg, 1980), 125–6.
68. Picker (ed.), *Tischgespräche*, 473–4.
69. Fröhlich (ed.), *Tagebücher*, II/4, entry for 30 May 1942, 406. See also ibid., entry for 23 May 1942, 343.
70. A. Hillgruber (ed.), *Staatsmänner und Diplomaten bei Hitler. Vertrauliche Aufzeichnungen über Unterredungen mit Vertretern des Auslandes 1939–1944*, 2 vols (Frankfurt am Main, 1967–70), vol. 1, 611; Jochmann (ed.), *Monologe*, 126; Picker (ed.), *Tischgespräche*, 282–3, 617; Fröhlich (ed.), *Tagebücher*, II/4, entry for 30 May 1942, 405.
71. Fröhlich (ed.), *Tagebücher*, II/4, entry for 24 May 1942, 361.
72. Ibid.
73. IfZ, MA 313, Bl. 2613144–48: Rede des Reichsführers-SS vor der deutschen Presse in Weimar am 4.12.1943, quotations on Bl. 2613148.
74. BA Berlin, NS 19/4014, Bl. 158–204: Rede des Reichsführers-SS am 21.6.1944 vor Generälen der Wehrmacht, here Bl. 172. See also ibid., Bl. 107–50: Rede des Reichsführers-SS vor Vertretern der deutschen Justiz am 25.5.1944.
75. Gellately, *Gestapo*, 227; Wagner, *Kriminalpolizei*, 338–43.
76. Jochmann (ed.), *Monologe*, 60, 125, 142, 272; Fröhlich (ed.), *Tagebücher*, II/4, entry for 23 May 1942, 343. The Nazi leadership's distrust of the Reich Ministry of Justice had been heightened in autumn 1941, during preparation for the trial of Prime Minister Eliáš; see Heiber, 'Justiz', *passim*.'
77. Picker (ed.), *Tischgespräche*, 182.
78. BA Berlin, R 3001/alt R 22/4162, Bl. 1–5: Arbeitstagungen der OLG Präsidenten und Generalstaatsanwälte, Vortrag Dr Schlegelberger, no date [31 Mar. 1942].
79. Schlegelberger to Hitler, 24 Mar. 1942, reprinted in B. Heiber, H. Heiber (eds), *Die Rückseite des Hakenkreuzes* (Munich, 1993), 243.
80. For these and other details on the Schlitt case, see Johe, *Justiz*, 172–4.
81. BA Berlin, R 3001/alt R 22/4162, Bl. 1–5: Arbeitstagungen der OLG Präsidenten und Generalstaatsanwälte, Vortrag Dr Schlegelberger, no date [31 Mar. 1942].
82. See, for example, Boberach (ed.), *Meldungen*, vol. 9, 3488.
83. Fröhlich (ed.), *Tagebücher*, II/3, entry for 20 Mar. 1942.
84. Noakes (ed.), *Nazism*, vol. 4, 518.
85. Picker (ed.), *Tischgespräche*, 282–3. The connection between the 1942 cut in rations and Hitler's obsession with 1918 is also made in Wagner, *Kriminalpolizei*, 334–5.
86. Domarus (ed.), *Hitler*, vol. II/2, 1865–77. See also Hirsch *et al.* (eds), *Recht*, 507–10; Kershaw, *Hitler. 1936–45*, 509–11.
87. Cited in Boberach (ed.), *Meldungen*, vol. 10, 3686. See also ibid., 3687; Lagebericht des Generalstaatsanwalts Celle, 31 May 1942, reprinted in Hirsch *et al.* (eds), *Recht*, 511–12; Lagebericht des OLG Präsidenten Hamm, 7 July 1942, reprinted ibid., 512–13; Kershaw, '*Hitler Myth*', 182–4.

88. ThHStAW, GStA bei dem OLG Jena Nr. 430, Bl. 178–83: Besprechung im Reichsjustizministerium am 6.5.1942.
89. Ibid., Bl. 184–95: Tagung der OLG Präsidenten am 5.5.1942.
90. Schlegelberger to Hitler, 6 May 1942, reprinted in Broszat, 'Perversion', 426–7.
91. Picker (ed.), *Tischgespräche*, 647. See also ibid., 473; Fröhlich (ed.), *Tagebücher*, II/4, entry for 30 May 1942, 405. For Hitler's views on Schlegelberger, see Picker (ed.), *Tischgespräche*, 222.
92. Dr Crohne, Bericht über die Rede des Reichsministers Dr Goebbels am 22.7.1942, reprinted in Broszat, 'Perversion', 437–9.
93. Fröhlich (ed.), *Tagebücher*, II/3, entry for 20 Mar. 1942, 504.
94. For Thierack's personal file, see BA Berlin, R 3001/alt R 22/Pers. 78253.
95. Hitler's political testament is reprinted and translated in Noakes (ed.), *Nazism*, vol. 4, 668–71. See also Fröhlich (ed.), *Tagebücher*, II/9, entry for 21 Aug. 1943, 335; ibid., entry for 23 Sept. 1943, 578; ibid., II/11, entry for 4 Jan. 1944, 47.
96. Fröhlich (ed.), *Tagebücher*, II/9, entry for 23 Sept. 1943, 578.
97. K. Bästlein, 'Vom hanseatischen Richtertum zum nationalsozialistischen Justizverbrechen. Zur Person und Tätigkeit Curt Rothenbergers 1896–1959', in Justizbehörde Hamburg (ed.), *'Für Führer, Volk und Vaterland...'*, 74–145.
98. Jochmann (ed.), *Monologe*, 347–54, quote on 348–9; BA Berlin, R 43 II/1560 b, Bl. 68: Erlass des Führers über besondere Vollmachten des Reichsministers der Justiz, 20 Aug. 1942. For Hitler's table talk of 20 August 1942, see also L. Gruchmann, 'Hitler über die Justiz. Das Tischgespräch vom 20. August 1942', *VfZ* 12 (1964), 86–101.
99. For one such example, see Staatspolizeileitstelle Düsseldorf to Aussendienststellen, no date [1943], reprinted in Bundesminister der Justiz, *Justiz*, 270.
100. Evans, *Rituals*, 914–16, table 1.
101. BA Berlin, R 3001/alt R 22/1160, Bl. 25–66: Statistisches Reichsamt, *Die Entwicklung der Kriminalität im Deutschen Reich vom Kriegsbeginn bis Mitte 1943* (Berlin, 1944); ibid., R 3001/alt R 22/897, Bl. 216: Gesamtbelegung am 30.9.1944.
102. Weckbecker, *Sondergerichte*, 67–8, 770; Gruchmann, *Justiz*, 953, n. 51; Johe, *Justiz*, 92; Bästlein, 'Sondergerichte', 228; Oehler, *Rechtsprechung*, 248–9; Schmidt, *Oberlandesgerichtsbezirk Düsseldorf*, 155.
103. RJM to OLG Präsidenten, 13 Oct. 1942, reprinted in Bundesminister der Justiz, *Justiz*, 296–7. See also G. Schmitz, 'Die Vor- und Nachschaubesprechungen in Hamburg, 1942–1945' in Justizbehörde Hamburg (ed.), *'Von Gewohnheitsverbrechern'*, 447–70; Angermund, *Richterschaft*, 233–4.
104. Cited in Noakes (ed.), *Nazism*, vol. 4, 149.
105. Richterbrief Nr. 4, 1 Jan. 1943, reprinted in Ayaß (ed.), *'Gemeinschaftsfremde'*, 320–2.
106. Cited in Noakes (ed.), *Nazism*, vol. 4, 158.
107. Angermund, *Richterschaft*, 244–5; Niermann, *Strafjustiz*, 371–2.
108. For the figures, see Evans, *Rituals*, 917, table 2. The figures refer to Germany, Austria, and the annexed areas of France and Poland. See also Fröhlich (ed.), *Tagebücher*, II/4, entry for 24 May 1942, 361. The severity of sentencing was also a reaction to the assassination of Reinhard Heydrich on 27 May 1942 in Prague.
109. Hillgruber (ed.), *Staatsmänner und Diplomaten*, vol. 2, 255. See also Gellately, *Gestapo*, 216, 244–5.
110. For the general background, see Kershaw, *'Hitler Myth'*, 189–220; idem, *Popular Opinion*, 382–3.
111. For property crime during the war, see Wagner, *Kriminalpolizei*, 316–29.
112. Roth, 'Kriminalpolizei', 309.

113. The great majority of people sentenced as 'national pests', for example, came from the poorer sections of society; see U. Danker, 'Zum Schutz der "Volksgemeinschaft": Zur Arbeit des schleswig-holsteinischen Sondergerichts in statistischer Hinsicht sowie an den Beispielen Rundfunk – und Volksschädlingsverordnung', in idem, R. Bohn (eds), *'Standgerichte der inneren Front'. Das Sondergericht Altona/Kiel 1932–1945* (Hamburg, 1998), 39–87, here 63.

114. Angermund, *Richterschaft*, 210–12. For cases against postal workers, see Justizbehörde Hamburg (ed.), *'Von Gewohnheitsverbrechern'*, 355–63.

115. BA Berlin, R 3001/alt R 22/1160, Bl. 25–66: Statistisches Reichsamt, *Die Entwicklung der Kriminalität im Deutschen Reich vom Kriegsbeginn bis Mitte 1943* (Berlin, 1944); Wagner, *Kriminalpolizei*, 322; M. Hepp, '"Bei Adolf wäre das nicht passiert"? Die Kriminalstatistik widerlegt eine zählebige Legende', *Zeitschrift für Rechtspolitik* 32 (1999), 253–60, esp. 254. For the concern of legal officials about youth crime, see also H. Boberach, 'Die Berichte der Oberlandesgerichts-Präsidenten und Generalstaatsanwälte aus Hessen im Zweiten Weltkrieg', in F.-J. Düwell, T. Vormbaum (eds), *Recht und Nationalsozialismus* (Baden-Baden, 1998), 63–75, here 65–6.

116. BA Berlin, R 3001/alt R 22/1160, Bl. 25–66: Statistisches Reichsamt, *Die Entwicklung der Kriminalität im Deutschen Reich vom Kriegsbeginn bis Mitte 1943* (Berlin, 1944); Informationsdienst des Reichsministers der Justiz, 1944, reprinted in B. Oleschinski (ed.), *Gedenkstätte Plötzensee* (Berlin, 1995), 54–5.

117. Bästlein, 'Sondergerichte', 230–1.

118. Cited in A. Düsing, 'Abschaffung der Todesstrafe' (Ph.D., Freiburg University, 1952), 215. See also BA Berlin, R 3001/alt R 22/1160, Bl. 25–66: Statistisches Reichsamt, *Die Entwicklung der Kriminalität im Deutschen Reich vom Kriegsbeginn bis Mitte 1943* (Berlin, 1944); C. Rothmaler, 'Zum Urteil gegen Bertha K.', in Justizbehörde Hamburg (ed.), *'Von Gewohnheitsverbrechern'*, 366–79.

119. Marxen, *Volk*, 36, 42–3; Dörner, *'Heimtücke'*, 33, 144–5; Schlüter, *Urteilspraxis*, 175–82. German defendants also included 'ethnic Germans' from Austria, Alsace and the Sudetenland.

120. Wagner, *Kriminalpolizei*, 336–7.

121. BA Berlin, R 3001/alt R 22/4200, Bl. 71–318: Tagung der OLG-Präsidenten und Generalstaatsanwälte am 10. und 11.2.1943, here Bl. 172.

122. Ibid., R 3001/alt R 22/4062, Bl. 35a–37: Besprechung mit Reichsführer SS Himmler am 18.9.1942 in seinem Feldquartier. This agreement excluded Poles singled out for 'Germanisation'.

123. Ibid., R 3001/alt R 22/4199, Bl. 8–137: Besprechung mit den Chefpräsidenten und Generalstaatsanwälten am 29.9.1942, here Bl. 37. For the views of the Rostock general state prosecutor, see Michelberger, *Berichte*, 394–5.

124. BA Berlin, 99 US 2 FC 585, Microfilm 22933, Bl. 287: Thierack to Bormann, 13 Oct. 1942.

125. Ibid., 99 US 2 FC 588, Microfilm 22941, Bl. 62–4: RSHA to Höhere SS- und Polizeiführer, 5 Nov. 1942.

126. Ibid., Bl. 85–6: 13. Verordnung zum Reichsbürgergesetz, 1 July 1943; BA Berlin, R 3001/alt R 22/1160, Bl. 25–66: Statistisches Reichsamt, *Die Entwicklung der Kriminalität im Deutschen Reich vom Kriegsbeginn bis Mitte 1943* (Berlin, 1944); H. Grabitz, 'In vorauseilendem Gehorsam . . . Die Hamburger Justiz im "Führerstaat"', in Justizbehörde Hamburg (ed.), *'Für Führer, Volk und Vaterland . . .'*, 21–73, here 54.

127. BA Berlin, R 3001/alt R 22/4200, Bl. 71–318: Tagung der OLG-Präsidenten und Generalstaatsanwälte am 10. und 11.2.1943, here 95–8, quotation on 97–8. See also Herbert, *Fremdarbeiter*, 245.
128. BA Berlin, R 3001/alt R 22/1160, Bl. 25–66: Statistisches Reichsamt, *Die Entwicklung der Kriminalität im Deutschen Reich vom Kriegsbeginn bis Mitte 1943* (Berlin, 1944). For sentencing against Poles in general, see Majer, '*Fremdvölkische*', 619–23, 789–93.
129. BA Berlin, R 3001/alt R 22/4200, Bl. 71–318: Tagung der OLG-Präsidenten und Generalstaatsanwälte am 10. und 11.2.1943, here 89–98.
130. Majer, '*Fremdvölkische*', 676–78; Angermund, *Richterschaft*, 189–90.
131. For this view, see, for example, Gruchmann, 'Die "rechtsprechende Gewalt"', 89; Gellately, *Backing Hitler*, 173, 177.
132. BA Berlin, R 3001/alt R 22/897, Bl. 216.
133. Wagner, *Kriminalpolizei*, 384–93; Entwurf für ein Gesetz über die Behandlung Asozialer, 1 Feb. 1943, reprinted in Ayaß, '*Gemeinschaftsfremde*', 323–5. For Thierack's quotation, see BA Berlin, R 3001/alt R 22/4062, Bl. 28–33: Besprechung mit Reichsführer SS Himmler am 13.12.1942, here Bl. 31–2. For the wider background, see P. Wagner, 'Das Gesetz über die Behandlung Gemeinschaftsfremder', in *Beiträge zur Nationalsozialistischen Gesundheits- und Sozialpolitik*, vol. 6 (Berlin, 1988), 75–100; G. Werle, *Justiz-Strafrecht und polizeiliche Verbrechensbekämpfung im Dritten Reich* (Berlin, 1989), 619–80.

Chapter 6

1. See, for example, J.-C. Wagner, 'Das Außenlagersystem des KL Mittelbau-Dora', in U. Herbert et al. (eds), *Die nationalsozialistischen Konzentrationslager*, vol. 2 (Göttingen, 1998), 707–29, here 719–24.
2. RJM to Generalstaatsanwälte, 28 Oct. 1939, reprinted in Kosthorst, Walter (eds), *Strafgefangenenlager*, vol. 2, 1313–14.
3. BA Berlin, R 3001/alt R 22/1429, Bl. 76–9: R. Freisler, 'Arbeitseinsatz des Strafvollzuges im Dienste des Vierjahresplanes', *Deutsche Justiz*, 100 (1938).
4. Ibid., R 3001/alt R 22/1261, Bl. 177: GStA Bamberg, Lagebericht, 3 Feb. 1940. See also ibid., Bl. 158–9: GStA Hamm to RJM, 22 Nov. 1939.
5. Ibid., 61 Re 1/1528, Bl. 166: 'Strafgefangene leisten rationelle Arbeit', *Zeitungsdienst Graf*, 18 Sept. 1940.
6. For the statistics, see ibid., R 3001/alt R 22/1429, Bl. 145–6: Arbeitseinsatz der Gefangenen, no date. For the German economy, see Overy, *War*, 294.
7. BA Berlin, R 3001/alt R 22/245, Arbeitstagung am 23. und 24.4.1941, here Bl. 206.
8. See, for example, ibid., R 3001/alt R 22/1399, Bl. 20: Oberkommando des Heeres to Reichswirtschaftsminister, 20 Mar. 1941.
9. For some examples, see HStAD-Kalkum, Gerichte Rep. 321/758.
10. Noakes (ed.), *Nazism*, vol. 4, 185–6, 221–37; Herbst, *Deutschland*, 298–304, 319–20, 409–15.
11. BA Berlin, R 3001/alt R 22/1429, Bl. 177: RJM to Generalstaatsanwälte, 18 Mar. 1942; ibid., Bl. 320: Vermerk, no date [1942]; ThHStAW, GStA bei dem OLG Jena Nr. 430, Bl. 243–60: Arbeitstagung der Generalstaatsanwälte am 30.6. und 1.7. 1942.
12. BA Berlin, 99 US 2 FC 38593/47471 P, Bl. 277–9: Reichsminister Dr Thierack, 'Die Lage des Strafvollzugs im Jahre 1944', no date [1944].

13. Ibid., R 3001/alt R 22/1430, Bl. 29: GStA Dresden to Vollzugsanstalten, 3 Feb. 1943; Bericht des GStA Hamm, 9 June 1944, reprinted in Justizakademie NRW (ed.), *Zum Strafvollzug 1933–45*, source 26h.
14. BA Berlin, R 3001/alt R 22/5023, Bl. 11–12: Speer to Thierack, 8 Feb. 1944; ibid., Bl. 24: Vermerk über die Besprechung im Ministerium Speer am 22.2.1944; ibid., R 3001/alt R 22/2946, Bl. 18: RJM to Generalstaatsanwälte, 8 Mar. 1944; ibid., Bl. 20: Thierack and Speer to Rüstungsinspekteure and Generalstaatsanwälte, 12 May 1944.
15. IfZ, MA 192, Bl. 3249476–7: Rüstungskommando Augsburg to Reichsminister für Rüstung, 24 July 1944.
16. BA Berlin, R 3001/alt R 22/5023, Bl. 11: Speer to Thierack, 8 Feb. 1944. See also ibid., R 3001/alt R 22/1429, Bl. 233–4: Reichsminister für Bewaffnung to RJM, 13 July 1943.
17. Ibid., R 3/1602, Bl. 51: Speer to Thierack, 6 Jan. 1944; ibid., R 3001/alt R 22/1338, Bl. 302: RJM to Generalstaatsanwälte, 9 Mar. 1944.
18. ThHStAW, GStA bei dem OLG Jena Nr. 1049, Bl. 32, Bl. 106; ibid, GStA bei dem OLG Jena Nr. 1050, Bl. 217–18; BA Berlin, R 3001/alt R 22/5027, Bl. 23–6: Vorstand Untermaßfeld to RJM, 6 Mar. 1944.
19. ThHStAW, GStA bei dem OLG Jena Nr. 430, Bl. 264–76: Arbeitstagung am 30.6. und 1.7.1942, notes by GStA Wurmstich, here Bl. 275.
20. StAMü, GStA bei dem OLG München Nr. 51, Dienstaufsicht über die Vollzugsanstalten, 26 Mar. 1943; ibid., Dienstaufsicht über das Frauenzuchthaus Aichach, 31 Jan. 1944; IfZ, MA 624, Bl. 3664647–53: GStA Munich to RJM, 22 Jan. 1945.
21. BA Berlin, R 3001/alt R 22/4349, Bl. 27–9: Frauenstrafvollzug im Kriege, no date [June 1944].
22. Ibid., R 3001/alt R 22/1437, Bl. 436; ibid., R 3001/alt R 22/897, Bl. 14–15, 194. From 1941, figures include prisoners in Leitmeritz. From 1943, figures include prisoners from parts of the Danzig and Kattowitz districts.
23. Ibid., R 3001/alt R 22/4089, Bl. 99: Führerinformation Nr. 83, 23 July 1942; ibid., R 3001/alt R 22/5103, Reisebericht über die von Dr Hupperschwiller und Dr Gündner ausgeführte Dienstreise vom 22–30.3.1944; Krüger, 'Bombenräumkommandos', *passim*, quote on 33; Frenzel, *Gesprengte Fesseln*, 59–60; E. Christoffel, *Der Weg durch die Nacht. Verfolgung und Widerstand im Trierer Land während der Zeit des Nationalsozialismus* (Trier, 1983), 203.
24. For prison labour during the First World War, see Fleiter, 'Straf- und Gefängnisreformen'.
25. BA Berlin, 61 Re 1/1528, Bl. 166a: 'Strafvollzug, der Werte schafft', *Berliner Börsen-Zeitung*, 31 May 1942. See also ibid., 'Sträflinge arbeiten', *Frankfurter Zeitung*, 5 June 1942; ThHStAW, GStA bei dem OLG Jena Nr. 430, Bl. 243–60: Arbeitstagung der Generalstaatsanwälte am 30.6. und 1.7.1942, here Bl. 257.
26. See BA Berlin, Film 44184, Vernehmung von K. Engert, 5 Dec. 1946.
27. BA Berlin, R 3001/alt R 22/5016, Reichsminister Dr Thierack, Bl. 2–4: 'Der Arbeitseinsatz der Justizgefangenen im Kriege', no date [1944]. In December 1944, a version of this article was also sent to general state prosecutors and other leading legal officials; see ibid., R 3001/alt R 22/4003, Bl. 125. Ministry officials tried to prevent the publication of detailed reports about armaments production in penal institutions, on account of the potential security implications; see ibid., R 3001/alt R 22/1262, Bl. 79: RJM to Generalstaatsanwälte, 24 May 1944.
28. A copy of the film (*Arbeit und Strafvollzug in dem Zuchthaus Brandenburg-Görden*) is held at the Bundesarchiv Berlin, Abteilung Filmarchiv. From 1940, the Reich

Ministry of Education and the Reich Ministry of Justice had planned to put together an ambitious film project on the prison service, entitled 'A Prisoner's Day'. In 1942, shortly before filming was due to begin, the project was apparently shelved. The exact relationship between this project, and the above film about Brandenburg-Görden, is not clear. For details on the project, see BA Berlin, R 3001/9829. See also Möhler, 'Strafvollzug', 117–18; Hottes, 'Strafvollzug im Dritten Reich'; R. Plischke, 'Aus der Strafvollzugsbeamtenschule Bautzen', *BlGefK* 75 (1944), reprinted in Justizakademie NRW (ed.), *Zum Strafvollzug 1933–1945*, source 31b.

29. Angermund, *Richterschaft*, 239–40; JVA Tegel (ed.), *100 Jahre Justizvollzugsanstalt Tegel* (Berlin, 1998), 67.
30. BA Berlin, R 3001/alt R 22/4089, Bl. 54–5: Führerinformation Nr. 41, 12 June 1942; ibid., Bl. 112: Führerinformation Nr. 93, 30 July 1942.
31. Ibid., R 3001/alt R 22/1417, Bl. 59–63: Arbeitseinsatz der Sicherungsverwahrten, no date [1942].
32. ThHStAW, GStA bei dem OLG Jena Nr. 767, Bl. 8: RJM to Generalstaatsanwälte, 8 May 1943. See also JVA Straubing, RJM to Generalstaatsanwälte, 3 June 1943.
33. ThHStAW, GStA bei dem OLG Jena Nr. 432, Bl. 153–69: Niederschrift über die Tagung beim Reichsminister der Justiz am 19. und 20.10.1943.
34. BA Berlin, R 3001/alt R 22/4089, Bl. 278: Führerinformation Nr. 185, 14 Nov. 1944.
35. Ibid., R 3001/alt R 22/245, Arbeitstagung am 23. und 24. April 1941, here Bl. 202–3.
36. *Vereinheitlichung der Dienst- und Vollzugsvorschriften für den Strafvollzug im Bereich der Reichsjustizverwaltung*, Sonderveröffentlichung der *Deutschen Justiz* Nr. 21 (Berlin, 1940). For the background and legal relevance of these guidelines, see Quedenfeld, *Strafvollzug*, esp. 41–2.
37. BA Berlin R 3001/alt R 22/1429, Bl. 144: RJM to Generalstaatsanwälte, 29 Jan. 1941. Lines of work where prisoners could engage in acts of sabotage were to be excluded, according to Freisler.
38. For some of these general points, see Drobisch, 'Konzentrationslager', 289; StAMü, GStA bei dem OLG München Nr. 52, Zuchthaus Aichach to GStA Munich, 16 Sept. 1944.
39. Cited in Krüger, 'Bombenräumkommandos', 34.
40. W. Uhlmann, 'Antifaschistische Arbeit', *aus politik und zeitgeschichte*, vol. 18 (3 May 1980), 7–15. For similar cases, see A. Breidenbach, *Antifaschistischer Widerstand im Zuchthaus Remscheid-Lüttringhausen* (Remscheid, 1992), 13–14.
41. BA Berlin, R 3001/alt R 22/4372, Bl. 33–4: RJM to Generalstaatsanwälte, 12 Aug. 1940; ibid., R 3001/alt R 22/1263, Bl. 1–18: Besprechung im RJM am 11.9.1940.
42. Ibid., R 3001/alt R 22/245, Arbeitstagung am 23. und 24. April 1941, here Bl. 185.
43. ThHStAW, GStA bei dem OLG Jena Nr. 433, Bl. 22–34: Dienstbesprechung am 3. und 4.2.1944. See also Kosthorst, Walter (eds), *Strafgefangenenlager*, vol. 1, 1125; Scharf, 'Strafvollzug', 806–7.
44. Justizakademie NRW (ed.), *Zum Strafvollzug 1933–1945*, source 30a.
45. IfZ, MA 624, Bl. 3664986–7: Entweichungen von Gefangenen in der Zeit vom 1.4.1943 bis 31.3.1944.
46. ThHStAW, GStA bei dem OLG Jena Nr. 433, Bl. 22–34: Dienstbesprechung am 3. und 4.2.1944; BA Berlin, R 3001/alt R 22/1262, Bl. 64: RJM to GStA Kattowitz, 18 Feb. 1944.
47. BA Berlin, R 3001/alt R 22/1262, Bl. 84: Engert to Thierack, 23 Feb. 1944; ibid., Bl. 95: Ferngesprächsnotiz, 26 May 1944; ibid., Bl. 97: Nörr to Eggensperger, 1 June 1944; ibid., Bl. 100: RJM to Generalstaatsanwälte, 12 June 1944.

48. Ibid., Bl. 137: RJM to Generalstaatsanwälte, 12 Sept. 1944; ibid., Bl. 136: Vermerk, no date; ibid., Bl. 134: GStA Karlsruhe to RJM, 22 Aug. 1944.
49. BLHA, Ld. Br. Rep. 214 Forschungsstelle Zuchthaus Brandenburg Nr. 1, Bl. 262: 'Verschärfter Vollzug', 22 July 1949.
50. *Vereinheitlichung der Dienst- und Vollzugsvorschriften*, § 75.
51. PRO, WO 311/520, Vertrag zwischen der Rheinischen Kunstseide AG und dem Vorstand in Anrath, 15 Dec. 1941.
52. Ibid., Deposition of Florence P., 3 Mar. 1948.
53. Ibid., Statement of Leonard H., 17 Mar. 1948.
54. Ibid., Deposition of Agnes H., 3 May 1948. See also ibid., Deposition of Heinrich S., 11 June 1948.
55. HStAD-Kalkum, Gerichte Rep. 321/780, Bl. 18: RJM to GStA Düsseldorf, 18 June 1943; ibid., Bl. 39–40: Leitender Arzt Düsseldorf-Derendorf to GStA Düsseldorf, 12 May 1944.
56. BA Berlin, R 3001/alt R 22/1442, Bl. 125: Verpflegungssätze für Justizgefangene und Häftlinge in Konzentrationslagern, 16 Jan. 1940; ibid., 99 US 2 FC 38593/47471 P, Bl. 249–57: Reichsminister für Ernährung to Landesernährungsämter, 6 April 1944; Noakes (ed.), *Nazism*, vol. 4, 514.
57. For Bernau, see, for example, K. Reichel, *. . . um Dich zu befreien* (Berlin, 1975), 141.
58. BA Berlin, R 3001/alt R 22/1440, Bl. 291: Anmerkungen für die heutige Besprechung, 9 May 1940; ibid., R 3001/alt R 22/4371, Bl. 103–7: Semler, 'Ernährungs- und Beschaffungslage', 1 July 1942.
59. PRO, WO 311/520, Deposition of Eva H., 2 Apr. 1948.
60. For the food supply in Germany, see G. Corni, H. Gies, *Brot, Butter, Kanonen. Die Ernährungswirtschaft in Deutschland unter der Diktatur Hitlers* (Berlin, 1997).
61. BA Berlin, SAPMO, DY 54/V 277/1/15, Bericht der ehemaligen Gefangenen Anja K., no date [1946?]; Christoffel, *Weg*, 127; BA Berlin, R 3001/alt R 22/1440: Bl. 238: Straf- und Jugendgefängnis Stuhm, Erfahrungen über die Auswirkungen der Verpflegungsordnung, 9 Apr. 1940.
62. V. von Gostomski, W. Loch, *Der Tod von Plötzensee* (Frankfurt am Main, 1993), 105.
63. BA Berlin, R 3001/alt R 22/1443, Bl. 269–76: Besprechung über Ernährung und Arbeitszeit am 9.5.1940.
64. Ibid., R 3001/alt R 22/1440, Bl. 315: Anstaltsarzt Untermaßfeld, Bericht, 14 June 1940.
65. A. Grätz to Pfarrer Winzler, 5 May 1940, reprinted in Brandenburgische Landeszentrale (ed.), *Was bleibt*, 106–7.
66. BA Berlin, R 3001/alt R 22/1441, Bl. 272–3: Medizinalrat Hartung to GStA Celle, 15 Sept. 1941; ibid., R 3001/alt R 22/4371, Bl. 103–7: Semler, 'Ernährungs- und Beschaffungslage', 1 July 1942; Möhler, 'Strafvollzug', 229.
67. See, for example, BLHA, Pr. Br. Rep. 29 Zuchthaus Brandenburg Nr. 4014.
68. BA Berlin, R 3001/alt R 22/1337, Bl. 416: RJM to Generalstaatsanwälte, 4 May 1940; Michelberger, *Berichte*, 329; Gruchmann, *Justiz*, 742.
69. BLHA, Pr. Br. Rep. 29 Zuchthaus Brandenburg Nr. 6425, Karl K. to his brother, 7 Apr. 1940; ibid., Verfügung, 11 Apr. 1940; ibid., Karl. K to his brother, 26 Sept. 1942. For the weight losses in 1940 in Brandenburg-Görden, see BA Berlin, R 3001/alt R 22/1443, Bl. 269–76: Besprechung über Ernährung und Arbeitszeit am 9.5.1940.
70. ThHStAW, GStA bei dem OLG Jena Nr. 812, Bl. 217: RJM to GStA Jena, 24 Oct. 1941; 'Die selbstständigen Vollzugsanstalten', 348.
71. Möhler, 'Strafvollzug', 92–3.
72. See chapter 5, p. 221.

73. BA Berlin, R 3001/alt R 22/897, Bl. 14–15. The figure for female prisoners includes the Leitmeritz district, but excludes those permanently on outside labour.
74. Ibid., Bl. 134, 194; ibid., R 3001/alt R 22/1417, Bl. 53, 171–8. See also BA Berlin, R 3001/alt R 22/4349, Bl. 27–9: Frauenstrafvollzug im Kriege, no date [June 1944].
75. StAMü, GStA bei dem OLG München Nr. 51, Nachschau in Aichach, 30 Sept. 1940; ibid., Dienstaufsicht über die Vollzugsanstalten, 26 Mar. 1943; ibid., Dienstaufsicht über das Frauenzuchthaus Aichach, 3 Mar. 1945; 'Die selbstständigen Vollzugsanstalten', 349.
76. HStAD-Kalkum, Gerichte Rep. 321/1281, Bl. 81–3: Gefängnis Cologne to GStA Cologne, 18 June 1942.
77. See, for example, StAMü, Justizvollzugsanstalten Nr. 13807, Frauenstrafanstalt Aichach to GStA Munich, 6 Dec. 1942; BA Berlin, Film 41305, Bericht, Spitalverwalter Michael S., 5 July 1945; Scharf, 'Strafvollzug', 789–90.
78. StAMü, Justizvollzugsanstalten Nr. 13794, Werkführerin Hörmann to Vorstand, 23 Aug. 1941; ibid., Erklärung der Werkführerin Hörmann, 9 Mar. 1942; ibid., Nr. 1203, Rechtsanwalt Merkenschlager to Frauenstrafanstalt Aichach, 14 Aug. 1947; ibid., Nr. 4818, Direktion der Frauenstrafanstalt Aichach, 24 Aug. 1941; ibid., Nr. 2339, Frauenstrafanstalt Aichach to GStA Kassel, 15 Apr. 1944; ibid., Nr. 2400, Rotes Kreuz to Strafgefängnis Aichach, 3 Nov. 1952.
79. BLHA, Pr. Br. Rep. 29 Zuchthaus Brandenburg Nr. 817, Erwin Köbrich to his parents, 24 May 1942. The letter was held back by the authorities. Köbrich was taken to Buchenwald concentration camp on 21 December 1943.
80. BLHA, Pr. Br. Rep. 29 Zuchthaus Brandenburg Nr. 10126.
81. For some examples, see BA Berlin, Film 44837, Vernehmung von H. Linsenmeyer, 25 Nov. 1946; ZStL, VI 416 AR–Nr 1127/66, Bl. 112–42: Landgericht Lüneburg, Einstellungsverfügung, 10 May 1952, here Bl. 116.
82. BA Berlin, R 3001/alt R 22/5028, Bl. 37–41: Dr Reichert, 'Besuch in einem Zuchthaus', no date [1944?].
83. See Kosthorst, Walter (eds), *Strafgefangenenlager*, vol. 3, 2359–62.
84. BLHA, Ld. Br. Rep. 214 Forschungsstelle Zuchthaus Brandenburg Nr. 2, Bl. 40: Georg B. to Polizeidezernent B., 26 Aug. 1945. For some other examples, see BA Berlin, SAPMO, DY 54/V 277/1/29, Fragebogen Johannes E., no date [1946]; PRO, WO 309/151, Captain Williams, Case No 248, no date; ibid., WO 311/520, Deposition of Rosalie Weiss, 11 Mar. 1948; IfZ, Sp. 1.13., Spuchkammer Nord-Württemberg, Verfahren gegen Max K., 21 Dec. 1949; ThSTA Mgn., Vorstand der Strafanstalt Untermaßfeld P. 2, Aussagen vor dem Vorstand, 28–29 Nov. 1946; E. Weissenbach, Erlebnisbericht, 21 Mar. 1994, reprinted in Scharf, 'Strafvollzug', 836–41; Christoffel, *Weg*, 202.
85. ThHStAW, GStA bei dem OLG Jena Nr. 433, Bl. 398–404: Dienstbesprechung am 23. und 24.8.1944.
86. Ibid., GStA bei dem OLG Jena Nr. 230, Bl. 278: Zuchthaus Untermaßfeld to GStA Jena, 13 Nov. 1944; GStA Hamm, Niederschrift über die Besprechung mit den Vorständen, 17 Feb. 1944, reprinted in Justizakademie NRW (ed.), *Zum Strafvollzug 1933–1945*, source 31a.
87. BA Berlin, 99 US 2 FC 38593/47471 P, Bl. 320–3: RJM to Oberste SA-Führung, 16 Mar. 1944. See also ibid., R 3001/alt R 22/4372, Bl. 212: RJM to Generalstaatsanwälte, 6 June 1944; ibid., R 3001/alt R 22/1273, Bl. 162: RJM to Generalstaatsanwälte, 29 Apr. 1944. The overall number of party members transferred to penal institutions was presumably rather small. They were more likely to be employed at the front and in the armaments industry. The prison authorities were left with old or disabled men and women, who could not be occupied elsewhere.

88. Christoffel, *Weg*, 127; Scharf, 'Strafvollzug', 804.
89. BA Berlin, R 3001/alt R 22/5016, Bl. 12–19: 'Die Lage des Strafvollzugs im Jahre 1944', draft, no date [summer 1944]. See also ibid., R 3001/alt R 22/1262, Bl. 105: RJM to Generalstaatsanwälte, 18 June 1944; Frenzel *et al.*, *Gesprengte Fesseln*, 74.
90. StAMü, Justizvollzugsanstalten Nr. 13832, Bl. 63: Strafanstalt Bernau, Dienststrafverfügung gegen Maria U., 8 Mar. 1945.
91. For one example of many, see IfZ, ED 106/1, W. Hammer, 'Fingerzeige über Personen, Zustände und Vorfälle im ehemaligen Zuchthaus Brandenburg', 8 Dec. 1945.
92. RJM to Generalstaatsanwälte, 28 Oct. 1939, reprinted in Kosthorst, Walter (eds), *Strafgefangenenlager*, vol. 2, 1313–14; BA Berlin, R 3001/alt R 22/1337, Bl. 260: RJM to Generalstaatsanwälte, 26 Feb. 1941; *Vereinheitlichung der Dienst- und Vollzugsvorschriften*, § 183; Quedenfeld, *Strafvollzug*, 78–9.
93. PRO, WO 309/1292, Draft of Interim Report by Field Investigation Section War Crimes Group, no date; BA Berlin, SAPMO, DY 55/62/2/169, Josef F. to Amtsgericht Neuwied, 20 Dec. 1949.
94. BA Berlin, SAPMO, DY 55/V 278/6/592, Bl. 77–81: W. Hammer, 'Mußte das sein?', no date. For a similar description, see H. Frese, *Bremsklötze am Siegeswagen der Nation* (Bremen, 1989), 93.
95. IfZ, Sp. 1.13., Spruchkammer Nord-Württemberg, Verfahren gegen Max K., 21 Dec. 1949.
96. BA Berlin, R 3001/9936, Bl. 127: RJM to Generalstaatsanwälte, 10 Apr. 1940.
97. Ibid., R 3001/alt R 22/5028, Bl. 29–30: RJM to Chef der Reichskanzlei, 9 Jan. 1942.
98. ThHStAW, GStA bei dem OLG Jena Nr. 433, Bl. 236–7: GStA Jena to RJM, 30 May 1944. For the meeting itself, see ibid., Bl. 216–35: Chefbesprechung vom 23.–25.5.1944.
99. Ibid., Bl. 216–35: Chefbesprechung vom 23.–25.5.1944.
100. See, for example, IfZ, ED 106/79, Bl. 19: Auer to Hammer, 10 June 1953; Gélieu, *Frauen*, 178.
101. BA Berlin, R 3001/alt R 22/1429, Bl. 239: GStA Düsseldorf to RJM, 12 July 1943.
102. Cited in Christoffel, *Weg*, 203.
103. The figures are based on statistics from penal institutions in Ludwigsburg, Aichach, Ebrach, Zweibrücken, Siegburg, Straubing and Tegel. The prewar figures for Ebrach, Siegburg, Straubing and Tegel are estimates. See Strafvollzugsmuseum Ludwigsburg; StAMü, JVA 13768 (including dead children of female prisoners); BA Berlin, Film 41305; Scharf, 'Strafvollzug', 806; BA Berlin, SAPMO BY 5/V 279/94; JVA Straubing, Statistik Strafvollzugskanzlei, 3 Dec. 1947; JVA Tegel (ed.), *100 Jahre Tegel*, 72.
104. 'Wie mache ich ein Testament', *Der Leuchtturm* 18 (20 Dec. 1942).
105. RJM, Vermerk, 19 Apr. 1941, reprinted in Kosthorst, Walter (eds), *Strafgefangenenlager*, vol. 2, 1352. Civilian 'war offenders' regarded as less serious offenders, including younger offenders and those with shorter sentences, were taken to other prison camps; RJM to Generalstaatsanwälte, 4 Dec. 1940, reprinted ibid., 1349–50.
106. Suhr, *Emslandlager*, 122.
107. Auszüge des Untersuchungsrichters in Oldenburg, reprinted in Kosthorst, Walter (eds), *Strafgefangenenlager*, vol. 3, 2369; Suhr, *Emslandlager*, 129–30.
108. Auszüge des Untersuchungsrichters in Oldenburg, reprinted in Kosthorst, Walter (eds), *Strafgefangenenlager*, vol. 3, 2370–1. See also Suhr, *Emslandlager*, 127.

109. Cited in Schwurgerichts-Anklage gegen W. Schäfer vor dem Landgericht Oldenburg, 22 July 1950, reprinted in Kosthorst, Walter (eds), *Strafgefangenenlager*, vol. 3, 2506–46, here 2541–2. See also Auszüge des Untersuchungsrichters in Oldenburg, reprinted ibid., 2428–31.
110. Auszüge des Untersuchungsrichters in Oldenburg, reprinted in Kosthorst, Walter (eds), *Strafgefangenenlager*, vol. 3, 2439–40, 2442; Urteil Landgericht Oldenburg, 30 Sept. 1949, reprinted ibid., vol. 2, 2036–77, here 2066; Urteil Landgericht Berlin, 31 Oct. 1959, reprinted ibid., 2079–138, here 2115.
111. Schwurgerichts-Anklage gegen W. Schäfer vor dem Landgericht Oldenburg, 22 July 1950, reprinted in Kosthorst, Walter (eds), *Strafgefangenenlager*, vol. 3, 2506–46, here 2518; Auszüge des Untersuchungsrichters in Oldenburg, reprinted ibid., 2350; Suhr, *Emslandlager*, 142, 167.
112. RJM to Beauftragter des Reichsministers der Justiz im Emsland, 6 June 1940, 8 Mar. 1941, reprinted in Kosthorst, Walter (eds), *Strafgefangenenlager*, vol. 3, 2432–3, 2438–9.
113. See Auszüge des Untersuchungsrichters in Oldenburg, reprinted ibid., 2441.
114. Urteil Landgericht Oldenburg, 30 Sept. 1949, reprinted ibid., vol. 2, 2036–77, here 2044; Auszüge des Untersuchungsrichters in Oldenburg, reprinted ibid., vol. 3, 2444, 2456–7.
115. See, for example, ibid., vol. 3, 2804–5.
116. Urteil Landgericht Osnabrück, 8 Dec. 1942, reprinted ibid., 2840–44.
117. Beauftragter des Reichsministers der Justiz im Emsland to RJM, 10 Aug. 1942, reprinted ibid., vol. 3, 2813–15.
118. ThSTA Mgn., Zuchthaus Untermaßfeld Nr. 826, Vermerk über die Erörterung von Tat und Vorleben, 31 Mar. 1943.
119. Chef der Reichskanzlei to Reichsminister für Ernährung und Landwirtschaft, 25 Feb. 1941, reprinted in Kosthorst, Walter (eds), *Strafgefangenenlager*, vol. 1, 920; Leiter der Partei-Kanzlei to Gauleiter Lauterbacher, 25 May 1941, reprinted ibid., 921.
120. For labour in the Emsland camp, see Suhr, *Emslandlager*, 217–21.
121. A. Milward, *The Fascist Economy of Norway* (Oxford, 1972), 90–2, 272–8; K. Ottosen, 'Arbeits- und Konzentrationslager in Norwegen 1940–1945', in R. Bohn *et al.* (eds), *Neutralität und totalitäre Aggression. Nordeuropa und die Großmächte im Zweiten Weltkrieg* (Stuttgart, 1991), 355–68.
122. BA Berlin, R 3001/alt R 22/4089, Bl. 46–7: Führerinformation, Nr. 34, 5 June 1942.
123. For the quotation, see BA Berlin, SAPMO, BY 5/V 279/91, 'Die deutschen Strafgefangenenlager Nord/Nord-Norwegen', 1 July 1945. My general account of the prison camp North is based on ibid.; ZStL, VI 107 AR–Z 114/67, Bl. 251–67: Vermerk, Oberstaatsanwalt bei dem Landgericht Hamburg, 15 Mar. 1950; ibid., UNWCC, 3872/Cz/G/74, Bl. 1046–9: Czech charges against German War Criminals, Aug. 1946; H. Schluckner, 'Sklaven am Eismeer', in F. Ausländer (ed.), *Verräter oder Vorbilder? Deserteure und ungehorsame Soldaten im Nationalsozialismus* (Bremen, 1990), 14–40; Suhr, *Emslandlager*, 171–3; H.-P. Klausch, *Die Bewährungstruppe 500* (Bremen, 1995), 96–9. For the prisoner figures, see BA Berlin, R 3001/alt R 22/897, Bl. 98.
124. BA Berlin, R 3001/alt R 22/4053, Bl. 22: RJM to Oberkommando der Wehrmacht, 7 Mar. 1945.
125. Schluckner, 'Sklaven', 21.
126. BA Berlin, SAPMO, BY 5/V 279/91, 'Die deutschen Strafgefangenenlager Nord/Nord-Norwegen', 1 July 1945; Suhr, *Emslandlager*, 172.
127. ZStL, VI 107 AR–Z 114/67, Bl. 251–67: Vermerk, Oberstaatsanwalt bei dem Landgericht Hamburg, 15 Mar. 1950, here Bl. 261.

128. Kommandeur der Strafgefangenenlager to Strafgefangenenlager IV, 28 Oct. 1943, reprinted in Kosthorst, Walter (eds), *Strafgefangenenlager*, vol. 1, 963–5. A few hundred prisoners left camp North in 1943 and 1944 for reasons other than illness, mostly to 'prove themselves' on the battlefield; Klausch, *Bewährungstruppe 500*, 95.
129. BA Berlin, R 3001/alt R 22/5023, Bl. 24: Vermerk über die Besprechung im Ministerium Speer am 22.2.1944.
130. ThHStAW, GStA bei dem OLG Jena Nr. 636, Bl. 117: RJM to GStA Jena, 24 Apr. 1943.
131. Ibid., GStA bei dem OLG Jena Nr. 637, Bl. 55–6: RJM to Generalstaatsanwälte, 18 Apr. 1944.
132. BA Berlin R 22/897, Bl. 232.
133. Vorstand der Strafanstalten Emsland to Oberstaatsanwalt Bremen, 9 July 1948, reprinted in Kosthorst, Walter (eds), *Strafgefangenenlager*, vol. 1, 943–4; Urteil Landgericht Oldenburg, 30 Sept. 1949, reprinted ibid., vol. 2, 2036–77, here 2058–9; Suhr, *Emslandlager*, 169–70; BA Berlin, R 3001/alt R 22/5023, Bl. 24: Vermerk über die Besprechung im Ministerium Speer am 22.2.1944; ibid., R 22/897, Bl. 179.
134. For the last point, see Tuchel, *Konzentrationslager*, 340.
135. ZStL, Verschiedenes, 301 Cz, Nr. 184, Bl. 124–31: Besichtigung des Konzentrationslagers Auschwitz am 28.6.1944.
136. Ibid., Bl. 226–36: Tagung bei der Generalstaatsanwaltschaft in Bamberg vom 16.11.1944.
137. Pingel, *Häftlinge*, *passim* (for the Dachau figures, 81); Orth, *System*, *passim*; Suhr, *Emslandlager*, 132.

Chapter 7

1. IfZ, MA 193/2, Bl. 3668387–8: Vermerk, Stand 31.3.1943.
2. For these examples, see ZStL, Verschiedenes, 301 Cz, Nr. 184, Bl. 226–36: Tagung bei der Generalstaatsanwaltschaft am 16.11.1944; BA Berlin, SAPMO, DY 55/62/2/169, Josef F. to Amtsgericht Neuwied, 20 Dec. 1949; Friedrich, *Cottbus*, 8; Faralisch, 'Zeitzeugenberichte', 364; BA Berlin, R 3001/alt R 22/1337, Bl. 402: RJM to Generalstaatsanwälte, 28 July 1943.
3. For the separation orders, see BA Berlin, R 3001/alt R 22/1261, Bl. 338–9: Fünfte Änderung der Strafvollzugsordnung, 22 Dec. 1942; ThHStAW, GStA bei dem OLG Jena Nr. 757, Bl. 190: RJM to Generalstaatsanwälte, 24 July 1943.
4. BA Berlin, R 3001/alt R 22/1238, Bl. 151–64: RJM to Auswärtiges Amt, 5 Jan. 1938. See also ibid., R 3001/alt 22/5054, Entwurf einer Ausführungsverordung zum Strafvollstreckungsgesetz, May 1937.
5. *Vereinheitlichung der Dienst- und Vollzugsvorschriften*; BA Berlin, R 3001/alt R 22/1338, Bl. 110: RJM to Generalstaatsanwälte, 14 Sept. 1940; J. Eichler, 'Der Begriff des Erstbestraften', *BlGefK* 71 (1940–41), 291–5. According to the regulations, certain 'first imprisoned' penitentiary inmates could also be separated from other inmates.
6. BA Berlin, R 3001/alt R 22/1261, Bl. 1–3: Klemm to Thierack, 23 Oct. 1942, Anlage.
7. Ibid., Bl. 340–4: Denkschrift über den Trennungsgedanken im Strafvollzug, Nov. 1942; ibid., Bl. 338–9: Fünfte Änderung der Strafvollzugsordnung, 22 Dec. 1942.
8. Ibid., R 3001/alt R 22/4349, Bl. 27–9: Frauenstrafvollzug im Kriege, no date [June 1944].

9. See, for example, R. Herr, 'Erziehung und gegenerzieherische Kräfte in der Strafvollzugsanstalt. Ein Beitrag zu den Fragen des Sondervollzugs an Gestrauchelten' (Ph.D., University of Jena, 1943).
10. For the position of the Reich Ministry of Justice, see, for example, ThHStAW, GStA bei dem OLG Jena Nr. 430, Bl. 243–60: Arbeitstagung der Generalstaatsanwälte am 30.6. und 1.7.1942.
11. In 1929, there were 22 full-time teachers in Prussian penitentiaries alone. Ten years later, only 21 teachers were employed in all German penitentiaries. See *Statistik über die Gefangenenanstalten Preußen 1929*; BA Berlin, R 3001/9949, Bl. 60–1: Kräfte des Schuldienstes an besonderen Vollzugsanstalten, 27 Oct. 1939.
12. ThHStAW, GStA bei dem OLG Jena Nr. 433, Bl. 398–404: Dienstbesprechung am 23. und 24.8.1944.
13. Oleschinski, 'Gefängnisseelsorge', 383–7.
14. ThHStAW, GStA bei dem OLG Jena Nr. 1086, Bl. 115: Pfarrer in Ichtershausen to GStA Jena, 18 Jan. 1943.
15. Ibid., GStA bei dem OLG Jena Nr. 432, Bl. 153–69: Niederschrift über die Tagung bei dem Reichsminister der Justiz am 19. und 20.10.1943. See also BA Berlin, 99 US 2 FC 38593/47471 P, Bl. 258–62: P. Buchholz, Eidesstattliche Erklärung, Oct. 1946.
16. Cardinal Bertram to Thierack, 5 Nov. 1944, reprinted in *Akten der deutschen Bischöfe über die Lage der Kirchen 1933–1945*, vol. 6 (Mainz, 1985), 441–4.
17. BA Berlin, R 3001/alt R 22/1456, Bl. 2: Reichsminister der Justiz to Cardinal Bertram, no date [1944].
18. BA Berlin, R 3001/alt R 22/1259, Bl. 35: RJM to Generalstaatsanwälte, 12 Dec. 1944. For a more detailed account of this conflict, see Oleschinski, 'Gefängnisseelsorge', 387–91.
19. ThHStAW, GStA bei dem OLG Jena Nr. 1067, Bl. 118: RJM to Generalstaatsanwälte, 5 July 1943.
20. IfZ, Sp 1.13., Spruchkammer Nord-Württemberg, Verfahren gegen Max K., 21 Dec. 1949; WL, Reel EW 4, Bl. 4473–4: Bericht Philipp P., Apr. 1958; SL, Zuchthaus Ludwigsburg to Hausarzt, 14 Nov. 1944; ibid., Gefangenenstand ab Juli 1944; ibid., Totenbuch, 1851–1945. For a brief and rather flowery history of Hohenasperg, see A. Zink, 'Hohenasperg im Wandel der Zeit', *ZfStrVo* 1 (1950), Nr. 2, 3–8.
21. ThHStAW, GStA bei dem OLG Jena Nr. 1066, Bl. 154: Zuchthaus Gräfentonna to GStA Jena, 2 Oct. 1944.
22. Robert H. was sentenced to seven years' penitentiary after the war for his reign of terror; BLHA, Ld. Br. Rep. 214 Forschungsstelle Zuchthaus Brandenburg Nr. 32, Bl. 212–13: Urteil der Großen Strafkammer Neuruppin, 1 Oct. 1948; IfZ, MA 624, Bl. 3664699–704: Kammergerichtsbezirk Berlin to RJM, 15 Mar. 1945; Frenzel *et al.*, *Gesprengte Fesseln*, 46–8; P. Plattner, *Das Zuchthaus. Eine Ausstellung über das faschistische Zuchthaus Brandenburg* (Berlin, 1990), 76; BLHA, Pr. Br. Rep. 29 Zuchthaus Brandenburg Do. 19.
23. Cited in Maier, 'Strafvollzug', 971. See also ibid., *passim*. For a prison camp reserved largely for women with sentences of less than one year, see A. Rosenbaum, 'Das Frauenstraflager Flußbach', in Ministerium der Justiz Rheinland-Pfalz (ed.), *Justiz im Dritten Reich. Justizverwaltung, Rechtsprechung und Strafvollzug auf dem Gebiet des heutigen Landes Rheinland-Pfalz*, vol. 2 (Frankfurt am Main, 1995), 946–70.
24. Boberach (ed.), *Meldungen*, vol. 3, 791, 848–9; ibid., vol. 7, 2598–600; ibid., vol. 11, 4271–5; BA Berlin, R 3001/9934, GStA Stuttgart to RJM, 19 June 1940; ibid., R 3001/alt R 22/1238, Bl. 237–40: RJM, Vermerk, no date [1941]; ibid., R 3001/alt R 22/1239, Bl. 61: RJM, Vermerk, 16 Apr. 1943; ibid., Bl. 108–17: Strafvollstreckung gegen Angehörige

der Ernährungswirtschaft, no date [1943]; ibid., R 3001/alt R 22/1261, Bl. 349: Lagebericht GStA Nuremberg, 30 Jan. 1943; ibid., R 3001/alt R 22/3379, Bl. 117–19: GStA Munich to RJM, 31 July 1944.
25. For one example, referring back to the First World War, see Roesner, 'Buchkritik von A. Philipp, "Scotland Yard"', *BlGefK* 71 (1940), 100.
26. Cited in S.R. Welch, '"Harsh but Just?" German Military Justice in the Second World War', *German History* 17 (1999), 369–99, here 379.
27. For the Formation Dirlewanger, see H.-P. Klausch, *Antifaschisten in SS-Uniform* (Bremen, 1993), *passim*.
28. Quoted in Welch, 'German Military Justice', 377, 379. See also ibid., 378; Klausch, *Bewährungstruppe 500*, 14–15.
29. Quoted in Welch, 'German Military Justice', 378. See also ibid., 377–97; M. Messerschmidt, F. Wüllner, *Die Wehrmachtjustiz im Dienste des Nationalsozialismus* (Baden-Baden, 1987), 38–46; F. Wüllner, 'Der Wehrmacht "strafvollzug" im Dritten Reich. Zur zentralen Rolle der Wehrmachtgefängnisse in Torgau', in N. Haase, B. Oleschinski (eds), *Das Torgau-Tabu* (Leipzig, 1993), 29–44; Klausch, *Bewährungstruppe 500*, 128.
30. BA Berlin, R 3001/alt R 22/245, Bl. 63–75: Vortrag des Dr Lehmann, 23 Apr. 1941; F. Wüllner, *Die NS-Militärjustiz und das Elend der Geschichtsschreibung* (Baden-Baden, 1991), 104–5, 650–9; Klausch, *Bewährungstruppe 500*, 128, 256–8. In late April 1944, some 10,456 'war offenders' sentenced by military courts were held inside penal institutions; IfZ, MA 624, Bl. 3664437–8: RJM, Vermerk, no date.
31. Oberkommando der Kriegsmarine to RJM, 25 May 1943, reprinted in Kosthorst, Walter (eds), *Strafgefangenenlager*, vol. 2, 1381.
32. BA Berlin, R 3001/alt R 22/5015, Bl. 14–15: Aussetzung der Strafvollstreckung zum Zwecke der Bewährung, 21 Dec. 1940. See also ibid., R 3001/alt R 22/245, Bl. 63–75: Vortrag des Dr Lehmann, 23 Apr. 1941.
33. Klausch, *Bewährungstruppe 500*, 62–4.
34. Klausch, *Bewährungstruppe 500*, 82–5. See also BA Berlin, R 3001/alt R 22/5015, Bl. 36–40: Oberkommando der Wehrmacht, Verordnung zur Durchführung des Erlasses des Führers, 5 Apr. 1941.
35. Cited in Wüllner, *NS-Militärjustiz*, 721.
36. BA Berlin, R 3001/alt R 22/5015, Bl. 54–5: RJM to Generalstaatsanwälte, 10 July 1942; Klausch, *Bewährungstruppe 500*, esp. 92, 100, 110, 128, 184, 351.
37. Dörner, *Erziehung*, 275–8, quotation on 276. In 1942, some 816 young prisoners were taken to the army; BA Berlin, R 3001/alt R 22/1238, Bl. 306–7: Aussetzung der Strafvollstreckung zum Zwecke der Bewährung vor dem Feinde, no date [1943].
38. Bartov, *Hitler's Army*, 36–9.
39. H.-P. Klausch, *Die 999er. Von der Brigade 'Z' zur Afrika-Division 999* (Frankfurt am Main, 1986), 13–16; Wagner, *Kriminalpolizei*, 338–40.
40. Bartov, *Hitler's Army*, 44.
41. Klausch, *Die 999er*, 16–19; BA Berlin, R 3001/alt R 22/5015, Bl. 61: RJM, Vermerk, Sept. 1942.
42. BA Berlin, 99 US 2 FC 588, Mikrofilm 22941, Bl. 50–5: Besprechung am 9.10.1942; Klausch, *Die 999er*, 30. For one such list, see HStAD-Kalkum, Gerichte Rep. 321/611, Bl. 124: RJM to Wehrmeldeamt, 23 Feb. 1943.
43. BA Berlin, R 3001/alt R 22/5015, Bl. 156–7: RJM to Generalstaatsanwälte, Jan. 1944.
44. See ibid., R 3001/alt R 22/4054, Bl. 95: Zuchthaus Untermaßfeld to RJM, 2 Oct. 1942; ibid., Bl. 306–8: Zuchthaus Amberg, Auslese von Zuchthausgefangenen, 2 Dec. 1942.
45. Klausch, *Die 999er*, 22; idem, *Bewährungstruppe 500*, 58.

46. Klausch, *Bewährungstruppe 500*, 225–6, 262–3, 352–5.
47. BA Berlin, R 3001/alt R 22/4720, Bl. 44–5: Bormann to Thierack, 2 Sept. 1942.
48. Ibid., 99 US 2 FC 588, Mikrofilm 22941, Bl. 49: Dr Joël, Ausführungen des Reichsmarschalls vom 14.9.1942.
49. Ibid., Bl. 50–5: Besprechung am 9.10.1942; Klausch, *Antifaschisten*, 72.
50. BA Berlin, R 3001/alt R 22/5024, Bl. 10: GStA Celle to RJM, 26 Oct. 1942; ibid., R 3001/alt R 22/4045, Bl. 88: Zuchthaus Hameln to RJM, 29 Oct. 1942.
51. Ibid., 99 US 2 FC 38580/47458 P, Bl. 4767: Aussage von R. Hecker, 7 July 1947.
52. IfZ, MA 193/2, Bl. 3668387–8: Vermerk, Stand 31.3.1943.
53. O. Buchwitz, *50 Jahre Funktionär der deutschen Arbeiterbewegung* (Stuttgart, 1949), 178.
54. IfZ, MA 193/2, Bl. 3668387–8: Vermerk, Stand 31.3.1943. See also BA Berlin, R 3001/alt R 22/897, Bl. 118.
55. Habicht, *Zuchthaus Waldheim*, 211.
56. G. Schultze-Pfaelzer, *Kampf um den Kopf. Meine Erlebnisse als Gefangener des Volksgerichtshofes 1943–1945* (Berlin, 1948), 238; Frese, *Bremsklötze*, 105.
57. Reichel, *. . . um Dich zu befreien*, quotation on 149. See also ibid., 140. For beatings of Czech prisoners, see also BayHStA, StK 13944, Urteil Landgericht Regensburg, 28 Feb. 1949; ThSTA Mgn., Vorstand der Strafanstalt Untermaßfeld P. 2, Aussagen vor dem Vorstand, 28–29 Nov. 1946; BLHA, Ld. Br. Rep. 214 Forschungsstelle Zuchthaus Brandenburg Nr. 1, Bl. 237–8: 'Ein aufschlußreiches Dokument', 24 Dec. 1948.
58. ThSTA Mgn., Zuchthaus Untermaßfeld Nr. 695.
59. Ibid., Nr. 752.
60. ThHStAW, GStA bei dem OLG Jena Nr. 757, Bl. 194: Zuchthaus Untermaßfeld to GStA Jena, 5 Aug. 1943.
61. ThSTA Mgn., Zuchthaus Untermaßfeld Nr. 718; Reichel, *. . . um Dich zu befreien*, 108–12.
62. BA Berlin, R 3001/alt R 22/1262, Bl. 161: RJM to Generalstaatsanwälte, 10 Nov. 1944.
63. See, for example, ThHStAW, GStA bei dem OLG Jena Nr. 604, Bl. 99: Zuchthaus Gräfentonna to Staatspolizeileitstelle Prague, 10 June 1943.
64. Quoted in ThSTA Mgn., Zuchthaus Untermaßfeld Nr. 1392, Bl. 14: Führungs- und Schlußbericht, 27 Aug. 1942. See also ibid., Bl. 24: Gestapo Troppau to Zuchthaus Untermaßfeld, 20 Feb. 1943.
65. IfZ, MA 193/2, Bl. 3668387–8: Vermerk, Stand 31.3.1943.
66. Möhler, 'Strafvollzug', 166–7; BA Berlin, R 3001/alt R 22/1338, Bl. 26: GStA Cologne to RJM, 2 May 1941; ibid., R 3001/alt R 22/1278, Bl. 325: RJM to Oberkommando des Heeres, 20 May 1941.
67. L. Gruchmann, ' "Nacht-und Nebel"-Justiz. Die Mitwirkung deutscher Strafgerichte an der Bekämpfung des Widerstandes in den besetzten westeuropäischen Ländern 1942–1944', *VfZ* 29 (1981), 342–96; BA Berlin, 99 US 57991, R. Lehmann, Eidesstattliche Erklärung, 23 Dec. 1946; ibid., 99 US 2 FC 588, Mikrofilm 22942, Bl. 395–400: W. v. Ammon, Eidesstattliche Erklärung, 17 Dec. 1946; Broszat, 'Konzentrationslager', 407–8; E. Froidure, *Der Leidensweg der Kranken im Zwangslager Esterwegen* (Lüttich, 1945), partially reprinted in Kosthorst, Walter (eds), *Strafgefangenenlager*, vol. 3, 3029–55, here 3032; 'Einleitungstext und Kommentar', ibid., 2848–62. The various decrees are reprinted ibid., 2862–75.
68. Gruchmann, ' "Nacht-und Nebel" ', 356, 372–8.
69. IfZ, MA 624, Bl: 3664606: RJM, Vermerk, no date [1944].
70. BA Berlin, Film 44184, Vernehmung von K. Engert, 6 Dec. 1946; ibid., Film 44840,

Vernehmung von H. Mayr, 10 Apr. 1947; ibid., SAPMO, DY 54/V 277/1/15, Charlotte K. to Oberstaatsanwalt Dr Scheidges, 30 May 1946; ZStL, VI 416 AR–Nr 477/68, Bl. 61: RJM to Generalstaatsanwälte, 6 Mar. 1943; H. Jenner, 'Norwegische Gefangene vor dem Sondergericht Kiel', in R. Bohn, U. Danker (eds), *'Standgerichte der inneren Front'. Das Sondergericht Altona/Kiel 1932–1945* (Hamburg, 1998), 263–75, here 273.

71. Suhr, *Emslandlager*, 175–85, quotation on 179; Froidure, *Leidensweg*, partially reprinted in Kosthorst, Walter (eds), *Strafgefangenenlager*, vol. 3, 3029–55, quote on 3041; Bericht des Herrn Falloise, reprinted and translated ibid., 2965–7; 'Einleitungstext und Kommentar', ibid., 2848–62, 3551; British Military Court, Application of the Prosecution, 1947, reprinted ibid., 2982–96.
72. BA Berlin, R 3001/alt R 22/245, Arbeitstagung am 23. und 24.4.1941, here Bl. 181.
73. Cited in Wrobel, *Justiz*, 72. For Drendel, see Gruchmann, *Justiz*, 287.
74. BA Berlin, R 3001/alt R 22/897, Bl. 9–10.
75. Zarzycki, *Besatzungsjustiz*, 15–24.
76. BA Berlin, R 3001/alt R 22/1429, Bl. 145–6: Arbeitseinsatz der Gefangenen, no date; ibid., R 3001/alt R 22/897, Bl. 9–10.
77. HStAD-Kalkum, Gerichte Rep. 321/758, Bl. 278: Reichsstatthalter Posen to GStA Düsseldorf, 11 May 1942. See also ibid., Bl. 213: Zuchthaus Remscheid-Lüttringhausen to GStA Düsseldorf, 9 Mar. 1942. For Polish prisoners arriving in other penal institutions in the west, see ibid., Bl. 77: Gefängnis Wuppertal to GStA Düsseldorf, 10 June 1941; ibid., Bl. 86: Gefängnis Wuppertal to GStA Düsseldorf, 12 Mar. 1941.
78. Ibid., Bl. 93: RJM to GStA Düsseldorf, 20 June 1941; ibid., Bl. 278: Reichsstatthalter Posen to GStA Düsseldorf, 11 May 1942.
79. Herbert, *Fremdarbeiter*, 94.
80. ThSTA Mgn., Vorstand der Strafanstalt Untermaßfeld P. 2, Aussagen vor dem Vorstand, 28–9 Nov. 1946.
81. Cited in Suhr, *Emslandlager*, 54. Some Jewish 'war offenders' were also taken to the Emsland camp; see BA Berlin, R 3001/alt R 22/1261, Bl. 317: RJM, Vermerk, 13 June 1942.
82. RJM, Vermerk, 19 Apr. 1941, reprinted in Kosthorst, Walter (eds), *Strafgefangenenlager*, vol. 2, 1352; Suhr, *Emslandlager*, 54–5.
83. RJM, Vermerk, 15 Feb. 1941, reprinted in Kosthorst, Walter (eds), *Strafgefangenenlager*, vol. 2, 1343–4; Auszüge des Untersuchungsrichters in Oldenburg, reprinted ibid., vol. 3, 2406–7; Übersicht über die Verteilung der Todesfälle, ibid., 3577.
84. BLHA, Pr. Br. Rep. 29 Zuchthaus Brandenburg Nr. 3096; BA Berlin, 99 US 57991, Schlegelberger to Generalstaatsanwälte, 24 July 1941.
85. BA Berlin, R 3001/alt R 22/1422, Bl. 79: Streckenbach to RJM, 31 Aug. 1940.
86. Ibid., Bl. 75: GStA Stuttgart to RJM, 26 Sept. 1940. For Wagner, see Gruchmann, *Justiz*, 284–5.
87. BA Berlin, R 3001/alt R 22/1344, Bl. 17: RJM to Generalstaatsanwälte, 8 Oct. 1940. In the case of Polish prisoners serving longer sentences, this additional punishment was supposed to apply only in the first and last month of their sentence.
88. Ibid., R 3001/alt R 22/1422, Bl. 94: RJM to Generalstaatsanwälte, 18 Nov. 1940; Möhler, 'Strafvollzug', 144, note 550.
89. BA Berlin, R 43 II/1549, Bl. 61–3: Schlegelberger to Chef der Reichskanzlei, 17 Apr. 1941.
90. For the discussions in the Reich Ministry of Justice leading up to the regulations of 7 January 1942, see ibid., R 3001/alt R 22/1422, Bl. 143–8.

91. Ibid., R 3001/alt R 22/848, Bl. 171: Polenvollzugsordnung, 7 Jan. 1942. See also ibid., R 3001/alt R 22/4372, Bl. 114: RJM to Generalstaatsanwälte, 14 Jan. 1942. Poles chosen for 'Germanisation' were exempt from the regulations.
92. For Sosnowitz, see BA Berlin, R 137 V/4; ibid., R 137 V/5, Strafvollzugsstatistik, Berichtsjahr 1943; E. Kinder, 'Das "Stammlager Sosnowitz". Eine Fallstudie zum Strafvollzug nach dem "Polenstrafrecht"', in F.P. Kahlenberg (ed.), *Aus der Arbeit der Archive* (Boppard, 1989), 603–23. For Krone, see Weckbecker, *Sondergerichte*, 721, 745–6. For Rawitsch, see BA Berlin, R 3001/alt R 22/4049, Stammlager Rawitsch to RJM, 28 Oct. 1942. For the inmate numbers in the incorporated territories, see ibid., R 3001/alt R 22/897, Bl. 83.
93. Weckbecker, *Sondergerichte*, 721–2 (notes 7 and 8), 729, 737 (note 67), 796.
94. HStAD-Kalkum, Gerichte Rep. 321/780, Bl. 21: GStA Cologne to RJM, 25 June 1942. For the insignia, see BA Berlin, R 3001/alt R 22/1422, Bl. 105: RJM to Generalstaatsanwälte, 31 Oct. 1941.
95. HStAD-Kalkum, Gerichte Rep. 321/758, Bl. 116: GStA Düsseldorf, Vermerk, 24 Oct. 1941; ibid., Rep. 321/759, Bl. 94: Justizoberinspektor N., Bericht, 24 June 1942; ibid., Rep. 321/473, Bl. 22–5: GStA Düsseldorf, Besichtigung am 30.7.1942, 6.8.1942; BA Berlin, R 3001/alt R 22/1343, Bl. 22–3: GStA Düsseldorf to Dr Eggensperger, 15 July 1942.
96. IfZ, MA 193/2, Bl. 3668387–8: Vermerk, Stand 31.3.1943. From late autumn 1942, several thousand Polish prisoners were handed over to the police before they had completed their sentences; see Chapter 8.
97. Diary of Jan Dubbeld, translated and reprinted in Justizakademie NRW, *Strafvollzug 1933–1945*, source 28c.
98. BA Berlin, Film 44169, Vernehmung von B. Wein, 17 Dec. 1946.
99. Möhler, 'Strafvollzug', 231, 256–7.
100. BA Berlin, R 3001/alt R 22/1262, Bl. 41: RJM to Generalstaatsanwälte, 26 Mar. 1943.
101. For Mürau, see in particular V. Godula, 'Zivot veznu na Mírove', *Slezský Sborník* 67 (1969), 514–27 (I am very grateful to Dan Vyleta for translating this article). See also idem, 'Obeti z rad ceských veznu na Mírove v letech 1943–1945', *Slezský Sborník* 69 (1971), 195–202; IfZ, MA 624, Bl. 3664668–70: GStA Leitmeritz to RJM, 12 Mar. 1945; BA Berlin, R 3001/alt R 22/1417, Bl. 175. For Nazi policy towards other Poles with tuberculosis, see K.-H. Roth, '"Asoziale" und nationale Minderheiten', *Protokolldienst der Evangelischen Akademie Bad Boll* 31 (1983), 120–34, here 124–5.
102. Godula, 'Zivot', 520, 523.
103. BA Berlin, R 3001/alt R 22/4053, Bl. 15: RJM to Generalstaatsanwälte, 11 Mar. 1944.
104. Ibid., R 3001/alt R 22/1337, Bl. 158: RJM to Generalstaatsanwälte, 21 Aug. 1940; ibid., Bl. 153: Reichsministerium des Inneren to RJM, 1 Aug. 1940.
105. Ibid., R 3001/alt R 22/4053, Bl. 14: RJM to Generalstaatsanwälte, 21 Apr. 1943. For many individual examples of the transfer of Polish prisoners, see BA Berlin, Film 72522. At the end 1944, the method for transfer was slightly modified. Determined to maintain the economic output of penal institutions, the legal authorities got the police to agree that certain Polish prisoners, in particular those in key positions in the war industry, could be exempted from transfer to the police after completing their sentence and instead could remain inside penal institutions; BA Berlin, R 3001/alt R 22/1429, Bl. 322: Beauftragter für den Vierjahresplan to RJM, 23 Nov. 1944.

106. Scharf, 'Strafvollzug', 834–5. In this period, some Russian prisoners were also handed over to the police before their sentences had been completed; BA Berlin, 99 US 2 FC 588, Mikrofilm 22941, Bl. 126: Freisler to Müller, 26 June 1942.

Chapter 8

1. For the last point, see Gruchmann, 'Hitler', 86.
2. For the quotations, see ZStL, II 416 AR–Nr 2643/65, Bl. 117–21: Vernehmung von E. Eggensperger, 25 Jan. 1949; HHStAW, Abt. 468, Nr. 426/1, Bl. 200–3: J. Eichler, Vermerk, 17 Nov. 1948; ibid., Nr. 426/2, Bl. 153–5: Vernehmung von Emil M., 27 Jan. 1949. Eichler's claim that he raised objections to Thierack in the meeting does not seem credible.
3. Fröhlich (ed.), *Tagebücher*, II/5, entry of 15 Sept. 1942, 504; Thierack, Vermerk, Gespräch mit Dr Goebbels am 14.9.1942, reprinted in Ayaß (ed.), *'Gemeinschaftsfremde'*, 312; BA Berlin, R 3001/alt R 22/4062, Bl. 52–3: Thierack, Vermerk, Aussprache am 16.9.1942; K. H. Roth, ' "Abgabe asozialer Justizgefangener an die Polizei" – eine unbekannte Vernichtungsaktion der Justiz. Eine Dokumentation', in idem et al. (eds), *Heilen und Vernichten im Mustergau Hamburg* (Hamburg, 1984), 21–5.
4. BA Berlin, R 3001/alt R 22/4062, Bl. 35a-37: Besprechung mit Reichsführer SS Himmler am 18.9.1942 in seinem Feldquartier.
5. The content of this draft can be inferred from HStAD-Kalkum, Gerichte Rep. 321/1044, Bl. 120: RJM to Generalstaatsanwälte, 14 Sept. 1942. The only obvious changes made in the meeting between Himmler and Thierack concerned 'racial aliens'. Now, the transfer included all Jews (rather than Jews with sentences of more than three months), all Sinti and Roma (rather than Sinti and Roma with sentences of more than three years) as well as all Russians and Ukrainians (who had not been part of the draft).
6. BA Berlin, 99 US 2 FC 588, Mikrofilm 22941, Bl. 50–5: Besprechung am 9.10.1942. These minutes do not explicitly state that this provision was also to be valid for all 'reformable' penitentiary prisoners sentenced to security confinement (which was to commence after their initial imprisonment). However, this was in fact the case. Jung's suggestion was made at the meeting in Berlin on 29 September 1942 between Thierack and leading members of the German judiciary. For workhouses and some minor exceptions to the transfer, e.g. regarding prisoners of war and certain other foreigners, see ibid., Bl. 56–61: RJM to Generalstaatsanwälte, 22 Oct. 1942. For workhouses, see also Ayaß, *Arbeitshaus*, 321–2.
7. Jochmann (ed.), *Monologe*, 271.
8. See Himmler's notes in his diary for this meeting. In the margin, the entry is ticked, signifying that the topic had been raised with Hitler; BA Berlin, NS 10/1447, Bl. 78–89: Vortrag b. Führer, 22 Sept. 1942, here Bl. 88.
9. BA Berlin, R 3001/alt R 22/4199, Bl. 8–137: Besprechung mit den Chefpräsidenten und Generalstaatsanwälten am 29.9.1942, here Bl. 41.
10. BA Berlin, R 3001/alt R 22/4199, Bl. 8–137: Besprechung mit den Chefpräsidenten und Generalstaatsanwälten am 29.9.1942, here Bl. 38–41, 126. For the 'euthanasia' programme, see Friedlander, *Nazi Genocide*, 110–11. For a discussion of other possible motives for Hitler's 'halt order', see Burleigh, *Death and Deliverance*, 180.

11. ZStL, VI 415 AR–Nr 1310/63, Staatsanwaltschaft Berlin, Einleitungsvermerk, 30 Apr. 1965.
12. For Hecker, see BA Berlin, R 3001/alt R 22/Pers. 59371.
13. ZStL, II 416 AR–Nr 2643/65, Bl. 117–21: Vernehmung von E. Eggensperger, 25 Jan. 1949.
14. See, for example, BA Berlin, Film 44840, Vernehmung von R. Marx, R. Hecker, 25 Mar. 1947.
15. ZStL, VI 415 AR–Nr 1310/63, Staatsanwaltschaft Berlin, Einleitungsvermerk, 30 Apr. 1965; ThHStAW, GStA bei dem OLG Jena Nr. 431, Bl. 172–87: Tagung am 10. und 11.2.1943; BA Berlin, R 3001/alt R 22/1417, Bl. 141: Vermerk, Stand: 24.4.1943; ibid., R 3001/alt R 22/1262, Bl. 15: Abgabe asozialer Gefangener an die Polizei, no date [spring/summer 1943].
16. N. Wachsmann, ' "Annihilation through Labor". The Killing of State Prisoners in the Third Reich', *Journal of Modern History* 71 (1999), 624–59, here 645, note 88.
17. ThSTA Mgn., Zuchthaus Untermaßfeld Nr. 311.
18. BA Berlin, 99 US 2 FC 588, Mikrofilm 22941, Bl. 50–5: Besprechung am 9.10.1942. For Aichach, see StAMü, Justizvollzugsanstalten Nr. 1797; ibid., Nr. 1820, Nr. 7793, Nr. 9053, Nr. 9840, Nr. 10514, Nr. 10756.
19. BA Berlin, R 3001/alt R 22/1417, Bl. 141: Vermerk, Stand: 24.4.1943.
20. The one remaining inmate had been taken to another prison; BA Berlin, R 137 V/14.
21. Ibid., R 3001/alt R 22/1417, Bl. 141: Vermerk, Stand: 24.4.1943. Temporary exemptions from the transfer of Poles sentenced in the General Government (ibid., 99 US 2 FC 588, Mikrofilm 22941, Bl. 56–61: RJM to Generalstaatsanwälte, 22 Oct. 1942) were apparently later dropped. Regarding Russian prisoners, their number only seems to have increased towards the end of the war.
22. For the persecution of the Sinti and Roma, see M. Zimmermann, 'Ausgrenzung, Ermordung, Ausgrenzung', in A. Lüdtke (ed.), *'Sicherheit' und 'Wohlfahrt'. Polizei, Gesellschaft und Herrschaft im 19. und 20. Jahrhundert* (Frankfurt am Main, 1992), 344–70; Lewy, *Nazi Persecution*, here esp. 14, 43, 169; Gellately, *Backing Hitler*, 106–11. For the two quotations, see Dr Gürtner to Staatsanwälte, 13 Apr. 1935, reprinted in Ayaß (ed.), *'Gemeinschaftsfremde'*, 59–61; Heindl, *Berufsverbrecher*, 261.
23. BA Berlin, R 3001/alt R 22/1417, Bl. 141: Vermerk, Stand: 24.4.1943.
24. From March 1941, legal officials were to report all Jewish prisoners before their release to the local criminal police. From November 1941, the Gestapo was to be informed as well; Majer, *'Fremdvölkische'*, 652–3.
25. BA Berlin, R 3001/alt R 22/1338, Bl. 102: Eichmann to RJM, 29 Oct. 1941.
26. Cited ibid., R 3001/alt R 22/1238, Bl. 285: GStA Berlin to RJM, 25 Mar. 1942.
27. Ibid., Bl. 286: RJM to Generalstaatsanwälte, 16 Apr. 1942.
28. BA Berlin, R 3001/alt R 22/1238, Bl. 283: GStA Berlin to RJM, 4 Feb. 1942.
29. Ibid., R 137 V/14, GStA Kattowitz to Gestapo Kattowitz, 18 July 1942; ibid., Stammlager Sosnowitz to Gestapo Kattowitz, 30 Aug. 1942.
30. BA Berlin, Film 44320, Vernehmung von R. Hecker, 16 Jan. 1947; ibid., R 3001/alt R 22/1417, Bl. 141: Vermerk, Stand: 24.4.1943; HHStAW, Abt. 468, Nr. 426/14, Vernehmung von Samuel S., 29 July 1949.
31. BA Berlin, R 3001/alt R 22/4053, Bl. 14: RJM to Generalstaatsanwälte, 21 Apr. 1943.
32. ZStL, Sammelakte Nr. 27a, Antrag auf Eröffnung des Hauptverfahrens, 24 Nov. 1949; BA Berlin, R 3001/alt R 22/Pers. 55261; ibid., R 2/Pers. SG (ex. BDC), Karl Engert, Engert to Himmler, 7 Sept. 1940; ibid., R 3001/alt R 22/58, Geschäftsverteilungsplan; 'Karl Engert 65 Jahre', *Völkischer Beobachter*, 24 Oct. 1942.

33. On 18 September 1942, Himmler made a call to Hitler's headquarters, to say that Engert should not be appointed as head instructor of the Nazi Jurists League – presumably because it had been decided that he would be involved in the transfer instead; IfZ, F 37/2, 1942/II, Bl. 186: Telefongespräche des Reichsführers SS am 18.9.1942. Engert's role was also mentioned in a meeting on 9 October 1942 in the Reich Ministry of Justice; BA Berlin, 99 US 2 FC 588, Mikrofilm 22941, Bl. 50–5: Besprechung am 9.10.1942.
34. BA Berlin, Film 44184, Vernehmung von K. Engert, 6 Dec. 1946, 6 Feb. 1947; ibid., Film 44327, Vernehmung von G. Joel, 23 Oct. 1946.
35. For individual examples, see BA Berlin, 99 US 2 FC 588, Mikrofilm 22941, Bl. 89–102: Ebrach Penitentiary Prisoner Ledger; HHStAW, Abt. 468, Nr. 426/20, Strafanstalt Ludwigsburg, Individuelle Abgabe, 21 June 1948.
36. German political offenders had routinely been sentenced to lengthy spells of imprisonment, rather than to security confinement. And the handful of political prisoners who had received sentences of security confinement were individually examined as well; BA Berlin, 99 US 2 FC 588, Mikrofilm 22941, Bl. 56–61: RJM to Generalstaatsanwälte, 22 Oct. 1942.
37. IfZ, MA 624, Bl. 3664611–12: Anzeigen der Anstaltsvorstände, 7 Dec. 1942.
38. IfZ, MB 1, E. Niekisch to Deutsche Justizverwaltung, 8 Dec. 1948. See also BA Berlin, Film 44325, Vernehmung von A. Hupperschwiller, 6 Dec. 1946.
39. BA Berlin, R 3001/alt R 22/895, K. Engert, Tätigkeitsbericht der Abteilung XV, Stand vom 23.2.1944; Urteil Landgericht Wiesbaden, 24 Mar. 1952, reprinted in A.L. Rüter-Ehlermann *et al.* (eds), *Justiz und NS-Verbrechen. Sammlung deutscher Strafurteile wegen nationalsozialistischer Tötungsverbrechen 1945–1966*, 22 vols (Amsterdam, 1968–81), vol. 6, 267–367, here 315. In the first overview of inmates reported for examination, institutions which held women (Aichach, Cottbus, Jauer, Lübeck-Lauerhof, Laufen, Hagenau) were absent; IfZ, MA 624, Bl. 3664611–12: Anzeigen der Anstaltsvorstände, 7 Dec. 1942. For female penitentiary inmates, see also BA Berlin, 99 US 2 FC 588, Mikrofilm 22941, Bl. 50–5: Besprechung am 9.10.1942.
40. IfZ, MB 1, Vermerk über die Rücksprache mit Dr Brill, 3 Sept. 1949; HHStAW, Abt. 468, Nr. 426/19, Bl. 26: Vernehmung von Eduard N., 31 May 1949.
41. HHStAW, Abt. 468, Nr. 426/1, Bl. 171: Vernehmung von Simon L., 14 Oct. 1948.
42. ZStL, VI 416 AR–Nr 1127/66, Bl. 193–6: Vernehmung von Max F., 10 Nov. 1948.
43. BA Berlin, Film 44320, Vernehmung von R. Hecker, 16 Apr. 1947. See also IfZ, MB 1, Vernehmung von H. Peter, 13 July 1948; Urteil Landgericht Wiesbaden, 24 Mar. 1952, reprinted in Rüter-Ehlermann *et al.* (eds), *Justiz*, vol. 6, 267–367, here 315.
44. BA Berlin, Film 44184, Vernehmung von K. Engert, 5 Dec. 1946. See also ibid., Film 44325, Vernehmung von A. Hupperschwiller, 24 Jan. 1947; ZStL, VI 416 AR–Nr 1127/66, Bl. 174–80: Strafanstalt Remscheid-Lüttringhausen to GStA Düsseldorf, 27 Aug. 1947.
45. IfZ, MB 1, Vernehmung von H. Peter, 13 July 1948. For Peter, see also ZStL, Sammelakte Nr. 27a, Antrag auf Eröffnung des Hauptverfahrens, 24 Nov. 1949.
46. Quoted in ThSTA Mgn., Zuchthaus Untermaßfeld Nr. 789, Vermerk, 14 Sept. 1941. See also ThHStAW, GStA bei dem OLG Jena Nr. 604, Bl. 72: Zuchthaus Untermaßfeld to GStA Jena, 31 Mar. 1943.
47. IfZ, MB 1, Vernehmung von R. Hecker, 19 Jan. 1949.
48. ThSTA Mgn., Zuchthaus Untermaßfeld Nr. 802; for the quotation see Rudolf L. to his brother, 17 Jan. 1943.

49. BA Berlin, R 3001/alt R 22/895, K. Engert, Tätigkeitsbericht der Abteilung XV, Stand vom 23.2.1944.
50. More than 17,300 prisoners were part of the general transfer (Wachsmann, '"Annihilation"', 636, note 52), and by 23 February 1944, 2,464 inmates had been transferred as part of the individual transfer. By the end of the war, this figure had probably increased to about 3,000.
51. After the war, the Wiesbaden state prosecutor established the fate of a total of 2,292 prisoners who had been handed over to the police: 1,143 of them had died within three months of their transfer; ZStL, VI 415 AR–Nr 1310/63, Staatsanwaltschaft Berlin, Einleitungsvermerk, 30 Apr. 1965.
52. For this estimate, see Wachsmann, '"Annihilation"', 650, note 107.
53. IfZ, Fa 183, Bl. 63–4: SS Wirtschaftsverwaltungshauptamt to Reichsminister der Justiz, no date [1943].
54. IfZ, MB 1, Vernehmung von K. Engert, 5 Jan. 1949.
55. ZStL, VI 415 AR–Nr 1310/63, Staatsanwaltschaft Berlin, Einleitungsvermerk, 30 Apr. 1965; Orth, *System*, 172–3.
56. StAMü, Justizvollzugsanstalten Nr. 7719; ibid., Nr. 7610.
57. HHStAW, Abt. 468, Nr. 426/14, Vernehmung von Samuel S., 29 July 1949.
58. Cited in Weckbecker, *Sondergerichte*, 764.
59. BA Berlin, 99 US 2 FC 588, Mikrofilm 22941, Bl. 80: Stammlager Schieratz to Oberreichsanwalt, 15 Jan. 1943; ibid., Bl. 82: Staatspolizeistelle Litzmannstadt to Oberreichsanwalt, 25 Mar. 1943.
60. For the visits of Thierack and Rothenberger, see HHStAW, Abt. 468, Nr. 426/1, Bl. 227–32: Vernehmung von Dr K., 24 Nov. 1948; ibid., Nr. 426/2, Bl. 222–5: Vernehmung von Hans H., 20 Jan. 1949.
61. HHStAW, Abt. 468, Nr. 426/11, Bl. 62–3: Vernehmung von Josef B., 30 June 1949.
62. ZStL, Sammelakte Nr. 27a, Antrag auf Eröffnung des Hauptverfahrens, 24 Nov. 1949.
63. HHStAW, Abt. 468, Nr. 426/18, Bl. 23: Vernehmung von Johann B., 15 July 1949; ibid., Bl. 46: Vernehmung von Wilhelm S., 8 July 1949.
64. HHStAW, Abt. 468, Nr. 426/9, Bl. 133–4: Vernehmung von Paul K., 13 June 1949. See also H. Kaienburg, *'Vernichtung durch Arbeit'. Der Fall Neuengamme* (Bonn, 1990), 429.
65. There are differing reports as to what this sign looked like. According to Eugen Kogon, a former inmate in Buchenwald, it consisted of the green triangle for 'criminals' with the added letter 'S'; Kogon, *Der SS-Staat*, 72. By contrast, Wolfgang Sofsky states that the security confined had to wear the green triangle, pointing up; Sofsky, *Ordnung*, 141.
66. Pingel, *Häftlinge*, 185–7, 302. For the quote, see Geheimerlaß des Chefs der Sicherheitspolizei, 2 Jan. 1941, reprinted in ZStL, VI 415 AR–Nr 1310/63, Staatsanwaltschaft Berlin, Einleitungsvermerk, 30 Apr. 1965.
67. The postwar investigation by the Wiesbaden state prosecutor tracked down 580 survivors, out of a sample of 3,698 prisoners handed over to the police (including 3,139 security confined). In 1,406 cases, the fate of the prisoners could not be determined; ZStL, VI 415 AR–Nr 1310/63, Staatsanwaltschaft Berlin, Einleitungsvermerk, 30 Apr. 1965.
68. Urteil Landgericht Wiesbaden, 24 Mar. 1952, reprinted in Rüter-Ehlermann *et al.* (eds), *Justiz*, vol. 6, 267–367, here 283; BA Berlin, 99 US 2 FC 588, Mikrofilm 22941, Bl. 56–61: RJM to Generalstaatsanwälte, 22 Oct. 1942.

69. ThSTA Mgn., Zuchthaus Untermaßfeld, Nr. 13; ibid., Nr. 62, 66, 184, 227, 309, 414, 448, 564, 656, 664, 738, 756, 757, 802, 803, 1381, 1388, 1420, 1427, 1438, 1580, 1679. For the prison officials' knowledge, see also ZStL, VI 416 AR–Nr 1127/66, Bl. 112–42: Einstellungsverfügung, May 1952, here Bl. 127–8; ibid., Sammelakte Nr. 27a, Antrag auf Eröffnung des Hauptverfahrens, 24 Nov. 1949.
70. See, for example, IfZ, MB 1, E. Niekisch to Deutsche Justizverwaltung, 8 Dec. 1948.
71. BA Berlin, R 3001/alt R 22/4199, Bl. 8–137: Besprechung mit den Chefpräsidenten und Generalstaatsanwälten im RJM am 29.9.1942, quotation on Bl. 41.
72. BA Berlin, R 3001/alt R 22/5023, Bl. 11–12: Speer to Thierack, 8 Feb. 1944; ibid., Bl. 13–14: Thierack to Speer, 21 Feb. 1944. For Faber, see his personal file: BA Berlin, R 3001/alt R 22/Pers. 55468.
73. ThHStAW, GStA bei dem OLG Jena Nr. 812, Bl. 148: Sicherungsanstalt Gräfentonna to GStA Jena, 28 Dec. 1939.
74. BA Berlin, R 3001/alt R 22/1417, Bl. 61–3: Arbeitseinsatz der Sicherungsverwahrten, no date [1942]; ibid., Bl. 57: Arbeitseinsatz der Sicherungsverwahrten, 1941.
75. BA Berlin, R 3001/alt R 22/4049, Zuchthaus Kaisheim to RJM, 29 Oct. 1942; ibid., R 3001/alt R 22/4045, Bl. 55: Zuchthaus Ebrach to RJM, 29 Oct. 1942.
76. ZStL, VI 416 AR–Nr 1127/66, Bl. 259: RJM to Generalstaatsanwälte, 2 Nov. 1942.
77. See, for example, Robert Hecker's reminder in ThHStAW, GStA bei dem OLG Jena Nr. 431, Bl. 172–87: Tagung am 10. und 11.2.1943.
78. See, for example, ThSTA Mgn., Zuchthaus Untermaßfeld Nr. 659, RJM to Zuchthaus Waldheim, 12 Dec. 1944.
79. BA Berlin, R 3001/alt R 22/1417, Bl. 141: Abgabe an die Polizei, Stand: 24.4.1943. Some other prisoners were spared because they were classified as 'not transportable', due to serious illness. For one such case, see Buchwitz, *50 Jahre*, 191.
80. ZStL, VI 416 AR–Nr 1127/66, Bl. 274–7: Vernehmung von A. Faber, 2 Mar. 1948; ibid., Bl. 264–8: Vernehmung von H. Nolte, 20 Feb. 1948; ibid., VI 415 AR–Nr 1310/63, Staatsanwaltschaft Berlin, Einleitungsvermerk, 30 Apr. 1965. In late October 1942 there had been 1,053 security-confined inmates in Straubing; BA Berlin, R 3001/alt R 22/4049, Sicherungsanstalt Straubing to RJM, 29 Oct. 1942.
81. IfZ, MA 624, Bl. 3664757–60: OLG Hamm to RJM, Nachweisung über den Bestand am 31.12.1944. In the first half of 1943 alone, 567 Germans were sentenced to security confinement, according to the incomplete statistics. By 31 December 1944, there were a total of 2,711 security-confined inmates inside penal institutions. For these figures see ibid., Bl. 3664567: RJM, Vermerk, no date; BA Berlin, R 3001/alt R 22/1160, Bl. 25–66: Statistisches Reichsamt, *Die Entwicklung der Kriminalität im Deutschen Reich vom Kriegsbeginn bis Mitte 1943* (Berlin, 1944).
82. Bericht über Reg.-Rat Dr Engelhardt, 10 Jan. 1944, reprinted in Justizakademie NRW (ed.), *Zum Strafvollzug 1933–1945*, source 29g. See also GStA Düsseldorf to Ministerialdirigent Marx, 14 July 1939, reprinted ibid., source 29f; ZStL, VI 416 AR–Nr 1127/66, Bl. 174–80: Strafanstalt Remscheid-Lüttringhausen to GStA Düsseldorf, 27 Aug. 1947; IfZ, MB 1, GStA Düsseldorf to Zuchthaus Remscheid-Lüttringhausen, 14 July 1943; Breidenbach, *Widerstand*, 12–21.
83. This passage is based on two completed questionnaires, signed by the governor of the penal institution in Kassel-Wehlheiden on 29 March 1944. It seems likely that the same forms were widely used in 1942/3; ZStL, VI 416 AR–Nr 1127/66, Bl. 280–1.
84. ThSTA Mgn., Zuchthaus Untermaßfeld Nr. 13, Gericke to Oberstaatsanwalt Verden, 11 Mar. 1943. Engert's commission agreed and A. was put on the transport to Buchenwald on 18 April 1943.

85. BA Berlin, Film 44564, Vernehmung von Joseph P., 17 Dec. 1946; BA Berlin, 99 US 2 FC 38577/47455 P, Aussage von B. Wein, 28 Apr. 1947.
86. For the details, see Wachsmann, '"Annihilation"', 645, notes 88 and 89.
87. W. Eberhard, 'Zu neuen Wegen im Strafvollzug', *MSchriftKrim* 33 (1942), 59–68, here 64. See also idem, 'Zur Frage der ausmerzenden Erbpflege', *Psychiatrisch-Neurologische Wochenschrift* 45 (1943), Nr. 2, 9–11.
88. Cited in Domarus (ed.), *Hitler*, vol. II/2, 1923–4.
89. See, for example, Richterbrief Nr. 4, 1 Jan. 1943, reprinted in Ayaß (ed.), *'Gemeinschaftsfremde'*, 320–22.
90. For one example, see Urteil Landgericht Hamburg, 26 Jan. 1943, reprinted in Justizbehörde Hamburg (ed.), *'Von Gewohnheitsverbrechern'*, 291–6.
91. See V. Klemperer, *Ich will Zeugnis ablegen bis zum letzten. Tagebücher 1942–1945* (Berlin, 1995), 272.
92. BA Berlin, 99 US 2 FC 585, Microfilm 22933, Bl. 169–76: Rede Dr Rothenberger am 17.2.1943.
93. BA Berlin, 99 US 2 FC 585, Microfilm 22933, Bl. 142–68: Rede Dr Thierack am 5.1.1943; 'Neuordnung der Rechtspflege', *Völkischer Beobachter*, 8 Jan. 1943.
94. See, for example, BA Berlin, 99 US 2 FC 38577/47455 P, Aussage von B. Wein, 28 Apr. 1947.
95. StAMü, GStA bei dem OLG München Nr. 51, Dienstaufsicht über die Vollzugsanstalten, 26 Mar. 1943.
96. BA Berlin, Film 44184, Vernehmung von K. Engert, 5 Dec. 1946. For one such example, see the case of Max M. in BA Berlin, R 3001/alt R 22/1424, Bl. 14, 20–21.
97. IfZ, MB 1, Vernehmung von R. Hecker, 18 Jan. 1949. See also BA Berlin, 99 US 2 FC 588, Mikrofilm 22941, Bl. 56–61: RJM to Generalstaatsanwälte, 22 Oct. 1942. For local officials, see StAMü, GStA bei dem OLG München Nr. 52, Zuchthaus Aichach to Kreisleiter Schrobenhausen-Aichach, 27 June 1943; ThHStAW, GStA bei dem OLG Jena Nr. 812, Bl. 156: Sicherungsanstalt Gräfentonna to GStA Jena, 4 May 1940.
98. IfZ, Fa 183, Bl. 63–4: SS-Wirtschaftsverwaltungshauptamt to RJM, no date [1943].
99. *Der Leuchtturm*, vol. 18 (18 Oct. 1942).
100. HHStAW, Abt. 468, Nr. 426/16, Bl. 96: Vernehmung von Heinrich P., 1 June 1949; ibid., Bl. 7: Vernehmung von Georg B., 13 June 1949; ibid., Nr. 426/9, Bl. 43: Vernehmung von Johann E., 8 June 1949; StAMü, Justizvollzugsanstalten Nr. 5470, Franziska K. to her sister, 7 Feb. 1943; Niekisch, *Erinnerungen*, 351; IfZ, MB 1, Vernehmung von Franz S., 4 Oct. 1948. After the war, the Kaisheim prison chaplain claimed that he had not suspected that the prisoners would be exterminated in the camps; see ZStL, VI 416 AR–Nr 1127/66, Bl. 187–8: Josef S. to Oberstaatsanwalt Wiesbaden, 28 Oct. 1948.
101. Cited in A. Leo, *Briefe zwischen Kommen und Gehen* (Berlin, 1991), 281.
102. HHStAW, Abt. 468, Nr. 426/11, Bl. 30: Vernehmung von Josef B., 15 June 1949; ZStL, VI 416 AR–Nr 1127/66, Bl. 209–18: Oberstaatsanwalt Dortmund, Verfügung, 13 Mar. 1963, here Bl. 215–16.
103. ZStL, VI 416 AR–Nr 1127/66, Bl. 261: RJM to Generalstaatsanwälte, 16 Nov. 1942.
104. HHStAW, Abt. 468, Nr. 426/18, Bl. 46: Vernehmung von Wilhelm S., 8 July 1949.
105. ThSTA Mgn., Zuchthaus Untermaßfeld Nr. 1589, A. Weinberg to Zuchthaus Untermaßfeld, 27 Apr. 1943; ibid., Strafanstalt Untermaßfeld to A. Weinberg, 29 Apr. 1943.
106. JVA Straubing, Josefa W. to Sicherungsanstalt Straubing, 19 Feb. 1943. See also ibid., Christian W. to Pfarrer der Sicherungsanstalt Straubing, 10 Feb. 1943.

107. JVA Straubing, Vermerk, 21 Feb. 1943; ibid., Zuchthaus Straubing to Christian W., 20 Feb. 1943.
108. BA Berlin, 99 US 2 FC 588, Mikrofilm 22941, Bl. 56–61: RJM to Generalstaatsanwälte, 22 Oct. 1942; ibid., R 3001/alt R 22/895, K. Engert, Tätigkeitsbericht der Abteilung XV, Stand vom 23.2.1944; ThHStAW, GStA bei dem OLG Jena Nr. 431, Bl. 172–87: Tagung am 10. und 11.2.1943; IfZ, MB 1, Vernehmung von F.W. Meyer, no date; ZStL, VI 416 AR–Nr 1127/66, Bl. 257–8: GStA Hamm to Zuchthaus Münster, 12 Nov. 1942.
109. BA Berlin, R 3001/alt R 22/895, K. Engert, Tätigkeitsbericht der Abteilung XV, Stand vom 23.2.1944; IfZ, MB 1, Bl. 129–40: Vernehmung von A. Hupperschwiller, 17 Feb. 1948.
110. BA Berlin, R 3001/alt R 22/5103, Reisebericht Dr Gündner, 26 Jan. 1944. See also HStAD-Kalkum, Gerichte Rep. 321/682, Bl. 34: RJM to Generalstaatsanwälte, 20 Aug. 1943.
111. BA Berlin, R 3001/alt R 22/4349, Bl. 32–3: Feldpostbriefe der Strafvollzugsverwaltung, 'Sonderbehandlung der Asozialen', June 1944.
112. IfZ, Ms 361, W. Schwerdtfeger, 'Zuchthausjahre 1935–1945', 217–33, quotation on 227. See also BA Berlin, R 3001/alt R 22/895, K. Engert, Tätigkeitsbericht der Abteilung XV, Stand vom 23.2.1944; ibid., R 3001/alt R 22/5103, Reisebericht Dr Gündner, 26 Jan. 1944. For Engert's visit to Dynamit-A.G., see HStAD-Kalkum, Rep. 321/1028, GStA Cologne, Vermerk, 5 Jan. 1944.
113. BA Berlin, R 3001/alt R 22/895, K. Engert, Tätigkeitsbericht der Abteilung XV, Stand vom 23.2.1944.
114. Ibid., 99 US 2 FC 588, Mikrofilm 22941, Bl. 50–55: Besprechung am 9.10.1942.
115. 'Auszug aus dem Gesetz gegen gefährliche Gewohnheitsverbrecher', 184–9, 198–9. For the debate about diminished responsibility in the German Empire, see Wetzell, *Inventing*, 73–96. For the legal position and the treatment of the 'criminally insane' in Germany, see Müller, 'Verbrechensbekämpfung', 80–127.
116. Friedlander, *Nazi Genocide*, 173; Burleigh, *Death and Deliverance*, 183–7; R. Scheer, 'Die nach Paragraph 42 RStGB verurteilten Menschen in Hadamar', in D. Roer, D. Henkel (eds), *Psychiatrie im Faschismus. Die Anstalt Hadamar 1933–1945* (Bonn, 1986), 237–55, here 246–8; S. Schröter, *Psychiatrie in Waldheim/Sachsen (1716–1946)* (Frankfurt am Main, 1994), 104–8, 183, 225; BA Berlin, R 3001/alt R 22/1336, Bl. 2: 'Menschen vom Wahnsinn gepackt', *Volksgemeinschaft*, 17 Mar. 1937; F. Assmann, 'Betrachtungen über die auf Grund des Gesetzes vom 24.11.1933 zur Sicherung und Besserung in der Brandenburgischen Landesanstalt in Neuruppin untergebrachten geistig abnormen Rechtsbrecher' (Ph.D., University of Munich, 1939).
117. Estimate based on figures in Walter, *Psychiatrie*, 927, table A 105.
118. The two best accounts of the 'euthanasia' programme in English are Burleigh, *Death and Deliverance*, and Friedlander, *Nazi Genocide*.
119. Cited in Burleigh, *Death and Deliverance*, 89. See also Friedlander, *Nazi Genocide*, 173; Schröter, *Psychiatrie*, 130–1; Noakes, Pridham (eds), *Nazism*, vol. 3, 1017–18.
120. Gruchmann, *Justiz*, 502–34, quotations on 512, 530; BA Berlin, R 3001/alt R 22/245, Arbeitsagung am 23. und 24.4.1941. See also Bundesminister der Justiz (ed.), *Justiz*, 205.
121. IfZ, MB 1, Vernehmung von K. Engert, 5 Jan. 1949. For the 'euthanasia' selections, see Friedlander, *Nazi Genocide*, 75–83. For the link between the 'euthanasia' programme and the 'final solution', see ibid., esp. 295–302.
122. IfZ, MB 1, Vernehmung von K. Giese, 3 June 1948; BA Berlin, R 2/Pers. SG (ex. BDC), Kurt Giese. Giese later introduced Herbert Peter, a more junior member of the Chancellery of the Führer, to the murderous project.

123. Burleigh, *Death and Deliverance*, 238.
124. BA Berlin, R 3001/alt R 22/1336, Bl. 16: RJM to Generalstaatsanwälte, 10 Mar. 1943; ZStL, 109 AR–Nr. 13.683/87, Bl. 11–33: GStA Frankfurt, Antrag, 17 Dec. 1968. See also E. Klee, *Was sie taten – Was sie wurden* (Frankfurt am Main, 1986), 121–2, 183–4, 306.
125. Cited in Walter, *Psychiatrie*, 765. See also G. Aly, 'Medizin gegen Unbrauchbare', in *Beiträge zur Nationalsozialistischen Gesundheits- und Sozialpolitik*, vol. 1 (Berlin, 1985), 9–74, here 53–4.
126. BA Berlin, R 3001/alt R 22/1335, RJM to Generalstaatsanwälte, 2 July 1943.
127. ZStL, Verschiedenes, 301 Cz, Nr. 184, Reichsminister des Inneren to Leiter der Heil- und Pflegeanstalten, 8 Aug. 1943. For the general background, see also Burleigh, *Death and Deliverance*, 246–7.
128. Scheer, 'Hadamar', 245, 250–1; Schröter, *Psychiatrie*, 182–5; Müller, *Gewohnheitsverbrechergesetz*, 93; ZStL, 449 AR–Nr 1045/67, Bl. 206–10: Vernehmung von Johannes S., 9 Nov. 1961.
129. IfZ, MA 624, Bl. 3664573–4: Nachweisung über den Bestand der Gefangenen in Anstalten anderer Verwaltungen am 30.9.1944.
130. N. Emmerich, 'Die Forensische Psychiatrie 1933–45', in Arbeitsgruppe zur Erforschung der Geschichte der Karl-Bonhoeffer-Nervenklinik (ed.), *Totgeschwiegen 1933–1945* (Berlin, 1989), 105–23, here 111–12, 119.
131. BA Berlin, 99 US 2 FC 588, Mikrofilm 22941, Bl. 50–5: Besprechung am 9.10.1942.
132. See, for example, HHStAW, Abt. 468, Nr. 426/11, Bl. 77–8: Vernehmung von Josef E., 2 June 1949.
133. ThHStAW, GStA bei dem OLG Jena Nr. 732, Bl. 11: RJM to Generalstaatsanwälte, 15 Dec. 1943; ibid., Nr. 637, Bl. 101: RJM to GStA Jena, 21 June 1944. Inmates with subsequent security confinement were excluded from the transport.
134. IfZ, Sp. 1.15., Spruchkammerverfahren gegen das Personal des Arbeitshauses Vaihingen/Enz; ibid., Gh. 08.02., Urteil Landgericht Heilbronn, Ks 4/52.
135. IfZ, Gh. 08.02., Urteil Landgericht Heilbronn, Ks 4/52. After the war, the former head of the workhouse was sentenced to six years and six months in a penitentiary. For the mortality figures, see IfZ, Sp. 1.15., Spruchkammerverfahren gegen das Personal des Arbeitshauses Vaihingen/Enz.
136. Urteil Landgericht Wiesbaden, 24 Mar. 1952, reprinted in Rüter-Ehlermann *et al.* (eds), *Justiz*, vol. 6, 267–367, here 316.
137. ZStL, Verschiedenes, 301 Cz, Nr. 184, Bl. 226–36: Tagung bei der Generalstaatsanwaltschaft in Bamberg vom 16.11.1944, here Bl. 226–7.
138. Urteil Landgericht Wiesbaden, 24 Mar. 1952, reprinted in Rüter-Ehlermann *et al.* (eds), *Justiz*, vol. 6, 267–367, here 340–2.
139. Cited in Noakes (ed.), *Nazism*, vol. 4, 122. See also Evans, *Rituals*, 915–16, table 1.
140. Cited in Dörner, '*Heimtücke*,' 47.
141. RJM, Führerinformation Nr. 90, reprinted in Bundesminister der Justiz (ed.), *Justiz*, 228.
142. Informationsdienst des Reichsministers der Justiz, 1944, reprinted in Oleschinski (ed.), *Plötzensee*, 54–5.
143. See, for example, BA Berlin, R 3001/alt R 22/245, Bl. 45–6: Zusammenstellung der bei der Tagung am 20.3.1941 zu erörternden Punkte.
144. BA Berlin, 99 US 57991, Urteil Sondergericht Essen, 8 Mar. 1943; ibid., Oberstaatsanwalt bei dem Sondergericht Essen to RJM, 10 Mar. 1943; ibid., Staatsanwalt Gärtner to Oberstaatsanwalt Essen, 22 Mar. 1943. Such swift punishment by the special courts was not the norm. On average, several months

passed between the start of the judicial investigation and the sentence. See Weckbecker, *Sondergerichte*, 802; Oehler, *Rechtsprechung*, 293.

145. Cited in Schlüter, *Urteilspraxis*, 202. See ibid., 195–202, 224–5; Marxen, *Volk*, 36.
146. For Hitler's views, see BA Berlin, R 43 II/1538, Bl. 59: Lammers to Thierack, August 1943. For the number of institutions, see Anlage 1 zur RV vom 17.1.1945, reprinted in Fricke, *Justizvollzugsanstalt*, 106; Möhler, 'Strafvollzug', 59–60. The following penal institutions were included in 1945: Brandenburg-Görden, Breslau, Bruchsal, Cologne, Danzig, Dortmund, Dreibergen-Bützow, Dresden, Frankfurt-Preungesheim, Graz, Halle, Kattowitz, Königsberg, Munich-Stadelheim, Plötzensee, Prag-Pankratz, Posen, Stuttgart, Vienna, Weimar, Wolfenbüttel.
147. Lammers to Himmler, 27 Nov. 1942, reprinted in M. Viebig, *Das Zuchthaus Halle/Saale als Richtstätte der Nationalsozialistischen Justiz* (Magdeburg, 1998), 145; Evans, *Rituals*, 710–20.
148. ZStL, Verschiedenes, 301 Cz, Nr. 184, Bl. 226–36: Tagung bei der Generalstaatsanwaltschaft in Bamberg vom 16.11.1944.
149. PRO, WO 309/199, Dr Thümmler, Eidliche Aussage, 26 Aug. 1947; Plattner, *Das Zuchthaus*, 78.
150. For the quotations, see Fröhlich (ed.), *Tagebücher*, II/9, entry for 14 Sept. 1943, 507; H. Poelchau, *Die letzten Stunden. Erinnerungen eines Gefängnispfarrers* (Berlin, 1987), 49–50. For the general background, see von Gostomski, Loch, *Tod*, 15–36, here 35 for the estimate; Oleschinski (ed.), *Plötzensee*, 56–63.
151. Cited in Viebig, *Zuchthaus*, 52, 54. See also Evans, *Rituals*, 915–16, table 1.
152. E. Klee, *Auschwitz, die NS-Medizin und ihre Opfer* (Frankfurt am Main, 1997), 97–110.
153. BA Berlin, 99 US 2 FC 38593/47471 P, Bl. 235–6: W. Strelow, Eidesstattliche Erklärung, 22 Nov. 1946.
154. PRO WO 309/199, Vernehmung von Willi P., 11 Sept. 1945; ibid., R. Bimler, Eidliche Aussage, 23 Aug. 1947; ibid., Dr Thümmler, Eidliche Aussage, 26 Aug. 1947; Edith G., Aussage, 11 Sept. 1945, reprinted in Plattner, *Das Zuchthaus*, 86; Kriminalpolizei Brandenburg, Bericht, 31 Oct. 1945, reprinted ibid., 88.
155. Möhler, 'Strafvollzug', 62; Bundesminister der Justiz (ed.), *Justiz*, 238; IfZ, ED 106/79, Baron D., Erlebnisbericht, no date.
156. Poelchau, *Erinnerungen*, 48.
157. HStAD-Kalkum, Rep. 321/873, Bl. 2: RJM to GStA Cologne, 16 June 1942; BA Berlin, R 3001/alt R 22/1337, Bl. 4: Reichswirtschaftsminister to RJM, 8 Nov. 1944; ibid., SAPMO, DY 55/62/2/170, Walter Z., Zeugenaussage, 5 May 1947; IfZ, Ms 361, W. Schwerdtfeger, 'Zuchthausjahre 1935–1945', 197.

Chapter 9

1. K.-D. Henke, *Die amerikanische Besetzung Deutschlands* (Munich, 1995).
2. See, for example, Johnson, *Nazi Terror*, 346.
3. Kershaw, '*Hitler Myth*', 258; Henke, *Besetzung*, 86–7, 814–20, 844; Noakes (ed.), *Nazism*, vol. 4, 656–7. For the Himmler quotation, see Commander of the order police to the Governor of Lower Bavaria, 3 April 1945, translated and reprinted ibid., 658.
4. Orth, *System*, 286, 314–20. For one regional example, see B.-A. Rusinek, '"Wat denkste, wat mir objerümt han". Massenmord und Spurenbeseitigung am Beispiel

der Staatspolizeistelle Köln 1944/45', in Paul, Mallmann (eds), *Gestapo – Mythos und Realität*, 402–16.
5. Quoted in Paul, Primavesi, 'Verfolgung', 398–9. See also ibid., *passim*; Rusinek, 'Massenmord', 408–15.
6. Orth, *System*, 287, 296–9, 335–6; J. Fest, *Plotting Hitler's Death. The German Resistance to Hitler 1933–1945* (London, 1997), 311.
7. For one such example, see ThHStAW, GStA bei dem OLG Jena Nr. 825, Bl. 54: Frauenjugendgefängnis Hohenleuben to GStA Jena, 5 Dec. 1944.
8. Justizbehörde Hamburg (ed.), 'Von Gewohnheitsverbrechern', 418.
9. Cited in Bundesminister der Justiz (ed.), *Justiz*, 310. Mostly underlined in the original.
10. M. Gilbert, *The Second World War* (London, 1995), 637.
11. See, for example, Ludewig, Kuessner, *Sondergericht Braunschweig*, 39; W.-D. Mechler, *Kriegsalltag an der 'Heimatfront'. Das Sondergericht Hanover in Einsatz gegen 'Rundfunkverbrecher', 'Schwarzschlachter', 'Volksschädlinge' und andere 'Straftäter' 1939 bis 1945* (Hanover, 1997), 42–5.
12. Cited in Niermann, 'Strafjustiz', 38.
13. Urteil Hanseatisches OLG, 16 Jan. 1945, reprinted in Justizbehörde Hamburg (ed.), 'Von Gewohnheitsverbrechern', 404–8. See also G. Schmitz, 'Zum Urteil gegen Schlichting', ibid., 409–19.
14. BA Berlin, R 3001/alt R 22/4051, RJM to Generalstaatsanwälte, 12 Feb. 1945.
15. Decree on the Establishment of Drum-head Courts Martial, 15 Feb. 1945, translated and reprinted in Noakes (ed.), *Nazism*, vol. 4, 655–6.
16. Quoted in Henke, *Besetzung*, 845. See also ibid., 851–3; Wrobel, *Justiz*, 95.
17. HStAD-Kalkum, Gerichte Rep. 321/406, Bl. 169: RJM to Generalstaatsanwälte, 27 Aug. 1943. See also BA Berlin, R 3001/alt R 22/Pers. 54545.
18. BA Berlin, R 3001/alt R 22/4089, Bl. 280–1: Führerinformation Nr. 187, 9 Dec. 1944. See also ibid., R 3001/alt R 22/4051, Vermerk, 12 Oct. 1944; HStAD-Kalkum, Gerichte Rep. 321/886, Zuchthaus Rheinbach to GStA Cologne, 22 June 1944; ibid., Besprechung der Vollzugsreferenten, 27 Nov. 1944.
19. BA Berlin, 99 US 2 FC 38593/47471 P, Bl. 201–5: Richtlinien für die Räumung von Justizvollzugsanstalten, no date.
20. StK, 2 Ks 1/70 StA Kiel, Gutachten Prof. Dr Krausnick, 18 May 1971, here 20–2.
21. See, for example, BA Berlin, R 3001/alt R 22/4051, Vermerk, Entlassungen in Stettin, 30 Jan. 1945; ibid., Vermerk, Anruf des Staatsanwalts Büttner, 26 Jan. 1945, 31 Jan. 1945; ibid., 99 US 2 FC 38593/47471 P, Bl. 200: Engert to GStA Linz, 5 Feb. 1945; HHStAW, Abt. 468, Nr. 426/2, Bl. 153–5: Aussage von Emil M., 27 Jan. 1949.
22. BA Berlin, 99 US 2 FC 38593/47471 P, Bl. 201–5: Richtlinien für die Räumung von Justizvollzugsanstalten, no date. For the number of police detainees, see BA Berlin, R 3001/alt R 22/5094.
23. IfZ, MB 1, Vernehmung von K. Engert, 5 Jan. 1949.
24. Cited in StK, 2 Ks 1/70 StA Kiel, Gutachten Prof. Dr Krausnick, 18 May 1971, here 8.
25. ZStL, 211 AR–Nr 190/72, Bl. 910–1347: Urteil Landgericht Cologne, 28 Feb. 1980.
26. L. Gruchmann, *Totaler Krieg. Vom Blitzkrieg zur bedingungslosen Kapitulation* (Munich, 1991), 212–14.
27. BA Berlin, R 3001/alt R 22/897, Bl. 229–31; ibid., R 3001/alt R 22/1417, Bl. 171–7: Verzeichnis der selbstständigen Vollzugsanstalten, 1 Aug. 1944.
28. BA Berlin, R 3001/alt R 22/4052, Haftanstalt Preußisch Stargard to GStA Danzig, 23 Feb. 1945.

29. See, for example, BA Berlin, R 3001/alt R 22/4052, Vorstand Frauenjugendgefängnis Marienburg, Bericht über die Rückführung der Anstalt, 27 Feb. 1945.
30. Ibid., R 3001/alt R 22/4051, Leiter Strafgefängnis Wronke to RJM, 5 Feb. 1945; ibid., Leiter Strafgefängnis Wronke, Tagebuch; ibid., RJM, Vermerk, 25 Jan. 1945.
31. Ibid., GStA Breslau to RJM, 12 Feb. 1945.
32. IfZ, MA 625, Bl. 3666205–12: Vorstand Frauenzuchthaus Fordon to GStA Danzig, 28 Feb. 1945.
33. There are numerous graphic reports of the marches in BA Berlin, R 3001/alt R 22/4051; ibid., 4052.
34. IfZ, MA 193/1, Bl. 3666434–5: Verwaltungsassistentin Lakomy, Bericht, 6 Mar. 1945. For other reports of escapes, see various documents in BA Berlin, R 3001/alt R 22/4051; ibid., 4052.
35. Gruchmann, '"Nacht- und Nebel"', 393–5; ZStL, Verschiedenes, 301 Cz, Nr. 184, Bl. 226–36: Tagung bei der Generalstaatsanwaltschaft in Bamberg vom 16.11.1944, quotation on Bl. 236. See also BA Berlin, 99 US 2 FC 588, Mikrofilm 22942, Bl. 401–4: R. Hecker, Erklärung, 5 Jan. 1946; I. Sprenger, *Groß-Rosen. Ein Konzentrationslager in Schlesien* (Cologne, 1996), 117–18.
36. It is not clear whether the trek ever reached Buchenwald. See IfZ, MA 625, Bl. 3666115–16: RJM, Vermerk, 1 Feb. 1945; ibid., Bl. 3666101–13: GStA Kattowitz to RJM, 15 Feb. 1945; BA Berlin, R 3001/alt R 22/4051, Reisebericht Dr Gündner, no date [Feb. 1945]. For conditions in Groß-Rosen, see I. Sprenger, 'Das KZ Groß-Rosen in der letzten Kriegsphase', in U. Herbert et al. (eds), *Die nationalsozialistischen Konzentrationslager* (Göttingen, 1998), vol. 2, 1113–27, here 1114.
37. BA Berlin, 99 US 2 FC 588, Mikrofilm 22942, R. Hecker, Erklärung, 5 Jan. 1946.
38. W. Sailer, 'Das Zuchthaus Kaisheim während der letzten Kriegsmonate und der amerikanischen Besatzungszeit', *ZfStrVo* 35 (1986), 259–61.
39. BA Berlin, R 3001/alt R 22/5096, Bl. 43–4: GStA Düsseldorf to RJM, 14 Mar. 1945.
40. IfZ, MA 193/2, Bl. 3667945: RJM, Vermerk, 5 Feb. 1945. For the Berlin prison numbers in early 1945, see JVA Tegel (ed.), *100 Jahre*, 74.
41. BA Berlin, R 3001/alt R 22/4051, RJM to GStA Dresden, 6 Feb. 1945.
42. For two eyewitness accounts, see IfZ, ED 106/79, Bl. 232: Joachim von B. to Heinz K., 15 June 1952; Schultze-Pfaelzer, *Kampf*, 202–20.
43. BA Berlin, R 3001/alt R 22/4053, Bl. 17: RJM to Gebietsbeauftragter der Organisation Todt, 21 Nov. 1944; ibid., SAPMO, BY 5/V 279/91, H. Happe, 'Die deutschen Strafgefangenenlager Nord/Nord-Norwegen', 1 July 1945; Strafgefangenenlager Nord to Wehrmachtstransportoffizier in Narvik, 12 Mar. 1945, reprinted in Kosthorst, Walter (eds), *Strafgefangenenlager*, vol. 1, 971–3.
44. ZStL, VI 107 AR–Z 114/67, Bl. 251–67: Oberstaatsanwalt Hamburg, Vermerk, 15 Mar. 1950.
45. Urteil Landgericht Bochum, 18 May 1949, reprinted in Rüter-Ehlermann et al. (eds), *Justiz*, vol. 4, 617–30, quote on 622; Christoffel, *Weg*, 203–7. Warder Hans Brodowski was sentenced to six years in a penitentiary in 1949.
46. JVA Straubing, Autobiographie Hermann D.
47. BayHStA, StK 13944, Urteil Landgericht Regensburg, 28 Feb. 1949; BA Berlin, SAPMO, DY 54/V 277/1/29, Johannes E., questionnaire, no date [1946]; JVA Straubing, Strafvollzugskanzlei, Vermerk, 3 Dec. 1947; R. Kriß, *Im Zeichen des Ungeistes* (Berchtesgaden, 1995), 116–19. For camps, see Henke, *Besetzung*, 910–11.
48. For individual examples, see also Urteil Landgericht Frankfurt am Main, 4 Dec. 1950, reprinted in Rüter-Ehlermann et al. (eds), *Justiz*, vol. 7, 747–61; IfZ, Sp. 1.15,

Spruchkammerverfahren gegen das Personal des Arbeitshauses Vaihingen/Enz; Scharf, 'Strafvollzug', 764.
49. See, for example, HStAD-Kalkum, Gerichte Rep. 321/473, Bl. 177: Besichtigung des Zuchthauses Remscheid-Lüttringhausen am 7.1.1943.
50. See, for example, BA Berlin, R 3001/alt R 22/4051, RJM, Vermerk, 25 Jan. 1945; ibid., RJM, Vermerk, 26 Jan. 1945; ibid., GStA Breslau to RJM, 25 Jan. 1945; ibid., R 3001/alt R 22/4052, GStA Kattowitz to RJM, 15 Feb. 1945; IfZ, MA 625, Bl. 3666021–2: RJM, Vermerk, 22 Jan. 1945; HStAD-Kalkum, Gerichte Rep. 321/550, Bl. 160–4: Vorstand Strafgefängnis Anrath to GStA Düsseldorf, 31 Mar. 1945.
51. BA Berlin, R 3001/alt R 22/1262, Bl. 183–4: RJM to Generalstaatsanwälte, 7 Feb. 1945. See also ibid., R 3001/alt R 22/4051, RJM to Generalstaatsanwälte, 12 Feb. 1945.
52. StK, 2 Ks 1/70 StA Kiel, Gutachten Prof. Dr Krausnick, 18 May 1971, here 12–16a.
53. For this, and the preceding two paragraphs, see ZStL, Sammelakte Nr. 422, Urteil Landgericht Kiel, 2 Aug. 1971; A. Hohengarten, *Das Massaker im Zuchthaus Sonnenburg vom 30./31. Januar 1945* (Luxemburg, 1979); BA Berlin, R 3001/alt R 22/4051, RJM, Vermerk, 30 Jan. 1945; ibid., SAPMO, DY 54/V 277/1/10, Vernehmung von G. Rung, 16 Oct. 1946. For the cooperation between the different agencies of state and party, see also StK, 2 Ks 1/70 StA Kiel, Aussage Prof. Dr Krausnick, 18 May 1971, here 1011, 1024. For Hanssen, see BA Berlin, R 3001/alt R 22/Pers. 58943; ibid., Pers. 58944, Pers. 58947, Pers. 58951; ibid., R 2/Pers. SG (ex. BDC), Kurt-Walter Hanssen.
54. IfZ, Gh. 08.02, Urteil Landgericht Heilbronn, Ks 4/52.
55. M. Broszat, 'Grundzüge der gesellschaftlichen Verfassung des Dritten Reiches', in M. Broszat, H. Möller (eds), *Das Dritte Reich* (Munich, 1986), 38–63, here 63; Henke, *Besetzung*, 820–21.
56. BA Berlin, R 3001/alt R 22/4051, RJM to Chef der Sipo und des SD, 3 Feb. 1945; IfZ, MA 193/1, RJM, Vermerk, 3 Feb. 1945.
57. ZStL, VI AR–Z 81/68, Bl. 39–46: GStA Stettin to RJM, 10 Feb. 1945. Other sources speak of 34 or 36 prisoners being singled out.
58. BA Berlin, R 3001/alt R 22/4052, RJM, Vermerk, 16 Feb. 1945; ibid., GStA Stettin to RJM, 16 Feb. 1945; IfZ, MA 193/1, Bl. 3666841–8: Thierack to Gauleiter Schwede-Coburg, 5 Mar. 1945.
59. For Germany as a whole, see Noakes (ed.), *Nazism*, vol. 4, 517.
60. BA Berlin, SAPMO, DY 54/V 277/1/29, Johannes E., questionnaire, no date [1946]. See also ibid., Film 55272, L. Schirner, Eidesstattliche Erklärung, 8 Jan. 1947.
61. ThHStAW, GStA bei dem OLG Jena Nr. 637, Bl. 207–8: Zuchthaus Untermaßfeld to GStA Jena, 19 Mar. 1945; BA Berlin, R 3001/alt R 22/4051, Besichtigung der Strafanstalten Dreibergen-Bützow am 5.2.1945; Kriß, *Im Zeichen*, 109–10.
62. BayHStA, StK 13944, Urteil Landgericht Regensburg, 28 Feb. 1949.
63. BA Berlin, Film 55272, Vernehmung von L. Schirner, 20 Dec. 1946; ibid., R 3001/alt R 22/5094, Bl. 179: Frauenzuchthaus Aichach to RJM, 21 Mar. 1945; Sailer, 'Kaisheim', 260; JVA Straubing, Strafvollzugskanzlei, Vermerk, 3 Dec. 1947.
64. See ThHStAW, GStA bei dem OLG Jena Nr. 637, Bl. 207–8: Zuchthaus Untermaßfeld to GStA Jena, 19 Mar. 1945. For the weight of individual inmates, see, for example, ThSTA Mgn., Zuchthaus Untermaßfeld, Nr. 346, Nr. 1114, Nr. 1785, Nr. 2018.
65. Kriß, *Im Zeichen*, 112.
66. See BA Berlin, R 3001/alt R 22/4052, RJM, Vermerk, 22 Feb. 1945; ThHStAW, GStA bei dem OLG Jena Nr. 637, Bl. 193: Zuchthaus Untermaßfeld to GStA Jena, 5 Feb. 1945.
67. BA Berlin, R 3001/alt R 22/5094.

68. Ibid., R 3001/alt R 22/1266, Bl. 395: Vermerk, Besichtigung des Zuchthauses Hameln, 21 Feb. 1945; ibid., R 3001/alt R 22/4051, Vorstand Strafgefängnis Wronke to RJM, 10 Feb. 1945; Hohengarten, *Massaker*, 101; Friedrich, *Cottbus*, 22; HStAD-Kalkum, Gerichte Rep. 321/886, Besprechung der Vollzugsreferenten, 27 Nov. 1944.
69. Noakes (ed.), *Nazism*, vol. 4, 258–9. For the impact on penal institutions, see, for example, BA Berlin, R 3001/alt R 22/5096, Bl. 43–4: GStA Düsseldorf to RJM, 14 Mar. 1945.
70. BA Berlin, Film 41305, M. Söllner, Bericht über die Krankenabteilung des Zuchthauses Ebrach, 5 July 1945.
71. See, for example, ibid., R 3001/alt R 22/5096, Bl. 24–5: Unterbringung weiterer Gefangener in den Anstalten des Bezirkes Celle, 7 Mar. 1945.
72. Ibid., Bl. 52–3: Untersuchungshaftanstalten Leipzig-Bautzen to RJM, 23 Mar. 1945.
73. PRO, WO 309/151, Captain Williams, Case No 248; BA Berlin, SAPMO, BY 5/V 279/94, Bericht über das Zuchthaus Siegburg, no date. See also G. van der Stroom, *Duitse strafrechtspleging in Nederland en het lot der veroordeelden* (Amsterdam, 1982), 118.
74. Cited in Faralisch, 'Zeitzeugenberichte', 373.
75. BA Berlin, R 3001/alt R 22/28, Bl. 26–32: Reisebericht Dr Thierack, 29 Jan. 1945.
76. Viebig, *Zuchthaus*, 225; Fricke, *Justizvollzugsanstalt*, 42.
77. PRO, WO 309/199, Vernehmung von E. Lautz, 28 July 1947; ibid., Aussage von R. Havemann, 10 Apr. 1947; ZStL, VI 416 AR-Nr 1540/65, Bl. 356–8: Dienstliche Äußerung, K. Jaager, 5 Dec. 1958.
78. Oleschinski, 'Gefängnisseelsorge', 493. See also idem, 'Der Gefängnisgeistliche Peter Buchholz im Dritten Reich', *ZfStrVo* 42 (1993), 22–41, here 41.
79. Breidenbach, *Widerstand*, 21–7; Niermann, 'Strafjustiz', 39; idem, *Strafjustiz*, 362.
80. Kosthorst, Walter (eds), *Strafgefangenenlager*, vol. 3, 3089–98. The impostor and five of his accomplices were sentenced to death by a British court in 1946.
81. C. Letsche, 'Frühjahr 1945 im Zuchthaus Ludwigsburg', in VVN Ludwigsburg (ed.), *Streiflichter aus Verfolgung und Widerstand*, vol. 4 (1990), 20–2.
82. K. Heger, 'Prison Reform in the American Zone of Occupied Germany, 1945–52' (Ph.D., University of Maryland, 1996), 45, 102; H. Wentker, *Justiz in der SBZ/DDR 1945–1953* (Munich, 2001), 207–8, 212.

Chapter 10

1. For the last point, see the discussion in P. Voglis, 'Political Prisoners in the Greek Civil War, 1945–50: Greece in Comparative Perspective', *Journal of Contemporary History* 37 (2002), 523–40.
2. *Nuremberg War Crimes Trials Online*, CD-Rom (Seattle, 1995). See also J. Friedrich, *Freispruch für die Nazi-Justiz* (Berlin, 1998), 19–72; Wrobel, *Justiz*, 169–88; Bundesminister der Justiz (ed.), *Justiz*, 331–45. In total, ten of the defendants were sentenced. One of the others (Carl Westphal, an official from the Reich Ministry of Justice) killed himself before the trial had started. For suicides in general, see Henke, *Besetzung*, 964–5.
3. A. Rückerl, *NS-Verbrechen vor Gericht* (Heidelberg, 1982), 95–127, 174, 329. See also M. Broszat, 'Siegerjustiz oder strafrechtliche "Selbstreinigung"', *VfZ* 29 (1981), 477–544.

4. Bundesminister der Justiz (ed.), *Justiz*, 314–30, 353–63; Müller, *Furchtbare Juristen*, 204–6; M. von Miquel, 'Juristen: Richter in eigener Sache', in N. Frei (ed.), *Karrieren im Zwielicht. Hitlers Eliten nach 1945* (Frankfurt am Main, 2001), 181–237.
5. Bundesminister der Justiz (ed.), *Justiz*, 422–3; von Miquel, 'Juristen', 194; J. Friedrich, *Die kalte Amnestie. NS-Täter in der Bundesrepublik* (Frankfurt am Main, 1984), 161–6; B. Diestelkamp, 'Die Justiz nach 1945 und ihr Umgang mit der eigenen Vergangenheit', in idem, M. Stolleis (eds), *Justizalltag im Dritten Reich* (Frankfurt am Main, 1988), 131–49; Wrobel, *Justiz*, 188–91; H. Kramer, 'Das Nürnberger Juristenurteil (Fall 3) – eine Lektion für die Justiz der BRD?', in M. Hirsch *et al.* (eds), *Politik als Verbrechen* (Hamburg, 1986), 60–3.
6. N. Frei, *Vergangenheitspolitik. Die Anfänge der Bundesrepublik und die NS-Vergangenheit* (Munich, 1996), *passim*. See also C. Garner, 'Public Service Personnel in West Germany in the 1950s', in R.G. Moeller (ed.), *West Germany under Construction. Politics, Society and Culture in the Adenauer Era* (Ann Arbor, 1997), 135–95; R.G. Moeller, *War Stories. The Search for a Usable Past in the Federal Republic of Germany* (Berkeley, 2001), *passim*.
7. Rückerl, *NS-Verbrechen*, 139–51; K. Bästlein, ' "Nazi-Blutrichter als Stützen des Adenauer-Regimes" ', in H. Grabitz *et al.* (eds), *Die Normalität des Verbrechens* (Berlin, 1994), 408–43; D. Siegfried, 'Zwischen Aufarbeitung und Schlußstrich. Der Umgang mit der NS-Vergangenheit in den beiden deutschen Staaten 1958–1969', in idem *et al.* (eds), *Dynamische Zeiten: die 60er Jahre in den beiden deutschen Gesellschaften* (Hamburg, 2000), 77–113; U. Brochhagen, *Nach Nürnberg: Vergangenheitsbewältigung und Westintegration in der Aera Adenauer* (Berlin, 1999), esp. 258–76.
8. Friedrich, *Freispruch*, 641–51; Bundesminister der Justiz (ed.), *Justiz*, 453.
9. Kosthorst, Walter (eds), *Strafgefangenenlager*, vol. 3, 2860; PRO, WO 311/520.
10. See various judgments reprinted in Kosthorst, Walter (eds), *Strafgefangenenlager*, vol. 2, esp. 2081–138, 2331–2, 2516.
11. The quotations are taken from various judgments reprinted in Kosthorst, Walter (eds), *Strafgefangenenlager*, vol. 2, 1991, 2046, 2057 (for the witness Fu.), 2075, 2136; BayHStA, StK 13944, Urteil Landgericht Regensburg, 28 Feb. 1949.
12. Herbert Peter, also from the Chancellery of the Führer, was exempted from the trial because of illness and died in early 1953.
13. For the burning of the files, see BA Berlin, R 3001/alt R 22/4688, Bl. 49: Abteilungsleiterbesprechung am 31.1.1945; HHStAW, Abt. 468, Nr. 426/1, Bl. 138: Vernehmung von O. Gündner, 6 Nov. 1948.
14. BA Berlin, Film 44840, Vernehmung von R. Marx, R. Hecker, 25 Mar. 1947, 27 Mar. 1947.
15. Urteil Landgericht Wiesbaden, 24 Mar. 1952, reprinted in Rüter-Ehlermann *et al.* (eds), *Justiz*, vol. 6, 267–367, here 311. For Hecker's testimony, see IfZ, MB 1, Vernehmung von R. Hecker, 18 Jan. 1949. Hecker claimed that he had realised in spring 1943 that the prisoners were being killed. See also HHStAW, Abt. 468, Nr. 426/2, Bl. 153–5: Vereehmung von Emil M., 27 Jan. 1949.
16. Urteil Landgericht Wiesbaden, 24 Mar. 1952, reprinted in Rüter-Ehlermann *et al.* (eds), *Justiz*, vol. 6, 267–367, quotation on 338, 366–7.
17. Heger, 'Prison Reform', 36–124. For the quotation, see Maier, 'Strafvollzug', 972. For Krebs, see H. Müller-Dietz, 'Albert Krebs'.
18. Möhler, 'Strafvollzug', 28 (n. 49); 120; BA Berlin, Film 44840, Vernehmung von R. Marx, R. Hecker, 27 Mar. 1947. For chaplains, see Oleschinski, 'Gefängnisseelsorge', 452.

19. For Kraus, see StAMü, Justizvollzugsanstalten Nr. 13799. For the quotation, see Personal- und Befähigungsnachweis, 11 April 1944.
20. StAMü, Justizvollzugsanstalten Nr. 13779; ibid., Nr. 13816. See also BA Berlin, R 3001/alt R 22/Pers. Dr Hermann von Reitzenstein.
21. StAMü, Justizvollzugsanstalten Nr. 13807. For the quotations see Dienstbeurteilung, 30 Jan. 1943.
22. StAMü, Justizvollzugsanstalten Nr. 13822.
23. Law Nr. 1, reprinted in Bundesminister der Justiz (ed.), *Justiz*, 314–15; Evans, *Rituals*, 775–88; Müller, *Furchtbare Juristen*, 228–33; Müller, *Gewohnheitsverbrechergesetz*, 95–6; R.G. Moeller, 'The Homosexual Man is a "Man", the Homosexual Woman is a "Woman": Sex, Society, and the Law in Postwar West Germany', in idem (ed.), *West Germany under Construction. Politics, Society and Culture in the Adenauer Era* (Ann Arbor, 1997), 251–84.
24. Quedenfeld, *Strafvollzug*, 94–148; Schattke, *Geschichte*, 212–52.
25. For Rendsburg, see Hellmer, *Gewohnheitsverbrecher*, 375. See also Justizbehörde Hamburg (ed.), '*Von Gewohnheitsverbrechern*', 265.
26. Danker, 'Schutz', 76–7.
27. Cited in Müller, *Furchtbare Juristen*, 217.
28. For compensation for victims of the Nazi regime in general, see G. Saathoff, S. Schlegel, *Beratungsleitfaden NS-Verfolgung* (Cologne, 1995). For the foundation Memory, Responsibility and Future, see www.stiftung-evz.de. For the general background, see also Ayaß, '*Asoziale*', 212–16.
29. Müller, *Furchtbare Juristen*, 270.
30. F. Werkentin, *Recht und Justiz im SED-Staat* (Bonn, 2000), 10–11. See also Broszat, 'Siegerjustiz', 487–95.
31. B. Oleschinski, 'Die Abteilung Strafvollzug der Deutschen Zentralverwaltung für Justiz in der Sowjetischen Besatzungszone 1945–1949', *ZfStrVo* 41 (1992), 83–90, here 84–5; idem, 'Strafvollzug in Deutschland vor und nach 1945', *Neue Justiz* 2 (1992), 65–8, here 68; Wentker, *Justiz*, 211.
32. Order Nr. 00315, 18 Apr. 1945, reprinted and translated in A. von Plato, 'Zur Geschichte des sowjetischen Speziallagersystems in Deutschland', in S. Mironenko *et al.* (eds), *Sowjetische Straflager in Deutschland 1945 bis 1950*, vol. 1 (Berlin, 1998), 19–75, here 26–7. For the treatment of POWs, see L. Niethammer, 'Alliierte Internierungslager in Deutschland nach 1945', ibid., 97–116, here 112–15.
33. Oleschinski, 'Abteilung Strafvollzug', 85; Viebig, *Zuchthaus*, 100. For the involvement of German courts in cases against individuals accused of Nazi crimes, see F. Werkentin, *Politische Strafjustiz in der Ära Ulbricht: Vom bekennenden Terror zur verdeckten Repression*, 2nd edition (Berlin, 1997), 22.
34. J. Morré, 'Sowjetische Speziallager in Deutschland', unpublished manuscript in the possession of the author; von Plato, 'Geschichte', 32–3, 40–1, 53–6; Niethammer, 'Internierungslager', 98–108.
35. For the DJV, see Wentker, *Justiz*, *passim*. For a very brief summary, see F. Werkentin, 'Justizgeschichte in der SBZ/DDR 1945–1989', *Archiv für Sozialgeschichte* 42 (2002), 448–55, here esp. 449.
36. ThHStAW, Ministerium für Justiz Nr. 292, Bl. 3–5: Deutsche Zentrale Justizverwaltung to Landes- und Provinzialverwaltungen, 16 Oct. 1945. See also Wentker, *Justiz*, 203–7, 213–22; Oleschinski, 'Abteilung Strafvollzug', 83–4.
37. Wentker, *Justiz*, 207–13.
38. The transformation of the justice system is described in detail in Werkentin, *Politische Strafjustiz*, *passim*; Wentker, *Justiz*, *passim*; Pohl, *Justiz*, *passim*.

39. Werkentin, *Politische Strafjustiz*, 161–83, 325–9.
40. Evans, *Rituals*, 833–4.
41. On average, around 180 individuals (per 100,000 inhabitants) were imprisoned in East Germany between 1970 and 1990. In Nazi Germany, this figure was around 183 in 1936 (including concentration camps). In West Germany, the figure was 87 between 1970 and 1990. See J. Arnold, ' "Strafvollzug in der DDR". Ein Gegenstand gegenwärtiger und zukünftiger Forschung', *MSchriftKrim* 76 (1993), 390–404, here 395. For the Third Reich figures, see below.
42. Wentker, *Justiz*, 215, 369–92.
43. Wentker, *Justiz*, 381, 393–4 (quote on 393), 594; H. Mehner, 'Aspekte zur Entwicklung des Straf- und Untersuchungshaftvollzugs in der ehemaligen sowjetischen Besatzungszone (SBZ) sowie in den Anfangsjahren der DDR', *ZfStrVo* 41 (1992), 91–8; M. Bath, 'Strafvollzug in der DDR', *ZfStrVo* 38 (1989), 343–4.
44. For a comparison between the legal apparatus in East Germany and the Third Reich, see Pohl, *Justiz*, 307–26.
45. Ibid., 326–41.
46. M. Mazower, 'Violence and the State in the Twentieth Century', *American Historical Review* 107 (2002), 1158–78.
47. P.H. Solomon, *Soviet Criminal Justice under Stalin* (Cambridge, 1996), esp. 196–229, 299–334, 447–69. See also L. Radzinowicz, 'Penal Regressions', *Cambridge Law Journal* 50 (1991), 422–44, here 425–7; R. Service, *A History of Twentieth-Century Russia* (London, 1998), 228.
48. M. Jakobson, 'Die Funktionen und die Struktur des sowjetischen Gefängnis- und Lagersystems von 1928 bis 1934', in D. Dahlmann, G. Hirschfeld (eds), *Lager, Zwangsarbeit, Vertreibung und Deportation* (Essen, 1999), 207–21. This article summarises aspects of the same author's *Origins of the Gulag. The Soviet Prison Camp System 1917–1934* (Lexington, 1993). See also Service, *Russia*, 223–4; Solomon, *Soviet Criminal Justice*, 125; S. Wheatcroft, 'The Scale and Nature of German and Soviet Repression and Mass Killings, 1930–45', *Europe-Asia Studies* 48 (1996), 1319–53, here 1346.
49. B. Musial, *'Konterrevolutionäre Elemente sind zu erschießen'. Die Brutalisierung des deutsch-sowjetischen Krieges im Sommer 1941* (Berlin, 2000), 98–142.
50. See, above all, Solomon, *Soviet Criminal Justice*, passim. See also R. Pipes, *Legalised Lawlessness. Soviet Revolutionary Justice* (London, 1986); G.T. Rittersporn, 'Zynismus, Selbsttäuschung und unmögliches Kalkül: Strafpolitik und Lagerbevölkerung in der UDSSR', in D. Dahlmann, G. Hirschfeld (eds), *Lager, Zwangsarbeit, Vertreibung und Deportation* (Essen, 1999), 291–315; Service, *Russia*, 210–34; Jakobson, 'Funktion', 218; Wheatcroft, 'Scale', 1335–6.
51. M. Liepmann, *Amerikanische Gefängnisse und Erziehungsanstalten* (Mannheim, 1927); B. Freudenthal, 'Tagebücher der amerikanisch-englischen Studienreise', *BlGefK* 61 (1930), Sonderheft, 133–96.
52. See Figure 10, pp. 402–3; Düsing, 'Abschaffung', 244.
53. L.W. Fox, *The English Prison and Borstal Systems* (London, 1952), 118, 127, 183, 194–5, 232–3; Forsythe, *Penal Discipline*, 236; B. McKelvey, *American Prisons. A History of Good Intentions* (Montclair, 1977), 306–7, 314–15; Grünhut, *Penal Reform*, 208. For the German inmate figures, see Figure 1, pp. 392–3.
54. For non-custodial punishment in Europe, see P. O'Brien, 'The Prison on the Continent', in Morris, Rothman (eds), *Oxford History*, 199–225, here 210–11, 216.

55. For the German prison figures, see BA Berlin, R 3001/9920/2, Bl. 2; Figure 1, pp. 392–3 (the estimated total population at that time was around 64 million in 1927 and 68 million in 1936). For the US figures, see Grünhut, *Penal Reform*, 156. For the remaining figures, see BA Berlin, R 3001/alt R 22/1281, Bl. 334: Report of the International Penal & Penitentiary Commission, 1938.
56. Forsythe, *Penal Discipline*, 175, 201–14; 'General Observations', in Scott (ed.), *German Prisons*, 106–8; Grünhut, *Penal Reform*, 269–74; Fox, *English Prison*, 167–71; E. Rotman, 'The Failure of Reform. United States, 1865–1965', in Morris, Rothman (eds), *Oxford History*, 169–97, here, 183–5; S. McConville, 'The Victorian Prison: England, 1865–1965', ibid., 131–67, here 161.
57. M. Mancini, *One Dies, Get Another. Convict Leasing in the American South, 1866–1928* (Columbia, 1996), passim. See also McKelvey, *American Prisons*, 276.
58. A. Lichtenstein, *Twice the Work of Free Labor. The Political Economy of Convict Labor in the New South* (London, 1996), 152–95. See also Rotman, 'Failure', 176.
59. Grünhut, *Penal Reform*, 392; *Vorentwurf*, 357–8; C. Harding et al., *Imprisonment in England and Wales. A Concise History* (London, 1985), 238; McConville, 'Prison', 156.
60. Langelüddeke, *Entmannung*, 7–21; S. Kühl, *The Nazi Connection. Eugenics, American Racism, and German National Socialism* (New York, 1994), 51.
61. R. Proctor, *Racial Hygiene. Medicine under the Nazis* (Cambridge, Massachusetts, 1988), 97–8; Kühl, *Nazi Connection*, 46; Hansen, 'Denmark', 13–14; Forsythe, *Penal Discipline*, 158.
62. N. Roll-Hansen, 'Scandinavian Eugenics in the International Context', in idem, G. Broberg (eds), *Eugenics and the Welfare State. Sterilization Policy in Denmark, Sweden, Norway, and Finland* (East Lansing, 1996), 259–71; M. Hietala, 'From Race Hygiene to Sterilisation: The Eugenics Movement in Finland', ibid., 195–258, esp. 225–32.
63. Forsythe, *Penal Discipline*, 90; Grünhut, *Penal Reform*, 392, 402; BA Berlin, R 3001/9920/2, Bl. 2–3; Hietala, 'Race Hygiene', 239; Figure 9, pp. 400–1. I wish to thank Dr Stephen Garton (University of Sydney) for the information on Australia.
64. Cited in Möhler, 'Strafvollzug', 28.
65. See, for example, Union für Recht und Freiheit (ed.), *Strafvollzug*, 76; *Sopade*, vol. 3, 52; BA Berlin, R 3001/alt R 22/1292, Bl. 193: Hauptvogel to Dr Wingler, 6 Aug. 1935.
66. 'The Nazi Way with Prisoners', *The Times*, 21 Nov. 1935. See also BA Berlin, R 3001/alt R 22/1286, Bl. 449–75: Teilnehmerliste. One of the few Weimar prison reformers to be invited was the former Untermaßfeld governor Albert Krebs, who was allowed to participate by Erwin Bumke, with whom he had had a good personal relationship; A. Krebs, 'Begegnungen mit Harald Poelchau. Ein Erlebnisbericht', *ZfStrVo* 38 (1989), 67–73.
67. BA Berlin, R 3001/alt R 22/1285, Bl. 45–6: RJM, Vermerk, 21 May 1935.
68. Ibid., R 3001/alt R 22/1292, Bl. 359–74: Vorstand der SPD, Entwicklungstendenzen im Deutschen Strafvollzug, 1935. For the reception, see ibid., R 3001/alt R 22/1286, Bl. 260–5: J. Scharffenberg, 'Eine Anklageschrift an den Gefängniskongress in Berlin', *Arbeiderbladet*, 13 Aug. 1935; ibid., R 3001/alt R 22/1299, Bl. 182: Gesandtschaft Stockholm to Auswärtiges Amt, 9 Aug. 1935.
69. BA Berlin, R 3001/alt R 22/1299, Bl. 131: C.M. Craven, 'Berlin Congress on Penal Reform', *Manchester Guardian*, 3 Aug. 1935.
70. Ibid., Bl. 163: 'Ein Kongreß beginnt zu arbeiten', *B.Z. am Mittag*, 20 Aug. 1935; ibid., Bl. 168: 'Gürtner Ehrenpräsident', *Kölnische Zeitung*, 20 Aug. 1935; ibid., Bl. 200–3: Gesandtschaft Stockholm to Auswärtiges Amt, 27 Aug. 1935; 'Dr Goebbels on Nazi Methods', *The Times*, 24 Aug. 1935.

71. G.H.C. Bing, 'The International Penal and Penitentiary Congress, Berlin 1935', *The Howard Journal* 4 (1935), 195–8, here 195.
72. 'Criminal Law in Germany', *The Times*, 22 Aug. 1935.
73. 'Herr Thälmann. Foreign Visitors to Prison', *The Times*, 23 Aug. 1935.
74. BA Berlin, R 3001/alt R 22/4201, Bl. 77–9: Gutachten von Professor Dahm; ibid., Bl. 80–3: Gutachten von Dr Schmidt; ibid., R 3001/alt R 22/1292, Bl. 345–6: extract of an article by Graf Gleispach; 'Human Treatment of Criminals', *The Times*, 24 Aug. 1935. For the quotation, see ibid., R 3001/alt R 22/1300, Bl. 219: 'Der Strafvollzug', *Der Deutsche Justizbeamte*, 8 Sept. 1935.
75. See, for example, BA Berlin, R 3001/alt R 22/1300, Bl. 56: Deutsche Botschaft Washington, Bericht, 14 Sept. 1935; ibid., R 3001/alt R 22/1286: Bl. 370–1: RJM, Vermerk, 31 Aug. 1935; 'Penal Congress Meeting', *The Times*, 27 Aug. 1935.
76. 'Penal Congress Meeting', *The Times*, 30 Aug. 1935.
77. Cited in Möhler, 'Strafvollzug', 32. See also ibid., 31–2; BA Berlin, R 3001/alt R 22/1286, Bl. 332–6: Entschließungen des Kongresses, Dritte Sektion.

Conclusion

1. Broszat, *Staat Hitlers*, 403–4.
2. Quoted in Johnson, *Nazi Terror*, 219.
3. This last point is also emphasised in Noam, Kropat, *Justiz*, vol. 1, 283.
4. Burleigh, *Third Reich*, 162, 199.
5. See, more generally, W. Naucke, 'NS-Strafrecht: Perversion oder Anwendungsfall moderner Kriminalpolitik?', *Rechtshistorisches Journal* 11 (1992), 279–92.
6. See Figure 6, pp. 398–9.
7. Jenner, 'Norwegische Gefangene', 273–4.
8. Cited in Lagebericht des OLG Präsidenten Bamberg, 1942, reprinted in Bundesminister der Justiz (ed.), *Justiz*, 295.
9. See Wildt, *Generation*, passim.
10. Rede vor Generälen in Sonthofen, 5 May 1944, cit. in Smith, Peterson (eds), *Himmler*, 198.
11. On the approach of legal historians to the conflict between natural and positive law, see Stolleis, *Law*, 5–6.
12. Gesetz zur Änderung des Strafgesetzbuchs, 28 June 1935, reprinted in Hirsch *et al.* (eds), *Recht*, 455–6.
13. For criticism of the use by legal historians of the concept of the 'Dual State', see also M. Frommel, 'Verbrechensbekämpfung im Nationalsozialismus', in M. Stolleis (ed.), *Die Bedeutung der Wörter* (Munich, 1991), 47–64, here 58–9.
14. Weckbecker, *Sondergerichte*, 411.
15. For this claim, see, for example, Gruchmann, 'Die "rechtsprechende Gewalt"', 88.
16. Fraenkel, *Dual State*, quotes on 73, 40, 50, 51–2. Fraenkel's collected works have recently been published in Germany, where he taught after his return in 1951. See A. von Brünneck *et al.* (eds), *Ernst Fraenkel. Gesammelte Schriften*, 4 vols (Baden-Baden 1999–2000).
17. Leiter der Partei-Kanzlei to Chef der Reichskanzlei, 10 June 1942, reprinted in Broszat, 'Perversion', 430–1.
18. Noakes, Pridham (eds), *Nazism*, vol. 2, 574.

19. For dissatisfaction with the regime in 1934, see Frei, *National Socialist Rule*, 3–18.
20. Cited in Weckbecker, *Sondergerichte*, 801.
21. See K. Marxen, 'Strafjustiz im Nationalsozialismus', in B. Diestelkamp, M. Stolleis (eds), *Justizalltag im Dritten Reich* (Frankfurt am Main, 1988), 101–11.
22. For this analysis, see Marxen, *Volk*, 50–6, 87.
23. Stolle, *Geheime Staatspolizei*, 252–65; Paul, 'Private Konfliktregulierung', *passim*; Johnson, *Nazi Terror*, 363–4. For the arrests of 'professional criminals' and 'asocials' in the late 1930s, see Wagner, *Kriminalpolizei*, 254–98.
24. Marxen, *Volk*, 69.
25. Cited in Dörner, *'Heimtücke'*, 314. See ibid., 313–15.
26. For this point, see Tuchel, *Konzentrationslager*, 357, note 30.
27. See I. Kershaw, ' "Working towards the Führer". Reflections on the Nature of the Hitler Dictatorship', *Contemporary European History* 2 (1993), 103–18; D. Rebentisch, *Führerstaat und Verwaltung im Zweiten Weltkrieg* (Stuttgart, 1989), for the quotation 550.
28. Cited in Gruchmann, 'Rechtssystem', 91.
29. For a scathing attack on the 'positivism tale', see Müller, *Furchtbare Juristen*, 221–6, quote on 224.
30. Ludewig, Kuessner, *Sondergericht Braunschweig*, 303.

Bibliography

Archival Sources

Bayerisches Hauptstaatsarchiv

MF (Bayerisches Staatsministerium der Finanzen)
    67427

MInn (Bayerisches Staatsministerium des Inneren)
    71560   71571   71579

MJu (Bayerisches Staatsministerium der Justiz)

7149	22470–22473	22484	22489	22493
22495	22496	22498	22499	22504
22507–22510	22512	22515	22522	22523
22525	22535	22556	22616–22620	22663
22675	22686	22694	22726	22727
22847	22866			

StK (Staatskanzlei)
    13944

Bundesarchiv Berlin

NS 10 (Persönliche Adjutantur des Führers und Reichskanzlers)
    1447

Bibliography 489

NS 19 (Persönlicher Stab Reichsführer SS)
    4014

R 2/Pers. SG (former Berlin Document Centre)
    Wilhelm Crohne   Karl Engert   Kurt Giese   Kurt-Walter Hanssen
    Rudolf Marx

R 3 (Reichsministerium für Rüstung und Kriegsproduktion)
    1602

R 43 II (Reichskanzlei)

1537	1538	1549	1560 b

R 58 (Reichssicherheitshauptamt)

473	1027	2235

R 137 V (Stammlager Sosnowitz)

4	5	14

R 3001 (Reichsministerium der Justiz)

5603	5606	5611	5629–5632	5658–5660
5982	6094	6709	9803/64	9803/78
9819–9821	9829	9852	9854	9859
9862	9863	9882	9908	9919
9920/2	9923	9934	9936	9939
9945	9949	9957	9993	

R 3001/alt R 22 (Reichsministerium der Justiz)

28	131	245	706	721
734	848	895	897	945
946	1089	1157	1158	1160
1238	1239	1247	1259	1261–1263
1266	1273	1277	1278	1281
1285	1286	1292	1299	1300
1334–1338	1343	1344	1395	1399
1400	1417	1422	1424	1429
1430	1437	1438	1439	1440–1443
1451	1453	1456	1467	1469
2946	3379	4003	4045	4048
4049	4051–4054	4062	4085	4089
4162	4199–4201	4273	4277	4349
4371	4372	4552	4688	4720
5015	5016	5023	5024	5027
5028	5054–5055	5087	5094–5096	5103

R 3001/alt R 22/Pers. (Reichsministerium der Justiz, Personalakten)

54545	55261	55468	56247	57079
57132	53758	53759	58396–58400	58943
58944	58947	58951	59371	67687
78253	Edgar Schmidt		Rudolf Schwerdtfeger	
Hermann von Reitzenstein				

Bibliography

61 Re 1 (Reichslandbund, Generalia)
    1527   1528

62 DAF 3 (Deutsche Arbeitsfront, Zentralbüro)
    1786   1787   1808

99 US (Nuremberg trial documents)
    2 FC 585, Microfilm 22933   2 FC 588, Mikrofilm 22941
    2 FC 588, Mikrofilm 22942   2 FC 38577/47455 P
    2 FC 38580/47458 P   2 FC 38593/47471 P
    57991

Film (Nuremberg trial documents)
    14769   41305   44169   44184   44320
    44325   44327   44564   44837   44840
    55272   72522

SAPMO (Stiftung Archiv der Parteien und Massenorganisationen der DDR)
    RY 1
    1/I 2/3/163
    BY 5
    V 279/91   V 279/94
    DY 54
    V 277/1/10   V 277/1/15   V 277/1/29
    DY 55
    62/2/169   62/2/170   V 278/6/592

Geheimes Staatsarchiv Preußischer Kulturbesitz

Rep 84a (Preußisches Justizministerium)
    17608 (M)   17962 (M)

Hessisches Hauptstaatsarchiv

Abt. 468, Nr. 426 (Verfahren 2 Ks 2/51 StA Wiesbaden)
    1   2   9   11   14
    16   18–20

Institut für Zeitgeschichte, München

ED 106 (Archiv Walter Hammer)
    1   79   86

Fotokopiensammlung
    F 37/2   Fa 183   Fa 245/32

Gerichtsakten
    Gh 08.02.

Manuskripte
   Ms 361

Mikrofilmsammlung
   MA 192   MA 193/1   MA 193/2   MA 313
   MA 624   MA 625   MB 1

Spruchkammerakten
   Sp 1.13.   Sp 1.15.

Justizvollzugsanstalt Straubing

   Selected uncatalogued documents

Landesarchiv Berlin

   Rep 5 Acc 2863 (Kriminalbiologische Untersuchungsstelle)
      97   98   129

Landeshauptarchiv Brandenburg, Zweigarchiv Bornim

   Ld. Br. Rep. 214 (Forschungsstelle Zuchthaus Brandenburg)
      1   2   32

   Pr. Br. Rep. 4 A (Kammergericht, Personalia)
      396

   Pr. Br. Rep. 12 A (Landgericht Berlin)
      171

   Pr. Br. Rep. 29 (Zuchthaus Brandenburg)
      Do. 19   419   691   723   775
      776   817   826   1010   1210
      3096   4014   5117   5652   6425
      8152   10126

   Pr. Br. Rep. 29 (Zuchthaus Luckau)
      122   414

Max-Planck-Institut für Psychiatrie, Historisches Archiv, München

   GDA (Genealogisch-Demographische Abteilung)
39

Nordrhein-Westfälisches Hauptstaatsarchiv, Zweigarchiv Schloss Kalkum

   Gerichte Rep. 22 (Generalstaatsanwalt bei dem Oberlandesgericht in Köln)
      343

Gerichte Rep. 321 (Generalstaatsanwalt bei dem Oberlandesgericht in Düsseldorf)

406	473	550	571	611
682	758	759	780	873
878	886	975	1028	1030
1044	1140	1281		

Public Record Office, Kew

WO (War Office)

309/151	309/199	309/1292	311/520

Staatsanwaltschaft Kiel

2 Ks 1/70 StA Kiel

Staatsarchiv München

Justizvollzugsanstalten

13	24	27	29	30
38	40	47	61	252
412	461	699	1203	1797
1820	2339	2400	2950	3001
4818	5258	5470	6051	6234
7610	7719	7793	8223	9000
9053	9840	10514	10756	11660
12019	12333	12334	12338	12340
13685	13693	13704	13779	13789
13794	13807	13816	13822	13832

Generalstaatsanwalt bei dem Oberlandesgericht in München

49	51	52

Strafvollzugsmuseum Ludwigsburg

Selected uncatalogued documents

Thüringisches Hauptstaatsarchiv

Thüringisches Justizministerium

397	414	421	423	1337
1339	1340	1354	1364	1398
1573	1683	1707	1712	1716
1718	1719	1765	1768	1779
1781				

Personalakten Thüringisches Justizministerium
    Albert Krebs   Julius Mentzner   Max Vollrath
Generalstaatsanwalt bei dem Oberlandesgericht in Jena
    197   206   229   230   430–433
    604   636   637   690   701
    732   754   755   757   767
    812   825   855   856   997/1
    1049   1050   1066   1067   1069
    1071   1086

Ministerium für Justiz
    292

Thüringisches Staatsarchiv Meiningen

HSM Staatsministerium, Abteilung Justiz
    985

Der Vorstand der Strafanstalt Untermaßfeld
    P. 2

Zuchthaus Untermaßfeld
    2   13   44   62   66
    184   227   309   311   346
    347   366   414   448   564
    644   656   659   663   664
    695   718   738   752   756
    757   789   802   803   826
    1018   1114   1381   1388   1392
    1420   1427   1438   1569   1580
    1589   1679   1785   2018

Wiener Library, London

EW (Eyewitness Testimony)
    4   6   8

Zentrale Stelle der Landesjustizverwaltungen in Ludwigsburg

VI 415 AR–Nr 1310/63   II 416 AR–Nr 2643/65
IV 439 AR–Nr 3305/65   VI 416 AR–Nr 1540/65
1 J 13/65 (RSHA)   VI 416 AR–Nr 1127/66
VI 107 AR–Z 114/67   449 AR–Nr 1045/67
VI AR–Z 81/68   VI 416 AR–Nr 477/68
211 AR–Nr 190/72   UNWCC, 3872/Cz/G/74
109 AR–Nr 13.683/87   Sammelakte Nr. 27
Sammelakte Nr. 27a   Sammelakte Nr. 422
Verschiedenes, 301 Cz, Nr. 184

Primary Printed Sources

Akten der deutschen Bischöfe über die Lage der Kirchen 1933–1945, vol. 6 (Mainz, 1985).
Akten der Reichskanzlei. Die Regierung Hitler 1933–1938, part 1, vol. 2 (Boppard, 1983).
'Anregungen der Vereinigung der Preußischen Staatsanwälte zu Ersparnissen auf dem Gebiet der Justizverwaltung und Rechtsprechung', *Juristische Wochenschrift* 61 (1932), 917–18.
'Arbeitsgemeinschaft für Reform des Strafvollzugs', *BlGefK* 56 (1924–25), 121–5.
Aschaffenburg, G., *Das Verbrechen und seine Bekämpfung*, 3rd edition (Heidelberg, 1923).
—— 'Hahnöfersand', *MSchriftKrim* 15 (1924), 346–51.
—— 'Die Stellung des Psychiaters zur Strafrechtsreform', *MSchriftKrim* 16 (1925), 145–66.
—— 'Einheitlichkeit der Sicherungsmaßnahmen', *MSchriftKrim* 22 (1931), 257–65.
—— 'Gleichzeitige Anordnung der Entmannung und der Sicherungsverwahrung', *MSchriftKrim* 26 (1935), 385–8.
Assmann, F., 'Betrachtungen über die auf Grund des Gesetzes vom 24.11.1933 zur Sicherung und Besserung in der Brandenburgischen Landesanstalt in Neuruppin untergebrachten geistig abnormen Rechtsbrecher' (Ph.D., University of Munich, 1939).
'Auszug aus dem Gesetz gegen gefährliche Gewohnheitsverbrecher und über Maßregeln der Sicherung und Besserung', in *Gesetz zur Verhütung erbkranken Nachwuchses vom 14. Juli 1933. Bearbeitet und erläutert von A. Gütt, E. Rüdin, F. Ruttke*, 1st edition (Munich, 1934), 179–214.
Ayaß, W. (ed.), *'Gemeinschaftsfremde'. Quellen zur Verfolgung von 'Asozialen' 1933–1945* (Koblenz, 1998).
Bayerisches Obsorge Amt (ed.), *Die Gefangenenobsorge* (Lichtenau, 1928).
Bayerisches Staatsministerium der Justiz (ed.), *Der Stufenstrafvollzug und die kriminalbiologischen Untersuchungen der Gefangenen in den bayerischen Strafanstalten*, 3 vols (Munich, 1926, 1928, 1929).
Bayerisches Statistisches Landesamt (ed.), *Verbrechen und Verbrechertum in Bayern 1882 bis 1937* (Munich, 1944).
Begemann, G., 'Strafvollzug an Frauen', *BlGefK* 69 (1938–39), 202–6.
Behrle, A., *Die Stellung der deutschen Sozialisten zum Strafvollzug von 1870 bis zur Gegenwart* (Berlin, 1931).
'Bericht über die XVII. Versammlung zugleich Fünfzigjährige Jubiläumsfeier des Vereins der deutschen Strafanstaltsbeamten e.V. in Hamburg vom 25.–29. Mai 1914', *BlGefK* 48 (1914), 291–526.
Berkholz, S. (ed.), *Carl von Ossietzky. 227 Tage im Gefängnis. Briefe, Dokumente, Texte* (Darmstadt, 1988).
'Beschlossene Thesen auf der Augsburger Versammlung 1927', *BlGefK* 59 (1928), 5–9.
Bing, G.H.C., 'The International Penal and Penitentiary Congress, Berlin 1935', *The Howard Journal* 4 (1935), 195–8.
Birkigt, C., 'Die Wirkung der bei Kriegsausbruch erlassenen allgemeinen Amnestie', *BlGefK* 49 (1915), 161–6.
Birnbaum, K., *Die psychopathischen Verbrecher*, 2nd edition (Leipzig, 1926).
Boberach, H. (ed.), *Meldungen aus dem Reich, 1938–1945*, 17 vols (Herrsching, 1984).
Boeters, G., 'Ein dreißigmal bestrafter Exhibitionist', *MSchriftKrim* 24 (1933), 418–22.
Bondy, C., 'Zur Frage der Erziehbarkeit', *ZStW* 48 (1928), 329–34.
—— '"Geschlecht in Fesseln"', *MSchriftKrim* 20 (1929), 166–8.
—— 'Moritz Liepmann', *BlGefK* 61 (1930), 279–81.
—— 'Fortschritte und Hemmungen in der Strafvollzugsreform', *MSchriftKrim*, Beiheft 3 (Heidelberg, 1930), 90–102.

Borchers, P., 'Die Gefangenenarbeit in den deutschen Strafanstalten', *BlGefK* 54 (1921), 7–146.
Brandenburgische Landeszentrale für politische Bildung (ed.), *Was bleibt, ist die Hoffnung. Eine Briefdokumentation aus Brandenburger Konzentrationslagern, Zuchthäusern und Gefängnissen der NS-Zeit 1933–1945* (Potsdam, 1994).
Brandstätter, H., 'Verpflegung der Strafgefangenen', *MSchriftKrim* 23 (1932), 111–13.
—— 'Zur Situation der Strafvollzugsreform', *MSchriftKrim* 23 (1932), 431–2.
—— 'Erfahrungen im Strafvollzug an Gefangenen, die wegen Verstoßes gegen das Verbot der Internationalen Bibelforscher bestraft worden sind', *BlGefK* 70 (1939), 48–55.
Brenner, 'Internationale Kriminalistische Vereinigung', *Deutsche Richterzeitung* 24 (1932), 306–8.
Broszat, M. (ed.), *Kommandant in Auschwitz. Autobiographische Aufzeichnungen des Rudolf Höß* (Munich, 1963).
Buchwitz, O., *50 Jahre Funktionär der deutschen Arbeiterbewegung* (Stuttgart, 1949).
Bumke, E. (ed.), *Deutsches Gefängniswesen. Ein Handbuch* (Berlin, 1928).
—— 'Die Freiheitsstrafe als Problem der Gesetzgebung', in idem (ed.), *Deutsches Gefängniswesen*, 16–32.
Bund der Gefängnis-, Straf- und Erziehungsbeamten und -Beamtinnen Deutschlands (ed.), *Der Aufsichtsbeamte im Strafvollzuge* (no place, no date, around 1927).
—— *Probleme der Strafvollzugsreform* (Berlin, 1930).
Bundesminister der Justiz (ed.), *Justiz und Nationalsozialismus* (Cologne, 1989).
Burgmair, W. et al. (eds), *Emil Kraepelin. Kriminologische und forensische Schriften* (Munich, 2001).
Cleric, G.F. von, 'Das Sexualproblem im Strafvollzug', *MSchriftKrim* 20 (1929), 621–7.
Dahm, G., Schaffstein, F., *Liberales oder autoritäres Strafrecht?* (Hamburg, 1933).
Degen, R., *Der Strafvollzug in Stufen in den bayerischen Strafanstalten* (Straubing, no date, 1924–25).
—— 'Zur Einführung', in Bayerisches Staatsministerium der Justiz (ed.), *Der Stufenstrafvollzug und die kriminalbiologischen Untersuchungen der Gefangenen in den bayerischen Strafanstalten*, vol. 1 (Munich, 1926), 3–8.
Deimling, G., *Erziehung und Bildung im Freiheitsentzug* (Frankfurt am Main, 1980).
Der Leuchtturm, vol. 18 (1942).
'Die für den Strafvollzugsbeamten wichtigen, seit dem 30. Januar 1933 erlassenen Bestimmungen', *BlGefK* 66 (1935), Beilage zu Heft 3, 1–15.
'Die Preußentagung des Vereins der deutschen Strafanstaltsbeamten', *BlGefK* 62 (1931), 1–329.
'Die selbstständigen Vollzugsanstalten der Reichsjustizverwaltung', *BlGefK* 71 (1940), 338–54.
'Die Strafanstalten in Deutschland', Sonderheft zu Band 56 der *BlGefK* (Heidelberg, 1925).
'Die Wende im Strafvollzug!', *Der Strafvollzug* 23 (1933), 153–64.
'Diskussion', *MKG* 4 (1933), 267–76.
Döblin, A., *Berlin Alexanderplatz. Die Geschichte von Franz Biberkopf* (Munich, 1995).
Dohna, Graf zu, 'Besprechung von Gustav Aschaffenburg, Das Verbrechen und seine Bekämpfung', *MSchriftKrim* 14 (1923), 323–6.
Domarus, M. (ed.), *Hitler. Reden und Proklamationen 1932–1945*, 4 vols (Wiesbaden, 1973).
Dressel, G., *75 Jahre Freistaat Thüringen. Wahlen und Abstimmungsergebnisse 1920–1995* (Erfurt, 1995).
Dübbers, 'Vierjahresplan und Außenarbeit der Gefangenen', *BlGefK* 68 (1937–38), 365–9.
Dubitscher, F., 'Asozialität und Unfruchtbarmachung', *MKG* 5 (1938), 99–110.
Eberhard, W., 'Vergleich der Gewichtsverhältnisse bei Gefangenen des Zuchthauses und der Sicherungsanstalt in Brandenburg (Havel)-Görden', *BlGefK* 68 (1937), 470–5.
—— 'Zu neuen Wegen im Strafvollzug', *MSchriftKrim* 33 (1942), 59–68.

—— 'Zur Frage der ausmerzenden Erbpflege', *Psychiatrisch-Neurologische Wochenschrift* 45 (1943), Nr. 2, 9–11.
Echternacht, K., 'Modernes Strafrecht, Strafvollzug und öffentliches Gewissen', *MdRfW* 7 (1932), 18–25.
Eden, K., 'Prison Economy', in Scott (ed.), *German Prisons*, 47–53.
Eichler, J., 'Neuzeitlicher Strafvollzug', *ZStW* 48 (1928), 171–94.
—— 'Der Begriff des Erstbestraften', *BlGefK* 71 (1940), 291–5.
Eiden, H., 'Das war Buchenwald. Tatsachenbericht', in H. Gobrecht (ed.), *Eh' die Sonne lacht. Hans Eiden – Kommunist und Lagerältester im KZ Buchenwald* (Bonn, 1995), 207–64.
Ellering, E., 'Der Strafvollzug an Frauen', in Bumke (ed.), *Gefängniswesen*, 353–62.
Ellger, H., 'Der Strafvollzug in Stufen', *BlGefK* 57 (1926), 189–233.
Engelberg, von, 'Dem Gedächtnis Eugen von Jagemann's', *BlGefK* 57 (1926), 159–64.
Erfurth, E., 'Staatsbürgerliche Erziehung in der Gefängnisschule', *BlGefK* 46 (1912), 191–209.
'Erlass des Preussischen Ministeriums des Inneren vom 8.3.1907 die Anfertigung von Characteristiken Gefangener betreffend', *BlGefK* 43 (1909), 542–3.
'Ersparnisvorschläge des Preußischen Richtervereins', *Juristische Wochenschrift* 61 (1932), 916–17.
Exner, F., *Studien über die Strafzumessungspraxis der deutschen Gerichte* (Leipzig, 1931).
—— 'Der Vollzug der bessernden und sichernden Maßnahmen', in Frede, Grünhut (eds), *Reform*, 244–60.
—— 'Über Rückfall-Prognosen', *MSchriftKrim* 27 (1936), 401–9.
—— 'Wie erkennt man den gefährlichen Gewohnheitsverbrecher?', *Deutsche Justiz* 11 (1943), 377–9.
Fallada, H., *Strafgefangener Zelle 32. Tagebuch* (Berlin, 1998).
Fechenbach, F., *Im Haus der Freudlosen. Bilder aus den Zuchthaus* (Berlin, 1925).
Fetscher, R., 'Die Organisation der erbbiologischen Erforschung der Strafgefangenen in Sachsen', *BlGefK* 57 (1926), 69–75.
—— 'Zur Theorie und Praxis der Sterilisierung', *MKG* 4 (1933), 247–57.
Fickert, H., *Rassenhygienische Verbrechensbekämpfung* (Leipzig, 1938).
Finke, H., *Der Rechtsbrecher im Lichte der Erziehung* (Weimar, 1931).
—— 'Kastration von Sexualverbrechern', *BlGefK* 64 (1933), 130–65.
—— 'Der zukünftige Strafvollzug', *MSchriftKrim* 26 (1935), 537–40.
Finkelnburg, K.M., 'Die Psychologie des Gefangenen', in Preußisches Justizministerium (ed.), *Strafvollzug in Preußen*, 73–82.
Frank, H., 'Der Sinn der Strafe', *BlGefK* 66 (1935), 191–2.
—— 'Strafrechts- und Strafvollzugsprobleme', *BlGefK* 68 (1937), 259–68.
Frede, L., Grünhut, M. (eds), *Reform des Strafvollzuges* (Berlin, 1927).
—— 'Der Strafvollzug in Stufen', ibid., 102–36.
—— 'Der Strafvollzug in Stufen in Thüringen', *ZStW* 46 (1925), 233–48.
—— 'Zur Einführung', in *Gefängnisse in Thüringen. Berichte über die Reform des Strafvollzugs* (Weimar, 1930), 1–8.
—— 'Was soll aus dem Entwurf des Strafvollzugsgesetzes werden?', *MSchriftKrim* 22 (1931), 161–5.
Freisler, R., 'Ein Querschnitt durch die Fragen der Sicherungsverwahrung', ibid., 7–14.
Freisler, R., Schlegelberger, F. (eds), *Dringende Fragen der Sicherungsverwahrung* (Berlin, 1938).
Frese, H., *Bremsklötze am Siegeswagen der Nation* (Bremen, 1989).
Freudenthal, B., 'Maßregeln der Sicherung und Besserung', in P.F. Aschrott, E. Kohlrausch (eds), *Reform des Strafrechts* (Berlin, 1926), 153–72.

—— 'Die rechtliche Stellung der Gefangenen', in Bumke (ed.), *Gefängniswesen*, 141–6.
—— 'Tagebücher der amerikanisch-englischen Studienreise', *BlGefK* 61 (1930), Sonderheft, 133–96.
Fröhlich, E. (ed.), *Die Tagebücher von Joseph Goebbels*, part I: 1924–41, 4 vols (Munich, 1987).
—— *Die Tagebücher von Joseph Goebbels*, part II: 1941–45, 15 vols (Munich, 1993–96).
Fuchs, G., *Wir Zuchthäusler. Erinnerungen des Zellengefangenen Nr. 2911 im Zuchthaus geschrieben* (Munich, 1931).
Gaupp, R., 'Über den heutigen Stand der Lehre vom "geborenen Verbrecher"', *MSchriftKrim* 1 (1904), 25–42.
Gebert, 'Umfang der in Preußen geschlossenen Gefangenenanstalten', *MSchriftKrim* 23 (1932), 754–5.
Gehrmann, C., Kuttner, E., 'Parlament und Strafvollzug', in Preußisches Justizministerium (ed.), *Strafvollzug in Preußen*, 30–7.
Gentz, W., 'Der moderne Strafvollzug', *ZStW* 46 (1925), 129–52.
—— 'Berufsverbrecher', in Bumke (ed.), *Gefängniswesen*, 334–52.
—— 'Das Sexualproblem im Strafvollzuge', *ZStW* 50 (1929), 406–27.
Gerstenberg, B., 'Der gläserne Sarg. Erinnerungen an das Zuchthaus Brandenburg in den Jahren 1938–1940', *aus politik und zeitgeschichte* 18 (3 May 1980), 19–32.
Gesetz zur Änderung des Gesetzes zur Verhütung erbkranken Nachwuchses, 26 June 1935, Reichsgesetzblatt, part I, 773.
Gesetz zur Verhütung erbkranken Nachwuchses vom 14. Juli 1933. Bearbeitet und erläutert von A. Gütt, E. Rüdin, F. Ruttke, 1st edition (Munich, 1934).
Gieseler, H., 'Landesstrafanstalt Untermaßfeld. Die Einzelbehandlung auf der I. Stufe', in *Gefängnisse in Thüringen. Berichte über die Reform des Strafvollzugs* (Weimar, 1930), 82–96.
Großmann, K., 'Strafvollzug', in Deutsche Liga für Menschenrechte (ed.), *Acht Jahre Politische Justiz* (Berlin, 1927).
Grüllich, 'Der Gewohnheitsverbrecher nach dem Entwurfe des neuen Strafgesetzbuchs', *MSchriftKrim* 18 (1927), 671–8.
'Grundsätze für den Vollzug von Freiheitsstrafen vom 7. Juni 1923' *Reichsgesetzblatt*, part II.
Grünhut, M., 'Rechtliche Garantien im Strafvollzug', in Frede, Grünhut (eds), *Reform*, 17–30.
Gumbel, E.J., 'Strafvollzugsstatistik', *Die Justiz* 5 (1929/30), 690–703.
—— 'Strafvollzugsstatistik', *Die Justiz* 5 (1929/30), 738–58.
—— 'Strafvollzugsstatistik', *Die Justiz* 6 (1930/31), 21–42.
Haensel, W. 'Militärische Formen im Strafvollzuge', *BlGefK* 67 (1936), 166–70.
Hapke, E., 'Landesstrafanstalt Untermaßfeld. Die Behandlung in der Gemeinschaft der II. Stufe', in *Gefängnisse in Thüringen. Berichte über die Reform des Strafvollzugs* (Weimar, 1930), 96–105.
Hasse, A., 'Die Gefangenenanstalten in Deutschland und die Organisation ihrer Verwaltung', in Bumke (ed.), *Gefängniswesen*, 33–70.
Hau, C., *Lebenslänglich* (Berlin, 1925).
Heiber, B., Heiber, H. (eds), *Die Rückseite des Hakenkreuzes* (Munich, 1993).
Heimberger, J., 'Sterilisierung und Strafrecht', *MSchriftKrim* 15 (1924), 154–66.
—— 'Berthold Freudenthal', *BlGefK* 60 (1929), 232–7.
Heindl, R., *Der Berufsverbrecher. Ein Beitrag zur Strafrechtsreform* (Berlin, 1926).
Heinke, P., 'Der Strafvollzug in Sachsen nach dem 5. März 1933', *BlGefK* 65 (1934), 140–65.
Hellmer, J., *Der Gewohnheitsverbrecher und die Sicherungsverwahrung 1934–1945* (Berlin, 1961).

Hellstern, E.P., 'Bekämpfung des Verbrechertums. Strafvollzug in Stufen und soziale Fürsorge für Verbrecher', *MSchriftKrim* 17 (1926), 142–53.
—— 'Bekämpfung des Verbrechertums. Sicherungsverwahrung, nichtbegrenzte Strafzeit und Sterilisation', *Archiv für Psychiatrie und Nervenkrankheiten* 78 (1926), 705–30.
Hentig, H. von, *Strafrecht und Auslese* (Berlin, 1914).
—— 'Die Anpassung des Verbrechens an die Deflation', *MSchriftKrim* 18 (1927), 51–2.
—— 'Strafanstalten für junge Mütter', *MSchriftKrim* 18 (1927), 374–6.
—— 'Märchen von den 20% Erziehbaren', *MSchriftKrim* 23 (1932), 614–15.
Herrmann, H., 'Militärische Achtungsbezeugungen von Strafgefangenen im Verkehr mit den Gefängnisbehörden', *BlGefK* 50 (1916), 70.
Herr, R., 'Erziehung und gegenerzieherische Kräfte in der Strafvollzugsanstalt. Ein Beitrag zu den Fragen des Sondervollzugs an Gestrauchelten' (Ph.D., University of Jena, 1943).
Hillgruber, A. (ed.), *Staatsmänner und Diplomaten bei Hitler. Vertrauliche Aufzeichnungen über Unterredungen mit Vertretern des Auslandes 1939–1944*, 2 vols (Frankfurt am Main, 1967–70).
Hippel, R. von, *Die korrektionelle Nachhaft* (Freiburg im Breisgau, 1889).
—— 'Zum Reichsgesetz vom 24. November 1933', *BlGefK* 65 (1934), 1–16.
Hirsch, M., Majer, D., Meinck, J. (eds), *Recht, Verwaltung und Justiz im Nationalsozialismus. Ausgewählte Schriften, Gesetze und Gerichtsentscheidungen von 1933 bis 1945* (Cologne, 1984).
Hirsch, W., *Hinter Stacheldraht und Gitter. Erlebnisse und Erfahrungen in den Konzentrationslagern und Gefängnissen Hitlerdeutschlands* (Zurich, 1934).
Hitler, A., *Mein Kampf* (London, 1992), trans. R. Manheim.
Hoelz, M., *Vom 'Weißen Kreuz' zur roten Fahne* (Frankfurt am Main, 1984; first published 1929).
Hoffmann, A., *Unfruchtbarmachung und Kriminalität* (Leipzig, 1940).
Hornig, 'Die Bedeutung des Aufsichtsbeamten im Strafvollzuge', in Preußisches Justizministerium (ed.), *Strafvollzug in Preußen*, 201–10.
Janus, 'Rückblick – Ausblick', *Der Strafvollzug* 22 (1932), 169–75.
Jensch, N., *Untersuchungen an entmannten Sittlichkeitsverbrechern* (Leipzig, 1944).
Jochmann, W. (ed.), *Adolf Hitler. Monologe im Führerhauptquartier 1941–1944* (Hamburg, 1980).
Just, T., 'Rheinisch-Westfälische Gefängnis-Gesellschaft', *BlGefK* 44 (1910), 189–94.
Justizakademie des Landes NRW (ed.), *Zum Strafvollzug 1933–1945 und seiner Vorgeschichte in der Weimarer Republik* (Recklinghausen, no date).
Justizvollzugsanstalt Untermaßfeld (ed.), *Kurzbeschreibung* (Untermaßfeld, 1997).
Kaiser, J.-C., Nowak, K., Schwartz, M. (eds), *Eugenik, Sterilisation, 'Euthanasie'. Politische Biologie in Deutschland 1895–1945* (Berlin, 1992).
Kankeleit, O., *Die Unfruchtbarmachung aus rassenhygienischen und sozialen Gründen* (Munich, 1929).
Kisch, E.E. (ed.), *Max Hoelz. Briefe aus dem Zuchthaus* (Berlin, 1927).
Kleist, F., 'Der Lehrer in der Strafanstalt', in Preußisches Justizministerium (ed.), *Strafvollzug in Preußen*, 185–95.
Klemperer, V., *Ich will Zeugnis ablegen bis zum letzten. Tagebücher 1942–1945* (Berlin, 1995).
Knickenberg, A., '"Der Leuchtturm". Die Reichs-Gefangenenzeitung', *BlGefK* 72 (1941–42), 67–75.
Koch, C., 'Der soziale Gedanke im Strafvollzug', in Bumke (ed.), *Gefängniswesen*, 384–91.
Koerber, L. von, *Menschen im Zuchthaus* (Frankfurt am Main, 1930).

Kogon, E., *Der SS-Staat* (Munich, 1995).
Kosthorst, E., Walter, B. (eds), *Konzentrations- und Strafgefangenenlager im Dritten Reich: Beispiel Emsland*, 3 vols (Düsseldorf, 1983).
Kothe, A., 'Das Problem der Arbeit in den Gefangenenanstalten', *MSchriftKrim* 21 (1930), 342–8.
—— 'Zum künftigen Strafvollzug', *MSchriftKrim* 26 (1935), 127–35.
Kraepelin, E., 'Das Verbrechen als soziale Krankheit', in idem, *Vergeltungsstrafe, Rechtsstrafe, Schutzstrafe. Vier Vorträge* (Heidelberg, 1906), 22–44.
Krebs, A., 'Die Selbstverwaltung Gefangener in der Strafanstalt', *MSchriftKrim* 19 (1928), 152–64.
—— 'Der Erziehungsbeamte in der Strafanstalt', *ZStW* 49 (1928), 65–83.
—— 'Landesstrafanstalt Untermaßfeld. Wesen, Organisation und Grenzen des Vollzugs', in *Gefängnisse in Thüringen. Berichte über die Reform des Strafvollzugs* (Weimar, 1930), 69–81.
—— 'Tagung der "Arbeitsgemeinschaft für Reform des Strafvollzugs"', *ZfStrVo* 1 (1950), Nr. 6, 57.
—— 'Begegnungen mit Harald Poelchau. Ein Erlebnisbericht', *ZfStrVo* 38 (1989), 67–73.
—— 'Strafvollzug am Vorabend des Dritten Reiches', *ZfStrVo* 42 (1993), 11–16.
Kriegsmann, N., *Einführung in die Gefängniskunde* (Heidelberg, 1912).
Kriminalstatistik für das Jahr 1921 (Berlin, 1924).
Kriminalstatistik für das Jahr 1929 (Berlin, 1932).
Kriminalstatistik für das Jahr 1932 (Berlin, 1935).
Kriminalstatistik für das Jahr 1933 (Berlin, 1936).
Kriminalstatistik für das Jahr 1934 (Berlin, 1938).
Kriminalstatistik für die Jahre 1935 und 1936 (Berlin, 1942).
Kriß, R., *Im Zeichen des Ungeistes* (Berchtesgaden, 1995).
Krohne, K., *Lehrbuch der Gefängniskunde* (Stuttgart, 1889).
Krüger, N., '"Wenn Sie nicht ins KZ wollen . . .". Häftlinge in Bombenräumkommandos', *aus politik und zeitgeschichte* 16 (23 Apr. 1977), 25–37.
Lange, J., *Verbrechen als Schicksal. Studien an kriminellen Zwillingen* (Leipzig, 1929).
—— 'In welchem Falle und nach welchen Grundsätzen empfiehlt sich im modernen Strafsystem die Anwendung der Sterilisation durch Kastration oder durch Vasectomie oder Salpingectomie?', *ZStW* 55 (1936), 291–306.
—— and Exner, F., 'Bemerkungen zu Stumpfl: Erbanlage und Verbrechen', *MSchriftKrim* 27 (1936), 329–39.
Langenhan, 'Der Vierjahresplan und die Gefangenenarbeit', *BlGefK* 68 (1937), 294–6.
Leißling, E., 'Die Anstaltsdisziplin', *BlGefK* 64 (1933), 320–9.
Lenz, F., *Menschliche Auslese und Rassenhygiene* (Munich, 1921).
—— 'Rassenhygienische Gesichtspunkte', in Bayerisches Staatsministerium der Justiz (ed.), *Der Stufenstrafvollzug und die kriminalbiologischen Untersuchungen der Gefangenen in den bayerischen Strafanstalten*, vol. 2 (Munich, 1928), 81–6.
Leo, A., *Briefe zwischen Kommen und Gehen* (Berlin, 1991).
Leppmann, F., 'Querulantentum und Psychopathie', *BlGefK* 60 (1929), 215–31.
—— 'Geisteskranke und geistig Minderwertige', in Bumke (ed.), *Gefängniswesen*, 233–55.
Letsche, C., 'Frühjahr 1945 im Zuchthaus Ludwigsburg', in VVN Ludwigsburg (ed.), *Streiflichter aus Verfolgung und Widerstand*, vol. 4 (1990), 20–2.
Leuss, H., *Aus dem Zuchthause* (Berlin, 1903).
Lexer, E., 'Die Eingriffe zur Unfruchtbarmachung des Mannes und zur Entmannung', in *Gesetz zur Verhütung erbkranken Nachwuchses vom 14. Juli 1933. Bearbeitet und erläutert von A. Gütt, E. Rüdin, F. Ruttke*, 2nd edition (Munich, 1936), 319–26.

Liepmann, M., *Die neuen 'Grundsätze über den Vollzug von Freiheitsstrafen' in Deutschland* (Berlin, 1924).
—— *Amerikanische Gefängnisse und Erziehungsanstalten* (Mannheim, 1927).
—— *Krieg und Kriminalität in Deutschland* (Berlin, 1930).
—— 'Die Problematik des "Progressiven Strafvollzugs"', *MSchriftKrim*, Beiheft 1 (Heidelberg, 1926), 56–68.
—— 'Der Strafvollzug als Erziehungsaufgabe', in Frede, Grünhut (eds), *Reform* (Berlin, 1927), 1–16.
Liszt, F. von, 'Der Zweckgedanke im Strafrecht', in idem, *Strafrechtliche Aufsätze und Vorträge*, vol. 1 (Berlin, 1905), 126–79.
—— 'Kriminalpolitische Aufgaben', ibid., 290–467.
Lotz, L., *Der gefährliche Gewohnheitsverbrecher* (Leipzig, 1939).
Luz, W., *Ursachen und Bekämpfung des Verbrechens im Urteil des Verbrechers* (Heidelberg, 1928).
Martell, P., 'Zum Problem der Vorbestraften', *MdRfW* 7 (1932), 10–13.
Mayr, H., 'Die Sicherungsverwahrung in Süddeutschland', *MSchriftKrim* 27 (1936), 209–15.
—— 'Die Wiedereingliederung von Sicherungsverwahrten in die Volksgemeinschaft', *MGGE* 13 (1937–38), 140–4.
Mehlitz, 'Wie wird in der heutigen Zeit die Fürsorge für die Gefangenen betrieben?', *MdRfW* 7 (1932), 28–32.
Meywerk, 'Das soziale Verhalten entmannter Sittlichkeitsverbrecher nach der Haftentlassung', *MSchriftKrim* 29 (1938), 503–7.
Mezger, E., 'Der deutsche Strafgesetzentwurf von 1919', *MSchriftKrim* 13 (1922), 47–75.
—— 'Inwieweit werden durch Sterilisationsmaßnahmen Asoziale erfaßt?', *MKG* 5 (1938), 81–98.
Michaëlis, von, ' "Audiatur et altera pars!" ', *BlGefK* 51 (1917), 74–9.
—— 'Harrende Aufgaben', *BlGefK* 52 (1918), 68–71.
Michel, R., 'Zur Psychologie und Psychopathologie der Strafhaft', *MSchriftKrim* 15 (1924), 58–83.
Michelberger, H., *Berichte aus der Justiz des Dritten Reiches* (Pfaffenweiler, 1989).
Mittermaier, W., 'Der progressive Strafvollzug', *MSchriftKrim* 13 (1922), 270–3.
—— 'Zur Frage der Sicherungsverwahrung', *MSchriftKrim* 23 (1932), 673–6.
Möller, H., *Die Entwicklung und Lebensverhältnisse von 135 Gewohnheitsverbrechern* (Leipzig, 1939).
Muntau, J., 'Entlassenenfürsorge', in Preußisches Justizministerium (ed.), *Strafvollzug in Preußen*, 263–80.
'Nachruf auf Albert Poller', *BlGefK* 64 (1933) 344–8.
Neuhaus, A., 'Die Frau im Gefängnis', in Preußisches Justizministerium (ed.), *Strafvollzug in Preußen*, 114–33.
Neureiter, F., 'Die Organisation des kriminalbiologischen Dienstes in Deutschland', *MKG* 5 (1938), 21–8.
Niekisch, E., *Erinnerungen eines deutschen Revolutionärs*, vol. 1 (Cologne, 1974).
Niethammer, L. (ed.), *Der 'gesäuberte' Antifaschismus. Die SED und die roten Kapos von Buchenwald* (Berlin, 1994).
Noakes, J. (ed.), *Nazism 1919–1945. A Documentary Reader*, vol. 4 (Exeter, 1998).
Noakes, J., Pridham, G. (eds), *Nazism 1919–1945. A Documentary Reader*, 3 vols (Exeter, 1983–88).
Nöldeke, 'Buchbesprechung von W. Petrzilka, Persönlichkeitsforschung und Differenzierung im Strafvollzug', *MSchriftKrim* 21 (1930), 562–4.

Nuremberg War Crimes Trials Online, CD-Rom (Seattle, 1995).
Obenaus, W., *Die Entwicklung der preußischen Sicherheitspolizei bis zum Ende der Reaktionszeit* (Berlin, 1940).
Oertel, O., *Als Gefangener der SS* (Oldenburg, 1990).
Oerter, S., *Acht Jahre Zuchthaus* (Berlin, 1908).
Oleschinski, B. (ed.), *Gedenkstätte Plötzensee* (Berlin, 1995).
Ollmann, 'Der Einsatz der Strafgefangenen beim Bau der Ostmarkstraße', *BlGefK* 72 (1941–42), 53–61.
Ott, A., 'Gefangenen-Obsorge', *Das Bayernland* 37 (1926), 179–84.
Paterson, A., *A Report of Visits to some German Prisons and Reformatories in August 1922* (Maidstone, 1923).
Petrzilka, W., *Persönlichkeitsforschung und Differenzierung im Strafvollzug* (Hamburg, 1930).
Picker, H. (ed.), *Hitlers Tischgespräche im Führerhauptquartier* (Berlin, 1997).
Plattner, P., *Das Zuchthaus. Eine Ausstellung über das faschistische Zuchthaus Brandenburg* (Berlin, 1990).
Plättner, K., *Eros im Zuchthaus* (Berlin, 1929).
Plischke, R., 'Historische Rückblicke ins 18. und 19. Jahrhundert zum Stufenstrafvollzug', *MSchriftKrim* 19 (1928), 417–29.
Poelchau, H., *Die letzten Stunden. Erinnerungen eines Gefängispfarrers* (Berlin, 1987).
Polenz, M., 'Gefängnisarbeit', in Preußisches Justizministerium (ed.), *Strafvollzug in Preußen*, 214–23.
Preußisches Justizministerium (ed.), *Strafvollzug in Preußen* (Mannheim, 1928).
Radbruch, G., 'Die Psychologie der Gefangenschaft', *ZStW* 32 (1911), 339–54.
Radusch, 'Achtungsbezeugung von Strafgefangenen', *BlGefK* 51 (1917), 70–3.
Reichardt, 'Der Vorentwurf zu einem deutschen Strafgesetzbuch von 1909', *BlGefK* 44 (1910), 5–50.
Reichel, K., *. . . um Dich zu befreien* (Berlin, 1975).
Reichsjustizministerium (ed.), *Das Gefängniswesen in Deutschland* (Berlin, 1935).
Reichsminister der Justiz, *Entwurf eines Strafvollzugsgesetzes* (Berlin, 1927).
Reiß, A., 'Atem- und Körpergymnastik als Hilfsmittel zur geistigen und körperlichen Gesundung', *BlGefK* 55 (1923), 115–29.
Reuß, M., *Der Strafvollzug an Frauen* (Munich, 1927).
Rietzsch, O., 'Die Anordnung der Sicherungsverwahrung', in Freisler, Schlegelberger (eds), *Fragen*, 25–67.
Rinke, F., 'Die Gefängnisarbeit als Problem des Strafvollzugs und der Gewerbepolitik' (Ph.D., University of Cologne, 1926).
Rodenfels, H., 'Sittenstrolche und Verbrecher', *Neues Volk* 7 (1939), Nr. 4, 19–25.
Rohden, von, F., 'Gibt es unverbesserliche Verbrecher?', *MSchriftKrim* 24 (1933), 74–92.
Rösch, F., 'Landesstrafanstalt Untermaßfeld. Die III. Stufe als Selbstverwaltungsgruppe', in *Gefängnisse in Thüringen. Berichte über die Reform des Strafvollzugs* (Weimar, 1930), 105–12.
Roesner, 'Buchkritik von A. Philipp, "Scotland Yard"', *BlGefK* 71 (1940), 100.
Rothberg, A., 'Sicherungsverwahrung als Sondermaßnahme zur Bekämpfung des Gewohnheitsverbrechertums' (Ph.D., University of Bonn, 1930).
Rüter-Ehlermann, A.L., Fuchs, H.H., Rüter, C.F., Sagel-Grande, I. (eds), *Justiz und NS-Verbrechen. Sammlung deutscher Strafurteile wegen nationalsozialistischer Tötungsverbrechen 1945–1966*, 22 vols (Amsterdam, 1968–81).
Salomon, E. von, *Die Geächteten* (Berlin, 1931).

Schaefer, A., 'Die Widerstandskämpfer im Zuchthaus Brandenburg-Görden 1933–1945', *aus politik und zeitgeschichte* 18 (3 May 1980), 3–6.
Schairer, 'Aus der fünfzigjährigen Geschichte des Vereins, 1864–1914', *BlGefK* 48 (1914), 3–65.
Scherübl, M., 'Die Gefängnisschule', *Das Bayernland* 37 (1926), 176–9.
Scheurer, K., 'Der Vorentwurf zu einem deutschen Strafgesetzbuch vom Standpunkt des praktischen Strafvollzugs', *BlGefK* 44 (1910), 737–51.
Schiefer, K., 'Der Verwahrungsvollzug in der Sicherungsanstalt Waldheim', *BlGefK* 68 (1937), 448–65.
Schlotterbeck, F., *Je dunkler die Nacht, desto heller die Sterne* (Berlin, 1948).
Schluckner, H., 'Sklaven am Eismeer', in F. Ausländer (ed.), *Verräter oder Vorbilder? Deserteure und ungehorsame Soldaten im Nationalsozialismus* (Bremen, 1990), 14–40.
Schmidt, Eberhard, 'Kritisches zur Kritik am modernen Strafvollzuge', *MSchriftKrim* 22 (1931), 193–207.
Schmidt, Edgar, 'Strafvollzugsstatistik und Strafvollzugskritik', *Die Justiz* 6 (1930–31), 127–35.
—— 'Haushalt der Strafanstaltsverwaltung 1933', *Der Strafvollzug* 23 (1933), 164–72.
—— 'Der neue Strafvollzug', *Deutsche Justiz* 95 (1933), 638–40.
—— 'Aus der Statistik der preußischen Gefangenenanstalten', *Deutsche Justiz* 96 (1934), 1023–6.
—— 'Die Kosten des Strafvollzuges', *Deutsche Justiz* 96 (1934), 1346–7.
—— 'Treatment of Prisoners and of Habitual Offenders Sentenced to Preventive Detention', in Scott (ed.), *German Prisons*, 25–8.
—— 'Der kriminalbiologische Dienst im deutschen Strafvollzug', *BlGefK* 69 (1938–39), 164–77.
—— 'Sicherungsverwahrung in Zahlen', in Freisler, Schlegelberger (eds), *Fragen*, 105–13.
Schmitt, C., *The Concept of the Political* (New Brunswick, 1976).
—— 'Der Führer schützt das Recht', *Deutsche Juristen Zeitung* 39 (1934), 946–8.
Schneider, K., *Die psychopathischen Persönlichkeiten*, 2nd edition (Leipzig, 1928).
Schoetensack, A., Christians, R., Eichler, H., *Grundzüge eines deutschen Strafvollstreckungsrechts* (Berlin, 1935).
Schroeder, F., 'Die Landesfrauenstrafanstalt Aichach', *Das Bayernland* 37 (1926), 184–6.
Schröder, K., 'Die letzte Station', in F. Ausländer, (ed.), *Die letzte Station* (Bremen, 1995).
Schultze-Pfaelzer, G., *Kampf um den Kopf. Meine Erlebnisse als Gefangener des Volksgerichtshofes 1943–1945* (Berlin, 1948).
Schurich, J., *Lebensläufe vielfach rückfälliger Verbrecher* (Leipzig, 1930).
Schwandner, 'Die Tuberkulosenfrage in den Strafanstalten', *BlGfK* 45 (1911), 153–72.
—— 'Württembergische Gefängnis-Statistik 1913', *BlGefK* 48 (1914), 554–5.
—— 'Das Ende des Dualismus im preußischen Gefängniswesen', *BlGefK* 52 (1918), 47–60.
Schwerdtfeger, R., 'Gedanken über die Sicherungsverwahrung', *MGGE* 10 (1934–35), 81–6.
Schwerdtfeger, W., 'Ein Journalist wird zum Schweigen gebracht. Bericht des Gefangenen 825/36', in W. Uhlmann (ed.), *Sterben um zu leben. Politische Gefangene im Zuchthaus Brandenburg-Görden* (Cologne, 1983), 26–107.
Scott, H.C.B. (ed.), *German Prisons in 1934* (Maidstone, 1936).
Seibert, O., 'Invaliden-Sicherungsanstalten', *BlGefK* 69 (1938–39), 286–90.
Selbmann, F., *Alternative-Bilanz-Credo* (Halle, 1969).
Semler, H., 'Strafvollzug in festen Anstalten und in Lagern', *BlGefK* 70 (1939), 3–14.
Seyfarth, H., 'Strafvollzug und Kriegsdienst', *BlGefK* 49 (1915), 185–97.
—— '14. Jahresbericht des Deutschen Hilfsvereins für entlassene Gefangene für das Jahr 1917', *BlGefK* 52 (1918), 3–12.
—— 'Der Humanitätsgedanke im Strafvollzug', *MdRfW* 5 (1930), 67–82.

—— 'Durchhalten!', *MdRfW* 7 (1932), 130–1.
Siefert, E., *Über den unverbesserlichen Gewohnheitsverbrecher und die Mittel der Fürsorge zu ihrer Bekämpfung* (Halle an der Saale, 1905).
—— *Neupreußischer Strafvollzug. Politisierung und Verfall* (Halle an der Saale, 1933).
Sieverts, R., *Die Wirkung der Freiheitsstrafe und der Untersuchungshaft auf die Psyche des Gefangenen* (Mannheim, 1929).
—— 'Die preußische Verordnung über den Strafvollzug in Stufen vom 7. Juni 1929', *MSchriftKrim*, Beiheft 3 (Heidelberg, 1930), 129–51.
—— 'Die Arbeitsgemeinschaft für die Reform des Strafvollzugs. Tagungen 1929 und 1930', *ZStW* 51 (1931), 255–68.
—— 'Gedanken über Methoden, Ergebnisse und kriminalpolitische Folgen der kriminalbiologischen Untersuchungen im bayrischen Strafvollzug', *MSchriftKrim* 23 (1932), 588–601.
Smith, B., Peterson, A. (eds), *Heinrich Himmler Geheimreden* (Frankfurt am Main, 1974).
Sopade – Deutschland-Berichte der Sozialdemokratischen Partei Deutschlands 1934–1940, 7 vols (Salzhausen, 1980).
Staff, I. (ed.), *Justiz im Dritten Reich. Eine Dokumentation* (Frankfurt am Main, 1964).
Stammer, G., 'Krohne und sein Einfluss auf die Fortentwicklung des Gefängniswesens', *BlGefK* 46 (1912), 7–13.
Staiger, 'Über Sterilisation und Kastration', *BlGefK* 65 (1934), 31–9.
Starke, 'Die Behandlung der Gefangenen', in Bumke (ed.), *Gefängniswesen*, 147–77.
Statistik der zum Preußischen Ministerium des Inneren gehörenden Strafanstalten 1913 (Berlin, 1915).
Statistik der zum Preußischen Ministerium des Inneren gehörenden Strafanstalten 1916 (Berlin, 1918).
'Statistik des Gefängniswesens im Deutschen Reich', *Stenographische Berichte der Verhandlungen des deutschen Reichstags*, IV. Wahlperiode (1928), vol. 434, supplement 814.
Statistik über die Gefangenenanstalten in Preußen 1924–1929 (Berlin, 1927–31).
Statistisches Jahrbuch für das Deutsche Reich 1935–1941/42 (Berlin, 1935–41)
Stenographische Berichte über die Verhandlungen des deutschen Reichstags.
'Stenographischer Bericht', *BlGefK* 58 (1927), Sonderheft zur Augsburger Tagung des Vereins der deutschen Strafanstaltsbeamten, 118–389.
Stolzenburg, 'Die Entlassung aus der Sicherungsverwahrung', in Freisler, Schlegelberger (eds), *Fragen*, 83–94.
'Strafgefängnis Berlin-Tegel', in Scott (ed.), *German Prisons*, 73–8.
Strafgesetzbuch für das Deutsche Reich, 31st edition (Leipzig, 1926).
'Strafvollzug', *Deutsche Richterzeitung* 24 (1932), 182–3.
Strube, W., 'Wie müssen Haft-, Gefängnis- und Zuchthausstrafen umgewandelt werden, damit sie dem Rechtsempfinden des Deutschen Volkes entsprechen?', *BlGefK* 67 (1936), 365–77.
Stumpf, K., 'Vergleichende Darstellung der reichsrätlichen Grundsätze für den Vollzug von Freiheitsstrafen vom 7. Juni 1923', *BlGefK* 57 (1926), 170–88.
—— 'Abgrenzung der Vollstreckung und des Vollzugs der Strafen, insbesondere die Stellung der Strafvollzugsbehörden', *BlGefK* 63 (1932), 3–79.
Thälmann, E., *Zwischen Erinnerung und Erwartung* (Frankfurt am Main, 1977).
Thierack, O., 'Der Strafvollzug im Dienste der Volksgemeinschaft', *MGGE* 11 (1936), 209–15.
The Times (1935).
Toller, E., *Justiz* (Berlin, 1927).

The Trial of the Major War Criminals before the International Military Tribunal, Nuremberg 14.11.1945–1.10.1946, 42 vols (Nuremberg, 1947–49).
Uhlmann, W., 'Antifaschistische Arbeit', *aus politik und zeitgeschichte*, 18 (3 May 1980), 7–15.
Union für Recht und Freiheit (ed.), *Der Strafvollzug im III. Reich. Denkschrift und Materialsammlung* (Prague, 1936).
'Verein der Deutschen Strafanstaltsbeamten, Protokoll über die Mitgliederversammlung vom 20.12.1933', *BlGefK* 65 (1934), 42–5.
Vereinheitlichung der Dienst- und Vollzugsvorschriften für den Strafvollzug im Bereich der Reichsjustizverwaltung, Sonderveröffentlichung der *Deutschen Justiz* Nr. 21 (Berlin, 1940).
'Verordnung über den Vollzug von Freiheitsstrafen und von Maßregeln der Sicherung und Besserung die mit Freiheitsentziehung verbunden sind', *BlGefK* 65 (1934), Erstes Sonderheft, 1–21.
Viernstein, T., 'Der kriminalbiologische Dienst in bayerischen Strafanstalten', *MSchriftKrim* 17 (1926), 1–21.
—— 'Entwicklung und Aufbau eines kriminalbiologischen Dienstes im bayerischen Strafvollzug', in Bayerisches Staatsministerium der Justiz (ed.), *Stufenstrafvollzug*, vol. 1, 68–85.
—— 'Referat auf der Augsburger Tagung vom 3. Juni 1927', special print in the possession of the author.
—— 'Über Typen des verbesserlichen und unverbesserlichen Verbrechers', *MKG* 2 (1929), 26–54.
—— 'Die kriminalbiologischen Untersuchungen der Strafgefangenen in Bayern', *MKG* 3 (1931), 30–8.
—— 'Stufenstrafvollzug. Entlassenenfürsorge. Sicherungsverwahrung', special print in the possession of the author, *MdRfW* 7 (1932).
Voigtländer, E., 'Über den Strafvollzug an Frauen', *BlGefK* 68 (1937), 268–78.
Völker, H., 'Das System der Hausstrafen im modernen Strafvollzug' (Ph.D., University of Leipzig, 1931).
Völkischer Beobachter (1942).
Vorentwurf zu einem Deutschen Strafgesetzbuch (Berlin, 1909).
Weber, F., 'Erfahrungen in der Sicherungsanstalt', *BlGefK* 68 (1937), 429–48.
Wegner, A., 'Internationale Kriminalistische Vereinigung. Tagung der deutschen Landesgruppe in Hamburg, am 13. u. 14. Juni 1924', *MSchriftKrim* 15 (1924), 353–7.
Weissenrieder, O., 'Zur Geschichte des Besserungsgedankens im Vollzug der neuzeitlichen Freiheitsstrafe', *BlGefK* 56 (1924–25), 5–43.
—— 'Die Strafanstaltsbeamten', in Bumke (ed.), *Gefängniswesen*, 71–97.
—— 'Pastor Dr phil Seyfarth', *BlGefK* 60 (1929), 145–8.
—— 'Vorwort', *BlGefK* 64 (1933), 113–17.
—— 'Mitteilungen der Schriftleitung', *BlGefK* 66 (1935), 302–4.
—— 'Der Wachtmeisterkurs im Oberlandesgerichtsbezirk Stuttgart', *BlGefK* 67 (1936), 12–33.
Wilke, G., 'The German Criminal Law', in Scott (ed.), *German Prisons*, 11–13.
Wilmanns, K., *Die sogenannte verminderte Zurechnungsfähigkeit als zentrales Problem der Entwürfe zu einem deutschen Strafgesetzbuch* (Berlin, 1927).
Wingler, A., '1. Tagung der Gesellschaft für Deutsches Strafrecht, München 27–29. Oktober 1938', *BlGefK* 69 (1938–39), 305–12.
Wüllner, J., 'Das Verhalten der Gefangenen angesichts der zu erwartenden Sicherungsverwahrung und Unfruchtbarmachung', *MGGE* 10 (1934–35), 236–40.

Wutzdorff, E., 'Die Arbeit der Gefangenen', in Bumke (ed.), *Gefängniswesen*, 178–97.
Zentralvorstand der Roten Hilfe Deutschland (ed.), *Gefangen. Dreissig politische Juliamnestierte berichten über ihre Erlebnisse in deutschen Zuchthäusern* (Berlin, 1928).
Zink, A., 'Hohenasperg im Wandel der Zeit', *ZfStrVo* 1 (1950), Nr. 2, 3–8.
Zirker, O., *Der Gefangene. Neuland der Erziehung in der Strafanstalt* (Werther, 1924).
—— 'Erste Tagung der Arbeitsgemeinschaft für Reform des Strafvollzugs', *MSchriftKrim* 15 (1924), 102–5.

Secondary Printed Sources

Abrams, L., 'Prostitutes in Imperial Germany, 1870–1918: Working Girls or Social Outcasts?', in R.J. Evans (ed.), *The German Underworld. Deviants and Outcasts in German History* (London, 1988), 189–209.
Allen, W.S., *The Nazi Seizure of Power. The Experience of a Single German Town 1922–1945*, 2nd edition (London, 1989).
Aly, G., 'Medizin gegen Unbrauchbare', in *Beiträge zur Nationalsozialistischen Gesundheits- und Sozialpolitik*, vol. 1 (Berlin, 1985), 9–74.
—— and Heim, S., *Vordenker der Vernichtung* (Frankfurt am Main, 1993).
Anders-Baudisch, F., 'Aus der "Rechts"-Praxis Nationalsozialistischer Sondergerichte im "Reichsgau Sudetenland" 1940–1945', *Bohemia* 40 (1999), 331–66.
Angermund, R., *Deutsche Richterschaft 1918–1945. Krisenerfahrung, Illusion, politische Rechtsprechung* (Frankfurt am Main, 1990).
Arnold, J., '"Strafvollzug in der DDR". Ein Gegenstand gegenwärtiger und zukünftiger Forschung', *MSchriftKrim* 76 (1993), 390–404.
Ayaß, W., *Das Arbeitshaus Breitenau* (Kassel, 1992).
—— *'Asoziale' im Nationalsozialismus* (Stuttgart, 1995).
—— 'Die "korrektionelle Nachhaft". Zur Geschichte der strafrechtlichen Arbeitshausunterbringung in Deutschland', *Zeitschrift für Neuere Rechtsgeschichte* 15 (1993), 184–201.
Bartov, O., *Hitler's Army* (Oxford, 1992).
Bästlein, K., 'Vom hanseatischen Richtertum zum nationalsozialistischen Justizverbrechen. Zur Person und Tätigkeit Curt Rothenbergers 1896–1959', in Justizbehörde Hamburg (ed.), *'Für Führer, Volk und Vaterland . . .'*, 74–145.
—— 'Sondergerichte in Norddeutschland als Verfolgungsinstanz', in F. Bajohr (ed.), *Norddeutschland im Nationalsozialismus* (Hamburg, 1993), 218–38.
—— '"Nazi-Blutrichter als Stützen des Adenauer-Regimes"', in H. Grabitz, K. Bästlein, J. Tuchel (eds), *Die Normalität des Verbrechens* (Berlin, 1994), 408–43.
Bath, M., 'Strafvollzug in der DDR', *ZfStrVo* 38 (1989), 343–4.
Baurmann, M., 'Kriminalpolitik ohne Mass – Zum Marburger Programm Franz von Listzs', *Kriminalsoziologische Bibliografie* 11 (1984), 54–79.
Becker, P., 'Randgruppen im Blickfeld der Polizei. Ein Versuch über die Perspektivität des "praktischen Blicks"', *Archiv für Sozialgeschichte* 32 (1992), 283–304.
—— 'Der Verbrecher als "monstruoser Typus"', in M. Hagner (ed.), *Der falsche Körper. Beiträge zu einer Geschichte der Monstrositäten* (Göttingen, 1995), 147–73.
Berding, H., Klippel, D., Lottes, G. (eds), *Kriminalität und abweichendes Verhalten. Deutschland im 18. und 19. Jahrhundert* (Göttingen, 1999).
Berenbaum, M. (ed.), *A Mosaic of Victims. Non-Jews Persecuted and Murdered by the Nazis* (New York, 1990).

Berger, T., *Die konstante Repression. Zur Geschichte des Strafvollzugs in Preussen nach 1850* (Frankfurt am Main, 1974).
Berghahn, V., *Modern Germany*, 2nd edition (Cambridge, 1987).
Bessel, R., *Political Violence and the Rise of Nazism* (New Haven, 1984).
—— *Germany after the First World War* (Oxford, 1995).
Blasius, D., *Bürgerliche Gesellschaft und Kriminalität* (Göttingen, 1976).
Blau, B., 'Die Kriminalität in Deutschland während des zweiten Weltkriegs', *Zeitschrift für die gesamte Strafrechtswissenschaft* 64 (1952), 31–81.
Boberach, H., 'Die Berichte der Oberlandesgerichts-Präsidenten und Generalstaatsanwälte aus Hessen im Zweiten Weltkrieg', in F.-J. Düwell, T. Vormbaum (eds), *Recht und Nationalsozialismus* (Baden-Baden, 1998), 63–75.
Bock, G., *Zwangssterilisation im Nationalsozialismus* (Opladen, 1986).
—— 'Sterilisation and "Medical" Massacres in National Socialist Germany', in M. Berg, G. Cocks (eds), *Medicine and Modernity. Public Health and Medical Care in Nineteenth- and Twentieth-Century Germany* (Cambridge, 1997), 149–72.
Breidenbach, A., *Antifaschistischer Widerstand im Zuchthaus Remscheid-Lüttringhausen* (Remscheid, 1992).
Brochhagen, U., *Nach Nürnberg: Vergangenheitsbewältigung und Westintegration in der Ära Adenauer* (Berlin, 1999).
Broszat, M., *Der Staat Hitlers* (Munich, 1992).
—— 'Zur Perversion der Strafjustiz im Dritten Reich', *VfZ* 6 (1958), 390–443.
—— 'Siegerjustiz oder strafrechtliche "Selbstreinigung"', *VfZ* 29 (1981), 477–544.
—— 'Grundzüge der gesellschaftlichen Verfassung des Dritten Reiches', in idem, H. Möller (eds), *Das Dritte Reich* (Munich, 1986), 38–63.
—— 'Nationalsozialistische Konzentrationslager 1933–1945', in H. Buchheim, M. Broszat, H.-A. Jacobsen, H. Krausnick (eds), *Anatomie des SS-Staates* (Munich, 1994), 323–445.
Browder, G., *Hitler's Enforcers. The Gestapo and the SS Security Service in the Nazi Revolution* (Oxford, 1996).
Brünneck, A. von et al. (eds), *Ernst Fraenkel. Gesammelte Schriften*, 4 vols (Baden-Baden, 1999–2000).
Buchheit, G., *Richter in roter Robe* (Munich, 1968).
Bülow, C. von, 'Verurteilt nach Paragraph 175', *DIZ Nachrichten* 20 (1998), 42–8.
Burgmair, W., Wachsmann, N., Weber, M.M., '"Die soziale Prognose wird damit sehr trübe ...". Theodor Viernstein und die Kriminalbiologische Sammelstelle in Bayern', in M. Farin (ed.), *Polizeireport München* (Munich, 1999), 250–87.
Burleigh, M., *Death and Deliverance. 'Euthanasia' in Germany 1900–1945* (Cambridge, 1994)
—— *The Third Reich. A New History* (London, 2000).
—— and Wippermann, W., *The Racial State* (Cambridge, 1991).
Caplan, J., *Government without Administration* (Oxford, 1988).
Christoffel, E., *Der Weg durch die Nacht. Verfolgung und Widerstand im Trierer Land während der Zeit des Nationalsozialismus* (Trier, 1983).
Classen, I., *Darstellung von Kriminalität in der deutschen Literatur, Presse und Wissenschaft 1900 bis 1930* (Frankfurt am Main, 1988).
Corni, G., Gies, H., *Brot, Butter, Kanonen. Die Ernährungswirtschaft in Deutschland unter der Diktatur Hitlers* (Berlin, 1997).
Crankshaw, E., *Gestapo. Instrument of Tyranny* (London, 1956).
Crew, D.F., *Germans on Welfare. From Weimar to Hitler* (New York, 1998).
Czarnowski, G., 'Women's Crimes, State Crimes: Abortion in Nazi Germany', in M.L. Arnot, C. Usborne (eds), *Gender and Crime in Modern Europe* (London, 1999), 238–56.

Danker, U., 'Der Schutz der "Volksgemeinschaft": Zur Arbeit des schleswig-holsteinischen Sondergerichts in statistischer Hinsicht sowie an den Beispielen Rundfunk- und Volksschädlingsverordnung', in idem, R. Bohn (eds), *Standgerichte der inneren Front': das Sondergericht Altona/Kiel 1932–1945* (Hamburg, 1998), 39–87.

Davis, J.A., *Conflict and Control. Law and Order in Nineteenth-Century Italy* (London, 1988).

Delarue, J., *Geschichte der Gestapo* (Düsseldorf, 1964).

Dickinson, E.R., *The Politics of German Child Welfare from the Empire to the Federal Republic* (Cambridge, Massachusetts, 1996).

Diestelkamp, B., 'Die Justiz nach 1945 und ihr Umgang mit der eigenen Vergangenheit', in idem, M. Stolleis (eds), *Justizalltag im Dritten Reich* (Frankfurt am Main, 1988), 131–49.

Dölling, D., 'Kriminologie im "Dritten Reich"', in R. Dreier, W. Sellert (eds), *Recht und Justiz im 'Dritten Reich'* (Frankfurt am Main, 1989), 194–235.

Dörner, B., *'Heimtücke'. Das Gesetz als Waffe: Kontrolle, Abschreckung und Verfolgung in Deutschland 1933–1945* (Paderborn, 1998).

Dörner, C., *Erziehung durch Strafe. Die Geschichte des Jugendstrafvollzugs von 1871–1945* (Weinheim, 1991).

Dreßen, W., 'Westwall', in W. Benz et al. (eds), *Enzyklopädie des Nationalsozialismus* (Munich, 1997), 806.

Drobisch, K., 'Alltag im Zuchthaus Luckau 1933 bis 1939', in D. Eichholtz (ed.), *Brandenburg in der NS-Zeit. Studien und Dokumente* (Berlin, 1993), 247–72.

—— 'Konzentrationslager und Justizhaft. Versuch einer Zusammenschau', in H. Grabitz, K. Bästlein, J. Tuchel (eds), *Die Normalität des Verbrechens* (Berlin, 1994), 280–97.

—— and G. Wieland, *System der NS-Konzentrationslager: 1933–1939* (Berlin, 1993).

Dürkop, M., 'Zur Funktion der Kriminologie im Nationalsozialismus', in U. Reifner, B.-R. Sonnen (eds), *Strafjustiz und Polizei im Dritten Reich* (Frankfurt am Main, 1984), 97–120.

Düsing, A., 'Abschaffung der Todesstrafe' (Ph.D., Freiburg University, 1952).

Eiber, L., 'Die Verfolgung der Sinti und Roma in München 1933–1945', in idem (ed.), *'Ich wußte, es wird schlimm'. Die Verfolgung der Sinti und Roma in München 1933–1945* (Munich, 1993), 21–143.

Eichholz, E., 'Gefangenenseelsorge und nationalsozialistischer "Strafernst"', *Kirchliche Zeitgeschichte* 12 (1999), 172–88.

Eley, G., 'What Produces Fascism: Preindustrial Traditions or a Crisis of the Capitalist State?', *Politics and Society* 12 (1983), 53–82.

—— 'German History and the Contradictions of Modernity: The Bourgeoisie, the State, and the Mastery of Reform', in idem (ed.), *Society, Culture, and the State in Germany, 1870–1930* (Ann Arbor, 1996), 67–103.

Emmerich, N., 'Die Forensische Psychiatrie 1933–45', in Arbeitsgruppe zur Erforschung der Geschichte der Karl-Bonhoeffer-Nervenklinik (ed.), *Totgeschwiegen 1933–1945* (Berlin, 1989), 105–23.

Evans, R.J., *Rituals of Retribution. Capital Punishment in Germany, 1600–1987* (London, 1997).

—— *Szenen aus der deutschen Unterwelt* (Reinbek, 1997).

—— *The Coming of the Third Reich* (London, 2003).

—— 'In Search of German Social Darwinism', in M. Berg, G. Cocks (eds), *Medicine and Modernity. Public Health Care in Nineteenth- and Twentieth-Century Germany* (Cambridge, 1996), 55–79.

—— 'Anti-Semitism: Ordinary Germans and the "longest hatred"', in idem, *Rereading German History* (London, 1997), 149–86.

—— 'Hans von Hentig and the Politics of German Criminology', in A. Ebbinghaus, K.H.

Roth (eds), *Grenzgänge: deutsche Geschichte des 20. Jahrhunderts im Spiegel von Publizistik, Rechtsprechung und historischer Forschung* (Lüneburg, 1999), 238–64.

Faralisch, B., ' "Begreifen Sie erst jetzt, daß wir rechtlos sind?". Zeitzeugenberichte über den Strafvollzug im "Dritten Reich" ', in H. Jung, H. Müller-Dietz (eds), *Strafvollzug im 'Dritten Reich'. Am Beispiel des Saarlandes* (Baden-Baden, 1996), 303–79.

Fest, J., *Plotting Hitler's Death. The German Resistance to Hitler 1933–1945* (London, 1997).

Finzsch, N., Jütte, R. (eds), *Institutions of Confinement. Hospitals, Asylums, and Prisons in Western Europe and North America, 1500–1950* (Cambridge, 1996).

Finzsch, N., 'Elias, Foucault, Oestreich: on a Historical Theory of Confinement', in idem, R. Jütte (eds), *Institutions of Confinement* (Cambridge, 1996), 3–16.

Fleiter, A., 'Strafen auf dem Weg zum Sozialismus. Sozialistische Standpunkte zu Kriminalität und Strafe vor dem Ersten Weltkrieg', *Mitteilungsblatt des Instituts für soziale Bewegungen* 26 (2001), 105–38.

—— 'Straf- und Gefängnisreformen in Deutschland und den USA: Preußen und Maryland, 1870–1935' (Ph.D., University of Bochum, forthcoming).

Flitner, W., 'Ideengeschichtliche Einführung in die Dokumentation der Jugendbewegung', in W. Kindt (ed.), *Die Wandervogelzeit* (Cologne, 1968), 10–17.

Förster, M., *Jurist im Dienst des Unrechts. Leben und Werk des ehemaligen Staatssekretärs im Reichsjustizministerium, Franz Schlegelberger* (Baden-Baden, 1995).

Forsythe, W.J., *Penal Discipline, Reformatory Projects and the English Prison Commission, 1895–1939* (Exeter, 1990).

Foucault, M., *Discipline and Punish. The Birth of the Prison* (London, 1991).

Fox, L.W., *The English Prison and Borstal Systems* (London, 1952).

Fraenkel, E., *The Dual State. A Contribution to the Theory of Dictatorship* (New York, 1969; first published 1941).

Frei, N., *National Socialist Rule in Germany. The Führer State 1933–1945* (Oxford, 1993).

—— *Vergangenheitspolitik. Die Anfänge der Bundesrepublik und die NS-Vergangenheit* (Munich, 1996).

—— 'Wie modern war der Nationalsozialismus?', *Geschichte und Gesellschaft* 9 (1993), 367–87.

—— 'Zwischen Terror und Integration. Zur Funktion der politischen Polizei im Nationalsozialismus', in C. Dipper, R. Hudemann, J. Petersen (eds), *Faschismus und Faschismen im Vergleich* (Cologne, 1998), 217–28.

Frenzel, M., Thiele, W., Mannbar, A., *Gesprengte Fesseln. Ein Bericht über den antifaschistischen Widerstand und die Geschichte der illegalen Parteiorganisation der KPD im Zuchthaus Brandenburg-Goerden von 1933 bis 1945* (East Berlin, 1975).

Fricke, K., *Die Justizvollzugsanstalt 'Roter Ochse' Halle/Saale 1933–1945. Eine Dokumentation* (Magdeburg, 1997).

Friedlander, H., *The Origins of Nazi Genocide. From Euthanasia to the Final Solution* (Chapel Hill, 1995).

Friedländer, S., *Nazi Germany & the Jews. The Years of Persecution 1933–39* (London, 1997).

Friedrich, C., *'Sie wollten uns brechen und brachen uns nicht...'. Zur Lage und zum antifaschistischen Widerstandskampf weiblicher Häftlinge im Frauenzuchthaus Cottbus 1938–1945* (Cottbus, 1986).

Friedrich, J., *Die kalte Amnestie. NS-Täter in der Bundesrepublik* (Frankfurt am Main, 1984).

—— *Freispruch für die Nazi-Justiz* (Berlin, 1998).

Frisch, W., 'Das Marburger Programm und die Maßregeln der Besserung und Sicherung', *ZStW* 94 (1982), 565–98.

Frommel, M., 'Verbrechensbekämpfung im Nationalsozialismus', in M. Stolleis (ed.), *Die Bedeutung der Wörter* (Munich, 1991), 47–64.
Fulbrook, M., *German National Identity after the Holocaust* (Cambridge, 1999).
Gadebusch Bondio, M., *Die Rezeption der kriminalanthropologischen Theorien von Cesare Lombroso in Deutschland von 1880–1914* (Husum, 1995).
Gandert, G. (ed.), *Der Film der Weimarer Republik 1929* (Berlin, 1993).
Garbe, D., *Zwischen Widerstand und Martyrium. Die Zeugen Jehovas im 'Dritten Reich'* (Munich, 1993).
Garner, C., 'Public Service Personnel in West Germany in the 1950s', in R.G. Moeller (ed.), *West Germany under Construction. Politics, Society and Culture in the Adenauer Era* (Ann Arbor, 1997), 135–95.
Gay, P., *The Cultivation of Hatred* (London, 1994).
Gélieu, C. von, *Frauen in Haft* (Berlin, 1994).
Gellately, R., *The Gestapo and German Society. Enforcing Racial Policy 1933–1945* (Oxford, 1991).
—— *Backing Hitler. Consent and Coercion in Nazi Germany* (Oxford, 2001).
—— 'Allwissend und allgegenwärtig? Entstehung, Funktion und Wandel des Gestapo-Mythos', in G. Paul, K.-M. Mallmann (eds), *Die Gestapo. Mythos und Realität* (Darmstadt, 1995), 47–72.
—— 'The Prerogatives of Confinement in Germany, 1933–1945', in N. Finzsch, R. Jütte (eds), *Institutions of Confinement* (Cambridge, 1996), 191–212.
—— 'Denunciations in Twentieth-Century Germany: Aspects of Self-Policing in the Third Reich and the German Democratic Republic', *Journal of Modern History* 68 (1996), 931–67.
Gilbert M., *The Second World War* (London, 1995).
Giles, G., ' "The Most Unkindest Cut of All": Castration, Homosexuality and Nazi Justice', *Journal of Contemporary History* 27 (1992), 41–61.
—— 'Drink and Crime in Modern Germany', paper delivered at the symposium 'The Criminal and his Scientists', Florence, 15–18 October 1998.
Godula, V., 'Zivot veznu na Mírove', *Slezský Sborník* 67 (1969), 514–27.
—— 'Obeti z rad ceskych veznu na Mírove v letech 1943–1945', *Slezský Sborník* 69 (1971), 195–202.
Goffman, E., *Asylums. Essays on the Social Situation of Mental Patients and Other Inmates* (Chicago, 1971).
Gostomski, V. von, Loch, W., *Der Tod von Plötzensee* (Frankfurt am Main, 1993).
Grabitz, H., 'In vorauseilendem Gehorsam . . . Die Hamburger Justiz im "Führerstaat" ', in Justizbehörde Hamburg (ed.), *'Für Führer, Volk und Vaterland . . .'*, 21–73.
Grau, G. (ed.), *Hidden Holocaust? Gay and Lesbian Persecution in Germany 1933–45* (London, 1995).
—— ' "Unschuldige" Täter. Mediziner als Vollstrecker der nationalsozialistischen Homosexuellenpolitik', in B. Jellonnek, R. Lautmann (eds), *Nationalsozialistischer Terror gegen Homosexuelle* (Paderborn, 2002), 209–35.
Grebing, H., *Geschichte der deutschen Arbeiterbewegung* (Munich, 1970).
Gruchmann, L., *Justiz im Dritten Reich. Anpassung und Unterwerfung in der Ära Gürtner*, 2nd edition (Munich, 1990).
—— *Totaler Krieg. Vom Blitzkrieg zur bedingungslosen Kapitulation* (Munich, 1991).
—— 'Hitler über die Justiz. Das Tischgespräch vom 20. August 1942', *VfZ* 12 (1964), 86–101.
—— ' "Nacht-und Nebel" – Justiz. Die Mitwirkung deutscher Strafgerichte an der Bekämpfung des Widerstandes in den besetzten westeuropäischen Ländern 1942–1944', *VfZ* 29 (1981), 342–96.

—— 'Rechtssystem und nationalsozialistische Justizpolitik', in M. Broszat, H. Möller (eds), *Das Dritte Reich* (Munich, 1986), 83–103.
—— 'Die "rechtsprechende Gewalt" im nationalsozialistischen Herrschaftssystem', in W. Benz, H. Buchheim, H. Mommsen (eds), *Der Nationalsozialismus. Studien zur Ideologie und Herrschaft* (Frankfurt am Main, 1993), 78–103.
—— 'Franz Gürtner – Justizminister unter Hitler', in R. Smelser, E. Syring, R. Zitelmann (eds), *Die braune Elite*, vol. 2 (Darmstadt, 1993), 128–36.
Grünhut, M., *The Development of the German Penal System 1920–1932*, English Studies in Criminal Science, vol. 8 (1944).
—— *Penal Reform* (Oxford, 1948).
Grüttner, M., *Studenten im Dritten Reich* (Paderborn, 1995).
Habicht, M., *Zuchthaus Waldheim 1933–45. Haftbedingungen und antifaschistischer Kampf* (East Berlin, 1988).
Haffner, S., *Die deutsche Revolution 1918/19* (Munich, 1979).
Hannover, H., Drück-Hannover, E., *Politische Justiz, 1918–1933* (Frankfurt am Main, 1966).
Hansen, B., 'Something Rotten in the State of Denmark: Eugenics and the Ascent of the Welfare State', in G. Broberg, N. Roll-Hansen (eds), *Eugenics and the Welfare State. Sterilization Policy in Denmark, Sweden, Norway, and Finland* (East Lansing, 1996), 9–76.
Harding, C., Hines, B., Ireland, R., Rawlings, P., *Imprisonment in England and Wales. A Concise History* (London, 1985).
Harvey, E., *Youth and the Welfare State in Weimar Germany* (Oxford, 1993).
Heger, K., 'Prison Reform in the American Zone of Occupied Germany, 1945–52' (Ph.D., University of Maryland, 1996)
Heiber, H., 'Zur Justiz im Dritten Reich: Der Fall Eliáš', *VfZ* 3 (1955), 275–96.
Henke, K.D., *Die amerikanische Besetzung Deutschlands* (Munich, 1995).
Hensle, M.P., '"Rundfunkverbrechen" vor NS-Sondergerichten', *Rundfunk und Geschichte* 26 (2000), 111–26.
Hepp, M., '"Bei Adolf wäre das nicht passiert"? Die Kriminalstatistik widerlegt eine zählebige Legende', *Zeitschrift für Rechtspolitik* 32 (1999), 253–60.
Herbert, U., *Fremdarbeiter. Politik und Praxis des 'Ausländer-Einsatzes' in der Kriegswirtschaft des Dritten Reiches* (Berlin, 1986).
—— *Best. Biographische Studien über Radikalismus, Weltanschauung und Vernunft* (Bonn, 1996).
—— 'Von der Gegnerbekämpfung zur "rassischen Generalprävention"', in idem, K. Orth, C. Dieckmann (eds), *Die nationalsozialistischen Konzentrationslager. Entwicklung und Struktur*, vol. 1 (Göttingen, 1998), 60–86.
—— (ed.), *Nationalsozialistische Vernichtungspolitik 1939–1945* (Frankfurt am Main, 1998).
Herbst, L., *Das nationalsozialistische Deutschland 1933–1945* (Frankfurt am Main, 1996).
Hietala, M., 'From Race Hygiene to Sterilisation: The Eugenics Movement in Finland', in N. Roll-Hansen, G. Broberg (eds), *Eugenics and the Welfare State. Sterilization Policy in Denmark, Sweden, Norway, and Finland* (East Lansing, 1996), 195–258.
Hohengarten, A., *Das Massaker im Zuchthaus Sonnenburg vom 30./31. Januar 1945* (Luxemburg, 1979).
Hong, Y.-S., *Welfare, Modernity and the Weimar State, 1919–1933* (Princeton, 1998).
Hottes, C., 'Grauen und Normalität. Zum Strafvollzug im Dritten Reich', in Oberstadtdirektor der Stadt Hamm (ed.), *Ortstermin Hamm. Zur Justiz im Dritten Reich* (Hamm, 1991), 63–70.

—— 'Strafvollzug im Dritten Reich. Ein Beitrag zu seiner Darstellung und historischem Lernen aus der Geschichte', in Justizministerium des Landes NRW (ed.), *Justiz und Nationalsozialismus* (Düsseldorf, 1993), 169–213.

Hüttenberger, P., 'Heimtückefälle vor dem Sondergericht München 1933–1939', in M. Broszat et al. (eds), *Bayern in der NS-Zeit*, vol. 4 (Munich, 1981), 435–526.

Ignatieff, M., *A Just Measure of Pain. The Penitentiary in the Industrial Revolution 1750–1850* (London, 1989).

—— 'State, Civil Society and Total Institutions: A Critique of Recent Social Histories of Punishment', in S. Cohen, A. Scull (eds), *Social Control and the State. Historical and Comparative Essays* (Oxford, 1983), 75–105.

Jakobson, M., *Origins of the Gulag. The Soviet Prison Camp System 1917–1934* (Lexington, 1993).

—— 'Die Funktionen und die Struktur des sowjetischen Gefängnis- und Lagersystems von 1928 bis 1934', in D. Dahlmann, G. Hirschfeld (eds), *Lager, Zwangsarbeit, Vertreibung und Deportation* (Essen, 1999), 207–21.

Jasper, G., 'Justiz und Politik in der Weimarer Republik', *VfZ* 30 (1982), 167–205.

Jeffery, C.R., 'The Historical Development of Criminology', in H. Mannheim (ed.), *Pioneers in Criminology* (London, 1960), 364–94.

Jellonnek, B., *Homosexuelle unter dem Hakenkreuz. Die Verfolgung von Homosexuellen im Dritten Reich* (Paderborn, 1990).

—— 'Staatspolizeiliche Fahndungs- und Ermittlungsmethoden gegen Homosexuelle', in idem, R. Lautmann (eds), *Nationalsozialistischer Terror gegen Homosexuelle* (Paderborn, 2002), 149–61.

Jenner, H., 'Norwegische Gefangene vor dem Sondergericht Kiel', in R. Bohn, U. Danker (eds), *'Standgerichte der inneren Front'. Das Sondergericht Altona/Kiel 1932–1945* (Hamburg, 1998), 263–75.

Joerger, G., *Die deutsche Gefängnispresse in Vergangenheit und Gegenwart* (Stuttgart, 1971).

Johe, W., *Die gleichgeschaltete Justiz* (Frankfurt am Main, 1967).

John, J., 'Einführung', in idem (ed.), *Quellen zur Geschichte Thüringens. 1918–1945* (Erfurt, 1996), 17–53.

Johnson, E.A., *Urbanization and Crime. Germany 1871–1914* (Cambridge, 1995).

—— *The Nazi Terror. Gestapo, Jews & Ordinary Germans* (London, 2000).

Jung, H., Müller-Dietz, H. (eds), *Strafvollzug im 'Dritten Reich'. Am Beispiel des Saarlandes* (Baden-Baden, 1996).

Justizbehörde Hamburg (ed.), *'Für Führer, Volk und Vaterland...'. Hamburger Justiz im Nationalsozialismus* (Hamburg, 1992).

—— *'Von Gewohnheitsverbrechern, Volksschädlingen und Asozialen...'. Hamburger Strafurteile im Nationalsozialismus* (Hamburg, 1995).

JVA Straubing (ed.), *100 Jahre Justizvollzugsanstalt Straubing* (Straubing, 2001).

JVA Tegel (ed.), *100 Jahre Justizvollzugsanstalt Tegel* (Berlin, 1998).

Kaienburg, H., *'Vernichtung durch Arbeit'. Der Fall Neuengamme* (Bonn, 1990).

Kammler J., et al. (eds), *Volksgemeinschaft und Volksfeinde. Kassel 1933–1945* (Fuldabrück, 1984).

Kárný, M., 'Protektorat Böhmen und Mähren', in W. Benz et al. (eds), *Enzyklopädie des Nationalsozialismus* (Munich, 1998), 656–7.

Kater, M.H., 'Die ernsten Bibelforscher im Dritten Reich', *VfZ* 17 (1969), 181–218.

Kebbedies, F., *Außer Kontrolle. Jugendkriminalität in der NS-Zeit und der frühen Nachkriegszeit* (Essen, 2001).

Keldungs, K.-H., *Das Duisburger Sondergericht 1942–1945* (Baden-Baden, 1998).

Kershaw, I., *Popular Opinion & Political Dissent in the Third Reich* (Oxford, 1983).
—— *The 'Hitler Myth'. Image and Reality in the Third Reich* (Oxford, 1989).
—— *The Nazi Dictatorship. Problems and Perspectives of Interpretation*, 3rd edition (London, 1993).
—— *Hitler. 1889–1936: Hubris* (London, 1998).
—— *Hitler. 1936–45: Nemesis* (London, 2000).
—— 'The Persecution of the Jews and German Popular Opinion in the Third Reich', *Leo Baeck Institute Yearbook* 26 (1981), 261–89.
—— '"Working towards the Führer". Reflections on the Nature of the Hitler Dictatorship', *Contemporary European History* 2 (1993), 103–18.
Kersting, F.-W., *Anstaltsärzte zwischen Kaiserreich und Bundesrepublik* (Paderborn, 1996).
Kinder, E., 'Das "Stammlager Sosnowitz". Eine Fallstudie zum Strafvollzug nach dem "Polenstrafrecht"', in F.P. Kahlenberg (ed.), *Aus der Arbeit der Archive* (Boppard, 1989), 603–23.
Klausch, H.-P., *Die 999er. Von der Brigade 'Z' zur Afrika-Division 999* (Frankfurt am Main, 1986).
—— *Antifaschisten in SS-Uniform* (Bremen, 1993).
—— *Die Bewährungstruppe 500. Stellung und Funktion der Bewährungstruppe 500 im System von NS-Wehrrecht, NS-Militärjustiz und Wehrmachtstrafvollzug* (Bremen, 1995).
Klee, E., *Was sie taten – Was sie wurden* (Frankfurt am Main, 1986).
—— *Auschwitz, die NS-Medizin und ihre Opfer* (Frankfurt am Main, 1997).
Klepsch, T., *Nationalsozialistische Ideologie. Beschreibung ihrer Struktur vor 1933* (Münster, 1990).
Kleßmann, C., 'Hans Frank – Parteijurist und Generalgouverneur in Polen', in R. Smelser, E. Syring, R. Zitelmann (eds), *Die Braune Elite*, vol. 1, 4th edition (Darmstadt, 1999), 41–51.
Knobelsdorf, A., 'Das Bielefelder Landgericht 1933–1945', in Justizministerium des Landes NRW (ed.), *Justiz und Nationalsozialismus* (Düsseldorf, 1993), 47–101.
Koch, B., 'Das System des Stufenstrafvollzuges in Deutschland unter besonderer Berücksichtigung seiner Entwicklungsgeschichte' (Ph.D., Freiburg University, 1972).
Koch, H.W., *In the Name of the Volk. Political Justice in Hitler's Germany* (London, 1997).
Köhler, K., 'Zur Erinnerung an Berthold Freudenthal', *ZfStrVo* 44 (1995), 294.
Kramer, H., 'Das Nürnberger Juristenurteil (Fall 3) – eine Lektion für die Justiz der BRD?', in M. Hirsch, N. Paech, G. Stuby (eds), *Politik als Verbrechen* (Hamburg, 1986), 60–3.
Krebs, A., 'Von den Anfängen des Progressivsystems und den Vorschlägen Carl August Zellers', in H. Kaufmann, E. Schwinge, H. Welzel (eds), *Erinnerungsgabe für Max Grünhut* (Marburg an der Lahn, 1965), 93–110.
—— 'Lothar Frede. Leiter des Gefängniswesens in Thüringen von 1922–1933', in idem, *Freiheitsentzug. Entwicklung von Praxis und Theorie seit der Aufklärung*, edited by H. Müller-Dietz (Berlin, 1978), 240–51.
—— 'Die GmbH als Betriebsform der Arbeit in der Strafanstalt', ibid., 498–508.
Kreutzahler, B., *Das Bild des Verbrechers in Romanen der Weimarer Republik* (Frankfurt am Main, 1987).
Krohn, M., *Die deutsche Justiz im Urteil der Nationalsozialisten 1920–1933* (Frankfurt am Main, 1991).
Kühl, S., *The Nazi Connection. Eugenics, American Racism, and German National Socialism* (New York, 1994).

Lang, J. von, *The Secretary* (New York, 1979).
Langelüddeke, A., *Die Entmannung von Sittlichkeitsverbrechern* (Berlin, 1963).
Large, D.C. (ed.), *Contending with Hitler. Varieties of German Resistance in the Third Reich* (Cambridge, 1995).
Lassen, H.-C., 'Der Kampf gegen Homosexualität, Abtreibung und "Rassenschande". Sexualdelikte vor Gericht in Hamburg 1933 bis 1945', in Justizbehörde Hamburg (ed.), *'Für Führer, Volk und Vaterland . . .'*, 216–89.
—— 'Zum Urteil gegen Jacobsohn', in Justizbehörde Hamburg (ed.), *'Von Gewohnheitsverbrechern'*, 177–84.
Leukel, S., 'Reformvorstellungen zum Frauenstrafvollzug im deutschen Kaiserreich', paper delivered at the workshop 'Crime and Criminal Justice in Modern Germany', May 2001, German Historical Institute (Washington, DC).
Leuthold, G., 'Veröffentlichungen des medizinischen Schrifttums in den Jahren 1933–1945 zum Thema: "Gesetz zur Verhütung erbkranken Nachwuchses vom 14. Juli 1933"' (Ph.D., University Erlangen-Nuremberg, 1975).
Lewy, G., *The Nazi Persecution of the Gypsies* (Oxford, 2000).
Liang, H.-H., *Die Berliner Polizei in der Weimarer Republik* (Berlin, 1977).
Liang, O., 'Criminal-biological Theory, Discourse, and Practice in Germany, 1918–1945' (Ph.D., Johns Hopkins University, Baltimore, 1999).
Lichtenstein, A., *Twice the Work of Free Labor. The Political Economy of Convict Labor in the New South* (London, 1996).
Linck, S., *Der Ordnung verpflichtet: deutsche Polizei 1933–1949: der Fall Flensburg* (Paderborn, 2000).
Löffler, M., *Das Diensttagebuch des Reichsjustizministers Gürtner 1934 bis 1938* (Frankfurt am Main, 1997).
Lotfi, G., 'Stätten des Terrors. Die "Arbeitserziehungslager" der Gestapo', in Paul, Mallmann (eds), *Gestapo im Zweiten Weltkrieg*, 255–69.
Longerich, P., *Die braunen Bataillone. Geschichte der SA* (Munich, 1989).
—— *Politik der Vernichtung* (Munich, 1998).
—— *The Unwritten Order* (Stroud, 2001).
Ludewig, H.-U., Kuessner, D., *'Es sei also jeder gewarnt'. Das Sondergericht Braunschweig 1933–1945* (Braunschweig, 2000).
Lüdtke, A., *'Gemeinwohl', Polizei und 'Festungspraxis'. Staatliche Gewaltsamkeit und innere Verwaltung in Preußen, 1815–1850* (Göttingen, 1982).
Lüerßen, D., '"Moorsoldaten" in Esterwegen, Börgermoor, Neusustrum', in W. Benz, B. Distel (eds), *Frühe Konzentrationslager 1933–39* (Berlin, 2002), 157–210.
Mai, G., 'Thüringen in der Weimarer Republik', in D. Heiden, G. Mai (eds), *Thüringen auf dem Weg ins 'Dritte Reich'* (Erfurt, no date), 11–40.
Maier, F., 'Strafvollzug im Gebiet des nördlichen Teiles von Rheinland-Pfalz im Dritten Reich', in Ministerium der Justiz Rheinland-Pfalz (ed.), *Justiz im Dritten Reich. Justizverwaltung. Rechtsprechung und Strafvollzug auf dem Gebiet des heutigen Landes Rheinland-Pfalz*, vol. 2 (Frankfurt am Main, 1995), 851–945, 970–1006.
Majer, D., *'Fremdvölkische' im Dritten Reich* (Boppard, 1981).
Mallmann, K.-M., 'Kommunistischer Widerstand 1933–1945', in P. Steinbach, J. Tuchel (eds), *Widerstand gegen den Nationalsozialismus* (Bonn, 1994), 113–25.
Mancini, M., *One Dies, Get Another. Convict Leasing in the American South, 1866–1928* (Columbia, 1996).
Mannheim, H., 'Introduction', in idem (ed.), *Pioneers in Criminology* (London, 1960), 1–35.
Marxen, K., *Der Kampf gegen das liberale Strafrecht* (Berlin, 1975).

—— *Das Volk und sein Gerichtshof* (Frankfurt am Main, 1994).

—— 'Strafjustiz im Nationalsozialismus', in B. Diestelkamp, M. Stolleis (eds), *Justizalltag im Dritten Reich* (Frankfurt am Main, 1988), 101–11.

Mason, T., 'The Legacy of 1918 for National Socialism', in A. Nicholls, E. Matthias (eds), *German Democracy and the Triumph of Hitler* (London, 1971).

Mazower, M., 'Violence and the State in the Twentieth Century', *American Historical Review* 107 (2002), 1158–78.

McConville, S., 'The Victorian Prison: England, 1865–1965', in N. Morris, D.J. Rothman (eds), *The Oxford History of the Prison* (New York, 1995), 131–67.

McGowen, R., 'The Well-Ordered Prison: England, 1780–1865', in N. Morris, D.J. Rothman (eds), *The Oxford History of the Prison* (New York, 1995), 79–109.

McKelvey, B., *American Prisons. A History of Good Intentions* (Montclair, 1977).

Mechler, W.-D., *Kriegsalltag an der 'Heimatfront'. Das Sondergericht Hannover im Einsatz gegen 'Rundfunkverbrecher', 'Schwarzschlachter', 'Volksschädlinge' und andere 'Straftäter' 1939 bis 1945* (Hanover, 1997).

Mecklenburg, F., *Die Ordnung der Gefängnisse. Grundlinien der Gefängnisreform und Gefängniswissenschaft in der ersten Hälfte des 19. Jahrhunderts in Deutschland* (Berlin, 1983).

Mehner, H., 'Aspekte zur Entwicklung des Straf- und Untersuchungshaftvollzugs in der ehemaligen sowjetischen Besatzungszone (SBZ) sowie in den Anfangsjahren der DDR', *ZfStrVo* 41 (1992), 91–7.

Mehringer, H., 'Sozialdemokratischer und sozialistischer Widerstand', in P. Steinbach, J. Tuchel (eds), *Widerstand gegen den Nationalsozialismus* (Bonn, 1994), 126–43.

Merkl, P.H., *Political Violence under the Swastika* (Princeton, 1975).

Messerschmidt, M., Wüllner, F., *Die Wehrmachtjustiz im Dienste des Nationalsozialismus* (Baden-Baden, 1987).

Milward, A., *The Fascist Economy of Norway* (Oxford, 1972).

Miquel, M. von, 'Juristen: Richter in eigener Sache', in N. Frei (ed.), *Karrieren im Zwielicht. Hitlers Eliten nach 1945* (Frankfurt am Main, 2001), 181–237.

Moeller, R.G., *War Stories. The Search for a Usable Past in the Federal Republic of Germany* (Berkeley, 2001).

—— 'The Homosexual Man is a "Man", the Homosexual Woman is a "Woman": Sex, Society, and the Law in Postwar West Germany', in idem (ed.), *West Germany under Construction. Politics, Society and Culture in the Adenauer Era* (Ann Arbor, 1997), 251–84.

Möhler, R., 'Nationalsozialistischer Strafvollzug – ein interdisziplinäres Forschungsprojekt an der Universität Saarbrücken', in H. Müller-Dietz (ed.), *Dreißig Jahre Südwestdeutsche und Schweizerische Kriminologische Kolloquien* (Freiburg im Breisgau, 1994), 111–27.

—— 'Strafvollzug im "Dritten Reich": Nationale Politik und regionale Ausprägung am Beispiel des Saarlandes', in H. Jung, H. Müller-Dietz (eds), *Strafvollzug im 'Dritten Reich'. Am Beispiel des Saarlandes* (Baden-Baden, 1996), 9–301.

Morré, J., 'Sowjetische Speziallager in Deutschland', unpublished manuscript in the possession of the author.

Morris, N., Rothman, D.J. (eds), *The Oxford History of the Prison* (New York, 1995).

Müller, C., *Das Gewohnheitsverbrechergesetz vom 24. November 1933* (Baden-Baden, 1997).

—— 'Das Gewohnheitsverbrechergesetz vom 24. November 1933', *Zeitschrift für Geschichtswissenschaft* 47 (1999), 965–79.

—— 'Verbrechensbekämpfung im Anstaltsstaat. Psychiatrie, Kriminologie und Strafrechtsreform in Deutschland 1871–1933' (Ph.D., University of Essen, 2002).

Müller, I., *Furchtbare Juristen. Die unbewältigte Vergangenheit unserer Justiz* (Munich, 1989).
—— *Hitler's Justice* (London, 1991).
—— 'Der Weltbühnenprozeß von 1931', in S. Berkholz (ed.), *Carl von Ossietzky. 227 Tage im Gefängnis* (Darmstadt, 1988), 13–28.
Müller, Joachim, *Sterilisation und Gesetzgebung bis 1933* (Husum, 1985).
Müller, Jürgen, ' "Bekämpfung der Homosexualität als politische Aufgabe!" Die Praxis der Kölner Kriminalpolizei bei der Verfolgung der Homosexuellen', in H. Buhlan, W. Jung (eds), *Wessen Freund und wessen Helfer?: die Kölner Polizei im Nationalsozialismus* (Cologne, 2000), 492–517.
Müller, R., 'Der Fall Max Hoelz', *Mittelweg 36* 8 (1999), 78–94.
Müller-Dietz, H., *Strafvollzugsgesetzgebung und Strafvollzugsreform* (Cologne, 1970).
—— 'Das Marburger Programm aus der Sicht des Strafvollzugs', *ZStW* 94 (1982), 599–618.
—— 'Der Strafvollzug in der Weimarer Zeit und im Dritten Reich. Ein Forschungsbericht', in M. Busch, E. Krämer (eds), *Strafvollzug und Schuldproblematik* (Pfaffenweiler, 1988), 15–38.
—— 'Einleitung', in G. Radbruch, *Strafvollzug*, bearbeitet von H. Müller-Dietz (Heidelberg, 1993), 1–24.
—— 'Albert Krebs. Annäherungen an Leben und Werk', *ZfStrVo* 42 (1993), 69–76.
Muntau, J., *Strafvollzug und Gefangenenfürsorge im Wandel der Zeit* (Bonn, 1962).
Musial, B., *'Konterrevolutionäre Elemente sind zu erschießen'. Die Brutalisierung des deutschsowjetischen Krieges im Sommer 1941* (Berlin, 2000).
Naucke, W., 'Die Kriminalpolitik des Marburger Programms 1882', *ZStW* 94 (1982), 525–64.
—— 'NS-Strafrecht: Perversion oder Anwendungsfall moderner Kriminalpolitik?', *Rechtshistorisches Journal* 11 (1992), 279–92.
Naumann, K., 'Die Justizvollzugsverwaltung im Institutionengefüge des NS-Staats. Das Beispiel Kassel-Wehlheiden', *Hessisches Jahrbuch für Landesgeschichte* 52 (2002), 115–44.
Neliba, G., 'Wilhelm Frick und Thüringen als Experimentierfeld für die nationalsozialistische Machtergreifung', in D. Heiden, G. Mai (eds), *Nationalsozialismus in Thüringen* (Weimar, 1995), 75–95.
Nerdinger, W., (ed.), *Bauen im Nationalsozialismus. Bayern 1933–1945* (Munich, 1993).
Nicke, H.-J., *In Ketten durch die Klosterstraße. Leben und Kampf eingekerkerter Antifaschisten im Zuchthaus Luckau* (East Berlin, 1986).
Niermann, H.-E., *Die Durchsetzung politischer und politisierter Strafjustiz im Dritten Reich* (Düsseldorf, 1995).
—— 'Strafjustiz und Nationalsozialismus im OLG-Bezirk Hamm, 1933–1945', in Oberstadtdirektor der Stadt Hamm (ed.), *Ortstermin Hamm. Zur Justiz im Dritten Reich* (Hamm, 1991), 17–45.
Niethammer, L. (ed.), *Der 'gesäuberte' Antifaschismus. Die SED und die roten Kapos von Buchenwald* (Berlin, 1994).
—— 'Alliierte Internierungslager in Deutschland nach 1945', in S. Mironenko, L. Niethammer, A. von Plato, V. Knigge, G. Morsch (eds), *Sowjetische Straflager in Deutschland 1945 bis 1950*, vol. 1 (Berlin, 1998), 97–116.
Nipperdey, T., *Deutsche Geschichte. 1866–1918*, vol. 1 (Munich, 1990).
Noakes, J., 'Nazism and Eugenics: The Background to the Nazi Sterilization Law of 14 July 1933', in R. Bullen, H. von Strandmann, A. Polonsky (eds), *Ideas into Politics* (London, 1984), 75–94.
Noam, E., Kropat, W.-A., *Justiz und Judenverfolgung*, 2 vols (Wiesbaden, 1975).
Nutz, T., *Strafanstalt als Besserungsmaschine. Reformdiskurs und Gefängniswissenschaft 1775–1848* (Munich, 2001).

O'Brien, P., 'The Prison on the Continent. Europe, 1865–1965', in N. Morris, D.J. Rothman (eds), *The Oxford History of the Prison* (New York, 1995), 199–225.
Oehler, C., *Die Rechtsprechung des Sondergerichts Mannheim 1933–1945* (Berlin, 1997).
Oleschinski, B., 'Die Abteilung Strafvollzug der Deutschen Zentralverwaltung für Justiz in der Sowjetischen Besatzungszone 1945–1949', *ZfStrVo* 41 (1992), 83–90.
—— 'Strafvollzug in Deutschland vor und nach 1945', *Neue Justiz* 2 (1992), 65–8.
—— '"Ein letzter stärkender Gottesdienst . . .". Die deutsche Gefängnisseelsorge zwischen Republik und Diktatur 1918–1945' (Ph.D., Free University Berlin, 1993).
—— 'Der Gefängnisgeistliche Peter Buchholz im Dritten Reich', *ZfStrVo* 42 (1993), 22–41.
Orth, K., *Das System der nationalsozialistischen Konzentrationslager* (Hamburg, 1999).
Ortner, H., *Der Hinrichter. Roland Freisler – Mörder im Dienste Hitlers* (Vienna, 1993).
Ottosen, K., 'Arbeits- und Konzentrationslager in Norwegen 1940–1945', in R. Bohn et al. (eds), *Neutralität und totalitäre Aggression. Nordeuropa und die Großmächte im Zweiten Weltkrieg* (Stuttgart, 1991), 355–68.
Overy, R., *War and Economy in the Third Reich* (Oxford, 1994).
—— *The Nazi Economic Recovery 1932–1938* (Cambridge, 1996).
Panayi, P. (ed.), *Weimar and Nazi Germany. Continuities and Discontinuities* (Harlow, 2001).
Paul, G., 'Private Konfliktregulierung, gesellschaftliche Selbstüberwachung, politische Teilhabe? Neuere Forschungen zur Denunziation im Dritten Reich', *Archiv für Sozialgeschichte* 42 (2002), 380–401.
Paul, G., Mallmann, K.-M. (eds), *Die Gestapo – Mythos und Realität* (Darmstadt, 1995).
—— *Die Gestapo im Zweiten Weltkrieg* (Darmstadt, 2000).
Paul, G., Primavesi, A., 'Die Verfolgung der "Fremdvölkischen"', in Paul, Mallmann (eds), *Gestapo – Mythos und Realität*, 388–402.
Petersen, K., *Literatur und Justiz in der Weimarer Republik* (Stuttgart, 1988).
Peukert, D.J.K., *Die KPD im Widerstand* (Wuppertal, 1980).
—— *Grenzen der Sozialdisziplinierung. Aufstieg und Krise der deutschen Jugendfürsorge von 1878 bis 1932* (Cologne, 1986).
—— *The Weimar Republic. The Crisis of Classical Modernity* (London, 1993).
—— *Inside Nazi Germany. Conformity, Opposition and Racism in Everyday Life* (London, 1993).
—— 'Alltag und Barbarei. Zur Normalität des Dritten Reiches', in D. Diner (ed.), *Ist der Nationalsozialismus Geschichte?* (Frankfurt am Main, 1987), 51–61.
—— 'The Genesis of the "Final Solution" from the Spirit of Science', in D.F. Crew (ed.), *Nazism and German Society* (London, 1994), 275–99.
—— 'Working-class Resistance: Problems and Options', in D.C. Large (ed.), *Contending with Hitler* (Cambridge, 1994), 35–48.
Pick, D., *Faces of Degeneration. A European Disorder, c.1848–c.1918* (Cambridge, 1989).
Pingel, F., *Häftlinge unter SS-Herrschaft* (Hamburg, 1978).
Pipes, R., *Legalised Lawlessness. Soviet Revolutionary Justice* (London, 1986).
Plato, A. von, 'Zur Geschichte des sowjetischen Speziallagersystems in Deutschland', in S. Mironenko, L. Niethammer, A. von Plato, V. Knigge, G. Morsch (eds), *Sowjetische Straflager in Deutschland 1945 bis 1950*, vol. 1 (Berlin, 1998), 19–75.
Plett, A., 'Von Peine aus: Hanns Kerrl, eine Karriere im 1000-jährigen Reich', *Heimatkalender Peiner Land* 31 (2001), 59–68.
Pohl, D., *Justiz in Brandenburg 1945–1955. Gleichschaltung und Anpassung* (Munich, 2001).
Polster, B., Möller, R., *Das feste Haus. Geschichte einer Straf-Fabrik* (Berlin, 1984).
Post, B., 'Vorgezogene Machtübernahme 1932: Die Regierung Sauckel', in D. Heiden, G. Mai (eds), *Thüringen auf dem Weg ins 'Dritte Reich'* (Erfurt, no date), 147–82.

Pretzel, A., 'Vorfälle im Konzentrationslager Sachsenhausen vor Gericht in Berlin', in idem, G. Roßbach (eds), *Homosexuellenverfolgung in Berlin 1933–1945* (Berlin, 2000), 119–68.

—— and Kruber, V., 'Jeder 100. Berliner. Statistiken zur Strafverfolgung Homosexueller in Berlin', in A. Pretzel, G. Roßbach (eds), *Homosexuellenverfolgung in Berlin 1933–1945* (Berlin, 2000), 169–85.

Proctor, R., *Racial Hygiene. Medicine under the Nazis* (Cambridge, Massachusetts, 1988).

Projektgruppe für vergessene Opfer des NS Regimes (ed.), *Verachtet – verfolgt – vernichtet* (Hamburg, 1988).

Quedenfeld, H.D., *Der Strafvollzug in der Gesetzgebung des Reiches, des Bundes und der Länder* (Tübingen, 1971).

Radzinowicz, L., 'Penal Regressions', *Cambridge Law Journal* 50 (1991), 422–44.

Rafter, N.H., *Partial Justice. Women in State Prisons, 1800–1935* (Boston, 1985).

Rebentisch, D., *Führerstaat und Verwaltung im Zweiten Weltkrieg* (Stuttgart, 1989).

Rittersporn, G.T., 'Zynismus, Selbsttäuschung und unmögliches Kalkül: Strafpolitik und Lagerbevölkerung in der UDSSR', in D. Dahlmann, G. Hirschfeld (eds), *Lager, Zwangsarbeit, Vertreibung und Deportation* (Essen, 1999), 291–315.

Roll-Hansen, N., 'Scandinavian Eugenics in the International Context', in idem, G. Broberg (eds), *Eugenics and the Welfare State. Sterilization Policy in Denmark, Sweden, Norway, and Finland* (East Lansing, 1996), 259–71.

Rosenbaum, A., 'Das Frauenstraflager Flußbach', in Ministerium der Justiz Rheinland-Pfalz (ed.), *Justiz im Dritten Reich. Justizverwaltung, Rechtsprechung und Strafvollzug auf dem Gebiet des heutigen Landes Rheinland-Pfalz*, vol. 2 (Frankfurt am Main, 1995), 946–70.

Rosenhaft, E., *Beating the Fascists? The German Communists and Political Violence, 1929–1933* (Cambridge, 1983).

Roth, K.-H., '"Asoziale" und nationale Minderheiten', *Protokolldienst der Evangelischen Akademie Bad Boll* 31 (1983), 120–34.

—— '"Abgabe asozialer Justizgefangener an die Polizei" – eine unbekannte Vernichtungsaktion der Justiz. Eine Dokumentation', in idem, A. Ebbinghaus, H. Kaupen-Hass (eds), *Heilen und Vernichten im Mustergau Hamburg* (Hamburg, 1984), 21–5.

Roth, T., 'Die Kölner Kriminalpolizei', in H. Buhlan, W. Jung (eds), *Wessen Freund und wessen Helfer?: die Kölner Polizei im Nationalsozialismus* (Cologne, 2000), 299–366.

—— 'Die "Asozialen" im Blick der Kripo', ibid., 424–63.

Rothmaler, C., '"Prognose: Zweifelhaft". Die kriminalbiologische Untersuchungs- und Sammelstelle der Hamburgischen Gefangenenanstalten 1926–1945', in Justizministerium des Landes NRW (ed.), *Kriminalbiologie* (Düsseldorf, 1997), 107–50.

—— 'Zum Urteil gegen Bertha K.', in Justizbehörde Hamburg (ed.), *'Von Gewohnheitsverbrechern'*, 366–79.

Rothman, D.J., *The Discovery of the Asylum. Social Order and Disorder in the New Republic* (Boston, 1971).

—— 'Perfecting the Prison: United States, 1789–1865', in idem, N. Morris (eds), *The Oxford History of the Prison* (New York, 1995), 111–29.

Rotman, E., 'The Failure of Reform. United States, 1865–1965', in N. Morris, D.J. Rothman (eds), *The Oxford History of the Prison* (New York, 1995), 169–97.

Rückerl, A., *NS-Verbrechen vor Gericht* (Heidelberg, 1982).

Rusche, G., Kirchheimer, O., *Sozialstruktur und Strafvollzug* (Frankfurt am Main, 1981).

Rusinek, B.-A., '"Wat denkste, wat mir objerümt han". Massenmord und Spurenbeseitigung am Beispiel der Staatspolizeistelle Köln 1944/45', in Paul, Mallmann (eds), *Gestapo – Mythos und Realität*, 402–16.

Saathoff, G., Schlegel, S., *Beratungsleitfaden NS-Verfolgung* (Cologne, 1995).
Sagaster, U., *Die thüringische Landesstrafanstalt Untermaßfeld in den Jahren 1923–1933* (Frankfurt am Main, 1980).
Sailer, W., 'Das Zuchthaus Kaisheim während der letzten Kriegsmonate und der amerikanischen Besatzungszeit', *ZfStrVo* 35 (1986), 259–61.
Sarodnick, W., ' "Dieses Haus muß ein Haus des Schreckens werden . . .". Strafvollzug in Hamburg 1933 bis 1945', in Justizbehörde Hamburg (ed.), *'Für Führer, Volk und Vaterland . . .'*, 332–81.
Sauer, P., *Im Namen des Königs. Strafgesetzgebung und Strafvollzug im Königreich Württemberg von 1806 bis 1871* (Stuttgart, 1984).
Scharf, E., 'Strafvollzug in der Pfalz unter besonderer Berücksichtigung der JVA Zweibrücken', in Ministerium der Justiz Rheinland-Pfalz (ed.), *Justiz im Dritten Reich. Justizverwaltung, Rechtsprechung und Strafvollzug auf dem Gebiet des heutigen Landes Rheinland-Pfalz*, vol. 2 (Frankfurt am Main, 1995), 757–849.
Schattke, H., *Die Geschichte der Progression im Strafvollzug und der damit zusammenhängenden Vollzugsziele in Deutschland* (Frankfurt am Main, 1979).
Scheer, R., 'Die nach Paragraph 42 RStBG verurteilten Menschen in Hadamar', in D. Roer, D. Henkel (eds), *Psychiatrie im Faschismus. Die Anstalt Hadamar 1933–1945* (Bonn, 1986), 237–55.
Scheerer, S., 'Beyond Confinement? Notes on the History and Possible Future of Solitary Confinement in Germany', in N. Finzsch, R. Jütte (eds), *Institutions of Confinement* (Cambridge, 1996), 349–61.
Schenk, C., *Bestrebungen zur einheitlichen Regelung des Strafvollzugs in Deutschland von 1870 bis 1923* (Frankfurt am Main, 2001).
Schiller, C., *Das Oberlandesgericht Karlsruhe im Dritten Reich* (Berlin, 1997).
Schlüter, H., *Die Urteilspraxis des nationalsozialistischen Volksgerichtshofs* (Berlin, 1995).
Schmacke, N., Güse, H.-G., *Zwangssterilisiert, verleugnet – vergessen. Zur Geschichte der nationalsozialistischen Rassenhygiene am Beispiel Bremen* (Bremen, 1984).
Schmidt, Eberhard, *Einführung in die Geschichte der deutschen Strafrechtspflege*, 3rd edition (Göttingen, 1965).
——— *Zuchthäuser und Gefängnisse* (Göttingen, no date).
Schmidt, H., *'Beabsichtige ich die Todesstrafe zu beantragen'. Die nationalsozialistische Sondergerichtsbarkeit im Oberlandesgerichtsbezirk Düsseldorf 1933 bis 1945* (Essen, 1998).
Schmitz, G., 'Wider die "Miesmacher", "Nörgler" und "Kritikaster". Zur strafrechtlichen Verfolgung politischer Äusserungen in Hamburg 1933 bis 1939', in Justizbehörde Hamburg (ed.), *'Für Führer, Volk und Vaterland . . .'*, 290–331.
——— 'Die Vor- und Nachschaubesprechungen in Hamburg, 1942–1945' in Justizbehörde Hamburg (ed.), *'Von Gewohnheitsverbrechern'*, 447–70.
Schmuhl, H.-W., *Rassenhygiene, Nationalsozialismus, Euthanasie. Von der Verhütung zur Vernichtung 'lebensunwerten Lebens', 1890–1945* (Göttingen, 1987).
Schoppmann, C., *Nationalsozialistische Sexualpolitik und weibliche Homosexualität* (Pfaffenweiler, 1991).
Schorn, H., *Der Richter im Dritten Reich. Geschichte und Dokumente* (Frankfurt am Main, 1959).
Schröter, S., *Psychiatrie in Waldheim/Sachsen (1716–1946)* (Frankfurt am Main, 1994).
Schumacher, M., (ed.), *M.d.R.. Die Reichstagsabgeordneten der Weimarer Republik in der Zeit des Nationalsozialismus* (Düsseldorf, 1991).
Schütz, R., 'Kriminologie im Dritten Reich' (Ph.D., Johannes-Gutenberg University, Mainz, 1972).

Schwartz, M., *Sozialistische Eugenik. Eugenische Sozialtechnologien in Debatten und Politik der deutschen Sozialdemokratie 1890–1933* (Bonn, 1995).
—— '"Proletarier" und "Lumpen". Sozialistische Ursprünge eugenischen Denkens', *VfZ* 42 (1994), 537–70.
—— 'Kriminalbiologie und Strafrechtsreform. Die "erbkranken Gewohnheitsverbrecher" im Visier der Weimarer Sozialdemokratie', in Justizministerium des Landes NRW (ed.), *Kriminalbiologie* (Düsseldorf, 1997), 13–68.
Schwarz, G., *Die nationalsozialistischen Lager* (Frankfurt am Main, 1996).
Schwerk, E., *Die Meisterdiebe von Berlin* (Berlin, 2001).
Seidl, R., *Der Streit um den Strafzweck zur Zeit der Weimarer Republik* (Berne, 1974).
Service, R., *A History of Twentieth-Century Russia* (London, 1998).
Siegfried, D., 'Zwischen Aufarbeitung und Schlußstrich. Der Umgang mit der NS-Vergangenheit in den beiden deutschen Staaten 1958–1969', in idem, A. Schildt, K.C. Lammers (eds), *Dynamische Zeiten: die 60er Jahre in den beiden deutschen Gesellschaften* (Hamburg, 2000), 77–113.
Simon, J., 'Kriminalbiologie – theoretische Konzepte und praktische Durchführung eines Ansatzes zur Erfassung von Kriminalität', in Justizministerium des Landes NRW (ed.), *Kriminalbiologie* (Düsseldorf, 1997), 69–105.
Sládek, O., 'Standrecht und Standgericht. Die Gestapo in Böhmen und Mähren', in Paul, Mallmann (eds), *Gestapo im Zweiten Weltkrieg*, 317–39.
Sofsky, W., *Die Ordnung des Terrors: Das Konzentrationslager* (Frankfurt am Main, 1997).
Solomon, P.H., *Soviet Criminal Justice under Stalin* (Cambridge, 1996).
Sommer, H., *Literatur der Roten Hilfe in Deutschland* (Berlin, 1991).
Sparing, F., 'Zwangskastrationen im Nationalsozialismus. Das Beispiel der Kriminalbiologischen Sammelstelle Köln', in Justizministerium des Landes NRW (ed.), *Kriminalbiologie* (Düsseldorf, 1997), 169–212.
Spierenburg, P., 'Four Centuries of Prison History', in N. Finzsch, R. Jütte (eds), *Institutions of Confinement* (Cambridge, 1996), 17–38.
Sprenger, I., *Groß-Rosen. Ein Konzentrationslager in Schlesien* (Cologne, 1996).
—— 'Das KZ Groß-Rosen in der letzten Kriegsphase', in U. Herbert, K. Orth, C. Dieckmann (eds), *Die nationalsozialistischen Konzentrationslager* (Göttingen, 1998), vol. 2, 1113–27.
Stapenhorst, H., *Die Entwicklung des Verhältnisses von Geldstrafe zu Freiheitsstrafe seit 1882* (Berlin, 1993).
Stein, W.H., 'Überlegungen zum Forschungsstand: Geschichte der Justiz im Dritten Reich, regionale NS-Justiz-Forschung und juristische Zeitgeschichte', in Ministerium der Justiz Rheinland-Pfalz (ed.), *Justiz im Dritten Reich. Justizverwaltung, Rechtsprechung und Strafvollzug auf dem Gebiet des heutigen Landes Rheinland-Pfalz*, vol. 1 (Frankfurt am Main, 1995), 11–33.
Steinbach, P., Tuchel, J. (eds), *Widerstand gegen den Nationalsozialismus* (Bonn, 1994).
Stolle, M., *Die Geheime Staatspolizei in Baden* (Konstanz, 2001).
Stolleis, M., *The Law under the Swastika* (Chicago, 1998).
Stroom, G. van der, *Duitse strafrechtspleging in Nederland en het lot der veroordeelden* (Amsterdam, 1982).
Stümke, H.G., 'The Persecution of Homosexuals in Nazi Germany', in M. Burleigh (ed.), *Confronting the Nazi Past* (London, 1996), 154–67.
Suhr, E., *Die Emslandlager. Die politische und wirtschaftliche Bedeutung der emsländischen Konzentrations- und Strafgefangenenlager 1933–1945* (Bremen, 1985).

520 Bibliography

Telp, J., *Ausmerzung und Verrat: zur Diskussion um Strafzwecke und Verbrechensbegriffe im Dritten Reich* (Frankfurt am Main, 1999).
Terhorst, K.-L., *Polizeiliche planmäßige Überwachung und polizeiliche Vorbeugungshaft im Dritten Reich* (Heidelberg, 1985).
Thoms, U., '"Eingeschlossen/Ausgeschlossen". Die Ernährung in Gefängnissen vom 18. bis 20. Jahrhundert', in U. Spickermann (ed.), *Ernährung in Grenzsituationen* (Berlin, 2002), 45–69.
Todorov, T., *Facing the Extreme. Moral Life in the Concentration Camps* (London, 2000).
Tuchel, J., *Konzentrationslager. Organisationsgeschichte und Funktion der 'Inspektion der Konzentrationslager' 1934–1938* (Boppard, 1991).
—— 'Planung und Realität des Systems der Konzentrationslager 1934–1938', in U. Herbert, K. Orth, C. Dieckmann (eds), *Die nationalsozialistischen Konzentrationslager. Entwicklung und Struktur*, vol. 1 (Göttingen, 1998), 43–59.
Turner, H.A., *Hitler's Thirty Days to Power: January 1933* (London, 1997).
Uhl, K., 'Das "verbrecherische Weib" im Diskurs der Humanwissenschaften vom Kaiserreich bis zum "Dritten Reich"' (M.A. diss., Hamburg University, 1997).
Ullrich, V., *Der ruhelose Rebell. Karl Plättner 1893–1945* (Munich, 2000).
Usborne, C., *The Politics of the Body in Weimar Germany* (Houndmills, 1992).
Viebig, M., *Das Zuchthaus Halle/Saale als Richtstätte der Nationalsozialistischen Justiz* (Magdeburg, 1998).
Viehöfer, E., 'Palais Schütz und Roter Ochsen. Zur Baugeschichte des Ludwigsburger Gefängnisses', *Ludwigsburger Geschichtsblätter* 50 (1996), 61–94.
Voglis, P., 'Political Prisoners in the Greek Civil War, 1945–50: Greece in Comparative Perspective', *Journal of Contemporary History* 37 (2002), 523–40.
Voigt, J.H., 'Die Deportation – ein Thema der deutschen Rechtswissenschaft und Politik im 19. und frühen 20. Jahrhundert', in A. Gestrich, G. Hirschfeld, H. Sonnabend (eds), *Ausweisung und Deportation* (Stuttgart, 1995), 83–101.
Volkov, S., 'Kontinuität und Diskontinuität im deutschen Antisemitismus, 1878–1945', *VfZ* 33 (1985), 221–43.
Wachsmann, N., '"Annihilation through Labor": The Killing of State Prisoners in the Third Reich', *Journal of Modern History* 71 (1999), 624–59.
—— 'From Indefinite Confinement to Extermination. "Habitual Criminals" in the Third Reich', in R. Gellately, N. Stoltzfus (eds), *Social Outsiders in Nazi Germany* (Princeton, 2001), 165–91.
—— 'Between Reform and Repression: Imprisonment in Weimar Germany', *The Historical Journal* 45 (2002), 411–32.
Wagner, J.-C., 'Das Außenlagersystem des KL Mittelbau-Dora', in U. Herbert, K. Orth, C. Dieckmann (eds), *Die nationalsozialistischen Konzentrationslager*, vol. 2 (Göttingen, 1998), 707–29.
Wagner, P., *Volksgemeinschaft ohne Verbrecher. Konzeptionen und Praxis der Kriminalpolizei in der Zeit der Weimarer Republik und des Nationalsozialismus* (Hamburg, 1996).
—— 'Das Gesetz über die Behandlung Gemeinschaftsfremder', in *Beiträge zur Nationalsozialistischen Gesundheits- und Sozialpolitik*, vol. 6 (Berlin, 1988), 75–100.
—— '"Vernichtung der Berufsverbrecher". Die vorbeugende Verbrechensbekämpfung der Kriminalpolizei bis 1937', in U. Herbert, K. Orth, C. Dieckmann (eds), *Die nationalsozialistischen Konzentrationslager*, vol. 1 (Göttingen, 1998), 87–110.
Wagner, W., *Der Volksgerichtshof im nationalsozialistischen Staat* (Stuttgart, 1974).
Walter, B., *Psychiatrie und Gesellschaft in der Moderne* (Paderborn, 1996).

Weber, H., *Die Wandlung des deutschen Kommunismus*, vol. 2 (Frankfurt am Main, 1969).
Weber, M.M., *Ernst Rüdin. Eine kritische Biographie* (Berlin, 1993).
Weckbecker, G., *Zwischen Freispruch und Todesstrafe. Die Rechtsprechung der nationalsozialistischen Sondergerichte Frankfurt/Main und Bromberg* (Baden-Baden, 1998).
Wehler, H.-U., *Deutsche Gesellschaftsgeschichte*, vol. 3 (Munich, 1995).
Weindling, P., *Health, Race and German Politics between National Unification and Nazism, 1870–1945* (Cambridge, 1989).
Weinkauff, H., *Die deutsche Justiz und der Nationalsozialismus* (Stuttgart, 1968).
Weisbrod, B., 'Gewalt in der Politik. Zur politischen Kultur in Deutschland zwischen den beiden Weltkriegen', *Geschichte in Wissenschaft und Unterricht* 43 (1992), 391–404.
Weiss, S.F., *Race Hygiene and National Efficiency. The Eugenics of Wilhelm Schallmayer* (Berkeley, 1987).
Welch, D., *The Third Reich. Politics and Propaganda* (London, 1995).
Welch, S.R., '"Harsh but Just?" German Military Justice in the Second World War', *German History* 17 (1999), 369–99.
Wentker, H., *Justiz in der SBZ/DDR 1945–1953* (Munich, 2001).
Werle, G., *Justiz-Strafrecht und polizeiliche Verbrechensbekämpfung im Dritten Reich* (Berlin, 1989).
Wetzell, R.F., *Inventing the Criminal. A History of German Criminology, 1880–1945* (Chapel Hill, 2000).
—— 'Criminal Law Reform in Imperial Germany' (Ph.D., Stanford University, 1991).
Werkentin, F., *Politische Strafjustiz in der Ära Ulbricht: Vom bekennenden Terror zur verdeckten Repression*, 2nd edition (Berlin, 1997).
—— *Recht und Justiz im SED-Staat* (Bonn, 2000).
—— 'Justizgeschichte in der SBZ/DDR 1945–1989', *Archiv für Sozialgeschichte* 42 (2002), 448–55.
Wheatcroft, S., 'The Scale and Nature of German and Soviet Repression and Mass Killings, 1930–45', *Europe–Asia Studies* 48 (1996), 1319–53.
Wiener, M.J., *Reconstructing the Criminal. Culture, Law and Policy in England, 1830–1914* (Cambridge, 1990).
Wildt, M., *Generation des Unbedingten. Das Führungskorps des Reichssicherheitshauptamtes* (Hamburg, 2002).
Wilhelm, F., *Die Polizei im NS-Staat. Die Geschichte ihrer Organisation im Überblick* (Paderborn, 1997).
Willett, J., *The New Sobriety. Art and Politics in the Weimar Period 1917–1933* (London, 1982).
Witter, K., 'Funktion und Organisation der Zuchthäuser im kapitalistischen Deutschland, dargelegt am Beispiel des Zuchthauses Untermaßfeld, 1813–1945' (Diplomarbeit, Humboldt University, East Berlin, 1982).
Wolfgang, M.E., 'Cesare Lombroso', in H. Mannheim (ed.), *Pioneers in Criminology* (London, 1960), 168–227.
Wrobel, H., *Verurteilt zur Demokratie. Justiz und Justizpolitik in Deutschland 1945–1949* (Heidelberg, 1989).
Wüllner, F., *Die NS-Militärjustiz und das Elend der Geschichtsschreibung* (Baden-Baden, 1991).
—— 'Der Wehrmacht "strafvollzug" im Dritten Reich. Zur zentralen Rolle der Wehrmachtgefängnisse in Torgau', in N. Haase, B. Oleschinski (eds), *Das Torgau-Tabu* (Leipzig, 1993), 29–44.
Wysocki, G., 'Lizenz zum Töten. Die "Sonderbehandlungspraxis" der Stapo-Stelle Braunschweig', in Paul, Mallmann (eds), *Gestapo im Zweiten Weltkrieg*, 237–54.

Zarusky, J., 'Politischer Widerstand und Justiz im Dritten Reich', *Jahrbuch der Juristischen Zeitgeschichte* 1 (1999/2000), 36–87.
—— 'Gerichte des Unrechtsstaates', *Zeitschrift für neuere Rechtsgeschichte* 22 (2000), 503–18.
Zarzycki, E., *Besatzungsjustiz in Polen. Sondergerichte im Dienste deutscher Unterwerfungsstrategie* (Berlin, 1990).
Zeidler, M., *Das Sondergericht Freiberg. Zu Justiz und Repression in Sachsen 1933–1940* (Dresden, 1998).
Zimmermann, M., 'Ausgrenzung, Ermordung, Ausgrenzung', in A. Lüdtke (ed.), *'Sicherheit' und 'Wohlfahrt'. Polizei, Gesellschaft und Herrschaft im 19. und 20. Jahrhundert* (Frankfurt am Main, 1992), 344–70.

Index

Academy for German Law   74, 82, 170
Aggravated detention in penal institutions   80. *See also* Disciplinary punishment
Aichach penal institution: as case study   12; number of inmates   12, 241–2; during the economic depression   55; disciplinary punishment   88; political indoctrination   89; overcrowding (1934)   91, (1940)   241–2, (1945)   334; prison conditions (1930s)   93–5; school lessons   98; security confinement   132, 135–6, 137; Hedwig J.   137; punishment of relations between prisoners   148–9; Frieda R.   148; sterilisation   154, 156; Maria Schr.   154; Prisoner E.   162; Betty O.   162–3; anti-Semitism and Jewish prisoners   162–3; Ingeborg E.   163; prison inmates denounced to police   178–9; Hedwig S.   178–9; prisoners mobilised for military production (1942)   231; pregnant women   242; Henriette C.   242; prisoners sent to Auschwitz (1943)   289, 296; Gabriele M.   296; Therese N.   296; West Germany, personnel continuities with Third Reich   352–4
Air raids: effect on public morale   210, 220; prisoners deployed in bomb disposal   232, 235, 301; bombing of prisons during   247–8, 316, 323, 328; legal system disrupted by   321–2
Aktion T4 *see* 'Euthanasia' programme
Alcohol, link to disorder and crime   45, 47–8, 51, 52, 115, 134, 205, 294
Alcoholics: detention of   20, 129, 170; sterilisation and persecution of   150, 155–6
Alsace-Lorraine and Nazi legal terror   200
Altreich, definition of   197
Amberg penal institution   124
Ammon, von   273
Amnesties and early release   38–9, 43, 69–70, 261–2
Angermund, Ralph   9
Angriff, Der   80
'Annihilation through labour'   227–8, 283, 284–8, 296, 297, 299–306, 349–50, 378
Anrath penitentiary   237–8, 239, 348; Florence P.   237
Anti-Semitism   30, 76, 156–64, 175, 181, 193. *See also* Jews
Aschendorf sub-camp *see* Emsland camp
'Asocial' prisoners   48, 156, 210; singled out for 'annihilation through labour'   226, 284–8, 296, 378; transferred to concentration camps   284–5, 289, 292–8, 300–1, 302, 306–8

Association of German Prison Officials 32, 39, 79, 84, 128
Association of National Socialist German Jurists *see* BNSDJ
Association of Prison Warders 29, 61
Auburn penal institution (New York) 23
Auschwitz: Polish ex-convicts with TB sent to 282; prison inmates transferred to 289; Jewish prison inmates sent to 291–2, and murdered 296–7; Samuel S. 296–7; Polish prisoners murdered 297; 'criminally insane' murdered 312; Holocaust and 316; death marches from 320
Austria: and Nazi legal terror 199; prisoner escapes in 236

Bad Sulza concentration camp 179
Bavaria: prisoner population doubles (1919–23) 20; Weimar prison reforms opposed or ignored 30, 35, 62; criminal-biology in 50–1, 56; criminalisation of Sinti and Roma (1920s) 53; Nazis take control of judicial system 74; Gürtner as hardline Minister of Justice (–1932) 75; prison policy (1933) 79–80; phasing out of stages system 88; protective custody in penal institutions 168–9; denouncing political prisoners to police (1933) 177; overcrowding and starvation in prisons (1945) 334–5
Bayerische Ostmark camp *see* Ostmarkstraße prison camp
Bayreuth, as destination for the People's Court (1945) 329
Bayreuth penitentiary 273, 329
Belgian prisoners: in Germany 248, 272, 274, 328, 333; in Belgium 365
Benediktbeuern, Straubing satellite camp at 103
Beria, Lavrenty 362
Berlin penal institutions *see* Moabit, Plötzensee, Tegel
Bimler, Rudolf 317
BNSDJ 71, 74, 82
Bochum penal institution 240, 274, 329–30
Boeters, Gerhard 151
Bomb disposal squads, prisoners deployed in 232, 235, 301
Bondy, Curt 32, 63–4
Bonhoeffer, Dietrich 321

Born, Kurt 311
Bormann, Martin 38, 224, 258, 323, 332, 351, 382
'Born criminal', concept of 46–7, 88. See also 'Incorrigibles'
Bouhler, Phillipp 173–4
Brack, Viktor 310
Brandenburg (Havel): escape of penitentiary inmates (1920) 40; Rudolf Höß imprisoned (1920s) 38–9; 'euthanasia' killings 310
Brandenburg-Görden: as case study 11–12; militarisation of (1933–) 84; overcrowding (1934) 85; Nazi activists as warders 85–6; prison labour 99, 173; solitary confinement 119; political prisoners 120, 121, 122–3; security confinement 131–2, 134, 136–7; Jewish prisoners 163–4; Max H. 163–4; *Work and Imprisonment in the Brandenburg-Görden Penitentiary* (film) 233; liberties for trusted prisoners 235–6; penalties for escape 237; malnutrition 240, 243; treatment of TB victims 261; Robert H. 261; transfer of inmates to concentration camps 305; executions 316, 317, 336; Red Army liberates 336; conditions in GDR 360; model cells to impress international visitors (1935) 369
Brandstätter, Heinz 127
Brecht, Bertolt 42
Breslau penal institution 328
Brieg penitentiary 91, 328
Brodowski, Hans 330
Broszat, Martin 6
Bruchsal penal institution 23
Buber, Martin 42
Buchenwald concentration camp: inmates transferred to penal institutions 175; judicial proceedings against guards set aside 175; prison inmates transferred to 295, 299, and killed 298; 'criminally insane' murdered in 312
Buchwitz, Otto 269
Bumke, Erwin 25, 342, 370, 371

Camp North 252–4, 308, 377
Capital punishment: and Lex van der Lubbe 72–3; increasing use of 197, 198, 218, 220, 314–18, 376, 402–3 (*Fig.10*); for economic crimes 221;

and People's Court 222, 273, 315, 398–9 (*Fig.7*); Hitler attacks earlier failure to use 263; military courts impose 264; West Germany abolishes (1949) 354; East Germany retains 360; in England 364
Castration: under Habitual Criminals Law 70, 140–1, 268, 400–1 (*Fig.9*); Nazi pressure for 139–40; discussion in Weimar years 140; operations and impact 142–4; and homosexuals 146–7; western states' practice of 368
Celle penal institution 152, 269, 297
Central Agency for the Solution of National-Socialist Crimes 10, 347
Chemnitz penal institution 168
Chlabicz, Wladislaw 277
Civilian courts martial 322–3, 345
Civilians, contact with prison inmates: in the Weimar period 35, 38, 39, 41, 44, 81; in the Third Reich 81, 86, 89, 94, 100, 106, 121, 124, 133, 135, 163, 172, 235–6, 237–8, 240, 243, 251, 257, 273, 280, 305, 327, 330
Cologne penal institution (Klingelpütz) 143, 168, 242, 318
Communists: popular association with criminality 39–40; prison governors' loathing for (1920s) 39–40; hungerstrike in Lichtenburg (1921) 41; agitation for imprisoned activists in Weimar years 41–2; resistance and repression in Third Reich 113, 115–17, 118, 165–6; prison conditions for 118–24; Thälmann in Moabit prison 119, 370; response of prisoners to Hitler–Stalin Pact 122, 198; glorification in East Germany 122–3, 356; transferred from prisons to concentration camps 176, 180, 293–5. *See also* Political prisoners
'Community aliens': removal from society as Nazi aim 1, 68; violence against not treated as criminal 70; campaign against 112–64, 380; escalation of repression of 191, 192–3; ferocity of sentences against 284. *See also* 'Habitual criminals', Homosexuals, Jehovah's Witnesses, Jews, Political prisoners
Concentration camps: as expression of Nazi terror 6; deportation to without trial 68, 206; convicts sent to 124; 'early camps' (1933) 167;

number of inmates 169, 170, 185, 194, 211–12, 394–5 (*Fig.2*); growth under SS control 170; Ministry of Justice refuses to hand over prison inmates to 173; legal officials excluded from 175; prison inmates transferred to 175–83, 261–2, 282–3, 288–96, 328; replacing prisons as main site of imprisonment 211–12; forced labour and extermination 227–8; Reich Ministry of Justice officials visit 255–6, 296; and death camps 256; convicts murdered in 296–9, 304, 306, 311–12; mortality and murder (1945) 320, 321; West German courts find deportation of prison inmates to be lawful 351. *See also* Auschwitz, Bad Sulza, Buchenwald, Dachau, Fuhlsbüttel, Groß-Rosen, Mauthausen, Ravensbrück
Conscription of convicts 266–9
Consumer Regulations Penal Decree 196, 221
Corporal punishment *see* Disciplinary punishment
'Correction' of sentences *see* Police
Correctional Custody Law (Weimar draft) 20
Cottbus penitentiary 240, 273
Crime: moral panic regarding 18–20, 54–9, 69, 128; rate in Weimar 19–20, 33–4, 54–5; in pre-war Nazi Germany 69–70; in early war years 198; by young people and women during the war 221, 241–2. *See also* Political prisoners, Property crime, Sex offences, Young offenders
Criminal biology: in Weimar years 50–2, 56, 61; in Third Reich 129; Habitual Criminals Law based on principles of 129; petty criminals as 'biological inferiors' 134; and transfer of prison inmates to concentration camps (1942–) 294, 302. *See also* 'Incorrigibles', Viernstein
Criminal Code: in Prussia (1851) 21; drafts in German Empire and Weimar 22, 49–50, 128, 151, 375; in Germany (1871) 26, 130, 144; draft in Nazi Germany 82–3, 375; in Austria 199; in West Germany 354; in East Germany 356; in Norway 367; in Switzerland 367

Criminal Law Decree for Poles and Jews (1941)   203–4, 225, 314
Criminalisation: of enemies of Nazi regime   4, 70; of Communists   39–40; of non-conformist behaviour   69, 113–15, 373; of homosexuality   70, 145–6; of Jews and 'racial aliens'   157–9, 193–4; of sexual relations: with Jews   157–9, 163, with Poles   203–4, 205, with POWs   222
'Criminally insane' offenders: in Germany   155, 308–12; in the US   368. *See also* Mental asylums
Criminology and criminologists   25, 46–9, 51, 54, 56, 58, 98, 131, 133, 135, 140, 142, 143, 151, 152, 153, 196, 202, 303, 309, 364, 367, 369, 370, 375
Crohne, Wilhelm   76, 126, 160, 160–1, 174, 181, 216
Czechoslovakia: Hitler plans attack on (1938)   105; Nazi legal terror extended to   200; Czechs tried by People's Court   200, 315; fate of Czech prisoners   269–71, 286, 296, 324

Dachau concentration camp: establishment of (1933)   170; mortality in   188, 256; Reich Ministry of Justice official praises (1938)   255; 'criminally insane' murdered in   312
Dahm, Georg   59, 371
Daluege, Kurt   165
'Dangerous habitual criminals': and security confinement   128–39; and sterilisation   151–3; extermination of   210–11, 219–20, 225–6, 285, 286, 298, 303. *See also* 'Annihilation through labour', Habitual Criminals Law, 'Incorrigibles', Security confinement
Death penalty *see* Capital punishment
Decree against National Pests (1939)   196, 243, 315, 347
Decree against Violent Criminals (1939)   196
Decree concerning Exceptional Methods relating to Radio (1939)   195, 222, 270, 296, 334, 387
Decree for the Protection of People and State (1933)   166. *See also* Protective custody
Decree to Supplement the Penal Provisions for the Protection of the Military Strength of the German People (1939)   195–6. *See also* POWs
Degen, Richard   61
'Degeneracy' and 'degenerates'   20, 47–8, 52, 74, 112, 144, 147, 149, 152, 153, 169, 202, 203, 210, 294, 367, 375
Denunciations: role in Nazi terror   4, 114, 115, 159, 199, 386–7; inside penal institutions   90, 124–5, 148–9, 161, 163, 245, 250; of prison inmates to security confinement   131; of prison inmates to sterilisation   151, 156; of prison inmates to police   176–83, 204, 247 (*see also* 'Annihilation through labour')
Dimpfl, Anni   98, 178, 352, 353
Disciplinary punishment in prisons: in the German Empire   23; in the Weimar Republic   26, 29, 30, 31–2, 75; in the Third Reich   79, 80, 81, 82–3, 87–8, 90, 124, 135–6, 148–9, 162–3, 173, 174, 187, 237, 245, 260, 276, 279; in West Germany   355; compared with Western states   366, 367
Dörner, Bernward   115
Dreibergen-Bützow penal institution   355; Prisoner S.   355
Drendel, Karl   275
Dual State, Nazi Germany as   3, 378–83
Duisburg prison *see* Oberhausen-Holten prison camp
Dutch prisoners: in Germany   236, 272, 281, 328, 333; in the Netherlands   365, 368

East Germany *see* Germany, East
Eberhard, Werner   302–3, 352
Ebrach penitentiary   40, 182, 300, 334, 335; Joseph K.   182; Johannes E.   334
Egelfing-Haar asylum   310
Eichler, Johannes   352
Eichmann, Adolf   291, 347
Eicke, Theodor   369
Einstein, Albert   42
Eisenach prison   63, 127, 180, 181
Eisner, Kurt   40
Elgas, Karl   121, 179
Empire *see* Imperial Germany
Emsland prison camp: studies of   5, 12–13; establishment and operation   102–5; brutality   106–9, 188, 248–54, 377; *Kapo* system   107, 109, 188, 250;

Aschendorf sub-camp   108, 109, 337; Prisoner P.   108; security-confined inmates sent to   136; treatment of homosexuals   147, 149; Prisoner K. 149; Jews excluded from   160; 'war offenders' in   248; brutality of Esterwegen sub-camp   249, 251, 252, 274; death rate   251, 256, 398–9 (*Fig.6*); Richard L.   251; Wilhelm K. 251; prisoners deported to camp North   252–4; soldiers sent to 264–5; Herbert R.   266; probation troop   500 recruited from   265–6; *NN* prisoners   274; Polish prisoners 277; executions (1945)   337; postwar investigations of   348
Engelhardt, Karl   301
Engert, Karl   292, 294, 295, 296, 300, 304, 308, 311, 316, 325, 343, 396, 397
England, punishment and imprisonment in   22, 99, 364, 365, 366
Ensisheim penitentiary   236, 308
Erbkrank (film)   309
Escapes from penal institutions   36, 40, 85, 87, 236–7
Esterwegen sub-camp *see* Emsland prison camp
Eugenics   150, 152, 153, 302, 313–14, 368
'Euthanasia' programme   191, 223, 286–7, 309–11
Exner, Franz   58

Faber, August   299–300, 301, 352
Fechenbach, Felix   40–1, 42
Ferri, Enrico   46
Finkelnburg, Karl Maria   43–4, 51
First World War: Hitler and the 'lessons' of 97; rise in youth crime and female convicts   196, 241; prison labour 232; cuts in prison provisions   238; food provision for German population   239; operation of military courts   263; capital punishment   316. *See also* Revolution (1918)
Flensburg prison   86
Flossenbürg concentration camp   320, 321
Fordon penitentiary   326
Foreign workers   202–4, 205–6, 320–1
Foreigners: extension of Nazi terror towards   199–204, 211; prisoner numbers   257, 377; political prisoners   269–83. *See also* Czechoslovakia, Dutch prisoners, France, Norway, Poles, POWs, Soviet Union
Formation Dirlewanger   262–3, 265, 266, 268
Fortress, imprisonment in a   38
Foucault, Michel   7, 23–4, 51
Four-Year Plan, role of prison labour in 97, 99–101, 103, 110–11
Fraenkel, Ernst   3, 166, 379–83
France: prison camp in (1943–44)   254–5; French prisoners in Germany   238, 242, 272, 274, 328, 333
Frank, Hans   74–5, 82, 152, 201, 342, 370, 388
Franziska K. (Aichach)   136–7, 289
Frede, Lothar   27, 29, 64
Freiendietz penitentiary   163
Freisler, Roland: Weimar penal policy attacked by   74; as Prussian State Secretary for Justice (1933–34)   74, 96; appointed as German State Secretary for Justice (1934)   75–6; envisages prison as 'house of horror' (1933)   76; Four-Year Plan, deploys prison labour under   99, 100, 103; Emsland camp commended by   103; reluctance to release the security-confined   137, 138; discriminates against Jewish prisoners   161; and police 'corrections' of court sentences (1937)   171; supports Hitler's wish to exterminate criminals   193, 196; and special courts   197, 386; repression of Poles   204; as President of People's Court (1942–45)   216–17, 218; supports recruitment of young offenders for army (1941)   266; supports transfer of foreign civilians to German prisons (1941)   272–3; orders stricter treatment of Polish prisoners   278; champions execution of criminals   314; killed in air raid (1945)   321; at Prison and Penitentiary Congress (1935)   370, 371
Freudenthal, Berthold   28, 62, 364
Frick, Wilhelm   141
Führer-Informations   233–4
Fuhlsbüttel concentration camp   185
Fuhlsbüttel penitentiary   168

Garbe, Detlef   264
GDR *see* Germany, East
Gellately, Robert   3–4

Index

Gender balance: in German penal institutions 12, 24, 92, 241–2, 396–7 (*Fig.5*); in Nazi prison administration 93–4
General Government 200, 325
General state prosecutors, role and outlook 77
Gentz, Werner 48, 78, 358
Gericke, Johannes 63
German League for Human Rights 41, 42, 44
Germany, East (GDR): studies of Nazi prisons 5, 122–3; attempts to undermine West Germany 346; purge of Nazi legal officials 356–8; poor prison conditions in 358–9, 360–1; courts as instruments of political leadership 359–60
Germany, West: de-nazification of jurists 344–6, 347; trials and re-employment of Nazi legal officials 347–54; Habitual Criminals Law retained (without castration clause) 354; death penalty abolished 354; prison regulations, continuity and change 354–5; prisoners and compensation 356
Gestapo *see* Police
Giese, Kurt 311, 349
Glatz, as destination for prisoners with TB 260
Goebbels, Joseph 80, 89, 193–4, 195, 209, 210, 212, 213, 217, 285, 316, 370
Gollnow penitentiary 168, 333
Göring, Hermann 67, 69, 97, 103, 165, 166, 268–9
Gostomski, Victor von 239
Gräfentonna penal institution 82, 132, 135; Anna K. 306
Grasshof, Otto 128
Griebo prison camp 104, 109
Großmann, Kurt 41
Groß-Rosen concentration camp 320, 328
Groß-Strehlitz penal institution 44, 96, 328
Gruchmann, Lothar 3, 5, 9
Gündner, Otto 292, 308, 349
Gürtner, Franz: as Reich Minister of Justice (–1941) 71–3, 75, 168, 216, 219, 223, 380; as Bavarian Minister of Justice (–1932) 72, 75; supports Lex van der Lubbe 73; tries to draft new criminal code 82; accepts brutality at Emsland camp 108–9; persecution of Jehovah's Witnesses 126, 181–2; enthusiasm for security confinement 130–1, 138; awareness of poor conditions in security confinement 136; supports criminal-biology 140; and Sterilisation Law 152; signs Nuremberg Laws 158; and detention without trial in concentration camps 168, 169, 182; attempts to regulate treatment of police detainees 172–3, 174; refuses transfer of prisoners to concentration camps before sentence completed (1939) 173–4; and the legacy of 1918 194–5; objects to Decree concerning Exceptional Methods relating to Radio 195; endorsement of special courts (1939) 197; death (1941) 203; attempts to curb police 'corrections' 208; campaigns against 'Gypsy plague' 290; comes to support 'euthanasia' killings 310; at Prison and Penitentiary Congress (1935) 370, 371
Gustav T. (Remscheid-Lüttringhausen) 132, 133
Gütt, Arthur 152
Gypsies *see* Sinti and Roma

Habitual Criminals Law (1933) 70, 128–32; Weimar drafts for 128, 375; workhouse detention introduced under 129–30; application of principles of criminal biology 129; indefinite security confinement introduced under 130; castration introduced under 140, 146; sterilisation not included in 152, 153; detention in asylums introduced under 153, 155, 309; eugenic aims of 153; plans to adapt to total war 226; West Germany retains (without castration clause) 354; penalties under 400–1 (*Fig.9*)
Halle prison 357
Hamburg prison service 30, 33, 78. *See also* Fuhlsbüttel
Hammer, Walter 125, 245
Hanssen, Kurt-Walter 332
Hecker, Robert 288, 291, 294, 304, 349, 350, 351
Heindl, Robert 48–9, 130, 290
Hereditary Health Courts 150, 154, 155. *See also* Sterilisation Law

Heß, Rudolf   38, 279
Heuck, Christian   174
Heyde, Werner   310
Heydrich, Reinhard   170, 173, 194, 200, 315
Higher State Courts   116
Himmler, Heinrich: homophobia of   144; as head of police   169; establishment of Dachau (1933)   170; defends breaches of the law   170; attempts to 'poach' prison inmates   173–4; violent interrogations approved by   174; charged by Hitler with maintenance of order (1939)   194; execution of 'racial aliens'   205; orders execution of criminals   207, 210, 211; as Reich Minister of the Interior (1943)   211; 'racial aliens' to be dealt with by police (1942–)   223–4; secret address to legal officials (1944)   246; 'annihilation through labour' of prison inmates   285, 286, 292; orders summary execution of 'defeatists'   320; Gestapo given free hand to murder foreign workers (1945)   320; police designed to realise 'will of the Führer'   372; Hitler's closeness to   387
Hippel, Robert von   128
Hitler, Adolf: imprisonment in early (1920s)   37–8; attack on Weimar judicial system   57; demands brutal punishment of 'treason' (1933)   68; role of legal system in Nazi regime defined by   68–9; retains Gürtner as Reich Minister of Justice   72–5; decides to retain Criminal Code   83; *Mein Kampf*   88, 157, 192, 263; growing popularity in Third Reich   96, 118; and Four-Year Plan   97; favourably impressed by Emsland camp   103; decides against using prison labour to construct Westwall   105; determines on conquest of Czechoslovakia   105; left-wing opposition to be converted or exterminated (1926)   113; demands castration of sex offenders   140; campaign against homosexuals   145; sterilisation of 'habitual criminals' demanded by   152; anti-Semitism of   156–7; and Nuremberg Laws   158; perceives Communists as behind Reichstag fire   166; justifies killings during the Night of the Long Knives   168–9; backs SS control of concentration camps   170; supports transfer of security confined prisoners to SS (1939)   173; approval of police brutality   174; criminality, racial 'deviance' and political opposition merging in the mind of   192, 194; determination to avoid recurrence of revolution of 1918   192, 210, 211, 212, 217, 263, 285; welcomes executions of 'racial aliens' for sex with German women   205; 'correction' of court sentences through executions ordered by   207, 208, 212; demands extermination of selected criminals (1942)   210–11, 213–14, 217, 285, 286–7, 303; regards prisons as too soft (1942)   212; public attack on legal system in Reichstag (1942)   212–15, 223, 388; appoints Thierack as Reich Minister of Justice (1942)   215–16; prison labour designed to impress   233; calls for preferential treatment of 'national comrades'   258, 388; selected prison inmates to be released for military duties   262, 263, 265, 268; and 'euthanasia' programme   309, 310, 311; and capital punishment   316; and People's Court (1945)   328–9; relationship with legal system   387–9; 'working towards the Führer'   388
Hoegner, Wilhelm   151–2
Hoelz, Max   42–3, 44
Hohenasperg, as destination for prisoners with TB   260
Hohenleuben prison   84
Höhler, Ali   174
Holocaust   6, 191, 209, 211, 223, 291–2, 296, 310, 316, 378
Homosexuals: criminalisation of   70, 145–6; legal terror directed against   144–9, 374; numbers in concentration camps   144; Nazi homophobia   144, 148; numbers convicted by courts   145, 146; castration of   146–7; discrimination practised against prisoners   147–8; Weimar debate on homosexuality in prison   148; convicted prisoners excluded from military service   267, 268; and compensation in West Germany   356

Index

Höß, Rudolf 38–9, 43, 207
Howard, John 22
Hupperschwiller, Albert 292, 293, 294, 307, 349, 351

Ichtershausen penal institution 30, 33, 127, 259
Imperial Germany: modern school of criminal law 21–2; prison life 23–4; compared with pre-war Nazi prisons 94–5; prison labour 97–8, 102. *See also* First World War, Revolution (1918)
'Incorrigibles': as concept 22, 46–9, 130–1; identification and treatment of (1920s) 46–54, 56, 58–9; Nazi measures against (1933–39) 95, 128, 129, 130, 131; debate on sterilisation of 152; murder of during Second World War 219, 284, 298, 325; envisaged by Thierack to be left to the police 223, 225–6; western democracies' treatment of 367–8. *See also* Criminal biology, Security confinement

Jehovah's Witnesses: persecution and legal terror against 125–7; treatment inside prisons 127–8; prison inmates sent to concentration camps 180, 181–2, 183
Jews: extermination of 6, 191, 209, 211, 223, 291–2, 296–7, 310, 316, 378; pogrom (1938) 70, 156, 170, 171, 172, 185; persecution and legal terror 70, 156–9, 374; excluded from civil service 73; portrayed as political *and* racial threat 112; Nuremberg Laws 157, 158, 160, 181; discrimination against in prisons (1933–39) 160–4; deportations of ex-convicts to concentration camps 181, 290–1; treatment in prisons compared with concentration camps 188; Nazi onslaught on (1939–41) 192, 193, 194; Criminal Law Decree for Poles and Jews 203–4; courts excluded from punishment of 223, 224; transfer of 'asocial' prison inmates to police (1942–43) 285, 286, 290–2, 300; deemed legal in West Germany 351
Joël, Günther 268, 322
Joseph, Dr Martin 160
Judges: and destruction of rule of law 3, 69, 72–3, 131, 380; compliance and sympathies with Nazi regime 8, 71, 220, 389; political bias in Weimar Republic 37–8, 40, 76; trend towards more lenient sentencing before 1930s 58; stricter sentencing (early 1930s) 58; Hitler demands 'elasticity' of sentencing (1933) 69; sentencing of Jews 70, 158; sentencing of political dissent and resistance 70, 115–18, 126–7, 222; sentencing of property crime 70, 197, 220–1, 315, 377; personnel continuities (1933) 73; sentencing of 'habitual criminals' 130–1, 171–2, 303; sentencing of sex offences and homosexuals 140–1, 145–6, 222; and sterilisation policy 150; criticism of police and SS measures 171, 177, 205; and the legacy of 1918 195, 220, 322, 391; growing enthusiasm for custodial sentences 197, 218, 221, 246; growing use of death penalty 197, 218, 314–15, 376; and sentencing of Poles 201–3, 225; pressure from above for harsher sentencing 206, 208, 219, 314, 321, 390; attacked by Hitler 212–15; sentencing of 'criminally insane' offenders 309; fighting to the end 321–3; de-nazification in West Germany 351–4; de-nazification in East Germany 356
Judges' Letters 219
Jung, Friedrich 286
Junkers, prison labour for 230, 300

Kaisheim penitentiary 294, 300, 305, 334, 337; Simon L. 294
Kakuschky, Karl 133–4, 240, 289
Kandulski, Josef 119
Kapo system 107, 109, 121, 187, 188, 250, 253, 297, 298
Karel N. (Untermaßfeld) 163, 183
Kasimir P. (Essen) 315
Kassel-Wehlheiden penal institution 179–80; Friedrich Z. 179–80
Kerrl, Hanns 74, 75, 96, 176
Kershaw, Sir Ian 113, 161
Kisch, Egon Erwin 42
Klemm, Herbert 217, 321, 342, 344
Klingelpütz *see* Cologne
Klumker, Christian Jasper 63
Knops, Theodor 332, 352
Köbrich, Erwin 243
Kohl, Franz 31, 39
Kopal, Josef 270–1

Index 531

KPD *see* Communists
Kraepelin, Emil 21
Kraus, Martin 353
Krebs, Albert 63, 351
Krejsa, Bretislaus 270
Kreuzzeitung 45
Kripo *see* Police
Kriß, Rudolf 335
Krohne, Karl 24, 31, 82, 92
Krone penal institution 279–80, 327
Kürten, Peter 55–6, 140

Lammers, Hans-Heinrich 208, 285
Landsberg penal institution 38, 46
Lang, Fritz 56–7
Lange, Johannes 143
Law against Community Aliens (draft) 146, 225–6
Law against Dangerous Habitual Criminals and on Preventive and Rehabilitative Measures *see* Habitual Criminals Law
Law against Malicious Attacks on State and Party 114–15, 179
Law for the Prevention of Offspring with Hereditary Diseases *see* Sterilisation Law
Law for the Protection of German Blood and German Honour *see* Nuremberg Laws
Law for the Restoration of the Professional Civil Service 73
Law to Protect Young People from Harmful and Obscene Publications 20
Leipzig prison 335
Leske, Willy 139, 289
Letsche, Curt 337
Lex van der Lubbe 131
Lex Zwickau 151
Lichtenburg penitentiary 41
Liepmann, Moritz 27, 62, 364
Liszt, Franz von 21–2, 47, 48, 50, 130–1, 135
Lombroso, Cesare 46, 47
Lubbe, Marinus van der 72–3, 166, 207
Lubinski, Dagobert 305
Luckau penitentiary 84, 87, 120, 121, 122, 177, 326
Ludwigsburg penal institution 124, 260
Lüttringhausen penal institution *see* Remscheid-Lüttringhausen
Luxemburg, legal terror extended to 200

Magdalena S. (Aichach) 137, 289
Marquard-Ibbeken, Frau 93

Marquardt, Heinz 360
Marriage Health Law (1935) 139
Marriage Loan scheme (1933) 150
Marx, Rudolf 76, 82, 288, 292–3, 349–51
Mauthausen concentration camp 289, 294, 297–8, 312, 320; Mieczyslaw W. 297
Max K. (Untermaßfeld) 120, 179
Medical care *see* Prison doctors
Meininger Tageblatt 60
Mental asylums 20, 25, 51, 63, 143, 150, 153, 155, 223, 238, 249, 309, 310, 311, 312
Meyer, Friedrich Wilhelm 292, 349
Mikorey, Max 143
Military courts and penal code 263–4
Military order and discipline in prisons: in German Empire 23–4; in Weimar period 29, 31–3, 42, 59, 376; in Third Reich 83–4, 135, 376; in GDR 360
Moabit penal institution (Berlin): solitary confinement 23; criminal-biological examinations 51, 52, 134; castrations 142; Friedrich K. 142; imprisonment of Ernst Thälmann 370
Modern school of criminal law 20–2, 59, 75. *See also* Liszt
Möhler, Rainer 6
Morel, Augustin 47
Mühsam, Erich 42
Müller, Heinrich 288
Müller, Ingo 201
Münster penal institution 25
Mürau penal institution 260, 281–2
Munich-Stadelheim prison 37–8, 145
Muntau, Johannes 90

National Association of Catholic Prison Teachers 58
National prison guidelines (1923) 26–7, 31–2, 38, 81
National Prison Law (draft) 82–3
National prison regulations (1934) 80–2, 87–8, 354–5
National prison regulations (1940) 258, 259
Nazi movement: members' experience of imprisonment during Weimar period 37–9, 67; distrust of legal system (1933) 68–9; amnesty of activists (1933) 69–70; judges as members of 71; prison warders as militant members of 85–6; political indoctrination in prisons 89; prisoners murdered by activists of (1933–4) 174–5

Nebe, Arthur 288
Neumünster prison 174–5
Newspapers in prisons: in Weimar period 28, 41, 62–3; in Third Reich 89, 122, 123, 160, 235, 248, 305
Night of the Long Knives 145, 168–9, 175, 188
NN prisoners 271–4, 327–8, 342, 348
Noakes, Jeremy 385
Nörr, Sigmund 100
Normative State *see* Dual State
Norway: prison camp North 252–4, 308, 377; Norwegian prisoners 273, 333, 378
Nuremberg Laws 158, 160, 181, 374, 388
Nuremberg trials 342–4, 345, 347

Oberems prison camp 104, 109–10, 232
Oberhausen-Holten prison camp 280–1
Obrawalde asylum 312
Oertel, Otto 180
Oerter, Sepp 25
Office for Racial Policy 139–40
Olberg, Oda 48
Organisation Todt 252, 254, 255
Ossietzky, Carl von 41, 76, 102
Ostmarkstraße prison camp 105–6, 109, 147

Panopticon 11
Papenburg *see* Emsland prison camp
Paterson, Alexander 24, 371
Paul G. (Untermaßfeld) 162, 181
Penitentiaries compared with prisons 2
Pennsylvania system 23
People's Court (*Volksgerichtshof*): trials of men behind July 1944 plot 9, 222; establishment and operation 117; Thierack as President of 117, 216; imprisonment and death penalty imposed 198, 216, 218, 222, 315, 398–9 (*Fig.7*); extension of role in war 198, 376; Czech nationalists tried 200; Goebbels criticises judiciary to 215; Freisler as President of 216–17, 218, 321; punishment of 'defeatism' 222; trials of NN prisoners 273; US bomb damages (1945) 321; projected move 328–9; judges re-employed in West Germany 345; role in deterrence of population 386

Perleberg, Otto 19
Peter, Herbert 295
Peukert, Detlev 18, 29, 32, 53, 63
Pilnacek, Johann 243
Pohl, Oswald 304
Plättner, Karl 43
Plötzensee penal institution (Berlin) 19, 51, 84–5, 91, 134, 160, 239, 316–17
Poles: as prisoners in Nazi Germany 161, 274–83, 377; legal terror against 200–8, 223, 224–5; as foreign workers inside Germany 202–3, 205–6; Prison Regulations (1942) 278–9; prison inmates handed to police 282–3, 285, 286, 289–90, 300, and taken to Auschwitz and Mauthausen concentration camp 297; death penalty applied to 314–15; prisoner evacuations and killings in Nazi-occupied Poland 325–7. *See also* Criminal Law Decree for Poles and Jews
Police: as part of Prerogative State (Fraenkel) 3, 382; role and operation in Third Reich 68, 166–7, 169–71, 204–5, 211, 223–5, 290, 320–1, 372, 379; Hitler's support for 68, 211, 372; conflicts with legal authorities 89, 171–4, 177, 184, 204–8, 301; Nazis take control of (1933) 166; protective custody 166–7; preventive detention 167, 170; Himmler as head of 169; interrogations of prison inmates 174; arrests of prison inmates 176–83, 204, 247, 282–3; relationship with legal apparatus 184–5, 379–83; and 'educational work camps' 206; 'corrections' of court sentences 207–8, 212, 277–8; resists conscription of convicts 267; role in 'annihilation through labour' of prison inmates 285–306; include Jewish prison inmates in extermination policy (1942) 291; executions of prison inmates towards the end of the war 325, 326, 327, 332–3, 336–7
Police detainees, treatment inside penal institutions 168–9, 172–3, 204, 242
Political prisoners: privileged status in Weimar years 37–8, 40–1, 44, 116; amnesty for Nazi supporters (1933) 69–70; convictions of 70, 115–18, 126–7, 222, 376–7; as broad category 113–14; numbers of 117–18, 166–7,

269; prison conditions for German inmates 118–25, for foreign inmates 269–74; warders' attitude towards 120–1; contempt for criminal prisoners 124–5; transfer to concentration camps 176–82, 271, 293–5, 328; and death penalty 222, 315. *See also* Communists, Jehovah's Witnesses, Social Democrats

Positivism and German jurisprudence 8, 389

POWs 193, 196, 202, 209, 220, 222, 252, 256, 264, 357

Prague, courts and prison 200, 270

Prerogative State *see* Dual State

Preußisch Stargard prison 326

Preventive detention *see* Police

Priests, imprisonment of 125–6, 247–8

Prison and Penitentiary Congress (1935) 369–71

Prison camp North *see* Norway

Prison camp West *see* France

Prison camps 101–11, 248–55.

Prison chaplains 31, 33, 39, 51, 61, 78, 79, 84–5, 90, 160, 253, 259–60, 281, 305, 316, 352

Prison doctors and medical care 92–4, 109–10, 134, 238, 242, 250, 260, 274, 282, 302–3; pregnant prisoners 93, 242; 'euthanasia' programme 311; medical use of prisoners' corpses 316–17. *See also* Castration, Schemmel, Sterilisation

Prison evacuations: by German authorities (1944–45) 324, 325–31; by Soviet authorities (1941) 362–3

Prison food: in the German Empire 23, 90, 239; in the Weimar Republic 34, 40, 43, 62, 91; in the Third Reich 90–1, 94, 101, 162, 172, 238–40, 242, 243, 245, 246, 253, 255, 274, 275, 278, 279, 282, 326, 329, 334–5

Prison governors: selection and outlook 31, 39, 93; and Weimar reforms 31–2, 35; and revolution of 1918 36, 39, 391; transition to Third Reich 78; call for stricter prison service (1933) 79; strained relations with Nazi warders 85–6; and violence against inmates 87, 243, 313; and prisoner complaints 94; and German political prisoners 124, 127; and security confinement 128–9, 131, 138, 139; and sterilisation of prisoners 153; and Jewish prisoners 160–3; denunciations of inmates to the police 177–83, 271, 283, 291; prison labour for the war effort 230; participation in 'annihilation through labour' 299–306; role in targeting other 'asocial' inmates 306–7; and evacuations 324–5, 331, 333; denazification and re-employment in West Germany 347, 352; denazification in East Germany 357

Prison labour: Weimar Germany 28, 95, 98, 102–3; Third Reich 95–101, 103, 110–11, 228–38, 280–1; Empire and First World War 97–8, 102, 232; promoted to impress Nazi leadership 100, 102–3, 232–7; in prison camps 103–11, 252–5; escapes resulting from 110, 236; whether designed for extermination 227–8; in Poland 275–6. *See also* 'Annihilation through labour', Unemployment

Prison liberations by Allies 329, 330, 352, 336, 337–8

Prison overcrowding: in Weimar years 20, 34; in Third Reich 84–5, 91–2, 102, 119, 147, 161, 232, 241–2, 259, 275, 304, 330, 331, 334–5; in East Germany 358, 360; in US 366

Prison Regulations for Poles (1942) 278–9

Prison teachers: outlook and role in Weimar period 31, 32–3, 39; and criminal-biology 51; and security confinement (1932) 58; and Nazi propaganda 89; diminishing role in Third Reich 259

Prison warders: violence against prisoners 23, 86–7, 106–10, 120, 243–4, 249–51, 253, 274, 276–8, 308, 313, 330, 334; training and outlook 24, 88, 187; and Weimar reforms 28–9, 33, 243–5; transition to Third Reich 78; and prisoner escapes 84, 135, 236; militant Nazis employed as 85–6; and political prisoners 120–1; and Jewish prisoners 161–4; personnel shortages in war 244; participation in capital punishment 317–18, 336; involvement in murder of prisoners 327, 332–3, 337; and evacuations 327; re-employment in West Germany 352

Prisoner complaints 44–5, 79, 81, 94

Prisoner letters and visits *see* Civilians
Prisoner memoirs: as sources 10–11; popularity in Weimar Germany 42–3
Prisoner numbers 20, 34, 55, 70–1, 92, 185, 192, 194, 198, 218–19, 374, 376, 392–5 (*Figs 1–3*), 396–7 (*Fig.4*); penitentiary inmates compared with prison inmates 2, 218; in prison camps 101, 231; compared with concentration camps 185, 194, 211–12, 374, 394–5 (*Fig.2*); in satellite camps 231–2 compared with western countries 365–6
Probation battalion 999 266–8
Probation troop 500 265
'Professional criminals' 48–9, 56–7, 58, 182, 207–8, 267. *See also* Habitual Criminals Law, 'Incorrigibles'
Property crime 19, 23, 33–4, 52, 55, 56, 131, 133, 134, 194, 196, 202, 204, 220–2, 315, 336
Prostitution 20, 47, 48, 49, 129, 134, 137, 145, 146, 170, 194, 294
Protective custody *see* Police
Prussia: Criminal Code (1851) 21; prisons in Weimar years 30; Nazis take control of judicial system 74; personnel changes in Ministry of Justice (1933) 78; prison population shoots up (1933) 70–1; prison regulations (1933) 80; prison labour (1920s) 98, 102; Göring heads Ministry of Interior 165; preventive detention (1933) 167. *See also* Emsland prison camp
'Psychopaths': prison inmates labelled as 45, 110, 312, 325; and crime 47–8; ban on marriages of 139
Public morale: at outbreak of war 192–3; support for regime weakening 209–10, 220, 222; collapse of (1945) 319–20. *See also* Hitler, Revolution (1918)

'Race defilement': punishment for 157–9, 162, 163, 183, 290. *See also* Nuremberg Laws
'Racial aliens': as subset of 'community aliens' 112; Hitler's radical plans to deal with 193–4; duality of police and legal terror against 204–6, 223–4; at bottom of prison hierarchy 257, 258, 274–83; transfer from prisons to concentration camps 285–6, 288, 289–92. *See also* Jews, Poles, Sinti and Roma, Soviet Union
Radbruch, Gustav 25, 48
Rations *see* Prison food
Ravensbrück concentration camp 297
Rawitsch penal institution 280
Reich Military Court 195
Reichel, Kurt 270
Reichstag fire 72–3, 166, 380
Reichstag Fire Decree *see* Decree for the Protection of People and the State (1933)
Reitzenstein, Hermann von 352
Religion in prisons 30, 33; role in Third Reich 89, 259–60. *See also* Prison chaplains
Remscheid-Lüttringhausen penitentiary 32, 92, 132, 168, 232, 276, 281, 301, 305, 337
Rendsburg penal institution 132, 355
Reuland, Josef 247–8, 329
Revolution (1918): and prisons 36–7; in the memory of legal officials 39–40, 194–5, 220, 322, 391; Nazis' determination to avoid repeat of 192, 194–5, 210, 211, 212, 213, 217, 263–4, 267, 283, 285, 322, 325
Rheika factory *see* Anrath
Ringk, governor 283
Rodgau prison camp 103–4, 109–10, 147
Röhm, Ernst 145, 146
Roma *see* Sinti and Roma
Rosa S. (Aichach) 134–5, 289
Rosenberg, Alfred 89, 119
Roßbach, Gerhard 38, 39
Rote Fahne 41
Rote Hilfe 42, 44, 123–4
Rothenberger, Curt 217, 285, 303, 342, 344
Rottenburg prison 308
RSHA (Reich Security Head Office) 194, 278, 282, 288, 291, 328
Rüdin, Ernst 152–3
Ruhr-Chemie AG, prison labour at 280–1
Runckel, Curt 311
Russian prisoners *see* POWs, Soviet Union

SA: recruited to prison service 85–6, 244; brutality at Emsland prison camp 106–7, 188; Night of the Long Knives 145; violence against Communists 165–6; murders by in 'early camps' (1933) 167; Göring warns against excesses 169

Sachsenhausen concentration camp   378
Sass, Franz and Erich   57, 207–8
Satellite prison camps   101, 103, 104, 227, 231–2, 236, 241, 255, 275, 335
Saxony: Weimar prison reforms   30, 31; criminal-biology   51; Nazis take control of judicial system   74; change in prison regulations (1933)   80
Schäfer, Werner   107, 109, 249, 348
Schaffstein, Friedrich   59
Schemmel, Ludwig   94–5, 156, 162–3, 352, 353
Schieratz institution   276, 297; Johann K.   297
Schiffer, Eugen   358
Schlegelberger, Franz: as German State Secretary of Justice   72–3, 75; punishment of political opposition   114; as acting Reich Minister of Justice   203, 216, 223; punishment of Poles   203, 206, 277–9; seeks to win Hitler's approval   208, 212–15; Hitler's dislike of   215; retires (1942)   216; supports 'euthanasia' programme   310; postwar trial of   342, 343, 344
Schlichting, Max   322
Schlitt, Ewald   212–13, 214
Schmidt, Edgar   76, 77–8, 371
Schmitt, Carl   168
Schneider, Kurt   47
Schoetensack, August   82
Schweidnitz penal institution   328
Schwerdtfeger, Rudolf   86
Schwerdtfeger, Walter   121
SD (security service)   194, 209, 213, 220, 278, 325
Security confinement: roots in pre-Nazi years   49–50, 58, 133; practice in Third Reich   128–39; prisons dedicated to   132; inmate numbers   132, 171–2, 288–9, 400–1 (*Fig.9*); petty criminals in   133; release from   137–9; failed police attempts to gain control over   173–4; deteriorating conditions in   240–1; calls for killing of some inmates   249; inmates excluded from military service   267, 268–9; 'asocial' inmates taken to concentration camps (1942–)   285–6, 288–9. *See also* 'Annihilation through labour', Habitual Criminals Law, 'Incorrigibles'

Seitler, Rudolf   87
Selbmann, Fritz   122
Sex in Chains (1928)   148
Sex offences   112, 133, 139–44; homosexuals accused of   144–9; Jews accused of   157–9, 163, 380; Poles accused of   203–4, 205, 315; as relating to POWs   222
Seyfarth, Heinrich   60–1
Siefert, Ernst   60
Siegburg penal institution   308, 335–6
Sinti and Roma: criminalisation of in Bavaria (1920s)   53; camps for   101; prisoners denounced to Gestapo   176, 180; courts to be excluded from punishment of (1942–)   223–4; 'asocial' prison inmates transferred to concentration camps   285, 290, 300, deemed legal in postwar West Germany   351; Nazi persecution of   290; evacuations from prisons   324
Social Democrats: and Weimar prison and penal policy   25, 26, 27, 30, 33, 42, 48, 49, 61, 102; Gürtner's hostility to   72; assessment of Nazi prisons   81, 86, 90, 91, 186, 369; supporters locked up inside Nazi prisons   99, 123, 269, and transferred as 'asocial' to concentration camps   293; Hitler's hatred of   113; resistance and repression in the Third Reich   115–16, 159, 166; former supporters working as warders   120, 161; opposition to Communists   122; and sterilising prisoners (Weimar)   151–2; role in shaping GDR justice   358. *See also* Political prisoners
Social workers in penal institutions   27, 29, 31, 32, 33, 63, 80, 375
Soldiers inside penal institutions   252, 262–6
Solitary confinement   23, 25, 26, 119, 123, 127, 147, 235, 270, 295
Sonnenburg penitentiary   273, 332–3, 378
Sosnowitz penal institution   279, 290
Soviet Union: invasion of   208–9, 246, 265, 266; Soviet prisoners in Germany   281, 290, 333, 337; role in East Germany   358–9, 361; punishment and prison compared with Nazi Germany   361–4. *See also* Special camps
Special camps   357–8, 359

Special courts (*Sondergerichte*): establishment of 114; criminal procedure 114–15; extension of role 197–8, 218; Freisler acknowledges brutality of 197, 386; number of defendants before 400–1 (*Fig.8*)
'Special penal institutions' 2, 93
Special Wartime Penal Code 195, 222, 263–4
SPD *see* Social Democrats
Speer, Albert 103, 229, 230, 252, 254, 255, 299
SS: concentration camps run by 68; criticism of legal apparatus 69, 184; members as prison warders 85, 185, 244; early release of imprisoned members 90; and Emsland camps 102; attacks on homosexuals 144, 145; and Nazi terror 165–71, 320; failure to 'poach' prison inmates 174; involvement in killing prison inmates 174, 207, 208, 284, 285, 289, 296–8, 304, 312, 325, 327, 332–3, 336; offences by removed from jurisdiction of legal courts 175, 198; and genocide 192; prisoners in penal institutions 204; Special Formation Dirlewanger 262–3, 265, 266, 268; members as senior legal officials 275, 292, 322. *See also* Concentration camps, Heydrich, Himmler, Holocaust, SD
Stages system in penal institutions 26–7, 27–8, 34–5, 88
Stalin, Joseph 361, 362, 363
Stark, Ernst 352, 353–4
Stein penitentiary 332
Sterilisation: debate about in Weimar period 20, 58, 149; debate on application to criminals 149–53; practice in Nazi Germany 150; selection of prison inmates for 153–6; compensation for victims 356; US and Scandinavian practice 368
Sterilisation Law (1933) 140, 150, 152–3
Stieve, Hermann 317
Stolleis, Michael 157
Straubing penal institution 31, 34, 36, 39, 53, 56, 103, 131, 136, 151, 154, 301, 330, 334, 335; Hans D. 334
Strauß, Emil 19
Streckenbach, Bruno 278, 285, 288, 289, 309

Strict detention in penal institutions 80, 135, 245, 279. *See also* Disciplinary punishment
Study Group for Prison Reform 27–8, 29, 30, 32, 33, 35, 49–50, 51, 127; Nazis remove officials associated with 62, 63, 64; disbanded (1933) 78
Stuttgart penal institution 168
Sudetenland, Nazi legal terror extended to 199–200

Tapiau penal institution 132, 240–1
TB, prisoners suffering from 245, 248, 260–1, 280, 281–2, 335
Tegel penal institution (Berlin) 233; Leopold T. 283
Teschen penal institution 283
Thälmann, Ernst 119, 370
Theft *see* Property crime
Thierack, Otto-Georg: as president of People's Court 17, 117, 198, 216; as Minister of Justice in Saxony 74, 75, 80; appointed as Reich Minister of Justice (1942) 216–17, 388–9; continuity with Gürtner 216; pressure on judges 219; competes with police for severity 223–6; hands over 'racial aliens' to police 223–4; handling of Poles' criminal offences by courts 224–5; removal of 'incorrigibles' and 'racial aliens' from prisons 226, 285; Law against Community Aliens 226; 'mobilisation' of prison inmates for military production 229, 230, 233–4; and prisoner escapes 236; visits and praises concentration camps 255–6; and prison chaplains 259; initiates transfer of selected NN prisoners to police 273; support for 'annihilation through labour' 284–8, 299–300; close relationship with Engert 292; replaces officials in Reich Ministry of Justice 292; calls for extermination of 'habitual criminals' 303–4; orders summary execution of condemned prisoners 316, 336; drives legal terror (1945) 321; sets up civilian courts martial 322–3; Hamburg authorities punished for release of remand prisoners (1943) 323–4; evacuation of prisons 324, 333; orders burning of incriminating documents 349; suicide of (1946) 342

Index 537

Thuringia, prisons in Weimar period 27–9, 30, 33, 63–4. *See also* Untermaßfeld, Wurmstich
Toller, Ernst 42
Torgau army prison 266
Trunk, Hans 154
Trusties in penal institutions 121, 123, 257, 270
Tuberculosis *see* TB

Uhlmann, Walter 235–6
Ukrainian prison inmates, murder of 290
Unemployment: in penal institutions (1930s) 95–7; prison camps designed to relieve 102
United States: imprisonment in the 19th century 23; punishment and prison compared with Nazi Germany 365, 366–7
Untermaßfeld: as case study 11; in Weimar period: life inside 27–9, 30, 34, warders' resistance to reforms 28–9, right-wing attacks on reforms 45, 60, Nazi governor takes control 63; prison escapes (1930s) 85; assaults on prisoners 86; forced labour 100, 230–1; political prisoners 120; castration 141; Max W. 141; anti-Semitism 162, 163, 181; and concentration camp inmates 175; Walter A. 175; prison inmates denounced to police 178; Willi B. 178; malnourishment (1940) 239–40; Czech prisoners 270; Ladislaus K. 270; Engelbert S. 271; Richard F. 289; 'asocial' inmates transferred to concentration camps 295, 299; Otto A. 302; Arnold W. 306

Vaihingen workhouse 312–13; Prisoner P. 313
Vechta prison 91
Verl prison camp 109; Prisoner W. 109; Warder K. 109–10
Viernstein, Theodor 56, 129, 151, 154
Völkischer Beobachter 80, 292, 384, 386
Vollrath, Max 30
Vorwärts 19, 44

Wagner, Otto 278
Wagner, Patrick 223
Waldheim penitentiary 84, 92, 121, 124, 168, 335

War Economy Decree (1939) 196, 221, 324
War Offenders Decree (1940) 196–7, 248, 264
Warders *see* prison warders
Warsaw prison 325
Weimar Germany 17–64; contradictions of 18, 20, 22; crime 18–20, 25, 54–9; inflation 19–20; revolution and postwar crisis 20, 36; legal system dominated by conservatives 37; political unrest 37–41, 54–5; German League for Human Rights 41, 42, 44; 'incorrigible' criminals 46–54; 'professional' criminals 48–9, 56–8; economic depression 54–5; criminalisation of homosexuality 144–5
Weimar prison service: question of Nazi continuity with 4, 71–2, 78–9, 130, 133, 375; attacked as too soft 17, 45–6, 57–8, 59–61, 67, 77, 80, 81; reforms of 25–9; stages system 26–7, 27–8, 34–5, 88; social workers in 27, 29, 31, 32, 33, 63; legal status of inmates 28; local officials ignore and oppose reforms 28–9, 30, 33, 88; conditions inside 33–5, 40, 62–3; and revolution of 1918 36–7; and political offenders 37–43, 67; public criticism of harshness of conditions 40–6; riots and hunger strikes 40–2; during the economic depression 59–64; dismantling of reforms in Third Reich 75, 77–8, 80, 375–6; debate on homosexuality 148; attempts to re-introduce reforms in GDR 358. *See also* Study Group for Prison Reform, Untermaßfeld
Wein, Benedikt 281
Weinkauff, Hermann 8
Weissenrieder, Otto 51, 79
Werl penal institution 97, 132, 137, 299–300, 301, 313, 314
Wessel, Horst: killing of 119; accomplice in killing treated harshly in prison 119; convicted killer of murdered 174
Westwall, projected role of prisoners in building 105
Wiener Graben (Mauthausen concentration camp) 297
Wiesbaden, trial of Nazi prison officials (1951–52) 349–51

Wittenau asylum 312; Prisoner B. 312
Wittlich penal institution 26, 162, 180, 261; Eugen S. 162; Joseph O. 162; Richard B. 180–1
Wolfenbüttel penal institution 128
Workhouses 25, 53, 63, 129–30, 153, 176, 238, 285, 312–13
Wronke penal institution 326–7, 335
Wuppertal prison 141, 335
Wurmstich, Werner 183, 246–7

Young offenders 26, 58, 101, 176–7, 196, 241, 266

Zeigner, Erich 42
Zweibrücken penal institution 151, 154
Zwickau penitentiary 123